THIRD EDITION

Interpersonal Communication in Action

Basic Text and Readings

BOBBY R. PATTON
THE UNIVERSITY OF KANSAS

KIM GIFFIN
THE UNIVERSITY OF KANSAS

HARPER & ROW, PUBLISHERS, New York
Cambridge, Hagerstown, Philadelphia, San Francisco,
London, Mexico City, São Paulo, Sydney

1817

Photo credits: p. 1, Corry, DeWys; p. 12, Herwig, Stock, Boston; p. 17, Franken, Stock, Boston; p. 49, Franken, Stock, Boston; p. 52 Siteman, Stock, Boston; p. 58, Grace, Stock, Boston; p. 70 Vandermark, Stock, Boston; p. 107 Berndt, Stock, Boston; p. 111, Franken, Stock, Boston; p. 124, Burnett, Stock, Boston; p. 173, Weldon, DeWys; p. 176, Conrad, DeWys; p. 187, Menzel, Stock, Boston; p. 213, Hrynewych, Stock, Boston; p. 228, Grace, Stock, Boston; p. 231, Albertson, Stock, Boston; p. 267, Vandermark, Stock, Boston; p. 274, Hopker, Woodfin Camp; p. 281, Siteman, Stock, Boston; p. 287, Bernheim, Woodfin Camp; p. 317, Liftin, Woodfin Camp; p. 321, O'Neil, Stock, Boston; p. 325, Pines, Woodfin Camp; p. 335, Anderson, Woodfin Camp; p. 363, DeWys; p. 368, Holland, Stock, Boston; p. 375, DeWys; p. 407, DeWys; p. 413, Gross, Stock, Boston; p. 419, Leonard, Woodfin Camp.

Sponsoring Editor: Alan M. Spiegel
Project Editor: Holly Detgen
Designer: Helen Iranyi
Production Manager: Jeanie Berke
Photo Researcher: Myra Schachne
Compositor: Maryland Composition Company, Inc.
Art Studio: Vantage Art Inc.
Cover photo: Steve Eagle, Nancy Palmer

Interpersonal Communication in Action: Basic Text and Readings,
Third Edition

Library of Congress Cataloging in Publication Data
Main entry under title:

Interpersonal communication in action.

    Includes bibliographical references and indexes.
    1. Interpersonal relations. 2. Interpersonal communication. I. Patton, Bobby R., 1935–
II. Giffin, Kim, 1918–
HM132.P36 1981   302   80-17147
ISBN 0-06-045062-2

Brief Contents

Detailed Contents

APPENDIXES

INDEXES

Preface

The decade of the 1970s has been referred to as "The *Me* Generation." Along with the negative implications of selfishness was a growing awareness of personal responsibility and recognition of the personal choices that an individual must make. Probably the most significant choice that we make concerns our significant relationships. We choose our friends and intimates, the people with whom we will spend our time and energy. Possibly the 1980s will be known as "The *We* Generation."

This third edition reflects the growing awareness of people wanting to improve their capacities and skills of reacting to one another. This edition emphasizes direct applications of the principles of interpersonal communication to the lives of the readers. Although our perspective is humanistic in that the reader is required to make personalized choices in his or her interpersonal communication behaviors, we have been openly prescriptive at times. The purpose of this book remains as with our earlier editions, to provide valid data on interpersonal communication to the student who possesses no specialized background and to provide some insights for improving one's relationships with others.

The major thesis of this book is that the more we understand our own motives and communication behaviors, the greater is the likelihood that we can control them, rather than having them control us. Our humanistic conception of people places emphasis on choice and freedom. A person has the potential for delaying reactions to circumstances until the processes of rational thought indicate the relatively best course of action. People are free to the extent that they can control or direct their behaviors. Such freedom entails responsibility to ourselves and to others for the consequences of our acts.

Human communication involves a complex and simultaneous utilization of a number of channels: verbal, visual, tactile, and vocal. When one person is attempting to enlighten or evoke a response from another, words are only a part of the total message. The total actions of both sender and receiver influence how the message is transmitted and received. We shall draw from the work of research scholars in human communication to try to better understand the potential responses to messages.

We believe that the study of interpersonal communication is important in promoting awareness of our capabilities as communicators, and should contribute to personal development in at least three areas: functional intelligence, social decision-making, and self-expression. Such development requires both theory and the opportunity for practice of behaviors with feedback. People have the capacity for controlling and choosing among alternative patterns of communication behaviors. By understanding the interactive, ongoing process nature of interpersonal communication, it becomes possible to alter elements within the process with more predictable results. Such development obviously requires both theory and practice. It's not enough simply to know that certain behaviors "work" in obtaining goals; theory should provide an understanding of the "whys" of interpersonal communication.

Knowledge of the theory alone, however, is of little value unless a person has opportunities to engage in experiences that provide feedback and insights into his/her interpersonal communication. Within this textbook we have attempted to supply opportunities to put the theory into action. Readings have been selected that provide vivid examples of the state of theory in the various areas. In addition, we have provided personal experiences that we hope the reader will utilize.

In this third edition approximately one-fourth of the material is new. Much of the chapters on nonverbal communication and relationships is new; parts of other chapters have been freshly added and other parts rewritten. Essentially we have made four improvements:

1. The readings in this edition have been selected for their capacity to extend or illustrate major concepts presented in the chapters. There is now consequently less duplication of treatment in chapters and readings than in former editions. The readings now follow the chapter text and are clearly differentiated by double columns.

2. Application of theory is presented in the form of Action Steps—suggestions of ways in which the reader can personally experience in an active way those principles described in the chapters and readings. These Action Steps are new to this edition and are viewed as an integral part of the book in helping the reader make personal applications.

3. We have identified ten characteristics of interpersonal communication that are emphasized throughout the book. We identify these characteristics in the form of propositions in Chapter 1.

1. Communication is unavoidable and inevitable when people are aware of one another.

2. In interpersonal communication both the sender and the receiver of the meaning must be present.
3. Each person assumes roles as both sender and receiver of messages in interpersonal communication.
4. The choices that a person makes reflect the degree of that person's interpersonal communication competencies.
5. In interpersonal communication the sender and the receiver are interdependent.
6. Successful interpersonal communication involves mutual needs to communicate.
7. Interpersonal communication establishes and defines the nature of the relationship between the people involved.
8. Interpersonal communication is the means by which we confirm and validate self.
9. Since interpersonal communication relies on behaviors, we must be satisfied with degrees of mutual understanding.
10. Interpersonal communication is irreversible, unrepeatable and almost always functions in a context of change.

While we realize that scholars are still in the process of learning how people interact and communicate, we believe that our treatment of these propositions reflect the best of available research.

4. We have provided new additional material on interviewing, small group communication, and public speaking. Although the treatment of these communication processes is brief, we believe that they add significantly to the students' potential understanding of the special communication skills inherent in these contexts. This new material can help those teachers who wish to give their students of interpersonal communication at least a modest set of insights and experiences in these communication activities.

We have benefited from feedback to our earlier writing in the area of interpersonal communication. Students and teachers have provided useful information that has guided our efforts in this revised edition. We hope that our use of the model and characteristics of interpersonal communication will help provide a more cohesive treatment of the subject.

We are indebted to the scholars and researchers who permitted us to use their materials in our readings. The constructive critiques of our efforts by such colleagues as Lynn Phelps, Nancy Mihevc, Larry D. Miller, Jon Blubaugh, and Kevin McClearey are appreciated. Karen Bals and Marilyn Conboy typed the manuscript. Recognition is due to Larry Nadler for the preparation of the Indexes. We also wish to acknowledge Jim Quiggins and Jon Blubaugh, who prepared the Instructor's Manual to accompany *Interpersonal Communication in Action,* Third Edition. Finally, we thank our wives, Eleanor Nyquist Patton and Charlene May, who not only encouraged us but served as friendly critics.

BOBBY R. PATTON
KIM GIFFIN

Chapter 1
Understanding the Process of Interpersonal Communication

I N OCTOBER OF 1978, a Pacific Southwest Airlines 727 passenger plane approached the San Diego Lindbergh Field for landing. A small private plane, a Cessna, was circling in the area. The following dialogue transpired between the control towers and the two planes:[1]

> 8:59:30 A.M. CONTROL TO PSA: Traffic 12 o'clock (dead ahead). One mile, northbound.
> PSA: We're looking.
> 8:59:40 A.M. CONTROL TO PSA: Additional traffic 12 o'clock three miles north of field, northeast bound Cessna 172 climbing out of 1400 (altitude in feet).
> PSA: OK. We got that one.
> 9:00:15 A.M. CONTROL TO PSA: Traffic 12 o'clock three miles out of 1700.
> PSA: Traffic in sight.
> 9:00:30 A.M. CONTROL TO CESSNA: Traffic 6 o'clock (directly to rear of Cessna) two miles eastbound. PSA jet inbound to Lindbergh out of 3200. Has you in sight.
> CESSNA: [Response unintelligible.]
> 9:00:40 A.M. CONTROL TO PSA: Traffic 12 o'clock one mile. A Cessna.
> PSA: OK. We had him a minute ago.
> CONTROL: Roger.
> PSA: I think he passed off to our right.
> 9:01:45 A.M. CONTROL TO CESSNA: Traffic in your vicinity is a PSA jet. Has you in sight. He is descending toward Lindbergh.
> CESSNA: [No response.]

The planes had just collided, killing 150 people including all 135 aboard the 727 and people on the ground hit by falling remnants of the two planes.

What had gone wrong? Had the planes seen each other? How can we account for the report about "traffic in sight"?

This tragedy is a vivid example of the crucial role that communication plays in our lives. Our typical day-to-day conversations may not have life-or-death consequences, but misunderstandings and pain can easily be caused by a wrong choice of words or the wrong response at the wrong time. An extremely terrifying consequence of confusion of meanings, reported in *Harper's Magazine*

---

[1] As reported in *Time*, October 9, 1978.

in 1953, suggested that the mistranslation of a single word may have caused the bombing of Hiroshima and Nagasaki. The word *mokusatsu* has two meanings in Japanese. One is "to ignore," with intent to affront, and the other is "to ignore," meaning a mere withholding of comment. To a surrender ultimatum from the Allies, a message with the "no comment" meaning was prepared; the translator, however, applied the meaning of "refused to notice" as the message was passed on. The first interpretation could have led to surrender with face, whereas the second forced the Allies to take the drastic action required to end the conflict. According to W. J. Coughlin's report, if the misinterpretation of that one word had not occurred, the atom bombs would never have been dropped and Russia would never have entered the Pacific theater, paving the way for the Korean War.[2]

Communication. This word became an "in" term in the 1970s. We like to have catchall terms that allow us to disregard conceptual matters we do not care to deal with; thus we have "communication gaps," "communication breakdowns," and "failures to communicate," which tend to be abstractions of the highest order and actually do little to communicate. Every problem is not a "communication problem." The debates on the status of the Panama Canal and the changing U.S. policy toward China were based on conflicting desires that are not products of poor communication. Good communication is not a panacea for all the world ills, and disputes will not vanish if we communicate well, but much needless irritation and disruption can be reduced. We believe that this is an important preamble. When discussing communication we should be dealing with something specific. Such discussions should not be evasions or substitutes for looking at specific behaviors. Our goal in this chapter will be to discuss communication both generally, and in terms specific enough to bridge the gap between theory and an understanding of our personal behaviors.

Communication is basic to human existence—indeed, to all life itself. In fundamental terms all life around us demonstrates communication. We would go so far as to suggest that death is denoted by the absence of communication. A renowned professor of molecular biology and bacteriology at the University of California at Berkeley stated recently: "The capacity to communicate is a fundamental feature of living cells." He proceeded to discuss the ways cells communicate by means of hormones and nerve fibers.[3] *To live is to communicate.*

Photosynthesis and rejuvenation in plant life have been discussed in terms of communication. Animals—from insects to mammals—communicate by means of chemicals, movements, and sounds. People also use these modes of communication, but add a unique kind of language based on symbols. Communication scientist John R. Pierce states:

> Animals live without knowing how they live, and they communicate without knowing how they communicate. By and large, so do we. Unlike animals, however,

[2] W. J. Coughlin, "The Great MOKUSATSU Mistake: Was This the Deadliest Error of Our Time?" *Harper's Magazine*, March 1953.
[3] S. Stent, "Cellular Communication," *Scientific American*, 227 (1972): 43–51.

we speculate about how we live and how we communicate. Our better brain and our unique means of communication—language—make such speculation possible.[4]

Pierce's value judgments reflect the fact that a human is making the description. Using our "better brains" and our language, let us now speculate on how we communicate.

Communication as Process

Communication is a *process*, not a thing. This distinction is important; characteristic of our universe is the expectation of change—nothing is static. Communication scholar David Berlo has observed:

> If we accept the concept of process, we view events and relationships as dynamic, ongoing, ever-changing, continuous. When we label something as a process, we also mean that it does not have a beginning, an end, a fixed sequence of events. It is not static, at rest. It is moving. The ingredients within a process interact; each affects all of the others.[5]

Even to write about process tends to freeze it in terms devoid of life and change. You are reading a textbook that is an object, that has a beginning and an end. If these symbols written on the page generate thinking in you—and thereby change— then we have an operational process.

We define communication as *the generation and attribution of meaning.* This definition is broad enough to encompass nonhuman communication. Thus bees may perform a dance that signals other bees to go for nectar; a dog may show hunger by walking back and forth to the dog bowl. People may attribute meaning to elements in nature. For example, dark clouds signal the prospect of rain or bad weather; an unusual noise in the night stirs us to investigate. As we assign significance to phenomena or events around us, communication is taking place.

The source of the "communiqué" or *message* is the generator or sender. Such generation may be intentional or unintentional. People are unique in the extent to which their communication behaviors are intentional, that is, planned with an expectation of achieving a desired effect or eliciting a desired response. However, even between people the unintentional messages may carry more meaning than the planned ones. Other characteristics of human communication will be noted later.

Our definition of communication is broad enough to be applied to mechanistic, nonhuman models of communication. A model developed in the late 1940s presented communication as a linear concept, having a beginning and an end. Later scholars noted the importance of feedback and pointed out that communication should be viewed as circular rather than linear because the input and output circuits are mutually linked as a means of controlling the

[4] J. R. Pierce, "Communication," *Scientific American*, 227 (1972): 31.
[5] D. K. Berlo, *The Process of Communication* (New York: Holt, Rinehart and Winston, 1960), p. 24.

performance.[6] Berlo illustrates this concept of feedback by citing the example of a thermostat in a house and the furnace engaged in mutual interaction: "Continual communication occurs between the furnace and the thermostat. Each transmits messages, each receives messages. Each reacts to the message it receives."[7]

Communication is the process that promotes change among humans. People attempt to interpret the world and their role—to make sense out of the influx of perceptions—so they can order and assign significance to the various components of their environment. In Reading 1.2 at the end of this chapter, Dean Barnlund develops this thesis in detail. From this perspective of communication as process, let us now examine the human factor.

People as Communicators

We are writing with a humanistic viewpoint; we believe that people are active forces in their life situations. We believe that the individual is not just a receiver and interpreter of stimuli, but takes a role in determining the stimuli to which he or she will respond.[8] We are born into a world of strange sensory sensations. Lights, visual images, and strange sounds bombard the nervous system. Our early days are spent sorting out these sensations. The presence of certain people becomes recognized as a signal that physical needs will be fulfilled. Sounds also begin to take on meaning as words are repeated over and over again. Eventually we begin to behave in certain ways that exert influence on the environment. Babbling, cooing, and finally vocalizing "ma-ma" or "pa-pa" gain warm approving signals of positive acceptance from the elders. As we develop we become more sophisticated and discriminating as we attach meaning to phenomena, and we are more able to control our environments by initiating communication with others.

We expand our experiences and our expectations of others in terms of our cultural surroundings and the models of behavior that we encounter. Communication, with its intrinsic feedback, is the means by which we adjust ourselves to our environment and adjust our environment to meet our needs as human beings. We do not live simply as a result of the products of our own hands; we live through our interactions with others. Although we do interact with objects, animals, and environment and receive messages from them, these are relatively unimportant when compared to the interactions and relationships which we maintain with people. As psychologists H. W. Bernard and W. C. Huckins state:

> . . . Things are easier to manage. Things do not ascribe meanings or accord status. Neither do they judge or evaluate. They place no pressure to impress or to convince. This happens only as a result of the interaction patterns which one has

---

[6] N. Wiener, *The Human Use of Human Beings* (Boston: Houghton Mifflin, 1954).
[7] Berlo, *Process of Communication*, p. 110.
[8] This basic humanistic idea is called "dynamic psychology" by H. W. Bernard and W. C. Huckins, *Dynamics of Personal Adjustment* (Boston: Holbrook Press, 1971), p. 13.

with other individuals. These patterns and interpersonal relationships are established, maintained, and mediated through communication.[9]

In a deeper sense, the way we deal with others is what we become. John Stewart and Gary D'Angelo, in their book on interpersonal communication, put it this way:

The quality of our interpersonal relationships determines who we are becoming as persons. Interpersonal communication is not just one of many dimensions of human life; it is the defining dimension, the dimension through which we become human.[10]

The major thesis of this book is that the more we understand our own motives and communication patterns, the greater is the likelihood that we can control them, rather than having them control us. Controlling rather than being controlled can be seen in an example: A young woman politely and cheerfully asks a stranger for directions. The stranger responds gruffly and walks on. The young woman has the choice of being upset and angry, or of remaining cheerful and inquiring of another person. She chooses the latter course of action because she doesn't want to be controlled. You cannot "make me angry," unless I allow myself to be angry. It is possible for us to think and act rather than simply to react.

Our humanistic conception of people places emphasis on choice and freedom. A person has the potential for delaying reactions to circumstances until the processes of rational thought indicate the relatively best course of action. People are free to the extent that they can control or direct their behaviors. Such freedom entails responsibility to ourselves and to others for the consequences of our acts.

Human communication typically involves a complex and simultaneous utilization of several channels—verbal, visual, tactile, and vocal. When one person is attempting to enlighten or evoke a response from someone, words are only a part of the total message. The total actions of both sender and receiver influence how the message is transmitted and received. If the sender looks uncertain, or sounds intoxicated or disinterested, the potential response to a given message will vary. Dean Barnlund has observed that the complexity is such that whenever there is communication there are at least six "people" involved:

The person you think yourself to be; the man your partner thinks you are; the person you believe your partner thinks you are; plus the three equivalent "persons" at the other end of the circuit. If, with as few as four constants, mathematicians must cope with approximately fifty possible relations, then we, in studying communication, where an even greater number of variables is concerned, ought to expound with considerable humility. In this age of Freudian and non-Freudian analysis, of information theory specialists, of structural linguists, and so on, we are

[9] Bernard and Huckins, *Dynamics of Personal Adjustment*, p. 269.
[10] John Stewart and Gary D'Angelo, *Together: Communicating Interpersonally* (Reading, Mass.: Addison-Wesley, 1975), p. 23.

just beginning to unravel the mysteries of this terribly involved, and therefore fascinating, puzzle.[11]

As we discuss interpersonal communication, we distinguish it from two other categories of human communication.

1. Intrapersonal Communication. Signals are going continuously from all parts of your body to your brain. A throbbing in your stomach may suggest that you are hungry or that you have overeaten. Intrapersonal communication refers to the communication that transpires inside a person.

Other forms of intrapersonal communication include the perceptual notes we make, and the rationalizations and attitudes that determine our overt behaviors. Basic to all levels of communication is a developed consciousness of self. As psychologist Rollo May observes:

> The capacity for consciousness of ourselves gives us the ability to see ourselves as others see us and to have empathy with others. It underlies our remarkable capacity to transport ourselves into someone else's parlor where we will be in reality next week, and then in imagination to think and plan how we will act. And it enables us to imagine ourselves in someone else's place, and to ask how we would feel and what we would do if we were this other person. No matter how poorly we use or fail to use or even abuse these capacities, they are the rudiments of our ability to begin to love our neighbor, to have ethical sensitivity, to see truth, to create beauty, to devote ourselves to ideals, and to die for them if need be.[12]

May goes on to develop the thesis that fulfilling these potentials is the key to becoming a person.

Deep internal problems are the province of the psychologist and psychoanalyst. Our concerns are the intrapersonal influences on our overt behaviors with others. In Chapters 2 and 3 we shall discuss our needs to communicate and our intrapersonal perceptions and orientations as they *affect* our interpersonal communication. Although interpersonal communication will be our central focus, other levels of the process cannot be ignored.

2. One-way Communication. This level suggests the absence of feedback. Although we have opposed the linear view of the communication process, we should note that on one level the roles of sender and receiver tend to be fixed. For example, in a large lecture hall the speaker has a preplanned message and the members of the audience accept the role of listeners. Feedback in such a situation is less direct and depends on the speaker's inferential abilities. Applause or lack of attentiveness provides clues to the audience's receptiveness to the speaker.

Other types of one-way communication involve mass media. As we watch a speaker on television or listen to the radio, our feedback to the sender is indirect (ratings, letters, reviews). Written communication also fits this category.

---

[11] D. C. Barnlund, "Toward a Meaning-Centered Philosophy of Communication," *Journal of Communication*, 11 (1962): 202.
[12] R. May, *Man's Search for Himself* (New York: Norton, 1953), p. 75.

As you read this page, your means of providing feedback are limited. We are on the sender end of a continuum, and you are on the receiving end. In such one-way situations the receiver determines whether communication is to occur. It is your choice whether to continue reading or to listen (in an attempt to attribute meaning) to the words of the teacher.

In contrast to two-way communication (involving direct feedback, give-and-take, between sender and receiver), researchers have concluded the following:

1. Two-way communication takes much longer.
2. Two-way communication results in greater mutual understanding.
3. In one-way communication, the sender feels relatively confident; the receiver, uncertain or frustrated.
4. In two-way communication, the sender often feels frustrated or angry; the receiver, relatively confident.[13]

As Barnlund points out in Reading 1.2, although one-way communication is obviously required in certain situations, two-way communication promotes greater understanding and a more cooperative relationship.[14]

3. Interpersonal Communication.   This two-way level of communication is the focus of this text. With "interpersonal communication" we are concerned with the face-to-face interactions between people who are consistently aware of each other. Each person assumes the roles of both sender and receiver of messages, which involves constant adaptation and spontaneous adjustment to the other person. This definition describes the *focus* rather than the extent of interpersonal communication. A telephone conversation is basically interpersonal although we do not have the visual messages of face-to-face interactions. The definition is intentionally broad enough to permit us to consider *all* of the variables that we feel are significant. The absence of one or another of these variables will not necessarily keep such communication from being "interpersonal."

Even public speaking should be two-way and interpersonal in its best instances. The key difference is that public speaking can be preplanned to a greater extent than most of our daily interactions.

The Study of Interpersonal Communication

So thoroughly do we take our interpersonal communication for granted that it scarcely ever occurs to us to examine its nature. We usually learn to communicate without much conscious effort. Thus by the time we are mature enough to understand the symbolism of actions and sounds that provide the basis for our interaction with others, communication has become so much like

---

[13] H. J. Leavitt, *Managerial Psychology* (Chicago: University of Chicago Press, 1958), pp. 118–128.
[14] Barnlund, "Communication: The Context of Change." Reprinted in this text as Reading 1.2.

reflex behavior (e.g., breathing, coughing, or chewing) that it hardly occurs to us that there is anything to be understood.

Social and behavioral scientists have long been interested in human communication behaviors. There is the tacit admission that communication is the foundation for all of our interpersonal relationships; its relevance to and significance for our lives can hardly be overemphasized. Yet only recently have attempts been made to translate behavioral theories into research-based foundations for personalized growth and development.

Probably no one model will ever identify all the potential variables in interpersonal communication; even if it were possible to apply labels to all conceivable elements, the size and complexity of the model would make it useless. For our purposes, we must recognize that communication is a dynamic process, constantly changing, never static. All variables are constantly interacting with one another, modifying and adapting to all situational modifications. Although we may focus attention on one or another of the variables, we must remember the fluid nature of the total process. As we examine interpersonal communication from a number of perspectives, different models will be utilized to help clarify views of particular variables.

We have prepared a model that will provide an overview of our conception of the major ingredients in the process of interpersonal communication. This model is shown in Figure 1.1. Our model attempts to identify the elements in the interpersonal communication process comprising the heart of this book. Discussion of any one element at a given time is arbitrary; all the elements are interdependent, and a change in any one affects all others. We have elected to discuss them in the following order in this book:

1. We desire and seek out communication with others, which can be called the *communication imperative*. Each of us has personal needs that can be satisfied only by interaction with others. Personal growth and development, as well as our needs for controlling our environment, can be accomplished only with the help of other people. This imperative to communicate is the topic of Chapter 2.
2. We *perceive* the other person and, based on our habitual *orientation* to this person, we choose whether or not to initiate interaction. Is this person able to fulfill our personal needs of the moment? This topic is discussed in Chapter 3.
3. We attempt to share ideas by attributing meaning to *verbal messages*. Based on the mutual understandings of a code, we infer the thoughts of the other person. This topic, verbal messages, is the focus of Chapter 4.
4. We use *nonverbal communication* as both senders and receivers to establish and maintain relationships. This topic is discussed in Chapter 5.
5. We make an *environmental analysis* of such matters as the physical environment (place, time, space) and the social context (presence of others, cultural influences, etc.) and decide on appropriate behaviors. We discuss the interpersonal environment in Chapter 6.

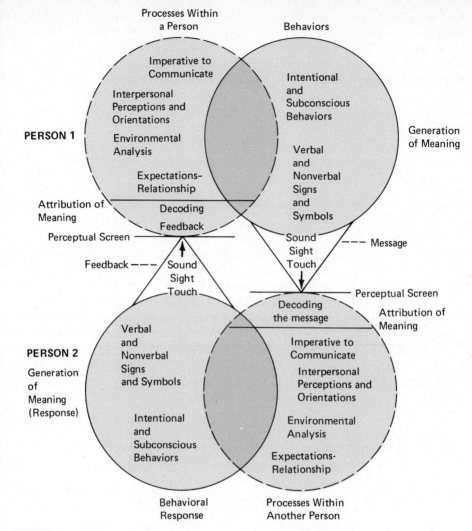

FIGURE 1.1. The circular process of interpersonal communication.

6. Based on the degree of mutual understanding, relationships tend to stabilize over time and we develop certain expectations. We evaluate these relationships in terms of cost/reward to our needs and decide to maintain, change, or terminate the relationships. The nature of the interpersonal relationship is discussed in Chapter 7.

Looking at our model of interpersonal communication, we see that processes are occurring within Person 1 that are reflected in his or her overt behaviors. An attempt is made to encode meanings by verbal and nonverbal signs and symbols. These messages are transmitted by means of sound, sight, and touch to Person 2. Not only are there a variety of complex motivations on the part of the communicator and a variety of messages generated by him/her at each moment, but the receiver of the message attributes meaning from an equally complex motivational system.

Each of us has a perceptual screen or filter through which we perceive the behavior of others. We "hear" what we want to hear, either laudatory or critical. Thus the complexity of both the sending and the receiving set makes communication a difficult human act. Of the many messages the individual may communicate, many of which he or she is unaware, he/she cannot know which are received by the other or whether the perceptual screen of the other distorts the message he/she attempted to convey.

The behavioral response of Person 2 generates a message back to Person 1 in the form of feedback that serves to monitor his/her subsequent communication. For example, an apparent lack of interest in the subject may cause the speaker to change subjects or adjust the message if he/she decodes the feedback with awareness. Thus we see the circular nature of the process.

We believe that the study of interpersonal communication is important in promoting awareness of our capabilities as communicators and should contribute to personal development in at least three areas: functional intelligence, social decision making, and self-expression. Such development requires both theory and the opportunity for practice of behaviors with feedback. People have the capacity for controlling and choosing among alternative patterns of communication behaviors. By understanding the interactive, ongoing, process nature of interpersonal communication, it becomes possible to alter elements within the process with more predictable results. Such development obviously requires both theory and practice. It is not enough simply to know that certain behaviors "work" in obtaining goals; theory should provide an understanding of the "whys" of interpersonal communication.

Knowledge of the theory alone, however, is of little value unless a person has opportunities to engage in experiences that provide feedback and insights into his or her interpersonal communication. Analogies can be made to any personal behavioral skill—writing, driving an automobile, or hitting a golf ball. The study of interpersonal communication is somewhat different, however, in that each individual must make personal judgments and choices about his or her behaviors. In some areas the criteria of excellence are not as specifically defined as in the case of other disciplines; there are no *absolute* rules of conduct. Personal growth and self-actualization must be generated within the individual. At this moment you are making a decision as to whether to continue reading; you are in control of your communicative behaviors.

As a summary to this point, we should reiterate our definition of interpersonal communication. We conceptualize interpersonal communication as the generation and attribution of meaning in face-to-face interactions between people who are consistently aware of each other and who assume roles of both sender and receiver of messages. A major goal of studying interpersonal communication is to become more aware of ourselves and our potentials as communicators. The importance of the elements in our definition will be seen as we now examine some of the characteristics of interpersonal communication.

One cannot *not* communicate.

Characteristics of Interpersonal Communication

We have chosen to state the ten characteristics and discussions that follow as propositions because of the realization that we are still in the process of learning how people interact and communicate. These ten characteristics are intended to serve as impetus for discussion rather than facts that should be accepted without question. Although we offer them tentatively, we believe that these ten characteristics reflect the best of available research and help to delineate the essence of interpersonal communication.

Proposition 1. Communication Is Unavoidable and Inevitable When People Are Aware of One Another. Whether or not a person chooses to talk or to act in the presence of another person, the other person will draw inferences and behave on that basis. As psychologists P. Watzlawick, J. H. Beavin, and D. D. Jackson state:

> . . . One cannot *not* communicate. Activity or inactivity, words or silence all have message value: they influence others and these others, in turn, cannot *not* respond to these communications and are thus themselves communicating.[15]

Our mere presence with another person carries some message. Even if that person says nothing, his/her presence alters the situation and all the interpersonal dynamics that transpire. Silence, in fact, is often quite significant. By withholding acknowledgment and reaction, one implies either a rejection or a disconfirmation of others. "The man at a crowded lunch counter who looks straight ahead, or the airplane passenger who sits with his eyes closed, are both communicating that they do not want to speak to anybody or be spoken to, and their neighbors usually 'get the message' and respond appropriately by leaving them alone."[16]

Whether or not we communicate with another person is then not for us to decide. The decisions and choices we make concern the nature of our communication. We are responsible for how others respond to us and the consequences of their reactions.

Proposition 2. In Interpersonal Communication, Both the Sender and the Receiver of Meaning Must Be Present. In other types of human communication the presence of both the message generator (sender) and the receiver is not required. In one-way communication I may write alone and you may read my message alone; I may record a message for you and you may hear it in my absence. In a large public meeting, your presence or absence most likely makes no difference to the speaker. Such is not the case with interpersonal communication.

We defined interpersonal communication as the face-to-face interactions between people who are consistently aware of each other. Thus, if I overhear a conversation unknown to the sender, I am not engaging in interpersonal communication. A mutual awareness of the other person makes communication inevitable. This factor will be developed in greater detail in Proposition 3. The important point here is that interpersonal communication cannot transpire without the presence and awareness of the parties involved.

Proposition 3. Each Person Assumes Roles as Both Sender and Receiver of Messages in Interpersonal Communication. As opposed to one-way communication, interpersonal communication requires constant adaptation and spontaneous adjustment to the other person. This give-and-take of *verbal*

---

[15] P. Watzlawick, J. H. Beavin, and D. D. Jackson, *Pragmatics of Human Communication* (New York: Norton, 1967), p. 48.
[16] Ibid., p. 48.

and *nonverbal* messages poses special problems for both parties. Based on personal experience, perceptions of the other person, and personal capabilities, the sender of the message selects and utilizes symbols in an attempt to elicit a desired response from the other person (or persons). The receiver, based on his/her knowledge of this person and similarities of experiences, attaches meaning to the symbols that may or may not correspond to the meaning intended by the sender. Ideally there would be total congruence between the two sets of meanings; but such is rarely the case.

The very process in which we arbitrarily make certain sounds or symbols stand for other things is societal in essence. We can, by mutual agreement, make anything stand for anything. This elementary "meaning of words" aspect of communication is important because arguments or disagreements may arise simply because A uses a word one way and B receives the word as if it meant something entirely different. This could happen when A says, "I was only a little late," and B responds, "You were not!"

By "meaning" we "mean" the sense of import that is signified by a linguistic message. Semanticists have, for purposes of clarity, used the analogy of a *map* and the *territory* it represents to describe the relationship between our verbal symbols and the reality for which they stand. The basic aspect of words and language is parallel to the map-territory analogy. Words are symbols that stand for something. The fact that the meanings of many words are shared by many people allows communication to occur.

Proposition 4. The Choices That a Person Makes Reflect the Degree of That Person's Interpersonal Communication Competencies. To talk about degree of competency obviously includes some value judgments. Throughout this book we shall attempt to make explicit the values that we think should govern our choices and their consequences.

After a comprehensive review of the literature, communication researchers Arthur Bochner and Clifford Kelly compiled three criteria by which interpersonal competency can be judged:

1. ability to formulate and achieve objectives,
2. ability to collaborate effectively with others (i.e. to be interdependent), and
3. ability to adapt appropriately to situational or environmental variations.[17]

How are these abilities developed? The chapters and readings that follow will merely scratch the surface. As we have already observed, reading about interpersonal communication is insufficient. You can learn only by examining and doing.

One of the values that we hold is that people should strive for authenticity in their relationships: to reflect true feelings, motivations, and desires, rather

[17] A. P. Bochner and C. W. Kelly, "Interpersonal Competence: Rationale, Philosophy, and Implementation of a Conceptual Framework," *Speech Teacher*, 23 (1974): 279–301.

than attempting to manipulate selfishly the other person. We agree with other commentators on the competencies that lead to better interpersonal relationships by deepening the emotional interchange and increasing understanding:

1. *Capacity to receive and send information and to express feelings reliably.* This competency includes sensitivity as well as the ability to listen and perceive accurately and fully.
2. *Capacity to evoke the expression of feelings.* This kind of listening encourages the other person to express thoughts, beliefs, and feelings that are typically inhibited.
3. *Capacity to process information and feelings reliably and creatively.* Points 1 and 2 deal with "sensitivity." This point introduces "diagnosis" as we abstract and order our interpersonal experiences.
4. *Capacity to implement a course of action.* Action skills are necessary in the implementation of the behaviors deemed appropriate by our diagnosis. For example, if a woman wants to be included more in the decision-making of a group, she must take a more active role.
5. *Capacity to learn in each of the above areas.* A person should cultivate a frame of mind that permits and encourages a constant analysis and interpretation of interpersonal experiences. This scrutiny of one's own and other's behavior will seem stilted at first and interfere with spontaneity, but is necessary for a time if we are to become more aware and competent.[18]

Proposition 5. In Interpersonal Communication, the Sender and the Receiver Are Interdependent.   The circular nature of interpersonal communication means that as we are attributing meaning to messages generated by the sender, we are simultaneously generating feedback messages to the sender that in turn influence subsequent message generation. The behaviors of the participants in interpersonal communication are so intertwined in the process that it is difficult to separate sender from receiver.

David Berlo distinguishes four levels of communication interdependence. He uses the term interaction to exemplify the highest level of interdependence. At this ideal level of interpersonal communication, Berlo states:

> When two people interact, they put themselves into each other's shoes, try to perceive the world as the other person perceives it, try to predict how the other will respond. Interaction involves reciprocal role-taking, the mutual employment of empathetic skills. The goal of interaction is the merger of self and other, a complete ability to anticipate, predict, and behave in accordance with the joint needs of self and other.[19]

Tied to this view of interdependence is our need for collective action. Communication researcher Donald Darnell has observed: "Because men collectively can affect the environment in ways that men individually cannot, because

---

[18] W. G. Bennis, E. R. Schein, F. A. Steele, and D. E. Berlew, *Interpersonal Dynamics: Essays and Readings on Human Interaction* (Homewood, Ill.: Dorsey, 1968), p. 671.
[19] Berlo, *Process of Communication*, p. 131.

the resources provided by the environment are apparently limited, and because the adaptive capacity of the individual man is limited, *men are interdependent.*"[20]

Proposition 6. Successful Interpersonal Communication Involves Mutual Needs to Communicate.   You may want to share with me the latest news about your brother in New Orleans. Unless I have some interest in the information, I may merely feign interest as I permit my mind to wander to other subjects. Because we both have controls over communicative behaviors, we choose whether to initiate contact, speak, or listen.

If you want to talk about you, and I only want to talk about me, we may be sending messages to reflect our ideas and feelings, with neither of us listening. The receiver ultimately determines whether genuine, functional communication is to transpire. Just as we may daydream or sleep during a dull lecture, we can shut out the other person in an interpersonal situation. A mutual reliance on listening and responding to visual cues can be distinguished from a one-way system in two ways.

First, receiving interpersonal messages, unlike reading or watching television, is a socialized activity. Instead of being able to shut out distractions and focus our attention, we are forced to respond to a variety of signals. Whereas we may choose the time and place to read or watch television, we have no such control over our interpersonal environment. Even after we have received shocking or distressing news, we are still placed in situations when accurate reception is important. For example, after hearing of an accident involving a loved one, important details may follow. A variety of emotional and social pressures influence our capability to attribute meaning.

A second distinction is that in interpersonal communication, again unlike reading, the sender controls the production of a message. Although we are each able to read at our own individual speed, we have no such control over the listening process. The speaker may rush and slur over words that are vital to the message, and we may have no opportunity to "rerun" the speech in order to correct our listening errors. For social reasons we respond as if we understood completely.

The message that the other person creates from what we send, and the interpretation given, will determine the reaction. Some communication problems that we attribute to the other person result because we fail to realize that they, not we, determine what they receive and act upon. If we are to understand their behavior, we must do so from their perspective. Our interaction can be improved if we understand that our acquaintances may not be spiteful or hostile; they just may not understand what we think we communicate.

Proposition 7. Interpersonal Communication Establishes and Defines the Nature of the Relationship Between the People Involved.   Our interpersonal communication not only conveys information, but at the same time, a

[20] D. K. Darnell, "Toward a Reconceptualization of Communication," *Journal of Communication*, 21 (1971): 7.

What relationships are indicated?

message is sent concerning the relationship between the communicants.[21] How I see and feel about myself and how I see and feel about you are communicated by our manner, our tone of voice, our posture, our eye contact, and all of our other nonverbal means, as well as through the words we use.

Researchers have labeled three stages of interaction: the *entry phase*, in which strangers meet and engage in general information based upon norms and rules appropriate to the particular situation; the *personal phase*, in which the communicants become more trusting of each other and attitudinal issues, personal problems, and basic values are revealed; and, the *exit phase* in which decisions are made about whether or not there will be future interactions.[22] These stages include two significant factors: reducing uncertainty and reciprocity. We reduce uncertainty and increase the predictability of the other person's and our own behavior as we get to know each other. At the same time, our patterns of communication tend to be reciprocal. If you're friendly, I'll be friendly and vice versa. Our trust, openness, and degree of self-disclosure must all be reciprocated if the interaction is to progress.[23]

Our nonverbal communication functions to describe the nature of the relationship. Our degrees of affection or hostility, equality, subordination, or

[21] Watzlawick, Beavin, and Jackson, *Pragmatics of Human Communication*, p. 49.
[22] C. R. Berger and R. J. Calabrese, "Some Explorations in Initial Interaction and Beyond: Toward a Developmental Theory of Interpersonal Communication," *Human Communication Research* 1 (1975): 99–112.
[23] I. Altman and D. A. Taylor, *Social Penetration: The Development of Interpersonal Relationships* (New York: Holt, Rinehart and Winston, 1973).

control are most likely to be displayed by our actions rather than our words. If a person expresses one thing in words and another nonverbally, we are often confused and will typically believe the nonverbal because it is harder to disguise and control. If you say you love me, but then choose to spend your available time with people other than me, I question your words.

Proposition 8. Interpersonal Communication Is the Means by Which We Confirm and Validate Self. Whenever one person attempts to initiate interpersonal communication with another, he or she has made an implicit request: "Please validate me as a person!" On the surface there is a request for recognition of the message content, while beneath the surface there is the implicit issue of the value of the person. In an interpersonal situation where two people are face-to-face, each aware of the presence of the other, if one even acts out a message such as a nod, it is impossible for the other to ignore that overture without giving an implied message in response. Ignoring someone is a response and implies that he/she does not exist as a person worthy of your consideration.

If there is consistent social confirmation, a strong, integrated self-identity will be developed and sustained. In such a case there is less need to seek confirmatory responses or to shield oneself from possible disconfirmation. Such a person can dare to receive feedback even if risks are involved.

Psychologists Bernard and Huckins point out, however:

> Too often interpersonal contacts remain impersonal and tentative. People lack self-validation and meaningful ties with others because the fear of rejection or disconfirmation prevents them from initiating such ties. By the way they manage their communications they literally furnish a basis for their own feelings of being left out and their lack of self-confirmation.[24]

Proposition 9. Since Interpersonal Communication Relies on Behaviors, We Must Be Satisfied with Degrees of Mutual Understanding. At this point we should distinguish between behaviors—the overt actions that we can see and hear—and the intrapersonal experiences that are invisible. Behavior would be what is recorded on a videotape machine. Alone it provides no interpretation of movements or sounds; the meanings are attached by the viewer-receiver. But behavior is merely the manifestation of a person's unique intrapersonal experience. As we use such words as interpersonal imperatives, perceptions, orientations, and relationships, we are evoking aspects of our experience, but they merge together in such ways as to make differentiation difficult. R. D. Laing, who has written extensively on the distinction between behavior and internalized experience, puts it this way: "Experience is man's invisibility to man."[25]

This distinction is important because although we are in effect cut off from one another in our private worlds of experience, interpersonal commu-

---

[24] Bernard and Huckins, *Dynamics of Personal Adjustment*, p. 273.
[25] R. D. Laing, *The Politics of Experience* (New York: Ballantine, 1967), p. 18. Another of Laing's works, *The Divided Self* (New York: Quadrangle, 1960), is devoted to describing versions of the split between experience and behavior.

nication becomes the bridge of contact. Because we believe we can attach personal meanings to our own behaviors, we have some control over the way others experience us. My behavior becomes your experience of me. But you cannot see my inner life (my experience), and your perceptions, thoughts, and feelings about me are simply projective aspects of your own inner life. Thus the impact we have on other people consists of the personal meanings they attach to our behaviors.

As we attribute meaning to the behavior of others, we are inferring with some degree of probability what is going on inside the person. We attach meanings to the behaviors that may or may not be valid. For example, an acquaintance fails to acknowledge and speak to you. You may infer that she is angry at you, while in reality she has just received disturbing news (the death of a loved one) and is not "seeing" anyone at that moment. Too often we are unaware of all the facets of an individual and respond habitually. We cannot read one another's minds so we have to settle for a degree of understanding.

Proposition 10. Interpersonal Communication Is Irreversible, Unrepeatable and Almost Always Functions in a Context of Change. This proposition is advanced in the writings of Dean Barnlund. In Reading 1.2 at the end of this chapter, he advances the thesis that communication is the basis of change in our views of the world and of ourselves: "What prompts communication is the desire for someone else to see our facts, appreciate our values, share our feelings, accept our decision. Communication is initiated, consciously or unconsciously, to change the other person."[26]

An important distinction is made in that reading between attempting to change the other person and attempting to manipulate the other person. In manipulation we treat the person like an object, a number, a customer, a vote, or a factor in production. Such communication is more "impersonal" than interpersonal.[27] We may respond to each other in terms of social roles rather than as people. Sometimes, such as in the entry phase of communication, and in brief contacts where we don't have the time or the energy to deal on a personal level, we choose to be impersonal. However, not all human interactions are, or have to be, mutually and unconsciously manipulative, and no one has to be a pawn in the process unless he/she remains unaware of its operation. We can quickly arouse defensiveness in a stranger or we can help contribute to the establishment of a friendly, trusting atmosphere.

The irreversible, unrepeatable nature of communication has been stated by Barnlund as follows:

> The distinction being suggested here is between systems that are deterministic and mechanical, and those that are spontaneous and evolutionary. One can start a motor, beat a rug, or return a book. But you cannot start a man thinking, beat your son, or return a compliment with the same consequences. The words of a

---

[26] Barnlund, "Communication: The Context of Change." Reprinted in this text as Reading 1.2.

[27] G. R. Miller believes that such a distinction is vital to a definition of interpersonal communication. "The Current Status of Theory and Research in Interpersonal Communication," *Human Communication Research*, 4 (1978): 164–178.

teacher, even when faithfully repeated, do not produce the same effect, but may lead to new insight, increased tension, or complete boredom. A moment of indifference or interest, a disarming or tangential remark, leave indelible traces.[28]

All of us, no doubt, regret words that we have spoken or things that we have done to other people. A single ill-chosen word may disrupt a relationship. Just as the clever lawyer knows, to "strike from the record" does not erase the impression made on a jury, we cannot take back our words or actions after the impact has been felt. The choices that we make determine the consequences that we have to be willing to accept.

From our discussion of these ten propositions, you will agree, we hope, that interpersonal communication is a complex process that cannot be taken for granted. In the eight chapters and their readings, we will focus attention on the elements presented in the model (Figure 1.1); examples and evidence in support of these ten propositions will be provided.

Summary and Preview of Readings

In this chapter we have examined the nature of interpersonal communication by looking at reasons for concern, ingredients in the process, and what we feel are basic characteristics. We believe that an individual should be an active force in determining the dynamics and nature of his or her interpersonal communication behaviors. As we become more conscious of the process, we are able to develop skills and competencies that will help us in our dealings with other people.

In the first reading that follows, Virginia Satir identifies four patterns of communication that can cause trouble: *placating, blaming, computing,* and *distracting.* She puts special emphasis on self-esteem (your "pot") and your need to have this pot refilled from time to time. When it is low, placating, blaming, and so on can occur. Avoiding or overcoming such problems should be included in your personal goals.

Dean Barnlund, whom we cited several times in this chapter, has been a pioneer in attempting to achieve more careful descriptions of the interpersonal communication process. In the second reading that follows, he not only provides his view of this process, but also identifies a special social value of human communication—its function as the criterion for changes in our views of our world and of ourselves. He points out that people nearly always talk in a context of change: "What prompts communication is the desire for someone else to see our facts, appreciate our values, share our feelings, accept our decisions."

[28] Barnlund, "Toward a Meaning-Centered Philosophy of Communication," p. 201.

Reading 1.1
Patterns
of Communication
Virginia Satir

After thirty years of listening to literally thousands of interactions among people, I gradually became aware of certain seemingly universal patterns in the way people communicated.

Whenever there was any stress, over and over again I observed four ways people had of handling it. These four patterns occurred only when one was reacting to stress *and at the same time* felt his self-esteem was involved— "his pot got hooked". In addition, the "hooked" one felt he could not say so. Presence of stress alone need not hook your pot, incidentally. Stress might be painful or annoying, but that isn't the same as doubting your own worth.

The four patterns of communication (which will be dealt with in detail later in this chapter) are: *placating, blaming, computing,* and *distracting.*

As I went into this more deeply I began to see that the self-esteem (pot) became hooked more easily when a

Reprinted by permission of the author and the publisher from Virginia Satir. *Peoplemaking.* Palo Alto, California: Science and Behavior Books, 1972.

person had not really developed a solid, appreciative sense of his own worth. Not having his own, he would use another's actions and reactions to define himself. If someone called him green, he would agree with no checking and take the other's comment as one fitting him. He was green because the other person said so. It's easy for anyone with doubts about his own worth to fall into this trap.

Do you know your internal feeling when your pot gets hooked? When mine does, my stomach gets knots, my muscles get tight, I find myself holding my breath, and I sometimes feel dizzy. While all this is going on I find that my thoughts concern the pot dialogue I am having with myself. The words are variations of "Who cares about me? I am unlovable. I can never do anything right. I am a nothing." Descriptive words for this condition are embarrassed, anxious, incompetent.

What I say at this point might be quite different from anything I am feeling or thinking. If I feel the only way out of my dilemma is to make things right with you so you will think I am lovable, etc., I will say whatever I think would fit. It would not matter if it were true or not. What matters is my survival, and I have put that in your hands.

Suppose, instead, I keep my survival in my hands. Then when my pot is hooked, I can say straight out what I think and feel. I might feel some initial pain at exposing my "weaknesses" and taking the risk that I believe goes with that, but I avoid the greater pain of hurting myself physically, emotionally, intellectually, socially, and spiritually, as well as avoiding giving you double-level messages.

It's important at this point to understand that every time you talk, all of you talks. Whenever you say words, your face, voice, body, breathing, and muscles are talking too. A simple diagram is as follows:

Verbal
    communication = words
Body/sound
    communication = facial expres-
                sion
                body position
                muscle tonus
                breathing
                tempo
                voice tone

What we are essentially talking about in these four patterns of communication are *double-level* messages. In all four instances your voice is saying one thing, and the rest of you is saying something else. Should you be interacting with someone who responds in double-level messages, too, the results of your interactions are often hurtful and unsatisfactory.

The troubled families I have known all have handled their communication through double-level messages. Double-level messages come through when a person holds the following views:

1. He has low self-esteem (low pot) and feels he is bad because he feels that way.
2. He feels fearful about hurting the other's feelings.
3. He worries about retaliation from the other.
4. He fears rupture of the relationship.
5. He does not want to impose.
6. He does not attach any significance to the person or the interaction itself.

In nearly all of these instances the person is unaware that he is giving double-level messages.

So the listener will be confronted by two messages, and the outcome of the communication will be greatly influenced by his response. In general, these are the possibilities: pick up the words and ignore the rest; pick up the non-word part and ignore the words; ignore the whole message by changing the subject, leaving, going to sleep, or commenting on the double-level nature of the message.

For example, if I have a smile on my face and the words, "I feel terrible," come out of my mouth, how will you respond? Picking up on the possibilities outlined in the last paragraph, you might respond to the words and say, "That's too bad," to which I can respond, "I was just kidding." Your second choice is to respond to the smile and say, "You look great," in which case I can say, "How can you say that!" Your third choice is to ignore the whole thing and go back to your paper, in which case I would respond, "What's the matter? Don't you give a damn?"

Your fourth choice is to comment on my double message: "I don't know what you're telling me. You're smiling, yet you tell me you're feeling bad. What gives?" In this case I have a chance to respond, "I didn't want to impose on you," and so on.

Let yourself imagine what kinds of results there could be if each of the above were the basis of communication between two people.

It is my belief that any family communication not leading to realness or straight, single levels of meaning cannot possibly lead to the trust and love that, of course, nourish members of the family.

Remember that what goes on in a moment in time between two people has many more levels than are visible on the surface. The surface represents only a small portion of what is going on, much in the same way that only a very small part of an iceberg is visible.

Thus in the following:

"Where were you last night?"
"You are always nagging me!"

Something is happening to each person in relation to himself. Something is happening to the perception by each of the other.

The ensuing direction of the relationship can go toward distrust, personal low pot, frustration, or, on the other hand, it can be the beginning of new depth and trust.

Let's take a closer look at these universal patterns of response people use to get around the threat of rejection. In all cases the individual is feeling and reacting to the threat, but because he doesn't want to reveal "weakness" he attempts to conceal it in the following ways:

1. *Placate* so the other person doesn't get mad;
2. *Blame* so the other person will regard you as strong (if he goes away it will be his fault, not yours);
3. *Compute* with the resultant message that you are attempting to deal with the threat as though it were harmless, and you are trying to establish your self-worth by using big words;
4. *Distract* so you ignore the threat, behaving as though it were not there (maybe if you do this long enough, it really will go away).

Our bodies have come to accommodate our feeling of self-worth whether we realize it or not. If our self-worth is in question, our bodies show it.

With this in mind I have devised certain physical stances to help people get in touch with parts of themselves that are obvious to other people but not to themselves. All I did was exaggerate and expand the facial and voice messages into the whole body and make it so exaggerated that nobody could miss it.

To help clarify the responses. . . , I have included a simple word-diagram with each descriptive section.

Placater

(1) Words	agree	("Whatever you want is okay. I am just here to make you happy.")
Body	placates	("I am helpless.")
Insides		("I feel like a nothing; without him I am dead. I am worthless.")

The *placater always* talks in an ingratiating way, trying to please, apologizing, never disagreeing, no matter what. He's a "yes man." He talks as though he could do nothing for himself; he must always get someone to approve of him. You will find later that if you play this role for even five minutes, you will begin to feel nauseous and want to vomit.

A big help in doing a good placating job is to think of yourself as really worth nothing. You are lucky just to be allowed to eat. You owe everybody gratitude, and you really are responsible for everything that goes wrong. You know you could have stopped the rain if you used your brains, but you don't have any. Naturally you will agree with any criticism made about you. You are, of course, grateful for the fact that anyone even talks to you, no matter what they say or how they say it. You would not think of asking anything for yourself. After all, who are you to ask? Besides, if you can just be good enough it will come by itself.

Be the most syrupy, martyrish, bootlicking person you can be. Think of yourself as being physically down on one knee, wobbling a bit, putting out one hand in a begging fashion, and be sure to have your head up so your neck will hurt and your eyes will become strained so in no time at all you will begin to get a headache.

When you talk in this position your voice will be whiny and squeaky because you keep your body in such a lowered position that you don't have enough air to keep a rich, full voice. You will be saying "yes" to everything, no matter what you feel or think. The placating stance is the body position that matches the placating response.

The *blamer* is a fault-finder, a dictator, a boss. He acts superior, and he seems to be saying, "If it weren't for you, everything would be all right." The internal feeling is one of tightness in the muscles and in the organs. Meanwhile the blood pressure is increasing. The voice is hard, tight, and often shrill and loud.

Good blaming requires you to be as loud and tyrannical as you can. Cut everything and everyone down.

As a blamer it would be helpful to think of yourself pointing your finger accusingly and to start your sentences with "You never do this or you always do that or why do you always or why do you never . . ." and so on. Don't bother about an answer. That is unimportant. The blamer is much more interested in throwing his weight around than really finding out about anything.

Whether you know it or not, when you are blaming you are breathing in little tight spurts, or holding your breath altogether, because your throat muscles are so tight. Have you ever seen a really first-rate blamer whose eyes were bulging, neck muscles and nostrils standing out, who was getting

Blamer

(2) Words	disagree	("You never do anything right. What is the matter with you?")
Body	blames	("I am the boss around here.")
Insides		("I am lonely and unsuccessful.")

Computer

(3) Words	ultrareasonable	("If one were to observe carefully, one might notice the workworn hands of someone present here.")
Body	computes	("I'm calm, cool, and collected.")
Insides		("I feel vulnerable.")

red and whose voice sounded like someone shoveling coal? Think of yourself standing with one hand on your hip and the other arm extended with your index finger pointed straight out. Your face is screwed up, your lips curled, your nostrils flared as you tell, call names, and criticize everything under the sun.... You don't really feel you are worth anything, either. So if you can get someone to obey you, then you feel you count for something.

The *computer* is very correct, very reasonable with no semblance of any feeling showing. He is calm, cool, and collected. He could be compared to an actual computer or a dictionary. The body feels dry, often cool, and disassociated. The voice is a dry monotone, and the words are likely to be abstract.

When you are a computer, use the longest words possible, even if you aren't sure of their meanings. You will at least sound intelligent. After one paragraph no one will be listening anyway. To get yourself really in the mood for this role, imagine that your spine is a long, heavy steel rod reaching from your buttocks to the nape of your neck, and you have a ten-inch-wide collar around your neck. Keep everything about yourself as motionless as possible, including your mouth. You will have to try hard to keep your hands from moving, but do it.

When you are computing, your voice will naturally go dead because you have no feeling from the cranium down. Your mind is bent on being careful not to move, and you are kept busy choosing the right words. After all, you should never make a mistake. The sad part of this role is that it seems to represent an ideal goal for many people. "Say the right words; show no feeling; don't react." ...

Whatever the *distracter* does or says is irrelevant to what anyone else is saying or doing. He never makes a response to the point. His internal feeling is one of dizziness. The voice can be singsong, often out of tune with the words, and can go up and down without reason because it is focused nowhere.

When you play the distracting role, it will help you to think of yourself as a kind of lopsided top, constantly spinning, but never knowing where you are going, and not realizing it when you get there. You are too busy moving your mouth, your body, your arms, your legs. Make sure you are never on the point with your words. Ignore everyone's questions; maybe come back with one of your own on a different

Distracter

(4) Words	irrelevant (the words make no sense)
Body	angular and off somewhere else
Insides	("Nobody cares. There is no place for me.")

subject. Take a piece of imaginary lint off someone's garment, untie shoelaces, and so on.

Think of your body going off in different directions at once. Put your knees together in an exaggerated knock-kneed fashion. This will bring your buttocks out, and make it easy for you to hunch your shoulders and have your arms and hands going in opposite directions.

At first this role seems like a relief, but after a few minutes of play, the terrible loneliness and purposelessness arise. If you can keep yourself moving fast enough, you won't notice it so much. . . .

As practice for yourself, take the four physical stances I have described, hold them for just sixty seconds and see what happens to you. Since many people are unaccustomed to feeling their body reactions, you may find at first that you are so busy thinking you aren't feeling. Keep at it, and you will begin to have the internal feelings you've experienced so many times before. Then the moment you are on your own two feet and are freely relaxed and able to move, you find your internal feeling changes.

It is my hunch that these ways of communicating are learned early in childhood. As the child tries to make his way through the complicated and often threatening world in which he finds himself, he uses one or another of these means of communicating. After enough use he can no longer distinguish his response from his feeling of worth or his personality.

Use of any of these four responses forges another ring in an individual's feeling of low self-worth or low pot. Attitudes prevalent in our society also reinforce these ways of communicat-ing—many of which are learned at our mother's knee.

"Don't impose; it's selfish to ask for things for yourself," helps to reinforce placating.

"Don't let anyone put you down; don't be a coward," helps to reinforce blaming.

"Don't be so serious. Live it up! Who cares?" helps to reinforce distracting.

At this point you may well be wondering if there is any hope for us at all if these four crippling modes of communication are all we have. Of course they are not.

There is a fifth response that I have called *leveling* or flowing. In this response all parts of the message are going in the same direction—the voice says words that match the facial expression, the body position, and the voice tone. Relationships are easy, free and honest, and there are few threats to self-esteem. With this response there is no need to blame, retreat into a computer, or to be in perpetual motion.

Of the five responses only the leveling one has any chance to heal ruptures, break impasses, or build bridges between people. And lest leveling seems too unrealistic to you, let me assure you that you can still placate if you choose, blame if you like, be on a head trip, or be distracting. The difference is you know what you are doing and are prepared to take the consequences for it.

So when you are leveling you apologize in reality when you realize you've done something you didn't intend. You are apologizing for an act, not for your existence. There are times when you need to criticize and evaluate. When you do this in a leveling way, you are evaluating an act, not blaming the person, and there is usually a new direction you have to offer. There are times when you're talking about intellectual kinds of things such as giving lectures, making explanations, giving directions, and so on, where precise word meanings are essential. When you are leveling in this area, you are still showing your feelings, moving freely while you're explaining. You aren't coming off like a machine. So many people who make their livings with their brains—scientists, mathematicians, accountants, teachers, and therapists—come off like machines and epitomize the computing response. In addition, there are times when you want to or need to change the subject. In the leveling response you can say what you want to instead of hopping all over the place.

The leveling response is real for whatever is. If a leveler says, "I like you," his voice is warm and he looks at you. If his words are, "I am mad as hell at you," his voice is harsh, and his face is tight. The message is single and straight.

Another aspect of the leveling response is that it represents a truth of the person at a moment in time. This is in contrast, for example, to a blaming response where the person is feeling helpless, but is acting angry—or is hurting, but is acting brave.

A third aspect of the leveling response is that it is whole, not partial. The body, sense, thoughts, and feelings all are shown, in contrast to computing, for example, where nothing moves but the mouth and that only slightly.

There is an integration, a flowing, an aliveness, an openness and what I call a *juiciness* about a person who is leveling. You trust him, you know where you stand with him, and you feel good in his presence. The position is one of wholeness and free movement. This response is the only one that makes it possible to live in an alive way, rather than a dead way.

Now, to help you distinguish more clearly between a given subject and the different ways of expressing oneself about that subject, let me present five ways of apologizing in the five ways of communicating. . . . Let's imagine that I have just bumped your arm.

Placating (looking down, wringing hands): "Please forgive me. I am just a clumsy oaf."

Blaming: "Ye gods, I just hit your arm! Keep it in next time so I won't hit it!"

Computing: "I wish to render an apology. I inadvertently struck your arm in passing. If there are any damages, please contact my attorney."

Distracting (looking at someone else): "Gee, some guy's mad. Must've got bumped."

Leveling (looking directly at the person): "I bumped you. I'm sorry. Are you hurt?"

Let's take another imaginary situation. I am your father, and there is something wrong in what you, my son, are doing.

Placating (coming up with a hushed voice, downcast face): "I'm—uh—uh—gosh, gee, Jim, I—am sorry—you feeling okay? You know—promise me you won't get mad—no, you're doing okay, it's just—maybe you could do a little better? Just a little, maybe? Hm?"

Blaming: "For Christ's sake, don't you know anything, you dumb cluck?"

Computing: "We are making a survey of our family efficiency. We find that in this department, namely with you, that efficiency is beginning to go down. Would you have any comments to make?"

Distracting (talking to his other son, standing next to Jim): "Say, Arnold, is your room about the same as Jim's? No, nothing wrong—I was just taking a walk through the house. Tell Jim to see his mother before he goes to bed."

Leveling: "Jim, your room is in bad shape. You haven't made your bed since yesterday. We need to stop, take a look, and see what's wrong."

It's anything but easy to break old habit patterns and become a leveler. One way in which you might be helped to achieve this goal is through learning what some of the fears are that keep you from leveling. To thwart the rejection we so fear, we tend to threaten ourselves in the following ways:

1. I might make a mistake.
2. Someone might not like it.
3. Someone will criticize me.
4. I might impose.
5. He will think I am no good.
6. I might be thought of as imperfect.
7. He might leave.

When you can tell yourself the following answers to the foregoing statements, you will have achieved real growth:

1. You are sure to make mistakes if you take any action, especially new action.
2. You can be quite sure that there will be someone who won't like

what you do. Not everyone likes the same things.
3. Yes, someone will criticize you. You really aren't perfect. Some criticism is useful.
4. Sure! Every time you are in the presence of another person, speak to him, and interrupt him, you impose!
5. So maybe he will think you're no good. Can you live through it? Maybe sometimes you aren't so hot. Sometimes the other person is "putting his trip on you." Can you tell the difference?
6. If you think of yourself as needing to be perfect, the chances are you will always be able to find imperfection.
7. So he leaves. Maybe he should leave, and anyway, you'll live through it.

These attitudes will give you a good opportunity to stand on your own two good feet. It won't be easy and it won't be painless, but it might make the difference as to whether or not you grow.

With no intention of being flippant, I do think that most of the things we use to threaten ourselves and that affect our self-worth turn out to be tempests in teapots. One way I helped myself through these threats was to ask myself if I would still be alive if all these imagined threats came true. If I could answer yes, then I was okay. I can answer yes to all of them now.

I will never forget the day I found out that lots of other people worried about these same silly threats as I did. I had thought for years I was the only one, and I kept myself busy trying to outwit them, and at the same time doing my best to conceal the threats.

My feeling was—what if somebody found out? Well, what if somebody did? We all use these same kinds of things to threaten ourselves.

By now you must realize that this isn't some kind of a magical recipe, but the leveling response is actually a way of responding to real people in real life situations that permit you to agree because you really do, not because you think you should; disagree because you really do, not because you think you won't make points unless you do; use your brain freely, but not at the expense of the rest of you; to change courses, not to get you off the hook, but because you want to and there is a need to do so.

What the leveling response does is make it possible for you to live as a whole person—real, in touch with your head, your heart, your feelings, and your body. Being a leveler enables you to have integrity, commitment, honesty, intimacy, competence, creativity, and the ability to work with real problems in a real way. The other forms of communication result in doubtful integrity, commitment by bargain, dishonesty, loneliness, shoddy competence, strangulation by tradition, and dealing in a destructive way with fantasy problems.

It takes guts, courage, some new beliefs, and some new skills to become a leveling responder. *You can't fake it.*

Unfortunately there is little in society that reinforces this leveling response. Yet people are actually hungry for this kind of straightness and honesty. When they become aware of it and are courageous enough to try it, distances between people are shortened.

I did not come to this formulation via religion or through the study of philosophy. I came to it through a tough, trial-and-error way, trying to help people who had serious life problems. I found that what healed people was getting them to find their hearts, feeling, their bodies, their brains, which once more brought them to their souls and thus to their humanity. They could then express themselves as whole people, which, in turn, helped them to gather feelings of self-worth (high pot), to nurturing relationships and satisfying outcomes.

None of these results is possible through the use of the four crippling ways of communication. I have found these, incidentally, as inevitable outcomes of the way authority is taught in families and reinforced by much of our society. What is so sad is that these four ways have become the most frequently used among people and are viewed by many as the most possible ways of achieving communication.

From what I have seen I've made some tentative conclusions about what to expect when I meet new groups of people. Fifty percent will say yes no matter what they feel or think (placate); 30 percent will say no, no matter what they feel or think (blame); 15 percent will say neither yes nor no and will give no hint of their feelings (compute); and $\frac{1}{2}$ percent will behave as if yes, no, or feeling did not exist (distracting). That leaves only $4\frac{1}{2}$ percent whom I can expect to be real and to level. My colleagues tell me I am optimistic, saying the leveling response is probably found in only 1 percent of our population. Remember this is not validated research. It is only a clinical hunch. In the vernacular it would seem we are all a bunch of crooks—hiding ourselves and playing dangerous games with one another.

At this point I want to make an even more drastic statement. If you want to make your body sick, become disconnected from other people, throw away your beautiful brain power, make yourself deaf, dumb, and blind, then using the four crippling ways of communication will in great measure help you to do it.

I feel very strongly as I write this. For me, the feelings of isolation, helplessness, feeling unloved, low pot, or incompetence comprise the real human evils of this world. Certain kinds of communication will continue this and certain kinds of communication can change it. What I am trying to do in this chapter is make it possible for each person to understand the leveling response so he can recognize and use it.

I would like to see each human being value and appreciate himself, feel whole, creative, competent, healthy, rugged, beautiful, and loving.

Despite the fact that I have exaggerated these different ways of communication for emphasis, and they may even seem amusing, I am deadly serious about the killing nature of the first four styles of communication.

Reading 1.2
Communication
The Context of Change
Dean C. Barnlund

Among the few universals that apply to man is this: That all men—no matter of what time or place, of what talent or temperament, of what race or rank—are continually engaged in making sense out of the world about them. Man, according to Nicholas Hobbs, "has to build defenses against the absurd in the human condition and at the same time find a scheme that will make possible reasonably accurate predictions of his own behavior and of the behavior of his wife, his boss, his professor, his physician, his neighbor, and of the policeman on the corner."[1] Although men may tolerate doubt, few can tolerate meaninglessness.

To survive psychically, man must conceive a world that is fairly stable, relatively free of ambiguity, and reasonably predictable. Some structure must be placed on the flow of impressions; events must be viewed from some perspective. Incoming sensations will be categorized, organized around some theme. Some facts will be noted and others neglected; some features will be emphasized and others minimized; certain relationships will appear reasonable, others unlikely or impossible. Meaning does not arise until experience is placed in some context.

Man is not a passive receptor, but an active agent in giving sense to sensation. The significance that any situation acquires is as much a result of what the perceiver brings to it as it is of the raw materials he finds there. Terms such as "personal constructs," "social schema," or "perceptual sets" have been used to identify the cognitive processes by which men render experience intelligible. As George Kelly notes, "Man looks at this world through transparent patterns or templets which he created and then attempted to fit over the realities of which the world is composed. The fit is not always good. But without such patterns the world appears to be such an undifferentiated

From Dean C. Barnlund, "Communication: The Context of Change," in Carl E. Larson and Frank E. X. Dance, eds., *Perspectives on Communication*, Shorewood, Wis.: Helix Press, 1968, pp. 24–40. Reprinted by permission.
[1] Nicholas Hobbs, "Sources of Gain in Psychotherapy," *American Psychologist*, (17, 1962), 74.

homogeneity that man is unable to make any sense out of it. Even a poor fit is more helpful to him than nothing at all."[2]

As the infant matures into adulthood he gradually acquires a picture of the world he inhabits and his place within it. Pervasive orientations—of trust or suspicion, of affection or hostility—are learned early, often at considerable pain, and through communication with significant other people. Every success or failure contributes in some way to his accumulating assumptions about the world and how it operates. Such cognitive predispositions are learned unconsciously, and most people are only vaguely aware of their profound effects. Yet they are, in the view of Roger Harrison, "the most important survival equipment we have."[3] Thus it is not events themselves, but how men construe events, that determines what they will see, how they will feel, what they will think, and how they will respond.

Such perceptual biases, taken together, constitute what has been called the assumptive world of the individual. The world men get inside their heads is the only world they know. It is the symbolic world, not the real world, that they talk about, fight about, argue about, laugh about. It is this world that drives them to cooperate or compete, to love or hate. Unless this symbolic world is kept open and responsive to continuing experience, men are forced to live out their lives imprisoned within the constructs of their own invention.

The worlds men create for themselves are distinctive worlds, not the same world. Out of similar raw materials each fabricates meanings according to the dictates of his own perceptual priorities. It is not surprising that nurtured in different families, informed by different sources, frightened by different dreams, inspired by different teachers, rewarded for different virtues, men should view the world so differently. The way men project private significance into the world can be readily illustrated. Here is a group of people asked to respond to an ordinary photograph showing adults of various ages, standing together, and looking up at a distant object. The experimenter asks, "What do you see?" "What does it mean?" Some of the viewers comment on the mood of the figures, reporting "grief," "hope," "inspiration," or "despair." Others notice the identity of the persons, describing them as "peasants," "members of a minority," "Mexicans," or "Russians." Still others see the "ages of man," a "worshipping family," or "three generations." Even at the objective level there is disagreement; some report three persons, some four, some five. When shown before lunch "hunger" is one of the first interpretations; after lunch this meaning is never assigned. A similar process of projection would seem to fit the varying reactions people have to a peace demonstration, Charles de Gaulle, a labor contract, the Hippies, or the Pill.

Two behavioral scientists, Hastorf and Cantril, studied the conflicting reactions of Princeton and Dartmouth students to a hotly contested game between their football teams. The students seemed not to have attended the same game, their perceptions were subservient to their personal loyalties.

[2] George A. Kelly, *The Psychology of Personal Constructs* (New York: W. W. Norton, 1955), pp. 8–9.
[3] Roger Harrison, "Defenses and the Need to Know," in Paul Lawrence and George V. Seiler, *Organizational Behavior and Administration* (Homewood, Illinois: Irwin and Dorsey), p. 267.

The investigators conclude: "It is inaccurate and misleading to say that different people have different attitudes toward the same 'thing.' For the 'thing' is *not* the same for different people whether the 'thing' is a football game, a presidential candidate, Communism, or spinach. . . . We behave according to what we bring to the occasion, and what each of us brings to the occasion is more or less unique. And except for these significances which we bring to the occasion, the happenings around us would be meaningless occurrences, would be 'inconsequential.'"[4]

While we are continually engaged in an effort after meaning, every perception is necessarily a private and incomplete one. No one ever sees all, for each abstracts in accordance with his past experience and emerging needs. Where men construe events similarly, they can expect to understand and agree readily; where they construe events differently, agreement is more difficult. In exploring the impact of cognitive styles upon communication, Triandis found that pairs of subjects who categorized objects similarly communicated more effectively than those who categorized them differently.[5]

Paradoxically, it is these differences in perception that make communication inevitable. If men saw the same facts in the same way, there would be no reason to talk at all. Certain rituals of recognition or flattery might interrupt the silence, but there would be no occasion for serious talk. There would be no experiences to share, no conflicts to negotiate. A simple experiment will demonstrate this idea. At the next conversational opportunity, agree completely, both in fact and feeling, with the person who has just expressed an opinion. (This is more difficult than many people imagine.) In a matter of seconds following this restatement, the conversation will grind to a halt, or someone will change the subject. The reason is clear: Where men see and feel alike there is nothing to share. Talk is primarily a means of confronting and exploring differences. Conversation moves from disagreement to disagreement, interrupted only occasionally to note areas of momentary concurrence.

It is not only inevitable that men communicate, but fortunate that they do so. The exposure to differences through communication, painful as it sometimes is, provides the only opportunity to test our private perceptions, to construct a total picture out of our separate visions, and to find new ways of negotiating unresolved problems.

Research on decision making illustrates how important communication is in improving human performance. Subjects in one of these studies solved a set of problems working alone, then through majority vote, and finally by discussing them in small groups.[6] The problems resembled those in everyday life; that is, they were difficult, emotionally involving, and presented a range of possible solutions. The results indicated that voting did not improve the quality of solutions reached by solitary effort, but group decisions were clearly superior to individual decisions. In some instances, groups of

[4] Albert Hastorf and Hadley Cantril, "They Saw a Game: A Case Study," *Journal of Abnormal and Social Psychology*, (49, 1954), 129–134.
[5] Harry Triandis, "Cognitive Similarity and Communication in a Dyad," *Human Relations*, (13, 1969), 175–183.
[6] Dean C. Barnlund, "A Comparative Study of Individual, Majority and Group Judgment," *Journal of Abnormal and Social Psychology*, (58, 1959), 55–60.

the least competent subjects were, through discussion, able to surpass the decisions made by the most talented person working alone. Subsequent research using executives in labor, government, education, and business confirmed these findings. Even groups composed of persons who were unable to solve *any* of the problems by themselves, made better group decisions than the most effective person working alone. That is, administrators with no ability to solve the test problems by themselves showed superior judgment when allowed to confer. Maximizing communicative opportunity produced superior judgments.

How can we account for these results? Careful study of the recorded conversations revealed a number of contributing factors: Groups had a wider range of information so that each person benefited from the knowledge of others. Every person had his own view of the problem, and sharing these perspectives enlarged the number of possible approaches. More solutions were proposed in the groups, supplying more alternatives from which to choose. The different biases of participants prevented any subject from suffering the consequences of his own prejudices. Finally, sharing opinions led to more critical examination of proposals. Where persons worked alone they could remain blind to their own errors, but groups quickly identified mistakes that would lead to wrong decisions.

After finishing the analysis, one further question arose: Why were the groups not infallible? Although this smacked of asking why men are not perfect, the question led to new findings. Two conditions accounted for most of the group errors. In some cases the groups lacked conflict, and, assuming that unanimity proved they were correct, did not discuss the problem. In others, despite the occurrence of conflict, the subjects lacked the patience or skill to resolve it, and compromised to avoid interpersonal antagonism. The absence of conflict or the inability to explore it prevented communication and thereby diminished the quality of decisions. In the vocabulary of science, communication among mature persons may be a necessary if not a sufficient condition for personal growth and social progress.

What, then, prevents men from transforming their differences into agreements? Why are facts so often distorted and disputed? What inhibits the flow of new ideas? What produces friction? Why is there so often an undercurrent of resistance when men talk? It is, I believe, because communication nearly always implies change. Aside from common social rituals, *men nearly always talk in a context of change.* What prompts communication is the desire for someone else to see our facts, appreciate our values, share our feelings, accept our decisions. Communication is initiated, consciously or unconsciously, to change the other person. If difference is the raw material of conversation, influence is its intent.

For most people, change is threatening. It is the old and familiar that is trusted; the novel and unknown that arouses alarm. "No one," John Dewey once wrote, "discovers a new world without forsaking an old one."[7] To change is to give up cherished values, to be left defenseless and forced to

---

[7] John Dewey, *Experience and Nature* (Chicago: Open Court Publishing Company, 1925), p. 246.

assume responsibility for a new organization of experience. The degree to which fear is aroused is usually proportional to the extent to which core values are placed in question. In some cases the fears may be quite specific, and can be articulated. More commonly, the threatened person is unable to identify the reason for his anxiety. Ordinarily threat arises from the source, the content, or the manner of communicating.

The mere presence of some people produces tension. Persons who are superior in age, power, wealth, appearance, esteem may create apprehension. Secretaries and lathe operators, medical interns and practice teachers are often incapable of accurate work while supervisors are observing their performance. There is evidence that people who control the destiny of others, such as parents, teachers, supervisors, provoke ego defensive reactions, quite apart from what they may say. The same seems to be the case for those who interrupt or reverse the direction of self-growth.[8] Threatening people, Landfield found, are those who perceive us as we once were, or now are and no longer wish to be.[9] Even status signs—the policeman's uniform, the judge's gavel, the executive's desk, the physician's stethoscope, the psychologist's tests—can arouse fear before or during interpersonal encounters. The presence of threat, of course, affects the depth and accuracy of communication. A number of studies demonstrate that where superiors are feared, information is withheld or distorted.[10] Thus where human institutions proliferate status differences or personal habits aggravate them, communication may be more difficult because of the repressive context in which it occurs.

The substance of communication, that is, the subject being discussed, may also trigger defenses. A new fact tests an old fact; a new attitude challenges an existing one. New proposals may provoke fear of an unknown future, fear of possible failure, fear of loss of power or prestige. No matter how frustrating the present, its dangers are palpable and familiar. Time has permitted some adjustment to them. But to turn in new directions is to face a host of uncertainties. Even consideration of a new program implies an attack on those who created or support an existing program. "We tend to maintain our cognitive structures in relatively stable form," writes Joseph Precker, "and select and interact with those who do not attack these structures." When such encounters were unavoidable he found they aroused defensiveness or rejection of the attacker.[11] Any new or unassimilated thought challenges the assumptions on which behavior is based, and no one is so secure that he cannot be aroused at the thought of revising favored values. Thus, even where people are not initially hostile and try to avoid unnec-

[8] Jacob Hurwitz, Alvin Zander, and Bernard Hymovitch, "Some Effects of Power on the Relations Among Group Members," in D. Cartwright and A. Zander, Group Dynamics: Research and Theory (New York: Row Peterson, 1960).

[9] A. Landfield, "A Movement Interpretation of Threat," Journal of Abnormal and Social Psychology, (49, 1954), 529–532.

[10] See, for example, John Thibaut and Henry Riecken, "Authoritarianism, Status, and the Communication of Aggression," Human Relations, (8, 1955), 113–133; Arthur Cohen, "Upward Communication in Experimentally Created Hierarchies," Human Relations, (11, 1958), 41–53; William Read, "Upward Communication in Industrial Hierarchies," Human Relations, (15, 1962), 3–16.

[11] Joseph Precker, "The Automorphic Process and the Attribution of Values," Journal of Personality, (21, 1953), 356–363.

essary friction, the topic, because of its emotional significance, may trigger resistance.

Beyond the source and content lies the manner in which men talk. One cannot separate who is speaking and what is talked about from the way differences are expressed. Matter and manner interact to produce meaning. Although all men have their own rhetoric, preferring some interpersonal strategies to others, a number of techniques that complicate communication can be identified.[12] Since interpersonal attitudes are conveyed both by verbal and nonverbal codes, any discrepancy in these codes may be regarded as a warning signal. Warm words are spoken in a cold voice. Frank statements are offset by calculating glances. Expressions of respect are contradicted with every interruption. Against the deceit that is evident in a confusion of codes, men become apprehensive and guarded in their own messages.

An attitude of infallibility discourages communication. The dogmatic assertion of difference leaves no opportunity for influence to move in both directions. Where men claim, "There is only one conclusion," "It all boils down to," "The only course of action is," there will be negligible exploration of differences. The person who is impervious to the words of others while demanding sympathetic consideration of his own denies his associates any significant role in communication. They are forced to disregard their experience, deny their feelings, censor their thoughts. Since unquestioned statements are untested statements, the dogmatic person appears to be more interested in triumph than in truth.

Messages that convey a manipulative purpose also subvert communication. A calculated use of argument, a carefully phrased idea, a solicitous manner, a restrained reaction, all indicate that someone is being maneuvered into a predetermined position. Sooner or later the manipulated recognizes his manipulator. He begins to feel regarded as an object, not as a person. He becomes suspicious, emotionally tense, and verbally devious himself. That the manipulator is sometimes unaware of his own desires to control others, does not reduce the threat he poses for them.

Information normally flows between communicants in both directions: The man who speaks also listens. But often, through deliberate design or personal preference, interaction is blocked so that one person sends all the messages, the other only receives them. The captain commands, the soldier obeys; the teacher lectures, the student takes notes. A letter from a friend who is an educational consultant in India illustrates how far it is possible to carry this kind of communicative irresponsibility. His daughter, raised in one of the great cattle provinces of Western Canada, is attending school in India.

Thora came home the other day doggedly repeating to herself, "A cow is a big animal with four legs and two horns. It is the most useful of all animals. The feet of the cow are called hoofs." I asked what she was doing, repeating this over and over again, and she replied

[12] Efforts to identify nonfacilitating techniques may be found in Jack Gibb, "Defensive Communication," *Journal of Communication*, (11, 1961), 141–148; in Frank Miyamoto, Laura Crowell, and Allan Katcher, "Communicant Behavior in Small Groups," *Journal of Communication*, (7, 1957), 151–160; and in Phillip Lichtenberg, "Emotional Maturity as Manifest in Ideational Interaction," *Journal of Abnormal and Social Psychology*, (51, 1955), 298–301.

that this was nature study and she had to memorize the cow. The teacher will not tolerate improvised replies, but the students must jump up smartly beside their desks and repeat exactly what was copied from the blackboard the day before. It sounds fantastic, but the end of the system is to stifle initiative, destroy creativity and engender a violent dislike for learning.[13]

One-way communication implies, of course, that meanings in the nervous system of one person can be deposited in the nervous system of another. Unfortunately communication is not this simple. Men differ not only in experience, but in their habits of speech as well. The only way to arrive at common meanings is through mutual accommodation. Each must share some responsibility for calibrating his words and intentions with the other.

Limiting communication to the sending of messages impoverishes the process and renders at least one participant impotent. Studies by Leavitt and Mueller illustrate some of the difficulties that attend one-way communication.[14] Persons attempting to give even the simplest instructions found their orders were inaccurately executed, that errors of interpretation could not be corrected, and that this condition produced extremely low morale. It is not difficult to estimate the cause of the low morale: For someone to receive confusing or complicated information and to be unable to clarify it, especially when it affects his performance or status, can be unnerving. Since all messages are ambiguous in some respect, cutting off efforts to

confirm their meaning leaves the receiver without protection in a potentially punishing situation.

A threatening atmosphere is probable, also, in encounters in which one of the communicants maintains considerable emotional distance. The person who is coldly objective or who refuses to disclose his own feelings is likely to be viewed with suspicion. To be treated as a set of facts or as a problem to be solved, rather than as a human being, seldom contributes to interpersonal rapport. Such emotional distancing creates, to use a phrase of Martin Buber's, an I-It rather than an I-Thou relation. One is not likely to approach or expose himself to an unresponsive facade. It is safer to remain on guard in the company of those who are themselves guarded. Any verbal indiscretion or spontaneous revelation may give an advantage or be used against one. As interaction continues, participants draw farther and farther apart from any real confrontation with their differences.

The most familiar form of threat is found in a highly evaluative communication context. There is continual appraisal. Remarks are judged rather than understood. Conversation becomes cross-examination. Criticism may be given directly through attack, or indirectly through sarcasm or innuendo. (The latter, because of its ambiguity, is far harder to handle.) Compliments seem only slightly less corrupting than insults, for in one case the receiver modifies his behavior to gain further rewards and in the other to avoid further punishments. In either case he is encouraged to distort his judgment. It becomes hazardous to be honest, to be open, to be original. Ideas are suppressed and remarks tailored

---

[13] Personal correspondence.
[14] Harold Leavitt and Ronald Mueller, "Some Effects of Feedback on Communication," *Human Relations*, (4, 1951), 401–410.

to fit the expectations of others. The result is to diminish honest contribution to the conversation, and to isolate men from their own experience.

A more subtle form of threat occurs when conversation is converted into a struggle over identity. At one level, talk flows around a common interest or problem; at another, communication becomes a competition for status. Participants present their credentials and challenge those of others. In organizational life these claims relate to the respective power, intelligence, skill, or rank of the communicants. But even in ordinary encounters, men verbally compete to determine who is in better physical condition, who has the more talented children, who can consume more alcohol, or who is more attractive to the opposite sex. Communication becomes an occasion for asserting and validating personal identity rather than for testing what we know. Status-reminding phrases, such as "I've devoted years to this matter," "I've had much more experience," or "You wouldn't be able to appreciate," are likely to invite reaction in kind. "Once the 'proving' syndrome is present," according to Paul Goodman, "the boys are quite out of touch with the simplest realities."[15] People who constantly remind us of who they are and of who we are—especially when who they are is superior, and who we are is inferior—threaten the concept we have of ourselves. When identity is challenged, few have enough insight or strength to resist. What might have become a productive conversation turns into an interaction of roles and of facades. Even the expression of affection can turn into a competitive affair:

"I love you," she said.
"I adore you," he said.
"I love you more," she said.
"More than what?" he said.
"Than you love me," she said.
"Impossible," he said.
"Don't argue," she said.
"I was only . . ." he said.
"Shut up," she said.[16]

In short, the prospect of communication may threaten people for a number of reasons: because such interactions occur with persons endowed with considerable power and status; because the underlying purpose is to change perceptions that have personal significance; because the communicative approach prevents a full and sympathetic exploration of differences. Any one of these factors alone can produce an undercurrent of tension in human affairs; but in many instances all three combine to arouse deeper anxiety.

Through all there runs a common theme. Though manifested differently, there is always a challenge to the personal integrity and self-respect of the person in communication. To talk to some people is dangerous because they control what it is possible for us to be and do. To talk about some topics is hazardous for it exposes one to differences in attitude and feeling. To talk in some ways is disturbing for one must guard continually against being exposed and attacked. But it is at the intersection of all three that men are most vulnerable: where a sensitive topic must be discussed with a powerful person in an emotionally charged atmosphere.

---

[15] Paul Goodman, *Growing Up Absurd* (New York: Random House, 1960), p. 206.

[16] John Ciardi, "Manner of Speaking," *Saturday Review*, (December 23, 1967).

During a lifetime of painful encounters people acquire an extensive repertoire of defensive strategies.[17] At low levels of stress men tend to remain open to new facts, flexible in interpretation, creative in response. As the perceived threat increases, they narrow their vision, resist certain kinds of information, distort details to fit their own biases, even manufacture evidence to bolster their preconceptions. The old, whether appropriate or not, is favored over the new. Anxiety is aroused when a person, in encounters with others, confronts perceptions that are beyond his capacity to assimilate. As Gregory Bateson has suggested, "This is a terrifying moment . . . , you've been climbing up a ladder, you knew it was an unsound ladder and now you're asked to step off it and you don't really know there's going to be another ladder—even if the ladder you were on was a rather unsound one. This is terror."[18] Defenses protect the individual against facts that might otherwise undermine the system of assumptions that give stability and significance to his experience.

Not all defending behavior, of course, is defensive. Most men hold tentative conclusions about many issues. We believe that certain ways of looking at the world and at ourselves have some credibility. At any time we may voice these opinions. If, when confronted with opinions that differ from our own, we can explore these differences quietly, comfortably, thoroughly, and with the aim of testing the validity of our own beliefs, then we are only defending an opinion to reach more reliable conclusions. However, if when confronted with disagreement, we find it difficult to examine that thought or feeling, find the opposing view arousing us emotionally, find our hearts racing and our minds frantically seizing upon arguments, find we cannot reply calmly and without antagonism, the reaction is probably defensive. Words are being used to protect rather than to test private judgment.

Some defensive techniques are conscious; most of them are unconscious. Each person has his own hierarchy of tactics to which he retreats when faced with inadmissible perceptions. These defenses, provoked in a context of change, constitute the major barriers to communication among men. When attacked, as Paul Tournier notes, "Each of us does his best to hide behind a shield."

For one it is a mysterious silence which constitutes an impenetrable retreat. For another it is facile chit-chat so that we never seem to get near him. Or else, it is erudition, quotations, abstractions, theories, academic argument, technical jargon; or ready-made answers, trivialities, or sententious and patronizing advice. One hides behind his timidity, so that we cannot find anything to say to him; another behind a fine self-assurance which renders him less vulnerable. At one moment we have recourse to our intelligence, to help us to juggle with words. Later on we pretend to be stupid so that we cannot reply. . . . It is possible to hide behind one's advanced years, or behind one's university degree, one's political office, or the necessity of nursing one's reputation. A woman can hide behind her startling beauty, or behind

---

[17] Men defend themselves intrapersonally as well as interpersonally. The principal forms of such inner defense—introjection, identification, repression, denial, regression, reaction-formation, displacement—will not be treated here. It is the character of defensive behavior in interpersonal relationships that is our major concern.

[18] Gregory Bateson, lecture at San Francisco State College, 1959.

her husband's notoriety; just as, indeed, a husband can hide behind his wife.[19]

One of the principal forms of defense is to avoid communicative contact altogether. It is unlikely that anyone reading these words has not, on some occasion, deliberately avoided certain persons. It may have been a teacher, a parent, a supervisor, or, depending on circumstances, anyone with the ability to contradict, to embarrass, to attack us. Selective communication—Whites talking with Whites, Republicans with Republicans, Generation with Generation, Physicians with Physicians—greatly reduces the prospect of having to cope with discrepant or damaging points of view.

Even when contact cannot be avoided, it is possible to resist exposure by remaining silent. If a person does not speak he cannot expose himself or his judgments to public scrutiny. By retreating into his own private world he can remain untouched by the worlds of others. Theodore Newcomb has identified the process of communicative avoidance, whether of persons or topics, as "autistic hostility."[20] Confrontation is avoided to protect prevailing attitudes. In talking together people run the risk of understanding one another, hence of having to alter existing prejudices. Fraternizing with the enemy or socializing with competitors is traditionally avoided lest one become incapable of manipulating and mistreating them on other occasions.

A kind of psychic withdrawal is also possible. In this case the person never really presents himself as he is. According to Ronald Laing, "He never quite says what he means or means what he says. The part he plays is always not quite himself."[21] Where this withdrawal occurs, there is often an undercurrent of nonverbal signs that express defensive feelings. Recent research shows that people who wish to avoid communication choose to sit at a greater distance from others than those who wish to interact.[22] Tension-reducing body movements and gestures which serve no instrumental purpose increase.[23] Any act, from smoking a cigarette to doodling on a note pad, may reflect developing resistance. Research on mutual glances shows that eye contact is reduced when persons are in competitive, embarrassing, or critical encounters with others.[24] Thus many nonverbal indicators may convey the defensive attitudes of another person.

Just short of the verbal forms of resistance lies the noncommital reply. Such phrases as "Uh-huh," "I guess so," "Maybe," and "Oh yeah," fill the void left by a preceding question, but reveal little of the thought or feeling of the respondent. They provide an escape route, for at the moment of utterance they convey only an ambiguous neutrality; later, according to the shifting intent of the speaker, they may be given a variety of meanings.

Yet men also talk to protect themselves from confronting differences.

[19] Paul Tournier, The Meaning of Persons (New York: Harper & Row, 1957), p. 219.
[20] Theodore Newcomb, "Autistic Hostility and Social Reality," Human Relations, (1, 1947), 69–86.

[21] Ronald Laing, The Divided Self (Chicago: Quadrangle, 1960).
[22] Howard Rosenfeld, "Effect of Approval-Seeking Induction on Interpersonal Proximity," Psychological Reports, (17, 1965), 120–122.
[23] Maurice Krout, "An Experimental Attempt to Determine the Significance of Unconscious Manual Symbolic Movements," Journal of General Psychology, (51, 1954), 121–152.
[24] Ralph Exline and Lewis Winters, "Affective Relations and Mutual Glances in Dyads," in S. Tomkins and C. Izard (eds.), Affect, Cognition, and Personality (New York: Springer, 1965).

Words become a substitute for, rather than a means to, understanding. People spin verbal cocoons around themselves that disquieting ideas cannot penetrate. One person describes it this way: "If, for example, I can talk at such an abstract level that few can determine what I am saying, then I must have high intelligence. This is especially true if no one can understand me. The reason I could not communicate was that I did not want to."[25] Men often talk compulsively, and through long and frequent repetitions leave others no chance to reflect on what was said, to explore their own reactions, or to answer objections. Opponents are overwhelmed and defeated in a rush of words. Sometimes this takes the form of counterattacks, with the defensive person placing the burden of proof upon the opposition. By turning attention to others and exposing their weakness he hopes to hide his own vulnerability.

Conversational detours around painful topics are not uncommon. This may be done consciously, as in the case of the hostess who steers talk away from religious or political topics. More commonly it is done unconsciously by people who are unaware of the threat they seek to avoid. The essential point of a remark is disregarded, and some tangential or entirely new thought is introduced. Parents who fear discussing sex with their children, or supervisors who prefer not to know about critical failures of their subordinates, often rely upon topical control to neutralize communication. Each time a threatening or sensitive comment is made talk is turned abruptly in a new direction. Men have become so skillful

[25] Personal correspondence.

at defensively diverting conversation into painless channels that some are able to avoid meaningful interaction on nearly every vital issue that touches their lives.

Men also hide from each other through communicating by formula. Talk is prompted not by inner necessity, but by social convention. Everyone is familiar with the meaningless phrases used in social greetings. But this same verbal game may be extended to cover more serious encounters. Phrases are uttered and repeated, but when examined turn out to be empty. Flattery substitutes for frankness. There is much moralizing and sloganizing. Instead of examining differences, communicants obscure them in large abstractions that permit a multitude of interpretations. A kind of doubletalk preserves the illusion of confrontation while preventing it from ever occurring. There is often an interaction of roles rather than of persons. When people speak as parents, professors, as physicians, or as political candidates, listeners are likely to discount or mistrust much of what is said. Their remarks are seen as a consequence of their position, not of their personal experience. Of all the defenses, this currently seems most disruptive of efforts to reach across races and generations.

There is also the use of indirection. Instead of speaking frankly, men speak in double meanings. At the explicit level, one idea is transmitted; at the implicit level another idea, often the opposite. The most familiar forms include kidding and sarcasm. Humor, despite its high reputation as a form of recreational communication, often serves defensive and destructive ends. Verbal indirection is almost an unassailable stratagem, for anyone who takes the implied meaning seriously may be accused of projecting false interpretations of it. With a few oblique comments, efforts to openly explore differences may be totally blocked.

Defensive behavior is characteristic of some men all of the time, and of all men some of the time. Everyone must build the house of his own consciousness to interpret events around him. It is this "personal cosmology" that stands between us and the unknown and unacceptable. With such a guidance system events become recognizable and comprehensible. Those who perceive reality on different terms—as everyone does—alarm us because they shake the stability of our system. Defenses, note Kahn and Cannell, "are designed in large part to help us to protect ourselves against making some undesirable revelation or against putting ourselves in an unfavorable light. They are man's methods of defending himself against the possibility of being made to look ridiculous or inadequate. And in most cases we are not content merely to avoid looking inadequate, we also want to appear intelligent, thoughtful, or in possession of whatever other virtues are relevant to the situation from our point of view."[26] Confronted with difference, men may deny it, obscure it, confuse it, or evade it in order to protect their own assumptive world against the meanings of others.

Unfortunately, to the extent that men insulate themselves from the worlds that others know, they are imprisoned within their own defenses. They become blind to the limits of their own knowledge, and incapable of incorporating new experience. They are forced to repeat the same old ways of thinking because they result from the same old ways of seeing. Interaction loses the significance it might have. "This shutup self, being isolated," writes Ronald Laing, "is unable to be enriched by outer experience, and so the whole inner world comes to be more and more impoverished, until the individual may come to feel he is merely a vacuum."[27] Without access to the experience and perceptions of others, the individual deprives himself of the raw material of growth. Defenses corrupt the only process by which we might extend and deepen our experience. Until we can hear what others say, we cannot grow wiser ourselves.

To appreciate the full significance of incomplete communication in organizational life, another factor must be added. It is this: The higher men rise, the fewer the problems with which they have direct contact, and the more they must rely on the words of others. Unfortunately, as men assume greater power their higher status increases the difficulty in obtaining reliable accounts from others, and increases their own capacity to shield themselves from unpleasant information. Given a superior who prefers reassurance and a subordinate who fears to speak out, there is every reason to expect censored and distorted reports. Yet it is imperative that those in high places cope with realities rather than defensive fantasies.

What, then, can be done to create conditions in which men are not afraid to communicate? How can the destructive cycle of threat and defense be

---

[26] Robert Kahn and Charles Cannell, *The Dynamics of Interviewing* (New York: Wiley, 1957), 6.

[27] Laing, *op cit.*, 75.

broken? Are there conditions that encourage men to respond to each other more creatively, so that differences can widen and deepen human experience? Can self-protective encounters be converted into self-enriching ones?

To reduce defenses, threat must be reduced. Such threats, as suggested earlier, spring from the source, the content, or the manner of communicating. Where it is the person who threatens, it is usually because differences in status exist, are introduced, or accentuated. For this reason groups and organizations ought regularly to review their internal structure to see if differences in authority are essential to or destructive of effective performance. Differences in rank are often multiplied or emphasized without regard for their inhibiting and distorting effects on the flow of information and ideas. Studies of organizational behavior suggest that those marked by severe competition for status often have serious problems of communication.[28] Status barriers, however, may dissolve in the face of facilitating interpersonal attitudes.

Where the threat arises from different perceptions of problems and policies, there are ways of rendering these differences less disruptive. Proposals can be made as specific as possible to counteract fears of an uncertain future; they can be introduced gradually to reduce the amount of risk involved; they can be initiated experimentally so that failure can be remedied; they can include guarantees against the loss of personal prestige and power. Every new idea, since it is an implicit criticism of an old idea, may disturb those responsible for the

prevailing view; but it is possible to innovate without attacking unnecessarily those associated with former policies.

Neither the source nor the subject, however, is as critical as the climate in which interaction occurs. Communication as a physical fact produces no magic; words can lead toward destructive or productive outcomes depending on the attitudes that surround them. Where the object is to secure as complete, as frank, as creative an interaction of experience as possible, the following attitudes would seem to promote communication in a context of change.

Human understanding is facilitated where there is a willingness to become involved with the other person. It means to treat him as a person, not as an object; to see him as a man, not as a number, a vote, or a factor in production. It is to regard him as a value in himself, rather than a means to some other value. It is to prize his experience and his needs. Most of all, it is to consider and explore his feelings. In practical terms it means one is willing to take time, to avoid interruptions, to be communicatively accessible. Dozens of superficial and fragmentary conversations do not encourage a meeting of minds. There must be as much respect for his experience as we expect for our own. Since it is the loss of self-esteem that men fear most, such respect can do much to reduce the motivation for defensive interaction.

Communication is facilitated when there is a frank and full exposure of self. It is when men interact in roles, speaking as they believe they should rather than as they feel, that communication is often corrupted. In the

[28] Read, *op cit.*

words of Sidney Jourard, "We say that we feel things we do not feel. We say that we did things we did not do. We say that we believe things we do not believe."[29] We present, in short, persons that we are not. As one person retreats behind his false self—performing his lines, weighing his words, calculating his movements—the danger signs are recognized. Rarely does the other person fail to detect them. In an atmosphere of deceit, his suspicion is aroused and defenses go up. He begins to edit his thoughts, censor his feelings, manipulate his responses, and assume the rituals and mask of his office. Not only does communication stop, but mistrust lingers on to corrupt future encounters. Afterwards each says to himself, "I don't believe him," "I don't trust him," "I will avoid him in the future." This pattern accounts for much of the communicative isolation of parent and child, teacher and student, Black and White. It may also be the reason why interaction is so often accompanied by an undercurrent of strain, for it takes considerable energy to sustain both a false and a real self.

In contrast, defenses tend to disintegrate in an atmosphere of honesty. There are no inconsistent messages. What is said is what is known, what is felt, what is thought. Pretenses are dropped and contrivance ceases. Instead the effort is to express, as spontaneously and accurately as possible, the flow of thought and feeling. In the absence of deceit, there is less reason to distort or deny in reply. A genuine interaction of experience can occur. Much of the tension goes out of personal relationships. Communication becomes something to seek rather than something to avoid. Through talk it becomes possible to learn more about ourselves and more about the issues we face as men.

The willingness to be transparent leads to a further condition that promotes healthy interaction. In social encounters men see their purposes in many ways: some as manipulative, some as dominating, some as competitive, some as impressive, some as protective. People seldom talk for more than a few moments without exposing their underlying communicative strategy. Most of our defenses are designed to prevent damage to the symbolic self that occurs in the face of these depreciating motives. But an attitude of mutuality can also be heard, and heard loud and clear. This attitude is manifest in many ways: whenever there is patience rather than impatience, whenever there is a tentative rather than dogmatic assertion of opinion, whenever there is curiosity rather than indifference for alternative views, whenever there is a creative rather than inflexible approach to arguments. Where there is a feeling of mutual involvement among communicative equals, defenses are unlikely to interfere with the pursuit of new meanings.

Understanding is also promoted when people assume their full communicative responsibilities. Now what does that mean? Simply that one will listen as well as speak, that he will try to understand as well as try to be understood. There is little doubt among specialists that listening is by far the harder communicative task. Then why is it so often assigned to the younger, the weaker, the less competent? Usually it is the student who must

[29] Sidney Jourard, *The Transparent Self* (New York: Van Nostrand, 1964).

understand the teacher, the employee who must understand the supervisor, the patient who must understand the doctor, the young who must understand the old. In response to an essay "On Being an American Parent," one college student wrote the following lines as part of a "Letter to the Editor."

> Your paragraph under "Listen" very well sums up what I'm trying to say. I could never tell my parents anything, it was always "I'm too busy . . . too tired . . . that's not important . . . that's stupid . . . can't you think of better things. . . . " As a result, I stopped telling my parents anything. All communication ceased.
>
> I have only one important plea to parents. . . . *Listen, listen,* and *listen again.* Please, I know the consequences and I'm in hell.[30]

In instance after instance, the heavier communicative burden is forced upon the weaker, and the easier load is assumed by the stronger. It is not surprising that such exploitation should occasionally arouse defensive reactions.

Research in the behavioral sciences gives consistent support to the principle that two-way, as compared with one-way, communication produces more accurate understanding, stimulates a greater flow of ideas, corrects misunderstandings more efficiently, and yields a higher level of morale. Why, then, do men so often block feedback? Partly out of habit. In many interpersonal encounters listening means no more than a passive monitoring of the conversation, a time in which men prepare their next remarks. Partly we prevent feedback because of fear. It is upsetting to find

how confusing our instructions have been, how inconsistent our words and deeds, how irritating our actions sometimes are. Where receivers have been given a chance to talk back after long periods of following orders, they usually respond at first with hostility. Yet the easing of communicative restrictions, in most instances, quickly restores a constructive and cooperative relationship.

On the national scene these days we hear much about the need for more dialogue. Many are skeptical of this demand. Has there not always been the right of free speech, free access to the platform for every advocate? True, but freedom to speak is not freedom to influence. For genuine dialogue there must be someone to talk, but also someone to listen. To speak is an empty freedom—as racial clashes and political demonstrations should remind us—unless there is someone willing to hear. And to reply in ways that prove that what was said has made a difference.

Within the intimacy of the therapeutic relationship—where communicative principles are tested at every moment—this premise seems equally valid. Again, it is not the talking that appears to accomplish the cure but association with someone capable of hearing. To be with someone who is truly willing to listen, who concentrates sensitively on all that is said, is no longer to need defenses. Such listening, of course, involves the risk of change. No one can leave the safety and comfort of his own assumptive world and enter that of another without running the risk of having his own commitments questioned. Not only questioned, but perhaps altered. To communicate fully with another human

---

[30] *Time*, December 22, 1967, 7.

being, since it entails the risk of being changed oneself, is to perform what may be the most courageous of all human acts.

Communication is facilitated when there is a capacity to create a nonevaluative atmosphere. Defenses are provoked not so much by the expectation of difference, as by the expectation of criticism. "The major barrier to interpersonal communication," Carl Rogers has suggested, "is our very natural tendency to judge, to evaluate, to approve, or disapprove the statement of the other person or group." Under the surface of many, if not most, conversations there runs an undercurrent of censure. If we differ, one of us, usually the other fellow, must be wrong, must be stupid, must be incompetent, must be malicious. In so polarized a setting, where conversation becomes cross-examination, it is not surprising that men speak cautiously, incompletely, ambiguously; it is not surprising that with such critical preoccupations they listen suspiciously, partially, vaguely, to what is actually said. "The stronger our feelings," continues Rogers, "the more likely it is there will be no mutual element in the communication. There will be just two ideas, two feelings, two judgments, missing each other in psychological space."[31] When people recognize that they will not be forced beyond their own limits, when they see that their meanings will be respected and understood, when they feel that others will help in exploring difficult or dangerous experiences, they can begin to drop their defenses.

As the atmosphere becomes less evaluative, men are more likely to express and examine a wider range of differences without distortion. Where the intent is to comprehend rather than to attack, communication becomes a source of benefit rather than harm. In a permissive climate people feel comfortable, feel respected, feel secure enough to talk openly. "Conveying assurance of understanding," writes Anatol Rapoport, "is the first step in the removal of threat."[32] Research done on the attributes of helpful people indicates that they are easy to talk with, maximize areas open to discussion, minimize embarrassment, and seldom disapprove.[33]

In such trusting relationships men can develop empathy. They can participate in each other's experience, sharing the assumptions, the perspectives, and the meanings that events hold for them. This is not to insist that evaluation always be avoided, for decisions must be made about facts, theories, policies, even people. It is only to argue that mutual understanding should precede mutual evaluation. Problems cannot be solved until they are understood, and highly critical attitudes inhibit the communication of problems.

It appears that whether communication promotes understanding and affection, or blocks understanding and builds defenses, depends more on the assumptions than on the techniques of the communicator.[34] Or, rather, it is to say that technique cannot be divorced from assumption: As men assume, so will they communicate. Where men

[31] Carl Rogers, *On Becoming a Person* (Boston: Houghton Mifflin, 1961), p. 54.

[32] Anatol Rapoport, *Fights, Games and Debates* (Ann Arbor: University of Michigan Press, 1960).
[33] Edwin Thomas, Norman Polansky and Jacob Kounin, "The Expected Behavior of a Potentially Helpful Person," *Human Relations*, (8, 1955), 165–174.
[34] Dean C. Barnlund, *Interpersonal Communication* (Boston: Houghton Mifflin, 1968), pp. 613–641.

presume their knowledge to be complete or infallible, there is no communication or only a manipulative concern for others. Where men presume—as we know to be the case—that their knowledge is fragmentary and uncertain, genuine communication can occur. To recognize the limits of one's own facts and feelings is to become curious about the facts and feelings of others. At such moments men are likely to be open, honest, trusting, empathic, not because of some altruistic motive, but because it is the only way to correct and to extend their own perceptions of the world. Each stands to gain; the speaker because he can test what he believes and because it is rewarding to be understood; the listener because he can broaden his experience and because it is stimulating to understand.

Every significant human crisis begins or ends in a communicative encounter of one kind or another. It is here that differences are voiced. It is here that differences threaten. It is here that defenses are raised, and men embittered. But it is here, too, that differences may be welcomed. It is here that words may be heard. It is here that understanding may be reached, that men may cross the distance that divides them. "In my civilization," wrote Antoine de Saint Exupéry, "he who is different from me does not impoverish me—he enriches me."[35]

[35] Antoine de Saint Exupéry, *Airman's Odyssey* (New York: Reynal and Hitchcock, 1939), p. 420.

Action Steps: Applications

1. Both the chapter and the Barnlund reading discuss the differences between one-way and two-way communication. With your classmates attempt the following experiment:
   A. Have the instructor or someone designated prepare two simple drawings on two separate sheets of paper.
   B. Select a sender and place him/her either behind a screen or with his/her back to the class. Have the sender describe the drawing so that members of the class can reproduce it. No feedback is permitted and no sounds should be made.
   C. Select another sender to describe the second drawing. He/she may face the class, and questions and answers will be allowed.
   D. Compare your reactions and findings to those described in the chapter text and by Barnlund.
2. Meet in small groups (4–6 people) and discuss the types of problems that make it difficult for two people to understand each other. List at least five reasons for potential failures to communicate. Check your list against ideas cited in the chapter and the readings. Were any of the problems cited by Satir mentioned?
3. In your small group discuss the ten propositions as they are reflected in the two readings. How are these characteristics related to the

components in the circular process model of interpersonal communication (Figure 1.1)?

4. Work in pairs. For one minute, one of you should attempt *no* communication to the other (without leaving the room). The partner should keep time and just watch. Then reverse the roles. The minute will seem like a long time. Discuss with your partner how you felt in the two roles, what you saw your partner do and how you interpreted it, and your evaluation of Proposition 1.

5. A great deal of data in interpersonal communication can be labeled "common sense." In small groups, discuss whether what is common sense to one person is necessarily that to another. Select examples of commonsense statements from this book and compare your views.

6. Individually, assess your communication strengths and weaknesses. Be as honest with yourself as possible. In what areas are you satisfied and what areas would you like to change or improve? Write down three or four goals for yourself in this course. In small groups, share the goals that you feel comfortable discussing. We predict a great deal of similarity and mutual understanding in your group. Suggest ways that you might help one another attain these goals.

Chapter 2
Understanding Ourselves as Communicators

INTERPERSONAL COMMUNICATION is the means by which we confirm and validate self (Proposition 8). Interaction with other people is imperative if we are to achieve a sense of personal well-being. The quality of our interpersonal communication heavily influences our personal growth, psychological health, and our success in influencing our environment. Interaction is imperative because we cannot avoid people, and when we are with them we cannot *not* communicate; if we try to ignore the presence of others we only succeed in giving them a message that is disconfirming to them.

In this chapter we look at ways in which interpersonal communication contributes to our personal development and our efforts to control our social and physical environment. Such behavior is so automatic that, as adults, we rarely stop to analyze our motives. Our study of this process thus begins with an investigation of our motives for interacting with others. These are the essential first steps in the process and greatly influence ways in which we respond to each other.

Personal Development

As we grow we strive to make sense of the world around us, to detemine what is real and what is not real (illusory, imaginary), and we depend on other people to confirm our views. All of us want to have an identity, to be somebody, a person with a distinct feeling of who he or she is. As our self-image develops, we constantly evaluate it; if it seems to be good, we gain self-esteem—a very comfortable feeling. To the extent that our personal interaction with others is successful and confirming, we are able to grow, find our identity, gain self-esteem, and feel we are firmly in touch with reality.

THE SEARCH FOR SELF-IDENTITY

As very small children we become aware of parts of the world around us. We particularly become aware of our relationships to other people and tend to experience ourselves by noting their responses to us. Thus, a major need is to obtain a clear reflection of ourselves from others.

Relating to Other People.   Ordinarily we are most comfortable and happy when we feel that our relationships with others are dependable and friendly, that is, when we can count on being understood and warmly accepted. As small children we are greatly dependent on persons immediate to us, usually our parents or those who take care of us. The satisfaction of our needs depends almost entirely on our ability to establish a workable relationship with them. At this stage our thoughts about ourselves are greatly colored by the quality of this relationship.[1] As we grow older this factor continues to influence our views of ourselves.[2]

Most of us have been able to establish relationships with others that meet our needs and give us a fairly satisfactory self-image. The importance of this process may be demonstrated by looking at some persons who, for one reason or another, are unable to establish acceptable relationships. Such persons frequently develop great anxiety over their inability to relate adequately to others; they tend to feel helpless in the face of this problem without really knowing why.[3] They cling to unproductive ways of reaching out to others and seem unable to change to more productive methods.[4] They tend to be afraid, and feel inadequate, helpless, and alone.[5]

A case illustrating this problem was presented by Sidney Jourard in his book *Disclosing Man to Himself.* A man in his late twenties consulted Professor Jourard for help when he found he couldn't complete a thesis. They met a number of times; the young man was obsessed with his manliness and very tense. He told about his earlier life and an unsatisfactory relationship with his father. Then, during one session there was a prolonged silence, and the young man sat there with a look of desperation on his face. Jourard writes:

> I felt an impulse to take his hand and hold it. I pondered . . . and debated whether I should do such a thing. I did it. I took his hand and gave it a firm squeeze. He grimaced; and with much effort not to do so, he burst into deep, racking sobs.[6]

Experiencing Ourselves Through Other People's Responses to Us.   As we interact with other people we note their responses to us and, as a result, we experience ourselves in terms of their reactions. As long as these reactions are positive and supportive we get along pretty well; if they are varied, we tend to try to pay more attention to those that are pleasant.[7]

When most or all responses to us are negative, we suffer from unhappy feelings about ourself. In some cases we may be driven to make up, create, or imagine responses that are more pleasing. Erik Erikson describes a rather inventive high school girl who secretly sought the company of Scottish immigrant

---

[1] Cf. F. Fromm-Reichmann's review of this process in *An Outline of Psychoanalysis* (New York: Random House, 1955), pp. 113–120.

[2] See Erik Erikson, *Identity: Youth and Crisis* (New York: Norton, 1968), pp. 91–141.

[3] Cf. R. May, *The Meaning of Anxiety* (New York: Ronald Press, 1951).

[4] See, for example, H. S. Sullivan, "The Meaning of Anxiety in Psychiatry and in Life," *Psychiatry,* 11 (1948): 1–13.

[5] Fromm-Reichmann, *Psychoanalysis*, pp. 115–126.

[6] S. Jourard, *Disclosing Man to Himself* (New York: Van Nostrand Reinhold, 1968), p. 98.

[7] Cf. Erikson, *Identity: Youth and Crisis*, pp. 96–107.

The struggle to define ourselves.

neighbors, assimilating their dialect and social habits. With travel guides and history books, she reconstructed for herself a childhood in an actual Scottish township and made it quite convincing in her talks with newly arrived immigrants from that country. She referred to her American-born parents as "the people who brought me over here." In her discussions with Erikson she was calm and almost convincing. Finally, when he asked her how she managed to work out all the details of life in Scotland, she said, in a pleading Scottish brogue, "Bless you, sir, I needed a past." Her own unhappy childhood and her near-delusional attempts to create one that was more to her liking eventually came to be viewed in better perspective. The basis of the invention came to be seen as her attachment to one of the immigrant women who had given her more of the kind of love she needed than had her parents.[8]

Most of us don't go as far as this young woman in trying to improve our self-image. Some of us encourage a favorite nickname or paint a slightly enlarged or brighter picture of our past. In so doing, we attempt to give ourselves a better self-image by encouraging more favorable responses from others.

In our youth we seem to be struggling desperately to define ourselves. Some of us seem to know what we are, while others are most concerned about what they might hope to become. With respect to this process of identity formation, it is useful to note the contribution of George Herbert Mead; perhaps more than any other theorist he viewed the development of self-identity as the product of social interaction. Mead emphasized the importance of face-to-face interpersonal communication—how we respond to others and how they in turn respond to us. In this way we learn about ourselves; each interchange gives us cues about how others see us, and this shapes our view of ourselves. This process begins when we are small children and continues on; virtually all communication to us gives us indications of our importance, capabilities, potential, and inadequacies.[9]

The following description of this process of identity formation is given by Erikson:

> Identity formation . . . is a lifelong development largely unconscious to the individual and to his society. Its roots go back all the way to the first self-recognition: in the baby's earliest exchange of smiles there is something of a self-realization coupled with a mutual recognition.[10]

The process of identity formation via interaction with others, suggested by Mead, and Erikson, is largely a reflection of others' perceptions of us. C. H. Cooley coined the phrase "the looking-glass self," and H. S. Sullivan spoke of "reflected self-appraisal." These are graphic labels for this process.[11]

Obtaining a Clear Reflection from Others. The images of us reflected by others are sometimes vague or distorted. Our psychological comfort is increased greatly if, from such reflections, we can develop a clear and accurate picture of ourselves. It is particularly important that you and I each see ourself as *an individual*, somehow different from people around us. In a sense we tend to feel that we are real to the extent that we are unique.

One example is the case of identical twins; twins are often described in the literature on child development. Identical twins are, typically, dressed alike and

---

[8] Ibid., p. 174.

[9] G. H. Mead, *Mind, Self and Society* (Chicago: University of Chicago Press, 1934), pp. 144–164.

[10] E. Erikson, "The Problem of Ego Identity," *Psychological Issues*, 1 (1959): 47.

[11] Not all psychologists are in agreement on theories of the development of the self-concept. Here we are following the widely accepted theories developed by William James, C. H. Cooley, G. H. Mead, Harry Stack Sullivan, and Erik Erikson. For a detailed treatment of theories of self-concept, see C. Gordon and K. J. Gergen, eds., *The Self in Social Interaction* (New York: Wiley, 1968); see also M. R. Stein, A. J. Vidich, and D. M. White, eds., *Identity and Anxiety* (New York: Free Press, 1960).

treated alike by their parents, with friends and relatives doting on "how cute they are" and "how much they look alike." The search for identity is well illustrated when one objects to being dressed like, treated like, and especially *confused* with the other. In one such case a twin girl said, "I don't want to be like her; I want to be like me."

Handling Inconsistent Reflections. Sometimes other people reflect images of us that are inconsistent. For example, one of our actions may be characterized by two other people as two different behaviors, so incompatible that both *views* cannot be correct. Occasionally these inconsistent reflections of us are produced by understandably different views of us based on other peoples' differing perceptions. These ways of seeing us may be influenced by different backgrounds or experiences on the part of our friends or relatives. For example, a brother may admire one of our actions as a show of "independence," while a parent may criticize us for being "disobedient." As we grow and more frequently take stands, we may be applauded by some for our "determination" and resented by others for our "stubbornness."

Inconsistent or contradictory reflections of our image ordinarily cause us to be uncomfortable. We seek to organize these reflections somehow into a unified picture composed of elements that seem to us to belong together. Requesting and receiving clarification or explanation frequently can help to reduce inconsistencies. In this way direct interpersonal communication can reduce tension and anxiety concerning our self-image.

Using "Reference" Persons or Groups. As we compare reflections of us from various other persons, we tend to pay more attention to some people and less to others. We select those whose approval is more important to us—more credible as well as desirable. Sometimes these are individuals; more frequently they are groups, sometimes called *primary* or *reference groups*.[12] For most of us an important reference group is our immediate family.

In his book *Self and Society*, Nevitt Sanford reports on a large, in-depth study of college students and the influences of others on their lives. An illustrative example of the positive influence of a father is taken from interviews with a rather successful sophomore:

> "Mother was sick in bed a great deal of the time. I remembered her reading and singing to us. She devoted her last strength to us kids. I don't have those early recollections of my father. My first recollection of him as a father was one spring morning, when mother passed away. He came back to tell us. Of course, there is such a disparity between his age and mine. He is 77 now. Mother had 3 operations. The third time she left I was very distressed. It was like a premonition. The aunt across the street helped take care of us, when we got sick. Father spent all of his time with us after mother died. . . ."
>
> (*What things did you admire especially in your father?*) "Mostly, his attention to us

[12] For a detailed discussion see H. H. Kelley, "Two Functions of Reference Groups," in G. E. Swanson, T. M. Newcomb, and E. L. Hartley, eds., *Readings in Social Psychology* (New York: Holt, Rinehart and Winston, 1952), pp. 410–414.

kids was very admirable. He's very honest, so much so that he won't condone charge accounts. He's known throughout the country as a man whose word is as good as his bond. His greatest contribution was denying himself pleasures to take care of us kids."[13]

By way of contrast we may look at parts of an autobiography reported by Sanford given by a young man who, at the age of 21, had begun to serve a sentence of 10 to 20 years for armed robbery:

> "My first memory has to do with Dad beating Mother. It seems that Mother and Aunt Catherine, who in the meantime had arrived from Greece, were having an argument. I do not recall its exact nature. However, Dad entered the room cursing Mother. He called her a son of a bitch and an old whore, and kicked her in the stomach. I began to cry and felt extremely sorry for Mother, who with her hands pressed to her abdomen had fallen into one of the dining room chairs. . . .
>
> "Dad came home angry one night. Business had fallen off; he was discouraged and was thinking of closing the store. Mother said that it was too bad. If she said anything else, I cannot remember it. Dad swore at her. She ran from the table. Dad kicked back his chair and started for her. She ran out in the hall toward the piazza. Dad ran and kicked her. She cried, 'Don't.' He stood there and cursed. 'You son of a bitch of a whore, you dirty bastard.' I ran and put my hand on his leg and between sobs asked him not to hit Mother. He told me to get away from him and struck at me. I ran up the hall. Poor Mother, heavy with child, stayed on the piazza until he had become quiet and then with a red nose and a drawn, haggard face crept into bed, afraid to speak, afraid to open her mouth for fear that her husband would kick her. Years later, when he would begin to curse, this scene would unfold itself, and I would rise and for every vile epithet he used, call him one in return, while four young children sat and listened."[14]

Sanford suggests that the young offender has transferred his hatred of his father to the police and other authority figures in general and has come to view himself as a compulsively "bad" person, unable to behave in ways that will win social approval.[15]

These cases illustrate ways in which our relating to individuals can influence our self-concept. Groups can exercise such an influence in similar ways; they can be healthy or unhealthy; they can stimulate undue fear or distrust, inadequate or distorted interpersonal communication, vague or unsatisfying goals, and conflict over power or interpersonal influence. As such, they can exercise damaging influence on our self-image.[16] Most of us have some opportunity to choose the groups with which we will identify, although sometimes, perhaps in school or at work, our choices are limited. In such cases our best hope may be to try to improve those groups with which we are associated.

Regardless of whatever else it is, interpersonal communication is a basic human process, one entailing the direct impact of other people on ways in

[13] Nevitt Sanford, *Self and Society* (New York: Atherton, 1966), pp. 141–142.
[14] Ibid., p. 123.
[15] Ibid., pp. 123–124.
[16] J. R. Gibb, "Defense Level and Influence Potential in Small Groups," in L. Petrullo and B. M. Bass, eds., *Leadership and Interpersonal Behavior* (New York: Holt, Rinehart and Winston, 1961), pp. 66–81.

which we identify ourselves. Your own program for personal development should consider the impact on you of those groups with whom you associate. Such groups will tend to reflect major ethics of the surrounding society. Today our society's hallmarks are approval of scientific technology, a market economy, and a warfare state. You should consider these potential influences on your self-image. In so doing, you will need to reevaluate your reference groups with care. And after this has been accomplished, you will need to use interpersonal communication for further evaluation of your own self-image as it is reflected by those in whom you have the greatest confidence.

To the extent that our efforts are successful in providing us with a self-image that is clear, unique, and consistent, we know who we are and what we are. To the extent that we are not so successful, we continue to search for a personal identity. For most of us this search continues more or less throughout life. Each new experience, each change of environment, each unexpected reflection of our image from a new acquaintance can cause us to reconsider various parts of our self-concept. Inconsistencies can produce significant feelings of discomfort, even anxiety.

In succeeding chapters we will consider problems of interpersonal communication—problems that interfere with the reflection of our image as seen by others. For these reflections to be perceived accurately and interpreted correctly, it is imperative that we make optimum use of the process of interpersonal communication.

THE PURSUIT OF SELF-ESTEEM

Of all the factors that combine to make our lives worth living, we believe that self-esteem is one of the most important. Almost all of us are concerned about a feeling that we are seen, both in our own eyes and in the eyes of others, as admirable people. The specific criteria for esteem may vary considerably from one person to another, but the desire for approval is almost universal. In large measure the "pursuit of happiness" is the pursuit of self-esteem.

Numerous examples may be cited of persons who have given up wealth, position, and even life itself to achieve or maintain self-esteem. The usual basis of self-esteem is a self-image that is satisfying to us as individuals, even though this self-concept is influenced heavily by our image as it is reflected to us by others.

An astute observer of this process was George Bernard Shaw; at the same time he refused to allow himself to become completely trapped by it, maintaining his own personal position of judgment. A rather humorous description of Shaw's insight into the process as it affected himself is given by Erikson, with brief quotations from Shaw's own writings:[17]

> G. B. S. (for this is the public identity which was one of his masterpieces) describes young Shaw as an "extremely disagreeable and undesirable" young man, "not at all reticent of diabolical opinion," while inwardly "suffering . . . from simple

[17] G. B. Shaw, *Selected Prose* (New York: Dodd, Mead, 1952)

cowardice . . . and horribly ashamed of it." "The truth is," he concludes, "that all men are in a false position in society until they have realized their possibilities and imposed them on their neighbors. They are tormented by a continual shortcoming in themselves; yet they irritate others by a continual overweening. This discord can be resolved by acknowledged success or failures only: everyone is ill at ease until he has found his natural place, whether it be above or below his birthplace." But Shaw must always exempt himself from any universal law which he inadvertently pronounces, so he adds: "This finding of one's place may be very puzzling by the fact that there is no place in ordinary society for extraordinary individuals."

Shaw proceeds to describe a crisis at the age of twenty. This crisis was not caused by lack of success or the absence of a defined role, but by too much of both: "I made good in spite of myself, and found, to my dismay, the Business, instead of expelling me as the worthless imposter I was, was fastening upon me with no intention of letting me go. Behold me, therefore, in my twentieth year, with a business training, in an occupation which I detested as cordially as any sane person lets himself detest anything he cannot escape from. In March 1876 I broke loose." Breaking loose meant to leave family and friends, business and Ireland, and to avoid the danger of success to "the enormity of my unconscious ambition."[18]

Seeking Approval of Others.   As we develop a concept of ourselves, some elements will please us and likely, some will not. What we tend to seek most from others is approval that bolsters our belief in the desirable elements of our view of ourselves. Occasionally we find approval of those elements about which we have some misgivings, and we may conclude that they are more or less admirable after all. If, in the long run, the balance appears to be favorable, our self-esteem grows and becomes more secure.

In some cases a favorable balance is achieved only at great personal risk— or so it would appear. Most high school and college students are acquainted with the game of "chicken," usually played with speeding autos aimed for a head-on collision—until one or both drivers swerve, with special social notoriety (approval) for the one who does not (if he lives to collect his reward). Occasionally the chicken game is played by people with guns, as reported in Fresno, California:

> A barmaid and a bandit played a game of "chicken" with loaded pistols early yesterday and, although no shots were fired, the barmaid won.
> The action took place at The Bit, a proletarian beer and wine oasis on the southern fringe of town, where lovely Joan O'Higgins was on duty behind the bar.
> Suddenly a towering bandit walked into the establishment, ordered a beer, flashed a small pistol and commanded Miss O'Higgins to clean out the cash register.
> The barmaid placed $11 on the bar, an amount that failed to satisfy the bandit, whose height was estimated at six feet five.
> "Give me the rest," he demanded.
> Barmaid O'Higgins reached into a drawer for the main money bag and the .22 caliber pistol beneath it.
> She pointed the gun at the man and asked:
> "Now, what do you want to do?"

[18] Erikson, *Identity: Youth and Crisis*, p. 143.

Seeking approval.

The bandit, realizing that he had met his match in The Bit, blinked at the sight of the gun and left, leaving his beer and the $11 behind.[19]

Sorting Out Approval and Disapproval. Situations occur. We act or react, always hoping for approval from those whose opinion is important to us. However, responses from others usually include some approval and some disapproval—a mixed picture of our success.

In many cases we have a serious problem in determining what, if any, approval of us is being given. A response to our behavior may be inappropriate, apparently unrelated to our intention, and unmeasurable in terms of its approval of us. In other cases it may appear that our actions have produced no response whatsoever. Occasionally we are praised for things we do not do, or did not know we did. Sometimes a response is given in such a nonchalant fashion that we are totally unable to decide whether or not we are being approved.

We sort our way through mirage and reality of reflected approval and disapproval—an uneasy task at best. Difficult as it may be, we find ourselves doing it as best we can because it is of great importance to us. All in all, we seek for a favorable balance: Are we generally liked, occasionally loved, sometimes admired, and ordinarily respected?

Putting On an Act. Because the maintenance of self-esteem is important to us, and our primary device for evaluating our behavior is the approval of

[19] *San Francisco Chronicle*, July 14, 1966.

persons important to us, we tend to behave whenever we can in ways that produce approval and avoid acting in ways that bring disapproval. Many times we are tempted to act in ways that win approval but are not true to our own inner feelings or beliefs—to present a front, acting out something we are not. One young woman describes her behavior as follows:

> I somehow developed a sort of knack, I guess, of-well-a-habit-of trying to make people feel at ease around me, or to make things go along smoothly. . . . At a small meeting, I could help things go along nicely and appear to be having a good time. And sometimes I'd surprise myself by arguing against what I really thought when I saw that the person in charge would be quite unhappy about it if I didn't. . . . I just didn't stand up for my own convictions, until I don't know whether I have any convictions to stand up for. I haven't been really honestly being myself, or actually knowing what my real self is, and I've been just playing a sort of false role.[20]

We are often tempted to act as if we are something we are not in two ways: by hiding parts of ourselves and by pretending we are more than we really are. Neither deception works very well; both have serious consequences for our self-image. In the long run, although frequently tried, both are self-defeating.

When we perceive that parts of ourselves are eliciting disapproval, we may attempt to hide those parts—if we think it can be done. We then relate to others as "part-persons" rather than whole persons. For example, we may attempt to show no fear except when we are alone. Generally such attempts are ineffective; people usually see nonverbal signs of tension that are beyond our control, and these are communicated to persons close to us despite our efforts to "say nothing." However, there are two important consequences when we are successful at hiding parts of ourselves. The first is that our anger or fear is stored up inside us, possibly to influence our later responses to communication from others. These feelings may break out in ways we do not understand and that are not understood by others. Such "breakouts" (or "outbreaks") may not be perceived by us, but are easily seen by others.[21] In this fashion, later communication not related to the focus of our anger or fear may be influenced in such a way that others (and we) are confused. At best, such internalized anger and fear contribute to our problem of fighting off an ulcer.[22] Improved habits of being open and frank in our interpersonal communication can be personally helpful.

A second potentially damaging effect of hiding parts of ourselves is that we cause apprehension in those persons with whom we relate. Suppose as your employer I must tell you that you are failing to do your job adequately. Suppose I tell you and you show no adverse reaction—you smile, remain calm, say nothing, and go your way. My interpretation is that you are a cool one, that you maintain your calmness through stiff self-discipline and do not easily get out

---

[20] Reported by C. Rogers, "What It Means to Become a Person," in C. E. Moustakas, ed., *The Self* (New York: Harper & Row, 1959), p. 197.

[21] C. Rogers, *On Becoming a Person* (Boston: Houghton Mifflin, 1961), pp. 338–346.

[22] S. Jourard, *The Transparent Self* (New York: Van Nostrand Reinhold, 1964), pp. 184–185.

of control. But I also wonder if you'll lay low and stab me in the back when I'm not expecting it—I become suspicious of you! I wonder how many emotional stimuli you can take before you react; do you remain calm under stress until, at some point, you "break" and cannot be depended on at all? The point is this: You have given me no way to assess your emotional behavior; I perceive only part of you and suspect there is more. I have experienced you as only a part-person, and as such you do not seem to be real. I am confused and will be suspicious until I learn more about you. In the meantime, this attitude will tend to distort my perceptions of even your ordinary, everyday communication, which may be totally unrelated to the earlier event. In this fashion, interpersonal communication and personal relationships are distorted by attempts to hide parts of ourselves.

Often, we try to hide parts of our true selves by staying close to the "straight and narrow" ritualized patterns of interaction. We don't really believe in these rituals, but they appear to be safe, sometimes winning approval but seldom bringing disapproval. We try to be cautious, to pursue only the "tried and true" forms of interpersonal behavior: "I can't receive negative feedback if I only do as everybody else does." The effect on the other person is one of appraising you as only a part-person—too cautious, unnatural, and somewhat unreal. In some cases the other person becomes somewhat apprehensive, wondering when your real self may show and what it will be like—and to what extent it may prove to be a threat.[23]

The second form of deceptive interaction is to pretend we are something we are not. This approach includes attempts to communicate false messages about ourselves—to wear masks or to erect facades. This game can be carried to incredible extremes; we can even put forth a little of that part of ourselves that produces undesired responses and then deride, derogate, or castigate such behavior! Erving Goffman carefully analyzes such forms of pretense in his book *The Presentation of Self in Everyday Life*.[24] He draws a distinction between "expressions given" (genuine communication) and "expressions given off" (artificial communication) and cites an insightful and humorous example taken from a novel by William Sansom in which Preedy, a vacationing Englishman, makes his first appearance on the beach at a summer resort:

> But in any case he took care to avoid catching anyone's eye. First of all, he had to make it clear to those potential companions of his holiday that they were of no concern to him whatsoever. He stared through them, around them, over them— eyes lost in space. The beach might have been empty. If by chance a ball was thrown his way, he looked surprised; then let a smile of amusement lighten his face (Kindly Preedy), looked around dazed to see that there were people on the beach, tossed it back with a smile to himself and not a smile at the people, and then resumed carelessly his nonchalant survey of space. But it was time to institute a little parade of the Ideal Preedy. By devious handlings he gave any who wanted to look a chance to see the title of his book—a Spanish translation of Homer,

[23] Cf. E. Goffman, "On Face-Work: An Analysis of Ritual Elements in Social Interaction," *Psychiatry*, 18 (1955): 213–231.

[24] E. Goffman, *The Presentation of Self in Everyday Life* (Garden City, N.Y.: Doubleday, 1959).

INTERPERSONAL COMMUNICATION IN ACTION

classic thus, but not daring, cosmopolitan too—and then gathered together his beachwrap and bag into a neat sand-resistant pile (Methodological and Sensible Preedy), rose slowly to stretch at ease his huge frame (Big-Cat Preedy), and tossed aside his sandals (Carefree Preedy after all).[25]

Most of us recall times when we have behaved in a manner similar to Preedy's. We all play roles of one kind or another at various times. The important thing is to know when we are doing it—and to note the relative portion of our time devoted to such behavior. Are we ever truly ourselves?

Pretense and Self-defeat.   A number of points may be made about pretending to be what we are not. In the first place, it takes much energy and concentration; while focusing on our performance, we may miss clues to the way people are perceiving us. Goffman makes the point that many times people eventually discover that nobody is really watching these performances and in reality those around us could not care less.[26] Such performances, when ignored, can amount to a severe loss of time and effort—time during which a genuinely rewarding interpersonal relationship might have been achieved.

In the second place, such playacting must be good. Many a television comedy is based on a character's pretense to be something he is not, with himself being the only member of the group who does not know that all others see through his facade. We may laugh at a comic character in a play, but we hardly want people laughing at our silly performance in real life. We shall mention more damaging effects later, but it seems bad enough to have people meet us and go away saying to themselves, "What an ass!"

Most of us are incapable of carrying off our deception on the nonverbal level. By muscular tension, changes of posture, facial expressions, jerky gestures, tone of voice, or other behaviors usually beyond our control, we signal our anger, fear, surprise, elation, and other real feelings and attitudes.[27] Few of us are adept at maintaining poker faces in our interactions. People may tolerate our pretense, but they usually know it for what it is if they care at all to look. How, for example, would you be able to carry off a pretense that would deny the messages described as follows?

> In a sheltered corner of the room we stopped dancing altogether and talked, and what I distinctly remember is how her hands, beneath steady and opaque appraisal of her eyes, in nervous slurred agitation blindly sought mine and seized and softly gripped, with infantile instinct, my thumbs. Just my thumbs she held, and as we talked she moved them this way and that as if she were steering me. When I closed my eyes, the red darkness inside my lids was trembling, and when I rejoined my wife, and held her to dance, she asked, "Why are you panting?"[28]

A more damaging consequence of another person's penetration of our

---

[25] W. Sansom, *A Contest of Ladies* (London: Hogarth, 1956), pp. 230–232. (Copyright 1956 by William Sansom.)

[26] Goffman, *Presentation of Self*, pp. 6–14.

[27] P. Watzlawick, J. H. Beavin, and D. D. Jackson, *Pragmatics of Communication* (New York: Norton, 1967), pp. 62–67.

[28] J. Updike, *Pigeon Feathers* (New York: Crest Books, 1953), p. 176.

"cover" is that he or she cannot further depend on anything we do or say—suspicion haunts his or her every observation of our behavior ("What a phony!"). He or she may never give us an *obvious clue* of this suspicion, but a *subtle show* of a clue may be lost to us during our "performance." But when we need his or her confidence most—when we very much want real trust and accurate estimate of our potential, when we ask sincerely to be given a try—he or she will try others first, and we may be left alone with our pretenses, a lonely phony.

Even when our pretenses win approval, they tend to provide shallow satisfaction. Inside, we know we are a fraud; such self-knowledge is damaging to our self-esteem and eventually our self-concept. Even if we use deception successfully in our interpersonal communication, we have only misused such interaction to defeat ourselves.

In our final estimation, the most severe consequence of pretending to be something we are not is that it becomes a way of life. The more we pretend, the better we become at playing a part. And the better we are at playing parts the more we will try to solve our problems of interpersonal relations by pretense rather than by honestly facing issues and working out solutions based on reality. One phony bit of behavior thus produces another, and even if we convince many other people, we will be faced with the problem of trying to find our real self. "Who are you?" is the basic question asked of persons thought to be mentally disturbed. Unlimited pursuit of pretense in life can produce the seeds of madness.[29]

Changing Our Behavior. Instead of pretense, a better alternative for maintaining or increasing self-esteem is to attempt to make personal changes in our behavior, changes that honestly win approval and at the same time make our self-image more satisfying to us.

We are usually able to make adjustments to *severe* demands in our environment without too much difficulty; such changes are required for personal survival and, although not easy to make , they are eventually handled by most of us. Over a period of time we develop certain ways of relating to other people. These relationship patterns are discussed in detail in Chapter 3 under the heading, "Orientations Toward People." The point to be emphasized here is that once such habitual patterns have become established, they are difficult to change. Only through firm resolve and deliberate effort on our part can such changes ordinarily be accomplished.

In any case, an attempt to change our behavior should be our own decision, firmly based on our own personal conviction. We should carefully evaluate those persons whose responses to us have fostered consideration of such changes. In no case should we try to change just to please someone else if our own sensitivities are thus violated; this would be similar to the pretense approach discussed. In the long run, violation of our own values to please someone else will diminish our own self-esteem.

---

[29] H. Deutsch, "The Imposter: Contribution to Ego Psychology of a Type of Psychopath," *Psychoanalytical Quarterly*, 24 (1955): 483–505.

Identification of changes that we wish to make can be helped by discussing our actions with persons we trust. We can thus gain a clearer picture of ourselves through interpersonal communication. However, we must try to make sure that these images of ourselves are perceived accurately and reflected back honestly to us; thus, the process of interpersonal communication discussed in this book must be used in optimal fashion. Effective maintenance or improvement in self-esteem requires that we openly discuss our own behavior and that we seek and obtain honest feedback. And we must evaluate carefully any suggestions for change.

There can be no guarantee of continued self-esteem as we attempt changes. We must risk our self-esteem with each attempt to improve it. Our doubts about our self-worth can be dissipated only by putting them to the test of self-exposure and feedback. *In the long run, probably the best type of self-esteem is confidence in our ability to use this approach—confidence that we can maintain our self-esteem by using self-exposure and feedback.*

This procedure involves exposure of ourselves by initiating communication or by responding to the communication of others. It also involves *evaluative* feedback. By evaluative feedback we mean reflected appraisals of ourselves as exposed. These are useful for self-evaluation and making decisions to attempt self-change. Persons with excessive fears and very low self-esteem will be able to accept *only* feedback that is reassuring. Those with higher self-esteem can risk the acceptance of feedback that shows some weaknesses or unacceptable aspects of themselves. They can test their assumptions about real worth, acceptability, lovability, and value to other persons.

There are two general classes of communication feedback useful for evaluating self-worth. When people communicate, however impersonally, they give off subtle cues in the form of *indirect* feedback. *Direct* feedback consists of verbal statements describing explicitly one person's reactions to another.

Indirect feedback is often ambiguous. A smile may be a polite social habit. Aloofness may indicate disapproval, or it may indicate the other person's fear of his own self-exposure and consequent evaluation. The problem is magnified by a person's tendency to see what he expects to see, to be sensitive only to those cues that confirm his expectations.[30] Thus, if we are suspicious of our self-worth, we are more likely to note cues confirming our suspicions.[31]

Indirect feedback tends to be overgeneralized. It is frequently difficult to associate our feeling of rejection by another person with any one of our own specific acts. We tend to interpret such rejection of some minor part of our behavior as rejection of our whole self, or all parts of ourselves about which we have doubts. Indirect feedback does not provide for explanation, specificity, or justification. In addition, indirect feedback may reveal more about the other person than about us; consequently, when we are fearful we may rationalize a negative response from another person by attributing it to *their* weakness,

---

[30] M. Deutsch and L. Soloman, "Reactions to Evaluations by Others as Influenced by Self-Evaluations," *Sociometry*, 22 (1959): 93–122.
[31] J. W. Thibault and H. W. Rieken, "Some Determinants and Consequences of the Perception of Social Causality," *Journal of Personality*, 24 (1955): 113–133.

injustice, narrowness, or malice.[32] Such indirect feedback may be easily misinterpreted.

Direct feedback is potentially more useful for evaluating self-worth; however, it is useless, even harmful, if it is not frank and honest. Frank evaluations are difficult to obtain because of our cultural taboos. We tend to approve people who look for and respond to "some good in everyone." We think it is somehow wrong to look critically at and to speak openly to another person. Maslow notes that even our definitions of love do not ordinarily include an obligation to give open and honest interpersonal evaluation; he points out the irony of our willingness to let someone go on doing damage to himself and others, ostensibly "out of kindness."[33] Probably our own fear of hurting someone and receiving retaliation is our real motivation.[34] Requesting frank and honest evaluation of ourself from another person requires courage.

To increase self-esteem, positive reevaluation of oneself is needed. This reevaluation requires exposure plus awareness and honest responses on the part of another person. We may thus conclude that it is difficult for a person to achieve change in interpersonal behavior without interaction with honest persons.[35] Such relationships are to be prized and protected with great care.

We have given extensive consideration to the development of self-image and the achievement of self-esteem. We have done so deliberately because, in all of the areas in which interpersonal communication influences people, we can think of nothing more important. We believe that these elements are fundamental to most, if not all, human interaction.

REACHING FOR REALITY

In our development as people we are constantly trying to ascertain what is real, to find solid ground, to determine its dependability, and to penetrate those appearances of reality that are illusory products of our imagination. It is not by accident that a long-running Coca-Cola advertisement neglects to discuss the contents of the product but joyously proclaims that "It's the real thing," and in another commercial we are advised that "When you're out of Schlitz—you're out of beer," as if Schlitz were the only real beer in the world.

Many questions concerning reality in the world around us can be answered by our physical senses: We can reach out and touch the soft surface of a leaf; smell the perfume of a rose; see a fleecy, floating cloud; and feel a summer breeze gently on our skin. Other questions of reality cannot be answered simply by sight, smell, or touch. They concern the reality of interpersonal relationships and social competence. It is important to us to determine the reality of our relationships with other people, the quality of their opinion of us, and our

---

[32] F. Heider, *The Psychology of Interpersonal Relations* (New York: Wiley, 1958), pp. 169–173.
[33] A. H. Maslow, "Summer Notes on Social Psychology of Industry and Management," Non-Linear Systems, Inc., Del Mar, Calif., unpublished manuscript, 1962.
[34] W. G. Bennis et al., *Interpersonal Dynamics*, rev. ed. (Homewood, Ill.: Dorsey, 1968), pp. 35–39.
[35] Ibid., pp. 505–523.

competence in dealing with them. One writer on human relations has said that it takes two to see one.[36]

The quality of a relationship is difficult to assess and many times we express our concern about how well we are doing at getting along with others. For example, young people frequently ask: Does he (or she) "really" love me? Can I count on it—is it "for real"? Such questions are neither naive nor inconsequential; they are intensely important to all of us.

Perceiving Social Reality.   From the time we are small children we need to know how to get along in the world, to detemine what other people are like, how they view us, and how they tend to respond to our efforts to make our way through life. In effect, we are motivated to discover all we can about ourselves and the people around us through interpersonal communication. We are particularly concerned about learning to get along with others.

In 1954 Leon Festinger wrote an essay that provided the basis for a large number of research studies.[37] In this essay Festinger describes his view of the way a person confirms his impressions of his environment. Festinger identifies a continuum on which he places "physical reality" at one end and "social reality" on the other. Physical reality is said to involve such things as objects or surfaces, the perceptions of which an individual can validate with his physiological senses. Social reality is said to involve perceptions of such things as appropriate social behavior, judgments of a moral or ethical nature—those elements of reality we usually associate with attitudes, opinions, or beliefs. An opinion, attitude, or belief is said to be perceived by the individual as valid to the extent that it is anchored in (or reflected by) an approved reference group. For example, the validation of one's perception of himself as an "adequate communicator" would require, at least in part, positive feedback from other people.

There are many areas in which our perceptions of social reality need to be checked by comparison with those of others through interpersonal communication. We do this each time we change to a new environment; for example, when we enter a different school, take a new job, or become a new member of a group, we ask others about norm expectancies. In groups and organizations certain people may be identified as "norm givers"—those who take responsibility for giving us orientations. Frequently such people tell us how we are doing as we adjust to the new environment.

In thus comparing ourselves with others, we tend to seek information about persons who are somewhat similar to us. We seek information about people similar to us or even a little above us when the characteristic in question is highly valued—for example, the ability to do well on an examination.[38] We tend to seek information about those a little less confident than ourselves when evaluating our fear or our behavior in a situation we see as threatening.[39] We

[36] S. A. Culbert, "The Interpersonal Processes of Self-Disclosure: It Takes Two to See One," in J. T. Hart and T. M. Tomlinson, eds., *New Directions in Client-Centered Therapy* (Boston: Houghton Mifflin, 1968).

[37] L. Festinger, "A Theory of Social Comparison Processes," *Human Relations*, 7 (1954): 117–140.

[38] L. Wheeler, "Motivation as a Determinant of Upward Comparison," *Journal of Experimental Social Psychology Supplement*, 1 (1966): 27–31.

[39] J. M. Darley and E. Aronson, "Self-Evaluation vs. Direct Anxiety Reduction as Determinants of the Fear-Affiliation Relationship," *Journal of Experimental Social Psychology Supplement*, 1 (1966): 66–79.

tend to seek information about others who are closely similar to us when we have some reason to be unsure of our ability.[40] And, in the absence of information about other persons, we tend to make inaccurate and unstable self-evaluations.[41] This process of discovering socially approved norms of behavior never ends. We continuously want to be sure we are doing the right thing and doing it well, that is, doing it in a way that will win the continued cooperation of others in satisfying such needs.

As we search for socially approved norms, we find it necessary to resolve our confusion when receiving conflicting feedback from others regarding our behavior. Studies of this problem have generally been reported under the rubric of *resolving cognitive dissonance*. This general concept applies to all of our perceptions, those related to physical reality as well as the ones directly relating to our self-evaluations.

Three theories of cognitive consistency have received wide attention: the "balance theory" of Heider,[42] the "congruity theory" of Osgood,[43] and the "cognitive dissonance theory" of Festinger.[44] The three theories are somewhat different but have this in common: They assert that the normal condition of a person's attitudes is that of internal consistency between elements perceived as related and that attitude change is the reduction of dissonance generated by new communications about, or new perceptions of, an attitude object.

Perhaps an example taken from a research report can illustrate the use of interpersonal communication to resolve problems of conflicting feedback about our behavior. In a manufacturing plant that was part of a nationally known industrial complex, a small item was being produced under a federal government contract. This contract required that all workmen at the plant wear conspicuous identification badges at all times. Compliance with this ruling had been lacking; some of the men said they thought the brightly colored official badges "looked silly." Interviews showed that company officials were telling the men that the badges must be worn. An inventory of attitudes toward wearing the badges showed that most of the men held negative attitudes. The experimenters arranged for discussion of the topic by randomly selected groups of workmen; workmen not selected were treated as a "control" group—the basis for comparison. The experimental groups were asked to "meet and discuss the topic of identification badges"—no additional instructions or leadership were provided. The kind of communication used was not controlled by the experimenter (nor by management); details of the discussion sessions reflected the decisions of the individuals involved. It was inferred that there was sufficient cognitive dissonance to motivate group interactions; the group members did talk about the

[40] K. Hakmiller, "Need for Self-Evaluation, Perceived Similarity and Comparison Choice," *Journal of Experimental Social Psychology Supplement*, 1 (1966): 49–54.

[41] R. Radloff, "Social Comparison and Ability Evaluation," *Journal of Experimental Social Psychology Supplement*, 1 (1966): 6–26.

[42] F. Heider, "Attitudes and Cognitive Organization," *Journal of Psychology*, 21 (1946): 107–112; see also F. Heider, *The Psychology of Interpersonal Relations* (New York: Wiley, 1958).

[43] C. E. Osgood, G. J. Suci, and P. H. Tannenbaum, *The Measurement of Meaning* (Urbana: University of Illinois Press, 1957).

[44] L. Festinger, *A Theory of Cognitive Dissonance* (New York: Harper & Row, 1957).

badges and related considerations—federal contracts, rulings, need for individual identification, and so on.

The results showed that the persons in the experimental groups, who had discussed the badges for about an hour, showed significant changes in attitudes (favorable) as measured by posttesting. Their posttest attitudes were significantly different from the posttest attitudes of the control group, and the members of the experimental groups were later reported by the company officials to have significantly increased the incidence of badge wearing. Postexperiment interviews indicated that the men found that although the individual's evaluation of *himself* when he wore the badge was that he "looked silly," most persons' evaluation of the looks of another person's wearing the badge was that he did not "look silly"—given the contract conditions existing at that plant. In this experiment, it appeared that cognitive dissonance regarding badges was reduced by interpersonal communication.[45]

Determining the Quality of a Relationship. It is not easy to assess the quality of one's relationship to another person. Relationships seem to be full of little surprises. In the first place, we must interact to test a relationship, to produce evidence of its nature, its strength and dependability; and we must weigh this evidence with care. When we have noted the responses of others, we will need to compare our impressions with those of other observers. Such interaction requires a good working relationship.

Over time it is quite possible for people to change and, consequently, for a relationship to change. Because of new experiences or associations, people can change their degree of expertness on some operation, or their amount of power to influence, or even the nature of their own self-image. Such changes usually occur only in response to major environmental changes, but they do occur.

When former associates meet following a period of separation, it is quite important to reaffirm the previous relationship before continuing interaction. An assumption that a prior relationship is still in effect is inappropriate; a brief exploration of how the relationship is viewed currently can expose new and different perceptions or indicate that the old basis is a solid one, still in effect. Businessmen seem to find this procedure a bit awkward; however, teenagers in love seem to make it a daily occurrence—in fact, sometimes they seem to do little else as they interact with each other. This problem is particularly pertinent in a leader-follower relationship. People in authority roles (e.g., parents) seem to take for granted that a relationship with a subordinate will never change; such an assumption holds real danger in terms of interpersonal cooperation and personal satisfaction. An authority relationship needs to be reaffirmed periodically if the relationship is to be functionally effective. The nature of one's relationships to other people—subservient or influential, warmly accepted or coldly tolerated—can have considerable impact on one's view of oneself. One's psychological development, sense of well-being, and personal self-esteem

---

[45] K. Giffin and L. Ehrlich, "The Attitudinal Effects of a Group Discussion on a Proposed Change in Company Policy," *Speech Monographs*, 30 (1963): 337–379.

can be severely influenced. Accurate determination of the quality of such relationships depends heavily on effective use of interpersonal communication. On the basis of this line of reasoning, we see it supporting our theory that interpersonal communication must be viewed as a basic human imperative.

THE QUEST FOR CONFIRMATION

We have noted that as very small children our sense of self-identity is influenced by the way other people respond to us. As we grow and develop, we need to feel that our relationships with others are dependable, that we can count on them, and that they are friendly—that we are accepted. For our personal sense of well-being we need the responses of others to confirm our belief in ourselves—that we are acceptable persons.

At the very least it is necessary that we receive confirmation from a few persons significant to us, confirmation that we exist as human beings, with senses, feelings, and thoughts similar to those of other people. In this way we must feel that we are human. Without this degree of confirmation, life itself loses significance.

The Implicit Issue of Validation.   As we suggested in Chapter 1, whenever one person attempts to initiate interpersonal communication with another, he or she has made an implicit request: "Please validate me as a person." Ostensibly, there is a surface request for recognition of the person's message, admission that his/her ideas are worth considering. However, beneath the surface there is the implicit issue of the value of that person as a human being.

Suppose you are alone at a table in a crowded cafe. Another person *acts as if* he would like a place to eat—perhaps at your table. Note that this behavior, without any verbal interchange, has already implicitly raised the question of your recognition of his needs and feelings as a person. If you *act as if* you don't see him, you have implicitly answered his request, "Please validate me," in a negative way. The implicit issue of validation of a person as a human being is always present whenever two or more people are together, face-to-face, and their presence is obvious to anyone who is awake.

Confirmation of another human being as a person consists of responses indicating that he or she is a normal, healthy individual. *Disconfirmation* consists of responses suggesting that someone is ignorant, inept, unhealthy, unimportant, or, at worst, does not exist.

As children we like to have our parents give us things, but most of all we want them to *communicate* with us. We do not know for certain what we are until others (significant to us) tell us. We even prefer mild punishment to total indifference; in later life we can tolerate hate better than we can accept total neglect.[46] Even in the pain of being hated, we can at least know that we really exist. Socrates, condemned to death, faced condemnation with pride and honor; he believed that his death would affect important future acts of his countrymen.

[46] H. D. Duncan, *Communication and Social Order* (New York: Oxford University Press, 1962), pp. 271–273.

But if no one responds to our acts or thoughts, and we cannot live without thinking and acting, the incongruity between our needs and our world becomes unbearable. Under such circumstances, children aggress against their parents and teenagers test authority by violating rules. In extreme circumstances, a person may behave in extreme ways to obtain a response—any response—to establish his existence, regardless of the degree of antagonism or hostility his/her behavior will produce.

An unprovoked attack on another person can never be condoned; however, the terrible sense of loneliness, neglect, and the need for some kind of attention from others that instigates such an attack is pertinent to the study of interpersonal communication. Attempted destruction of oneself may be a call for help—for attention from and consequential interaction with others; it may also be the despondent conclusion that this need will never be met, that rewarding human interaction for such a person is impossible.

The important point is that almost every time we initiate communication, even on a nonverbal level, we are making an implied request: "Please confirm my viewpoint." Sometimes this request is actually spoken; usually, however, it is implied on the unspoken, nonverbal level. Sometimes it concerns our understanding of factual data or information; frequently it involves confirmation of an opinion. Always there is an implicit request for evaluation of us as a person. In this fashion we use interpersonal communication to form an impression of our self-identity. Consistent social confirmation provides greater freedom for the individual to be spontaneous and creative—to live; there is no great need to be concerned about every little criticism or evaluation of one's behavior. Such a person can dare to hear feedback about who and what he/she is and can frequently test the validity of his/her beliefs about himself/herself.

On the other hand, a person whose self-image is frequently disconfirmed will have a great need for information about it. Consider a young woman named Joan: She will need to hear feedback, but will fear it; she will seek it, and at the same time try to avoid it. Her self-image will suffer either way: If she hears negative evaluation no matter how slight, she will likely feel anxiety; if she avoids evaluation she will derogate herself for being a coward—she's "damned if she does and damned if she doesn't." A wise person once said, "To him who hath shall be given and from him who hath not shall be taken away." This principle applies to the maintenance of one's self-image. To a large extent theories of nondirective counseling developed by Carl Rogers are attempts to break this vicious circle of need, fear, and avoidance of possible image-building feedback.[47]

There is little question of the importance of the continuing need for interpersonal communication that confirms one's self-image. Once is never enough. People develop elaborate social rituals to reduce the probability of disconfirmation. Children are taught to become "tactful," to respond to other people in a way that does not challenge the validity of the self-image other people present in public.

[47] Rogers, *On Becoming a Person.*

Confirmation and validation.

Confirmation by Pleasant Recognition.   The purpose of much small talk is to acknowledge in a pleasant way the presence of another person. Commonly used greetings and friendly chatter are examples of a type of communication labeled "phatic communion."[48] We use such pleasant noises to signal that we welcome interaction, that we are friendly, or that we at least recognize the presence of the other person. In our culture such courtesies tend to be rather unimaginative: "Hello," "Nice day," "Howdy," "Hi." We call these greetings "noises" because no literal meaning is usually intended. If someone asks, "How are you?" he would indeed be surprised by even a brief medical report, however accurate. A precise response could be humorous, as when James Thurber was once asked, "How's your wife?" and he replied, "Compared to what?"

It should be obvious that pleasantries upon encountering another person are small but effective measures of confirmation. If you do not think this is true, stroll down the nearest campus walkway, giving each person you meet a warm, friendly smile. Check your own feelings when this overture is ignored— rewarded with a cold stare that in effect says, "Who (or what) do you think you are?" (And you only thought you were another human being out for a stroll.)

Studies have shown that simple failure to acknowledge a person's presence is painful if not insulting; few persons find comfort in situations lacking sociability.[49] The democratic act of social recognition may appear to be somewhat perfunctory or even artificial, but it is the action of individuals desiring to create little moments of pleasurable interaction, moments when the stresses of life are

[48] B. Malinowski, "The Problem of Meaning in Primitive Languages," Supplement 1 in C. K. Ogden and I. A. Richards, *The Meaning of Meaning* (New York: Harcourt Brace Jovanovich, 1923), pp. 296–336.
[49] Duncan, *Communication and Social Order*, pp. 20–24.

temporarily set aside and two persons may enjoy simply being together on a friendly basis. Such brief encounters are important to an individual's psychological well-being and enjoyment of life.

Confirmation by Sharing Personal Growth.   If two people have fairly good self-images and if their self-esteem is reasonably secure, they may engage in interpersonal communication that is growth producing and mutually confirming. Interpersonal exchange is then exhilarating; ideas bounce back and forth; response and feedback are openly given and easily accepted. The pleasure lies in the interaction, not simply in talking or listening. When such an instance occurs we are struck by the feeling, "Isn't he (or she) a wonderful person?" Such experiences actually *are* wonderful.

There can be a certain pleasure in exposing some of our more protected thoughts and feelings to trusted others. We take pleasure in articulating such thoughts; some of them may have been little understood by us until we started to express them, and they may take shape in ways we had not quite planned or even suspected. There is pleasure in having such thoughts and feelings become clearer as we gain honest feedback. Sometimes we feel that they must be reassessed or reshaped by us; sometimes we achieve solid confirmation from other persons.

There is also pleasure in seeing this happen to the other person, joy in participating in his/her personal growth and development. There is gratificaion in giving honest feedback when you feel it will not be misused. It is our belief that most families would like to have such relationships and that interpersonal communication of this order between parents and children would make parenthood worthy of the name.

Confirmation Through Shared Silence.   When personal growth and development have been shared and enjoyed, moments of silent communion are frequently the result. In such cases interpersonal communication has not stopped; the persons so involved are quite aware of each other's presence and feelings. There is an atmosphere of shared trust and confidence, one in which one's own feelings are secure and one's feelings about the other person are also secure. There is also a willing tolerance of the other person's need for silence, with security in knowing that their thoughts will give them pleasure. There is a ready willingness to offer independence to the other person—freedom to think as he wishes, to develop thoughts and feelings that may be shared at some future time or perhaps never shared.

Such nonverbal interpersonal communion is usually restful, frequently much more so than merely being alone. Some autobiographies and diaries will attest the value of such moments. Our own personal experiences corroborate this principle. Sometimes there was an environmental element, such as a sunset or the shadows creeping along the basin of the valley below. Sometimes such conditions seemed to offer an excuse to enjoy shared silence. But the thing that was later recalled with greatest pleasure was not the sunset or the valley, but the restful comfort of the moment of silence enjoyed together. Such moments of silent communion provide a yardstick to judge the quality of an interpersonal relationship.

Interpersonal Negotiation

We have discussed ways in which interpersonal communication aids us in our personal development. We have suggested that optimal use of this process is necessary in our struggle for personal identity, self-esteem, a sense of reality, and confirmation as human beings.

The second primary contribution of interpersonal communication is that it is useful in negotiating with other people as we seek to control our social and physical environment. Of course, other forms of communication assist us in this task—written communication, the mass media, and "one-way" speaker presentations to audiences. Even so, most significant negotiations are carried out in face-to-face two-way interactions.

Consideration of interpersonal negotiation exposes clearly one of a person's basic dilemmas: *How can I maintain my own personal freedom and obtain your needed assistance in achieving my personal goals?* Perhaps, with the single exception of the need for personal growth and development, there is no more important question for us to face in all of our life struggles. It is also a most difficult question because it is truly a dilemma: To the extent that assistance is obtained, almost always some element of personal liberty is given up; and to the extent that personal independence is achieved, assistance from others is lost. Small wonder that people throughout history have tried to slide between the horns of this dilemma by manipulation and even brainwashing the minds of others. We view such manipulative use of interpersonal communication as unethical—beneath the dignity of people's potential for relating to each other.

ACHIEVING OUR PERSONAL INDEPENDENCE

In some ways it appears that every new generation must win its independence from the preceding generations. To a large extent, this is true for every individual person. We start with other people doing things for us and keeping us from doing things that might hurt us. Later we are kept from doing things that might hurt others.

Achieving one's individual independence essentially consists of negotiating with others (1) to reduce their attempts to restrict us and (2) to diminish their efforts to keep us dependent on them. There are few arguments against these individual goals as such; interpersonal conflicts arise on how far they should be carried out. Interpersonal communication is useful in establishing agreement on fine lines of distinction concerning these boundaries.

If the people around us—parents, teachers, and other authority figures—are willing to allow us more and more freedom, our interactions with them will be cooperative. Our interpersonal communication can be exploratory, agreeable, and productive, giving them and us a deep sense of personal satisfaction. To the extent that they seem determined to keep us restricted or reliant on their help, we find ourselves attempting to persuade them that they are wrong and we are right. The optimal use of interpersonal communication can be of great value at exactly this point.

It is important to discuss with important others your needs and desires for increased freedom in a tentative, exploratory way before commitments have been made, "sides" have been chosen, and an atmosphere of conflict has settled on the scene. If we assume too early that they will never negotiate, that in no way can they be persuaded, then our struggle for personal independence may take the form of a "resistance movement," with heavy commitments on both sides and no expectation of resolution through interpersonal communication. Personal freedom is generally won in small stages—through little incidents and persistence. In negotiating with others, we should work on small items one at a time and not expect large gates to open all at once. But the keynote must be that voiced by Winston Churchill as he reviewed his early life and struggle: "Never give in!"[50] In the struggle for personal freedom, one must not give up just because progress is not rapid. As we get older we find that the struggle continues throughout life.

Achieving Freedom from Restrictions. In attempting to diminish personal restrictions placed on us, we must recognize that liberty does not mean absolute license; at no time in our lives will we be allowed to do whatever we please without considering the effect on others. Thus, in attempting to reduce restrictions placed on us by others, we should seek to identify those restrictions that we will, in turn, place upon ourselves. Our negotiation will thus consist of our offering to provide self-discipline as a replacement for their discipline. Such a trade—a substitution of one policy for another—can hardly be worked out with other persons at long distance unless interpersonal communication has previously set the stage for such negotiation.

Negotiation of a trade, giving something in return for something received, appears to be an almost universal form of social interaction. The process consists essentially of offers and responses, counteroffers and counterresponses, until either agreement is reached or one or both of the participants decide that no agreement is possible. Here again is life's basic dilemma: To get something new, I must give up something owned. If I cannot receive without giving, how can I avoid giving without receiving? Only by negotiation can the answer be obtained.

Reducing Our Reliance on Others. A difficult and sensitive problem in achieving personal independence is to diminish one's dependence on others. In our early life, we can't seem to wait until we are *capable* of doing things for ourselves. A little girl, 2 years old, fell asleep while playing in the basement. Her parents carried her upstairs and tucked her into bed, whereupon she awoke, jumped out of bed, said, "Me get in mine own bed," crawled back in and

---

[50] Churchill in his speech at the Harrow School, reported in D. Price and D. Walley, eds., *Never Give In* (Kansas City, Mo.: Hallmark Cards, 1967), p. 30.

went to sleep. Achieving capability is only part of the problem; being allowed to use this capacity, to do for oneself that which one can do, may be even more difficult. It seems that many people like to have others rely on them; such dependent-seeking behavior has been identified as a major personality variable.[51]

As we increasingly do more for ourselves, many persons are content to let us do so. A simple show of initiative can diminish some others' efforts to keep us reliant on them. Some of our associates will be most happy that we are no longer their burden and will encourage our efforts. But those few who want to keep us tied to them may be persistent. Frequently, they are persons about whom we care very much; the sensitive part of the problem is our desire to consider their feelings while simultaneously considering our own. It is precisely this kind of situation in which interpersonal communication may be the only way we can make any progress—by exposing our feelings and needs, showing concern for the sensitivities of the other person, offering suggestions, asking for feedback, and searching for possible areas of agreement.

A short time ago a man 35 years old came to inquire about our graduate program. He was pleased with our program but hesitated to leave his present job, working in his father's small business. We asked if his fear was that his father could not get along without his help. He said that was not the case; rather, he feared he would hurt his father's feelings if he ceased to depend on his father's help and made his professional success on his own. We listened while he mulled over his problem and suggested he talk it over with his father. A few days later we received a letter saying that he just couldn't talk to his father about it, that he felt his father couldn't accept his son's being on his own, and that, although he would very much like to become part of our graduate program, he would stay where he was. We later thought that perhaps this man belongs in his father's business; without more courage he probably is not capable of being free.

NEGOTIATING MUTUAL ASSISTANCE

A great amount of our time is spent in working out ways in which we, with one or more other persons, try to achieve desired goals that each of us, individually, cannot hope to accomplish. Usually such activities are identified as problem solving. People work with each other in two basic ways: (1) cooperating to solve mutual problems, or resolving shared concerns, and (2) trading help and resources. Both approaches involve the use of interpersonal communication.

Cooperating to Solve Mutual Problems. Many times people share a mutual concern; they talk it over, hoping to cooperate in reaching a resolution. This simple process is the essence of democratic action. It is cooperative in that all viewpoints are allowed to be voiced. It is purposive in that an attempt is

---

[51] R. B. Cattell, H. W. Eber, and M. W. Tatsvoka, *Handbook for the Sixteen Personality Factor Questionnaire (16PF)* (Champaign, Ill.: Institute for Personality and Ability Testing, 1970), pp. 85–86.

made to identify and resolve a problem felt by two or more people. In many cases, who takes part in these discussions—and who does not—is influenced primarily by the degree of concern mutually shared.

A concern shared with another person ordinarily involves the need for reaching agreement on a program of action that commits you and them to a way of assisting each other—sharing a load or responsibility. Such commitment allows each person to rely on the other for behaving in a way that is mutually beneficial. In many cases, the mutual concern requires a pooling of resources— material, energy, time, money.

Types of problems that require mutual assistance cover a wide range of conditions. A group of students and teachers may try to develop a new set of required courses for a major academic program. Two or three students living in an apartment may reach an agreement on the tasks of cooking and cleaning, and perhaps on ways of providing each with some personal privacy. Two families may share their resources and build a cabin on a lake. Six commuters may arrange a program of taking turns driving as well as schedules for picking up each member of the car pool. In each of these examples, there are certain common factors: Two or more people are identifying a mutual concern, analyzing a situation, and producing a desired program of action requiring certain behavior on the part of each individual.

Much of our lives is spent working with others, working out arrangements with them, developing new procedures for mutual benefit. The interpersonal problem-solving process involves two major types of behavior: (1) task-oriented behavior—identifying and analyzing a mutual problem, evaluating possible ways of trying to resolve it, and preparing to implement a selected solution; and (2) relating to each other in a decent human way—noting the way other persons *feel* about their ideas as well as just hearing the ideas, and listening for indications regarding the way they feel about *us* as well as how they feel about our ideas. *Task-oriented behavior* focuses on dealing with the problem. *Relating interpersonally* focuses on understanding each other as human beings.

Both types of behavior are essential for working out programs of mutual assistance. Neither type can be neglected if we are to be effective in resolving concerns shared with others. And a particularly vexing problem arises when elements of the two are confused, a common example being when open, honest *disagreement* on ideas is perceived as *personal dislike*. It is extremely unfortunate that the two are frequently confused. Only by efficient use of the process of interpersonal communication can such confusion ordinarily be dispelled.[52]

There can be honest *disagreement* on any step in the problem-solving process: on the nature or causes of the problem, on possible values of alleged solutions, on who can best do what in implementing a plan of action. Ample reason for sincere disagreement can include different sources or amounts of information, different personal experiences or observations, and different personal value systems.

Honest disagreement should be voiced, heard, and discussed; only in this

[52] For a detailed treatment of this and other factors in negotiating mutual assistance, see B. R. Patton and K. Giffin, *Decision Making Group Interaction* (New York: Harper & Row, 1978).

way can the full value of different backgrounds and resources be utilized. However, when such disagreement is misperceived as personal *dislike*, it usually elicits a defense of oneself *as a person*. The true value of the source of disagreement is lost entirely, and the problem-solving process is contravened—"shot down." *And for no adequate reason!* In addition, considerable interpersonal difficulty usually results. Sometimes this takes the form of retaliatory behavior—a show of *retaliatory* personal dislike. This, of course, is usually perceived correctly and reacted to immediately. Hostilities may consume endless time and energy: Friction may ebb and flow for minutes, sometimes days, even years. We should be deeply concerned about such waste of human potential. As authors of this book we are highly aware of this problem because we have observed it so often.

Proper use of the process of interpersonal communication can contribute greatly to the achievement of shared effort in solving mutual problems. Even more important, in our estimation, it is practically the only way that the confusion of honest disagreement with personal dislike can be resolved.

Trading Help and Resources.   A second way of negotiating mutual assistance is that of working out a trade. Such a trade requires giving something in return for something received. There are many interpersonal situations in which the persons involved are not likely to be entirely cooperative. More often than not, the goal of one or another individual contains both cooperative and competitive motivations. For example, suppose your car will not start on a cold morning. The relationship between you as owner and a mechanic as repairman is both cooperative and competitive. Both of you can benefit from negotiating an agreement in which the mechanic earns a fee and you achieve an auto that functions in cold weather. To this extent both of your motivations are cooperative. On the other hand, the terms of the agreement are competitive: The higher the mechanic's fee, the greater the relative cost to you (assuming the quality of his workmanship remains the same). Such interpersonal situations have been studied under the label "mixed-motive negotiations." Many human interactions fall into this category.

The study of negotiation, or bargaining, has usually focused on two questions: (1) For a specified set of conditions, what procedures are likely to be used by the participants? (2) What decision will likely be the outcome? The theory of games has been used to find answers to these questions.[53] Game theory as applied to negotiation situations rests on the assumption that individuals attempt to achieve the highest possible returns (in terms of each individual's value system) by interacting with others. If the theory of games is to provide insight into mixed-motive interactions, communication between the participants must be considered. In recent research, direct verbal communication has been studied as a part of the negotiation process. Research by Beisecker has explored the role of communication in mixed-motive negotiations.[54]

[53] For an introductory treatment of game theory, see A. Rapoport, *Two-Person Game Theory: The Essential Ideas* (Ann Arbor: University of Michigan Press, 1966).
[54] T. Beisecker, "The Use of Persuasive Strategies in Dyadic Interaction," unpublished PhD. dissertation, University of Wisconsin, 1968.

Beisecker has concluded that the potential impact of communication on the outcome of a negotiation is related to the degree that each participant can estimate the other's position. When participants have only limited knowledge of each other's utility values, or when these tend to change during interaction, understanding of such values can be achieved only with the aid of communication; estimates will tend to be valid to the extent that such communication is effective. Beisecker has also developed a theoretical analysis of the ways in which communication can aid participants in the pursuit of both cooperative and competitive goals.[55] Communication can be used cooperatively by two or more persons to produce a group decision that gives maximum satisfaction to all participants. The role of cooperative communication is to discover and increase areas of common interest; it provides a search process through which the participants identify previously unnoticed alternatives, reconsider criteria for evaluating alternatives, and strive for greater logical consistency among their utility (evaluative) systems. Most scholars who study this process have labeled it "problem-solving" discussion or interaction.

On the other hand, communication may be used competitively to distort the other person's perceptions of the situation in order to gain an individual bargaining advantage. Strategies for accomplishing this are numerous, including the following:

1. Misrepresentation of available alternatives
2. Misrepresentation of the utility values of various alternatives
3. Rejection of additional alternatives
4. Rejection of additional criteria for estimating the utility of alternatives
5. Insisting on the other person's need to achieve an agreement
6. Indicating high commitment to a demand for resolution.

There are additional strategies that could be identified. In each of the strategies the purpose is to alter the other person's perception of the outcome when a specific agreement is reached. Mothers and fathers seem to be altogether too adept at the use of these strategies in negotiating with their children.[56]

Competitive communication strategies are viewed here as unjust or "unfair" whenever attempts are made to distort another person's perception of a situation or the value system involved. On the other hand, *mutual efforts* in search of new alternatives, new value systems, or greater internal consistency are considered to be just and fair. Although they may produce differences of opinion, *efforts toward accurate or objective perception of a bargaining situation* are viewed broadly as a cooperative effort.

In our culture, deliberate distortion of the perceptions of another person is unethical. However, from time to time one may find it practiced. In many situations the participants possess simultaneous motivations to be both cooperative and competitive; sometimes one or the other is uppermost, and

[55] T. Beisecker, *The Role of Verbal Communication in Interpersonal Interaction: An Analysis from the Point of View of Games* (Lawrence: Communication Research Center, University of Kansas, 1969).
[56] For an insightful and interesting analysis of parental competitive communication strategies, see C. Russell and W. M. S. Russell, *Human Behavior* (Boston: Little, Brown, 1961), pp. 189–247.

sometimes the individual himself would be hard pressed to analyze his interpersonal motivations objectively. *To provide an opportunity for another person to alter his perceptions in a mutual search for a negotiated agreement is not unethical; however, to distort deliberately the perceptions of others is an irresponsible and unethical use of communication in an interpersonal situation.*

Cooperative communication can serve the participants' purposes in a mixed-motive situation by providing information needed by them. One of these purposes is to indicate to each other the utility value attached to each possible bargaining alternative; data can be given concerning such values and the firmness with which those values are held. Procedurally, this may take the form of one person offering to "settle" for certain considerations by the other, followed by the other person telling what he thinks of the offer.

A second purpose is served when each person indicates his perception of the interpersonal relationship between the participants: Can the other person be trusted as a source of pertinent information (e.g., does he bluff)? Does he view himself as a subordinate or superior to the other? Is one person heavily dependent on the other for needed information, or does he have access to a reliable outside source?

Finally, a useful purpose is served by discussion of the negotiation process itself: determination of an agenda, speaking order, speaker responsibilities, and data desired.

Much of the preceding discussion seems to imply that people negotiate mainly on matters of material value, and indeed much of the research on negotiation focuses on this type of bargaining. However, a great deal of interpersonal negotiation concerns matters less tangible, such as criteria for gaining personal regard, standards for determining status, procedures for showing recognition, and a host of other matters requiring social contracts or agreements if people are to achieve personal satisfaction from their interaction with others. Almost anything is likely to have utility value for someone somewhere; if it has such a value, one may have to negotiate with others in order for that value to be enjoyed.

The Inevitability of Interpersonal Communication

There appears to be little room for disagreement with the conclusion that interpersonal communication is inevitable. In the first place, we can hardly succeed in avoiding people even if we so desire. In the second place, if we are in the presence of others, we cannot *not* communicate. (Proposition 1. Communication is unavoidable and inevitable when people are aware of one another.)

WE CANNOT AVOID PEOPLE

In our culture it is difficult to be alone, to achieve privacy. More people are pressed together daily in tightly compact areas—apartment complexes, dormitories, suburban developments. Increased specialization of occupational roles makes us more interdependent, each upon the other. Advances in technology make people more mobile, make communication easier, make others more available to us—and, conversely, make us more available to them. A day alone at the seashore is for most of us a romantic dream; even an afternoon alone in one's room may require special measures involving telephone, signs on the door, and a bit of luck.

A major ethic of parenthood in our society is the socialization of children: Make sure that little Johnny learns to play and work with the other children. This project is often programmed to boundless limits—preschool, parties, dancing lessons, swimming teams, scouting, and so on, until parent and child are nearly exhausted.

Much of this activity is desirable and beneficial. Our point is not that it can be overdone; rather, that at least some of it cannot *not* be done. A child in our culture is going to be with people; probably even more so as an adult. This fact alone is important, and it holds great significance as it relates to this principle: When we are with other people, we cannot *not* communicate.

WE CANNOT AVOID RESPONDING TO OTHERS

There is no more important recent observation in the study of interpersonal communication than this: When we are with other people, and they are aware of our presence, we cannot *not* communicate. Its importance is more fully realized because of new investigations of nonverbal communication, body language, vocal intonation, and facial expression. We now know that when people try to communicate least they may be communicationg most. In terms of personal disconfirmation, such messages frequently have more impact on interpersonal relations than do occasional overt, verbal statements.

"NO RESPONSE IS A RESPONSE"

Perhaps we can best manifest this point by describing the experiences of people who have deliberately tried to give other people "no response." In the literature on child development there are careful studies of children who are identified as "autistic"—children who have shut themselves off from interaction with all other human beings. These children are typically passive, usually mute, frequently inert—almost deathlike.[57] It has often been noted that they give an impression of lonely desperation combined with an appearance of little old men or women possessing an inner silent wisdom. Most of them exhibit a profound withdrawal from contact with people, behaving as if others were not there, perhaps crouching in a corner, indifferent to all that goes on about them. Some of them endlessly repeat snatches of songs, phrases, or even lists of items, patiently refraining from expressing their own thoughts or making any personal commitments. Others make clucking or clicking noises, unused, however, for

---

[57] B. Bettelheim, *The Empty Fortress* (New York: Free Press, 1967), pp. 56–60.

interpersonal communication.[58] Occasionally, when approached (e.g., for medical attention), these children fight with inordinate strength and the violence of utter desperation. For the most part, however, they are unresponsive to the world around them. In many cases bodily functions are so constricted that special measures are necessary for feeding or elimination.[59] It would appear that they have attempted to blot out all stimuli, inner or outer, in order to avoid giving any response to their environment.[60]

Careful diagnostic examination separates these autistic children from those that are feebleminded or brain damaged. Their central nervous systems are normally and fully developed, and they possess all the necessary potential for human communication.[61] With treatment, they demonstrate that they understand language but fear people. With extended treatment, the majority of them take their place in society pretty much like normal people. Most autistic persons are children; without special treatment, they rarely live to be adults.[62]

Autism has been identified as a massive response to a catastrophic threat in early childhood. In almost every case the early development of autistic children includes the ordinary beginnings of speech, most of them having functioned in a fairly normal way at least for awhile. Then something happened that to them was frightening, and it involved, in some way, other people.[63] The perceived threat may have involved either physical or psychological danger. Consequently, these children have tried to shut out the world, sometimes closing their ears (and even their nostrils) with their fingers when approached by others.[64]

In their attempt to close out other people, autistic children try at great price to avoid the inevitability of interpersonal communication; they seem to be saying, "If I don't respond, they can't hurt me."[65] Actually, they are aware of others but are "passionately indifferent."[66]

We Cannot *Not* Communicate When We Are With Others.   Although autistic children have tried almost beyond endurance, they have not succeeded in giving "no response" to those about them.[67] Their response is negative and mostly nonverbal, but their unspoken message is clear to strangers seeing them on the street whenever they stray from home or institutions.[68] They are readily seen as "different" and in trouble. Their autism is real and easily identified, not by what they say verbally but by what they say nonverbally in bodily expression and behavior. Studies by R. A. Spitz and others have well documented the principle that if small children are denied human warmth and attention they

---

[58] Ibid., pp. 100, 364–365.
[59] Ibid., pp. 57–60.
[60] Ibid., pp. 160–161, 205.
[61] Ibid., pp. 4–5.
[62] Ibid., pp. 89–90, 413–421.
[63] Ibid., pp. 43–45.
[64] Ibid., pp. 161–162.
[65] Ibid., p. 46.
[66] Ibid., p. 89.
[67] Ibid., pp. 89–90. To some extent Kanner disagrees, saying that they *do not relate* to persons. See L. Kanner, "Early Infantile Autism," *Journal of Pediatrics*, 25 (1944): 211–217.
[68] Bettelheim, *Empty Fortress*, pp. 356–357.

will sicken and die.[69] The same is generally true of autistic children. Formal treatment generally consists of a demonstration of warmth and acceptance, along with efforts to reduce the source of fear or anxiety. The road to recovery actually commences, however, when these children *initiate* interaction, that is, when they actively start to try to deal with the world around them.[70]

We opened this chapter with the statement that personal development and psychological health require human interaction. The experiences of those who have tried to deny this principle serve to prove its merit. Fortunately, most of us readily acknowledge the dictum that interaction with others is unavoidable and interpersonal communication inevitable. We strive to use and improve it for purposes suggested in the earlier sections of this chapter.

Summary and Preview of Readings

We try to achieve a personal identity by relating to other people, experiencing ourselves through their responses to us. We strive to obtain a clear reflection of our image from others, comparing and evaluating inconsistent or contradictory reflections. We learn to rely primarily on "reference" persons or groups in whom we have the most confidence.

We try to achieve self-esteem by developing a self-image that is pleasing to us. A pleasing self-concept is one that elicits approval from those persons we trust. We tend to monitor and modify our behavior in ways that obtain more approval and less disapproval. We are frequently tempted to "put on acts" that gain applause, hiding parts of our true selves or acting as if we are something that we are not. Careful consideration of such performances shows that they are likely to be self-defeating. Instead, sincere efforts to change our ways of relating to others may lead to personal growth and increased self-esteem.

As we grow and develop we are always in search of reality—"the real thing"—especially in terms of our relationships to other people. To test social reality, we need to make optimal use of the process of interpersonal communication. We must expose our true selves to a trusted other person, request and obtain honest feedback, and check our perceptions of this feedback with the person giving it. Through this process of exposure, feedback, and checking perceptions, we can assess the reality of our relations with others, at least to the extent that they and we are honest.

The quest for confirmation of ourselves as persons—human beings—is a lifelong process. Each time we are in the presence of another person, we implicitly ask for validation of ourself as an acceptable person. If the other person is important to us, denial by him/her can seriously discredit our belief in ourself. Conversely, confirmation may be derived from pleasant recognition by others, from sharing our personal growth with another trusted person, and by spending comfortable moments in silent communion with that person.

[69] See R. A. Spitz, "The Psychogenic Diseases in Infancy," in *The Psychoanalytical Study of the Child* (New York: International Universities Press, 1951), vol. 6, pp. 255–275.
[70] Bettelheim, *Empty Fortress*, pp. 89–94, 405–413.

The second major contribution of interpersonal communication is its use in negotiating with others. Through interpersonal negotiation, we seek to control our social and physical environment. We negotiate to achieve our personal freedom—freedom from restrictions placed on us by others and reduction of our reliance on them. We also negotiate with others in cooperative efforts to solve mutual problems. In mixed-motive (partially cooperative, partially competitive) situations, we negotiate "trades" of help and resources.

For the reasons just summarized, interpersonal communication is a basic human imperative. In our culture it is inevitable. As our society is presently constituted, we cannot avoid people; and when two or more people meet, the implicit issue of personal confirmation is raised. This implied request cannot be avoided: "Please respond to me as a human being." Any effort to avoid giving a response *becomes* a response, even if not intended as such. In this way the human imperative of interpersonal communication is unavoidable; it is bound to happen. The attendant question thus arises: How well do we understand and use this process?

In the first reading that follows, "I Think I Am, Therefore I Am," Ellen J. Langer and Carol S. Dweck explore the way your interaction with others is influenced by how you talk to yourself. They suggest that you tend to become *what you expect to become* because you *interpret* the responses of others in ways that fit your own expectations. This is a most interesting and significant idea with respect to self-achievement and self-esteem. You should read and think about their article with care.

You may believe you can think *unrealistic* thoughts about yourself and get away with it; that is, you may think you are not attractive when you are or influential when you are not, and successfully convince yourself that you are what you think. If so, read carefully the second article, "Communication Within," by John O. Stevens. He asks you to become more aware of your own reality—who and what you really are. Only by grounding your self-image in your actual feelings and behaviors can you achieve satisfactory relationships with others. Stevens suggests specific ways of getting in touch with yourself, of becoming more clearly aware of who you really are. We suggest that after you have achieved such awareness, you should focus on your positive attributes in order to implement Langer and Dweck's ideas about positive thinking.

I Think I Am, Therefore I Am

Self-concept

Ellen J. Langer and Carol S. Dweck

> Human reason needs only to will
> more strongly than fate and she is fate.
> —Thomas Mann

Who is it that is free of feelings of insecurity? Is it the rich, the very bright, the athletic, the actor or comedian, the person that you envy the most? We maintain that there are few, if any, of us who have a truly satisfying self-concept. People occasionally put on a good show and seem to others to be on top of it all, but these very same people often think: "If they only knew the real me."

We see others with their public faces

on, and we are usually not permitted to view the feelings of inadequacy that lurk beneath. Thus we pick up positive information about other people's self-esteem and dwell on the negative information we have about ourselves. We are bound to suffer by the comparison.

Some anecdotal evidence comes from a brief interchange that was recently shared with us. The conversation was between two faculty members of a prestigious university in the East. One of the professors is a member of a minority group and as a result has a great deal of empathy for the minority

From Ellen J. Langer and Carol S. Dweck, *Personal Politics: The Psychology of Making It*, © 1973, pp. 29–37. Reprinted by permission of Prentice-Hall, Inc., Englewood Cliffs, New Jersey.

students. He commented that it was really rough for the men and women coming from the ghettoes to the university because of the feeling that they weren't "really" bright enough. They felt that they were faking it. They faked their way into the school and were therefore fearful that their success would vanish if they let down their masks for more than a moment. The other faculty member was somewhat amazed because it was her belief that these were the students who were most secure. She thought they must be secure because they had a harder fight up the ladder—they must know by now that they are competent. Prior to this conversation her sympathies were basically with the students who were both members of the majority group and wealthy. These were the people who never really had to work for anything. They could never be sure they could make it on their own—that if "mommy and daddy" weren't around they wouldn't crumble.

Then who is secure? People who recognize their assets and who realize the control they have over their own lives. These are the people who do not see themselves merely as victims or beneficiaries of circumstances.

Many insecure people tend to minimize the role that their true abilities and efforts played in determining success. They tend to emphasize external factors or factors beyond their control and view the successes as somehow unearned or undeserved. Many popular pseudoexplanations feed these myths:

It's not *what* you know but *whom* you know.

He was born with a silver spoon in his mouth.

He had it made, or: He was born under a lucky star.

Either you've got it or you don't.

When applied to yourself, they could be damaging. They lead one to believe that these are the only factors at work; they make no mention of the individual's beliefs and attitudes about himself and how they contribute to his success. For example, success is often attributed to "connections": Brad thought he got into college because his father knew the dean; Hal thought he was promoted to supervisor because his boss, Catherine, was interested in "getting to know him better." There is *no* accomplishment which a clever enough person can't explain away by finding some extenuating circumstance. But what does this buy you—anxiety because you have to keep up the act or frustration because you're not as good as you think you "should" be? Connections may get you in—but rarely are they enough to keep you in. And what makes you so sure that all those other people made it without help?

By not focusing your attention on the effort you've expended to attain the goal or the clever way *you* brought about the positive consequences, you deny yourself that pat on the back you deserve; the pat on the back we all so desperately need. That is, by attending to external or uncontrollable influences, as suggested in the clichés presented, you may well prevent yourself from attaining a sense of worth.

In a similar way, common statements may masquerade as explanations of failure:

He was cursed from the day he was born.

He was born on the wrong side of the tracks.

Again no mention is made of how a person's belief about his worth contributes to failure when, in fact, this may be a much more important influence than curses or tracks.

We are suggesting an alternative position: You are what you think you are.

Of course, learning is involved in this process. You can't just say "I want to make myself a malted. Poof! I'm a malted!" Phrased differently, our position is: You are what you've learned to be; you view things (including yourself) in the way you've learned to view them. Moreover, you've taught other people how to view you. In the rest of this chapter we will demonstrate how your expectation for yourself can become a self-fulfilling prophecy—how the prediction of failure begets failure and the prediction of success begets success. We will show you how you can change these expectations in order to act in more adaptive ways and bring about more rewarding consequences.

. . .

The Virtuous Circle of Success

Some of us are lucky enough to have been trained early to see ourselves in a positive light. As Freud put it: "A man who has been the undisputable favorite of his mother keeps for life the feeling of conqueror, that confidence of success that often induces real success."[1]

The person who has a high regard for his assets and abilities and who

[1] From Ernest Jones, *Life and Works of Sigmund Freud* (Garden City, N.Y.: Doubleday-Anchor Books, 1963), p. 6, Basic Books Edition.

believes he will succeed will act in ways consistent with his expectations. He has learned to make the best bet; that is, he has learned to focus on the positive alternatives. How does this attitude increase the likelihood of success? This may be understood by conceptualizing the process in four stages:

1. Expectation. An individual defines a goal for himself. His expectation refers to how certain he is that he will reach that goal.

A forty-five year old divorcé, Dennis, is contemplating having an affair with Marcia, the company's "fresh-out-of-college" research assistant.
Assume for the moment that Dennis expects to be successful in his pursuits.

2. Behavior in the Situation. A person tends to work harder and more consistently when he is fairly certain that his efforts will pay off. Thus an expectation of success will lead to greater effort in the situation, which, of course, will increase the chances of succeeding.

Because this is the first time Dennis has attempted to date anyone his daughter's age, and he is bent on succeeding, he proceeds with a plan that took him a good deal of time to think out and put into action. He obtains information about the project Marcia is currently working on. After gaining a fair degree of familiarity with the subject matter, he initiates a conversation with her. While strolling through her lab one day, he stops to ask her a few interesting questions about the research. He begins to make frequent visits with the timing of each visit getting later and later in the day. Surprisingly enough, on Friday he appears at 4:45 and after a short conversation, he asks, "Marcia, if you're not doing anything else, would you like to have dinner with me tonight?"

3. View of the Outcome. This stage involves deciding whether you succeeded or failed by comparing the outcome of the situation to the goal you initially defined for yourself. Often outcomes cannot be clearly labelled "success" or "failure." On such occasions expectations will determine whether you see it one way or the other. In general, an expectation of success makes you more likely to accept the positive alternative and see the outcome as a success. . . . this can maximize the probability of future success.

> How did Marcia respond to Dennis's invitation? Consider some of the answers she might have given, and note the view that Dennis took of each outcome.
>
> "Yes, I'd love to," she replies. Dennis, pleased with his success, quietly offers a sigh of relief.
>
> "Gee, I'd really love to, but I've made other plans. Maybe some other time." Dennis, sorry she didn't say "yes," is still sort of encouraged by her opening remark.
>
> "No," she hesitates. "I really can't, but thanks anyway." This is clearly a setback for Dennis.

4. Attribution. This refers to the reason one finds to explain the outcome that has occurred. On the one hand, you may attribute success or failure to some characteristic of yourself (intelligence, ability, looks, age, personality), or to some aspect of your behavior in the situation (such as amount of effort or tactic used). Alternatively, you may attribute the outcome to something external to yourself, such as luck or fate, characteristics of the situation (the difficulty of the task, the weather, failing equipment, etc.) or the influence of another person, organization, or institution. An individual generally chooses his attributions in a way which lends support to his initial expectation. [See Figure 1.]

If a person has an expectation of success, he can maintain his positive self-concept and expectation of subsequent success. He can do this by either attributing the failure to some aspect of his behavior that he can change (like the amount of effort or strategy) or to some external factor that may be different next time (like the other person's mood). Or he may write it off as a one-in-a-million occurrence.

After thinking about this issue, we happened to be watching the Dick Cavett Show. The championship chess match between Bobby Fischer and Boris Spassky was going to take place within a few months and Cavett asked

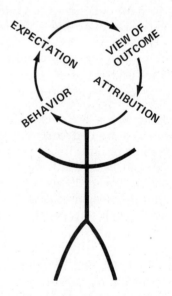

FIGURE 1.

his guest, Fischer, what it would do to his ego if he lost. To the audience's amusement and our delight, the confident Fischer replied, "I would consider it a fluke."

Taking a positive view of the outcome (as in stage 3) or making attributions that maintain a positive self-concept is not equivalent to rationalizing or lying to oneself. The person who takes a positive view is not ignorant of the negative alternatives. He simply knows that in many cases the positive alternatives are just as likely to be true and that by taking this approach to the situation he maximizes his payoffs.

Oddly enough, though, people are inclined to believe negative outcomes and alternatives are somehow more truthful. Even the most confident people will occasionally have "secret" fears of inadequacy and feel that they are faking it.

A failure might be seen as providing a glimpse of the "real you." On the other hand, a person with no confidence who experiences a success rarely believes he has found his true self.

By and large, the person who has a positive self-concept can find reasons for a failure that allow him to continue to pursue his goal with the same motivation, and perhaps with new information to help him. He may even view the setback as challenging. The same person experiencing success takes it as a confirmation of his expectation and feels confident of success in subsequent situations.

When Dennis hears that Marcia is eager to dine with him, he attributes it to the effort he made in combination with his winning personality and youthful charm.
While Dennis is less pleased to encounter "Gee, I'd love to but I've made other plans. Maybe some other time," he chooses to believe that she would indeed at least like to, but honestly had a prior engagement. Consequently, his expectation of eventual success has not much changed. His subsequent reactions to her remain friendly and after a few days he asks her out again.

"No, I really can't but thanks anyway" sounds pretty final to Dennis. However, one "No" does not a failure make. Dennis decides to attribute the rejection to something he can change, like the particular strategy he used (maybe I asked her too late in the week, maybe I asked her too abruptly, or maybe I gave her the impression that all I talk about is work). While not wishing to make a pest of himself, Dennis accepts the setback as a challenge and prepares to set a new plan into action. His persistence may pay off, even if Marcia initially had no intention of embarking on a romantic relationship with Dennis. By spending more time with him she is more likely to recognize his assets and overcome initial hesitations. Ultimately, even if she does reject him, since he is basically sure of himself, he is likely to attribute the rejection to something that is not devastating to his self-esteem. "She thinks I'm too old for her," "Maybe she's inhibited by the fact that I have a daughter her own age," "She may have a rule about not getting involved with anyone at work," "An attractive girl like that probably has a boyfriend already," "I wonder if she thinks that I couldn't take a girl her age seriously and that I just wanted to play around."

Remember, he has no way of being sure what her real intentions were. He can choose to focus on those that will make him miserable, or just as easily he can focus on alternatives that are not unpleasant for him. One is just as apt to be correct as the other, but one approach leads to far less grief.

Communication Within

John O. Stevens

Many psychologists talk about how it is healthy to develop a strong ego, a good self-concept, a strong character, etc. Any such image of myself is a fantasy, an idea. To the extent that I am preoccupied with this fixed idea of myself, I lose touch with the flow of my actual present experiencing. At best a strong self-image will cause me to become a rigidly predictable, socially useful automaton—a person who identifies with an *idea* of myself instead of with the *reality* of my actual feelings, experiences, and actions. My living becomes split between image and reality, between what I think I am and what I am.

I also become fragmented in another way: As soon as I try to achieve a goal, I become prey to fears of failure. If I want to impress you with what a nice guy I am, I begin to fear that you'll think me a louse. The more I fear your bad opinion, the more I will try to convince you that I am a good guy. Hopes and fears feed and grow upon each other, and each of these two opposing fantasies takes me farther from the reality of my experiencing at the moment.

It is possible to re-establish communication between these fragments of myself and gradually work toward recognizing and relinquishing my images, and toward regaining contact with my actual experiencing and my real responses. When I am in solid contact with ongoing reality, living in a flexible flowing with events as they really are, I have no need for a "self-concept" or a "strong ego" to tell me what I am like or what I "should" do. This is the Zen teaching of "no-mind." If my "mind" is empty of images, ideas, intentions, prejudices, and demands, then—and only then—can I be in touch with my actual experiencing of the world, balanced and centered in the present moment of my sensing and responding.

Full awareness of my experience

requires complete acceptance of that experience as it is. Any demands—by myself or others—to be different than I am, reduces my contact with what I actually experience. This begins the falsification of my life through acting differently than I feel and playing roles. I might try to be nicer or tougher than I feel to impress others, or "society" might demand that I act tougher or more tender than I feel, less or more sexual than I feel, etc. The next experiment gives you an opportunity to become aware of some of the demands that you place on yourself, and how you are split between what you are and what you demand of yourself. If possible, do this in a small group and ask someone to read the instructions to you; if not, read through the instructions and then try the experiment alone by yourself.

Demand and Response (Topdog-Underdog)

Sit comfortably and close your eyes. . . . Now imagine that you are looking at yourself, sitting in front of you. . . . Form some kind of visual image of yourself, sitting there in front of you, perhaps as if reflected in a mirror. . . . How is this image sitting? . . . What is this image of yourself wearing? . . . What kind of facial expression do you see? . . .

Now silently criticize this image of yourself as if you were talking to another person (If you are doing this experiment alone, talk out loud.) Tell yourself what you should and shouldn't do. Begin each sentence with the words, "You should—" "You shouldn't—" or their equivalent. . . . Make a long list of criticisms. . . . Listen to your voice as you do this. How does your

voice sound? . . . How do you feel, physically, as you do this? . . .

Now imagine that you change places with this image. Become this image of yourself and silently answer these criticisms. . . . What do you say in response to these critical comments? . . . And what does your tone of voice express? . . . How do you feel as you respond to these criticisms? . . .

Now switch roles, and become the critic again. As you continue this internal dialogue, be aware of what you say, and also how you say it—your words, your tone of voice, and so on. . . . Pause occasionally to just listen to your own words in your mind and experience them. . . .

Switch roles whenever you want to, but keep the dialogue going. Notice all the details of what is going on in you as you do this. . . . Notice how you feel, physically, in each role. . . . How do these two speakers differ? . . . Do you really talk *to* each other, or do you avoid real contact or confrontation? . . . Are you listening to each other as well as talking, or are you only broadcasting and not receiving? . . . How do you feel about this other speaker as you talk? . . . Tell this to the other speaker, and see what he or she responds. . . . Do you recognize anyone you know in the voice that criticizes you and says "You should—"? . . . What else are you aware of in this interaction? . . . Bring this awareness into the conversation between you. . . . Continue this silent dialogue for a few minutes longer. . . . Do you notice any changes as you continue the dialogue? . . .

Now just sit quietly and review this dialogue. . . . As you look back, is there anything else about this conversation that you notice? . . .

In a minute I'm going to ask you to open your eyes and come back to the group. I want each person, in turn, to share your experiences with the group in as much detail as possible. I want you each to express what happened in your dialogue in *first-person present tense, as if it were happening now:* "As the critical person, I feel strong and I say 'You shouldn't goof off so much. You ought to work harder,'" or whatever your experience is. Open your eyes now and do this. . . .

Probably you experienced some kind of split or conflict, some division between a powerful, critical, authoritative part of you that demands that you change, and another less powerful part of you that apologizes, evades, and makes excuses. It is as though you are divided into a parent and a child: the parent, or "topdog," always trying to get control to change you into something "better" and the child, or "underdog," continually evading these attempts to change. As you listened to the voice that criticized and made demands on you, you may have recognized that it sounded a lot like one of your parents. Or it might have sounded like someone else in your life who makes demands on you—your husband or wife, a boss, or some other authority who controls you. If you do recognize someone specific in this dialogue, it is valuable to continue the dialogue as if you are speaking directly to this person.

At the same time, I want you to realize that everything that you experience in this dialogue happens in your own head. Whether your dialogue is with another specific person or with "society," it occurs in your own world of fantasy. When the other speaks in this dialogue, it is not "society" or an actual person who speaks, but your *image* of this other. Whatever occurs in your fantasy dialogue goes on between different parts of *yourself*. If there is a conflict in your dialogue, this conflict is between two parts of yourself, even if you alienate and disown one part and call it "society," "mother," "father," etc. We usually assume that our problems and conflicts are with *other* people, so we struggle to be free of their demands, and don't realize how much of the conflict is actually *within* us. . . .

There are real problems in the world, and I can really deal with these problems only when I am clear in myself about how I feel and what I want to do. When I am in conflict, I identify partly with my own feelings and wants and partly with fantasies that conflict with this awareness—ideas about what I should be, catastrophic expectations, fears of what others will do, etc. Much of my communication and activities are directed toward myself instead of toward the world. To the extent that I do this, I become ingrown, autistic, and isolated from others. My energy becomes divided and in opposition, so that very little energy is available for my struggles with the real world. When I participate in outside conflicts before I have cleared up the conflicts within me, I just create more conflict both inside and outside.

As long as I believe that my conflict is only with someone or something outside myself, I can do very little except complain about it, or try to change or destroy it. When I realize that much of the conflict is within me, then I can do something much more productive. I can take responsibility for my own difficulties, and stop blaming the world for problems that are my own. I can seek to discover more about these different and conflicting parts of myself, identify with them, and learn from them. The first step in this process is to become aware of the autistic activity that goes on in my "mind" or fantasy life. The next step is to direct it outward, so that the autistic self-to-self activity becomes relational self-to-other activity. As I direct this activity outward toward the world, it becomes more explicit and more detailed. Often I can discover who these messages are really intended for, or where they come from.

Listening to Yourself

Everyone says, "I tell myself," [but] nobody says, "I listen to myself." So try listening to yourself for a change. Begin by paying attention to the thoughts going on in your head, and simply observe them. . . . Now begin to say these thoughts, but like very soft whispering, so the words barely get past your lips. . . . Now say them a bit louder. . . . and keep increasing the volume until you reach your normal speaking level. . . . Imagine that you are actually talking to someone. . . . Continue to say your thoughts, and pay attention to what is communicated by the sound of your voice. . . . What is your voice like? . . . Is it strong or weak, clear or unclear, harsh or mellow, etc.? . . . Is it judging, complaining, angry, pleading? . . . Does this voice sound like anyone that you know? . . . Who might these words be directed to? . . . Choose some person to say these words to. Imagine that you actually do this, and see whether they fit. . . . How do you feel as you talk to this person? . . . Does this person reply to what you say? . . . Now quietly absorb your experience for a little while. . . .

The value of this is that although you are actually still talking to yourself, you do it as *if* you were talking to someone else. As you do this, your autistic activity becomes more relational, and you begin to regain contact with the world and your own experience. When you develop this into a dialogue, each side of a conflict contrasts with the other and clarifies it.

You can really do a lot for yourself through having these dialogues. You do have to be willing to suffer the unpleasantness of experiencing and expressing both parts of the conflict, and the two parts have to be willing to confront, encounter, and communicate honestly with each other. It is best if you can find a time or place where you can talk out loud, and bring your physical postures and movements into the dialogue. Often the tone of voice, a pointing finger, a frown, a fist, slumped shoulders, etc. express much more about what is going on in the dialogue than the words. Try to be aware of your total experience as you do this. As long as the dialogue is not just empty words but expresses your real feelings and experience, then as you become more and more deeply aware of these feelings and experiences, some change and development will take place.[1]

Any time you are aware of a conflict of opposites in yourself, or between yourself and someone else or something else, you can use this kind of fantasy dialogue to get communication started between the conflicting parts. In a previous experiment, the conflict is between what you are and what you "should be." For most people this is

[1] See *Gestalt Therapy Verbatim*, by Frederick S. Perls, and *Don't Push the River*, by Barry Stevens, for examples of such dialogues.

like an argument or struggle between a parent and a child. As long as this conflict continues to be a battle for control—with the "parent" preaching and threatening, and the "child" apologizing and evading—nothing will change. If you can really identify with both sides of this conflict you can gradually begin to understand more about the conflict between them. As your understanding of both sides grows, the interaction between them will gradually change from fighting and avoiding each other, into more contact and communication. As the two sides start to listen to each other and learn from each other, the conflict will decrease and can even come to resolution.

Usually we are unbalanced because we identify mostly with one side of a conflict and don't realize our part in the opposing side. As both sides become clear and as we identify with both sides, we become more balanced and centered. We can act more from this balanced center, instead of from one of the conflicting sides. Resolution of conflict releases the energy that has been locked up in the struggle between the opposing sides, and this energy then becomes available in increased vitality and a sense of clarity, strength, and power. *This process is not something that can be forced or manipulated.* It is what happens by *itself*, when you deepen your identification with, and your awareness of, both sides of a conflict.

Letting Go of the "Past"

All of us carry around parts of our "past" with us in the form of memories. Our memories, even if they are exact images of previous things and events, are *images* and not the events themselves. Often these images and fanta-

sies that we call memories are quite different from the things and events that actually happened. Some people are so burdened with the past, and so involved in their memories, that they have very little involvement with the present. If you want to reduce your involvement with your memories you can invest yourself in them in the same way as any other fantasy; you can discover what awareness is hidden in these fantasies through identification and dialogue. Your involvement in the memory does something for you, and before you can let go of this memory you will have to find out what it does for you—what need is served by hanging onto it.

You might be escaping from a present that is unsatisfactory in some way to a memory of a time that was more fulfilling. If so, you can discover what it is that you are missing in your life now. If you can realize that the satisfactions of memory are a pale substitute for the satisfactions of reality, then you can face the challenge of working toward making the present more satisfactory for you, instead of retreating into memory.

If the memory is unpleasant, there is probably an unfinished situation in which you held back and have not expressed yourself fully. By investing yourself in this unfinished situation you can rediscover these unexpressed feelings and actions and let them complete themselves. The next experiment can give you an experience of working with this kind of unfinished situation.

Yes—No Situation

Lie down on your back and find a comfortable position. . . . Close your eyes, and keep them closed until I ask you to open them. . . . Let go, and get in touch with your body. . . . Notice any discomfort you feel, . . . and see if you can change your position so that you are more comfortable. . . .

Now focus your attention on your breathing. . . . As you become aware of your breathing, does it change? . . . Without interfering with your breathing, just observe it and be aware of it in detail. . . .

Now imagine that your whole body is like a balloon that slowly fills as you breathe in, and becomes very taut and stiff when you have a full breath. . . . and then slowly releases as you breathe out, so that you are completely released when your lungs are empty. . . . Do this three or four times. . . .

Now just be aware of your natural breathing. . . . and imagine that each breath washes some of any remaining tension out of your body, . . . so that you become even more released with each breath. . . .

Now remember a specific situation in which you said "Yes" but you really wanted to say "No." Try to visualize this situation as if it were happening now. . . . Where are you? . . . What are your surroundings like, and how do you feel there? . . . Who is there with you and what has just been said? . . . Really invest yourself: Get in touch with being in the situation, and relive it as if it were occurring now. . . .

Now focus on the moment when you say "Yes." What tone of voice do you use as you say "Yes," and how do you feel as you do this? . . . What does it do *for* you to say "Yes"? . . . What do you gain by saying "Yes"? . . . And what do you *avoid* by saying "Yes"? . . . How do you feel about saying "Yes" in this situation?

Now go back to the moment just before you said "Yes." Now say "No," and say anything else that you didn't express previously.

What tone of voice do you use as you say "No," and how do you feel as you do this? . . . How does the other person respond to you after you say "No"? . . . How do you feel now, and what do you reply to this person? . . .

Now change places and become the person to whom you said "No." What are you like as this person? . . . And how do you feel? . . . As this person, what do you say, and what tone of voice do you use? . . .

Now become yourself again and continue the dialogue. . . . How do you feel as yourself now, and how is this different from how you feel as the other person? . . . Do you feel more powerful as yourself, or as the other person? . . . Speak directly to this person, and tell him about how you are different from him. . . .

Become the other person again, and continue this dialogue and interaction. . . . Try to really get into the full experience of being this other person. . . . Continue this dialogue and switch places on your own each time the other person begins to reply, so that you always identify with the one who is speaking. . . . How are the two of you interacting now—are you fighting and arguing, or do you begin to communicate with each other? . . . What are you aware of that you are *not* expressing—what are you holding back? . . . Now express how you feel toward each other. . . . If this is too difficult for you, at least say to the other "I am still holding back," and then say something about this holding back. . . . Continue this dialogue for a few more minutes. Get even more into the experience of being these two people and exploring how you interact. . . .

Take a little while to quietly absorb your experience. . . . In a minute I'm going to ask you to open your eyes and relate your experience to the others in the group in first-person present tense, as if it were happening to you now. For example: "I'm reading in the living room: I'm very tired and my wife comes in and asks me to go to the store," etc. Be sure to include how you feel saying both "yes" and "no" in this situation, what it did *for* you to say yes or no, and what you learned from the dialogue after you said "no." Open your eyes now and share your experiences with the group. . . .

When I ask you to remember this kind of situation, whatever emerges is an event that is still alive in your memory because there is energy still invested in it. By re-experiencing it in the present through identification and dialogue, you can discover what is unfinished and unexpressed, and assimilate both the experience and the energy that is bound up in it. There is a real parallel between taking in an experience and eating food. If you only gobble without chewing thoroughly, it sits inside you and continues to give you trouble until you vomit it up or digest it. Until you digest and absorb any food, the energy in it is not available to you, and the same is true of any experience you have. Probably you were not able to fully digest this experience of saying "yes" when you really wanted to say "no" but I hope you got some experience of chewing and digesting. You can return to this or any other experience repeatedly, until you really chew it up, experience it, and absorb it.

In this particular experiment you can also get quite a lot of understanding of your compliance behavior—what actually goes on when you comply with another person's wishes although you would really prefer not to. Try to realize what complying does *for* you, as well as what it does *to* you. Realize that when you comply, you do it *for yourself*—to get love and approval, to avoid a quarrel, or so that you can think of yourself as "nice" or "capable," etc. There are some people who spend most of their lives complying, others who spend most of their lives *not* complying, and some who give the appearance of complying, but actually don't. Very few people take time to fully realize what goes on in them as they comply. If you are really aware of what goes on in you when you comply, then you can work through the opposing forces within you and realize whether you *really* want to comply in a particular situation or not. In this way you can become more flexible, and free to act according to the actual situation and how you really feel. The extremes of compliance are the conformist who *always* complies and the rebel who *never* complies. Both are equally trapped in a rigid response to the outside demands of parents, society, etc. The conformist believes that he always has to do the approved thing, while the rebel believes he always has to *not* do the approved thing so that he can be "free." Full awareness of how you trap yourself can bring real freedom as you re-identify with this power you have given away to others—the power to respond honestly and directly without the need of outside support, approval or permission.

. . .

Most of us still hang onto our parents and other significant people in our lives in this way, continuing to ask for their approval and support long after we are capable of making our own decisions—and often long after they are dead. Almost all of us have a great many unfinished situations with our parents and many unexpressed feelings toward them. These situations and feelings are more bits and pieces of history that clutter our lives. These unfinished situations interfere with your present relationships with parents, because to the extent that you hang onto previous situations, you lose contact with what is happening now. You are partly in contact with your memory fantasies of your parents and yourself, and only partly in touch wih the reality of you and your parents *now*. Even in less intense relationships with friends and acquaintances, you are more likely to meet your memories of them than to meet them as they are now. Until you can deal with these unfinished situations and accept and express the feelings that you have held back, you will continue to be stuck with these burdens, and also stuck in your static relationship with your parents. I have seen seventy-year-olds still tied up in a bitter struggle with their memories of long-dead parents. It is hard work to deal with these unfinished situations, but until you do, you will continue to think of yourself as a child who needs support from a parent or someone else. Maturing is discovering that you are capable of your own support and that you are no longer a child who needs support and approval from parents. The next experiment can get you started on clearing up some of the unfinished situations that you have with your parents.

Parent Dialogue

Sit comfortably and close your eyes. . . . Visualize one of your parents, sitting facing you. Take some time to really see your parent sitting there in front of you, and make contact with him or her. How is he sitting? . . . What is he wearing? . . . What kind of facial expression does he have? . . . Notice all the details of your parent in front of you. . . . How do you feel as you look at your parent? . . . Now begin by being completely honest with your parent. Express all the things that you never told him and say these directly *to* him as if you were actually talking to him now. Express everything that comes to your mind—resentments you held back, anger you were afraid to show, love that you didn't express, questions that you never asked, etc. Be aware of how you feel as you do this, and notice if you begin to tense your body somewhere, etc. Be sure you stay in contact with your parent as you do this. Take about five minutes to do this. . . .

Now become your parent, and respond to what you have just said. As your parent, how do you reply to what your child just said? . . . Be aware of how you feel as you do this. . . . How do you feel toward your child? . . . Now tell him how you feel toward him, and tell him what you think of him. . . . What kind of relationship do you have with him? . . .

Switch places again and become yourself. How do you respond to what your parent just said? . . . What do you say now, and how do you feel as you say it? . . . Tell him how you feel toward him now, and tell him what you think of him. . . . How do you experience this relationship? . . . Now tell him what you need and want from him. Take some time to tell him exactly and specifically what you want him to do for you, and be aware of how you feel as you do this. . . .

Now become your parent again. As parent, what do you reply to this expression of needs and wants from your child? . . . How do you feel as you do this? . . . What understanding do you have of what he is asking for? . . . Have you experienced anything similar in your life? . . . Now tell your child what you need and want from him. . . .

Switch places and become yourself again. How do you respond to what your parent just said? . . . Do you have any better understanding of him now? . . . Now tell him what it does for you to hang onto him in fantasy like this. . . . What do you gain by holding onto all these unfinished feelings toward your parent? . . .

Now become your parent again and respond to this. . . . What do you say in reply? . . . What is your relationship like now? . . . Is any understanding developing, or is it still mostly fighting and conflict? . . .

Switch places and become yourself again. How do you respond to what your parent just said? . . . How do you experience your relationship, and what understanding do you have of your parent's situation? . . . Tell him whatever understanding you have of him now. . . .

Now I want you to tell your parent what you appreciate in him. No matter how difficult your relationship is, there must be something about him that you appreciate. Tell him about these things now, and be specific and detailed. . . .

Now become your parent again. How do you respond to these appreciations? . . . Can you really accept them, or do you minimize or reject them? . . . Now express your appreciations of your child. Tell him in detail what you appreciate in him. . . .

Now become yourself again. How do you respond to the appreciations you just got from your parent? . . . How do you feel toward each other now? . . . Continue this dialogue on your own for some time, and switch back and forth between being yourself and your parent whenever you want to. Pay attention to what is going on in this interaction and make this explicit. For instance, if you realize that the parent is scolding and blaming, point this out and demand that he express himself more directly. Notice when you are tense and holding back, and express yourself more fully. See how much you can express and clarify about this relationship. . . .

It takes time to clarify a relationship, and often you will arrive at a place where both sides are stuck in an unyielding deadlock. As you become more aware of the details of this deadlock, it will gradually become more flexible; when you become fully aware of the conflict, it will disappear. This may take many sessions of struggling, but each time there can be some clarification and deepening of awareness. Eventually you can arrive at letting go of parents, giving up your demands that they be different, and forgiving them for their faults, and what they did or didn't do for or to you. You can recognize that they couldn't be other than they were, and that even "forgiving" is irrelevant. Perhaps hardest of all is to let go of a lost relationship. When an important person in your life has died or left you, he continues to exist in your fantasies as if he were still alive. In a kind of self-hypnosis, you continue to be involved with a dead relationship. When you can complete this dead relationship and say good-bye, you can wake up from your hypnosis and become involved with the living people around you.

One of the ways we give away our power to be ourselves is by hypnotizing ourselves with the words that we use to describe our own actions. We put ourselves to sleep and become less aware of our own feelings and wishes. Whenever I say "I should—" I am hypnotizing myself with this demand. I tend to assume that this demand is reasonable, legitimate, and not open to question; I lose the realization that I can choose whether to accept the demand or not. I also lose awareness of my own response to this demand— my resentment, resistance, dislike, etc. My resistance and resentment still exist—even though I have lost awareness of it—and will continue to frustrate my attempts to change myself into what I "should" be. An earlier experiment focuses on this conflict. The next experiments focus on other ways that we hypnotize ourselves.

I Have to—I Choose to—

Pair up with someone else, and sit facing this person. Throughout the experiment, maintain eye contact and talk directly to this person. Take turns saying sentences to each other that begin with the words "I have to—" Make a long list of things that you have to do. (If you do this experiment alone, say these sentences out loud and imagine that you are saying them to some person you know.) . . . Take about five minutes to do this. . . .

Now go back to all the sentences you just said and replace "I have to—" with "I *choose* to—" and take turns saying these sentences to your partner. Say exactly what you said before except for this change. I would like you to realize that you do have the power of making a choice, even if that choice is between two undesirable alternatives. Take time to be aware of how you experience saying each sentence that begins with "I choose to—" Then repeat this sentence and immediately add any sentence that comes to you next. For example: "I choose to stay with my job. I feel safe and secure." Again take about five minutes to do this. . . .

Now take a few minutes to tell each other what you experienced as you did this. Do you have any actual experience of taking responsibility for your choices—any feeling of waking up a little from your self-hypnosis, any discovery of more power and possibilities? . . .

I Can't—I Won't—

Now take turns saying sentences to your partner that begin with the words "I can't—" Take about five minutes to make a long list of things that you can't do. . . .

Now go back to all these sentences you just said and replace "I can't—" with "I *won't*—" and take turns saying these sentences to your partner. Say exactly what you said before, except for this change, and then take time to be aware of how you experience saying each sentence. Is this really something impossible—or is it something possible that you refuse to do? I want you to become aware of your capability and your power of refusal. Then repeat this sentence that begins "I won't—" and immediately add any sentence that comes to you next. Take about five minutes to do this. . . .

Now take a few minutes to tell each other what you experienced as you did this. Did you experience any feeling of strength as you took responsibility for your refusal by saying "I won't"? What else did you discover? . . .

I Need—I Want—

Now take turns saying sentences to your partner that begin with the words "I need—" Take about five minutes to make a long list of your needs. . . .

Now go back to all these sentences you just said and replace "I need—" with "I *want*—" and take turns saying these sentences to your partner. Say exactly what you said before, except for this change, and then take time to be aware of how you experience saying each sentence. Is this something you really need or is it something that you want, but can easily survive without? I want you to realize the difference between something that you really need, like air and food, in contrast to other things you want that are very pleasant and nice, but not absolutely necessary. Then repeat this sentence that begins "I want—" and immediately add any words that come to you next. Take about five minutes to do this. . . .

Now take a few minutes to tell each other what you experienced as you did this. Did you experience any sense of lightness or freedom as you realized that some of your "needs" are really only conveniences and not necessities? What else did you become aware of? . . .

I'm Afraid to—I'd Like to—

Now take turns saying sentences to your partner that begin with the words "I'm afraid to—" Take about five minutes to make a long list of things that you are afraid to try. . . .

Now go back to all these sentences and replace "I'm afraid to—" with "I'd *like* to—" and take turns saying these sentences to your partner. Say exactly what you said before, except for this change, and then take time to be aware of how you experience saying each sentence. What is it that attracts you toward this risk, and what is the possible gain? I want you to realize that many of your fears hold back the satisfaction of important wants. Then repeat this sentence that begins "I'd like to—" and immediately add any sentence that comes to you next. Take about five minutes to do this. . . .

Now take a few minutes to tell each other what you experienced as you did this. Did you become aware of some of the wants and possible gains that your fears prevent you from reaching? . . . What else did you become aware of? . . .

Whenever I say "I have to" "I can't" "I need" or "I'm afraid to" I hypnotize myself into believing that I am less capable than I really am. "I have to" makes me a slave, "I can't" and "I'm afraid to" make me a weakling, and "I need" makes me helpless and incomplete. Whenever I say "I choose to," I affirm that I have the power of choice, even when I continue to choose in the same way as before. Whenever I say "I won't," I affirm my power of refusal, and often become aware of large reservoirs of hidden and disguised power to resist. Of course, it is possible for me to say "I won't" in a meek, small voice, so that it is clear to anyone that my real feeling is "I can't." When this happens, I can become aware of my tone of voice and take responsibility for this expression of myself as well. It is my willingness to identify fully with my experience and my actions, and be responsible for what I feel and do, that brings a sense of power and capability. When I say "I want," I can realize that although many of the things I desire might be very pleasant and comfortable, they are conveniences, not necessities. I can actually get along very well without them. I may even realize that the satisfactions of some of the things I try so hard to get are not worth half the effort I spend in trying to get them. When I say "I'd like to—" I can realize that I'm experiencing attraction as well as fear. I can then realize the possible gain as well as the possible loss in what I am afraid to attempt. I can realize that every risk has positive aspects as well as negative ones.

One aspect of growth is the discovery that many things are possible and that there are many alternatives in coping with the world and satisfying your wants. The real problem is that most people *believe* they are not capable and *believe* that there are no alternatives. We are in contact with our *beliefs*, and not in contact with reality. Rather than interact with reality and take certain risks, we hypnotize ourselves with our fantasies of what isn't possible, and the catastrophes that would happen if we tried alternatives, etc. Be aware of what you say and how you speak, and see if you can discover other ways that you hypnotize yourself into believing that you are less than you are—less capable, less feeling, less strong, less intelligent, etc.

We normally express our feelings and experiences through our body posture and movements. In some strongly emotional experiences, our entire body is involved. In joy, our whole body tends to be mobilized into activity—smiling, dancing, singing, etc. In fear, our whole body either becomes immobilized and tense, or explodes into actively running away. With other experiences, only parts of our body express what we are feeling. Perhaps only my mouth smiles, my nose wrinkles in disgust, my foot taps out my impatience, or tension in my neck or fist expresses my anger.

Most of us avoid experiencing certain feelings and other aspects of our experience which are uncomfortable or painful, or which might bring about an unpleasant response from other people in our environment. When I avoid awareness of what I am feeling, I also have to avoid awareness of how my body is expressing the feeling. Usually this involves partial or complete stopping of the movements that would normally express the feeling. If I feel angry and begin to make a fist and tense my arm and shoulders to hit, I can only stop this expression by tensing the muscles that oppose this movement. The resulting tension is still a signal to me that something is seeking expression, so I may also avoid being aware of this tension by directing my attention elsewhere and losing awareness of these areas of my body.

If I want to regain awareness of what I feel, it is often useful to reverse this process by deliberately focusing attention on the parts of my body that are tense or have very little feeling. By exploring the areas of tension or lack of sensation in my body, I can recover awareness of these feelings. The next experiment can give you some experience of doing this.

Face Awareness

Close your eyes, . . . find a comfortable position, . . . and become aware of your face. . . . Be aware of the sensations coming from the different areas of your face. . . . Where do you feel tension or tightness? . . . What parts of your face can you feel distinctly? . . . And which parts do you feel very vaguely or not at all? . . . Notice what part of your face emerges most strongly into your awareness, . . . and focus your attention on this part of your face. . . . Become more and more aware of this part of your face, and see what feeling, expression or movement emerges as you do this. . . . Let this part of your face do whatever it wants to do, and focus your attention on whatever develops out of this. . . . What does this part of your face express? . . . If this part of your face could talk to you silently, what would it say? . . . Now imagine that you become this part of your face and identify with what this part of your face expresses. As this part of your face, what do you say? . . . Really get into the experience of being this part of your face. . . . What is your life like? . . . And what do you do? . . . How do you feel, and what is it that you are trying to express? . . .

In a minute or so, I'm going to ask you to open your eyes and share your experience with the others in the group. Express your experience in the first-person present tense, as if it were happening now. Describe in detail what you are aware of in your face and show this in your facial expression. Go on to describe what develops as

you focus your attention on a part of your face, intensify the expression, and then what you experience as you identify with this part of your face. . . .

We meet and communicate with others mostly through the face, and the face is particularly important in communicating feelings and emotions. If you are willing to occasionally take a few moments to become really aware of your face, you can regain contact with what is going on in you at the time that is not being expressed. For instance, you might find your nose wrinkling in disgust, or your eyes holding back tears, or your mouth beginning to smile. Whatever you become aware of, realize that this is a part of your experience, another part of your life that you can regain and use—but only if you become deeply aware of what is held back.

You can become more aware of what is held back in any part of your body through this noticing and identification. You can also use a dialogue between parts of your body to deepen the experience of identification and discover how the different parts of your body are related to each other. The next experiment can give you an experience of this.

Hand Dialogue

Close your eyes, and keep them closed until I ask you to open them. Find a comfortable sitting position that allows you to use both your hands. Get in touch with your physical existence. . . . Turn your attention away from the outside world and become aware of your body. . . . Notice which parts of your body emerge into your awareness, . . . and notice which parts of your body you are not very much aware of. . . .

Now bring your hands together in your lap in any way that is comfortable for you. Focus your attention on your hands. . . . Get in touch with your hands. . . . Become aware of the sensations that are coming from your hands. . . . What is the physical relationship between your hands? . . . Are your hands interacting in any way? . . . Let your hands begin to move a little, as if they were interacting or having a silent conversation. . . . How do your hands move, and how do they feel? . . .

Now I want you to give words to this silent conversation. Imagine that you become your right hand, and that you are silently speaking to your left hand. . . . As right hand, what do you say to left hand? . . . And what does left hand answer? . . . How do you feel as right hand? . . . How are you different from left hand? . . . Tell left hand how you are different. . . .

Now identify with your left hand. Become left hand, and continue this conversation. . . . Tell right hand how you feel as left hand, and how you are different from right hand. . . . What do you say as left hand, and what does right hand answer? . . . What is going on between you? . . .

Now become right hand again. Continue this dialogue between your hands for four or five minutes. Continue to focus your attention on your hands and find words for how they interact and relate to each other. Identify with one hand and feel how it is to be that hand speaking directly to the other hand. Switch back and forth between your hands whenever you wish. If you get stuck, say to the other hand "I'm stuck" or "I have nothing to say to you," and see what the other hand replies. Keep the interaction going and see what develops. . . .

Keep your eyes closed for a little while longer. Sit silently and absorb whatever you have just experienced. . . . What went on between your hands? . . . What did you experience while identifying with your hands? . . .

In a minute I'm going to ask you to open your eyes and share your experiences with the group. Express your experiences in first-person present tense, as if the dialogue were happening now: "As right hand, I am covering left hand; I feel confident and protective, and I say to left hand—" Really express your experiences in detail. Don't talk *about* your hands; *become* your hands. Don't talk in the past tense "I *was*;" talk in the present tense "I *am*." Now open your eyes and tell your experiences to the others in the group. . . .

Almost everyone experiences some differences between their hands, and often these differences are quite impressive. Usually the right hand expresses what we think of as "masculine" aspects of personality—strength, activity, dominance, etc. Usually the left hand expresses what we think of as "feminine" aspects of personality—warmth, tenderness, weakness, etc. In some people the two hands are comfortable with their differentness: This differentness is a basis for interdependence and cooperation, as in a healthy relationship. In other people this differentness is mostly a source of conflict and disagreement. Sometimes the hands, or other parts of the body, express a continuing battle between the two sides of such a conflict. This continuing partial expression causes some parts of the body to be in continual or repeated activation and tension. This continued misuse of a body part without awareness often leads to distortion of its function, and if it is overlooked, can cause destructive physical changes and disease. We all misuse our bodies in some way, and we all suffer from some degree of such psychosomatic disease. A great many difficulties—from "ordinary" aches, pains, and headaches to really crippling and killing diseases like ulcers, asthma, and arthritis—*can* be entirely a result of this unawareness and misuse of the body. Even when there is a distinct physical cause for a disease, our misuse of the diseased part is often a predisposing factor that makes this part break down, or that makes the disease much worse than it would otherwise be. See what you can learn about what is expressed in your own aches, pains, or other symptoms in the next experiment.

Symptom Dialogue

Close your eyes and think of some physical symptom that bothers you. If possible, think of a symptom that you can feel right now. If you can't feel any discomfort right now, think of a symptom that bothers you regularly or repeatedly, and see if you can re-create the feeling of that discomfort. Focus your attention on this symptom and seek to be more aware of it in detail. . . . Exactly what parts of your body are affected, and what different sensations do you feel in these body parts? . . . Pay particular attention to feelings of pain and tension. . . . See if you can fully accept any discomfort you feel, and let it into your awareness. . . . See if you can increase this symptom. . . .

Be aware of how you increase this symptom. . . . and now see if you can reduce it by letting go in some way. . . . Take a little more time to explore this symptom some more and become more aware of it in detail. . . .

Now *become* this symptom. As this symptom, what are you like? . . . What are your characteristics and what do you do to this person? . . . Now talk to this person and tell him what you do to him and how you make him feel. . . . As this symptom, what do you say to him? . . . What is your attitude, and how do you feel? . . .

Now become yourself again and talk back to this symptom. . . . What do you answer, and how do you feel as you answer? . . . What is going on between you? . . .

Now become the symptom again and continue the dialogue. . . . How do you feel now as this symptom, and what do you say? . . . Now tell this person what you do *for* him. . . . In what way are you useful to him, or do you make his life easier in some way? . . . What do you help him avoid? . . . What else can you say? . . .

Now become yourself again. What do you answer now? . . . Continue this dialogue for awhile and switch back and forth, so that you identify with whoever is speaking at the time. See what you can learn from each other as you continue this dialogue. . . .

Now keep your eyes closed and silently absorb this experience for awhile. . . . Now open your eyes and share your experience in first-person present tense, as if it were happening now. . . .

A symptom often has a great deal to tell you, if you take the time to pay attention to it and listen to the messages it sends you. At the same time that it is sending you messages, it is also sending messages to the people around you. A symptom is not just an expression of an alienated part of yourself, it also has powerful effects on others. See what you can learn about this from the next experiment.

Symptom—Other Dialogue

Close your eyes and again become aware of the same symptom that you worked with in the previous experiment. . . . Get really in touch with all the details of this symptom. . . . See if you can become aware of additional details that you didn't notice before. . . . Again see if you can exaggerate this symptom. . . . And be aware of how you exaggerate it—what do you do, and what muscles do you tense? . . .

Now *become* this symptom and identify with it. What are you like, and how do you feel? . . . What are your characteristics? . . . What do you do and how do you do it? . . . Now continue to be this symptom and talk to the people in your environment. Talk to parents, friends, boss, wife, children—anyone that you affect—and tell them how you affect them. . . . What do they do because of you? . . . Tell them what you do to them and see what they reply. . . . Take some time to explore how you, as symptom, affect others. . . .

Now become yourself again and say the same things to these people as *yourself*. Take responsibility for what you do. For example, "I use my headaches to make you do things I don't want to do," or whatever your situation is. . . .

Now open your eyes and share your experience in first-person present tense as if it were happening now. . . .

Some symptoms are created or exaggerated primarily to influence others and manipulate them into certain responses. Some people suddenly get a headache whenever they don't want to face a chore or difficulty, so others have to help them. Even a symptom with a specific external cause, such as a broken leg, can be used to get more care and attention than is really necessary—and some people have an amazing ability to collect broken bones and other injuries. A symptom is an ideal way to manipulate others. It is something that I can't be held responsible for; it prevents me from doing certain things and it pressures others into doing them for me.

One of the most important things to learn about a symptom is what it does for *you*. Does it keep you out of trouble, give you a rest from overwork, take you out of unpleasant activities that you don't say "No" to, bring attention from others, give you "deserved" punishment, help you avoid unpleasant tasks, etc.? Whatever you find the symptom does for you, you might explore some means other than diseasing yourself that would achieve the same result. If you become ill in order to get a rest, perhaps you could be aware of your exhaustion, and take a rest before illness forces you to. If your symptom gets you care and attention from others, perhaps there is some other way that you could ask for this care and attention. Often when such an alternative is found, the symptom improves suddenly or disappears.

You can use a fantasy dialogue with *anything* in your life that gives you trouble, either in reality or fantasy. If you are trying to stop smoking, you can have a dialogue with a pack of cigarettes. If you find yourself angry at a car that keeps breaking down, you can have a dialogue with the car. If you discover a conflict or separation in a fantasy trip, you can have a dialogue between these parts, whatever they are. For instance, you could have a dialogue between your rosebush and anything that significantly affects it. Particularly important is anything that threatens or frustrates and anything that supports or protects in any way. Have a dialogue with the people who pick your roses, the fense that shuts you off from the sun's warmth, the bugs that eat your leaves, the greenhouse that protects you, or the grandmother that takes care of you. You can also have dialogues between parts of the rosebush that seem quite different—between the tiny fibrous roots and the thick stems, between the beautiful blossoms and the ugly thorns, between the half of the roots that are in soil and the half that are wiggling in the air, etc. Dialogues with things or qualities that are absent or vague can be particularly valuable. Have a dialogue with the roots you can't feel, the water that is missing from the dry soil, etc.

Every time you experience one of these dialogues you can discover a little more about your life and become a little less fragmented. You can discover more about your difficulties, especially what you gain from these difficulties and how much you contribute to them. As you deepen your awareness of your own functioning, you will feel more centered, and your life will become much simpler and less confusing. As you take more responsibility for what you do, you will gradually be able to act much more directly and honestly, and your actions will become much more effective and less destructive and self-defeating.

Action Steps: Applications

1. Answer the question "Who am I?" by writing all the answers that come into your mind on a sheet of paper. Share these answers with a few of your classmates and give each other feedback on how you perceive each other. Are you satisfied with how well you know yourself?
2. Attend a meeting of some campus problem-solving group, such as a planning group for a dormitory or house party; while you are participating in this group, as an experiment follow very carefully "straight and narrow" patterns which reflect generally "what everybody believes." After you have done this for one meeting, if one member of the group is a good friend tell him/her what you have been doing and how you plan to be different during the next meeting. Ask for his/her help and support during the next meeting as you attempt to do more than "just what everybody expects."
3. With two of your classmates write a three-person skit in which one "actor" presents only a small part of himself and the other "actors" try to obtain more information from him about himself. Ask your teacher

if you may present this skit to the class. Have the class give you feedback on whether or not they know people who behave this way in real life and how they respond to such persons.

4. With a particularly good friend or helpful classmate, mutually attempt to share some of your more protected thoughts and feelings about yourself. Strive especially for clarity as you try to express these thoughts and feelings. Listen very carefully to the responses the other person gives as you talk about yourself. Pay close attention to responses which indicate that some of your notions about yourself seem to be unwarranted. Discuss ways in which you can achieve growth and maturity by behaving differently. Note new perceptions of yourself as you begin to think about adopting some of these new behaviors.

5. Meet in small groups (4–6 people). Using Langer and Dweck's model for the "virtuous circle of success," contrast a model for the "vicious circle of failure." Use the same four stages and show how Dennis can assure himself of failure with Marcia.

6. After you have tried the private experiments suggested by Stevens, meet in small groups to discuss your reactions. Work in pairs on the exercises labeled: "I have to—I choose to—," "I can't—I won't—," "I need— I want—," and "I'm afraid to— I'd like to—." Discuss your experiences with the group.

Chapter 3
Perceiving People and Responding to Them

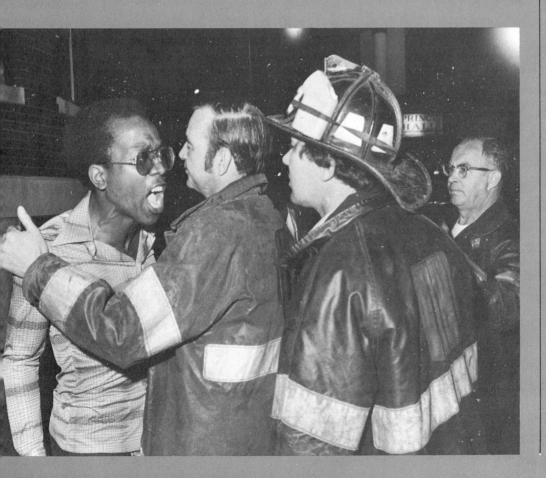

T HE FIRST STEP in communicating with another person is to form some impression of him/her. This impression directs our reactions to that person and thus influences the course of our interpersonal communication. This process of forming impressions of others and making judgments about them we have labeled interpersonal perception; our characteristic responses to people are our orientations. In this chapter we shall examine the processes of interpersonal perception and making characteristic responses in keeping with our personal needs.

The Process of Interpersonal Perception

We tend to take our perceptions of others for granted without considering why and how we form them and whether they are right. We thus select our friends without conscious realizations of why; we choose whom to ask for a date, and even marriage partners, without analyzing why we find ourselves attracted to each other.

The significance of attention to interpersonal perception has been stated by British psychologist Mark Cook:

> Everyday "informal" judgments of others can have far-reaching effects such as marriage; the same is even more true of "professional" judgments. People are selected for jobs or higher education, etc., often on the basis of an interview in which the interviewer forms, on the basis of a fifteen-minute encounter, an opinion of the person's suitability, and, in the process, affects that person's life for years to come. Interviewers often never consider whether they are right or not, but rather have a firm belief in their own infallibility. Is this justified? If not, does it not follow that the interview should be abandoned as a form of assessment? The interview is the most important single type of "professional" perception of others, but there are many more. Psychiatrists decide what is wrong with patients and have complete confidence in the correctness of the (often highly unlikely) conclusions they draw. Social workers do the same for their "clients." School teachers give assessments of their pupils' ability and often of their behaviors, with complete confidence in their own judgment. The police and the courts decide whether someone has committed an offense or whether witnesses are telling the truth, and are confident that their verdicts are correct.[1]

[1] M. Cook, *Interpersonal Perception* (Middlesex, England: Penguin, 1971), pp. 13–14.

The process of perception is generally believed to accomplish two things:

1. People record the diversity of data they encounter in a form simple enough to be retained by their limited memory; and
2. They mentally go beyond the data given to predict future events, and thereby minimize surprise.[2]

These two accomplishments of perception, selective recording and prediction, become the basis for forming our impressions of other people. In forming our impression of others, we observe their actions and expressive movements, we notice their voices, and we note what they say and do as they respond to us and other stimuli. From this data we make inferences about their cognitions, needs, emotions and feelings, goals, and attitudes. Our actions toward them and prediction of future interactions are guided by these judgments. Simultaneously the other person is making judgments about us that will direct subsequent communications to us. If our judgments of each other are correct, genuine communication can be established and effective interaction becomes possible. If, however, our observations or predictions of each other are incorrect, communication is hampered and difficulties may develop in our interpersonal relations.

As with other variables in the process of interpersonal communication, our person perceptions (i.e., our perception of another's personality) are never static; we are constantly in a state of modification and reevaluation. The flawless boyfriend of last week may now be the most despicable villain of the twentieth century. As we have greater and more diverse opportunities for interaction, our perceptions undergo change.

In essence, the process can be outlined as follows: We process the available data (our sensory bases of judgment); we define the other person and build expectations of future behavior (encoding simplification—stereotyping); in an attempt to achieve consistency of beliefs, expectations, and predictions, we choose what we see, process, and internalize (congruency and selective perception); our expectations help determine our behavior toward the other person (estimated relationship potential); and our behavior often significantly affects the behavior of the other person (reciprocal perspectives). We shall now examine this process in detail.

OUR SENSORY BASES OF JUDGMENT

Sight, sound, touch, and smell are our avenues of contact with other people. While other animals rely heavily on smell, people tend to place greater emphasis on the other sensors. As Mark Knapp observes:

Generally, Americans do not rely on their sense of smell for interpersonal cues unless perspiration odor, breath, or some other smell is unusually strong. Ironically, however, hundreds of thousands of dollars are spent by American men and women each year on deodorant sprays and soaps, mouth washes, breath mints, perfumes,

[2] J. S. Bruner, "Social Psychology and Perception," in E. Maccoby, T. M. Newcomb, and E. L. Hartley, eds., *Readings in Social Psychology* (New York: Holt, Rinehart and Winston, 1958), pp. 85–94.

aftershave lotions, and other artificial scents. The so-called "natural" scent seems to have low priority at this time point in our cultural development.[3]

In the absence of systematic studies of human perceptual responses to odor, we shall turn our attention to the other sensory bases of judgment.

Sight. As we have already suggested, visual communication, when people are together, is inevitable and basic to the establishment of a relationship. The study of nonverbal communication is tied closely to the visual signals exchanged between people.

Eye contact between people may establish the initial contact. As one sociologist suggests:

> Of the special sense organs, the eye has a uniquely sociological function. The union and interaction of individuals is based upon mutual glances. This is perhaps the most direct and purest reciprocity which exists anywhere. . . .
>
> This mutual glance between persons, in distinction from the simple sight or observation of the other, signifies a wholly new and unique union between them. . . . By the glance which reveals the other, one discloses himself. By the very act in which the observer seeks to know the observed, he surrenders himself to be understood by the observer. The eye cannot take unless at the same time it gives.[4]

Thus the dynamic nature of the visual interaction is indicated. We have all traded glances with a stranger across a room. Our desire for communication will determine whether we seek or avoid this visual contact.

In recent years, the role of eye contact in interpersonal communication has been the subject of considerable research. Knapp summarizes the research as follows:

> Eye contact is influenced by a number of different conditions: whether we are seeking feedback, need for certain markers in the conversation, whether we wish to open or close the communication channel, whether the other party is too near or too far, whether we wish to induce anxiety, whether we are rewarded by what we see, whether we are in competition with another or wishing to hide something from him, and whether we are with members of a different sex or status. Personality characteristics such as introversion/extroversion may also influence eye behavior.[5]

Another part of our impression of another person is based on his/her facial features and expressions. Studies confirm that people tend to agree in attributing certain personality traits to faces. This perceptual agreement amounts to a sort of cultural stereotyping. For example, the use of cosmetics and other grooming aids has been demonstrated to affect our judgment of women. At the time of the research, the amount of lipstick worn was perceived as relating to sexuality, while bowed lips gave the impression of being conceited,

---

[3] M. L. Knapp, *Nonverbal Communication in Human Interaction* (New York: Holt, Rinehart and Winston, 1972), p. 76.

[4] G. Simmel, "Sociology of the Senses: Visual Interaction," in R. E. Park and E. W. Burgess, eds., *Introduction to the Science of Sociology* (Chicago: University of Chicago Press, 1921), p. 358.

[5] Knapp, *Nonverbal Communication*, p. 138.

The dynamic nature of visual interaction.

demanding, immoral, and receptive to the attentions of men.[6] These perceptual judgments change, as evidenced by our culture's altered response to long-haired men.

Some facial expressions are so fleeting that we respond to them subconsciously. These have been labeled "micromomentary" expressions and have been studied by film or videotape run in slow motion. At 4 frames per second instead of the usual 24, psychologists have noticed as many as $2\frac{1}{2}$ times as many changes of expression, some lasting only $\frac{1}{5}$ of a second. These expressions seem especially significant in conflict situations. If a person wishes to appear confident but feels fearful, some of the fear is released through these flickering expressions.[7] In the current vernacular, this person would thus give off *"bad vibes."* Someone truly confident and consistent in the micromomentary expressions would be a source of *"good vibes."* Such research lends support for our thesis of the need for genuineness and lack of artificiality in our interpersonal relations.

In addition to facial expressions, other visual cues are given us in a person's gestures and other expressive movements. Subtle cues tend to be tied to individual cultures, but certain acts seem to have near-universal meaning. The elocutionists of the nineteenth century worked out detailed scientific analyses of the overt expressions of our various feelings and emotions. This

[6] P. F. Secord, "Facial Features and Inference Processes in Interpersonal Perception," in R. Tagiuri and L. Petrullo, eds., *Person Perception and Interpersonal Behavior* (Stanford, Calif.: Stanford University Press, 1958), pp. 300–318.

[7] E. A. Haggard and K. S. Isaacs, "Micromomentary Facial Expressions as Indicators of Ego Mechanisms in Psychotherapy," in L. A. Gottschalk and A. H. Auerback, eds., *Methods of Research in Psychotherapy* (New York: Appleton, 1966).

mechanistic approach for training public speakers has long been disdained as artificial and unnatural, but the fact remains that visually we are constantly communicating, either reinforcing or distracting from any messages being sent vocally.

Some people are more expressive than others in their visual communication. The highly animated person may appear more open and involved in the act of communicating, but even the stiff, rigid, aloof person cannot conceal himself for long. The person who shrugs his shoulders or waves his hands while speaking without facial emotion may only be reflecting a cultural heritage, yet the receiver of the message will react as if these expressive movements are cues to the personality. The animated talker is likely to be judged as "forceful," while the immobile speaker is thought to be "controlled" and "cold."

Jurgen Ruesch defined three classifications of a nonverbal codification system that indicate the scope of behaviors constituting nonverbal communication:

> *Sign language* includes all those forms of codification in which words, numbers, and punctuation signs have been supplanted by gestures; these vary from the monosyllabic gesture of the hitchhiker to such complete systems as the language of the deaf.
>
> *Action language* embraces all movements that are not used exclusively as signals. Such acts as walking and drinking, for example, have a dual function: on one hand, they serve personal needs, and on the other, they constitute statements to those who perceive them.
>
> *Object language* comprises all intentional and nonintentional display of material things, such as implements, machines, art objects, architectural structures and—last but not least—the human body and whatever clothes or covers it. The embodiment of letters as they occur in books and on signs has a material substance, and this aspect of words has to be considered as object language.[8]

Of the three classes named, action language is probably the least consciously performed and the richest source of communication in interpersonal relationships. Although we often communicate by gesture and material objects, we tend to be more conscious of these than we are of the natural stream of movements we perform when we go about our business of living. This topic is discussed in greater detail in Chapter 5.

Sound. We hear a voice for the first time on the telephone or radio and quickly assess our response to the speaker. Low, deep voices of males are perceived as indicators of strength, sophistication, maturity, and general appeal. The male with a high-pitched voice has a burden in our society. U.S. soldiers serving in Vietnam sometimes laughed at the orders delivered in a falsetto voice by a Vietnamese officer. In one study 18 male speakers read uniform manuscripts from prepared texts to an audience of 600 people by means of audio recording. The audience, who did not know the speakers and could not see them, was asked to match certain personality data including photographs

---

[8] J. Ruesch and J. Kees, *Nonverbal Communication* (Berkeley: University of California Press, 1956).

and sketches of people to the voices of the speakers. The experimenters concluded that the voice alone conveys some correct information in choosing among age and general personality sketches. Individual personality traits and photographs were matched less accurately. Members of the audience tended to respond in a uniform manner if incorrect in their judgments and when stereotypes were perceived from the voice (as through accents), all features of the stereotype were attributed to the speaker.[9]

A subsequent study verified that, whether we like it or not, our voices do elicit stereotyped personality judgments that may or may not be valid. In response to tape-recorded voices, freshmen students at the University of Iowa attributed personality characteristics to the speakers in terms of vocal attributes. Among the many findings,

> thinness in female voices cued perceptions of increased immaturity on four levels: social, physical, emotional, and mental, while no significant traits were correlated to thinness in the male voice. Males with throaty voices were stereotyped as being older, more realistic, mature, sophisticated, and well adjusted; females with throatiness were perceived as being less intelligent, more masculine, lazier, more boorish, unemotional, ugly, sickly, careless, inartistic, naive, humble, neurotic, quiet, uninteresting, and apathetic.[10]

In the face-to-face encounter, the vocal communication, rather than the fact of being isolated, is but one of the ingredients of the interaction. The question then becomes one of congruency. As with the micromomentary expression studies, we unconsciously note whether the words, vocal signals, and movements carry the same message. If there is conflict, the nonverbal aspects tend to speak closer to the truth because they are, to a great extent, unconsciously performed. We shall note later the potential inaccuracies of such judgment.

Touch. Tactile communication plays an ambivalent role in the lives of most of us. On the one hand, it is critical in our interpersonal relations as we affirm, encourage, support, and show love and tenderness. Moreover, widespread positive responses to exercises involving touch in encounter groups reflect a yearning for physical contact. A study controlling the conditions for interaction revealed the following comparative descriptions:

> *Verbal*—"distant, noncommunicative, artificial, insensitive, and formal."
> *Visual*—"artificial, childish, arrogant, comic, and cold."
> *Tactile*—"trustful, sensitive, natural, mature, serious, and warm."[11]

Touch thus seems to be trusted in interpersonal relations more than are other modes of communication.

On the other hand, however, our culture places strict limitations on tactile interactions. A handshake and pat on the back are acceptable among business

[9] G. W. Allport and H. Cantril, "Judging Personality from Voice," *Journal of Social Psychology*, 5 (1934), 37–55.

[10] D. W. Addington, "The Relationships of Selected Vocal Characteristics to Personality Perception," *Speech Monographs*, 35 (1968): 499–502.

[11] J. P. Bardeen, "Interpersonal Perception Through the Tactile, Verbal and Visual Modes," paper presented to the International Communication Association, Phoenix, Ariz., 1971.

associates. Affectionate pats and embraces are reserved for intimate moments. Ashley Montagu suggests, "Perhaps it would be . . . accurate to say that the taboos on interpersonal tactuality grew out of a fear closely associated with the Christian tradition in its various denominations, the fear of bodily pleasure."[12] This attitude restricting touch is a cultural one. Montagu states:

> There are clearly contact people and non-contact people, the Anglo-Saxon peoples being among the latter. Curious ways in which non-contactuality expresses itself are to be seen in the behavior of members of the non-contact cultures in various situations. It has, for example, been observed that the way an Anglo-Saxon shakes hands constitutes a signal to the other to keep his proper distance. In crowds this is also observable. For example, in a crowded vehicle like a subway, the Anglo-Saxon will remain stiff and rigid, with a blank expression on his face which seems to deny the existence of other passengers. The contrast on the French Metro, for example, is striking. Here the passengers will lean and press against others, if not with complete abandon, at least without feeling the necessity either to ignore or apologize to the other against whom they may be leaning or pressing. Often the leaning and lurching will give rise to good-natured laughter and joking, and there will be no attempt to avoid looking at the other passengers.[13]

Interpersonal perception by touch, then, is quite restricted. The handshake is the most common contributor to first impressions. One college administrator has suggested that the handshake is his most significant signal in whether he is interested in getting to know a new acquaintance. A firm, natural handshake from a warm hand is his expectation. The problem with such judgments is that, like other responses to nonverbal communication, they are intuitive and without foundation; the validity of such judgments must therefore be questioned.

THE ACCURACY OF OUR JUDGMENTS

As we have suggested, few people realize that they are constantly making judgments about others, and even fewer consider that they may be wrong about others much of the time. A basic fact to consider is that we differ in our perceptions of people. Just as witnesses at an accident note different phenomena, we may respond to different aspects of a person. William V. Haney suggests and discusses five variables that affect our responses: differing environments, differing stimuli, differing sensory receptors, differing internal states, and differing evoked sets (see Reading 3.2). Thus we vary in our ability to perceive the attitudes, intentions, feelings, needs, and wishes of others.[14] Since even slight misjudgments may cause difficulties in communicating, it is truly amazing that we do as well as we do.

As we observe the behavior of others, we merely infer with some degree of probability what is going on inside the person. How well we infer depends upon the quality of the cues, how well we know the person, and our capabilities

---

[12] A. Montagu, *Touching: The Human Significance of the Skin* (New York: Perennial Library, 1972), p. 273.

[13] Ibid., pp. 303–304.

[14] W. V. Haney, "Perception and Communication," *Communication and Organization Behavior*, rev. ed. (Homewood, Ill.: Irwin, 1967), pp. 51–77.

as judges. We have all perhaps known people about whom we could not tell in certain situations whether they were serious or joking; the cues supplied were inadequate for our purposes.

As we interact with people we see or hear them do certain things; from these observed behaviors we infer or guess that they have certain personality characteristics, motives, or intentions. For example, we may see them smile and conclude that they are "friendly." This process of inferring traits or intentions is known as *attribution* and has recently become the focus of much interest and study in social psychology.

In the development and testing of attribution theory, research has tended to support the following principles: (1) much of the behavior of others that can be observed is trivial or incidental and is not valuable for drawing conclusions regarding personality or intentions—we must be carefully tentative in the attribution process; (2) the observable behavior of others is often neatly designed to mislead or deceive us; and (3) their actions are often determined by external factors beyond their control and *not* by their internal states, personalities, or intentions. As a result of these limiting factors in the attribution process, we must use it with care; however, our experience tells us that in large measure it often works for us very well. This is essentially true for attribution of general dispositions or intentions on the bases of numerous observations over extended periods of time. Further research has indicated that we can sharpen the use of the attribution process if we pay special attention to two types of behavior: (1) that for which the observed person could have had only one or at most a very few possible reasons (for example, a young man marries a crabby, stupid, ugly, old woman who is *wealthy*), and (2) behavior that deviates markedly from widely accepted social norms (for example, a middle-aged bachelor cooks all his food over an open fire in the middle of the living room).

A college instructor felt ill and abruptly left class in the middle of a discussion. At the next class meeting the students were asked by the instructor why they thought he had left. Responses included such reactions as: The instructor was angered over the low quality of the discussion and left in disgust; he had an appointment; he thought he had arrived at a good stopping point; he wanted to give the class more preparation time; and he was reacting emotionally to one of the comments made by a member of the class. None of the class guessed the true reason, but all were willing to make inferences concerning the behavior witnessed.

It seems that the experience, and the learning that accompanies it, are vital in making accurate judgments of others. Small children become quite adept at "reading" their parents for indications of "how far to go" before actual punishment becomes imminent. Cues of punishment threat are often interpreted with great accuracy. The child, however, is not yet a discriminating observer and may try unsuccessfully to generalize from his parents to all adults. In kindergarten, attempts to cajole the teacher through baby talk and acting "cute" may prove inappropriate responses to threatened discipline.

Intelligence as well as maturity should obviously be related to our skill in judging people. Two kinds of capacity (relevant to our judgment of others) are correlated with intelligence: the ability to draw inferences about people from observations of their behavior; and the ability to account for observations in terms of general principles or concepts. A researcher arranged to have some 700 pupils in elementary and secondary public schools see a silent movie. Two scenes of the film depicted a boy engaged in "good" activities, while two others reflected "bad" behavior. The children were asked to write their opinions of the boy. Expert judges then classified these responses as inferences (if the student attempted to go beyond the action shown on the screen) and concepts (if the student attempted to explain both the good and the bad behavior by introducing conceptual notions that accounted for the diversity). This analysis revealed that the older the child, the greater the number of inferences and conceptual applications. On the average, the girls slightly exceeded the boys at all ages in the number of inferences made.[15]

There is also abundant evidence that, other things being equal, one can judge people with whom he has a common background of experience more accurately than he can judge unknown persons. Members of the same sex or age category, or the same national, ethnic, or religious groups are better judges of one another than would be an outsider. This advantage may result from sharing the same sets of norms, including the meanings attached to special gestures and speech mannerisms, as well as other forms of interpersonal responses. For example, the "straight" social scientist may have difficulty interpreting responses in an interview with groups of students who label themselves "freaks." Facetious and satirical responses may be accepted as genuine unless the interviewer becomes adept at recognizing the subtle non-verbal signals. Similarly, an American who first-names everyone as soon as he meets him will probably be more fully understood by another American who recognizes him as a compatriot and who has similar habits than by an Englishman to whom such habits may be strange. Such familiarity goes beyond mere stereotyped accuracy; the more one knows about any set of phenomena, the more sensitive one becomes to small differences within that set. This fact would account for the ability of men and women to understand the behavior of members of their own sex better than that of members of the opposite sex.

Our backgrounds also affect the ways that we simplify data about people for determining our response to them. We shall now look into this process.

ENCODING SIMPLIFICATION—STEREOTYPING

As we perceive other people and proceed to encode our impressions, the necessity of classifying the data for memory storage forces us to generalize and simplify. These classifications of people are commonly called "stereotypes." These "pictures in the head," as Walter Lippmann once described stereotypes, permit us to classify quickly and easily, providing ready-made compartments in which to place people. This phenomenon of stereotyping helps to explain why

[15] E. S. Gollin, "Organizational Characteristics of Social Judgment: A Developmental Investigation," *Journal of Personality*, 26 (1958): 139–154.

we may be "unjust" or "biased" in our reactions to social practices, institutions, and other cultures, as well as to people. The simplification involved may blind us to the innumerable differences among the members of our self-imposed classification based on such categories as age, race, socioeconomic status, national origin, and sex. This sign was on the Mexican border entrance at Tijuana a few years ago:

NOTICE
MEN WITH LONG HAIR
ARE NOT ALLOW TO
ENTER MEXICO, DUE TO
PROBLEMS CAUSED
BY LONG HAIR
PEOPLE. DON'T
INSIST ON COMING
ACROSS. AVOID
BEING SENT TO
JAIL.

The sign leading into Mexico says a great deal about police experiences with "long-hairs" in Tijuana. The conclusion was reached that long hair is a signal that there is likely to be trouble. Before dismissing this example for its naivete and grammatical errors, consider the techniques used by airlines to detect potential "skyjackers." Surveillance and searches of people with certain characteristics have often been used.

An important point to remember concerning stereotyping is that this categorical mode of perceiving people is not a fault found only among prejudiced people. It is done by all of us, due to the very nature of our perceptual processes. Our judgment of the competitiveness of a particular Jew, the intelligence of someone with a thick southern accent, or the honesty of a used car dealer, is merely the application to specific individuals of traits associated in our minds with a group. For example, consider your inferences about the driver of a car with a bumper-sticker proclaiming: "America—Love it or leave it." The attorney who refuses to accept bearded men on a jury, the school board that refuses to hire unmarried men over 30, the employer who restricts applicants to white, Anglo-Saxon Protestants, and the black who views all policemen as brutal, are all engaged in stereotyping, applying categories, and predicting future behavior based on these categories.

Stereotyping simplifies perceptual judgments by extending generalizations concerning one aspect of a person (for example, age) to force him/her to assume all characteristics that we associate with this grouping. Obviously, such judgments ignore the differences among people that we feel make us unique individuals. Stereotyping involves a "probabilities" game that tends to govern our impressions until additional behavioral data are generated. While all of us are guilty of stereotyping people in terms of certain characteristics, the practice has two serious adverse effects.

1. Stereotyping Limits Our Perceptions of the Gradations of Differences Among People. We are forced to think in "allness" terms; rather than looking for differences, we fit people into a category and use it as a basis for explaining all their behaviors. One such limitation is based on bipolar dichotomies. It is much easier to dismiss an individual totally for one character trait of which we disapprove than to consider the divergent facets of each individual that we encounter. Thus, all drinkers may be viewed as sinners, and the president of the United States is either a "good" or a "bad" president, a judgment often based on party label.

In many ways our society promotes this two-value orientation of other people. Our television and movie heroes are often portrayed as all good, while villains are viewed without redeeming qualities (although we have gained some overt sophistication in dispensing with the white hats on our cowboy heroes and the black hats on the villains and occasionally making the villain a hero). Our two-party political system and our fraternity/sorority–independent splits are facets of such an orientation. When we view people as either American or un-American, saved or damned, wholesome or degenerate, we narrow our perceptual capacities with these labels. To force a person into honest-dishonest, dependable-undependable, clean-dirty, sane-insane, liberal-conservative categories ignores the numerous possible degrees between the two extremes.

Similar to this dichotomized view of people is a special category of perception behavior known typically as "the halo effect." Acting as a type of filter to our sense perceptions, a strong, favorable view of a person gives us a mental set for judging all his behaviors. As a hypothetical example, consider the behavior of Will Gray, a young history professor and basketball enthusiast. Professor Gray was elated to learn that the university's new basketball star—known for his speed and ball handling—had enrolled in his European history course. Gray took every opportunity to discuss basketball with the young man, and so great was his admiration for his student's basketball talent that he failed to notice that the young man's work was below the standards of most of the other students in the class. When other students complained, Professor Gray attributed their reactions entirely to jealousy. Conversely, if we have a generally unfavorable impression of a person (labeled by an undergraduate student "the horns effect"), we may judge him/her unusually low in all personality traits. In both cases we are exaggerating the homogeneity of the personality of the individual. We are guilty of oversimplifying our perceptions.

2. Stereotyping Serves to Perpetuate Self-fulfilling Myths About People. If we perceive a person as untrustworthy and treat him/her as such, we tend to *make* the person less trustworthy. This phenomenon of forcing people to fit our definition of them will be discussed later in greater detail, but here we should note how by forcing people into categories we perpetuate erroneous "truths" about them.

A contemporary case in point is the claim that women, by nature, are the "weaker sex," that they are not built to perform physical labor. As a result we encourage women to spend their lives reinforcing this "weakness" rather than trying to compensate for it. We do this by teaching women not to be aggressive and not to be physically competitive in such activities as baseball, track, weight lifting, and tree climbing. Political scientist Warren Farrell cites some of the effects:

> To create a myth of weak women when that myth suits economic purposes and destroy it when it does not is a highly cynical use of human potential and aspiration. If this is a form of cynicism, it perpetuates every socializing agent: television commercials of women with whiter wash for the satisfaction of role number one (woman as a fulfilled washing machine) and soap manufacturer's budget; for role number two (woman as a fulfilled sex object) our woman is transformed into a seductive tigress to be had along with an over-horsepowered, convertible sports car—"a machine made for a man."[16]

This self-fulfilling myth extends to our interpretations of behaviors of men and women who are essentially alike. When a man has a picture of his family on his desk it is a reflection of a solid family man. A picture on a woman's desk reflects a woman more concerned with her home than her job—"a doting mother at heart." When a man's desk is cluttered he is thought a busy, overburdened executive; when a woman's desk is cluttered she is a disorganized, scatterbrained female. When a man talks about his colleagues *he* is engaged in constructive criticism or office politics; when a woman does the same, *she* is catty.

Such myths help account for antifeminine prejudice even among women. In a study at the University of Connecticut, 40 college women were given the same writing selection to evaluate, but half of them were told that it was by John T. McKay, while the other half were told it was by Joan T. McKay. John was rated as much more intelligent and persuasive than Joan, even though there was no difference in the material other than the author's name.[17] Because we do have a penchant to react initially on the basis of stereotypes, it is important that we recognize this tendency and realize that our perceptions of people are filtered.

SELECTIVE PERCEPTION AND CONGRUENCY

"We see what we want to see and hear what we want to hear." This exaggerated simplification does have an element of truth. *Selective perception* refers to the choices we make in attributing meaning to the infinite number of signals generated by another person; *congruency* is the term we use to indicate an accurate matching of experiencing and awareness. A number of studies bear on these phenomena.

A significant experiment by Solomon Asch attempted to determine how people form impressions of personality. The experimenter read to some college students a number of characteristics that were said to belong to an unknown person. For example, one list included such adjectives as "energetic," "assured," "cold," "inquisitive," "talkative," "ironical," and "persuasive." After the list was

[16] W. T. Farrell, "The Resocialization of Men's Attitudes Toward Women's Role in Society," paper presented to the American Political Science Association, Los Angeles, September 9, 1970.
[17] P. A. Goldberg, "Are Women Prejudiced Against Women?" *Transaction*, April 1968, pp. 28–30.

repeated a second time, the subjects were instructed to write a description of their impression of this person. One student wrote:

> He impresses people as being more capable than he really is. He is popular and never ill at ease. Easily becomes the center of attraction at any gathering. He is likely to be a jack-of-all-trades. Although his interests are varied, he is not necessarily well versed in any of them. He possesses a sense of humor. His presence stimulates enthusiasm and very often he does arrive at a position of importance.

Another subject reported:

> He is the type of person you meet all too often: sure of himself, talks too much, always trying to bring you around to his way of thinking, and with not much feeling for the other fellow.

Thus, the discrete terms of the list were organized into a single, unified personality. The subjects even gained impressions about characteristics not mentioned ("He possesses a sense of humor"). Asch summarized his study as follows:

> When a task of this kind is given, a normal adult is capable of responding to the instruction by forming a unified impression. Though he hears a sequence of discrete terms, his resulting impression is not discrete.[18]

The complexities and contradictions in people may be too great, however, to permit a unified impression to emerge. Another experiment involved a motion picture showing a young woman in five different scenes, designed to portray divergent aspects of her personality. In the first scene she is shown being "picked up" in front of a shabby hotel; in the second she is going to a bar with a man different from the one who had "picked her up"; the third scene shows her giving aid to a woman who has fallen down a public stairway; the fourth shows her giving money to a beggar; and the final scene shows her walking and talking with another young woman. The film was shown to a group of college students, and they were asked to write their impressions of the woman's personality. The investigators then divided the responses into three categories:

1. *Unified.* The major character qualities of sexual promiscuity and kindness were able to be integrated by 23 percent of the respondents.
2. *Simplified.* Forty-eight percent of the subjects retained only one of the two major character qualities.
3. *Aggregated.* Twenty-nine percent of the subjects kept both major character qualities but failed to unify their impression.

Therefore, less than one-fourth of the students were able to achieve an organized impression of the divergent bits of information.[19]

The importance of first impression in our interpersonal relationships was

---

[18] S. E. Asch, "Forming Impressions of Personalty," *Journal of Abnormal and Social Psychology*, 41 (1946): 256–290.

[19] E. S. Gollin, "Forming Impressions of Personality," *Journal of Personality*, 23 (1954): 65–76.

confirmed by a series of studies by social psychologist Abraham S. Luchins. As Rubin (Reading 3.1) reports, two paragraphs were read separately to different groups of subjects. In one paragraph Jim was portrayed as extroverted and in the other as introverted. Those who heard the first paragraph pictured Jim as friendly and somewhat extroverted; subjects hearing only the second paragraph correctly viewed Jim as more introverted. To determine the importance of the first impression of a person, the two paragraphs were combined in two patterns—one citing the extrovertive data first and the other citing the introvertive first. Consistently, the data presented first had the greater impact on the subjects' perception of Jim. On the trait of "friendliness," for example, 90 percent of the people who heard the first paragraph noted Jim to be friendly, as did 71 percent of the subjects hearing the combined paragraph with the extrovertive data first. Only 25 percent of the subjects who heard only the second paragraph thought Jim to be friendly; 54 percent of the people who heard the combined paragraph with the introvertive data first considered Jim friendly. Thus, with the only variable being the order of the data presentation, the composite impression of Jim differed markedly.[20]

Possibly, the first information perceived about a person gives us a "mental set" that we consider more basic than subsequent data. If in our minds we initially accept Jim as friendly, we may create special circumstances to account for his latter actions. Perhaps he had a bad day at school or is otherwise bothered by something. We try to fit the conflicting pieces of data together by inferring what is going on inside Jim. On the other hand, if we initially react to Jim as unfriendly, we may view his later actions as merely fulfilling some ulterior base motive. Consider how our impression of Jim would greatly affect our response to and communication with him.

Since we have a stake in avoiding dissonance, our expectation/prediction helps us choose what we see, process, and believe. Thus we can better account for the findings comparing the work of "John McKay" and "Joan McKay."

When a person first comes in contact with another person a variety of nonverbal and verbal messages are exchanged. The initial moments of contact between strangers tend to be especially important. As the old adage proclaims: "You only get one chance to make a good first impression." Communication researcher Charles Berger states:

> We believe that the first few minutes of verbal and nonverbal communication between strangers may determine, at least under some conditions, whether persons will be attracted to each other, and by implication, whether the persons involved in the interaction will attempt to communicate at a future time.[21]

Some researchers argue that what people communicate during their first four minutes of contact is so crucial that it will determine whether strangers will remain strangers or become acquaintances, friends, lovers, or lifetime mates.

[20] Abraham S. Luchins, "Primacy-Recency in Impression Formation," in Carl Hovland et al., *Order of Presentation in Persuasion* (New Haven: Yale University Press, 1957).
[21] C. R. Berger, "The Acquaintance Process Revisited: Explorations in Initial Interaction." Paper presented to the International Communication Association, April 1974.

Leonard and Natalie Zunin write:

> Why *four* minutes? It is not an arbitrary interval. Rather it is the *average* time, demonstrated by careful observation, during which strangers in a social situation interact *before* they decide to part or continue their encounter. By watching hundreds of people at parties, offices, schools, homes, and in recreational settings, I discovered that four minutes is approximately the minimum breakaway point—the socially acceptable period that precedes a potential shift of conversational partners.[22]

Berger questions the accuracy of the four-minute estimate, and in a systematic study of initial interaction he discovers that the content of the first few minutes between strangers is dominated by "demographic" data, that is, information about the backgrounds of the people (hometowns, families, academic majors, etc.). This concern suppresses the opportunity to pass other kinds of information during the first few minutes. After about five minutes, these demographic comments decrease and content shifts to topics of attitudes, opinions, and other people. Other topics, such as hobbies, future plans, and personality discussions are rare during the first ten minutes of interaction.[23]

Attraction. An initially favorable or unfavorable impression of another person can seriously influence your perception of their various characteristics. We define *attraction* as a positive attitude or liking for another person. Research has indicated that geographical proximity tends to influence perceived attractiveness. Other research has established a relationship between liking a person and perceived similarity to oneself—common interests, beliefs, and attitudes. But it is not clear if we tend to like people because they are like us, or if we tend to think they are like us (perceive them thus) because we find them attractive.

Research has quite clearly shown that the single most important factor in influencing initial positive attitudes between people is perceived physical attractiveness. Perception of physical appearance has significant impact on first impressions. Many times other characteristics are neglected, ignored, or perceptually distorted to accommodate an impression of physical desirability. In our culture we often try to remind ourselves to look beyond this first impression, to give proper balance to other personal characteristics. Even so, studies tend to indicate that beauty or handsomeness is also perceived as good, intelligent, and worthwhile. This topic of first impressions is discussed more fully in Reading 3.1.

ESTIMATED RELATIONSHIP POTENTIAL

When we encounter new people, we process our perceptions consciously and unconsciously and decide whether a relationship is possible and desirable. Look around you in class. By now you may have formed some friendships that mean a great deal to you, while there may be other members of the class that

---

[22] L. Zunin and N. Zunin, *Contact: The First Four Minutes* (New York, Ballantine, 1973), p. 6.
[23] Berger, "Acquaintance Process."

you would like to get to know better. Conversely, there may be members of the class that do not interest you in the least. In each case you have calculated an ERP (estimated relationship potential).

What sort of people have the greatest attraction to you? Even folk adages offer contradictory general rules: "Opposites attract," while "Birds of a feather flock together."

While there are also conflicting data from social researchers, there is a general finding of a positive relationship between similarities and attraction. Perception plays a major role here: People will tend to like those who possess attitudes similar to their own; concurrently, people will *perceive* themselves as being more similar to those they like, and less similar to those they abhor, than they really are.[24]

The relationship must be by mutual agreement; people tend to like those who like them. One study attempted to determine why people seek out people like themselves and avoid dissimilar ones.[25] The researchers reasoned that individuals might more often choose to associate with people different from themselves if they were not afraid of being disliked. When the other person is unknown, we are afraid that our behavior will be unacceptable and fear "being ourselves." In the study, college students were informed that they had been assigned to one of several groups set up to discuss why people dream. The students could elect to participate in a group of students similar to themselves or in a group composed of such people as psychologists, factory workers, and so on, quite different from the student population. The variable was the information given the students as to whether members of the dissimilar group would probably like or dislike them; some were told to select a group in which the members were likely to like them. As we might guess, those students who had been assured that everyone would find them likable were more willing to join with dissimilar people, greatly preferring dissimilar groups. Those students who had been told that they would probably not be liked were more anxious to join student groups made up of people like themselves. It was also found that if students were told that it was important to talk with people who would like them, they more often chose to interact with similar than with dissimilar people. Apparently they assumed that similar people were more likely to like them than dissimilar people.

The ERP with a given person is generated by our own feelings of self-esteem and our interpersonal needs as well as the qualities, traits, behaviors, or inferred attitudes of the other person. Sara Kiesler devised an experiment to determine the relationship of male self-esteem to his choice of a romantic partner. The male subjects were paid to participate in the study, which involved initially taking an intelligence test. Impressions of raised or lowered self-esteem were created by the experimenter's response to the test performance. During a planned break in the experiment, a girl who was a confederate in the

[24] E. Berscheid and E. H. Walster, *Interpersonal Attraction* (Reading, Mass.: Addison-Wesley, 1969), pp. 69–70.
[25] E. Walster and G. W. Walster, "Effect of Expecting to Be Liked on Choice of Associates," *Journal of Abnormal and Social Psychology*, 67 (1963): 402–404.

The relationship must be by mutual agreement; people tend to like those who like them.

experiment was introduced to each subject as a coed from a nearby college. The girl's physical appearance was altered to fit one of two conditions—attractive or unattractive—by such techniques as makeup, clothing, and heavy glasses (in the unattractive condition). The girl would be friendly and show interest in the boy subject. If the subject asked for a date or behaved in such a way as to suggest future interest, he was rated upward on an index of "romantic behavior." The conclusions were as predicted: Subjects with raised self-esteem displayed more romantic behavior toward the girl when she appeared to be highly attractive than when she was made to appear unattractive; the lowered-self-esteem subjects displayed more romantic behavior toward the girl when she seemed unattractive than when she was made to appear highly attractive.[26] Another study has shown that individuals who consider themselves (and are judged to be) socially desirable (physically attractive, personable, wealthy, famous, etc.) require that a romantic partner also be more socially desirable than the average.[27]

[26] S. B. Kiesler and R. L. Baral, "The Search for a Romantic Partner: The Effects of Self-Esteem and Physical Attractiveness on Romantic Behavior," in K. Gergen and D. Marlow, eds., *Personality and Social Psychology*, (Reading, Mass.: Addison-Wesley, 1970).

[27] E. Walster, V. Aronson, D. Abrahams, and L. Rottman, "Importance of Physical Attractiveness in Dating Behavior," *Journal of Personality and Social Psychology*, 5 (1966): 508–516.

This emphasis on physical attractiveness and social status in determining the degree of acceptance on the ERP scale makes it difficult for less attractive people in our society. A university coed has stated:

> One of the greatest troubles is that men here, as everywhere, I guess, are easily overwhelmed by physical beauty. Campus glamor girls have countless beaux flocking around them, whereas many companionable, sympathetic girls who want very much to be companions and, eventually wives and mothers, but who are not dazzling physically, go without dates and male companionship. Many who could blossom out and be very charming never have the opportunity. Eventually, they decide that they are unattractive and become discouraged to the point that often they will not attend no-date functions where they have their best (and perhaps only) opportunity to meet men. I will never understand why so many men (even, or maybe particularly, those who are the least personally attractive themselves) seem to think they may degrade themselves by dating or even dancing with a girl who does not measure up to their beauty standards.[28]

We may agree cognitively that "beauty is only skin deep," but the evidence suggests that physical attractiveness is a major contributor to the ERP of new acquaintances.

RECIPROCAL PERSPECTIVES

A few years ago a popular song pondered whether "she looked back to see if I looked back to see if she looked back." Communication problems can occur when people disagree in their interpretations of their responses to one another. We are here concerned with the question: Do you see me responding to you in the same way I see me responding to you? Further, will how I see you accepting (or not accepting) my views of me affect my further responses to you? To complicate matters more, you are also responsive to your view of my perception of you. Thus we are greatly affected by our reciprocal perspectives.

Our behavior as response to other people significantly affects their subsequent behaviors in our presence. R. D. Laing and his associates have constructed a hypothetical example of how perceptions of greed and meanness "spiral":

> Jack feels Jill is greedy. Jill feels Jack is mean. That is, Jack feels Jill wants too much from him whereas Jill feels Jack does not give her enough. Moreover Jack feels that Jill is mean as well as greedy. And Jill feels that Jack is greedy as well as mean. Each feels that the other has and is withholding what he or she needs. Moreover, Jack does not feel he is either greedy or mean himself, nor does Jill. Jack, however, realizes that Jill thinks he is mean, and Jill realizes that Jack thinks she is greedy. In view of the fact that Jack feels he is already over-generous, he resents being regarded as mean. In view of the fact that Jill feels that she puts up with so little, she resents being regarded as greedy. Since Jack feels generous but realizes that Jill thinks he is mean, and since Jill feels deprived and realizes that Jack thinks she is greedy, each resents the other and retaliates. If, after all I've put

---

[28] Quoted in E. W. Burgess, P. Wallin, and G. D. Schultz, *Courtship, Engagement and Marriage* (Philadelphia: Lippincott, 1953), pp. 63–64.

up with, you feel that I'm greedy, then I'm not going to be so forebearing in the future. If, after all I've given to you, you feel I'm mean, then you're not getting anything from me any more. The circle is whirling and becomes increasingly vicious. Jack becomes increasingly exhausted by Jill's greed and Jill becomes increasingly starved by Jack's meanness. Greed and meanness are now so confused in and between each and both that they appear to take on a life of their own. Like two boxers dominated by the fight that they are themselves fighting, the dyad, the system, the marriage, becomes "the problem" to each of the persons who comprise it, rather than they themselves.[29]

Both parties are thus caught in a spiral that destroys the potential for the relationship.

Responding to people in terms of stereotyped roles promotes a similar spiral of adversity. Betty and Theodore Roszak have depicted in vivid terms the mutually destructive effects of reciprocal responses in terms of masculine/feminine roles:

He is playing masculine. She is playing feminine. He is playing masculine because she is playing feminine. She is playing feminine because he is playing masculine. He is playing the kind of man that she thinks the kind of woman she is playing ought to admire. She is playing the kind of woman that he thinks the kind of man he is playing ought to desire. If he were not playing masculine, he might well be more feminine than she is—except when she is playing very feminine. If she were not playing feminine, she might well be more masculine than he is—except when he is playing very masculine. So he plays harder. And she plays . . . softer.[30]

Envy poisons an opportunity for love. The spiral continues until:

Her femininity, growing more dependently supine, becomes contemptible. His masculinity, growing more oppressively domineering, becomes intolerable. At last she loathes what she has helped his masculinity to become. At last he loathes what he has helped her femininity to become.[31]

Thus the reciprocal perspectives force both parties into roles and behaviors that destroy the relationship.

On a more positive level, the Jack Gibb study of defensive and supportive behaviors suggests how the characteristic climates of small groups influence individual behaviors. Defensive behaviors increase general defensiveness that serves to impair the accuracy of our perceptions. As we become emotionally involved, we tend to lose perspective. Conversely, as Gibb states:

The more "supportive" or defense reductive the climate, the less the receiver reads into the communication distorted loadings which arise from projections of his own anxieties, motives, and concerns. As defenses are reduced, the receivers become better able to concentrate upon the structure, the content and the cognitive meanings of the message.[32]

[29] R. D. Laing, H. Phillipson, and A. R. Lee, "The Spiral of Reciprocal Perspectives," in K. Giffin and B. R. Patton, eds., *Basic Readings in Interpersonal Communication* (New York: Harper & Row, 1971), p. 219.
[30] B. Roszak and T. Roszak, *Masculine/Feminine* (New York: Harper & Row, 1969), p. vii.
[31] Ibid., p. viii.
[32] J. R. Gibb, "Defensive Communication," *Journal of Communication*, 11, No. 3 (September 1961): 142.

Thus to a great extent we create the "other" person in our relationships. This phenomenon will be discussed further in Chapter 7.

Orientations Toward People

Closely related to our perception of others is our system of typical responses. In our modern environment most of our actions immediately or ultimately are reactions to other people. We must be able to anticipate, for example, how an instructor views the process of living—what his experiences mean to him, and how he goes about relating to us and to others.

Our purpose here is to review systematic approaches to the analysis of interpersonal orientations, that is, ways in which individuals are usually oriented toward other people as they attempt to communicate with them. There are several systematic approaches that scholars have developed. Each is slightly different, indicating that this field of study is in the process of being explored and has not as yet become well stabilized; each systematic approach, however, provides some additional insight into possible improvement of one's interpersonal communication habits.

OPEN- AND CLOSED-MINDEDNESS

Milton Rokeach theorized one framework for examining a given person's interpersonal orientation—a continuum extending from closed-mindedness to open-mindedness, depending on the characteristic way in which an individual receives and processes messages from others.[33] The general degree to which a person will change his/her attitude toward an object or concept after hearing another person's orientation toward that object or concept is the basis of a scale from open- to closed-mindedness. Extreme closed-mindedness is identified as dogmatism. A dogmatic person is described as follows:

1. Likely to evaluate messages on the basis of irrelevant inner drives or arbitrary reinforcements from external authority, rather than on the basis of considerations of logic;
2. Primarily seeking information from sources within his/her own belief system—for example, "the more closed-minded a Baptist, the more likely it is that he/she will know what he/she knows about Catholicism or Judaism through Baptist sources";
3. Less likely to differentiate among various messages coming from belief systems other than his/her own—for example, an "extremely radical rightist may perceive all nonrightists as communist sympathizers";
4. Less likely to distinguish between information and the source of the information and likely to evaluate the message in terms of his/her perceptions of the belief system of the other person.

[33] Milton Rokeach, *The Open and Closed Mind* (New York: Basic Books, 1960).

Essentially the "closed" person is one who rigidly maintains a system of beliefs, who sees a wide discrepancy between his/her belief system and those belief systems that are different from his/hers, and who evaluates messages in terms of the "goodness-of-fit" 'with his/her own belief system.

It should be readily apparent that the "openness" or "closed-mindedness" of an individual is an index to his/her interpersonal orientation. In like manner it is an indicator of the way this person will interpret another person's attempts to communicate with him/her.

COOPERATIVE–UNCOOPERATIVE BEHAVIOR

Another conceptual framework for examining our characteristic responses to people is in terms of attempts to be either cooperative or uncooperative. In Chapter 2 we noted the interpersonal needs of all people. Some of us attempt to fulfill these needs with the *help* of others, while some of us move at the *expense* of others.

Obviously all situations do not call for cooperative behaviors. When we are engaged in purchasing an automobile, we are in effect competing to reduce the margin of potential profit for the salesperson. In such situations our gain is at the expense of the other party. Other situations, however, involve the potential for mutual gain since we are seeking compatible goals; for example, planning a vacation with the family may involve conflicting ideas, but the outcome of the best possible trip for all is shared mutually. Regardless of situation, some people display orientations of willingness to cooperate or an inherent tendency to compete.

Basic to this orientation is the degree of trust that we feel toward other people. If we fear others and their motives, we are likely to respond in a defensive, uncooperative manner. Only when we trust—are willing to rely on people to achieve a desired objective in a risky situation—is cooperation possible.[34] Such trust can be shown from a classic example that has been labeled "the prisoner's dilemma":

> Two suspects are taken into custody and separated. The district attorney . . . points out to each that he has two alternatives: to confess to the crime the police are sure they have done or not to confess. If they both do not confess then the district attorney states that he will book them on some trumped-up charge . . . if they both confess, they will be prosecuted, but he will recommend less than the most severe sentence; but if one confesses and the other does not, then the confessor will receive lenient treatment for turning state's evidence, whereas the latter will get the "book" slapped at him.[35]

Compare the above situation with disarmament talks. Trust is essential if we are going to be cooperative and disarm. The risk is high, and if we misjudge, the loss will be gigantic! The difference is one of fighting a war or negotiating

[34] For a detailed discussion of the dimensions of trust, see K. Giffin, "Interpersonal Trust in Small Group Communication," *Quarterly Journal of Speech*, 53 (1967): 224–234.
[35] R. D. Luce and H. Raiffa, *Games and Decisions: Introduction and Critical Survey* (New York: Wiley, 1957), p. 95.

for peace. Willingness to cooperate is obviously then tied to the amount of risk involved and the desirability of the goal.

Some people are more competitive than others and tend to view all interpersonal relationships in terms of winning or losing. Morton Deutsch studied this orientation in a game situation.[36] To cooperate meant mutual gain for both parties, while individual gains as a result of a competitive orientation were made at the other's expense.

From Deutsch's work and that of his students, the following inferences can be drawn concerning interpersonal cooperation:

1. A cooperative (or noncooperative) orientation on the part of the individual will influence his tendency toward actual cooperative behavior.[37]
2. Communication between the speaker and listener will tend to increase the likelihood of cooperation between them, especially if they express their intentions and expectations of each other and indicate their plan of reacting to violations of their expectations.[38]
3. Increased social power over another person increases the likelihood of the powerful person cooperating with the person over whom he has power.[39]
4. A person will tend to cooperate with another person if he knows they both dislike a specified third person.[40]
5. Cooperative persons tend to have personalities which can be characterized as below average in authoritative or dogmatic orientations.[41]

This basic interpersonal orientation applies to many social situations where mutual trust and cooperation are vital, as in husband-wife relations, pupil-teacher interactions, and in a theater where there is a fire.

INTERPERSONAL RESPONSE TRAITS

A slightly more elaborate classification of interpersonal styles has been developed by Karen Horney.[42] She classified people into three types according to their interpersonal response traits: (1) moving toward others; (2) moving against others; and (3) moving away from others. According to Horney's system, going toward others ranges from mild attraction to affiliation, trust, and love. Such a person shows a marked need for affection and approval and a special need for a partner, that is, a friend, lover, husband, or wife who is to fulfill all

---

[36] M. A. Deutsch, "Trust and Suspicion," *Journal of Conflict Resolution*, 2 (1958): 265–279.

[37] M. A. Deutsch, "The Effect of Motivational Orientation upon Trust and Suspicion," *Human Relations*, 13 (1960), 123–139.

[38] J. Loomis, "Communication, the Development of Trust, and Cooperative Behavior," *Human Relations*, 12 (1959): 305–315.

[39] L. Solomon, "The Influence of Some Types of Power Relationships and Game Strategies upon the Development of Interpersonal Trust," *Journal of Abnormal and Social Psychology*, 61 (1960): 223–230.

[40] J. N. Farr, "The Effects of a Disliked Third Person upon the Development of Mutual Trust," paper presented to the American Psychological Association Annual Conference, New York, 1957.

[41] M. Deutsch, "Trust, Trustworthiness, and the F Scale," *Journal of Abnormal and Social Psychology*, 61 (1960): 138–140.

[42] K. Horney, *Our Inner Conflicts* (New York: Norton, 1945).

expectations of life and to take responsibility for good and evil. This person "needs to be liked, wanted, desired, loved; to feel accepted, welcome, approved of, appreciated; to be needed, to be of importance to others, especially to one particular person; to be helped, protected, taken care of, guided."[43]

Behavior identified as going against others ranges from mild antagonism to hostility, anger, and hate. Such a person perceives that the world is an arena where, in the Darwinian sense, only the fittest survive and the strong overcome the weak. Such behavior is typified by a callous pursuit of self-interest. The person with this interpersonal orientation needs to excel, to achieve success, prestige, or recognition in any form. According to Horney, such a person has "a strong need to exploit others, to outsmart them, to make them of use to himself." Any situation or relationship is viewed from the standpoint of "what can I get out of it?"[44]

Behavior characterized as going away from others ranges from mild alienation to suspicion, withdrawal, and fear. With this orientation, the underlying principle is that one never becomes so attached to anybody or anything that he or it becomes indispensable. There is a pronounced need for privacy. When such a person goes to a hotel, he rarely removes the "Do Not Disturb" sign from outside his door. Self-sufficiency and privacy both serve his outstanding need, the need for utter independence. His independence and detachment have a negative orientation, aimed at not being influenced, coerced, tied, or obligated. To such a person, according to Horney, "to conform with accepted rules of behavior or to additional sets of values is repellant. . . . He will conform outwardly in order to avoid friction, but in his own mind he stubbornly rejects all conventional rules and standards."[45]

Horney summarizes the three types as follows:

> Where the compliant type looks at his fellow men with a silent question, "Will he like me?"—and the aggressive type wants to know, "How strong an adversary is he?" or "Can he be useful to me?"—the detached person's concern is "Will he interfere with me? Will he want to influence me or (will he) leave me alone?"[46]

Most of us display more than one of these interpersonal response patterns at different times toward various people. However, it is quite surprising how easily we can classify our acquaintances on the basis of their choice of words: "Will they like me?"—"I wonder if I can beat him (or use him)?"—or, "Will they interfere with me or let me alone?"

ORIENTATIONS BASES ON INTERPERSONAL NEEDS

Although all the orientations discussed relate to the needs of the people involved, a more elaborate and systematic approach has been advanced by William Schutz.[47] The major premise of this theory is that people need people;

[43] Ibid., pp. 50–51.
[44] Ibid., p. 65.
[45] Ibid., p. 78.
[46] Ibid., pp. 80–81.
[47] W. C. Schutz, *FIRO: A Three-Dimensional Theory of Interpersonal Behavior* (New York: Holt, Rinehart and Winston, 1958).

and each person, from childhood on, develops a fundamental interpersonal relations orientation. Schutz posited three fundamental dimensions of interpersonal behavior: inclusion, control, and affection. His analysis of the results of a large number of research studies—parental, clinical, small group—shows convergence in their discovery of the importance of these three areas and demonstrates how a measure of these three variables can be used both to test a variety of hypotheses about interpersonal relations and to understand and predict interpersonal communication behavior.

Each of these three areas can be divided into two parts: the behavioral characteristics that the individual actively *expresses* toward others and the degree to which he *wishes* such behavior to be directed toward him.

Inclusion concerns the entrance into associations with others. The need for inclusion involves being interested in other people to a sufficient degree that others are satisfactorily interested in oneself. Behavior aimed at gaining inclusion is seen as an attempt to attract the attention and interest of others.

The need to *control* includes the ability to respect the competence of others and the need to be respected by others. It is the need to feel adequate and reliable. Control behavior implies decision-making and is identified by such terms as "authority," "influence," "dominance," "submission," and "leadership."

Affection, unlike inclusion and control, occurs primarily between two people (at a time). It includes the need to love and to be loved. Degrees of affectionate behavior are implied in the terms "friendliness," "caring," "liking," "hate," "loving," and "emotional involvement."

To have satisfactory interpersonal relationships, according to Schutz, in each of these three areas *the individual must establish a balance between the amount of behavior he actively expresses and the amount he desires to receive from others.*

We believe that Schutz's theory is significant because it establishes the groundwork for understanding the basis of a relationship between people. From his theory, we can infer that others respond to us within a framework of the role we indicate they should play in our interpersonal relationship. They can then make a choice to play that role or not to respond to us in the way that we intend. For example, if we show a desire to control other people, they will respond according to their willingness to be controlled or refuse to respond to our messages. Of course, they may initiate new communication concerning the role we have identified for them to play.

Summary and Preview of Readings

As we come into contact with one another, we receive sensory signals that establish the basis for our communication. The attempts at communication will be guided by our interpretation of these signals. These signals and the interpretations establish the basis of our "interpersonal perception." By interpersonal perception we mean the way individuals view and evaluate each other in direct interaction; this encompasses the interrelationships between the perceiver, the person perceived, and the external contextual variables to be discussed in Chapter 6.

While all of our sense receptions form the basis for a variety of perceptual cues, interpersonal perception differs from our perception of objects in at least two ways: First, unlike objects, other people are perceived as having motives that influence their behaviors; second, the person being perceived is simultaneously perceiving the other person and may alter his/her behaviors accordingly.

When one person responds in a specific way to another person, this manner of response might be termed a type of interpersonal orientation. However, the concern of this chapter has been with the way in which a person or persons generally respond to other people—an interpersonal life-style. We might say our interest is on the wholesale, rather than the retail, level. Sets of typical interpersonal responses may be identified, classified, observed, and analyzed. Basic classifications of interpersonal response sets are commonly recognized by all of us: We note that a person is generally cooperative or competitive, generally open to new friends and ideas, or usually closed to these situations. Individuals may orient themselves toward other people to satisfy interpersonal needs identified as inclusion, control, and affection. A case is made for the proposition that these needs, as described, constitute a conceptual system that is helpful in the prediction and explanation of interpersonal behavior.

In the first article that follows, "The Rise and Fall of First Impressions," Zick Rubin emphasizes the importance of other people's first impressions of us. More than most of us think, and for longer than we think, first impressions influence the ways people respond to us. Rubin identifies interpersonal behaviors that influence these first impressions.

In William V. Haney's article, "Perception and Communication," he indicates that, in general, "what you see is what you get." By this he means that we respond to people in terms of how we see them whether that is what they "really" are or not; for us, our perception of them *is* our reality. If we see people as posing a threat to us (even if they are not threatening), we tend to behave defensively. Haney offers specific suggestions for coping with defensive behavior and avoiding it when it is necessary.

INTERPERSONAL COMMUNICATION IN ACTION

The Rise and Fall of First Impressions

How People Are Perceived

Zick Rubin

Master, shall I begin with the usual jokes
That the audience always laugh at?
—Aristophanes, *Frogs*

The acknowledged superstar of the 1971 baseball season was a twenty-one-year-old Oakland Athletics pitcher named Vida Blue. Signed for his first full major league season for the comparatively paltry salary of $14,750, Blue proceeded to leap to the heights, winning the starting assignment in the All-Star Game, the American League's Most Valuable Player Award, and the Cy Young Award for the best pitcher in the league. After a prolonged hold-out he finally signed for the 1972 season for a reported salary of some $60,000, representing an annual raise

of about 300 percent. Some writers were calling him the greatest left-handed pitcher who ever lived—better than Grove, better than Koufax.

There is no doubt that Blue had a superb 1971 season, finishing the year with a won–lost record of 24–8 and leading the league with an earned-run average of 1.82. But this meteoric rise to fame seemed to be based not only on what he did, but also on the *order in which he did it*. Beginning the season in relative obscurity, Blue proceeded to win ten of his first eleven decisions, four of them with shutouts. By late May he was leading the league in earned-run average (1.01), strikeouts (78), shutouts (4), and complete games (8). He continued on the same course through June, July, and early August, accumulating an amazing won–lost record of 22–4. His chances to become a thirty-game winner looked excellent. In late August and September, however, Blue's fortunes took a downward turn. After winning his first three games in August, he proceeded to lose four of his last five decisions. During the stretch between August 15 and September 26, three days before the end of the season, he managed to win only a single game. Whereas he had led the league in four major categories in late May, he ended the season on top in only one, earned-run average—and even this index had worsened over the course of the season.[1] In 1972 Blue's performance continued to decline. Although the Athletics won the American League pennant and World Series, Blue's record was a disappointing 6–10, and he did not pitch well in the series.

There are many possible explanations for Blue's decline toward the end of the 1971 season, including the facts that his teammates were not getting as many runs for him and that he was pulled out of several games that he might have won. But without denying Blue's legitimate right to the acclaim he received, one might well speculate that it would not have been quite so great if his season had progressed in reverse order, starting with a mediocre record of 5–4 after the first two months and only gradually building up to his final 24–8. Blue's tremendous acclaim at the end of the 1971 season illustrates what social psychologists call a "primacy effect" in person perception. The general principle is that first impressions establish the mental framework in which a person is viewed, and later evidence is either ignored or reinterpreted to jibe with this framework.

But whereas first impressions are often extremely powerful they do not always determine our ultimate opinions of people. In the fall of 1971 a college quarterback named Gary Wichard was widely reported to be near the top of the draft lists of several professional football teams. Although Wichard played for a small college, C. W. Post, he had performed outstandingly through most of his college career. A month before the professional draft, however, Wichard played in the Senior Bowl game and performed poorly. As a result, he was not selected until the sixteenth round of the pro draft, by the Baltimore Colts. George Young, the Colts' personnel director, explained the management's reasoning: "One of our maladies is that we tend to overlook consistency and Gary had that. Like any other business, it's a matter of what you have done lately."[2] The case of Gary Wichard illustrates what social psychologists call a "recency effect," in which later information outweighs or replaces a previously performed impression.

Primacy and recency effects are of importance not only to the baseball or football scout, but also to the student and practitioner of liking and loving. As sociologists George J. McCall and J. R. Simmons observe, "we interact, not with individuals and objects, but with *our images* of them."[3] These images go beyond our perception of the other person's physical characteristics or overt actions to our inferences about

---

[1] Vida Blue's statistics were obtained from the *Official Baseball Guide for 1972* (St. Louis: Sporting News, 1972)

[2] *The New York Times*, February 6, 1972.
[3] George J. McCall and J. R. Simmons, *Identities and Interactions* (New York: Free Press, 1966), p. 106.

his underlying personality traits and abilities. These inferences are never perfectly objective or reliable, but they are necessary to allow us to predict the other person's future behavior and to develop our own strategy of relating to him. In this chapter we will survey research on the ways in which people perceive other people. A central focus will be the attempt to distinguish between the cases of Vida Blue and of Gary Wichard—that is, to specify the factors that lead to the perpetuation of first impressions and those that lead to their downfall.

Reputations and Stereotypes

We often begin to form our impression of another person even before we meet him. Before going out on a blind date, people are briefed about the date's characteristics by their fixer-uppers. Before attending the first lecture of a course, students learn something about the professor from students who took the course the previous year. Professors similarly obtain advance information about their students. In each case the other person's reputation, regardless of whether or not it is in fact justified, is likely to shape the way the person is perceived when he is later encountered. In most cases, the direction of this impact is that of the primary effect—that is, we are primed to see a person as living up to his reputation.

In a pioneering experiment conducted in the late 1940s, social psychologist Harold Kelley[4] arranged to have students in a social science course at M.I.T. told that their class would be

taken over for the day by a new instructor, whom they would be asked to evaluate at the end of the class period. Before the instructor was introduced, the students were given a biographical note about him to read. Unbeknownst to the students, two versions of the sketch were employed. The sketch that was distributed to half of the students read as follows:

> Mr. —— is a graduate student in the Department of Economics and Social Science here at M.I.T. He has had three semesters of teaching experience in psychology at another college. This is his first semester teaching Economics 70. He is 26 years old, a veteran, and married. People who know him consider him to be a rather warm person, industrious, critical, practical, and determined.

The other half of the students read the following description:

> Mr. —— is a graduate student in the Department of Economics and Social Science here at M.I.T. He has had three semesters of teaching experience in psychology at another college. This is his first semester teaching Economics 70. He is 26 years old, a veteran, and married. People who know him consider him to be a rather cold person, industrious, critical, practical, and determined.

The two descriptions differ in but a single word: In the first sketch the instructor is described as "warm" and in the second as "cold." After the students had read the sketch, the instructor appeared and led the class in a twenty-minute discussion. During the discussion an observer recorded how often each student made a comment or asked a question. After the instructor had left the room, the students were asked to rate him on a set of

[4] Harold H. Kelley, "The Warm-Cold Variable in First Impressions of Persons," *Journal of Personality*, 1950, *18*, 431–439.

adjective scales and to write a brief description of him. The results were striking. Although all of the students had been exposed to the same person at the same time, those who had been told that he was reputed to be "warm" rated him as substantially more considerate, informal, sociable, popular, good-natured, humorous, and humane than those who had been forewarned that he was "cold." Identical behaviors of the instructor were apparently interpreted quite differently by the students in the two conditions. Kelley noted, for example, that "several 'cold' observers described him as being '. . . intolerant: would be angry if you disagree with his views . . .'; while several 'warm' observers put the same thing this way: 'Unyielding in principle, not easily influenced or swayed from his initial attitude.' "

The instructor's reputation also influenced the students' willingness to interact with him: 56 percent of the "warm" subjects entered the class discussion, while only 32 percent of the "cold" subjects did so. As this result suggests, once a negative first impression of another person is formed, we may avoid further contact with him. Such avoidance, in turn, is likely to foreclose our opportunity to revise or correct the impression. Theodore Newcomb has labeled this unfortunate phenomenon "autistic hostility," and suggests that it applies to relationships between groups as well as between individuals.[5]

There are many analogous examples of the impact of a person's reputation upon our impression of him. If a girl is told in advance that her blind date is extremely witty, she will be primed to categorize his remarks as witty ones. If the same date were billed as solemn and humorless, the same "witty" remarks might well fall flat. This is the secret of many comedians. Since they have the reputation of being uproariously funny, people are predisposed to laugh at practically everything they say. Similarly, in the first game of the recent world chess championship, an overeager Bobby Fischer made a "beginner's blunder," seizing a pawn in a way that trapped his own bishop behind enemy lines. But for some time afterward the commentators, awed by Fischer's reputation, insisted that the move was part of a winning combination that was simply too deep for anyone else to fathom. (Unfortunately for Bobby, then-champion Boris Spassky did not make this interpretation. After an initial double-take, he coolly proceeded to capture the bishop and win the game.) "In social perception," Fritz Heider writes, "the act is in many cases assimilated to the origin. Acts or products are colored by the qualities of the person to whom they are ascribed."[6]

The impact of a person's reputation on the way we view him is mirrored in the way we view entire groups of people. Black people are often expected to be musical, Italians to be emotional, football players to be unintelligent. In some cases these group expectations, known as *stereotypes*, have a factual basis, in the sense that on the average members of the group conform to the expectation to some degree. In other cases they have no factual basis whatsoever. In any event, when it comes to forming impressions of an individual

[5] Theodore M. Newcomb, "Autistic Hostility and Social Reality," *Human Relations*, 1947, *1*, 69–87.

[6] Fritz Heider, "Social Perception and Phenomenal Causality," *Psychological Review*, 1944, *51*, 358–374.

member of the group, the expectations produced by knowledge of this group membership are too frequently dead wrong. Nevertheless the expectations persist, with powerful effects upon our evaluations of individuals. Ex-pitcher Jim Bouton made this observation in his diary of a major league season:

> I'm not sure I'm going to like Don Mincher. It's prejudice, I know, but everytime I hear a Southern accent I think: Stupid. A picture of George Wallace pops into my mind. It's like Lenny Bruce saying he could never associate a nuclear scientist with a Southern accent.[7]

In addition to their membership in religious, ethnic, occupational, or regional groups, people may be stereotyped on the basis of their physical appearance. In his *Eminent Victorians*, Lytton Strachey described Dr. Thomas Arnold in the following terms:

> Such was the man who, at age 33, became headmaster of Rugby. His outward appearance was the index of his inward character: Everything about him denoted energy, earnestness, and the best intentions. His legs, perhaps, were shorter than they should have been; but the sturdy athletic frame, especially when it was swathed (as it usually was) in the flowing robes of a Doctor of Divinity was full of an imposing vigor; and his head, set decisively upon the collar, stock, and bands of ecclesiastical tradition, clearly belonged to a person of eminence. The thick, dark clusters of his hair, his bushy eyebrows and curling lower lip—all these revealed a temperament of ardour and determination. His eyes were bright and large; they were also obviously honest. . . .

As social psychologists Albert Hastorf,

David Schneider, and Judith Polefka note, "Many of the characteristics noted are the results of inferences by the author, yet they are cast as if they were just as clear and as given in experience as the individual's physical height."[8] Vigor is inferred from a sturdy frame, determination from a firm lip, honesty from bright eyes. Jim Bouton makes the same sort of inferential leap: "Before the first workout, Joe Schultz, the manager (he's out of the old school, I think, because he *looks* like he's out of the old school, short, portly, bald, ruddy-faced, twinkly-eyed), stopped by while I was having a catch."[9]

As in the case of other stereotypes, the assumed links between appearance and personality may be wholly idiosyncratic, as when a person encounters someone who looks like an old friend and assumes that the physical resemblance extends to his temperament as well. In other cases the links have achieved a large degree of cultural acceptance. Fat people are often assumed to be jolly, men with moustaches to be villainous, women with bowed lips to be seductive. Sometimes the stereotypes can be traced to metaphorical or functional assumptions. People with thin lips ("tight-lipped") may be typecast as reticent, people with "coarse" skin as insensitive, and people with high foreheads (and therefore presumably more brain room) as intelligent.[10] I have a rather low fore-

[7] Jim Bouton, *Ball Four* (New York: Dell, 1971), p. 52.

[8] Lytton Strachey's description of Dr. Arnold is from *Eminent Victorians* (New York: Modern Library, 1933), as cited by Albert H. Hastorf, David J. Schneider, and Judith Polefka in *Person Perception* (Reading, Mass.: Addison-Wesley, 1970), p. 10. Hastorf et al. are quoted from p. 11.

[9] Bouton, p. 13.

[10] The inference of personality traits from physical features is discussed by Paul F. Secord, "Facial Features and Inference Processes in Person Perception," in Renato Tagiuri and Luigi Petrullo (Eds.), *Person Perception and Interpersonal Behavior* (Stan-

head myself and look forward to growing bald as a means of gaining an aura of intellect.

In its most general form the stereotyping process refers to our pervasive tendency to fill out our impressions of other people on the basis of assumptions about which characteristics tend to co-occur. When some people are told that someone is unsuccessful, for example, they may assume that he is unintelligent as well, even though they have no direct evidence for the assumption. A woman may be attracted to tall men not because she values tallness itself, but because she has somewhere along the line acquired the notion that tall men are more likely to be successful. Psychologists call a person's set of assumptions about which characteristics of others are likely to co-occur his "implicit personality theory." Each of us has such a theory, even though we may be unable to spell it out explicitly. As a result, each of us, whether consciously or not, engages in stereotyping to a greater or lesser degree. We go beyond the information directly known about another person to a mental construction of what he must be like.

Social psychologists Seymour Rosenberg and Russell Jones recently made use of a computational technique called multidimensional scaling to explore in detail one man's personality theory. The person they chose was the American novelist Theodore Dreiser.[11] They began by carefully recording each description of a physical, social, or psychological trait applied by Dreiser to each of 241 different characters in his collection of sketches, *A Gallery of Women.* They proceeded to construct an elaborate map of the dimensions underlying Dreiser's descriptions, based on an analysis of which combinations of traits tended to be applied to the same characters. One of the most central dimensions that emerged from their mapping was that of "male–female." In other words, one would know a good deal about all other aspects of a Dreiserian character's personal traits if one knew only the character's sex. Female characters were likely to be described as attractive, charming, defiant, intelligent, cold, and clever. These characteristics may reflect Dreiser's own predilection [for] "attractive, unconventional women" and his reliance on female literary agents. On the other hand, the mapping revealed that Dreiser reserved for men the traits of sincerity, genius, and greatness, perhaps revealing something of the novelist's conception of himself.

Rosenberg and Jones also discovered a notable absence of a basic split between the positive and negative aspects of people in Dreiser's descriptions. "Good" and "bad" traits were as likely as not to co-occur in the same characters. This conclusion jibes with Granville Hicks's observation that "there are no contemptible persons in Dreiser's novels. Although at times he professed a Nietzschean scorn of the masses . . . he instinctively made the best case possible for any person he wrote about."[12] Former Green Bay Packer guard Jerry Kramer illustrated

ford: Stanford University Press, 1958). A related discussion is provided by Solomon Asch, "The Metaphor: A Psychological Inquiry," in the same book.

[11] Seymour Rosenberg and Russell Jones, "A Method for Investigating and Representing a Person's Implicit Theory of Personality: Theodore Dreiser's View of People," *Journal of Personality and Social Psychology,* 1972, *22,* 372–386.

[12] Granville Hicks, "Theodore Dreiser and 'the Bulwark,'" in A. Kazin and C. Shapiro (Eds.), *The Stature of Theodore Dreiser* (Bloomington: Indiana University Press, 1965), p. 229.

a similar transcendence of the good–bad polarity when he described his coach, the late Vince Lombardi, as "a cruel, kind, tough, gentle, miserable, wonderful man whom I often hate and often love and always respect."[13]

Kramer's description is probably a good deal more accurate than any description that stressed only Lombardi's toughness or only his compassion. Nevertheless, it violates a basic organizing principle inherent in most people's implicit personality theories. The principle is that the "social personalities" of other people, as created by our thoughts about them, should be tied up in neat, uncontradictory packages. It is summed up in Heider's influential theory of cognitive balance:

> We want to attain orderly and stable evaluations; we want to find the good and the bad distributed in a simple and consistent fashion. The codification in terms of positive and negative value is simpler when the positive features are grouped into one unit and the negative ones in another unit. For instance, there is a tendency to see only the positive traits in a person we like. . . . If we hear that a person we like has done something we dislike, we are confronted with a disharmonious situation, and there will arise a tendency to change it to a more balanced situation; for example, we can refuse to believe that the person performed this negative action.[14]

Several studies have documented Heider's proposition that we tend to see the people we like as having almost exclusively positive traits and those whom we dislike as having almost exclusively negative traits. For example,

college students in Kentucky and California were recently asked to describe "liked" and "disliked" persons with whom they were well acquainted by choosing words from a list of two hundred adjectives.[15] There proved to be quite general agreement among the students that liked people were energetic, considerate, happy, intelligent, and truthful, whereas disliked people were complaining, insincere, narrow-minded, quarrelsome, and self-centered. Thus we may view liking and disliking as themselves giving rise to stereotypical images of others, sometimes known as positive and negative "halo effects." There is, to be sure, a chicken-and-egg problem here. Do we consider another person to be energetic, considerate, and intelligent because we like him, or do we like him because we value his qualities of energy, consideration, and intelligence? The evidence suggests that in fact the causal link goes in *both* directions: from liking to favorable evaluation, and from favorable evaluation to liking.

Seeing What You're Looking For

The decision as to which pigeonhole to put a person in depends not only on expectations based on his reputation or group membership, but also upon the perceiver's own needs and values. Studies of the perception of physical objects have proven that perception is an active, constructive process, rather than a passive one in which external stimuli automatically impinge themselves upon our consciousness.

---

[13] Jerry Kramer, *Instant Replay* (New York: Signet, 1969), p. xii.
[14] Heider, "Perceiving the Other Person," in Tagiuri and Petrullo, p. 25.

[15] Albert J. Lott, Bernice E. Lott, Thomas Reed, and Terry Crow, "Personality-trait Descriptions of Differentially Liked Persons," *Journal of Personality and Social Psychology*, 1970, *16*, 284–290.

This process is powerfully affected by our physical and psychological needs. Men who have not eaten for long periods of time, for example, display the "mirage effect" of seeing hazy objects as food or eating utensils. Poor children—for whom we may suppose that the value of money is greater—reportedly see coins as being larger than rich children do. As explained by psychologist Jerome Bruner, our needs and values have the effect of making certain of our mental pigeonholes more available for use than others.[16]

The tendency to see what you are looking for, sometimes called "perceptual accentuation," becomes even more striking when it comes to forming impressions of other people. The link between value and perceived size documented in the coin-size study also applies to the perceived size of other people. Two-thirds of a sample of Californians who planned to vote for John F. Kennedy in 1960 perceived him as being *taller* than Richard M. Nixon, while more than half of those planning to vote for Nixon perceived Nixon as being at least as tall.[17] A man's height indeed seems to be associated with his ascribed value in our society, a phenomenon which one sociologist has recently denounced as "heightism."[18]

(The association between women's heights and their value is less clear. One study found that there was a significant correlation between students' expressed liking for President Johnson and their estimates of his height, but that no such link between height estimates and liking existed for Lady Bird.)[19]

A recent experiment conducted by social psychologists Walter Stephan, Ellen Berscheid, and Elaine Walster probed the impact of sexual arousal on perceptual accentuation.[20] The subjects, male undergraduates at the University of Minnesota, thought they were taking part in two unrelated experiments. In the "first experiment," half of the subjects read a description of a highly arousing seduction scene. The other subjects read a highly nonarousing description of the sex life of herring gulls. In the "second experiment," each of the young men was asked for his impressions of an attractive coed on the basis of her photograph and a rather uninformative self-description that she had purportedly provided on a questionnaire. As Stephan and his colleagues had predicted, the sexually aroused subjects rated the girl as being significantly more attractive than unaroused subjects did. The men indeed "saw" what they wanted to see.

The Minnesota researchers also varied whether or not the subject anticipated that he would actually meet the girl he rated, as part of a research

[16] Studies of the effects of the perceiver's needs upon perception include David C. McClelland and John W. Atkinson, "The Effect of Different Intensities of the Hunger Drive on Perception," *Journal of Psychology*, 1948, *25*, 205–222; and Jerome S. Bruner and C. C. Goodman, "Value and Need as Organizing Factors in Perception," *Journal of Abnormal and Social Psychology*, 1947, *42*, 33–44. These and other studies representing what came to be called the "new look in perception" were analyzed by Bruner in "On Perceptual Readiness," *Psychological Review*, 1957, *64*, 123–152.

[17] Harold H. Kassarjian, "Voting Intentions and Political Perception," *Journal of Psychology*, 1963, *56*, 85–88.

[18] Saul D. Feldman, "The Presentation of Shortness in Everyday Life—Height and Heightism in American Society: Toward a Sociology of Stature,"

a paper presented to the American Sociological Association meetings, 1971.

[19] Charles D. Ward, "Own Height, Sex, and Liking in the Judgment of Heights of Others," *Journal of Personality*, 1967, *35*, 381–401.

[20] Walter Stephan, Ellen Berscheid, and Elaine Walster, "Sexual Arousal and Heterosexual Perception," *Journal of Personality and Social Psychology*, 1971, *20*, 93–101.

INTERPERSONAL COMMUNICATION IN ACTION

program on dating. Half of the men in each of the arousal conditions were told that the girl they were to rate was their randomly assigned blind date, while half were told that they had been assigned to a date with someone else. The coed was perceived as most sexually receptive—the specific traits rated included "amorous," "willing," and "non-inhibited"—by men who were sexually aroused and also expected to have a date with her. Thus the men's impressions were influenced not only by their sexual needs, but also by their expectations as to whether the coed might be able to satisfy them.

Our needs and values seem to have two interrelated effects on person perception. First, one focuses attention on those aspects of the other person that are relevant to what one is looking for and consequently ignores other less relevant characteristics. Football scouts sort prospects in terms of size and speed and ignore most of their other human characteristics. Cabdrivers notice little about a fare other than cues related to the amount of his probable tip. "A young man may think of females almost exclusively as objects possessing some degree of the multidimensional attribute 'desirability,'" McCall and Simmons write. "He is surprised to learn that they must also budget their money, defecate, and have dental checkups, as he himself does."[21] Second, one tends to magnify or accentuate those characteristics of the other person that are relevant to one's needs. Just as hungry people may perceive food as tastier, sexually aroused people may perceive available sexual partners as sexier. An especially striking instance of perceptual accen-

tuation goes by the name of "idealization," and is associated with the state of being in love. The process has not been well researched by social scientists, but it was described by Stendhal a century and a half ago:

> Why is one so carried away by each fresh beauty that one discovers in the person one loves?
> The reason is that each fresh beauty gives you the full satisfaction of a desire. If you want her to be sentimental, she is sentimental; later you want her to be proud like Corneille's Emile, and although these qualities are probably incompatible, she immediately seems to acquire the Roman spirit.[22]

It may be speculated that in love, especially in its early stages, we tend to see what we are looking for to the fullest degree.*

The perceptual tendencies that we have examined so far often lead to perceptual distortions. By placing people in pigeonholes, we obscure the fact that people's personalities typically do *not* form neat, consistent packages. All of us in fact share with Vince Lombardi the human characteristics of inconsistency: We are good in some respects, bad in others, and vastly changeable in many. Nevertheless, as Heider suggests, we are strongly motivated to form consistent, stable impressions of others. When we categorize people on the basis of reputations and stereotypes, we sacrifice some degree of accuracy for the sake of efficient information storage and retrieval. "Too often it happens," a cab-driving sociologist admitted, "that a fare tabbed as

---

[21] McCall and Simmons, *Identities and Interactions,* p. 115.

[22] Stendhal, *On Love* (New York: Grosset & Dunlap University Library, 1967), p. 33.

* "To be in love," H. L. Mencken wrote, "is merely to be in a state of perceptual anaesthesia—to mistake an ordinary young man for a Greek god or an ordinary young women for a goddess."

a Sport (big tipper) turns out to be a Stiff (non-tipper), that a Blowhard matches his words with a generous tip, or that a Lady Shopper will give fifteen or even twenty cents."[23] Nevertheless, the imperfect predictive system provided by our stereotypes is in many instances preferable to no predictive system at all. As McCall and Simmons suggest, "We must . . . inquire into the *quality,* not the existence, of stereotyping."[24]

The process of perceptual accentuation may also have its uses. It may in fact be profitable for a hungry man to perceive food as more appetizing than it "really" is, or for a sexually aroused person to overestimate the receptiveness of a prospective partner. These distortions may help the aroused person to marshal his best efforts in pursuit of his goal. In other cases, however, we are motivated to see not what we most desire but what we are most afraid of. The paranoid makes "sense" out of his environment by viewing friendly people as hostile and taking smiles for scowls. The anti-Semite is especially likely to perceive other people as being Jewish, even when they are not. As Gordon Allport has suggested, "It is important to the prejudiced person to learn the cues whereby he may identify the enemy."[25] We may also see the opposite of what we are looking for as a hedge against our failure to obtain it. Thus I would predict that especially timid or insecure men would be likely to *underestimate* the sexual receptiveness of their assigned dates in the Minnesota study, as a means of shielding themselves against possible rejection.

From Acts to Dispositions

In forming impressions of people, we are commonly called upon to make inferences about people's underlying abilities and dispositions on the basis of their overt actions. But the degree to which such inferences can safely be made depends on the context in which the action takes place. Imagine that you are observing another person pacing back and forth. He takes ten steps in one direction, pauses momentarily, turns around, takes ten steps in the other direction, and continues the process uninterruptedly for over an hour. If you observed the person behaving this way in his home or office you might well conclude that he is an extremely nervous sort of fellow, perhaps with a host of personal problems to boot. Having inferred this much about his underlying disposition, you would not be too surprised to find him shaking slightly the next time you were to see him, and you would be inclined to approach him, if at all, with some trepidation. But if you observed the pacing man in a different situation—the waiting room of a hospital maternity ward, for example—he would no longer seem to be a basically nervous person. It would be apparent only that his wife was having a baby, probably her first, and that he was behaving as any prospective father would under such circumstances. And if you observed the same pacing man in a

[23] Fred Davis, "The Cabdriver and His Fare: Facets of a Fleeting Relationship," *American Journal of Sociology,* 1959, *65,* 158–165.
[24] McCall and Simmons, p. 116.
[25] Gordon Allport is quoted from *The Nature of Prejudice* (Reading, Mass.: Addison-Wesley, 1954), p. 133. Research on the identifiability of Jews is summarized by Henri Tajfel in "Social and Cultural Factors in Perception," in Gardner Lindzey and Elliot Aronson (Eds.), *Handbook of Social Psychology,* rev. ed., vol. 3 (Reading, Mass.: Addison-Wesley, 1969), pp. 328–331.

guard's uniform outside of Windsor Castle, his pacing would convey even less information about him. In such a case you would know what he does for a living, but would be able to make no inferences at all about his personality.

Making inferences from acts to dispositions involves processes of *attribution*.[26] Specifically, the perceiver must decide to what extent the action is caused by qualities of the actor himself and to what extent it is caused by the role or situation in which the actor finds himself. A basic attributional principle which is illustrated by the case of the pacing man is that the less socially desirable or "appropriate" a person's actions, the more informative they are about his enduring personal dispositions. "Deviations—almost any deviation—from the rules of propriety," sociologist Gerald Suttles observes, "leave us with the impression that someone has behaved out of choice. Such actions are almost invariably attributed to something basic and essential to the individual; a sort of unalterable and irrepressible force."[27] When a person behaves in ways that are fully appropriate to the situation he is in, on the other hand, the perceiver is more likely to see his actions as constrained by his circumstances rather than as revealing his distinctive personal qualities.

An experiment conducted by social psychologist Edward Jones and his colleagues demonstrated the operation of the principle of appropriateness.[28] Subjects listened to a taped interview between a psychologist and a student applying for a job. On two versions of the tape the applicant presented himself to the interviewer as the sort of person who would be personally well suited to the listed job requirements. On two other versions he presented himself as having a rather different sort of temperament from that called for by the job. The subjects perceived the applicant who behaved "appropriately" in neutral and uncertain terms. They found it difficult to form any confident impressions about his underlying personality. When the applicant behaved "inappropriately," on the other hand, subjects were confident that his "real personality" corresponded to the way he had presented himself in the interview.

We can often deal quite successfully with other people on the level of social roles or standards of propriety. The cabdriver and his fare do not need to know much about one another to insure a successful interaction. But especially when we are considering more permanent relationships, it becomes important to keep an eye out for inappropriate, "out-of-role" behaviors from which the other person's dispositions can be reliably inferred. Observing that a girl is well dressed at a debutante ball or stoned at a pot party does not provide much information

[26] Theory and research on attribution processes was spurred by Fritz Heider's paper on "Social Perception and Phenomenal Causality," cited above, and his larger work, *The Psychology of Interpersonal Relations* (New York: Wiley, 1958). Influential subsequent papers include Edward E. Jones and Keith E. Davis, "From Acts to Dispositions: The Attribution Process in Person Perception," in Leonard Berkowitz (Ed.), *Advances in Experimental Social Psychology*, vol. 2 (New York: Academic Press, 1965), and Harold H. Kelley, "Attribution Theory in Social Psychology," in David Levine (Ed.), *Nebraska Symposium on Motivation, 1967* (Lincoln: University of Nebraska Press, 1967).

[27] Gerald D. Suttles is quoted from "Friendship as a Social Institution," in George J. McCall and others, *Social Relationships* (Chicago: Aldine, 1970), p. 102.

[28] Edward E. Jones, Keith E. Davis, and Kenneth J. Gergen, "Role Playing Variations and Their Informational Value for Person Perception," *Journal of Abnormal and Social Psychology*, 1961, *63*, 302–310.

about how she will behave under other circumstances. If the girl was wearing bluejeans at the ball or smoking only cigars at the pot party, her actions would provide better clues of her underlying dispositions.

In general, we are more highly motivated to attribute a person's acts to his enduring dispositions than to situational factors because such dispositional attributions best serve our desire to predict his future behavior. Our desire to make dispositional attributions often gets the better of us, leading us to underestimate the importance of situational factors. The sociologist Gustav Ichheiser provides one such example:

> We are passing by the army barracks and see how a sergeant is handling his subordinates. He barks his commands, snaps at any attempted questions on the part of his men, listens to no excuses or explanations and is downright rude. Now, confronted with this type of behavior, we are not, as a rule, inclined to say to ourselves or to others, "This man is performing certain functions defined by the context of military regulations and standards. He is behaving in a way which corresponds to expected and stereotyped norms of behavior in this type of social role." Rather, we tend to react in a way which, on the verbal level, would sound something like this: "The man is rude," or "The man has such-and-such personality characteristics which make him behave in this way."[29]

This underestimation of situational factors reflects what Heider called "behavior engulfing the field." We are led to believe that the debater really believes his arguments or that the ath-

lete endorsing hair tonic is really sold on the brand, even when their behavior can be more adequately accounted for by such situational factors as debating rules or large fees. "We take raw material too literally," Heider writes, "without taking into account additional factors that may influence it."[30] In doing so we are led to infer enduring dispositions from actions that in fact reflect responses to special conditions. This perceptual bias, as we shall see, has the effect of bolstering the primacy effect.

Getting Off on the Right Foot

What can you say about a person who is intelligent, industrious, impulsive, critical, stubborn, and envious? That he is a walking mass of contradictions? That he has a split personality? That he is just an ordinary guy with a run-of-the-mill mixture of "desirable" and "undesirable" characteristics? The last of these possibilities would probably be most accurate, but none of them corresponds to what most people actually say about such a person. Instead they attempt to integrate all of the person's traits into a single, unambivalent impression. And the overall impression that is formed often depends on the order in which the information about him is obtained. Social psychologist Solomon Asch initiated research on such "order effects" in the 1940s, utilizing a procedure in which adjectives describing a hypothetical person are read one at a time to subjects.[31] Asch found that a person

[29] Gustav Ichheiser, "Misunderstandings in Human Relations: A Study in False Social Perception," *American Journal of Sociology*, 1949, *55*, Part 2, p. 27.

[30] Heider, "Social Perception and Phenomenal Causality."

[31] Solomon Asch, "Forming Impressions of Personality," *Journal of Abnormal and Social Psychology*, 1946, *41*, 258–290.

described as "intelligent, industrious, impulsive, critical, stubborn, and envious" was evaluated by subjects in considerably more positive terms than a person introduced as "envious, stubborn, critical, impulsive, industrious, and intelligent." The descriptions provided by two of Asch's subjects illustrate what happened:

A. *Intelligent . . . envious.* The person is intelligent and fortunately he puts his intelligence to work. That he is stubborn and impulsive may be due to the fact that he knows what he is saying and what he means and will not therefore give in easily to someone else's idea which he disagrees with.

B. *Envious . . . intelligent.* This person's good qualities such as industry and intelligence are bound to be restricted by jealousy and stubbornness. The person is emotional. He is unsuccessful because he is weak and allows his bad points to cover up his good ones.

These subjects apparently used the earlier adjectives in the list to create a framework within which the later adjectives were interpreted: The stubbornness of a man who is already known to be intelligent and industrious is interpreted as integrity, while the stubbornness of a person already known to be envious is seen in a much less favorable light. Thus, Asch obtained a primacy effect.

Psychologist Abraham Luchins, employing fuller descriptions of a person's behavior, provided a further demonstration of the primacy effect.[32] Luchins constructed two paragraphs about a young man named Jim. They

read as follows:

Paragraph E. Jim left the house to get some stationery. He walked out into the sunfilled street with two of his friends, basking in the sun as he walked. Jim entered the stationery store which was full of people. Jim talked with an acquaintance while he waited for the clerk to catch his eye. On his way out, he stopped to chat with a school friend who was just coming into the store. Leaving the store, he walked toward school. On his way out he met the girl to whom he had been introduced the night before. They talked for a short while, and then Jim left for school.

Paragraph I. After school Jim left the classroom alone. Leaving the school, he started on his long walk home. The street was brilliantly filled with sunshine. Jim walked down the street on the shady side. Coming down the street toward him, he saw the pretty girl whom he had met on the previous evening. Jim crossed the street and entered a candy store. The store was crowded with students, and he noticed a few familiar faces. Jim waited quietly until the counterman caught his eye and then gave his order. Taking his drink, he sat down at a side table. When he had finished his drink he went home.

When high school and college students were given either Paragraph E by itself or Paragraph I by itself they had no trouble forming an unambivalent impression of Jim. Students who read Paragraph E (for "extroverted") unanimously viewed Jim as a sociable, outgoing, and friendly person. They visualized him as physically well developed and athletic, as walking erect and briskly, and as thinking well of himself. When asked what Jim would do when he was bypassed in favor of another customer at a barber shop, they indicated that he would stand up

[32] Abraham S. Luchins, "Primacy—Recency in Impression Formation," in Carl Hovland and others, *The Order of Presentation in Persuasion* (New Haven: Yale University Press, 1957).

and assert his priority. Students who read Paragraph I (for "introverted"), on the other hand, viewed Jim as shy, reserved, and unfriendly. They pictured him as having an average or below-average build, as walking slowly or with poor posture, and as feeling inferior to other people. When ignored at the barber shop, he would just sit there and wait. In the crucial conditions of his experiment, Luchins presented subjects with *both* paragraphs, run together to form a single continuous passage. One group of subjects read the new paragraph in the E-I order, another group in the I-E order. They were then asked to answer the same set of questions about Jim. The subjects in the E-I condition consistently described Jim as an extroverted, friendly person, while subjects in the I-E condition described him as shy and introverted. The subjects apparently attributed a stable disposition to Jim on the basis of his initial actions. His later contradictory actions could then be written off to special circumstances. Some of Luchin's E-I subjects decided, for example, that Jim was essentially a friendly person, but that he had had an unusually bad day at school.

A recent series of experiments by Edward Jones and his colleagues also documented the power of first impressions.[33] Subjects observed a fellow student (the "performer") attempt to solve a series of multiple-choice problems, of the sort that appear on tests of intellectual ability. The items were described as being of equal difficulty. The performer, in fact a confederate of the researchers, always answered fifteen of the thirty problems correctly. In one experimental condition, however, his successes were concentrated among the earlier items, and his performance tapered off toward the end. Jones called this the "descending" condition. In the "ascending" condition, on the other hand, his performance steadily improved over the course of the trials. Afterward the subjects were asked to recall how many correct answers he had given and predict how well he would do on a second series of trials. In four experiments conducted along these lines, primacy effects were consistently found. On the average, subjects judging the "descending" performer—the laboratory analogue of Vida Blue—recalled him as solving more of the problems than did students observing the "ascending" performer, even though the number of problems actually solved in the two conditions was identical. The "descending" performer was also expected to do better on a second series of trials than his "ascending" counterpart, and was judged to be the more intelligent.

As Jones and George R. Goethals note, intellectual ability is generally viewed as a stable disposition rather than a changeable state.[34] Since the subjects were told that the problems were of equal difficulty, they probably expected the performer's successes and failures to be more or less equally spaced over the course of the trials. The proportion of successes in the first few trials could be taken as a good indication of the performer's ability

[33] Edward E. Jones, Leslie Rock, Kelly G. Shaver, and Lawrence M. Ward, "Pattern of Performance and Ability Attribution: An Unexpected Primacy Effect," *Journal of Personality and Social Psychology*, 1968, 10, 317–340.

[34] Edward E. Jones and George R. Goethals, *Order Effects in Impression Formation: Attribution Context and the Nature of the Entity* (New York: General Learning Press, 1971). I am indebted to that paper for several of the ideas in this chapter.

and thus provide a basis for pigeon-holing him. The subjects then apparently distorted or ignored the later evidence which contradicted their initial expectations.

Given the power of first impressions to shape lasting opinions, it is often wise for a person who wishes to make a particular impression to present himself in that way from the outset of the relationship. Having done so, he may later be able to reveal other sides of himself with greater impunity. Erving Goffman notes that some teachers take this view:

> You can't let them get the upper hand or you are through. So I start out tough. The first day I get a new class in, I let them know who's boss. . . . You've got to start off tough, then you can ease up as you go along. If you start out easy-going when you try to get tough, they'll just look at you and laugh.[35]

The strategy of getting off on the right foot is sometimes complicated, however, by the fact that a person who initially presents himself *too* positively will be regarded by others as immodest or intimidating. Sociologist Peter Blau observes that in group situations "impressive qualities make a person attractive in one sense and unattractive in another, because they raise fears of rejection and pose a status threat for the rest of the group."[36] . . . Other people may respect the highly impressive person, but they will find it hard to work up much affection for him. A common technique for handling this problem is for the person to begin by letting his impressive qualities be known,

but once he has done so to reveal some of his shortcomings. "Having impressed us with his Harvard accent and Beacon Hill friends," Blau writes, "he may later tell a story that reveals his immigrant background."[37] Johnny Bench, the star catcher of the Cincinnati Reds, has mastered the essentials of this strategy:

> As a rule, Bench does not subscribe to baseball's unwritten code of modesty, but he is nicely measured about it: He is given to understatement ("I've got a little ability") when he thinks you know better, and to fervid overstatement when he thinks you do not ("I can throw out any runner alive").[38]

Even outright blunders may increase the attractiveness of a person if his admirable qualities have already been documented. Elliot Aronson and his co-workers asked Minnesota students to listen to a tape recording of a fellow student trying out for the school's College Bowl team.[39] The contestant performed either brilliantly or at a mediocre level, and then—as enacted on the tape heard by half of the subjects—clumsily spilled his cup of coffee all over himself. The blunder had the effect of decreasing the subjects' rated liking for the mediocre contestant, but it increased their liking for the brilliant contestant. When imposing people reveal weaknesses they emphasize their common ties with the rest of us mortals and may be liked better as a result. One of the least predictable consequences of the Bay

[35] Erving Goffman, *The Presentation of Self in Everyday Life* (Garden City, N. Y.: Doubleday Anchor Books, 1959), p. 12.

[36] Peter M. Blau, *Exchange and Power in Social Life* (New York: Wiley, 1964), p. 43.

[37] Blau, p. 48.

[38] William Barry Furlong, "Johnny Bench: Supercatcher for the Big Red Machine," *New York Times Magazine*, August 30, 1970.

[39] Elliot Aronson, Ben Willerman, and Joanne Floyd, "The Effect of a Pratfall on Increasing Interpersonal Attractiveness," *Psychonomic Science*, 1966, 4, 227–228.

of Pigs fiasco was an upsurge in President Kennedy's popularity rating in the polls. As the coffee-spilling experiment suggests, however, when an ordinary person blunders it only makes him appear ignorant or clumsy. It is only after a person has gotten off on the right foot that he can afford to stumble.

But What's He Done Lately?

For all of the importance of first impressions, our images of other people are nevertheless highly susceptible to change. "A playwright's only as good as his last play," and the same standard is often applied to racehorses, boxers, and psychological researchers. Even the opinionated Jim Bouton is capable of changing his mind, and admitting it:

> One of the dumb things I do sometimes is form judgments about people I really don't know. Case history: Jack Hamilton, pitcher, Cleveland Indians. He was with the Angel organization last year and played with me in Seattle, which is where I got to know him. Before that I played against him in the minors and considered him stupid, a hard-throwing guy who didn't care whether or not he hit the batter. In the majors I figured him for a troublemaker because he used to get into fights with Phil Linz. Nobody fights with Phil Linz.
> Then, when Hamilton hit Tony Conigliaro in the eye a couple of years ago and put him out for the season, I thought, boy, this guy is some kind of super rat. But when I played with him in Seattle I found he was just a guy like everybody else, honestly sorry he'd hit Conigliaro, a good team player, a friendly fellow who liked to come out early to the park and pitch batting practice to

his kids. All of which made me feel like an ass.[40]

It is in part because admitting that one's first impression of another person was wrong makes one "feel like an ass," to borrow Bouton's felicitous phrase, that first impressions are often so impervious to change. The desire to achieve consistent evaluations of others may stem not only from the desire for perceptual harmony, as stressed by Heider's balance principle, but also from our reluctance to admit that our initial opinions were mistaken. Consequently, it may sometimes be possible to minimize the impact of first impressions by reminding people to keep their minds open, that all the evidence is not yet in. Luchins found, for example, that the strength of the primacy effect in subjects' evaluations of Jim was reduced when they were advised in advance to be sure to take into account all of the information to be presented.[41] Paradoxically, it is sometimes the case that the most recent information one has obtained about another person is weighted most heavily when it contrasts sharply with one's previously formed impression. Thus, Jim Bouton may end up perceiving Jack Hamilton as *especially* friendly precisely because he had previously considered him to be a super rat. Against the sinister background of Bouton's initial impression, Hamilton's otherwise unremarkable actions, like pitching batting practice to his kids, take on an aura of virtual saintliness.

A central determinant of whether one's impressions of other people will be governed by primacy or recency is

[40] Bouton, *Ball Four*, p. 77.
[41] Luchins, "Experimental Attempts to Minimize the Impact of First Impressions," in *The Order of Presentation in Persuasion.*

one's set of assumptions about which characteristics of people tend to be stable and which are susceptible to change. We typically view other people as capable of growth, development, or modification in at least certain respects. We may not be too surprised, for example, to note large shifts in interests, personality, and abilities from one year to the next among children or adolescents. In such cases our evaluation of the other person is likely to rely heavily on the most recent information, which, in effect, supersedes any previous evidence. The fact that Senator Edward Kennedy was able to overcome his undergraduate cheating incident and may even be able to rise above the stigma of Chappaquiddick suggests that in at least some instances people are willing to view moral lapses as temporary or mutable. On the other hand, the difficulties encountered by many ex-mental patients in finding jobs, . . . illustrated in the . . . case of Senator Thomas Eagleton's removal as the Democratic vice-presidential candidate, may reflect an implicit theory that mental and emotional illnesses reflect stable and inherently unchangeable predispositions.

The cases of Vida Blue and Gary Wichard may also be distinguished on the basis of such attributions of stability. The early information on Vida Blue may in fact have been more easily generalized to predictions about his later performance than the early information on Gary Wichard. After all, Blue's early string of victories had been in the majors, against the very teams that he would continue to face in the future. He had demonstrated that he could do it. For a healthy twenty-one-year-old pitcher, such a demonstration might well be construed as evidence of

an underlying ability that would persist for a considerable period of time. As a result of this dispositional attribution, the contradictory later information could not easily offset the power of the first impression. In the case of Gary Wichard, on the other hand, the early impression was based on his performance at C. W. Post, against relatively weak opponents. Thus, it might be attributed to the situation, that of small-college football, rather than to a stable ability that would continue to be displayed in the professional ranks. When it came to dealing with the pass rush of gargantuan professional linemen, Wichard might rise to the occasion, get even better, or fall by the wayside. In light of this perception of changeability, the safest course for the perceivers of Gary Wichard was to give heaviest weight to what he had done lately.

The Self-fulfilling Prophecy

The importance of impressions of other people goes far beyond their role in the perceivers' own mental lives. Like secret wishes at a birthday party, our impressions of others have ways of making themselves come true. If, for example, we perceive another person as friendly, we are likely to behave warmly toward him. And this behavior on our part may in turn have the effect of *making him* friendly. If, on the other hand, we perceive another person or group of people as being hostile, we may well react toward him in such a way as to make him so. Ichheiser notes that individuals often have no choice but to play the social roles that are assigned to them by others:

The ex-convict . . . may return to his community with a new view of himself and a determination to become a good citizen, [but] the opinions the people of the community hold of him and ex-convicts in general often prevent his accomplishing his good aims. Instead, in bitterness and resentment, he often gives up the struggle and becomes what the community expected—a hardened criminal. Sometimes, too, the situation is reversed. The ex-convict comes back, hardened, embittered, and with his worst characteristics emphasized. Some one or several persons take an interest in him, play up his better qualities, and through encouragement he comes to be what they see him as—a good citizen.[42]

A more personal example is provided by J. R. Simmons:

> . . . My informant rented a room for several days from a middle-aged woman. After seeing her only briefly, and before he had spoken with her, he "intuited" that she was a warm, accepting person who was filled with psychic strength and goodness. When he first talked with her a couple hours later, his manner was far more friendly and patronizing than usual. He showed interest in her collection of antiques, asked about her children, and ended up by saying he felt she was a wonderful person and he wanted to rent from her, partly because they would have a chance to talk together. During the next few days, the writer had a chance to question other tenants and neighbors about the landlady. They described a fairly caustic gossiper who was unreasonably strict about the use of electricity, and of her property and grounds. Her attitude toward the writer was taciturn. But she responded graciously to my informant's open friendliness. She sought him out to talk with on several occasions, she inquired if there was enough light in his room for late reading and supplied him with a table lamp, etc. In her behavior

toward him, my informant's intuition certainly seemed correct.[43]

A striking experimental demonstration of the impact of images upon reality was provided by Robert Rosenthal, a social psychologist, and Lenore Jacobson, an elementary school principal.[44] At the start of a school year teachers were given lists of those students in their classes who had been identified by a special aptitude test as probable academic "late bloomers." The lists were in fact entirely unrelated to any test results. They were arrived at by a process of random selection. At the end of the year the children's intelligence was tested. It was found that those children who had been identified as "late bloomers" in fact showed significantly greater gains in I.Q. scores than those children who had not been listed. The teachers had unwittingly given differential treatment to their "late bloomers," perhaps encouraging them more, or listening to them more attentively. Whatever it was that the teachers did, it had the effect of making their expectation come true. For obvious ethical reasons Rosenthal and Jacobson did not create parallel experimental conditions in which teachers were told that particular students had been identified as dullards. But just such conditions are often created in educational situations in which teachers hold the expectation that children in particular schools, particular tracks, or of particular backgrounds lack the ability to go far academically. This expectation, too, bears the seeds of its own fruition.

---

[42] Ichheiser, p. 30.

[43] J. R. Simmons, "On Maintaining Deviant Belief Systems: A Case Study," *Social Problems*, 1964, 11, 250–256.

[44] Robert Rosenthal and Lenore Jacobson, *Pygmalion in the Classroom* (New York: Holt, Rinehart and Winston, 1968).

The sociologist Robert Merton has labeled this phenomenon the "self-fulfilling prophecy." He defines it as "a false definition of the situation evoking a new behavior which makes the originally false conception come true." Merton continues, "The specious validity of the self-fulfilling prophecy perpetuates a reign of error. For the prophet will cite the actual course of events as proof that he was right from the very beginning."[45] The self-fulfilling prophecy thus lends further weight to the power of first impressions to shape the course of interpersonal relationships. On balance, first impressions seem at least as likely to confirm and perpetuate themselves than to decline and fall under the weight of later information. As a result, the process of repudiating unearned reputations and smashing erroneous stereotypes is often an exceedingly difficult one. The case is not a hopeless one, however.

[45] Robert K. Merton, *Social Theory and Social Structure* (New York: Free Press, 1957), p. 423.

Reading 3.2
Perception and Communication
William V. Haney

"This is nothing. When I was your age the snow was so deep it came up to my chin." (Reprinted from *Redbook* by permission.)

Dad is right, of course—*as he sees it.* And in this seemingly innocuous self-deception lies one of the most interesting and perhaps terrifying aspects of human experience: *We never really come into direct contact with reality.* Every-

From William V. Haney, *Communication and Organizational Behavior*, rev. ed., Homewood, Ill.: Richard D. Irwin, Inc., 1976, pp. 51–77. Reprinted by permission of the publisher.

thing we experience is a manufacture of our nervous system.

For practical purposes we should acknowledge that there is a considerable range of similarity between reality and one's perception of it. When an engineer is measuring, testing, and the like, usually with the aid of precise gauges and instruments, his perceptions may be an extremely close approximation of reality. This is basically why bridges, tunnels, and skyscrapers not only get built but generally stay built.

But when the engineer, or anyone else, is relating to and communicating with other human beings—when he is operating in a world of feelings, attitudes, values, aspirations, ideals, and emotions—he is playing in a very different league and the match between reality and perceptions may be far from exact.

Just what is going on and just what is this concept "perception" we have been alluding to so casually? "Perception" is a term we perhaps shouldn't be using at all. There seems to be very little agreement as to what it entails. It evidently is a complex, dynamic, interrelated composite of processes which are incompletely and variously understood. Allport, for example, describes some 13 *different* schools of thought on the nature of perception, listing, among others, core-context theory, gestalt theory, topological field theory, cell-assembly, and sensory-tonic theory.[1] In the face of such irresolution I will be so bold as to define perception in unsophisticated language as the process of *making sense out of experience—of imputing meaning to experience.*[2]

Obviously what kind of "sense" one makes of a situation will have great bearing on how he responds to that situation, so let us examine the phenomenon more closely.

[1] F. H. Allport, *Theories of Perception and the Concept of Structure* (New York: John Wiley & Sons, Inc., 1955).

[2] Perception has been defined as "the more complex process [as distinguished from sensation] by which people select, organize, and interpret sensory stimulation into a meaningful and coherent picture of the world." B. Berelson and G. A. Steiner, *Human Behavior: An Inventory of Scientific Findings* (New York: Harcourt, Brace & World, Inc., 1964), p. 88.

A Model of Perception

March and Simon suggest a model (see Figure 1) which seems well supported by research. First of all, they regard man as a complex, information-processing system—"a choosing, decision-making, problem-solving, organism that can do only one or a few things at a time, and that can attend to only a small part of the information in its memory and presented by the environment."[3]

They argue that one's behavior, through a short interval of time, is determined by the interaction between his *internal state*[4] (which is largely a product of one's previous *learning*) at the beginning of the interval and his *environment.*

When the interval is very short only a small part of one's internal state and a small part of his environment will be active, i.e., will significantly influence his behavior during the interval. In information theory terms, the eye can handle about 5 million bits per second, but the resolving power of the brain is approximately 500 bits per second. *Selection* is inevitable. How, then, are these active parts determined? As stated above, they are selected through the interaction of one's internal state and his environment at the beginning of

[3] J. G. March and H. A. Simon, *Organizations* (New York: John Wiley & Sons, Inc., 1958), p. 11.

[4] His internal state is mostly contained in his memory which "includes [but is not limited to] all sorts of partial and modified records of past experiences and programs for responding to environmental stimuli." Thus, the memory consists, in part, of:

a) Values or goals: criteria that are applied to determine which courses of action are preferred among those considered.

b) Relations between actions and their outcome; beliefs, perceptions, and expectations as to the consequences that will follow from one course of action to another. . . .

c) Alternatives: possible courses of action. Ibid., pp. 10–11.

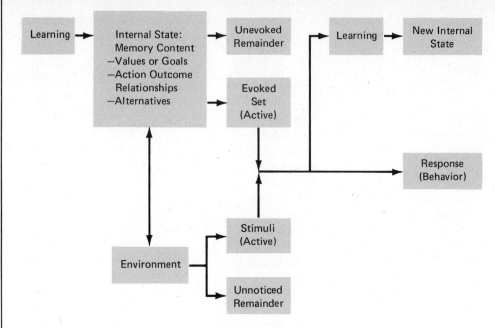

FIGURE 1.

the time interval. The active part of the internal state is called the set[5] which is evoked by the environment, leaving the *unevoked remainder* which plays no significant role in affecting the behavior at that time. Similarly, the active part of the environment is selected by the internal state and is called the *stimuli*; the residue is the "unnoticed" remainder. Munn gives a relevant illustration:

> I once had a colony of white rats in the attic of the psychology building. One afternoon I found several rats outside of their cages. Some were dead and partly eaten. It occurred to me that, however the rats had escaped, they must have been eaten by wild rats. I went downstairs to get some water and was climbing the stairs again when I saw before me, and directly in front of the cages, a large wild gray rat. It was

standing tense and trembling, apparently having heard me ascend the stairs. Very slowly I raised a glass jar that was in my right hand, and aimed it at the rat. Much to my surprise, the animal failed to move. Upon approaching the object, I discovered it to be a piece of crumpled-up-grayish paper. Without the set induced by my suspicion that gray rats were in the attic, I should undoubtedly have seen the paper for what it was, assuming that I noticed it at all.[6]

Let us examine Munn's behavior, asserting a chain of *sets* and *stimuli*. To start at an arbitrary point, he was *set* to notice the white rats among other reasons because they were presumably why he went to the attic in the first place. Thus, the partly eaten white rats readily became *stimuli* which in turn triggered still another *set*—the expec-

[5] Set is generally regarded as the readiness of the organism to respond in a particular way.

[6] Norman L. Munn, *Psychology: The Fundamentals of Human Adjustment* (Boston: Houghton Mifflin Co., 1947), p. 327.

tation of wild gray rats Any part of his environment which bore a reasonable resemblance to a wild gray rat thus became a candidate for becoming his new *stimuli*. The crumpled paper qualified. It was not only selected as a *stimulus* (supposedly it had been part of the "unnoticed remainder" of the environment on his first trip to the attic) but was interpreted as a wild gray rat.

The result of the interplay of environment and internal state is one's *response* (behavior) and his *internal state* at the beginning of the next time interval. This new internal state can be considered as modified by the *learning* derived from the experience of the previous interval

Just what is active or passive in one's internal state and environment is a function of time, among other factors. For a very short period, there will be very few active elements in set and stimuli. For a longer period, a larger portion of the memory content will likely be evoked and a large number of environmental events will influence behavior at some time during the interval. Thus, phrases such as "definition of the situation" and "frame of reference" are more appropriate than "set" in discussing longer time periods.

If one's response is a function of interrelated variables it follows that a variation in any or all of them would normally affect the response. Therefore we shall examine some of these variables in greater detail.

DIFFERING ENVIRONMENTS

Hold up a die between us. If you see three dots I will see four. As obvious as it should be, the phenomenon of differing environments, which would preclude our receiving the same stimuli, seems to contribute to a great deal of unnecessary and destructive conflict.

I have had the rewarding experience of serving for several years as a consultant to the Federal Mediation and Conciliation Service. Any number of the commissioners, men who are constantly concerned with union-management controversies, have asserted to me that a significant portion of the lack of communication, understanding, and harmony between the two parties stems from the simple fact that neither side is given full and direct access to the private environment—including the pressures, complexities, and restrictions—of the other. Thus, from the very outset of the negotiation the parties are exposed to substantially different environments and therefore are, in many respects, responding to different stimuli.

DIFFERING STIMULI

Presume a mutual environment and there is still no guarantee that your responses and mine will be influenced by the same stimuli. Our respective evoked sets will have a considerable bearing on which parts of the environment will significantly impinge upon us as stimuli. Munn's story of the rat is a case in point.

DIFFERING SENSORY RECEPTORS

Another reason why parts of the environment either never become stimuli or are experienced differently is that our sensory "equipment" varies. It has long been recognized that individuals differ markedly in sensory thresholds and acuity. While there has been gratifying progress in the prevention, correction, and amelioration of sensory limitations there is still much to be learned.

An interesting demonstration of differing sensory equipment is to give a bit of paper to each person in a group and request each to determine the taste of the paper. The group does not know it but the paper is impregnated with phenylthiocarbamide (PTC). If the group is representative, a significant portion will experience a distinctly bitter sensation. But some will taste it as sweet, others as sour, and still others as salty. And about half will find it utterly tasteless!

PTC, a chemical used by geneticists to trace hereditary traits, reveals dramatically that we simply do not all inherit identical sensory apparatus. Add to this variations of the nervous system due to disease and injury and it is clear that our senses are inclined to be neither infallible nor uniform. I have a personal example to contribute in this regard. I have had a few mild disputes with my wife who "alleged" a shrill whistle in the television set. Since I did not hear it I denied that it existed. Somewhat later I had an audiometric examination and discovered that, like many others who were around artillery during the war, I had lost the capacity to hear tones of extremely high pitch.

DIFFERING INTERNAL STATES

One's *internal state* is the product of his *learning processes* and it is obvious that the "lessons" acquired by one person can differ markedly from those of another. Imagine a number of individuals observing a man drinking liquor. If the observers are candid and sufficiently representative we can expect a gamut of reactions. Some will regard

the man as sinful; others as extravagant. Others will associate his drinking with friendliness and congeniality. Some will view it as a character flaw—a way of avoiding unpleasantness, running from problems. Still others may perceive it as a relaxant. And people in the distilling industry—and the Alcohol and Tobacco Tax Division of the Internal Revenue Service—may relate it to a job!

For a more dramatic example of the role of learning compare cultures. One's culture is an extraordinarily effective teacher. First, it teaches us unrelentingly—every waking moment. Second, it is a most subtle, even insidious teacher—which detracts not at all from its effectiveness. Immersed in it constantly, we are seldom conscious of what it has been teaching us until we contrast its lessons with those taught by other cultures. The perceptive traveler, for example, as he visits countries learns a good deal about *himself* and the special lessons his culture has taught him.

For example, anthropologists tell us that we learn from our respective cultures how to perceive a misbehaving child. This is revealed by how we speak to the child. English-speaking people generally consider misbehavior as "bad" or "naughty," a suggestion of immorality, and admonish the child with "Johnny, be *good!*" Italian- and Greek-speaking people say the equivalent. The French, however, tend to say "Jean, sois sage!"—be wise. Their culture teaches that the child who misbehaves is being stupid, foolish, imprudent, injudicious. The Scandinavians have another concept expressed by the Swedish, "Jan, var snell!" and the Norwegian, "Jan, ble snil!"—be *friendly*, be *kind*. Germans have learned still differently. With them it is "Hans, sei artig!"—*get back in step. Sei artig* is literally "be of your own kind" —in other words, "conform to your role as a child."[7]

Clearly, individuals from these various cultures could observe the same child misbehaving but regard him very differently because they had been *trained* to do so. Grant that different people learn different "lessons" from life and it is readily apparent that individualized learning plays a subtle but critical role in one's communication with others.

DIFFERING EVOKED SETS

One's set, according to the model, is dependent upon three other variables: that which is available in the internal state, the stimuli which trigger the set, and, though less directly, the processes of learning. March and Simon clarify the role of learning in this regard:

> When one of these elements (values or goals, action-outcome relationships and alternatives) is evoked by a stimulus, it may also bring into the evoked set a number of other elements with which it has become associated through the learning process. Thus, if a particular goal has been achieved on previous occasions by execution of a particular course of action, then evocation of that goal will be likely to evoke that course of action again. Habitual responses are extreme instances of this in which the connecting links between stimulus and response may be suppressed from consciousness. In the same way, the evoca-

tion of a course of action will lead by association to evocation of consequences that have been associated with the action.[8]

This helps to account for the apparent self-perpetuating nature of sets which others have observed.

> Our concept of causal texture implies that definitions and relations, once they have been adopted, influence interpretations of subsequent events. Early definitions of the conditions under which a task will be accomplished are apt to take precedence over later definitions.[9]
>
> . . . The tendency to distort messages in the direction of identity with previous inputs is probably the most pervasive of the systematic biases.[10]

Sebald confirmed a hypothesis "that largely only those meanings are being perceived and recalled which reinforce images."[11] He also suggested "that selective distortion takes place in order to screen out dissonant features—features which are apt to disturb preconceived images."[12]

The concept of differing sets helps to explain the abyss which so frequently separates superiors and subordinates. A man looking downward in an organization may often have a very different set from the man below him looking up. For example, Likert reports that 85 percent of a sampling of foremen estimated that their men

---

[7] L. Sinclair (ed.), "A Word in Your Ear," *Ways of Mankind* (Boston: Beacon Press, 1954), pp. 28–29. For a fascinating account of cultural differences interfering with interpersonal communication, see E. T. Hall, *The Silent Language* (Garden City, N.Y.: Doubleday & Co., Inc., 1959).

[8] March and Simon, op. cit., p. 11.

[9] H. B. Pepinsky, K. E. Weick, and J. W. Riner, *Primer for Productivity* (Columbus, Ohio: The Ohio State University Research Foundation, March, 1964), p. 54.

[10] D. T. Campbell, "Systematic Error on the Part of Human Links in Communication Systems," *Information and Control*, Vol. 1 (1958), p. 346.

[11] H. Sebald, "Limitations of Communication: Mechanisms of Image Maintenance in the Form of Selective Perception, Selective Memory and Selective Distortion," *Journal of Communication*, Vol. XII, No. 3 (September, 1962), p. 149.

[12] Ibid.

"felt very free to discuss important things about the job with my superior." However, only 51 percent of their men shared this view.[13] Seventy-three percent of the foremen felt they "always or almost always get subordinates' ideas" on the solution of job problems. Only 16 percent of their subordinates agreed with this appraisal.[14] Ninety-five percent of the foremen said they understood their men's problems well but only 34 percent of the men felt that they did.[15]

The gulf between superiors' and subordinates' sets is documented further by Maier[16] who reports a study of 35 pairs from four large firms. A pair consisted of a manager, third echelon from the top, and one of his immediate subordinates. Each partner in each pair was questioned regarding the subordinate's job. On only one aspect was there substantial agreement—the content of the subordinate's duties. However, there was little agreement on the order of importance of these duties. There was only fair agreement on the job's requirements and almost complete disagreement on their priority ranking. Finally, there was virtually no agreement on the problems and obstacles of the subordinate. These findings were discussed with all participants. Several months later a questionnaire was sent to each participant asking if the superior and his respective subordinate had gotten together to discuss their differences. Only 22 pairs replied. Six of them agreed that they had gotten together; nine agreed they had not; and seven pairs could not agree on whether they had or had not gotten together![17]

IN SUMMATION

The perception model suggests why it is impossible for one to be in simple direct contact with reality, why he lives in a personalized world and why, in the words of St. Paul, "We see through a glass darkly." Indeed, there are a number of interrelated variables (differing environments, stimuli, sensory receptors, internal states, and evoked sets) which intervene between perception and reality. Thus, individuals are led to respond differently to events and, in general, complicate the process of communication enormously—particularly *if the role of such factors is ignored or misunderstood.*

> . . . The prime obstacle of every form of communications . . . is simply the fact of *difference.* On this point most serious students of communication are in agreement, the great gap in background, experience, and motivations between ourselves and those with whom we would communicate.
>
> It is a gap that will remain. . . . But if we cannot close the gap, we must at least acknowledge it. For this acknowledgement of difference is the vital preface to all the efforts that follow. . . .[18]

Defensiveness

The "acknowledgement of difference"—a simple phrase but how difficult to practice! Perhaps the most appropriate adjective to describe much

---

[13] Rensis Likert, *New Patterns in Management* (New York: McGraw-Hill Book Co., 1961), p. 47.

[14] Ibid., p. 53.

[15] Ibid., p. 52.

[16] N. R. F. Maier, "Breakdown in Boss-Subordinate Communication," *Communication in Organizations* (Ann Arbor, Mich.: The Foundation for Research on Human Behavior, 1959).

[17] The reader may wish to test the influence of sets upon him by viewing perceptual (*not optical*) illusions.

[18] "Is Anybody Listening," *Fortune*, September 1950, p. 83. The emphasis is mine.

of the behavior of people communicating and relating to one another in organizational settings would be *defensive*. A fundamental reason for defensive behavior appears to be the inability of so many people to *acknowledge differences*—differences between their perceptions and reality and differences between their perceptions and those of others. Their prevailing, albeit largely unconscious, presumption is that "the world is as I see it." He who harbors this notion will find life continuously threatening for there are many others who share his notion—but not *his "world!"* Such people find it perpetually necessary to protect their "worlds" and to deny or attack the other fellow's.

Admittedly, the premise that one deals only indirectly and often unreliably with reality can be disturbing. To those who crave a certain, definite, and dependable world (and that includes all of us in varying degrees) the admission that we respond only to *what it appears to be* rather than *what it is* necessarily lessens our *predictability* about the "real world." Even those who *intellectually accept* the perception model and the roles that stimuli, set, learning, and so on, play in determining responses may have difficulty converting the concept into performance. A good test of the extent to which one has truly internalized such awareness occurs when he becomes emotionally involved with others.

For instance, suppose you and I work in the same organization and we observe one of our colleagues taking home company supplies—such as paper pads, paper clips, and pencils—not in large quantities but it is obvious to us that he will not use them exclusively for official purposes. He will let the children have them, use them for his private affairs, and so on.

Now, let us say that you are the product of a rigorous, religious upbringing. It is likely that you will be *set* to regard Joe as dishonest. But suppose that I have had none of your training and that the only part of my background that is particularly relevant was the three years I spent in the Army in World War II. There I learned a code that was unwritten but very pervasive. It was in effect, "You may rob the Army blind! but you must not steal a nickel from another serviceman." I would be quite inclined to regard Joe as honest and could readily consider his acquisitions as normal perquisites.

Let us examine the *communication* issue. (Permit me to disregard the moral issue without denying that there is one.) Consider the tremendous difficulty you and I would have in discussing Joe if in our increasingly vehement statements—"Joe's dishonest!" "No, he's not!"—we failed to realize that neither of us was talking about *Joe*. We were talking about *you* and *me* and our *respective* "inside-the-skin" experiences. Our respective worlds were different from the outset and there was no reason to expect them to be identical—and no *rational* reason to have to protect them. Why, then, did we protect them so ardently?

Let us begin with an assertion: Most reasonably mature people can tolerate fairly well differences in value judgments, opinions, attitudes, points of view—*so long as they can recognize them as such*. If I can realize that your "reality" is not the same as mine then your statement about *your* "reality" is no threat to *mine*.

But no one can tolerate differences

on matters of objectivity—matters which submit to corroborable measurement and are capable of general agreement. To illustrate, suppose you and I have a mutual superior and he comes to us and says: "This may sound silly but I'm serious. I want you two to estimate the length of that 2 × 4 over there (about 20 feet away) on the ground. You have to estimate because you can't use any kind of measuring device and you can't get any closer to it than you are now. Now, I want a good estimate and only one between you—so get to it!"

(Now suppose the piece of lumber is actually 7 feet long but neither of us knows this.) So we start sizing up the situation and you say, "Looks about 6½ or 7 feet." And I say, "No, no—you're way short—that's a lot closer to 14 feet!" Unless you had admirable constraint you would probably blurt out, "You're crazy!"

Now, why were you moved to feel I was crazy?

Was it not partly because my statement was at least a slight threat to your sense of reality and, therefore, your sanity? In other words if (I said *if*) I were indeed right—i.e., if the board actually were 14 feet and everything were twice as big as you perceive it—would you not begin to have serious misgivings about *your* "contact with reality"? "You're crazy!" then, is your understandable if impulsive way of defending yourself against an attack on your sanity.

Actually, we would be unlikely to have such a disparity (unless one or both of us *were* losing touch with reality) because our perceptual lessons, when we initially learned to perceive the inch, the foot, and the yard, were likely to have been very similar re-gardless of where or when we learned them. And even if we were to disagree on matters such as distance, speed, and weight we could resolve our differences by using standardized measuring devices.

But when we encounter Cezanne and Dali, Tolstoi and Faulkner, Mozart and Cole Porter, we are unlikely to have had identical learning experiences and where is the "standardized measuring device"? Will someone resolve a controversy with "Why, that Van Gogh is 87 percent beautiful"? Even professional critics are unable to provide universally acceptable and applicable criteria.

The point is that not only can we not tolerate differences in matters of objectivity (but what differences there may be are generally minor or resolvable by objective measurement) but we cannot accept differences on matters of subjectivity (value judgments, opinions, and so on) if we unconsciously *treat* them as matters of objectivity. There are many important aspects of our lives such as art, music, architecture, religion, politics, morals, fashions, food, economic and political theory, which (1) are taught to us in standardized lessons and (2) are not, by and large, measurable by standardized scales or gauges. It is in such areas that we find it easiest to threaten one another. And when one is threatened he tends, if he does not run, to fight back—the threatener is now threatened and bootless conflict generally follows.

Defensiveness appears to be so pervasive and potentially so destructive to organizational communication and interpersonal relationships that we shall examine it in more detail in terms of the communicator's *frame of reference*.

FRAME OF REFERENCE

Frame of reference is the term March and Simon used for longer intervals of time in lieu of "set." It has been defined as:

A system of standards or values, usually merely implicit, underlying and to some extent controlling an action, or the expression of any attitude, belief, or idea.[19]

Carl Rogers offers several propositions[20] which serve as a rationale for the validity and utility of the frame of reference construct.

1. Every individual exists in a continually changing world of experience of which he is the center.

Rogers holds that each of us is at the core of his own world and everything else is happening, developing, occurring about him (not unlike Ptolemy's homocentric notion of the earth as the center of the universe). It is painfully obvious that man is the most egocentric organism on earth, and surely no one can be more self-centered than the human infant. The baby will outgrow much of this, of course, but hardly all of it. But it would seem that one who is approaching emotional maturity has already recognized that egocentrism is a substantial part of being human. Once one accepts this frailty he is in an excellent state to begin to compensate for it and to grow beyond it. The truly arrogant person, however, is the man or woman who has never made and perhaps cannot make this admission. For so long as one can shield himself from a recognition of his fallibility, he need not expend energy in growing and he need not submit to the unknowns and possible pain of *change*.

2. The individual reacts to his world as he experiences and perceives it and thus this perceptual world is, for the individual, "reality."

Rogers put quotes around *reality* to indicate that it is not the "real" reality. Consider these definitions of perception: "The point of reality contact, the door to reality appraisal,"[21] the "structuring of stimuli"[22] and the "organization of stimuli";[23] and "the way in which the person structures his world and himself."[24] But regardless of how invalid and incomplete it may be, one's personalized reality is the only one he has and therefore the only one to which he responds.

3. The individual has one basic tendency and striving which is to actualize, maintain, and enhance himself.

Rogers writes of the *actualizing tendency* as "the inherent tendency of the organism to develop all its capacities in ways to serve to maintain or enhance the organism. It involves not only the tendency to meet . . . 'deficiency needs' for air, food, water, and the like, but also more generalized activities. . . . It is development toward autonomy and

[19] H. B. English and A. C. English, *A Comprehensive Dictionary of Psychological and Psychoanalytical Terms* (New York: Longmans, Green & Co., 1958).

[20] Paraphrased from C. R. Rogers, *Client-Centered Therapy* (Boston, Mass.: Houghton Mifflin Co., 1951), pp. 483, 484, 487, 494.

[21] G. S. Klein, "The Personal World Through Perception," *Perception, An Approach to Personality*, eds. R. R. Blake and G. V. Ramsey (New York: The Ronald Press Co., 1951), pp. 328–329.

[22] C. M. Solley and G. Murphy, *Development of the Perceptual World* (New York: Basic Books, Inc., Publishers, 1960), p. 26.

[23] F. A. Beach, "Body Chemistry and Perception," Blake and Ramsey, op. cit., p. 56.

[24] U. Bronfenbrenner, "Toward an Integrated Theory of Personality," ibid., p. 207.

away from heteronomy, or control by external forces."[25] He subscribes to Angyal's statement: "Life is an autonomous event which takes place between the organism and the environment. Life processes do not merely tend to preserve life but transcend the momentary status quo of the organism, expanding itself continually and imposing its autonomous determination upon an ever-increasing realm of events."[26]

More specifically, Rogers refers to *self*-actualization. We will discuss his concept of the self-image later in this chapter and for the moment will merely suggest that much of the individual's perceiving is in the service of preserving or enhancing his self-image.

According to Frenkel-Brunswik:

It would appear that we do not always see ourselves as we are but instead perceive the environment in terms of our own need. Self-perception and perception of the environment actually merge in the service of these needs. Thus, the perceptual distortions of ourselves and the environment fulfill an important function in our psychological household.[27]

The role of *needs* and *motivation* in influencing perception and therefore behavior is clearly important. . . .

4. Therefore, the best vantage point for understanding another's behavior is from that person's internal frame of reference.

This conclusion follows logically from Rogers' preceding propositions but this does not necessarily make it easy to utilize the frame of reference concept. The individual's internal frame of reference *is* his subjective world. "Only he knows it fully. It can never be known to another except through empathic inference and then can never be perfectly known."[28]

Probably the greatest single deterrent to one's accurately visualizing another's frame of reference is his *own*. An analogy will suggest why this is so.

ANALOGY OF THE BOX

Visualize each of us as the sole and constant tenant of a box with a top, a bottom, and four sides. There is just one window in this box—one's frame of reference, loosely speaking—through which he views the outside world.

A Restricted Window. This suggests immediately that one's view is restricted—he cannot see what is happening in back of him, above, to the sides, and so forth. One obviously cannot be ubiquitous and therefore his view is inevitably limited. But there is another restriction that he can overcome to an extent—the *size* of the window. We all have our "narrownesses"—our areas of naivete. I, for example, was born and reared in a suburb. Suppose you are a country boy and we go out to a farm. We could share the same environment but I would expect that your stimuli and evoked sets would greatly outnumber mine. You would have the preparation, the memory content, to make so

[25] C. R. Rogers, "A Theory of Therapy, Personality, and Interpersonal Relationships, as Developed in the Client-Centered Framework," *Psychology: The Study of a Science*, Vol. 3, *Formulations of the Person and the Social Context*, ed. Sigmund Koch (New York: McGraw-Hill Book Co., 1959), p. 196.

[26] A. Angyal, *Foundations for a Science of Personality* (New York: Commonwealth Fund, 1941).

[27] Else Frenkel-Brunswik, "Personality Theory and Perception," chap. 13 in Blake and Ramsey, op. cit., p. 379.

[28] C. R. Rogers, "A Theory of Therapy . . . ," op. cit., p. 210.

much more significance out of the experience than I.

But I have the capacity to learn. Given the time and provided I have the motivation I can acquire some of your sophisticaion. In short I can *expand* my window.

Stained-Glass Window. Not only is one's window frame restricted (but expandable largely at his will) but it also does not contain a pane of clear glass. It is rather like a stained-glass church window with various peculiarly shaped, tinted, and refracting lenses. In one's frame of reference these lenses are his experiences, biases, values, needs, emotions, aspirations, and the like. They may all be distorting media to an extent but are we powerless to overcome these distortions? Hardly, but let us establish one point first.

Does anyone grow up with a clear window? Can anyone be without bias for example? Quite unlikely, for everyone had to be born at a particular time and in a particular place. Thus he was exposed to particular people and situations all of whom and which taught him *special* lessons regarding values, customs, mores, codes, and so on.

But again man has viability and the capacity to adjust and compensate—he can *clarify* his window. A pencil in a glass of water appears to bend abruptly but if one *understands* something about the nature of refraction he can compensate for the distortion, aim at where the pencil appears not to be, and hit it. So it is more profoundly with a man himself—if he can *understand himself* he can *compensate* for his distorted frame of reference, and, in effect clarify his window.

THE SELF-IMAGE

But there is at least one extremely formidable obstacle in the way of a man's truly understanding himself. We return to Carl Rogers for this. A key concept of the Rogerian therapeutic approach is the premise that as a person grows up he develops a *self-image* or *self-concept*—a picture of himself. Hayakawa asserted: "The mode of human behavior is not self-preservation but self-concept. The self-concept is who you think you are and the self is who you are. Values determine people's self-concept and self-concept determines social experience."[29] Rogers uses *self, concept of self,* and *self-structure* as terms to refer to

the organized, consistent conceptual gestalt composed of perceptions of the characteristics of the "I" or "me" and the perceptions of the relationships of the "I" or "me" to others and to various aspects of life, together with the values attached to these perceptions. It is a fluid and changing gestalt, a process. . . . The term self or self-concept is more likely to be used when we are talking of the person's view of himself, self-structure when we are looking at this gestalt from an external frame of reference.[30]

On Coping with Guilt. The self-image helps to explain how one copes with guilt.

One of man's most compelling needs is the need to justify himself. Moreover, most of us tolerate guilt very poorly. Guilt is painful—acutely so. Therefore, as pain-avoidance organisms most of us have highly facile and sophisticated means for eliminating or

[29] S. I. Hayakawa, participating in the 1965 Student Symposium, "Spectrum of Perspectives," Northwestern University.

[30] C. R. Rogers, "A Theory of Therapy. . . ," op. cit., p. 200.

diminishing the pain of guilt. Test this assertion, if you can tread a painful route, by tracing back to an event in which you did something that you *knew* was *wrong*; that you *could not justify* by rationalizing that the end warranted the means; and that was *not beyond your control*.

Most of us have great difficulty remembering such events objectively and yet almost all of us have been guilty of them. The pain of guilt is so noisome that we have developed great skill in justifying our behavior before, during, or after the act.

At the core of this behavior appears to be the overriding motive to "actualize, maintain, and enhance" one's self-image. It is clear that the individual can distort experience to satisfy this powerful need. For example, suppose Mike treats Tom unjustly—at least as Tom perceives it. Tom will likely become angry and want revenge. If Tom were to analyze himself he might find that what he wants most of all is for Mike to experience remorse, true contrition—the pain of guilt—at least commensurate with the pain he inflicted upon Tom. However, Mike as a pain-avoider has already begun to justify his behavior and is unlikely, therefore, to tender a sincere apology. Failing to receive evidence of Mike's acceptance of his own guilt, Tom may be moved to retaliate in kind or to attempt to wrench an apology from Mike. In either event, Tom's behavior, as Mike perceives it, is sufficiently obnoxious to complete his self-justification. "You see how Tom is acting? That _____ deserved to be treated that way in the first place!"

No matter how unreasonable, irrational, or immoral another's behavior may appear to us it is generally a good

assumption that it is quite reasonable, rational and moral *in his world*. Epictetus wrote: "The appearances of things to the mind is the standard of action of every man."

One's self-image is perhaps most profoundly important to the individual in the sense that it serves as *his contact with himself*. In fact, when he talks or thinks about *himself* he is usually not referring to his limbs, torso, and head but rather to an abstraction he usually labels as "my *self*." Thus, it is by his self-image that he *knows* himself.

Images of Others.   But we also need to know and understand others and thus we form images of them as well—particularly those with whom we are most interdependent—parents, spouse, children, superiors, subordinates. Such image formation, whether one is conscious of it or not, requires considerable energy output and the marshaling of much psychological intelligence about the individual of whom one is forming an image. The prime motive for the effort is that we need to build a good base for understanding and predicting the behavior of the other person. And only by predicting the other's behavior reasonably accurately can we confidently control our own behavior and deal effectively with the other person.[31] This helps to explain why one becomes confused and upset when an-

[31] The process we call *forming impressions of personality* is sometimes called *person perception*, Bruner [J. S. Bruner, "Social Psychology and Perception," *Readings in Social Psychology*, eds. E. Maccoby, T. M. Newcomb, and E. L. Hartley (3rd ed.; New York; Henry Holt, Inc., 1958), pp. 85–94] has argued that the "process of perception tends, in general, to accomplish two things: (1) a recording of the diversity of data we encounter into a simpler form that brings it within the scope of our limited memory; (2) a going beyond the information given to predict future events and thereby minimize surprise." Roger

other's behavior suddenly contradicts his image of that other person. He has lost or risks the loss of his base for predicting and thus for controlling himself in dealing with the other.

And this holds even when the other's behavior is *more favorable* than anticipated. Suppose you have a superior—a father, a teacher, a boss—who is a veritable tyrant. And suppose one day he greets you with a broad smile, a friendly clap on the back, and an encouraging comment. Is your initial response—"Wonderful, the old buzzard has finally turned over a new leaf!" Or is it—"What's he up to now!" As a friend in business put it, "You can work for an s.o.b.—provided he's a *consistent* s.o.b.! It's the one who turns it on and off unpredictably that gives you the ulcers!"

Self-image Challenged. Now if we are troubled by another person's jeopardizing our predictability about him, then how much more traumatic is it for one to have his own *self-image* challenged. He stands the risk of losing the ability to predict, control and *know* himself. It is difficult to imagine a

greater internal upheaval than suddenly not to *know oneself—to lose contact with oneself*. It may not be inaccurate to say that our mental institutions are filled with people who have lost contact with themselves more or less permanently.

It is no wonder, then, that the loss of a self-image is generally warded off at almost any cost. And yet few of us have gone through life unscathed. Anyone who has experienced a deeply traumatic experience at one time or another—whether related to a parent, a spouse, a child, school, religion, vocation, narcotics, alcoholism, job security, illness, injury, lawsuit—will probably find on retrospection that his self-image was being severely threatened.

A Personal Case. My own experience is a case in point. As a high school freshman I hit upon chemical research for a career. I suppose this was encouraged by an older boy I admired who also aspired to chemistry. He had built a laboratory in his basement so, of course, I had to have one too. I remember collecting hundreds of jars and bottles and scores of other treasures that might somehow be useful in my lab. I can also recall spending hour after hour thoroughly enjoying mixing potions of every description—and some beyond description. (I recall without quite so much relish the time I brewed some chlorine and nearly gassed myself unconscious!)

I *devoured* the chemistry course in my junior year. I must admit feeling rather smug during this period for I had a ready answer to the recurrent question, What are you going to be? Most of my friends had either a hazy

Brown, *Social Psychology* (New York: The Free Press, 1965), p. 611.

Social psychologists, in particular, have been concerned with how we perceive or infer the traits and intentions of others. For a sampling of experimental and theoretical works in "social perception" or "person perception" see: I. E. Bender and A. H. Hastorf, "On Measuring Generalized Empathic Ability (Social Sensitivity)," *Journal of Abnormal and Social Psychology*, Vol. 48 (1958), pp. 503–506; V. B. Cline and J. M. Richards, Jr., "Accuracy of Interpersonal Perception—A General Trait?", *Journal of Abnormal and Social Psychology*, Vol. 60 (1960), pp. 1–7; F. Heider, *The Psychology of Interpersonal Relations* (New York: John Wiley & Sons, Inc., 1958); W. C. Schutz, *FIRO: A Three-Dimensional Theory of Interpersonal Behavior* (New York: Holt, Rinehart & Winston, Inc., 1960); R. Taft, "The Ability to Judge People," *Psychological Bulletin*, Vol. 52 (1955), pp. 1–23; R. Tagiuri and L. Petrullo (eds.), *Person Perception and Interpersonal Behavior* (Stanford, Calif.: Stanford University Press, 1958).

answer or none at all. My self-image in this regard was forming and solidifying.

I was graduated from high school during World War II and immediately entered the service. Somehow the Army gave little shrift to young men who were long on aspiration but short on experience and consequently I had three years of singularly nonchemical experience—but this did not dissuade me. Finally, the war ended and I was discharged. I immediately enrolled in a chemical technology program at a university reputed for this field.

Suddenly, reality began to catch up with my self-image. I had not realized that a chemist was also expected to be a pretty fair mathematician. I had done well enough in high school math courses but the last three years were nonmathematical as well as nonchemical. At any rate I foolishly disregarded the math refresher course (my self-image said I didn't need a "crutch") and charged headlong into college algebra where I was in competition with fellows fresh from high school math. While I was rusty, it would be unfair to say that I didn't get the math; I did get it but about a week after the exams, which is poor timing! Net result—the first *D* I had ever received in my life. What was the consequence—did I trade in my self-image for a new model? Hardly; rather than yield, I fought tenaciously and found a ready explanation for my plight: Aside from the Army's causing me to "forget my math" the instructor "had it in for me." Among other evidence he had a Scottish name and I was convinced he was anti-Irish!

I was practicing what some writers call "perceptual defense," a form of perceptual distortion which "demonstrates that when confronted with a fact inconsistent with a stereotype already held by a person, the perceiver is able to distort the data in such a way as to eliminate the inconsistency. Thus, by perceiving inaccurately, he defends himself from having to change his stereotypes."[32] Haire and Grunes suggest that we "blinder" ourselves to avoid seeing that which might trouble us.[33] As communication authority David K. Berlo paraphrased the Bible—"Seek and ye shall find—whether it is there or not!"

The next quarter? A *C* in math. This instructor had an Irish name but he didn't like me either! In the middle of the third quarter and another math *D*, my self-image had withstood all the onslaught from harsh reality that it could. And for two to three weeks (at the time it seemed like six months) I was in a state of unrelieved depression. I became very nervous and had difficulty eating, sleeping, and studying (which only intensified my problem). Figuratively, a large section of my self-image had been shot away and *I had nothing to replace it.* The most appalling aspect of the experience was that I realized that *I didn't know myself.* To give the story a happy ending I took a battery of aptitude tests, changed to another major, and very gradually began to construct another self-image.

Resistance to Image Change. Anyone who has undergone such a trauma will understand why the individual generally resists image change—par-

[32] S. S. Zalkind and T. W. Costello, "Perception: Some Recent Research and Implications for Administration," *Administrative Science Quarterly*, September, 1962, p. 227.

[33] M. Haire and W. F. Grunes, "Perceptual Defenses: Processes Protecting an Original Perception of Another Personality," *Human Relations*, Vol. 3 (1958), pp. 403–412.

ticularly sudden change. And herein lies one of the greatest obstacles to the full development of an effective communicator and, for that matter, an effective person. The central premise of an excellent book[34] by psychiatrist Karen Horney is that the neurotic process is a special form of human development which is the antithesis of healthy growth. Optimally, man's energies are directed toward realizing his own potentialities. But, under inner stress, he becomes estranged from his *real self* and spends himself creating and protecting a false, idealized self, based on pride, but threatened by doubts, self-contempt, and self-hate. Throughout the book the goal of liberation for the forces that lead to true self-realization is emphasized.

Take the case of a high school friend. After graduation he, too, went into the service but was more fortunate (in a sense), for the Army put him through three years of an engineering curriculum. Then the war was over and he was discharged. But he decided he did not care for engineering and could not bring himself to take a final year of course work to earn an engineering degree. And yet he could not bear the thought of starting all over again in another field. The net result was that, for all practical purposes, he did nothing. He took a clerical job in a nearby insurance firm and has been there for 20 years. Through the years, his perhaps largely unconscious philosophy of life has evidently been: "I can't stand another failure [he probably regarded not completing the engineering degree as a failure] and one

sure way not to lose a race is not to enter it." In sum, here is a man who apparently has protected his self-image at the cost of a stunted life.

The handicap of inaccurate self-knowledge and the unwillingness to reconstruct a more realistic self-image seem to be very widespread. In 15 years of organizational research and consulting I have known scores, if not hundreds of men, particularly in the middle echelons of their organizations, who seemed to have all the requisites for continued success: intelligence, education, experience, drive, ability, ambition. But they lacked one vital thing— *they did not know themselves.* The image they held of themselves was pitifully out of phase with that which they were projecting to others. They seemed chronically annoyed and/or bewildered by the reactions of others to them. What was happening? As unrealistic as their self-images were it was nevertheless too threatening to entertain contrary cues from other people. Fending off the reactions of others variously as "those malicious/crazy/misinformed/ornery/perverse/stupid people!" they had been successful in perpetuating and even reinforcing their respective self-myths. Thus, they ineffectualized themselves; squandered their nervous energies in a kind of internal conflict, protecting their fallacious self-images.[35] The masterful Robert Burns captured the poignancy of self-deception almost two centuries ago.

Oh wad some power the giftie gie us

[34] Karen Horney, *Neurosis and Human Growth: The Struggle Toward Self-Realization* (New York: W. W. Norton & Co., Inc., 1950).

[35] This is why Brouwer was moved to write: "Manager development means change in the manager's self-image." Paul J. Brouwer, "The Power to See Ourselves," *Harvard Business Review*, Vol. 42, No. 6 (November-December, 1964), p. 156.

To see oursels as ithers see us!
It wad frae monie a blunder free
us,
    An' foolish notion.

On Coping with Defensiveness

We have discussed defensive behavior as a critical obstacle to effective interpersonal communication. What, in the final analysis, are people defending *against*? In a word, *perceived threat*—the threat of change or harm to their self-images, to their personalized worlds. This would suggest that whatever reduced perceived threat would reduce the need to defend against it—to enable one to reduce his defenses accordingly. What threat-reducing techniques or approaches, then, are available to us?

After an eight-year study of recordings of interpersonal discussions, Jack Gibb delineated two communication climates—one threatening ("defensive"); the other nonthreatening ("supportive"). (See Table 1.) Incidentally, Gibb's "supportive climate" is quite in keeping with Likert's "supportive relationship" and McGregor's Theory Y.

Gibb defined his paired categories of perceived behavior as follows.[36]

> *Evaluation.* To pass judgment on another; to blame or praise; to make moral assessments of another; to question his standards, values and motives and the affect loadings of his communications.
>
> *Description.* Nonjudgmental; to ask questions which are perceived as genuine requests for information; to present "feelings, events, percep-

[36] "Defensive Communication," *Journal of Communication*, Vol. 11, No. 3, Sept., 1961, pp. 142–148.

Table 1 Categories of Behavior Characteristic of Supportive and Defensive Climates in Small Groups

Defensive Climates	Supportive Climates
1. Evaluation	1. Description
2. Control	2. Problem orientation
3. Strategy	3. Spontaneity
4. Neutrality	4. Empathy
5. Superiority	5. Equality
6. Certainty	6. Provisionalism

Source: Jack R. Gibb. "Defensive Communication," *Journal of Communication,* Vol. 11, No. 3 (Sept. 1961), p. 143.

tions, or processes which do not ask or imply that the receiver change behavior or attitude."

Control. To try to do something to another; to attempt to change an attitude or the behavior of another—to try to restrict his field of activity; "implicit in all attempts to alter another person is the assumption of the change agent that the person to be altered is inadequate."

Problem Orientation. The antithesis of persuasion; to communicate "a desire to collaborate in defining a mutual problem and in seeking its solution" (thus tending to create the same problem orientation in the other); to imply that he has no preconceived solution, attitude, or method to impose upon the other; to allow "the receiver to set his own goals, make his own decisions, and evaluate his own progress—or to share with the sender in doing so."

Strategy. To manipulate others; to use tricks to "involve" another, to make him think he was making his own decisions, and to make him feel that the speaker had genuine interest in him; to engage in a stratagem involving ambiguous and multiple motivation.

Spontaneity. To express guilelessness; natural simplicity; free of deception; having a "clean id"; having unhidden, uncomplicated motives; straightforwardness and honesty.

Neutrality. To express lack of concern for the welfare of another; "the clinical, detached, person-is-an-object-of-study attitude."

Empathy. To express respect for the worth of the listener; to identify with his problems, share his feelings, and accept his emotional values at face value.

Superiority. To communicate the attitude that one is "superior in position, power, wealth, intellectual ability, physical characteristics, other ways" to another; to tend to arouse feelings of inadequacy in the other; to impress the other that the speaker "is not willing to enter into a shared problem-solving relationship, that he probably does not desire feedback, that he does not require help and/or that he will be likely to try to reduce the power, the status, or the worth of the receiver."

Equality. To be willing to enter into participative planning with mutual trust and respect; to attach little importance to differences in talent, ability, worth, appearance, status, and power.

Certainty. To appear dogmatic; "to seem to know the answers, to require no additional data"; and to regard self as teacher rather than as co-worker; to manifest inferiority by *needing to be right*, wanting to win an argument rather than solve a problem, seeing one's ideas as truths to be defended.

Provisionalism. To be willing to experiment with one's own behavior, attitudes, and ideas; to investigate issues rather than taking sides on them, to problem solve rather than debate, to communicate that the other person may have some control over the shared quest or the investigation of ideas. "If a person is genuinely searching for information and data, he does not resent help or company along the way."

It would appear that if one were to offer another the most supportive climate possible his behavior should be descriptive, problem oriented, spontaneous, and so on, and should avoid attempting to evaluate, control, employ stratagems, and so forth. But the situation is a bit more complex.

First of all, the above are *perceived behaviors.* Therefore, the *perceptions* of the *perceivers* rather than the *intentions* of the perceived will be the final arbiter as to how defensive or supportive the perceiver regards the climate. Moreover, as a person becomes more defensive he becomes less able to assess accurately the motives, values, and emotions of the other person. Conversely, as he grows less defensive, the more accurate his perceptions become.[37]

The more "supportive" or defense reductive the climate, the less the receiver reads into the communication distorted loadings which arise from projections of his own anxieties, motives, and concerns. As defenses are reduced, the receivers become better able to concentrate upon the structure, the content and the cognitive meanings of the message.[38]

Another qualification on Gibb's classifications is that while the defensive

[37] J. R. Gibb, "Defense Level and Influence Potential in Small Groups," L. Petrullo and B. M. Bass (eds.), *Leadership and Interpersonal Behavior* (New York: Holt, Rinehart, and Winston, 1961), pp. 66–81.
[38] J. R. Gibb, "Defensive Communication," op. cit., p. 142.

categories *generally* arouse defensiveness and the supportive categories *ordinarily* generate defense reduction, the degree to which these responses occur depends upon the *individual's level of defensiveness* as well as the *general climate of the group at the time*.[39]

Still another qualification is that the behavior categories are *interactive*. For example, when a speaker's behavior appears *evaluative* it ordinarily increases defensiveness. But if the listener feels the speaker regards him as an *equal* and was being direct and *spontaneous*, the evaluativeness of the message might be neutralized or not even perceived. Again, attempts to *control* will stimulate defensiveness depending upon the degree of *openness* of the effort. The suspicion of hidden motives heightens resistance. Still another example, the use of *stratagems* becomes especially threatening when one attempt seems to be trying to make strategy *appear spontaneous*.

OPENNESS

A central theme running throughout Gibb's findings is the importance of *openness*—the willingness to be receptive to experience. Rogers considered openness as the polar opposite of defensiveness.

In the hypothetical person who is completely open to his experience, his concept of self would be a symbolization in awareness which would be completely congruent with his experience. There would, therefore, be no possibility of threat.[40]

One who is open to experience evaluates threat more accurately and tolerates change more graciously. This is why the frame of reference concept can be so helpful in reducing defenses and in keeping them low. Because the frame of reference obviates the mine-is-the-only-valid-world presumption it makes defense of one's personalized world unnecessary. Nondefensive, one is not compelled to attack or counterattack—thus he is more able to contribute to a supportive climate in his relations with others.

In a supportive climate people are more able to explore their own and each other's decision premises[41] and thus get down to the real grounds of controversy (or to discover that there was no real basis for conflict). Even if there are genuine differences, under conditions of openness people find themselves more capable of dealing with them maturely.

Rogers offers this practical suggestion:

The next time you get into an argument with your wife, or your friend, or with a small group of friends, just stop the discussion for a moment and for an experiment, institute this rule. "Each person can speak up for himself only after he has first restated the ideas and feelings of the previous speaker accurately, and to that speaker's satisfaction." You see what this would mean? It would be necessary for you to really achieve the other speaker's frame of reference—to understand his thoughts and feelings so well that you could summarize them for him. Sounds simple, doesn't it? But if you try it you will discover it one of the most difficult things you have tried to do. However, once you have been able to see the

---

[39] J. R. Gibb, "Sociopsychological Processes of Group Instruction," N. B. Henry (ed.), *The Dynamics of Instructional Groups* (Fifty-ninth Yearbook of the National Society for the Study of Education) (1960), Part II, pp. 115–135.

[40] C. R. Rogers, "A Theory. . . ," op. cit., p. 206.

[41] H. A. Simon, *Administrative Behavior* (2d ed.; New York: The Macmillan Co., 1957).

other's point of view, your own comments will have to be drastically revised. You will also find the emotion going out of the discussion, the differences being reduced, and those differences which remain being of a rational and understandable sort.[42]

Summary

We have depicted human behavior as the product of the internal state of the individual and the environment in which he finds himself. His behavior, then, is only indirectly a response to reality. One who cannot tolerate this basic uncertainty of life and assumes *his world is the only real world* may find that "world" in almost constant jeopardy. Closed and defensive he may respond to the "threats" with irrational attack and/or flight.

We have conceded that many organizations are populated to an extent with more or less defensive (and thus often aggressive) people. Therefore, the challenge to anyone who aspires to be an effective leader or member of an organization (or more broadly, wishes to live an emotionally mature and deeply satisfying life) might be phrased as follows:

1. Can he come to accept that *his* and everyone else's "reality" is subjective, incomplete, distorted, and unique? Can he, therefore, muster the courage to become open and nondefensive—to permit even contrary cues to reach him and to begin to revise, update, and make more valid his self-image?

2. Having clarified his own frame of reference can he learn to assess accurately the frames of reference of others? Can the manager, for example, realize the simple but profound truth that his subordinates' worlds have him in it as a boss—his world does not?

[42] C. R. Rogers, "Communication: Its Blocking and Its Facilitation," a paper originally prepared for delivery at the Northwestern University Centennial Conference on Communications, held in Evanston, Illinois, October 11–13, 1951. Reproduced here from the Northwestern University *Information*, Vol. XX, No. 25.

Action Steps: Applications

1. Working in groups, prepare a brief questionnaire that you think can categorize members of the class. Some categories may be: What jobs have you held? What are your hobbies? What are your career plans? How serious are you? Compare your evaluations of one another and identify cues that might be misleading from your behavior.

2. Eye behavior is one of the most potent elements in our nonverbal behavior. Our normal eye contacts last only about a second and we are quite careful about how and when we look someone directly in the eye. Intercultural communication researchers have noted the differences between cultures and subcultures in the amount and types of interpersonal eye contacts (see Chapter 5). What have you noted of these differences? As an exercise, work in pairs and sit facing each other for a period of about three minutes, saying nothing and looking each other

intently in the eyes. Discuss your reactions. What were you able to communicate?

3. Compile a list of current bumper stickers. Put them in various combinations and determine your stereotype of the driver. What stickers are considered totally contradictory?

4. What are the assumptions concerning "reality" and the "nature of the world" that underlie Haney's analysis of perception theory? Relate this view back to Chapter 1 and the readings from Satir and Barnlund.

5. Meet with a group of your classmates whom you don't know well. Go around the group and focus on each person. Express inferences about them that extend beyond what you see and already know. Are they rich, poor, married, industrious, etc.? State the basis for your guesses. Have the person then confirm or correct the guesses made.

6. Relate the concept of the self-fulfilling prophecy as presented in Reading 3.1 with the "virtuous circle of success" discussed in Reading 2.1.

Chapter 4
Encoding and Decoding Verbal Messages

W E GATHER, share, give, and receive information through words. We establish, continue, or terminate relationships by words. The process by which we arbitrarily make certain sounds or symbols stand for ideas is societal in essence. We can, by mutual agreement, make anything stand for anything. In this chapter we examine some of the problem areas involved in people's attempts to communicate by words. Recall Proposition 9: Since interpersonal communication relies on behaviors, we must be satisfied with degrees of mutual understanding.

Characteristics of Language

The first fragmentary utterances of a small child who is just learning to speak indicate the interpersonal nature of human speech. Swiss psychologist Jean Piaget distinguished two functions of speech for the child: the social and the egocentric. In social speech, "the child addresses his hearer, considers his point of view, tries to influence him or actually exchanges ideas with him." In egocentric speech, "the child does not bother to know to whom he is speaking, nor whether he is being listened to. He talks either to himself or for the pleasure of associating anyone who happens to be there with the activity of the moment."[1] Other investigations have concluded that the bulk of the child's speech, approximately 90 percent, is social.[2] The work of the Russian psychiatrist L. S. Vigotsky suggests that even the monologues labeled by Piaget as "egocentric" are actually directed toward others. When Vigotsky placed a child who demonstrated the characteristics of "egocentric" speech (babblings, incomplete sentences) in isolation, in a very noisy room, or among deaf-and-mute children, the child's speech dropped off considerably. Vigotsky concluded that the child believes his speech is being understood by others, and when external conditions make speaking difficult or when feedback is lacking, he stops speaking.[3] The child does not initially clearly differentiate his/her perception of the world from the world as perceived by others. He/she seems to believe that everyone else perceives and understands the world just as he/she perceives and understands

---

[1] Jean Piaget, *The Language and Thought of the Child* (New York: Harcourt Brace Jovanovich, 1926), p. 26.

[2] G. A. Miller, *Language and Communication* (New York: McGraw-Hill, 1951), pp. 155–156.

[3] L. S. Vigotsky, "Thought and Speech," *Psychiatry*, 2 (1939): 29–54.

it; thus, others must understand his/her highly idiosyncratic language. This tendency, as we shall see, is not completely restricted to the child, and it lies at the heart of many communication problems. The most important point, however, is that according to available experimental data, all speech is a form of interpersonal behavior.

The child attaches meanings to visual and verbal phenomena and, in effect, works to "break the code." As we have noted, however, all language and all codes are arbitrary. Mutual understandings as to the meanings assigned to symbols are entirely by agreement and consent. There is usually no connection between the sound or series of letters in a word and the "thing" in reality except what is arbitrarily attached by human beings. Semanticists have used the analogy of a *map* and the *territory* it represents to describe the relationship between our verbal symbols and the reality for which they stand. We shall now examine in some detail those characteristics of language that potentially cause us problems in our interpersonal communication.

1. WORDS HAVE DIFFERENT MEANINGS TO DIFFERENT PEOPLE

Generally we think of words as having two kinds of meaning or two kinds of definition. One is the connotative, or associative, definition. The other is the denotative, or operational, definition. The latter kind of meaning refers to the thing or event, a phenomenon to which the word refers. This denotative definition is what we would point to if asked to define a word without being able to speak or use any other words. Such denotative meanings are reasonably stable; they are common to science (H_2O), business (debit), industry (arbitration), and to each profession. They mean about the same to everyone, but problems can develop if agreements are not reached. For example, if someone asked you "What class are you in?" it would be useless to respond unless you knew whether he was referring to class in school or social standing. Even in as restricted an area as parliamentary procedure, to "table" a motion in the United States means to put it aside, while in England it means "Let's bring it up for discussion."

Consider numerous possible meanings in the following story:

> Struck by a sign in a plumber's window ("struck"?) reading "Iron Sinks," a wag went inside to inform the merchant that he was fully aware that "iron sinks." The storekeeper, ready to play the game, inquired, "And do you know that time flies, sulphur springs, jam rolls, music stands, Niagara Falls, concrete walks, wood fences, sheep run, holiday trips, rubber tires, the organ stops . . . ?" But by then the wag had had enough and fled.

Such multiple meanings inherent in our language force us to consider context and nonverbal cues to give us more exact meaning. The educated adult uses, in daily conversation, only about 2,000 of the more than 600,000 words in the English language. Of these 2,000, the 500 most frequently used words have over 14,000 dictionary definitions. Even the term *meaning*, which we have attempted to define, has 18 groups of meanings in one dictionary. Further, our language is constantly changing, adding new words, and modifying definitions

The context and nonverbal cues are important to a message.

as usage changes. Figure 4.1 shows dictionary definitions ascribed to the word "love."

Dictionary definitions do not tell the complete story, however. Social psychologist Joost A. M. Meerloo cites some of the potential meanings that the statement "I love you" may convey:

This is no essay on love and no profound treatise on the variations of feelings of tenderness. I only want to show how much semantic difficulty there is in the expression "I love you"—a statement that can be expressed in so many varied ways. It may be a stage song, repeated daily without any meaning, or a barely audible murmur, full of surrender. Sometimes it means: I desire you or I want you sexually. It may mean: I hope you love me or I hope that I will be able to love you. Often it means: It may be that a love relationship can develop between us or even I hate you. Often it is a wish for emotional exchange: I want your admiration in exchange for mine or I give my love in exchange for some passion or I want to feel cozy and at home with you or I admire some of your qualities. A declaration of love is mostly a request: I desire you or I want you to gratify me, or I want your protection or I want to be intimate with you or I want to exploit your loveliness. Sometimes it is the need for security and tenderness, for parental treatment. It may mean: My self-love goes out to you. But it may also express submissiveness: Please take me as I am, or I feel guilty about you, I want, through you, to correct the mistakes I have made in human relations. It may be self-sacrifice and a masochistic wish for dependency. However, it may also be a full affirmation of the other, taking the responsibility for mutual exchange of feelings. It may be a weak

love (luv), *n.*, *v.*, **loved, lov·ing.** —*n.* **1.** the profoundly tender or passionate affection for a person of the opposite sex. **2.** a feeling of warm personal attachment or deep affection, as for a parent, child, or friend. **3.** sexual passion or desire, or its gratification. **4.** a person toward whom love is felt; beloved person; sweetheart. **5.** (used in direct address as a term of endearment, affection, or the like): *Would you like to see a movie, love?* **6.** a love affair; amour. **7.** (*cap.*) a personification of sexual affection, as Eros or Cupid. **8.** affectionate concern for the well-being of others: *a love of little children; the love of one's neighbor.* **9.** strong predilection or liking for anything: *her love of books.* **10.** the object or thing so liked: *The theater was her great love.* **11.** the benevolent affection of God for His creatures, or the reverent affection due from them to God. **12.** *Chiefly Tennis.* a score of. zero; nothing. **13.** a word formerly used in communications to represent the letter L. **14. for love, a.** out of affection or liking; for pleasure. **b.** without compensation; gratuitously: *He took care of the poor for love.* **15. for the love of,** in consideration of; for the sake of: *For the love of mercy, stop that noise.* **16. in love (with),** feeling deep affection or passion for (a person, idea, occupation, etc.); enamored of: *in love with life; in love with one's work.* **17. make love, a.** to embrace and kiss as lovers. **b.** to engage in sexual intercourse. **18. no love lost,** dislike; animosity: *There was no love lost between the two brothers.* [ME; OE *lufu*; c. OFris *luve*, OHG *luba*, Goth *lubō*]
—*v.t.* **19.** to have love or affection for: *All her pupils love her.* **20.** to have a profoundly tender or passionate affection for (a person of the opposite sex). **21.** to have a strong liking for; take great pleasure in: *to love music; She loves to go dancing.* **22.** to need or require; benefit greatly from: *Plants love sunlight.* **23.** to make love to; have sexual intercourse with. —*v.i.* **24.** to have love or affection, esp. for one of the opposite sex. [ME *lov(i)en*, OE *lufian*; c. OFris *luvia*, OHG *lubōn* to love, L *lubēre* (later *libēre*) to please; akin to LIEF]
—**Syn. 1.** tenderness, fondness, predilection, warmth, passion, adoration. **1, 2.** LOVE, AFFECTION, DEVOTION all mean a deep and enduring emotional regard, usually for another person. LOVE may apply to various kinds of regard: the charity of the Creator, reverent adoration toward God or toward a person, the relation of parent and child, the regard of friends for each other, romantic feelings for one of the opposite sex, etc. AFFECTION is a fondness for persons of either sex, that is enduring and tender, but calm. DEVOTION is an intense love and steadfast, enduring loyalty to a person; it may also imply consecration to a cause. **2.** liking, inclination, regard, friendliness. **19.** like. **20.** adore, adulate, worship.
—**Ant. 1, 2.** hatred, dislike. **19, 20.** detest, hate.

FIGURE 4.1. Definition of love. (From *The Random House Dictionary of the English Language*, unabridged edition, p. 849. Copyright © 1971 by Random House, Inc. Reprinted by permission of the publisher.)

feeling of friendliness, it may be the scarcely even whispered expression of ecstasy. "I love you"—wish, desire, submission, conquest; it is never the word itself that tells the real meaning here.[4]

Even greater numbers of problems result from the connotative meaning of a word or expression than from the denotative. While the denotation gives sharpness and accuracy to a word, its connotations give it power. Our most familiar words are rich with connotations—mother, Watergate, the president. The connotation may even be so strong that it erases the denotation, and, for the individual, only the connotation then has significance.

The connotative meaning of a word is the thought, feeling, or ideas that we have about the word, the things we say about the word when asked to define

[4] J. A. M. Meerloo, *Conversation and Communication* (New York: International Universities, 1952), p. 83.

it. The words "factory worker" denote a person who earns his living by performing productive tasks in a building where many persons are organized to produce a product at a cost below what other people will pay for it. However, the words connote certain feelings and emotions. To some people, "factory worker" may mean a lazy, irresponsible, and apathetic person hostile to management. To others it may connote an honest, good man who is exploited, unjustly treated, and deprived of any freedom and opportunity to exercise responsibility and judgment. In the course of a lifetime, the denotations of words change but little, while their connotations alter with our experience.

To some extent, the individual experiences of each of the approximately 300 million English-speaking people differ from all others. Every second of our lives we are experiencing something that is not exactly the same experience as any other we have had before, or that anyone else has had. Each individual has certain personal connotations derived from his/her experience with objects, persons, or ideas that are the referents of the words he/she uses. General connotations are those accepted as the typical reaction of a majority of people; thus most people in our society regard "war" with fear and abhorrence. Being able to anticipate a person's reaction to a word allows some people to manipulate another by the simple use of that word.

Virtually all words have both denotative and connotative dimensions. The type and degree of reaction to words will vary from person to person. Meanings reside not in the words, but in the minds of people using them.

2. WORDS VARY IN THE DEGREE OF ABSTRACTION

A second major aspect of words and language is that words, like thoughts and conceptions, vary in degree of abstraction; words are symbols used to represent a generalized category of things, experiences, or ideas. The symbols vary from indicating a total class ("foreigners"), to a particular class ("Spaniards"), to a specific member of the class ("Juan Martinez"). S. I. Hayakawa depicted the principle of abstracting with his story of "Bessie," a cow. If we perceive in front of us a living organism, we respond, based on our previous experiences with other similar animals, by labeling the creature we are seeing a "cow." The cow is at the same time unique (different from all other living creatures in certain respects) and a member of a class ("cows").[5]

This characteristic of language permits people to avoid one another in arguments by retreating from one level of abstraction to another. Teachers and politicians are often adept at handling difficult questions by changing the level of abstraction when pushed as to specifics. The more abstract we become, the more we are relying on "what is in our heads" rather than any sort of denotative reality.

When dealing with concrete empirical referents (denotative definitions)—such as "book," "tree," "Illinois"—we have generally agreed-on referents; highly abstract terms such as "justice," "obscenity," and "public welfare" are less likely

[5] S. I. Hayakawa, *Language in Thought and Action* (New York: Harcourt Brace Jovanovich, 1964), pp. 173–180.

to have common referents. In general, the more abstract a word, the greater the ambiguity and the greater the chances of misunderstanding.

Hayakawa cites a course in aesthetics in a large midwestern university

in which an entire semester was devoted to Art and Beauty and the principles underlying them, and during which the professor, even when asked by students, persistently declined to name specific paintings, symphonies, sculptures, or objects of beauty to which his principles might apply. "We are interested," he would say, "in principle, not in particulars."[6]

Wendell Johnson labeled the linguistic phenomenon of a person's remaining more or less stuck at a certain level of abstraction "dead-level abstracting." As an example of a persistent low-level abstracting, he cites the following:

Probably all of us know certain people who seem able to talk on and on without ever drawing any very general conclusions. For example, there is the back-fence chatter that is made up of he said and then I said and then she said and I said and then he said, far into the afternoon, ending with, "Well, that's just what I told him!" Letters describing vacation trips frequently illustrate this language, detailing places seen, times of arrival and departure, the foods eaten and the prices paid, whether the beds were hard or soft, etc.[7]

This example contrasts sharply with the persistent, high level of abstraction of the professor cited by Hayakawa. Usually our speech demonstrates a constant interplay of higher- and lower-level abstraction, as we adapt quickly up and down the abstraction ladder.

High-level abstractions are quite useful when they are related to sensory experience and demonstrate relationships and order. On the other hand, these abstractions can be dangerous as merely evocative terms standing for anything or nothing. The most highly valued terms in our language (love, beauty, truth, etc.) can either be maps without territories or can point to specific experiences and feelings. Stuart Chase summarizes the point as follows:

When we use words as symbols for the abstraction that we "see," they are an abstraction of an abstraction. When we use generalizations like chairs-in-general, or "household furniture," we abstract again. The semantic moral is to be conscious of these abstraction levels, and not to lose sight of the original chair.[8]

Harry Truman was never a man to mince words. A constituent once wrote him about the postmen's motto "Neither snow, nor rain, nor heat, nor gloom of night stays these couriers from the swift completion of their appointed rounds" and asked what it meant. "It means," replied Truman, "they deliver the mail in the wintertime."

3. LANGUAGE IS, BY ITS VERY NATURE, INCOMPLETE

Millions of people, when reporting their experiences, use the same meager store of accepted symbols. Each common word symbol must, therefore, be used

[6] Ibid., p. 189.
[7] W. Johnson, *People in Quandaries* (New York: Harper & Row, 1946), p. 270.
[8] S. Chase, *Power of Words* (New York: Harcourt Brace Jovanovich, 1954), p. 55.

to cover a wide range of "meanings." Obviously, the categorized symbols omit details.

In Chapter 3 we discussed our perceptual tendency to simplify by the use of black–white categories and stereotyping. This characteristic of perception is reflected in our language. We are ill equipped linguistically to describe gradations of differences, so we describe someone as either lazy or industrious, unable to categorize him/her in any unique fashion.

To be of any value, language must categorize and omit unique details; but this characteristic forces us to overgeneralize. If we fail to recognize that words are only generalized symbols, we are in danger of making certain invalid assumptions:

1. We may assume that one instance is a universal example: "Nobody likes me." "All women are . . ." "This always happens to me." "Nothing ever turns out right."
2. We may assume that our perceptions are complete: "Yes, I already know about that."
3. We may assume that everyone shares our feelings and perceptions: "Why didn't you do it the right way?" "Why would anyone eat in that horrible restaurant?"
4. We may assume that people and things don't change: "That's the way she is!"
5. We may assume that characteristics we attribute to people or things are truly inherent: "That picture is ugly." "He's a selfish person."
6. We may assume that our message is totally clear to someone else: "You know perfectly well what I mean." "You heard me!"[9]

Although generalizations are potentially dangerous, they cannot be avoided because language is a body of generalizations. Absolutely perfect interpersonal communication is impossible to achieve because our language is inherently incomplete. Yet there are degrees of incompleteness, and as communicators we should recognize that we are always functioning at levels of probability of understanding. The incomplete nature of our language makes it easy for us to misunderstand one another.

4. LANGUAGE REFLECTS NOT ONLY THE PERSONALITY OF THE INDIVIDUAL, BUT ALSO THE CULTURE OF HIS/HER SOCIETY

We have noted that an individual's language behavior necessarily reflects basic features of his/her personality and that individual experiences and attitudes contribute to different reactions to words. Language, having developed in the context of a certain culture, of necessity reflects that particular culture. As a derived system of human solutions to recurring human events, experiences, and conditions, culture constitutes a system of social organization that differ-

[9] For other examples, see V. Satir, *Conjoint Family Therapy* (Palo Alto, Calif.: Science and Behavior, 1968), pp. 65–70.

entiates and integrates human interaction and provides guides to behavior and motives to conform.

Language gives us innumerable insights into a culture. As an example of how language mirrors a culture, a study was made of the figures of speech in the language of the Palaun people of the western Pacific. Because figures of speech are a means of making the abstract concrete, such an analysis provides unique insights into a culture. To Palauns, a beautiful woman is a "comet." Because maternal descent is more greatly valued than paternal descent, superlative expressions reflect this organizational bias. "Largest" is *delad a klou* ("mother of large") and "highest" is *delad a ngarabub* ("mother of up").[10]

Even subcultures have language behaviors that distinguish one from another. Although we tend to discount class differences in our own society, a team of investigators examined social-class speech differences of people surviving an Arkansas tornado. Ten people were classified as middle class by virtue of one or more years of college education and a moderate income. Ten other respondents were matched with them on such factors as age, race, and residence, but were able to be classified as lower class on the basis of income and education (no schooling beyond elementary school). Analyses of the transcribed tape-recorded interviews revealed the following differences:

1. Almost without exception, descriptions of the tornado and its aftermath by lower-class participants were given as seen through their own eyes; middle-class respondents, however, described the actions of others as the others saw them.
2. Lower-class respondents demonstrated a relative insensitivity to differences between their perspective and that of the interviewer. For example, surnames were used without identification, and pronouns like "we" and "they" had no clear referents. By comparison, middle-class respondents used contextual clarification of their perspective in an attempt to consider the listener's role.
3. Whereas middle-class respondents used overall frames to organize their entire account, lower-class respondents were basically disorganized, giving segmental, limited accounts. Connections between incidents were obscure because respondents tended to wander from one incident to another.

It could be concluded that lower-class respondents perceive in more concrete terms and that their speech reflects these more concrete cognitions. However, as the investigators ask:

> Does his [the lower-class person's] speech accurately reflect customary "concrete" modes of thought and perception, or is it that he . . . is unable to convey his perception? . . . One concludes that speech does in some sense reflect thought. The reader is perhaps best left at this point to draw his own conclusions. . . .[11]

[10] R. W. Force and M. Force, "Keys to Cultural Understanding," *Science*, 133 (1961): 1202–1206.
[11] L. Schatzman and A. L. Strauss, "Social Class and Modes of Communication," *American Journal of Sociology*, 60 (1955): 329–338.

There is the great temptation to render value judgments on the language development and behavior of various subgroups, instead of viewing language differences as merely reflections of cultural differences. The imposition of linguistic rules to formulate language into predictable sound patterns and a well-ordered grammatical structure and formal vocabulary facilitates analysis and description of the language, but does not provide a basis for qualitative judgments. A case of such a linguistic assumption can be noted in the following:

> The syntax of low-income Negro children differs from standard English in many ways, but it has its own internal consistency. Unfortunately, the psychologist, not knowing the rules of Negro non-standard English, has interpreted these differences not as the result of well-learned rules but as evidence of "linguistic underdevelopment." He has concluded that if black children do not speak like white children they are deficient. One of the most blatant errors has been a confusion between hypotheses concerning language and hypotheses concerning cognition. For this reason, superficial differences in language structures and language styles have been taken as manifestations of underlying differences in learning ability. To give one example, a child in class was asked, in a test of simple contrasts, "Why do you say they are different?" He could not answer. Then it was discovered that the use of "do you say," though grammatically correct, was inappropriate to his culture. When he was asked instead, "Why are they different?" he answered without any hesitation at all.[12]

Such assumptions evolve because of misconceptions of what language is and how it functions.

Because language thus reflects a particular culture, problems abound when cross-cultural communication is attempted. Although words may mean different things to different people within a cultural grouping, at least some consensus and predictability is possible. The predictability is far less and the potential for misunderstanding is far greater in dealing with nonnative speakers. A young mother from the Middle East, for example, phoned a friend in extreme distress: Something must be wrong with her child because her two usual baby-sitters were *afraid* of her baby. She had called the sitters and both had told her, "I'm sorry, but I'm afraid I can't sit with your child tonight." If we fail to recognize the diverse ways in which the different peoples of the world have attempted to cope with the universal problems of adapting to their environment we lay the groundwork for misunderstanding and conflict.

5. LANGUAGE CREATES A "SOCIAL REALITY"

It is ridiculous to consider language a neutral medium of exchange. Specific words are selected for our use because they do affect behavior. Words call forth internal experiences as if by hypnotic suggestion. The role of language in contributing to people's problems and potential solutions can be shown to contribute to dangerous misconceptions and prejudices.

The color of a person's skin, for example, is tied to plus-or-minus words that inevitably condition our attitudes. The words "black" and "white" in

[12] J. C. Baratz, "The Language of the Ghetto Child," *The Center Magazine*, 1 (1969): 32.

Western culture are heavily loaded—"black" with unfavorable connotations and "white" with positive values. Ossie Davis, black actor and author, concluded after a detailed study of dictionaries and Roget's *Thesaurus* that the English language was his enemy. In the *Thesaurus* he counted 120 synonyms for "blackness" and noted that most of them had unpleasant connotations: "blot, blotch, blight, smut, smudge, sully, soot, becloud, obscure, dingy, murky, threatening, frowning, foreboding, forbidden, sinister, baneful, dismal, evil, wicked, malignant, deadly, secretive, unclear, unwashed, foul, blacklist, black book, black-hearted," and so on, as well as such words as "Negro, nigger, and darky."[13]

In the same book, 134 synonyms for the word "white" are cited; they have such positive connotations as "purity, cleanliness, birth, shining, fair, blonde, stainless, chaste, unblemished, unsullied, innocent, honorable, upright, just, straightforward, genuine, trustworthy, honest," and so on. Orientals fare little better than blacks because "yellow" calls forth such associative words as "coward, conniver, baseness, fear, effeminacy, fast, spiritless, timid, sneak, lily-livered," and so on.

Because colors are not truly descriptive of races, color designations are more symbolic than descriptive. It seems reasonable and likely that our racial attitudes have been affected by our language. Our culture is not unique in this regard. In the Chinese language, "yellow" is associated with "beauty, openness, flowering, and sunshine," whereas "white" connotes "coldness, frigidity, blood-lessness, absence of feeling, and weakness." Similarly, in many African tongues "black" has associations of "strength, certainty, and integrity," whereas "white" is associated with "pale, anemic, untrustworthy, and devious."

Our language can also be shown to be sexist in nature. Feminist writer Jean Faust observes:

> All the titles, all the professions, all the occupations are masculine. They are weakened when they are made feminine by the addition of ess, ette. And man insists that these suffixes be used; he knows the power of language. He knows that language can control not only behavior, but thought itself. Words can determine the function, the very being of a person. Hence the awkwardness of lady novelist, sculptress, authoress, etc. *The New York Times* reached a low in its history when, on January 15, 1969, in the heat of the Great Jockey Controversy, it referred to girls who wish to ride horses in races as "jockettes."[14]

One indication of the sexism of our language is in the grammatical use of personal pronouns. In most cases when the pronoun "he" is used, "he or she" is actually meant. To repeat the referent (e.g., "the speaker recited the speaker's speech") is extremely awkward; further, to state "The speaker recited his or her speech" is confusing. In this book we have made conscious efforts to include "he/she" and "his/her" references to people. Because of our awareness of the

[13] This study of the effect of language on our prejudices was conducted at Pro Deo University in Rome. It is reported and evaluated by N. Cousins, "The Environment of Language," *Saturday Review*, April 8, 1967, p. 36.

[14] Jean Faust, "Words That Oppress," *Women Speaking*, April 1970.

effect of language, we feel that such attempts are needed in lieu of a new glossary of personal pronouns.

The point is, the lack of a single pronoun for "he or she" forces a distinction in the case of an individual whose sex is not known and makes no difference. It forces emphasis on differences between the sexes, instead of similarities, instead of accepting one common humanity (huwoman/manity?).

Understanding One Another

As we attempt to elicit reponses from other people, we seek to describe or "display" our thoughts in such ways that the receiver is able to identify with our thoughts. This process depends on both effective transmission and effective reception of the messages.

SPEAKING

As the encoder of the message, the speaker has certain responsibilities. Implicit in our discussion has been the assumption that words matter; the choice of words in the interpersonal relationship makes a difference to the people involved. If we want a child to move from a particular chair, we ask him/her to move. If at first words and vocal emphasis do not impress him/her, we may try to cajole the child out of the chair or, as a last resort, threaten or physically remove him/her. In our adult world, because most of the action we desire from others cannot be induced by the direct threat of force, we must rely on words and nonverbal communication to achieve any manipulation of others.

Any attempt to manipulate people must be considered on ethical as well as pragmatic grounds. Interpersonal behavior depends to a great extent on persuasive symbol manipulation designed to achieve certain actions from others, based on some kind of psychological consent. Such efforts might be viewed as unethical when we judge that the action called for will be advantageous to the persuader at the expense of the other person. The information, if deliberately distorted, can be viewed as constituting unethical behavior.

A business firm, in an automated effort to be personal, sent a letter to the Speech and Drama Department at the University of Kansas:

Dear Mr. Department,
Did you know that the Department family name was recorded with a coat of arms in the heraldic archives—and while there are 60 million households in the United States, fewer than 212 of them are Department households.

The letter goes on to offer Mr. Department of Lawrence, Kansas, a coat of arms and "the entire report on the Department family documented and printed on parchment paper suitable for framing."

Skilled salesmen become adept at selecting the key words that appeal to our motives, fears, and desires. Motivational selling has progressed to a fine art with its near-scientific procedures. The encyclopedia salesman may induce us to buy because we think we are getting something for nothing, because we want an educated environment for our children, or because his product will make a significant contribution to our lives.

Word association is a common device in eliciting a desired response. A brewer was considering using the word "lagered" to describe his beer and conducted a word-association test. Only one-third of the people tested gave such responses as "ale," "beer," or "stout." Another third gave such responses as "tired," "drunk," "slow," and "dizzy," while the remaining participants had no response to the word. Thus the word was discarded.

The "social reality" created by words can be used to control the minds of people. For example, a Soviet dictionary is reported to define "religion" as

> a fantastic faith in gods, angels and spirits . . . a faith without any scientific foundations. Religion is being supported and maintained by the reactionary circles. It serves for the subjugation of the working people and for building up the power of the exploiting bourgeois classes. . . . The superstition of outlived religion has been surmounted by the Communist education of the working class. . . .[15]

In a similar vein, Hungarian Communists are reported to have taught their children the following Sovietized version of the Nativity:

> There was once a poor married couple who had nothing to eat or dress in. They asked the rich people for help but the rich people sent them away. Their baby was born in a stable and covered with rags in a manger. The day after the baby was born, some shepherds who had come from Russia brought the baby some gifts. "We come from a country where poverty and misery are unknown," said the shepherds. "In Russia the babies grow in liberty because there is no unemployment or suffering." Joseph, the unemployed worker, asked the shepherds how they had found the house. The shepherds replied that a red star had guided them. Then the poor family took to the road. The shepherds covered the little baby with furs, and they all set out for the Soviet paradise.[16]

Are any of us so very different from the Soviet propagandist as we entice, seduce, and coerce (all "loaded" words) others to view the world as we want them to see it? As individual senders of messages, we select the words designed to have the greatest desired effect on the listener. When we want to make a side trip, we tell our fellow traveler that the trip is "only about 100 miles"; but if the idea came from our companion and we oppose it, we protest, "Why, that trip is over 100 miles!" Virtually every utterance that we make reflects a coloring of reality to reflect our feelings, attitudes, and values.

Our language usage creates attitudes and behaviors that would not otherwise occur. The exact words that we use at any particular time reflect our attitudes, feelings, and desires at that time. The same woman may be referred to as "young woman," "young lady," "miss," "hey-you," "girl," even "broad," or worse, depending on the feeling and intent of the speaker.

Columnist Sydney Harris has frequently used what he labeled "antics with

[15] *Time*, January 29, 1951, p. 62.
[16] *Newsweek*, September 21, 1953, p. 62.

semantics" to demonstrate how our attitudes determine the words we select:

> I lost the match because I was "off my form"; you lost because you were "over-confident"; he lost because he was "too cocky." The academic expert I agree with is a "scholar"; the academic expert I disagree with is a "pedant." When our statesmen say what they do not really mean, they are exercising "diplomacy"; when their statesmen say what they do not really mean, they are engaging in "guile."[17]

One of the cruelest practices in our labeling process is the remark that tags a person—sometimes for life. Putting a label on a child can influence his entire life; for example, "piggy-fats," "brains," "porky," "gimpy," or "bat" can have the effect of encouraging the victim either to live up to the label or to reject the title by changes in behavior. "Clumsy John" may be clumsy for years unless he is able to forget his label. The labels "juvenile delinquent" and "ex-con" may brand people for life.

LISTENING

We spend far more time as receivers of messages than as senders. Just as the sender attempts to elicit a response from the receiver, the receiver must attempt to interpret the genuine meaning in the message. In the interpersonal verbal transaction, the receiver fulfills the role of listener.

We have become quite adept at not listening. In a society in which we are constantly bombarded with noise, we learn to close our minds to such distortions. Our brain picks and selects those cues having genuine significance. This capacity to shut out and ignore insignificant noise is a genuine blessing, but it can lead to listening habits that can adversely affect the capability for interpersonal communication. The listener actually determines whether communication will take place. For any reason we can, as receivers, shut the speaker off mentally.

Part of the problem can be attributed to the disparity between our thought speed and the rate of a speaker. Whereas we speak in the vicinity of 125–175 words per minute, our thought rate is far greater. We may use this spare time to "detour," to make brief excursions away from the subject, then come back to listen. Unlike the reader who loses his or her chain of concentration and rereads the section missed, however, the listener may have no opportunity for reiteration. The differential between thought speed and speech rate tempts us into the bad habits of daydreaming, shutting out the speaker, and impairing the flow of communication.

A leading authority on listening believes that much bad listening results from an emotional reaction to certain words or ideas that blots out the rest of the message. Consciously watch for the times when you tend to tune out a speaker because you fail to like his/her personality or ideas. Even if our goal is to argue the speaker down, we owe it to ourselves to listen fully. Notice the words or thoughts that make you stop listening. Today some people develop static when hearing such words as "pot," "chauvinist," "freak," or "Republican."

---

[17] Sydney Harris, "Last Things First," syndicated column appearing in the *Chicago Daily News*, December 18, 1962.

More people must listen than speak.

And there are special terms that jar persons involved in certain fields and distort their listening judgment. A man who has been having trouble with a newly purchased house may go "deaf" at the mention of leaks, termites, or contractors; his interest perks up, but he hears mainly his own jangled thoughts. Similarly, a person who has been speculating in the stock market may tune out anyone who mentions losses, sharp drop, or sell-off.[18] Thus, we filter incoming stimuli and perceive only those parts of the total pattern that fit our general or specific orientations (biases).

An additional problem for the listener is to distinguish between observational statements and statements of inference. A speaker may be reporting his/her perception of reality ("That man lives in a brown house") or drawing inferences ("That man is proud of his house"). Observational and inferential statements are extremely difficult to distinguish because grammar, syntax, and pronunciation offer no clues to the differences. Likewise, the inference may be made with such vocal dynamics and certainty that the "truth" of the statement may go unquestioned. In Chapter 3 we noted the willingness of students to infer motives for the instructor's departure from the classroom ("He had another meeting"), all of which were wrong. Inferences are necessary for our behavior and communication, but problems may develop when we tacitly assume that statements of inference are totally factual.

[18] R. G. Nichols and L. A. Stevens, *Are You Listening?* (New York: McGraw-Hill, 1957), pp. 90–94.

FEEDBACK

The accomplishment of mutual understanding between encoder and decoder can be determined only by feedback. Because of the numerous sources of error and distortion in the message, it is often valuable to check back to see if understandings exist. Among the possible problems are the following:

1. The encoded message may not be the same as the message intended by the speaker, or it may be garbled or unclear.
2. The receiver's perception of the speaker's motives or goals may influence the way the message is interpreted.
3. The words in the message may have different meanings to the receiver than to the sender, or they may have no meaning at all for the receiver.
4. The listener's attention might be diverted at a crucial time during transmission.
5. Expectations of the relationship may be confused.

You can probably add to this list. The point is that there are so many pitfalls that we owe it to ourselves to provide adequate feedback to one another if we are to have any hope of gaining understanding and rapport.

Summary and Preview of Readings

In this chapter, we discussed the characteristics of language that make effective communication difficult to achieve. Words have different meanings to different people; words vary in their degree of abstraction; and language is by nature incomplete, reflects the culture of a person's society, and creates a "social reality." These factors all contribute to misunderstandings between people, so we must be satisfied with degrees of mutual understanding.

Words play an important part in every human relationship. They are among the tools used to establish bonds between people and may clarify or obscure ideas, unify or alienate people. As senders and receivers of verbal messages, we must be aware of the potential problems and be constantly on guard to insure understanding.

We are concerned with the listener as well as the speaker. In the first article that follows, "Words and Deeds," examples of the problems that listeners have in trying to interpret what a speaker means are cited. The author, Peter Farb, presents a strong case for the strategic role that language plays in our lives. As we choose to use certain words, we calculate the impact they will have on the listener.

In "Verbal Contact," Leonard Zunin and Natalie Zunin analyze the strategies used in the first four minutes of contact with a new person. The adage "You only get one chance to make a good first impression" is strongly suggestive of the impact our words make on first contact. As you read this article, reflect back to Proposition 10: Interpersonal communication is irreversible, unrepeatable, and almost always functions in a context of change.

Words and Deeds

Peter Farb

Speech cannot emerge as an utterance until it has first passed through the filter of a speech situation—and also through the filter of the personality of the speaker, who is himself a composite of beliefs, attitudes, and misconceptions that can distort a message and increase the unpredictability of the language game. We all unconsciously assume that the speaker believes what he is saying and that he bothers to speak because he feels he has something worth communicating. Therefore, a speaker who utters nonsense has violated a basic covenant between speaker and listener (unless, of course, a conspiratorial wink or an ironic tone of voice signals the listener that the speaker is only joking). A speaker who says *I am silent* has uttered an impossible statement. He has broken the covenant and converted speech into nonsense in much the same way that the clowns in the film *Blow-Up* played tennis—without a ball.

Most listeners are amazingly trusting, and their lack of discrimination about a speaker's credibility can be observed at any social gathering. Imag-ine that a speaker states—in an earnest, conversational tone of voice and with a perfectly straight face—something devoid of any significance in that speech situation, such as *The green seas hastened furiously colorless this morning.* His listeners will undoubtedly be confused about what to make of the statement. They may assume that he is imparting some fascinating natural-history lore or they might think that he is making a witty observation which they are too dense to understand. Whatever the explanations that pass through the minds of the listeners, the point is that they attempt interpretations just because they assume every utterance has significance.

Because listeners so obviously place their trust in speakers, the question might well be asked: To what extent is that faith justified? Several years ago a series of experiments was carried out at Princeton University to examine how reliably speakers conveyed instructions to their listeners. Pairs of five-year-old children were separated from sight of each other by screens and provided with identical sets of building blocks. One child, acting as the speaker, selected a block at random and attempted to describe it to his unseen partner; the other child, acting as the listener, tried to find the described block. The speaker then described a second block to the listener, and so on, until all six blocks had been stacked. The game obviously was a very simple one—except for one factor. The planners of the experiment had intentionally printed intricate designs on the blocks to make them very difficult to describe. Therefore, a listener's ability to build a stack of blocks in the correct sequence depended completely upon his partner's ability to describe what the blocks looked like.

The children—all alert and intelligent students from Princeton nursery schools—failed miserably at this game. Nor did they improve after the game was played several times. The problem was not that the game was too difficult, for the same youngsters did very well when pictures of animals were substituted for the intricate designs. Clearly, the reason for the failure was the inability of the speakers to describe the designs well enough for the listeners to stack the blocks in the correct order. Tape recordings of the children's conversations, made while they tried to stack the blocks, explained the failure. The speakers had described the designs in a private language that was as opaque to their listening partners as the screens that separated the pairs of players. One child, for example, described an intricate design as a *sheet*. When asked by the experimenter what he meant, the child replied, "Have you ever noticed when you get up in the morning the bedsheet is all wrinkled? Well, sometimes it looks like this." The child's description of the design in terms of a rumpled bedsheet had great significance for him—but it was, obviously, totally useless information to

his partner, who had no such private association.

Children, of course, are less aware than adults of the limitations of the listener. Adult speakers have learned that the sounds they utter must be clearly understood by the listener, that they must be combined into words which are arranged grammatically in sentences—and that the meaning conveyed must be mutually intelligible. The adult speaker realizes that he is somewhat like a transmitter that broadcasts messages to a listener on a very narrow wavelength, so he tries to send his message in forms of speech that can be received by the listener and decoded without static. But sometimes inconsiderate or neurotic speakers encode their thoughts in a language almost as private as the child's description of an intricate design in terms of a bedsheet. They speak with little regard for the effect the utterance will have on the listener, and thus their speech is nonsocial. The result is utter confusion and a total breakdown in communication.

Some parents might argue that the child who described the design as a bedsheet was using language in a poetic way. Parents often feel pride when they hear their child use a strange metaphor, and they may envision him as the next generation's T. S. Eliot or Ezra Pound. They feel that if the poet Gerard Manley Hopkins could write a line like "sheer plod makes plough down sillion shine," then a child is certainly entitled to describe an intricate design as a bedsheet. The difference between Hopkins and the child, though, is major. Hopkins' line is admittedly obscure, but it resulted directly from his awareness as a craftsman of how an obscure image might trigger an emotion in a perceptive reader, tuned to the restricted wavelength Hopkins was broadcasting on. No one, though, could ever hope to decode the child's description of the intricate design as a bedsheet. It was uttered with no consideration for any listener at all. The child simply emitted a nonsocial statement which could never be more than gibberish to his partner. The same block-stacking experiment, carried out with older children and with college students, showed that increasing age brings increasing accuracy. Apparently, as a child grows older, he learns to put himself into the listener's place and to modify his descriptions accordingly.

In the block-stacking experiment, the blame for failure clearly lay with the speaker. But a breakdown in communication can also be caused by the listener. In the same way that optical illusions distort a picture, auditory illusions distort speech; both kinds of illusions are misjudgments about external reality. Every listener during his waking day compensates for auditory illusions. Consider a conversation carried on at a crowded cocktail party. Someone speaks to a listener through canapés and slurps of a beverage; the listener's attention is diverted by the jostling of people nearby, by noisy laughter and chatter, perhaps by music blaring from a record player. The listener could not possibly hear every syllable uttered by the person speaking to him. Yet he somehow utilizes the syllables that reach him during moments free from interfering noise to put together what he does hear into complete statements.

Ingenious experiments conducted by a psychologist and a zoologist at the University of Wisconsin, Richard and Roslyn Warren, have gone far toward illuminating how such auditory illusions work. The Warrens first recorded on tape the sentence *The state governors met with their respective legislatures convening in the capital city.* Then they carefully snipped out of the tape the syllable *gis* in *legislatures* and substituted a cough. When listeners serving as test subjects heard the altered tapes, they unconsciously blocked out the cough and restored the missing *gis* to *legislatures.* Even when the listeners were afterward told that a syllable had been deleted from the sentence, and the tape was played for them again, they still could not distinguish the missing sound. Apparently the process of listening entails the storage of incomplete information in the memory until the entire statement is heard, after which the listener unconsciously supplies what the context tells him must be a missing element.

The Warrens next experimented with auditory illusions free from context. Instead of dealing with complete and meaningful sentences, they recorded the single word *tress* on a loop of tape so that it was repeated over and over again without pause, 120 times a minute. They anticipated that a listener, after hearing *tresstresstresstress . . .* for a few minutes, would merge the sounds to form an illusory word such as *rest* or *stress.* But they were surprised to discover how much greater the auditory illusions were. One listener heard *tress* distorted into eight illusory forms, among them *stress, dress, Joyce, florist,* and *purse.* The listeners obviously were unwilling to believe that they heard a speaker repeat just a single word—so they unconsciously attempted to organize speech sounds into words and sentences.

Further experiments have shown that auditory illusions are much more common than optical illusions. An optical illusion can occur only in certain ambiguous cases in which line, perspective, light, or color distorts the appearance of an object. Auditory illusions, however, are much more unpredictable. They affect some listeners more than others and they vary from speech situation to speech situation. They can occur with any sound or word and they are not restricted to ambiguous cases—which adds yet another element of chance to the language game.

A listener's appraisal of a speaker is influenced not only by the speaker's way of phrasing the message and the listener's illusions about it but also by the speaker's "tone of voice." No protestation by a speaker that he is uttering the truth is equal to the nonverbal confirmation of his credibility contained in the way he says it. A man who says *I love you* to a woman is using a grammatical utterance to convey an attitude; but the woman, if she has any sense, will pay more attention to the accompanying vocal phenomena than to the words. The array of vocal phenomena that every speaker commands is known as "paralanguage," and it consists of such things as pitch, intensity, stress, tempo, and volume.

Contrary to what many people believe, no listener can judge the emotions expressed by a speaker of an unknown language just by noting his paralanguage. Old jungle movies often included lines like "I can't understand a word the beggars are saying, but I don't like the way they're saying it"— even though such an observation is inherently false because each speech community has its own rules for the expressive use of paralanguage. When an American visitor innocently interprets an Egyptian's paralanguage as signifying mere annoyance, he is seriously underestimating the intensity of the emotion. The Egyptian is most likely signaling that he is vengeful and that the American had better be careful.

Everyday experience seems to indicate a connection between paralanguage and personality, and between paralanguage and occupational roles. Most people are intuitively aware that speakers have "old" or "youthful" voices, that they sound "sad" or "self-satisfied." As soon as people step into their professional capacities they assume stereotyped "tones of voice," as is obvious to anyone who listens carefully to the speech of ministers, lawyers, undertakers, sports commentators, disc jockeys, and street vendors. A minister usually sounds like a minister because of paralanguage traits specific to that calling: a narrow range of pitch, frequent use of monotone, overpreciseness in pronunciation, regular rhythm, fairly slow tempo, and deep resonance of the voice.

Even the simplest statement may convey meanings through paralanguage that a sensitive listener detects without quite realizing how he does it. To examine the meanings often hidden in utterances, a team of linguists and psychiatrists collaborated on a remarkable project—a microscopic analysis of the speech interaction between a young woman and a psychiatrist, the words they used, their tone of voice and stress patterns, their pauses and coughs and hesitations. So detailed was the analysis that only the first five minutes of the interaction filled an entire book. This is what took place in merely the first few seconds:

> The scene is a psychiatrist's office. A young woman enters and he says to her, "What brings you here?" The woman hesitates for a moment, then emits a brief, throaty sigh; she drawls her words as she replies, "Everything's wrong. I get so—irritable, tense, depressed."

Since the psychiatrist is trained in the strategies of the language game, presumably his utterances are calculated. When he says *What brings you here?* he apparently intends to evoke a certain kind of response from the young woman. His first statement does indeed set the tone for the interaction. Three of the four words he uses—*what, you,* and *here*—are words that linguists call substitute, or pronominal, forms. They can easily be substituted for other words, and therefore they are basically noncommittal. Instead of these pronominal forms, the psychiatrist might have said *What problems bring you so upset to a psychiatrist's office?* But if he had begun the conversation that way, he would clearly be starting off on the wrong track. He would appear to be saying that he already concluded the woman has problems, that her face plainly reveals the intensity of her emotions, and that she is in an office that treats mentally ill people—which is certainly too much for him to convey before the woman has even spoken. Instead, he chose to use neutral pronominal forms and allow the story to emerge from the woman.

A close look at the stress pattern of the psychiatrist's opening sentence is revealing. He placed stress only on the word *here,* and even that was very slight. If the stress had been very strong—*what brings you HERE?*—he might have appeared to express sur-

prise that the woman was seeing a psychiatrist, which would have been unfitting, since he did not yet know anything about her. If he had chosen to place stress elsewhere in the sentence—such as *WHAT brings you here?* or *What brings YOU here?*—he might have seemed to imply amazement that the woman had the same sort of problems as the disturbed people he treats. The word *you* also is significant. He uses it as the object of the sentence, sympathetically indicating that the woman may have come to him because of external pressures that were victimizing her rather than because of problems in her own personality. If, instead, he had used *you* as the subject of the sentence—such as *Why have you come here?*—he would appear to be blaming the woman for having the leading role in whatever her problems are.

It is now the woman's turn to speak. She hesitates, emits a sigh, and finally says *Everything's wrong.* She drawls her words slightly, which is not the way someone who speaks spontaneously would utter them. Like most people who visit a psychiatrist for the first time—or who go to an interview for a job, meet with a client or customer, or even testify in a law case—she has rehearsed the opening of her story. She no doubt thinks she is being very clever, but her hesitation, sigh, and drawl have given her away.

Her next sentence confirms that she is dramatizing a conversation opener she has memorized. The way she utters the words *I get so* is particularly important. She clips the *so* by closing her vocal cords, then holds a pause before she speaks the three adjectives that are her symptoms: *irritable, tense, depressed.* The absence of *and* between the last two adjectives is a further indication that she is delivering a prepared speech; spontaneous conversation surely would insert an *and* in a string of adjectives. The psychiatrist's first question had been carefully posed to leave open the possibility that the woman had come to see him because of external pressures rather than because of problems stemming from her own personality. But the woman does not accept this opportunity to appear blameless. Instead of making external forces the subject of her sentence—such as *People make me irritable, tense, depressed*—she acknowledges at least partial responsibility for whatever is troubling her by saying *I get so.*

In only a few seconds and through the utterance of a total of a dozen words, two people have entered fully into a speech interaction. Each has heard the sound of the other's voice. The psychiatrist has shown himself to be open-minded, fair, willing to listen. The woman had come to the office with her mind made up to play a part in a drama she had written in advance, yet she displays a willingness to face up to her problems. The rest of the conversation can now proceed fruitfully, as in fact it did.

The microanalysis made plain that considerable interaction took place between the two speakers beneath the mere surface of the way their sentences were grammatically constructed. But in certain rare cases, speakers apparently disregard grammatical constructions altogether and utter what can be considered either gibberish or divine words, depending upon the listener's religious orientation. The second chapter of the Acts of the Apostles in the New Testament relates that the disciples waited in Jerusalem after the resurrection of Jesus. On the day of Pentecost they joined in prayer, when suddenly

> there came a sound from heaven as of a rushing mighty wind, and it filled all the house where they were sitting.
>
> And there appeared unto them cloven tongues like as of fire, and it sat upon each of them.
>
> And they were all filled with the Holy Ghost and began to speak with other tongues, as the Spirit gave them utterance.

Such extemporaneous utterances of incomprehensible sounds, which listeners often assume to be foreign languages, is known among various Christian sects as "speaking in tongues" and among linguists by the technical term "glossolalia." The important thing about glossolalia in the context of this chapter is that it dramatically reveals the unqualified faith that listeners place in a speaker, no matter how incoherent his utterances may be.

Glossolalia is today an important feature of various Pentecostal denominations, as it has been at one time or another of fundamentalist sects, Mormons, Shakers, Spiritualists, the Catholic Apostolic Church, and others. These sects differ in the details of their creeds, but most believe that a Christian needs a "baptism" in the Holy Spirit, an event made manifest by the sudden ability to utter the divine speech of tongues. Believers consider glossolalia to be a "gift of tongues" because the speaker has been selected by God to make a pronouncement in this strange speech to an assembly of worshipers. Since the speaker's utterance is incomprehensible, other members of the assembly have a different "gift"— that of translating what was said into conventional language.

The Acts of the Apostles further reports that the multitudes who heard the strange tongues came from all over the Roman Empire, and that each listener thought that the disciples were speaking in his own language. The belief that a speaker in tongues utters words in languages unknown to him, languages both living and dead, has persisted to this day, but the cases that have been investigated show the belief to be unfounded. Any resemblance to a foreign language is usually in the mind of the listener, not on the tongue of the speaker. If a speaker in tongues utters a long chain of nonsense syllables, simply by the laws of chance some of these syllables will sound like words in foreign languages. And once a listener thinks he detects a few words from a particular foreign language, he would tend to "hear" many more words resembling those in that language. Actual cases do exist in which a speaker has uttered fragments from real languages he never learned—but these cases stem from a completely different phenomenon, known as "cryptomnesia," or "hidden memory." The English poet Samuel Taylor Coleridge, for example, told of an illiterate maid who, in a delirium, spoke in Latin, Greek, and Hebrew. It was later learned that she had unconsciously assimilated these languages from a former employer who read aloud passages in them.

Several characteristics distinguish glossolalia from other speech phenomena such as gibberish, nonsense rhymes, and disguised languages. Glossolalia is usually a sudden and spontaneous utterance, not something memorized or planned in advance. Unlike the random sounds of gibberish, the utterances of glossolalia are structured and follow many of the rules of the speaker's own language, even though the speaker is not aware of it. For an idea of what speaking in tongues sounds like, here are the first few lines of an utterance by a twenty-year-old New England women:

> yah-muh-nuh kee-tuh see-yuh-nah-yuh-see yah-muh-nuh kee-tuh see-yuh-nah-yuh-see ah-nuh-kee-yah-nuh tee-yah-sah-nah-yah ah-nah-kee-yah-tah-nah see-yuh-nah-yuh-see

At first glance the utterance appears disorganized (except for a number of repetitions), incomprehensible, and even exotic. All the syllables end in vowels that are repeated constantly, which might give an impression of "primitiveness" to those listeners who have learned about exotic languages from the dialogue in Hollywood jungle movies. But a closer look makes several things clear. The utterance uses an extremely limited number of vowels and consonants—*t, k, m, n, s, y, ee, ah,* and *uh*—all of which are familiar sounds in English. Not a single foreign sound can be found, such as the rolled French *r* or the gargle-like German *ch.* And the sounds are combined into extremely simple syllables that occur in numerous English words. In fact, the pattern of the entire utterance, its stresses and intonation, is comparable to what one might hear in a typical English sentence.

It is clear that the woman who spoke in tongues was a native speaker of English. And her pronunciation and other clues reveal that she probably spent most of her life in the area between Hartford, Connecticut, and Springfield,. Massachusetts. She was attempting to speak a new language—actually, to create utterances in a religious speech situation—yet the resources at her disposal could never be more than those linguistic habits she had stored up as a native New Englander. Some examples of glossolalia are, of course, more strange than this one, but that proves only that the speaker has a wider exposure to different kinds of languages from which he could unconsciously borrow sounds and syllable patterns. Were an American farmer in Minnesota named Ole Svenson to speak in tongues, we would naturally expect that some of his utterances would be borrowed from Swedish, a language which he no doubt heard his parents or grandparents speak.

If glossolalia were merely some aberration of particular religious sects, or if it were characteristic only of people with neurotic tendencies, then little reason would exist for interest in it. But speech acts similar to speaking in tongues have been discovered around the world in many different kinds of cultures and in many different languages, both modern and ancient. In ancient Egypt magicians were accustomed to uttering senseless strings of sounds; four hundred prophets are said to have spoken incoherently before the gates of Samaria in 853 B.C.; similar sorts of speech acts are known to have occurred in ancient India and China, among the American Indians, in much of Africa. Those who speak in tongues, though, probably display no more neurotic tendencies than does the general population. Linguists are interested in glossolalia because it bears directly on a human being's ability to create a new language by distorting his native speech and by employing other kinds of speech he may have consciously or unconsciously learned. Glossolalia emphasizes that human

speakers use their sound-making abilities in unconventional ways. Other forms of language play—verbal dueling, nonsense rhymes, children's verses, disguised languages, and so forth . . . also confirm that people often speak in ways that have no "meaning" but instead serve other functions.

For the moment, though, what is of interest is that certain speech communities allow, and even encourage, speakers to utter nonsense. Furthermore, these communities put a premium on incomprehensible utterances, regarding them as more inspired or supernatural than conventional statements. The fact that glossolalia thrives only in speech communities that approve of it demonstrates the extent to which a speaker requires audience approval. The speaker in tongues gradually learns how to use his new speech within the environment of the speech community of his religious denomination and how to adjust his utterances according to its conventions—just as a child reared in a more traditional denomination learns to say his prayers in a low voice.

A speaker with a firm conviction, who is reinforced by his speech community, is a difficult person to change. So long as he knows that other people exist who approve of what he says, he can encounter the disbelief of the world with unwavering faith in his own statements. A true believer in any cult is unshakable—whether he puts his faith in a miracle diet, a drug, a way to make plants grow by prayer, the teachings of a guru, or a political perspective that sees a Fascist or Communist conspiracy in the most innocent transactions. Quote evidence against his opinions and he will deride its authenticity. Apply the strict rules of logic and he will reply that logic is irrelevant. No matter how devastating the attack upon him, the speaker will successfully protect his opinions—so long as he knows that fellow believers support him.

But what will happen if this speaker commits himself irrevocably to his opinions by staking his livelihood or even his survival on them—and then finally receives undeniable proof that he was wrong? Will he finally come to his senses and stop speaking the way he did previously?.

An answer to these questions was accidentally provided some years ago. Psychologists at the University of Minnesota read a newspaper report about a housewife who claimed she had received messages from another planet that foretold destruction by flood at 7:00 A.M. on December 21. Here was a woman who had publicly uttered very controversial opinions and who had assembled a group of fellow believers. She would be forced to commit herself to some kind of action to escape the deluge which she herself foretold—and her opinions would be clearly demonstrated as true or false by whether or not the deluge occurred at the time specified. The Minnesota researchers infiltrated the housewife's group to observe events as they developed; their report is a fascinating study in depth of speakers who are committed to their own utterances.

During the few months before the December 21 deadline, the housewife, Mrs. Keech, attracted a small group of believers in her community of Lake City and elsewhere (all persons and places mentioned in the study were given fictitious names). One of her followers, Dr. Armstrong, was a physician in nearby Collegeville; he spread Mrs. Keech's message among a group of students, known as "The Seekers," who met regularly at his home to discuss spiritual matters. Throughout the fall the Lake City and Collegeville groups held joint meetings to prepare themselves for salvation. They spoke passionately of their convictions; they committed themselves irrevocably to them by giving away their possessions and by resigning from their jobs. As the day of the deluge approached, Mrs. Keech announced that the believers should gather at her house to await a visitor from outer space. He would arrive precisely at midnight on December 20–21, escort them to a flying saucer, and take them to a place safe from the flood.

By late afternoon on December 20, most of the believers had gathered in Mrs. Keech's living room. The only absentees were some of the college students, who had gone home to await the cataclysm with their families during the Christmas vacation. Mrs. Keech instructed the believers in the correct way to greet the visitor and she revealed the passwords that would allow them to board the saucer. As the minute hand approached midnight, the believers sat quietly in the living room, their coats on their laps. The clock chimed midnight, then the hours passed—and nothing happened. The time for salvation had come and gone, the cataclysm was due in a few hours, but no visitor arrived from outer space to save them. The believers discussed the messages received by Mrs. Keech; they re-examined their interpretation of them and offered various explanations for what might have gone wrong. At 4:00 A.M. Mrs. Keech broke down and cried bitterly. Then, three quarters of an hour later she announced that she had just received a new message. The cataclysm had been called off.

The believers stood firm in the face of the utter failure of Mrs. Keech's predictions. They phoned the news media to tell of God's grace in calling off the deluge, and they even increased their efforts to win converts to a belief that had already been demonstrated false. In other words, they attempted to maintain their beliefs by convincing others that the messages really were true; after all, if new believers could be enlisted, then apparently the messages were still believable. In contrast, the students from Collegeville who had gone home to await the deluge with their families acted quite differently. They were in the presence of nonbelievers who ridiculed their opinions. When these students learned of the failure of the prophecy, most reacted by giving up their beliefs completely, and some even concealed their previous association with Mrs. Keech.

The contrasting reactions of the Lake City group and the students demonstrated how vital audience support is for a speaker's expression of his convictions. All conditions were the same for the two groups—with but a single exception. The Lake City group was constantly in the presence of fellow believers when the deluge failed to occur; rather than being shaken from their beliefs, they stuck to them more stubbornly. The students, though, faced the aftermath of December 21 alone. Lacking the support of other believers to reinforce their statements, they stopped uttering them and even denied having made them.

All of his waking day the human chatters, grumbles, argues, mutters, implores, pontificates. He asks questions and furnishes answers when other people ask him questions; he emits pat phrases and clichés; he inquires about people's health and he comments about the weather, although he usually cares about neither. Man the Talker besieges the eardrums with an arsenal of speech—but at no time does he utter random collections of idle words or completely spontaneous statements. No matter what he says, he always had other choices. He might have expressed the same thought in a different way, said something quite different altogether, or even remained silent. In short, every language offers its speakers an array of strategies with which they can play the language game.

Reading 4.2
Verbal Contact
Leonard Zunin and
Natalie Zunin

We talk, we sing, we cry or moan, we make simple sounds of joy or despair, we read and we write; all of these are forms of verbal communication, depending on words and sounds. We also touch, embrace, fondle, gesture or merely look another person in the eye; these are nonverbal contacts. Our ways of seeing, listening and touching are often intertwined, and how we handle the mixture will be apparent as the Contact story unfolds.

Except in special therapeutic groups where people touch before they are formally introduced, the primary means of communication between friends and strangers is verbal. Just as there are voiceprints to scientifically identify speech patterns (so we can determine who is the *real* Howard Hughes), there is also a wide variety of conversational types. In fact, some people can be identified and classified according to certain categories of verbal initiative and response.

For example, there are the agreement addicts who nod or mumble "yes" to almost anything you say until it seems certain they are either human sponges or incapable of original thought. In contrast are the disagreement zealots who come on strong in less than four minutes, usually to inflate their own egos with bursts of hot air. If such a character happens to agree with a few of your points, he'll rearrange their importance. The conversation-dominator has a mental chart, and you may be steamrollered if you try to change the subject. You also know the jokers who take the Don Rickles approach and attempt to put you down with barbs that may or may not be poisoned.

With experience you learn to recognize these patterns in the conversation game. Some are quite fixed, some boring, others are engaging. However, as you examine the various ways people interact with words, you find several constants. First, effective communication is based on sincerity. Ways with words may be unsuccessful, even by sincere, mature individuals, if those words do not *project* warmth. Appearance is also an essential (nonverbal) influence, since the face and body create a supporting or contradictory image as the mouth speaks.

In addition, a conversational contact may win friends and influence people in one situation, while the same verbal approach in other circumstances may be disastrous. For instance, your uncle, the prominent attorney, may come on with a formal demeanor in legal circles and gain both respect and admiration. The same gentleman at a birthday party for your teenage daughter may seem stand-offish or even insulting unless he tempers his formality to fit the more relaxed social surroundings.

I am not suggesting that you stand there analyzing your conversational gambits in any mechanical manner, but it seems reasonable that an awareness of the patterns you use will improve your contact with others, whether a situation is familiar or threatening.

The word-ways, or conversational techniques, discussed in this chapter apply to encounters with strangers as well as to ongoing, intimate relationships. Do you or your wife, husband, lover or good friends usually open a conversation with questions, complaints, compliments or banal observations? It may not matter, if the usual interchange is satisfying, but if your spouse is often irritated, or if you are beginning to feel indifference to routine greetings, a deeper look at the influence of communication on your relationships may be indicated. It is precisely this sort of probing which this book aims to stimulate, to help you develop renewed awareness of all your contacts, intimate, social or business.

As you consider the modes of contact examined in this chapter, weigh the effectiveness of your own conversation game. Can you allow warmth and fondness for someone to show in your voice without being threatened or threatening? Do your words and inflections create positive, negative, or neutral reactions from friends or strangers? Stop, look and listen to yourself—and to everyone you talk with. I predict you're in for some enlightening (maybe startling) surprises.

Word-Ways with Strangers

When you meet a stranger, the outcome within four minutes will be one of the following:

1. Both of you will indicate, perhaps indirectly, that you want to continue talking.
2. Both of you will prefer to taper the conversation off and end it as soon as it seems acceptable.
3. One of you may want to go on, while the other doesn't. (These feelings may not be conveyed, depending on one's skill in showing them.)

Do you recognize the symptoms of a blossoming or a waning conversation? Do you know the signals, especially those that are devious? I asked myself some of the same questions not long ago during an airline flight to a speaking engagement. I had settled down, my briefcase on my lap, going over a number of papers. The seat immediately next to me was empty. One seat over at the window was a pleasant-looking woman in her late fifties. She appeared to be reading a magazine, but I realized that, with some regularity, she was glancing my way. I saw her glancing at my papers on the seat between us; these were notes concerning a law and psychiatry seminar.

Finally, she opened up with, "You're a doctor, I see by the 'M.D.' on your briefcase. Do you do any work with the courts?"

"Sometimes," I replied, explaining that I was interested in problems of legal psychiatry.

"My son's an attorney," she volunteered, clearly hoping to continue the chat, but I was preoccupied. I smiled cordially and returned, with a nod, to my work. I had not totally rebuffed her, and it was evident her urge to continue the contact was stronger than her sympathy for my preoccupation. In several minutes she interjected, "I have another son who's a dentist."

"My wife is a dental assistant," I remarked; and we both smiled as I tried to concentrate on my notes.

Her strong desire to talk was obvious, and her congenial manner was appropriate for the situation. At that moment there was no way I could discern the degree of need this woman had to make contact with me. She returned to intermittently reading and glancing in my direction.

Then abruptly she blurted, "My brother took his life yesterday. I'm going to his funeral."

With that I chose to set aside my sheaves of paper and respond with sincere concern. She had made contact with me via a major accounting of facts, seasoned by her emotions. In our conversation, I believe I was able to give her some temporary solace, which only occurred because she clearly reached out for contact. I was glad she had.

Instinctively, this lady knew she had failed to gain my attention for more than a minute through the mode I refer to as *the search for mutual interests*. Her intuition or her experience led her to make the *provocative statement* about her brother, another approach we will discuss, and thereby she "hooked" me into her life for a brief interval. Though she could not precisely anticipate my feelings, she had apparently received both verbal and nonverbal signs that there was favorable potential in perseverance.

While human behavior cannot be programmed in computer fashion, nor can we expect sequential directions for contact such as those for building a model airplane, there are many basic modes of conversation. You may use some of these already, and others may prove valuable to break the ice with strangers. At least, the following modes will give you ideas of your own to work out.

1. The Search for Identifying Data. In this category fall the preliminary questions about name, rank and serial number. If this verbal quest is stretched too far, personality characteristics and emotional overtones may be overlooked or restricted. Thus an opening gambit of this type should be short and sweet, followed by more intimate fact-finding. Here's a digested version of a typical "I.D." conversation that seems to bloom:

J: Hello, my name is Joe. What's yours?
N: Nan.
J: That's a lovely name. Do you live near here?

N: Not far away, in the Valley. What's your last name?

J: It's Keppie. Before you ask, it's spelled K-e-p-p-i-e.

N: Thanks. That's an unusual name; is it German?

J: Yes; my dad was born in Germany, but I was born in Cincinnati. Where are you from?

N: New York City; can't you tell by my accent?

J: You've lost it—if you ever had one. Have you ever been married?

N: Nope; have you?

J: Almost, a few years ago; but we chickened out.

N: What do you do in real life?

J: *(laughing)* I'm a film distributor.

From this point he tells the name of his company; she says some of their movies were amusingly dirty; he counters with an offer to see a preview a few nights hence; she asks a few details; and then they settle into fewer facts and more feeling about mutually agreeable subjects. They both avoid making data-gathering seem like an inquisition and seek to discover more about each other than plain facts. Joe and Nan soon find many things they have in common, which can well stimulate a relationship onward and upward.

2. Existential and Personality Topics. In Joe and Nan's conversation, when topics shifted to attitudes, likes and dislikes, or any subject in which they reflected an evaluation of their lives and times, they began offering insights into their personalities. Feelings you have about or get from someone are always being added to basic facts. As you discover the many

views you share about everyday life, you learn something about your differences as well. Those differences may seem insurmountable or a pleasant challenge.

Alex and Cindy are in their late teens. Their first four minutes are somewhat condensed here, as an example of dialogue in this category:

A: Hi, I'm Alex.

C: Hi, Alex; I'm Cindy.

A: I'm having a great time, how about you?

C: Yeah, this party is groovy. Do you like the music?

A: I dig it, but sometimes my feet get tangled when I dance to it.

C: Right, I used to have the same problem. Now I improvise. I seemed to get the hang of it.

A: Maybe I could try improvising, but I'd really rather hold a girl close when I dance.

C: I know what you mean. Let's put on something slower and try.

They're dancing; they talk about singers and music for awhile. The conversation then turns to college, parents, finances, cars, television, movies and all the really important things of their generation.

By "existential" I mean subjects closely involved with your own existence which, in discussion, are colored by personality. Hints about what a person is "really like" are revealed in this way, providing someone is not trying consciously to mask or distort.

I want to stress that during and after initial contact, you must sum up all the feelings and facts you absorb about another individual and average these within your own reality frame of reference. Otherwise, you may be misled—and it happens all the time. In other words, because someone shares an interest or delight in animals, ballet, foreign films, or politics with you, your needs and values may still not be similar enough to make a binding relationship later. The first four minutes of *any* contact is a kind of audition; information and impressions are exchanged and filtered through both mind and senses. As self-confidence and self-knowledge develop, so does our ability to evaluate our assumptions. With practice, we become more accurate, thus decreasing our chances for disappointment.

A few other random questions that combine personality and existence may cover early childhood, recreation, child rearing, and anything that can be answered without statistics. Try one of these if you like: Would you consider yourself happy? Are you happily married? What would you like to do with the rest of your life? Any of them, or similar queries, can open up all sorts of personality doors.

3. Identifying Data Offered Spontaneously. This category is an offshoot of the first one but may be reserved for strangers who seem difficult to turn on. If someone appears worth getting to know but lapses into silence quickly, you might open and then probe:

YOU: We moved from Connecticut only a few months ago, and I'm just getting used to California weather. Have you ever lived in the East?

SOMEBODY: Yes, and I hated driving in snow.

YOU: I was used to it. Actually, I had an opportunity to open a new branch of my company out here, and the Coast seemed appealing. I'm an electrical engineer. What do you do?

SOMEBODY: I'm in insurance.

YOU: I have a good friend in Stamford who handled all my insurance, but he's too far away to help me much now.

If that last statement, or something equally provocative, doesn't get a rise from another individual who can recognize the opportunity to make a friend and a client at the same time, the contact may be hopeless. In other circumstances, topics such as househunting, family vacations, or information volunteered about many mutual interests of life, may help strike a spark. Once you open, remember to give the other person a chance to talk, even if he or she is naturally reticent. There are people who might be categorized as conversational bores, but if you are adept at contact, you won't meet one. By that I mean you will be able to *manipulate* verbal communication to switch topics and hold your own—for at least four minutes. If you are really stuck, you can tactfully move away and begin anew.

Incidentally, manipulation has objectionable connotations in contemporary parlance, but I consider it in positive terms. Without approaching a semantic maze, to manipulate is to lead constructively, if not entirely altruistically. If you ask a child to wash his hands (when he's preoccupied having fun in a sandpile), or suggest to your mate that it's time to turn off the TV and make love (in the middle of an absorbing movie), you are manipulating contact for mutually worthwhile reasons. The words you choose, your timing, facial expressions, grooming, dress and body language—all are phases of creative manipulation. The word gets its offensive significance when it is associated with extremely selfish motives.

4. Spontaneous Offering on the Existential and Personality Level. This is a variation of the second category, particularly appropriate for the hard-to-reach contact with whom you hope a personal note might lead to give-and-take. If both of you can be revealing without feeling vulnerable or ridiculous, there could be gratifying response. Here are a few phrases offering connotations that could be discussed in more depth:

> I was always a shy kid.
> I really like parties best when they're not too crowded.
> I like to drink, but three's my limit.
> I've thought of getting married, but I don't know if I'm ready.
> I wonder what it would be like to be single again, even for a short time?
> I'd love to learn to sail (or ski, dance, play the guitar, etc.).

5. The Art of Compliments. When you offer a sincere compliment to a stranger (or somebody close, for that matter), you are saying, "I like you," or "something about you is special." Most people react positively to compliments because it's hard to resist being liked. However, your admiration should not be expressed in phony superlatives which will seem transparent. The receiver may suspect ulterior motives which are unwelcome or, at least, premature. Everyone has some positive attributes about which you can make realistic compliments within initial contact.

In the male-female contact, compliments may carry seductive connotations, which is fine if you express them with open honesty. Here is a montage interchange that points up the potential winning ways of words:

HE: *(after introductions and amenities)* I was noticing that beautiful necklace you're wearing. Is it an heirloom?

SHE: It's an ivory cameo my grandmother brought from France a long time ago. You have very sharp eyes!

HE: Thanks, I like the way you wear it—a lovely setting.

SHE: I'm glad you noticed.

HE: I make jewelry as a hobby, but nothing as fine as your cameo.

SHE: How interesting. Do you make it for fun or to sell?

HE: Just for kicks. I'm a dentist and I have all the equipment in the office for casting in gold to make rings and things.

SHE: I'll bet you're very good at it. Do you have any samples here?

HE: My wife's wearing a pin I'll show you later.

At this point mutual admiration has flowered, and they continue to converse about hobbies, children, and a cruise one couple is planning. They like each other and they show it before the four-minute mark. This is not necessarily a seductive exchange; it represents the warmth and interest which people can offer and enjoy in a short interval.

6. Talking About Here-and-Now Surroundings. This is another spin-off from the search for personal and existential information. You attempt to make contact through comments on the moment, usually not controversial. At a party, for instance, he mentions how casually everyone is dressed, and she says it's nice to be informal. She complains about cigar smoke, and he offers to put out his cigarette, though she says it isn't necessary. They talk about the furniture and the food, the hostess and her problems, or the background music. A quick survey of the milieu in which they live indicates enough in common to continue contact in a more congenial setting.

You can consciously originate conversational topics about the here-and-now shared temporarily with someone, and expand the scope of verbal communication to the outer limits of serendipity.

7. Focus on the External World. A conversational path sometimes leads away from the personal and into the world around us. If it isn't bogged down on an unrewarding topic, such an exchange can also reveal things not easily apparent about other people as well as ourselves. Often this sort of encounter occurs in the midst of another conversation, and the external world becomes an excellent vehicle for initial involvement. Later you might segue into more familiar topics with emotional overtones.

I watched a foursome interrelate recently at a reception that followed a lecture I gave. Two men were talking about an automobile race, and the wife of one accused them of being fascinated by blood and guts of accidents. A third man nearby countered that it was the driver's skill which most men found exciting, leading the first man to ask if the newcomer drove a sports car. He admitted owning a Jaguar XKE, and was thereby included in the conversation with little more effort. They went on commenting on TV coverage of races and the highlights of a Can-Am competition that had been run a few days before. I drifted away as they were telling the woman that movie stars rarely do their own driving in the racing movies she had seen.

This group shared opinions and took impressions of each other according to values expressed about a sport in which none of them participated. World affairs, local scandals, space exploration, the ups and downs of the stock market, and dozens of other "out there" subjects are also handy ways to make verbal contact, which can refocus on the personal later.

8. The Search for Mutual Interests or Acquaintances. One of the most frequent modes for establishing communication with a new acquaintance is to find friends or interests in common. Your son goes to the same school his son does; she lives in a neighborhood where you have friends; he knows a doctor who plays tennis at the courts where your daughter plays, etc., etc. There's always a linkage in every crowd between strangers who have seen, or been, or know, or have dealings with someone you know. If a proud father shows you some good snapshots of his children, even when you have no offspring to compare, you may discover you both enjoy photography or use the same brand of camera.

Mutual friends or interests are a temporary device, however, and contact that begins in this category usually needs more depth to continue. There's a reverse twist as well, when you search for the similar and come up with opposites that may breed antagonism. Bach and Deutsch mention this in *Pairing*:

> We do not encourage pairers to seek out differences. But we tell them not to shy away from potential partners just because great polarities exist. When they do exist, we advise that the pairers not sweep them under the rug and emphasize what similarities they find between them. If the differences are confronted, the interest that is generated is likely to be warm and intriguing. The experience can be enriching because each is attempting to pair not only with an individual, but with another world as well.

9. The Creative Gibe. There's a bit of sarcasm in us all, and the urge to greet others with benevolent insults sometimes seems fitting. I call this the *creative* gibe because, to have a positive effect, it must be well-intended and have a touch of humor. It may also be the technique by which a person of limited self-confidence feels he can "come on strong," but such gambits may be embarrassingly transparent. However, pleasant sarcasm helps open a contact to a more revealing dimension than innocuous chatter.

Keep in mind that every gibe or playful insult involves a risk. People can be turned off or embarrassed by what sounds like your lack of sensitivity. It is advisable to have the measure of another person, at least through instinct, before resorting to sarcasm in the first four minutes. On the other hand, you might *enjoy* taking chances. A friend once told me how he met his future wife over the punchbowl at a wedding reception, which is usually a delightful place to make new contacts. He related, "I had seen her from a distance and thought she was gor-

geous, but a little haughty. We finally met at the punchbowl and I guess I was trying to cover a lack of self-confidence when I asked, 'Do you always drink so much?' She was startled but answered, 'How would you know? Have you been counting?' I was actually being presumptuous, but I came up with something flip that kept the conversation open, and she was intrigued. I knocked off the insults pretty fast, but the first one worked!"

Many characters in fiction or on TV seem to relate swimmingly through sharp quips, but only professional entertainers and the lighthearted young can pull of the creative gibe with that kind of consistency. However, it's one way of seeking new acquaintances if you're willing to take that kind of risk.

Barbara Walters summarized this scene well in her book, *How to Talk with Practically Anybody About Practically Anything* (Doubleday, 1970), and her observation applies to both sexes: "Don't make the adolescent mistake of trying to impress a man by insulting him. It doesn't demonstrate that you're hard to get, just hard to like."

10. The Humorous Approach. Choosing something funny you saw or heard as an entree to conversation in the first four minutes can smooth the way to further contact, if your remarks are in good taste—and really humorous. Most people respond well to the light touch, though it is advisable not to stay with jokes or comic remarks very long. They are often impersonal, and could keep others at a distance. Most people avoid the traveling salesman prototype who comes on with vulgar and boring jokes, though he still appeals to kindred characters. If your humorous monologues last awhile, and you can hold an audience, perhaps you should consider a career in show business!

11. Social Graces in Action. The most elementary display of courtesy or social grace is as nice a way as any to make contact with friend or stranger, though it may only be the prelude to a four-minute interval. Some word-ways include:

> May I light your cigarette?
> Please sit next to me—I've been wanting to meet you.
> That glass looks very empty; shall we wander over to the bar?
> May I get you a chair?
> You have a couple of buttons undone in the back of your dress; may I close them for you?

12. The Hobby and Fad Approach. While youngsters may still play party games, unfortunately adults usually don't feel relaxed enough to enjoy themselves in such icebreakers (though charades may make a comeback someday). As a substitute, you might pursue your own hobby-game-fad interests through conversation about handwriting analysis, astrology, palmistry, the psychological effects of color, or improvisational theater games. Because these reflect your personality and tastes, they can induce others to open up more freely than a discussion of the weather can. Personal diversions and interests find response from strangers, either because they have similar interests or are intrigued by yours.

For instance, a couple met at a social gathering and he remarks on the beauty of her hands. "May I hold one?" he asks, "Palm reading is my hobby." She willingly extends a hand, and borrowing on his amateur knowledge of palm reading, he says something like: "These lines show you're a fairly outgoing person, and that long curve indicates you have a warm personality." He may take a few guesses that she was once a tomboy or has philosophical leanings, and they both play the next stages of the conversation game by ear.

Just talking about a hobby or a current enthusiasm that you share with someone can be an excellent means of positive contact, even if you don't get everyone in the room involved.

13. Can You Tell Me . . . ? Spontaneous contact through asking for help or information might be functional (you may just *be* lost and need directions), or it could be an opening gambit that is sincere but unnecessary. It does give the other person a chance to show how clever he is by offering aid, which could begin to close the gap you had as strangers. There are a number of "Can you tell me?" openings for the social situation, including:

> —where you got the cigarette case? It's beautiful.
> —who your veterinarian is, the one you mentioned cured your dog of worms?
> —the best way to get home from here? I had an awful time finding the place.
> —how you mix these drinks. They taste just like the ones I had on an Italian cruise last summer.

Everyone enjoys a situation in which he can show off naturally, even if the subject is trivia. However, don't use this gambit too often, or you may find yourself catalogued as a "professional waif." You don't need the helpless game to make contact with a legitimate question.

14. Verbalizing the Nonverbal. Since people are usually flattered when they are observed and/or admired, indicating this can be a conversational opener. "I notice that you seemed so quiet sitting here in the corner of the couch. Is anything wrong you'd like to talk about?" That may be a nosy way of encounter, but everyone is looking for a shoulder to cry on at one time or another.

You might also comment on clothes and grooming, the fact that somebody talks with their hands, or any other feature or gesture which deserves a positive response. The fact that you *noticed* is the key to many a contact door. Of course, you must be sincere; you shouldn't be critical. And if you start with flattery, keep it crisp and ringing true. How you verbalize about the nonverbal can turn a four-minute contact into a decisive friendship or even more.

15. You Remind Me of. . . . This opening phrase is rather lame if not in earnest; but, when someone says, "You remind me of my sister (brother, boyfriend, uncle or army buddy)," your interest perks up long enough to find out why. But the person who is often told he or she looks like Paul Newman or Raquel Welch may not be surprised; the reply you get may indicate whether the conversation is worth continuing. A sincere "You remind me of . . ." works best when the reference is unfamiliar to the other individual and you add a few exotic details.

16. Self-apology. Opening lines such as—

I didn't realize how people would be dressed here; I feel so uncomfortable with this dress on.

I'm sorry to be so late but the television was broken and I had to wait for the repairman.

Please don't ask about my hands; I'm a mechanic and I can never get the grease off them entirely.

None of these sincere regrets are prone to generate much interest from other people so avoid them if possible. You tend to demean yourself. Apologies are appropriate for many situations, but don't lean on them expecting a sympathetic response; there are many better ways to achieve positive contact. On the other hand, such an opening gives you the opportunity to put somebody else at ease if that gesture seems temporarily useful.

17. The Effective Accident. The cliché in this category is the lady who drops her handkerchief, hoping it will attract the attention of a charming gentleman whom she would like to meet. An "accidental" collision with someone in order to make verbal contact is another sally. Any casually planned mishap may backfire because it seems contrived, but in fact and fiction this mode has launched many four-minute meetings which grew into more intimate relationships. This approach also offers the bumper and the bumpee immediate physical contact, which could result in solace being offered that might bring people closer together.

18. The Whimsical Hook-In. The most prevalent use of whimsy is "putting someone on," usually by distorting reality in a humorous way. By exaggerating we gain attention and individuality, *providing* we are not malicious or harmful to anyone. Friendly teasing often results in friendly response. In a short time, the deception is usually realized or signaled, and the aftermath of your gambit is enjoyed out in the open. Of course, if you deceive someone intentionally only to impress them, feelings will be hurt because of your dishonesty, and you are more apt to make an enemy, not a friend.

The put-on can also be useful to "steer" a conversation that you find turning in an unpleasant direction. For example, at a party I met a woman who was so vehement in her fact-gathering that it seemed like a cross-examination. She had heard me mention Puerto Rico, and when she asked bluntly what I had been doing there, I told her I was lecturing to the crime commission, which I was. She bore in with more questions, turning me off further. I elected to tell her I was an experienced criminal who had never been caught, but was so expert that the authorities called upon me to brief law enforcement officers. She was impressed enough to take a step backwards. Later I told her who I actually was, and she apologized for coming on so strongly. (Again this gambit was placed in the open because the attempt was whimsy, not deceit.)

Many put-ons center around identity misrepresentation or far-out observations ("This is the best coffee I've had since my outfit captured a cappucino machine in Naples"), reversals of role or opinion, or excessive flattery. References to physical attributes (beautiful legs, handsome profile), or sexuality in its many forms ("My wife knows about my mistress, but says . . .") can be intriguing in early conversation. How you handle the subject of sex in good taste will depend on the time, place, and company you're with. You run the risk of discovering, after it's too late, how your whimsical hook-in was accepted or rejected if people are reluctant to continue the conversation or invite you back again.

19. The Provocative Hook-In. Both whimsy and the creative gibe are forms of provocation, but the shading in this category is concerned with a projection of identity or personality impudence. You may recall the meeting of Jenny and Oliver in *Love Story,* by Erich Segal (Harper & Row, 1970), which is a classic of deft provocation. The Harvard hero meets a "bespectacled mouse type" girl in the Radcliffe library where she's working behind the desk. He asks for a certain book, and she counters by suggesting he look in his own school library. He ruminates to himself that Radcliffe girls have an exaggerated impression of their own intelligence, and asks for the "goddamn book" again. She cautions him about using profanity, calling him "Preppie," and adds that he looks "stupid and rich." He is challenged to rejoinder:

"What the hell makes you so smart?" I asked.

"I wouldn't go for coffee with you," she answered.

"Listen—I wouldn't ask you."

"That," she replied, "is what makes you stupid."

Segal uses the creative insult to provoke and hooks the reader into his story just as his protagonists hook in to each other.

Provocation can also have negative aspects, as a friend once explained when he said, "I tell myself I'm testing response and learning more about people, which is partially true; but I can't escape the realization that provocation is also an attention-getting mechanism. Why not just say what's real and not fall into this exaggerated pattern?"

Provocation, whimsy, humor and the creative gibe are all approaches to contact which I would label, "Handle with care," though they can be fun and effective.

In Summary

If your manner of verbal communication expresses genuine interest in someone else, in their work, clothes, travels, accomplishments, lifestyle, physical appearance, values, etc., and you approach with warmth, contact is easily extended beyond four minutes. Since interpersonal relations can't be scored like a basketball game, you have to *sense* how a contact starts and proceeds. You know that modes of conversation are intermixed. Questions, answers, compliments, jokes, opinions, and careful listening as well, all add up to making a connection—finding things and feelings in common. If there were actually a rigid, step-by-step formula for applying contact modes, we'd all be bored quickly and look for variations. The modes described above merely point out directions contact may take, based on typical situations. Your own self-confidence is also vastly important and will be discussed later.

Here are three outstanding aspects to understanding all verbal contact:

1. *Recognize the importance of the initial few minutes.* We tend to take contacts for granted, especially with close friends and relatives. We need to realize the significance of words, inflections and subliminal signals others give us— or we give out.

2. *Be aware of your word-ways.* Most of us meet and greet—and we may realize what we're saying and what others tell us—but we are not fully conscious of the modes applied as described in this chapter or of the possible variations and alternatives. It's a little like knowing all the moves of chess, but using only a few of them to play the game.

3. *Evaluate your word-ways and make changes.* If we do take initial relationships for granted, and we are not aware of contact techniques, we may be making ineffectual contact in the same way, over and over. Try to analyze the effectiveness of your verbal approaches. Do you converse according to an automatic pattern? You need to know the way of words and your own ability to use them with hard-to-reach strangers, loved ones who seem to talk but say nothing, or whenever verbal relationships seem to need improvement.

Think about this: It is impossible to be in the presence of another person and *not* make contact. Even in total silence, in open hostility, in any effort to be left alone, there is contact, however tenuous or strained. Sitting next to a stranger on a plane or a park bench, there is always an atmosphere of awareness, even without verbal communication. Add words and feelings, realize how many people relate from beneath masks they try to keep invisible, and think of the many options for contact which we enjoy—and which can motivate us as we try to move others.

Vicarious experience helps boost morale, so I'll conclude this chapter with a story I found heartening. It concerns an Eastern college dean who visited me in California to discuss setting up a workshop program in his hometown. He arrived at lunchtime, checked into his hotel, and proceeded to the large restaurant where he sat alone. Nearby he noticed three men in animated conversation. Casually he approached their table, with drink in hand and a smile on his face, which is a blend of Richard Burton and David Niven. "Excuse me," he said cordially, "would you mind if I joined you just for the company? You all sound so congenial."

Before he could offer another word of introduction, one of the three stood up, tossed his napkin on the table, and hissed fiercely at the dean, "You damned people from L.A. are all alike! I'm getting the hell out of this place!"

With that, he left abruptly, followed by his two companions, all of them glaring as though they had been kicked in the shins.

"What did you do then?" I asked, With a wry smile, he told me, "Well, I saw three other men at another table, and slowly—a bit more cautiously—I made the same request of them."

"What happened?" I asked with hesitation.

My friend smiled and responded, "They said, 'Yes, please sit down and join us,' and introduced themselves. I spent the time very pleasantly and I appreciated even that brief contact with some of the natives,"

The dean had refused to accept the first rebuff as a token of his own inadequacy, and, like the rider who is thrown, he got back on the horse. He had both confidence in his ability to make positive contact and motivation to continue his quest for simple social exchange. It is evident that he had been successful in meeting strangers in unfamiliar surroundings before, or he might have retreated and perhaps brooded alone, or, at best, withdrawn to ponder ways of amending or improving his approach to launching the first four minutes with complete strangers.

Action Steps: Applications

1. Meet in groups of five or six students. Have each group originate a word that has a justifiable meaning to the group. The members may choose, at random, one member of another group and give him/her the word to define. He/she may in turn immediately give the definition or take the option of conferring with other group members. The originating group may challenge this definition. Discuss criteria for judgment.

2. Have designated members of your group prepare brief, narrative stories. Send five members of your group out of the room and read someone's story. As the students return to the room one by one, have the story passed along, and note how the message changes. Ideas may be dropped, added, or modified. Discuss your capabilities as listeners and determine some of the causes for bad listening.
3. Collect some letters to the editor from your school and local newspapers. Observe the language usage and what it tells you about the sender of the message. As groups, generalize your reactions to the techniques employed.
4. Brainstorm a list of words that can cause communication problems between people of different reference groups (examples: "heavy," "gross," "chick," "dude," "hip"). To whom might these words cause difficulties—foreign students, older people? How do such words originate?
5. Compare your lists of potential problem words with Farb's analysis of misunderstanding in his reading. Are his suggestions for listening and clarifying realistic?
6. Farb discusses how vital audience support and reinforcement are to the expression of convictions. Based upon the example of Mrs. Keech's followers, discuss with your classmates current and recent "cults" such as the followers of Reverend Moon, the People's Temple of Jim Jones, and Synanon. As projects, you may wish to read about the tactics of persuasion of such groups.
7. With a group of your classmates review the ten propositional characteristics of interpersonal communication cited in Chapter 1. Relate these propositions to this chapter and the readings.

Chapter 5
Using Nonverbal Communication

COMMUNICATIVE BEHAVIOR ordinarily consists of actions involving many elements: perceiving one another; considering and using space, rooms, furniture, and time; and interacting with both nonverbal and verbal behavior. For purposes of studying these factors, we will consider them one at a time. The order in which we look at them is quite arbitrary. They usually occur in sets, all at once. We have chosen to discuss them in the order in which they come to our attention upon meeting someone for the first time: we may have, at that time, thoughts and/or feelings that we need to express; we meet in a physical setting; we are more or less aware of our social environment; as we meet, nonverbal behavior that carries meaning inevitably occurs; and we may employ verbal behavior involving a linguistic code. In previous chapters we have discussed personal needs to communicate, the person perception process, and the use and influences of environmental factors. In the next two chapters we will consider interpersonal behaviors that aid us in expressing ourselves to one another.

If you and one of us were to meet and talk, you would notice sights and sounds that in your mind would have certain meanings. The nonverbal and verbal behavior you observed would be a series of events. Based upon your awareness of these events, you would interpret them in terms of various possible messages. In essence, interpersonal communication consists of making meaning out of events. We seek to make sense out of what we see and hear.

Communication without words makes up a large part of the meanings shared between people. Sometimes people are unwilling or unable to express their true feelings and desires in words, or they may even be unaware of these feelings. Yet everyone conveys messages by the way they use their bodies and through their facial expressions, gestures, touch, and tone of voice.

We distrust much of the recent writing on "body language" that has attempted to assign psychodynamic meanings to particular facial expressions or explain what a woman's crossing her legs "means." We are not concerned with simplistic views of using nonverbal communication in such a way as to manipulate another person, to gain popularity, or to be able to "read a person like a book." Instead, we are concerned with nonverbal communication in the context of the total relationship between people.

In Chapter 3 we discussed the perceptual channels of sight, sound, and touch and noted Jurgen Ruesch's three classifications of nonverbal codifications (sign language, action language, and object language). Although scholars disagree on the definitional limits of verbal and nonverbal communication, we make the distinction to indicate that communication in addition to words occurs and has profound effects on people.

The interlacing of fingers, twist of a foot, slump of a shoulder, curl of a lip, direction of a gaze, or tilt of the head are instances of what we call nonverbal behavior. All can occur simultaneously or separately, with or without words, spontaneously or by contrivance during an interaction or when an individual is alone. Our concern is with the communicative functions of nonverbal behavior during an exchange with a person as part of a relationship.

The Interface of Verbal and Nonverbal Interaction

I may say the sentence "I don't know where I'm going to have dinner tonight" in a variety of ways. I may be seeking information on good restaurants or I might be angling for an invitation. By my intonation, the context, the relationship between the two of us, and the various nonverbal cues I'm providing, you infer what I mean. Even "Good morning" can convey a number of meanings. One "Good morning" may indicate timidity, awareness of subordinate status, anxiety as to how the greeting will be received, and so on. Another may convey condescension, awareness of power position, rejection, hostility, and the like. The key is making sense out of the verbal and nonverbal messages to arrive at a congruent perception of a transaction.

Congruent messages contain information from a number of channels to be combined harmoniously, agreeably, and consistently into one clear meaning. Messages from both verbal and nonverbal cues form redundant statements as clusters of behaviors reinforce and complement one another. For example, after a difficult task is completed, a woman might express a congruent message of relief by saying, "Thank heaven that's done," relaxing her body as she eases into a chair, exhaling a full, audible sigh, and resting her arms lightly beside her body.

When the verbal and nonverbal aspects of the message do not fit, the receiver must somehow translate the data into a single message. A husband— for example, one who has been working in the yard—comes into the house and says to his wife in an irritable tone of voice, "Damn it, the shovel handle broke!" The wife must then, with great agility and skill, go through the following process in her mind:

1. He is reporting on the condition of the shovel.
2. I know he is irritated. His "Damn it" and the tone of his voice make this clear.
3. Is he blaming me for the condition of the shovel? If he is criticizing me, what does he think I should do—apologize, help him, or what?
4. Maybe he is criticizing himself and is frustrated by the broken handle. If so, what is he asking me to do—sympathize, just listen, or what?

5. Since I know from living with him that he has little patience with malfunctions, he is probably just irritated at the situation and is asking me primarily to sympathize with him.
6. Now how can I communicate that I am genuinely sympathetic—listen quietly, offer to help, bring his coffee, offer suggestions? How can I best communicate my conscious concern and interest?

Had the husband merely said, "I'm having a hard time in the yard; bring me a cup of coffee," the wife would have had little difficulty assessing the message. She would still be in the position of deciding whether to agree to the husband's request, but at least she would not be in doubt about what he wants of her.[1]

Behavior in an interpersonal situation speaks as effectively as words and is more readily accepted. Nonverbal communication similarly establishes the basis for interaction in the animal world and for animal interaction with humans. In research with bottle-nosed porpoises, investigators have noted the unique way the porpoise attempts to establish a relationship with humans. The animal tries to take a person's hand in its mouth and gently squeeze the hand in its powerful jaws, which contain razor-sharp teeth. If the human will submit to this demonstration, the porpoise seems to accept the act as a message of complete trust. Its next move is to reciprocate by placing the forward, bent portion of its body, roughly equivalent to the human throat—its most vulnerable area—on the person's hand, foot, or leg, thereby signaling its trust in the friendly intentions of the person. Similarly, a cat routinely establishes a demonstration of trust through the ritual of throwing itself on its back, exposing its jugular vein to younger cats or cats from outside its own territory. The taking of the jugular vein in the jaw of the other cat establishes an "I-shall-not-attack-you" message that serves to define the relationship.[2]

While language can be used to communicate almost anything, however abstract, nonverbal behavior is rather limited in range. It is usually used to communicate feelings, liking, and preferences and to reinforce or contradict the verbal message. It may also add a new dimension to the verbal message, such as when a salesman describes his product to a client and simultaneously conveys, nonverbally, the impression that he likes the client.[3]

Nonverbal messages can, like linguistic ones, be misinterpreted. For example, a husband may find himself suspected of an unconfessed guilt if he spontaneously presents his wife with a bouquet of flowers. Sometimes we are confused in trying to interpret the meaning of growing pale, trembling, sweating, or stammering by a person who is being questioned. It can be interpreted as unmistakable proof of guilt, or it may merely be the behavior of an innocent person going through the experience of being suspected and realizing his fear may be interpreted as guilt. We add to the potential confusion

[1] This exchange and analysis is suggested by Virginia Satir, *Conjoint Family Therapy* (Palo Alto, Calif.: Science and Behavior Books, 1967), p. 79.
[2] P. Watzlawick, J. H. Beavin, and D. D. Jackson, *Pragmatics of Human Communication* (New York: Norton, 1967), p. 104.
[3] Albert Mehrabian, "Communication Without Words," *Psychology Today*, February 1968, p. 53.

by our propensity to "play games" with our outward manifestations of feelings. Some of us have become good "poker faces" and are temporarily able to conceal our genuine feelings.

The ways we interpret another person's reactions to us in the form of nonverbal messages determine our relationship with him/her. This person's acceptance of us in turn causes us to accept him/her. The cues are constantly being reinterpreted and reanalyzed at our subconscious level as the basis for future interaction. Because the nonverbal behaviors tend to be less conscious, we tend to believe them even more than the linguistic messages if the two are incongruent. Recent work with lie detectors shows the impact of our unconscious nonverbal communication behaviors. These detectors record physiological changes, such as pulse and perspiration changes, that cannot be controlled by the person being tested.

It is important to note that verbal communication is usually more or less conscious; often it is not deliberate, but it usually involves conscious cognitive effort. On the other hand, nonverbal communication may be either conscious or non-conscious. When we are conscious of our nonverbal communication we deliberately use signs to signify our intended meaning. Artful use of posture, gestures, tones, and body language may assist others to interpret meaning from our actions. Non-conscious behavior of a nonverbal kind ordinarily operates whether we want it to or not—in fact, frequently in spite of our wishes. For the most part it serves very well in helping others to interpret our meanings, motives, and intentions in limited circumstances. Ordinarily you should not have to worry about your non-conscious nonverbal behavior so long as you wish to be honest with others. In such cases, it will tend to take care of itself and serve its purposes well in helping others to understand you. For most of us it does not serve us well when we are dishonest, dissembling, and trying to deceive one another. Even little children seem to be able to discern deceit—unless you have consummate skill in "acting."

As we meet and interact we are constantly interpreting each other's actions, both verbal and nonverbal, to help us make judgments about what the other person is thinking, feeling, wanting, or intending. We interpret the other's actions by ascribing meaning that "makes sense." Certain acts are taken to signify certain attitudes, motives, or feelings. In passing, we should be careful to point out that the "meaning" of such acts is in the observer's head, not in the acts as such, although it may appear that certain acts have "certain meanings." The study of this process has recently become an important interest of communication scholars. This interest has come to be called *semiology*, the science of signs.

The Science of Signs: Semiology

In human interaction acts can be taken to signify events, thoughts, attitudes, motives, intentions, and feelings. Students of semiology are interested in the nature of this process—how it works. Such study is relatively new to students of communication, having been developed in the last fifteen years. Semiology as a science is rather less than exact, although it has a long tradition in the medical profession: the diagnosis of diseases from *symptoms*.

If you have ever been diagnosed as having any disease other than the "flu" you know that a symptom or sign stands for or refers to something else, usually something more important than the symptom itself. Thus, a basic concept of semiology is the idea of the *sign*. Very simply, a sign stands for something other than what it is. A complicating factor is that any specific sign can signify more than one thing. Students of semiotics are interested in three broad questions: (1) How does the use of signs affect or influence perceivers (*pragmatics*); (2) what is the system of the code employed—the form of statements received by observers of signs (*syntactics*); and (3) how are signs interpreted to mean specific things or sets of things—ideas, events, attitudes, and so on (*semantics*). We will discuss each of these branches of semiology very briefly. It should be understood that each of them refers both to nonverbal and verbal communicative acts. Although in the present chapter our primary interest is in nonverbal communication, our discussion of semiology here is clearly related to our discussion of verbal communication in Chapter 4.

Pragmatics.   As the name of this approach to the study of semiology would indicate, a very practical (or pragmatic) question is this: How does the use of signs influence us to do, think, or feel certain ways. Scholars who pursue this issue are concerned with the results of the use of signs—their effect on us. How and to what extent do people respond to symbol systems? For example, what effects do advertising, news releases, slogans, and television have on people? What are their effects on children? Can the use of words, symbolic actions, and slogans seriously influence public opinion? Government officials? One another in conversation? As we shall see in a later section of this chapter, nonverbal behavior in the forms of personal appearance, vocal tones, facial expressions, eye contact, and "body language" can have important influences on us as we engage in interpersonal communication.

Syntactics.   The format of a statement which we perceive as being made by another person can make a difference to our ability to interpret such signs. We are most easily made aware of complexity and awkward word order (as illustrated in the sentence immediately preceding this one). However, nonverbal communication also employs a format in the use of signs which, if violated, can lead to misinterpretation or confusion. For example, suppose you and a woman friend are going to the theater; you drive by to pick her up and she is dressed in a track suit, athletic socks, and jogging shoes. Obviously she isn't ready and you infer it will be at least a few minutes before you can depart together. Now, if she were in an evening dress, hair neatly combed, with athletic socks and jogging shoes on her feet, the message you infer is not so clear. Is she ready to go that way? How well do you feel you really know this woman?! The format of her nonverbal behavior causes you to be confused, or at least to hesitate in ascribing meaning to what you see.

Semantics.   The third question asked by students of semiology is, What does a specific sign refer to? What is the nature of the meaning intended by the person who chose to use such a sign? How can you be sure?

The answers to these questions of semantics lie in three more or less separate areas. In the first place, a sign can signify something because it resembles it. We call such a signifier an *icon* (from the Greek word for simile) because the sign is *like* something else. It can look like it, smell like it, feel like it, or taste like it. For example, suppose you meet someone wearing a T-shirt with a drawing of your school symbol on it—perhaps a wildcat, tiger, or lion. There are numerous inferences you might draw about the wearer of such a shirt, many of which are interesting and useful to you for further interaction, but mostly tenuous. Icon signs often cannot be taken at face value; the intended meaning (if any) and the inferred meaning may not match.

A second way in which semantic meanings may be inferred from signs is when the signifying event or circumstance was *caused by* another event or circumstance. We call such a sign an *index* of the event or situation thus signified. For example, suppose you come into a gymnasium locker room, dressed in a basketball suit and shoes, holding your nose which is bleeding profusely. We would tend to infer that you had an accident or a rough game of basketball (or some similar sport—perhaps tennis, handball, soccer, etc.). As you can see, *indexical* signs are somewhat tenuous—not for certain, but frequently very useful.

A third way in which semantic meanings may be inferred, and by far the most often used in human communication, is from *symbolic* signs. Symbol systems do not work by resembling something (although sometimes this occurs as an additional factor), or by being caused by an event or circumstance; they work simply by arbitrary agreement or social custom. The word "woman" does not look like a woman, is not caused by a woman, but by social agreement has come to stand for or refer to (in English) an adult female human being. *Symbols* are the essence of natural human languages, and we have discovered their essential use in Chapter 4 in our discussion of verbal communication. However, nonverbal symbols can help us infer meaning through arbitrary use of social conventions. Traffic signs may provide an interpretation of their meaning even if snow has covered the verbal (words) on them; uniforms may be taken to provide meaning about those who wear them; by agreement (social convention) even a "meaningless grunt" can be taken as a sign of recognition when given by a hard-shelled, mean, old professor (sometimes that's all the affection for another human such a person ever shows—at least, in front of students).

The unlimited opportunity to invent and use arbitrary symbols is uniquely human; it has allowed us to communicate meaning far beyond rudimentary limits. We can speak of ideals, fantasies, unrealized hopes, and even unrealistic fears through the use of arbitrary symbol systems. They have helped us develop statistics, calculus, chemistry, history, religion, physics, astronomy, stocks and bonds, organizations, nations, governments, laws, and even mythology; the list is endless.

Perhaps, as humans, we owe our greatest of all debts to those who have, before and along with us, developed symbol systems. Even so, ascribing meaning to symbols as we see or hear them used in our presence carries inherent risks and problems. Symbols can refer to things that are thought to exist but cannot be found; we can think we know their meaning when we do not; and we can use such symbols as if we meant one thing when, in fact, we mean something else. In addition, we can use words as if they signified something when, in fact, they are meaningless, a "sound full of fury, signifying nothing." Languages may thus be viewed as a special kind of sign system, and other sign systems, in part, may be used in place of language.

Both nonverbal and verbal (word) communication employ all three types of semantic use of signs: iconic, indexical, and symbolic. All three are useful in nonverbal communication, but the first two are of primary utility. Thus there is an inherent risk in signs employed in nonverbal communication because iconic and indexical signs are less definite, more ambiguous, and more subject to erroneous interpretation than symbolic systems. On the other hand, they are often viewed as more dependable because they are less easily manipulated; it is more difficult to communicate deceitful or artificial iconic and indexical signs than it is to use dishonest words.

As students of semiology we should be interested in how the total process of communication works and we should be especially interested in codes and symbol systems. When we try to determine what a sign *means*, we should try to discover *all* of its meanings—iconic, indexical, and symbolic. We should be aware of all that is happening to us when we hear our friend say, "The Minnesota North Stars *put out* the Atlanta Flames last night, 4 to 3."

We should be careful not to interpret an icon on a T-shirt as if it were an index (caused by some underlying motive or emotion). We should not attribute to a symbol that we hear the same strong value we might attribute to an icon or index. Is a woman on television beautiful *because* she uses Revlon (or Kinney shoes, Regal cookware, Salem Lights, etc.)? Is a presidential candidate handsome *because* he is a Democrat? Or is he honest *because* he has an innocent smile? What, if anything, is the *meaning* of long hair, white shirts, wide shoulders, soft smiles, a trim figure, a strong handshake, slumping posture, twisting fingers, a firm step, or eyes that are wide open? In essence, what are the various meanings we can reasonably attribute to nonverbal behaviors?

Nonverbal Communication Behaviors

There are many nonverbal actions to which we might attribute meaning as we meet and interact with another person. When we talk we rarely trust the words alone. We shift our weight, wave our arms, frown or smile, and convey our words in varying tones. When we are in the presence of other people, as we noted in Chapter 2, we cannot *not* communicate. Meanings may be attributed to the ways we straighten our clothing, read a magazine, manipulate a cigarette or a coffee cup. Interest in such nonverbal behavior has increased a great deal in the past several years. As yet, however, there are varying opinions concerning the classifications of nonverbal behavior and the generalizations that may be made about them.

In Reading 6.1, Edward and Mildred Hall identify different nonverbal behaviors with the "distance zones" involved. At close or "intimate" zones, the head, pelvis, eyes, and trunk can be brought into actual contact; there is also an exchange of heat and body odors and an ability to see sensitive shifts in eye movements and facial expressions. As the distance increases into the "public" zones, nonverbal communication plays a less precise role.

How do these classifications of the Halls relate to an interpersonal relationship? Obviously, in a love or friendship relationship, the intimate distances are far more likely to be experienced. In such relationships, greater reciprocity is desirable. Close contact with another person who is physically passive or rigid, who avoids eye contact, who turns his/her head away, and who does not reciprocate can certainly not be identified as a relationship of intimacy or responsiveness.

In another analytic study, Paul Ekman and Wallace V. Friesen developed a classification of nonverbal behaviors based on *origin*, circumstances of *usage*, and interpersonal significance or *coding*.[4] They describe five generic classes of nonverbal behavior: (1) emblems, (2) illustrators, (3) affect displays, (4) regulators, and (5) adaptors. These classifications are defined and discussed in Reading 5.1.

Ekman and Friesen's classification helps us to understand and identify certain types of nonverbal coding. Good friends, lovers, and spouses may be able to communicate on an intuitive or subliminal level with a flick of the head, an eye glance, or a special movement that conveys great meaning to the partner. As the relationship grows, all facets of nonverbal communication become more synchronized and more concrete in their meanings. Whether our partner is upset, detached, or "with us," we are able to notice this without using words.

In another attempt at classification, Mehrabian identified three dimensions of nonverbal behavior: *evaluation, potency, and responsiveness*.[5] In positive interaction situations, there is an increase in positive evaluation, as indicated by a closer position, more forward lean, more eye contact, and more direct orientation. There also seems to be an increase in potency, which is reflected in postural relaxation. Increased responsiveness in positive social relationships is indicated by more facial expressions and more active vocal mannerisms. In an ongoing relationship, we are constantly communicating an evaluation of the other person in either a positive or a negative way by our nonverbal responses.

Scholars who are working on the development of theory of nonverbal communication are not entirely in agreement regarding the classification of nonverbal behaviors. Thus, we have rather arbitrarily grouped these behaviors under four headings: (1) personal appearance, (2) vocal tones, (3) eye and facial movements, and (4) body posture and gestures.

[4] Paul Ekman and Wallace Friesen, "The Repertoire of Nonverbal Behavior: Categories, Origins, Usage, and Codings," *Semiotica*, 1 (1969): 49–98.

[5] Albert Mehrabian, "A Semantic Space for Nonverbal Behavior," *Journal of Consulting Psychology*, 34 (1970): 248–257.

Personal Appearance. There is considerable evidence that the general impression one forms of another person has significant influence on the way we respond to that person.[6] One of the most important factors in such an early impression is one's general appearance. Studies have shown that appraisals of others are made easily and with little conscious awareness. In a few minutes perceivers form an image of another person that will guide their responses. In a study by Barker, for example, strangers who had no opportunity to interact verbally showed significant agreement with each other in their impressions of personality traits. Preferences for working together were correlated with these impressions. After several months of working with one another, 55 percent of these subjects reported the same impressions and working-partner choices.[7]

Clothing, cosmetics, and jewelry often represent a personal choice and are frequently taken as clues to the way people will respond to us in certain circumstances. Clothes and personal effects serve many purposes—protection, concealment, sexual attraction, group or organization affiliation, status, role, and self-expression. One study found significant correlations between clothing choices and personal behavior. Subjects scoring high in *decorative* dress were found to be conventional, conforming, and submissive, while those high on *economy* in dress were responsible, efficient, and precise.[8]

Clothing retailers and advertisers believe that dress is a way of expressing one's self-concept. A study by Compton of clothing choices and desired self-image tended to support this belief.[9] Further studies have shown an association between dress and perceived status with consequent differences in response behavior.[10] There is some evidence that persons are influenced by perceived differences in status clothing; in a well-known study, pedestrians were more influenced to cross "against the traffic lights" by well-dressed (high status) persons doing so than by poorly dressed persons.[11] Even small items of personal appearance may influence observers' responses. One study has shown that the use of lipstick affected potential responses of males to females.[12] Another study has suggested that wearing glasses may produce more favorable judgments of intelligence and industriousness.[13]

Although the studies completed to date can only be taken to be suggestive of a relationship between personal appearance (including apparel) and predictable interpersonal response behavior, it is quite clear that ordinarily we are

[6] See, for example, Leonard Zunin and Natalie Zunin, *Contact: The First Four Minutes* (New York: Ballantine, 1973) pp. 6–10.

[7] Roger Barker, "The Social Interrelations of Strangers and Acquaintances," *Sociometry*, 5 (1942): 169–179.

[8] L. Aiken, "The Relationship of Dress to Selected Measures of Personality in Undergraduate Women," *Journal of Social Psychology*, 59 (1963): 119–128.

[9] N. Compton, "Personal Attributes of Color and Design Preferences in Clothing Fabrics," *Journal of Psychology*, 54 (1962): 191–195.

[10] R. Hoult, "Experimental Measurement of Clothing as a Factor in Some Social Ratings of Selected American Men," *American Sociological Review*, 19 (1954): 324–328.

[11] M. R. Lefkowitz, R. Blake, and J. Mouton, "Status Factors in Pedestrian Violation of Traffic Signals," *Journal of Abnormal and Social Psychology*, 51 (1955): 704–706.

[12] W. McKeachie, "Lipstick as a Determiner of First Impressions of Personality: An Experiment for the General Psychology Course," *Journal of Social Psychology*, 36 (1952): 241–244.

[13] G. Thornton, "The Effect of Wearing Glasses upon Judgments of Personality Traits of Persons Seen Briefly," *Journal of Applied Psychology*, 28 (1944): 203–207.

influenced by it in a fairly dependable way. An interesting example of this principle was demonstrated by Schauer.[14] Subjects including students, police cadets, and school teachers, judged persons whose apparel *did not match* to be *less credible* than persons whose attire matched. "Matching" elements included beards, sport jackets, fringed leather shirts, "dress slacks," blue jeans, and "dress shirts." When apparel did not appear to present a clear, composite picture, observers reflected doubt and suspicion.

At present, we do not have research that provides a clear, complete index of the way dress and appearance can be taken as dependable *indexical* (cause and effect) or symbolic signs of potential interpersonal responses of others. However, as *iconic* signs, we rely upon uniforms, gross differences in clothing, and general appearance as signs of status, authority, knowledge, and general response behaviors.

Vocal Tones.   Actors and their audiences have long had great respect for the extent and nuances of feeling that can be expressed by the voice alone. Most of us have a similar respect, and we are often more willing to trust a person if we can hear his/her voice when a statement is made than if the same substantive information is conveyed in writing, provided we judge the vocal indications to be favorable. To some extent we are interested in judging personality patterns as we listen to another's voice. To a great degree, however, we are interested in noting emotional states of one another. Generally, our judgment of the current emotional state of another person will be based as much on the tone of voice as on what is said. Such a judgment is very likely to have a significant effect upon our interaction with that person.

The earliest studies of the voice alone indicated that age, sex, bodily build, intelligence, and occupation might be dependably judged from vocal differences. Efforts to find a significant relationship between vocal characteristics and major personality factors have been somewhat tenuous.[15] Only recently have more carefully selected samples of voice usage and more precise specification of personality factors produced support for the voice/personality relationship.[16] For example, introverted female speakers have been found to be low in variation of pitch, force, and rate. Introverted males were found to have breathy, muffled, high-pitched voices.

Probably of more immediate value in interpersonal communication have been studies of *stereotypes* of voice usage. That people use such stereotypes may be objectionable on moral or ethical grounds; however, the fact that they are used is an important consideration as we meet and interact with one another. Negative listener attitudes are often associated with low-volume, high-pitched voices of males and with husky, harsh, low-pitched voices of females. It is

[14] P. M. Schauer, "Some Effects of Variations in Personal Appearance and Apparel on Judgments of the Credibility of Potential Sources of Communication." Unpublished M.A. Thesis, The Pennsylvania State University, 1975.

[15] Ernest Kramer, "Personality Stereotypes in Voice: A Reconsideration of the Data," *Journal of Social Psychology*, 62 (1964): 247–251.

[16] J. C. Weaver and R. J. Anderson, "Voice and Personality Interrelationships," *Southern Speech Communication Journal*, 38 (1973): 262–278.

unfortunate that opportunities for employment and/or advancement are influenced by attitudes toward such vocal variations; there are recorded instances where employers apparently have judged the potential success of applicants on such bases.[17] Other studies have shown that these attitudes are essentially culture-based, not inherent in most cultures.[18] Because these attitudes are the result of cultural accidents or social prejudice, they are subject to change if a society wants them changed.

Of even greater practical significance in interpersonal communication is the value of the voice as a cue of the current emotional state of a person as we meet and interact. Early studies by Fairbanks and Pronovost demonstrated that internal states of fear, anger, and grief were expressed with different vocal rates, pauses, and pitch.[19] Later studies showed that ten emotional states could be identified reliably by voice quality alone.[20] Considerable differences have been noted in the capacity (at least in ordinary circumstances) to use vocal variations in pitch and force (volume); for each individual a general "base line" of ordinary variation must be considered. Even so, experimental evidence clearly indicates that vocal qualities accurately convey indications of a current emotional state. Love, fear, and hate are most easily identified.

Of particular interest to the student of communication is the judgment of the credibility of a speaker made by a listener. Considerable evidence has been found that judgments of credibility are linked to a speaker's vocal behavior—"firmness" (force) and avoidance of nonfluencies (*uh, er,* etc.), as well as pleasing tones (pitch and resonance). The amount of trust listeners offer to speakers appears to be increased as a more "conversational" style and use of the voice is achieved.[21]

As we continue to discuss various nonverbal communication behaviors it would be well to remind you that seldom does one of them occur alone. Vocal usage is reinforced (or confused) by facial expression, gestures, posture, and other behaviors. In any given instance all of them should be noted collectively and a judgment of a person's attitudes, ideas, and intentions made on the basis of an integrated response to all of them together.

The Face and Eyes. Of all the nonverbal behaviors in interpersonal communication, very probably those involving the face and eyes are the most important in interpreting the meaning that events have for one another, particularly the event engaged in by persons meeting and interacting. Specifically, the mutual glance or meeting of the eyes and the exchange of mutual

[17] Robert Hopper and Frederick Williams, "Speech Characteristics and Employability," *Speech Monographs,* 40 (1973): 296–302.

[18] Howard Giles, R. Bourkis, P. Trudgill, and A. Lewis, "The Imposed Norm Hypothesis: A Validation," *Quarterly Journal of Speech,* 60 (1974): 405–410. See also W. E. Lambert, R. C. Hodgson, R. C. Gardner, and S. Fillenbaum, "Evaluational Reactions to Spoken Languages," *Journal of Abnormal and Social Psychology,* 60 (1960): 44–51.

[19] Grant Fairbanks and Wilbur Pronovost, "An Experimental Study of the Pitch Characteristics of the Voice During the Expression of Emotion," *Speech Monographs,* 6 (1939): 87–104.

[20] James Davitz, *Communication of Emotional Meaning* (New York: McGraw-Hill, 1964), pp. 23–27.

[21] W. Barnett Pearce and F. Conklin, "Nonverbal Vocalic Communication and Perceptions of a Speaker," *Speech Monographs,* 38 (1971): 235–241.

smiles set the tone for the encounter and influence the interaction behavior that follows.

The smile has been identified as the most primitive of human responses and the earliest evidence of recognition and acceptance of another person.[22] In one experimental study, approval-seeking persons gave significantly more smiles than avoidance-seeking persons.[23]

The significance of the mutual glance in interpersonal communication was given an early emphasis (1921) by a sociologist, George Simmel. He called it the purest form of reciprocity: "By the same act in which the observer seeks to know the observed, he surrenders himself to be understood."[24] The mutual glance is a way of indicating degree of willingness to be involved with another person, as well as the absence of fear, hostility, or suspicion; it is a primary display of readiness to communicate. Averting the eyes is a basic way of attempting to insulate oneself from appeals, arguments, commands, threats, and affection of others. Studies by Exline have shown that persons being praised increase the frequency of their glances while persons given negative criticism avert their eyes.[25] He also found that women use eye contact in interpersonal communication more than men, and that persons high in affiliative or affection needs tend to return glances more often.[26] Other studies have shown that persons requested to talk about themselves use far more visual contact with persons who show nonverbal approval,[27] and that they use significantly less eye contact while answering embarrassing questions.[28]

There is some evidence that emotional states of a person can be identified by observing the face and eyes in live, expressive communication; however, familiarity with that person's usual behavior is helpful. Even so, identification of inner emotional states from facial expressions alone is rather undependable.[29] Still, it is quite clear that certain parts of the face tend to be used more than other parts to express various emotional states: the eyes to show surprise and the mouth to signal disgust.[30]

Mutual glances have been shown to aid in defining the nature of a desired interpersonal relationship. The two basic relationship dimensions, degree of dominance-submissiveness, and of hostility-affection, are communicated.[31] Such

[22] K. Goldstein, "The Smiling of the Infant and the Problem of Understanding the 'Other,'" *Journal of Psychology*, 44 (1957): 175–191.

[23] Howard Rosenfeld, "Instrumental Affiliative Functions of Facial and Gestural Expressions," *Journal of Personality and Social Psychology*, 4 (1966): 65–72.

[24] George Simmel, "Sociology of the Senses: Visual Interaction," in R. Park and E. Burgess (eds.), *Introduction to the Science of Sociology* (Chicago: University of Chicago Press, 1921), p. 358.

[25] Ralph Exline and L. Winters, "Affective Relations and Mutual Glances in Dyads," in S. Tomkins and C. Izard (eds.), *Affect, Cognition and Personality* (New York: Springer, 1965).

[26] Ralph Exline, "Explorations in the Process of Person Perception: Visual Interaction in Relation to Competition, Sex, and Need for Affiliation," *Journal of Personality*, 31 (1963): 1–20.

[27] J. Efran and A. Broughton, "Effect of Expectancies for Social Approval on Visual Behavior," *Journal of Personality and Social Psychology*, 4 (1966): 103–107.

[28] Ralph Exline, D. Gray, and D. Schuette, "Visual Behavior in a Dyad as Affected by Interview Content and Sex of Respondent," *Journal of Personality and Social Psychology*, 1 (1965): 201–209.

[29] Allen Dittman, *Interpersonal Messages of Emotion* (New York: Springer, 1973), pp. 78–80.

[30] Paul Ekman, W. V. Friesen, and S. S. Tomkins, "Facial Affect Scoring Technique: A First Validity Study," *Semiotica*, 3 (1971): 37–58, 113–114.

[31] Ralph Exline, "Visual Interaction: The Glances of Power and Preference," in J. Cole (ed.), *Nebraska Symposium on Motivation, 1971* (Lincoln, Neb.: University of Nebraska Press, 1972), pp. 163–206.

use of mutual glances serves to monitor and control the interaction, guiding the participants in their responses to one another.[32]

To make a useful interpretation of other persons' mutual glances, you will need to take into account their sex, the nature of the task in which you are engaged, and their desire to maintain a friendly relationship with you. Research has shown that generally women spend more time looking at other women than men. Both women and men spend *less* time looking at each other if they are more concerned with maintaining a friendly relationship than if they are concerned primarily with completing a task, and they look at each others' eyes *more* if they are competitively oriented toward achieving a task.[33]

Gazing into another person's eyes may be perceived as a warm, affectionate gesture if the relationship is warm and affectionate; however, between strangers or new acquaintances it may be viewed as a prelude to combat! Studies of animals show that a direct gaze into their eyes signals a threat unless mitigated by friendly vocal signals and/or touch (petting, etc.). Centuries of evolution have produced a ritualization of glaring and looking away. Glaring is used by dogs and monkeys to threaten and control, and looking away is used as a signal of submission.[34] Some experiments suggest that this signal system is similarly employed by people.[35] Arousal of hostility by prolonged eye contact (e.g., staring) varies considerably from culture to culture. Prolonged eye contact is rather common among white Americans; it tends to arouse hostility among black Americans, South Americans, and Southern Europeans.[36]

We should remind our readers once again that interpretation of eye contact and facial expression should be done in conjunction with other nonverbal behaviors, especially vocal tones and gestures.

Posture, Gestures, and Body Language. The human body is quite versatile, capable of expressing a wide variety of feelings and ideas. Ray Birdwhistell, one of the early pioneers in the study of "body language," identified 60 elements of behavior that would be reacted to as different and separate from each other.[37] A problem of interpreting these behaviors is that they function as continuous variables, not as individually discrete interpretable behaviors. In a somewhat gross way they can be interpreted usefully: for example, Howard Rosenfeld has found that persons seeking the approval of others use more head nods and gestural activity.[38]

Posture alone can convey useful information. It will, in the first place, indicate activity being pursued that might deny or diminish an opportunity for interpersonal communication—for example, getting into an auto, starting its

---

[32] Michael Argyle, *Social Interaction* (New York: Atherton Press, 1969).
[33] Exline, "Explorations in the Process of Person Perception," pp. 1–20.
[34] Ibid.
[35] Phoebe Ellsworth, J. M. Carlsmith, and A. Henson, "The Stare as a Stimulus to Flight in Human Subjects," *Journal of Personality and Social Psychology*, 21 (1972): 203–211.
[36] Marianne LaFrance and Clara Mayo, "Gaze Direction in Interracial Dyadic Communication," paper presented at the Eastern Psychological Association Convention, Washington, D.C., May 1973.
[37] Ray Birdwhistell, *Kinesics and Contexts* (Philadelphia: University of Pennsylvania Press, 1970).
[38] Howard Rosenfeld, "Effects of an Approval-Seeking Induction on Interpersonal Proximity," *Psychological Reports*, 17 (1965): 120–122.

motor, and so on. More specifically, posture can communicate two conditions that may influence interaction: (1) attitudes toward a person or object, and (2) an internal emotional state.[39]

In a long series of studies, Mehrabian found that posture can indicate reliably two basic attitudes: (1) attention (to a person or object) and (2) relaxation.[40] Attention was indicated primarily by leaning forward or toward the person or object, and relaxation by leaning backward with accompanying variety (less uniformity) in arm and leg positions. The *attentive* style is used toward people who are liked, of higher status, or currently more important; it is used by females more than by males. The *relaxed* style is used toward persons of lower status, toward females more than toward males, and to a person of the opposite sex more than to a person of the same sex. Other studies have suggested that persons who are dominant in a relationship tend to stand or sit erect; compliant or submissive persons tend to be less erect with head often lowered or tilted up toward the dominant person.[41] Albert Scheflen has concluded from a long series of studies that when two people of opposite sex meet and interact they often go through a series of postural shifts similar to those of courtship behavior; the second reading following this chapter describes these behaviors.

Body posture has been found to show the *intensity of an emotional state* although facial expression conveys more information about the emotion (fear, joy, anger) being experienced.[42] Extreme emotions can thus be identified when people are severely disturbed; for example, those suffering deep depression tend to droop and sit listlessly looking at the floor.[43]

As we meet one another and engage in interpersonal communication, general postural behavior acts as an extension of gestures, wider in scope and usually longer in duration than gestures, but narrower and shorter than use of space, spatial positions, and relationships (for example, how close to one another we stand or sit).

Gestures, particularly hand and arm movement (but including other elements of body movement: head nodding, slumping, foot shifting, etc.) perform several functions: illustrating an idea, expressing an emotional state, and signaling by using a conventional or agreed-upon sign.

Illustration of an idea or object is usually connected to verbal speech. Nonverbal illustrations are *iconic*: that is, they show movements or relationships (shape, distance) with hands, arms, or other parts of the body that show *similarity* to an object or condition. They are especially useful in describing an idea that is difficult or inconvenient to describe in words, by use of pointing, showing

---

[39] Michael Argyle, *Bodily Communication* (New York: International Universities Press, 1975), p. 276.

[40] Albert Mehrabian, "The Inference of Attitudes from the Posture, Orientation and Distance of a Communicator," *Journal of Consulting and Clinical Psychology*, 32 (1968): 296–308.

[41] Michael Argyle, V. Salter, H. Nicholson, M. Williams, and P. Burgess, "The Communication of Inferior and Superior Attitudes by Verbal and Nonverbal Signals," *British Journal of Social and Clinical Psychology*, 9 (1970): 221–231.

[42] Paul Ekman and Wallace Friesen, "Head and Body Cues in the Judgment of Emotion," *Perceptual and Motor Skills*, 24 (1967): 711–724.

[43] G. B. Rozenberg and J. Langer, "A Study of Postural-Gestural Communication," *Journal of Personality and Social Psychology*, 2 (1965): 593–597.

Gestures express emotional states and are often connected with verbal messages. What would you infer is being said/ Why are the men in the background smiling?

tempo or rhythm, showing body movements: spatial relationships, and direction.[44] One study has shown that people who have *greater* verbal facility also use *more* gestures.[45]

Although facial expressions generally are more dependable for inference of an emotional state, gestures and hand movements also display emotions. These movements are often diffuse, otherwise meaningless, and often idiosyncratic (peculiar to individuals).[46] Hand movements especially convey the level of excitement of a speaker—hands waving, clutching each other, straining. Anxious speakers often show such nonverbal signs that are not intended to communicate, and attempts are often made to conceal them.

Gestures, especially hand movements, may reveal feelings and emotional states that persons don't intend to reveal.[47] Many of these feelings or attitudes

[44] Jean Graham and Michael Argyle, "A Cross-Cultural Study of the Communication of Extra-Verbal Meaning by Gestures," *International Journal of Psychology*, 24 (1975): 21–31.
[45] J. C. Baxter, E. P. Winter, and R. E. Hammer, "Gestural Behavior During a Brief Interview as a Function of Cognitive Variables," *Journal of Personality and Social Psychology*, 8 (1968): 303–307.
[46] Paul Ekman and Wallace Friesen, "Nonverbal Behavior in Psychotherapy Research," *Research in Psychotherapy*, 3 (1968): 179–216.
[47] Maria Rudden, "A Critical and Empirical Analysis of Albert Mehrabian's Three-Dimensional Theoretical Framework for Nonverbal Communication," Ph.D. dissertation, Pennsylvania State University, 1974, pp. 12–22.

are directed toward oneself.[48] Self-directed gestures may include covering the eyes, touching or covering part of the face, and other hand movements designed to groom or hide parts of one's body. Such movements are frequently indicative of shame or embarrassment.[49] One research team asked subjects to view a film and then to (1) describe their feelings *honestly* in an interview and (2) *dishonestly* in another. Observers were able to identify *twice as many* self-directed motions when the subjects gave *dishonest* reports; further, they rated the dishonest reports significantly lower in credibility.[50]

On the other hand, many people are quite aware that small, unobtrusive movements may reveal more of their emotions or feelings than they wish to reveal. To compensate they may be fairly clever at deliberately using other movements to convey a contradictory impression; for example, artifices may be used to show confidence in order to conceal real anxiety. In such a case, gestures that can usually be taken as *indexical* (the *result* of an inner emotional state) are being faked; such gestures should be interpreted only with considerable care.

As we have seen, gestures can be used to illustrate ideas and may be an index of an inner emotional state. A third way gestures aid interpersonal communication is by signaling, that is, using a conventional symbol that has an agreed-upon meaning. Paul Ekman and Wallace Friesen, probably the foremost researchers in this area, have identified nonverbal acts that have a direct verbal counterpart as *emblems*.[51] Well-known emblems are hand-raising in an auction signaling a bid, or traffic officers' hand signals for stop or go. In addition to emblems, however, there are conventional or symbolic gestures that have no direct verbal counterpart—for example, handshakes, salutes, clasped hands (double-fist) waved above one's head. Some of these conventional signals may be iconic in nature or origin, such as giving the "sign of the cross," and may be used in ceremonial or religious settings. Some of them may be given additional meaning by the manner in which they are performed—for example, degree of pressure in a handshake, or who salutes first when salutes are conventional.

Occupational groups often develop systems of conventional or symbolic signals where conditions of noise or distance make verbal signals difficult or inappropriate—for example, crews in airline terminals or broadcasting studios.

Languages for the deaf employ both iconic and symbolic signals. These languages may have a single signal for a complex idea—for example, "heavy rain is coming"—or a signal may be used for one word, such as "go." In addition, signals are used for each letter of the alphabet to spell out significant or difficult words. In these nonverbal communication systems, the vocabulary is often quite large, yet the communication is surprisingly rapid.

Nonverbal intercultural communication is ordinarily best achieved with the use of *iconic* gestures, for example, pointing or using motions that represent

---

[48] N. Freedman and S. P. Hoffman, "Kinetic Behavior in Altered Clinical States: Approach to Objective Analysis of Motor Behavior During Clinical Interviews," *Perceptual and Motor Skills*, 24 (1967): 527–539.
[49] Ekman and Friesen, "The Repertoire of Nonverbal Behavior," pp. 49–98.
[50] Paul Ekman and Wallace Friesen, "Hand Movements," *Journal of Communication*, 22 (1972): 353–374.
[51] Ekman and Friesen, "The Repertoire of Nonverbal Behavior," pp. 49–52.

an action such as eating. Interpersonal communication between persons knowing no common verbal language is not easy but is often surprisingly effective by use of iconic gestures.

Body Contact.   Touching another person is one of the most primitive and important means of nonverbal interpersonal communication. The most valuable use of physical contact is to establish and enjoy interpersonal relationships.

Touching and all forms of physical contact communicate interpersonal attitudes and inner emotional states. Touching is particularly valuable in communicating degrees of personal intimacy. If feelings are mutual it can produce increased emotional arousal and feelings of heightened intimacy.

Touch often has a sexual meaning, usually conditioned in part by one's culture; certain kinds of touching between various types of persons are regarded primarily as sexual signals in some cultures. Degree of contact between two persons can imply a certain level of intimacy—by frequency of touch, duration, and how much clothing is in the way.

Touching and body contact have different significance for various age groups depending on the sex and relationship of the persons involved; such behavior is usually governed by a strong set of cultural rules. Infants cling to their mothers and for them it is a primary means of communicating. At adolescence contact with parents is much reduced, especially beyond the age of about twelve years; a study by Jourard found that few college students were touched anywhere beyond their hands and arms by their parents.[52] He found that 75 percent of English male students had been touched by girlfriends on their head, arms, and torso; 75 percent of females had been touched by boyfriends on head, neck, arms, and knees; and over 50 percent on legs and torso (this study was done in 1963).

The body contacts related to sex have a biological basis and are greatly similar in most cultures; however, each culture imposes cultural rules about what people may do when they are unmarried, engaged, and married. Desmond Morris suggests that in Western culture couples normally go through the following 12 stages in this order (though one or more may be omitted):

1. eye to body
2. eye to eye
3. voice to voice
4. hand to hand
5. arm to shoulder
6. arm to waist
7. mouth to mouth
8. hand to head
9. hand to body
10. mouth to breast

---

[52] Sidney M. Jourard, "An Exploratory Study of Body Accessibility," *British Journal of Social and Clinical Psychology*, 5 (1963): 221–231.

Physical contact communicates attitudes and inner emotional states.

   11. hand to genitals
   12. genitals to genitals[53]

This hierarchy is an interesting example of structured (syntactical) meaning within a system of nonverbal behavior; going from one behavior to another too fast (or too slowly) or skipping may have negative meaning and consequent negative interpretation.

     In a field study Mary Henley found that men touched women much more frequently than women touched men, and much more than either sex touched

[53] Desmond Morris, *Intimate Behavior* (London: Cape, 1971).

persons of the same sex; also, in other relationships higher status persons did much more touching of lower status persons, for example, doctors and patients, lawyers and clients, and teachers and students.[54]

We have indicated that body contact is used to communicate nurturant attitudes and feelings toward children and dependents and to communicate attitudes toward sex in a relationship. A third use of body contact in a relationship is to express hostility and/or aggression. Aggression is a fairly normal response to attack, frustration, and a perceived threat. Human infants kick and beat with their fists; these aggressive tendencies may be either strengthened or reduced during childhood. To a large extent the increase or reduction is a result of cultural norms: children wrestling, parents spanking, youths engaging in boxing, judo, military training, and so on. In Western culture aggression by body contact is to some extent replaced by verbal, symbolic interaction—but not entirely, by any means.

Body contact, particularly touching, is a basic biological way of expressing interpersonal attitudes. In adult life these forms of nonverbal communication are often replaced by use of gestures and verbal symbols.

Use of Feedback

To understand fully the use of nonverbal behaviors in interpersonal communication we must remember that it is constantly changing and flowing, one fleeting movement following another with similarly fleeting cues making impressions not fully realized by the observer, but adding to the impressions and interpretations of one another's attitudes, feelings, and communicative meanings. In addition, responses are given to responses to responses, and so on, so that, as changes in nonverbal behaviors are noted, they provide feedback and constant little changes in the general impressions and interpretations of one another's meanings.

In addition to the ebb and flow of body communication, verbal communication is used to check these impressions and interpretations of meaning. Verbal inquiries about attitudes and feelings may act as checks on impressions picked up from nonverbal cues. In a review of research involving both modes of communication, Kanzer concluded: "Only an intellectual bias and misunderstanding proposes that vocalized expression must somehow be higher . . . than other forms."[55] When contradictory messages are concurrently given by verbal and nonverbal communication, confusion results. When they concur, we as observers are more certain of the other person's attitudes and meanings. Feedback, both verbal and nonverbal, is an important adjunct to nonverbal communication.

---

[54] Mary Henley, "Status and Sex: Some Touching Observations," *Bulletin Psychonomic Society*, 2 (1973): 91–93.

[55] F. Kanzer, "Verbal Rate, Eyeblink, and Content in Structured Psychiatric Interviews," *Journal of Applied Psychology*, 61 (1960): 341–347.

Summary and Preview of Readings

In this chapter we have reviewed semiology, the science of signs, as a basis for considering the essential elements of both nonverbal and verbal communication. We have noted that communicative signs may be *iconic, indexical,* or *symbolic*; this principle applies to nonverbal communication as well as to verbal communication.

We have examined the use of nonverbal behaviors for communicating in four somewhat arbitrarily chosen areas: personal appearance, vocal tones, the face and eyes, and "body language" of posture and gestures. In each case we focused on the type of behavior employed and the kinds of messages that may be conveyed. We concluded our chapter with an emphasis on the value of feedback in enhancing nonverbal communication behavior.

In Reading 5.1, Mele Koneya and Alton Barbour describe ways in which nonverbal behaviors are ordinarily interpreted in interpersonal communication. Their discussion may be viewed as a description of the applications of the principles we have presented.

In Reading 5.2, Albert E. Scheflen focuses on a much narrower but very interesting target—the use of nonverbal behavior in courtship and "quasi-courtship" situations. In Scheflen's article, his use of three words to identify certain types of communication situations may be new to you. He uses the word "discourse" to refer to most common interaction between two or more people; he also uses the word, "orientation" to refer to the way in which a listener turns his/her body more or less toward another person; the word "quasi" (in conjunction with courtship) is used to indicate seemingly, somewhat like, but not actual courtship. Scheflen also refers (in his article) to two psychiatrists, Whitaker and Malone, whose nonverbal behavior he has studied; these persons were more fully described in an earlier part of Scheflen's book from which this reading was taken.

What the Body "Says"

Mele Koneya and
Alton Barbour

> There was speech in their dumbness, language in their
> very gesture.
> —Shakespeare, *The Winter's Tale*

If there were such a thing as a "people watchers' society," this chapter could be regarded as a field guide to "people watching." It should at least give you new ways of looking at each member of the crowds of people you encounter in a lifetime (or, if you're a big city dweller, a daytime). You may even be surprised by the regularities in appearances you discover along with the expectations you have for behavior associated with the appearances.

Just as the Audubon Society of bird watchers provides information on how to identify and differentiate the great number of birds its members might observe, we hope to provide you with key aspects of human physical appearances. From this, however, we don't

From Mele Koneya and Alton Barbour, *Louder Than Words . . . Nonverbal Communication*, 1976, pp. 27–43. Reprinted by permission of Charles E. Merrill Publishing Co., Columbus, Ohio.

want you to start lumping people together in neat box-like categories. And don't entertain any notions about collecting and stuffing people! Instead, we want you to get in touch with the internal processes by which you discriminate one individual from another and make judgments, no matter how short-lived this might be, about persons you meet before they have begun to speak.

Let's carry the analogy to the Audubon Society's program of bird watching a bit further. No matter how many pictures or verbal descriptions of birds you might absorb as a society member, you eventually will have to, and most probably will want to, view birds in their natural habitats. Likewise with people watching, you will want to station yourself in the field settings of human beings with a good vantage point from which you can see without being seen.

As you begin to look for specimens from your vantage point, you will notice them in a certain sequence according to their distance from you. First you will see them from a far distance and then you will see them so close that you could touch them. What are the aspects of appearance that you are likely to see at each of these distances?

At the far distance you would probably notice such things as size and shape, dressed versus undressed, and certain colors of skin and garments, walking styles and speed. At a closer distance you would begin to notice any missing or crippled limbs and such things as age, sex, hair styles, degree of baldness, beardedness, and hats. You would then begin to notice clothing styles, shoes or their absence, and general facial features such as nose shapes, scars, eyeglasses, etc. Finally, at the closest range, you would notice such things as jewelry, emblems, badges, tattoos, and specific facial expressions such as frowns, smiles, and "dead pans." As he or she passes you might then notice such things as a company name, club sign or insignia on the back of the individual's shirt, jacket, or coat. At each distance you might find yourself forming judgments about the people you observe. Shape might tell you one thing, color another, clothing another, and so forth. It's very unlikely that no message at all would be read by you.

This chapter on what the body "says," i.e., what messages we attribute to the body, its parts, and its adornments, is organized to reflect the probable sequences outlined above for "people watching." We hope you will be motivated to do some "field trip-ping" and to reflect on the opinions you make of people from their appearances.

A Classroom Experiment

In a course in nonverbal communication the teacher arranged for a visit by a person unknown to the class members. Before the visitor arrived the students were given copies of a personality rating sheet with forty scaled items including such things as height, age, wealth, education, energy level, health, sociability, sexiness, courage, sincerity, and lawfulness.[1] The scale was arranged with two extremes of each of the items so that looks were shown as ranging from "good looking" to "ugly." The students were instructed on the use of the sheet and were told that when the visitor arrived he would take a seat in the front of the room facing the students but initially would not speak to them. In the first phase of the experiment the students were to complete the rating sheet solely on the basis of the nonverbal information they read from the visitor's physical appearance. After this the visitor would stand and walk around the room among the students. The students would then have a chance to record new impressions on the rating sheet. When this phase was completed the visitor would return to the front of the room where he would answer simple and direct questions about himself such as "What kinds of things do you like to read?", "What kind of car do you drive?", "Do you paint or play an instrument?", etc.

[1] This personality rating sheet was used by one of the authors and drawn from page 19 of the Teacher's Manual accompanying James McCroskey, Carl E. Larson and Mark L. Knapp, *An Introduction to Interpersonal Communication* (Englewood Cliffs, N.J.: Prentice-Hall, 1971).

Again, the students would note any changes in their impressions on the rating sheet.

The visitor[2] arrived and the experiment went off as planned. The experiment proved interesting to the students for the changes in the ratings which were noted as additional information became available. Standing and walking gave new information on such things as height and age while verbal responses to questions gave a variety of supportive or contradictory information for those items not easily answered from physical appearance alone. Also of interest was the fact that only two students out of the group of twenty-six complained at the beginning of the experiment of any difficulty they foresaw in being able to make valid scaled judgments about a person on the basis of so little verbal information or documentation of any sort. The bulk of the class responded to the forty items as if the answers were written all over the visitor.

Perhaps the most interesting aspect of this experiment came from a spontaneous twist to its conclusion and wrap-up. The visitor, a student acquaintance of the teacher, was chosen to be in the experiment because his name and facial features presented some degree of incongruity (if you prefer a "heavy" word). Before identifying the visitor by name at the end of the experiment the teacher playfully decided to ask the class to vote on the visitor's first and last names from lists of names which he quickly improvised on the chalkboard. Each respective list carried the visitor's actual first and last

names. Incidentally, the visitor's real first and last names were Russian in origin while the visitor had a considerable North-west American Indian ancestry which showed in his facial features. Several teachers, including the one who conducted the experiment, had met the student and thought he looked more Indian than Russian (which meant he fit their mental image of what Indians look like better than their mental image of what Russians look like). It was expected that the class in which the experiment was conducted would also have similar mental images or stereotypes, e.g., that people who look Indian must have Indian names and that people who have Russian names must look Russian.

In addition to the visitor's real name the first names list included such ordinary names as "George" and "Bill" but also included "Nanook," a name associated with an old Hollywood Eskimo film, to mislead the students whose school was geographically close to Alaska. No first name emerged as a clear-cut winner of the election but two people actually thought the visitor's name should be Nanook. The visitor remained silent and poker-faced throughout the voting in order not to encourage the students toward any one choice.

The last names list included "Schwartz" and "O'Reilly" as well as the visitor's Russian name and one, "Saskatchewa" which was supposed to sound Indian. No one voted for the names "Schwartz" and "O'Reilly" but a few were hooked by "Saskatchewa." The class was indecisive in its voting and appeared to be suspicious that there was some sort of surprise awaiting them. Indeed, the class was surprised to learn the visitor's real names

[2] The visitor was a student by the name of Ross Soboleff who agreed to participate in the experiment which was conducted in a nonverbal communication class taught at the University of Oregon by one of the authors.

and a following discussion revealed some mental sets these students, and probably many other people, have regarding physical appearances.

How We Look at Others

The fact that two dozen students could willingly undertake to judge forty personality traits from a person's physical appearance was important in itself and may say quite a bit about the mental sets which provide filters on how we look at others. Some could argue that the class members were merely playing the "good student game" of complying with a teacher's request no matter how far out it might be. However, the discussion did not reveal this nor does the history of the use of this particular personality rating exercise.

Most people strongly deny that they are bigoted because bigotry is an undesirable attribute in our culture. Therefore, they also deny that they prejudge people from appearances without speech or written information. For example, consider the expressions, "Don't judge a book by its cover," and "Beauty is only skin deep." The truth appears to be that we all make prejudgments to some degree. The narrow-minded person makes prejudgments and defends them no matter how much new and clarifying information comes his/her way. The open-minded person allows the prejudgment based on physical appearances to fade as reliable additional information becomes available. That's the essential difference between the two— not the absence or presence of prejudgment mechanisms but the durability of the impression. Another way

of saying it is, "It's not what we know but how we know it."

Here's what the experiment contributed to the support of this premise. When the teacher asked why no one chose the names "Schwartz" or "O'Reilly" many students responded that the visitor didn't look like a "Schwartz" or an "O'Reilly." The teacher brought the issue to a head and trapped the students when he asked "What does a 'Schwartz' or an 'O'Reilly' look like?" No one could really say. Nevertheless, they all acknowledged that these were ethnic names, one Jewish and the other Irish and that the person bearing such a name would be expected to be a member of the name's ethnic group. Therefore, saying that a person does not look like "Schwartz" or "O'Reilly" is the same as saying that a person does not look Jewish or Irish. The students in this class experiment are not radically different from the population-at-large. Don't we all carry mental sets or very general "ballpark" descriptions of what various ethnic group members should look like? Isn't there a "Schwartz" range and an "O'Reilly" range of physical features somewhere in the back of our minds? Again, the open-minded will allow for exceptions to the range but still may register surprise at the misfit of name and appearance. One of the authors of this book has a name which conjures up images of Hawaiians or Japanese to people who receive his name before he makes an "in person" visit to them. Actually, the name is of Albanian derivation and when people meet him after hearing or seeing his name they are surprised that he isn't at least Hawaiian. In sarcastic moments he has dealt with the surprise by saying, "Are you relieved or disappointed?"

Do you have any black friends with names ending in "ski"? Would it seem funny to you to discover one? Some black people, incidentally, have recently begun to react to the awkward names that were fixed upon them in slavery days and are seeking out more authentically African names.

What about Color?

Notwithstanding the fact that when Julius Caesar's armies occupied England, the ancient Britons painted their bodies blue for religious reasons, and that body dyes are widely used by many primitive peoples for magical reasons, and that some racial groups show changes in facial color when blushing, humans cannot change their colors as chameleons do. Human skin color is usually able to show through any efforts to mask it including the wonders of modern cosmetics. Accordingly, some groups of humans, especially those who are known as blacks and browns, can be distinguished at distances. Other groups, such as Japanese, Chinese, and Caucasians do not have skin color which contrast with each other at great distance. As a result, some of the exaggerated color categories used by the majority white population in this country are difficult to understand. For example, how many of us have ever really seen an American Indian who had red skin or Orientals who had yellow skin?

Japanese, Chinese, and American Indian people exhibit ranges of skin color within the race that we call "Caucasian." Even "white" when applied to Caucasians as a group is a very abstract generalization. Very few Caucasians the world over are really white in color

and some are as dark as those peoples anthropologists refer to as Negro. Some anthropologists maintain that the Ainu, an Oriental-looking people of Japan, and the dark-skinned Bushmen of Australia, and most of the inhabitants of India are Caucasian. If this is the case, white Caucasians may indeed be a smaller minority than is now recognized. A white anthropologist who was living with a native culture in the South Pacific was asked, "When are you going home, red man?"

When you engage in people watching be sure to notice how many people you think you can classify ethnically or racially at long range as opposed to the number you think you can classify only at close range. Don't overlook the ones you can't classify at all. Then consider how this external and eternal identification affects how persons behave and are perceived. What are the advantages and disadvantages of conspicuous color and what are the advantages and disadvantages of bland color? There's a big difference in the implications of labels such as "black lawyer" and "white teacher" when contrasted with the terms "a lawyer who happens to be black" and "a teacher who happens to be white." The difference has to do with the order in which a person is perceived and with why it is necessary at all to include color in a descriptive term. If people are seen first by their group color affiliation and second as individuals they might be expected to behave in a way which typifies our impression of the whole group. We might not know how to deal with expressions of individuality and may even inhibit or ignore them when they appear. Professor Irving Lee once said that we discriminate against people to the extent we fail to discriminate between them.

Very often the differences we perceive in members of groups other than our own are smaller than the differences each individual member perceives in him/herself. For example, there are many subgroupings in the "Spanish surname" classification of the U.S. Census Bureau. Puerto Ricans, Cubans, Mexican Americans, Spaniards, Filipinos, and South and Central Americans are thrown together into that classification. To many "Anglos" or persons other than the Spanish surnamed the subgroups within the larger classification are very similar if not completely indistinguishable. But to the many subgroups themselves there are vast differences and a great deal of resentment emerges when these differences are ignored. For the many individuals in these subgroups, too, there is a need to be seen as free-thinking and acting persons who do not always go along with the group on every political and social matter.

However, from anything presented thus far the conclusion should not be made that ethnic and racial groups do not enjoy their separate identities. On the contrary, most want to preserve distinctions in clothing styles, customs, cooking, and language. It's just that the members of these groups usually want to be seen as individuals, too.

Incidentally, an arrangement of adjectives which describe physical features and abilities together, such as "former black pitching ace" also creates linguistic problems for people not familiar with our language and habits. A foreign visitor may very well wonder what the word "former" refers to as he translates the words. It could easily be suspected that the person being referred to by the term is no longer black instead of an inactive and retired pitcher.

The lesson from this discussion for the student of nonverbal communication is that even when our verbal descriptions do not include color or other physical feature words it is very likely that we nonverbally take them into account. This taking-into-account may very well influence what we hear another person saying and may even keep us from getting close enough to engage the other person in a conversation.

Body Shapes

"Keeping in shape" is an activity which preoccupies many weight and cardiac watchers in America. The assumption is that a good shape is a characteristic of good health. It may very well be; at least it makes for a healthy appearance, and we belong to a culture which puts great emphasis on the way things look. A determining factor in the success of actors and actresses and models whose careers require them to be sex symbols is the body shape they have and maintain. When a man uses both hands to draw the outline of an hour glass in the air while talking about a woman, he is indicating an ideal shape—small waist, large hips and large bust.

Like all verbal language the term "keeping in shape" can have humorous uses. When an overweight person explains that he or she jogs to "keep in shape" you know that's not true. What the overweight person is really doing is working toward a new shape while *losing* the old one. There's also a person we know who copes with a flabby waist-line which he says disappears when he sucks in his stomach and chest. He therefore claims not to have a weight problem so much as he has a shape problem. The extra pounds would be tolerable if they weren't so shapeless. We use the euphemism "weight" to avoid the more accurate terms "fat" or "obesity."

The point of all this is that shape is an important aspect of our appearance and we communicate through our shapes while reading things into the shapes of others. There are desirable shapes which many of us aspire to in the belief that these will keep us looking young, healthy, romantic, successful, and above all, attractive to others. Since we read these qualities into the desirable shapes of others we can safely assume that others would read them into our shapes.

"Being in bad shape" is a figure of speech which gets attached to a variety of bad health and poor financial conditions. Incidentally, the use of an attribute of physical appearance to describe nonphysical conditions partly shows the extent to which nonverbal things are used to express verbal things. We will encounter several more later on in the book.

Body shape is a nonverbal message which has not received a great deal of systematic study because until recently no one took early studies seriously. A study of the relationship between body shapes and personality traits was scoffed at when it first appeared.[3] It sounded to academicians too much like the sort of stuff newspapers and popular magazines feature to create reader interest

and to increase circulations. Since the early study was placed in such a poor light there was reluctance on the part of many researchers to continue in that direction. This work identified three basic groups of body shape characteristics and recognized that any one person may have features from all three groups. The names and characteristics of the basic groups are:

1. *The Endomorph:* Soft and round with excess fatty tissue and an apparently greater amount of flesh than bone.
2. *The Mesomorph:* Hard, angular and muscular, athletic, with some boniness but no excess fat.
3. *The Ectomorph:* Tall, thin, frail, with more bone than flesh and hardly any fatty tissue.

Silhouettes of typical male members of these three groups have been shown to subjects in a study designed to see what "messages" were seen in the types.[4] The results of the study indicated that characteristics were attributed to the three body types as follows:

Endomorph or fat person: old fashioned, short, weaker and not in as good health as the other types, warmhearted and sympathetic, good-natured and agreeable, dependent on and trusting of others, more talkative than others.

Mesomorph or muscular person: stronger, more masculine, younger, taller than endomorphs, better looking, more adventurous, more mature in behavior and self-reliant. We think of criminals as being mesomorphic.

Ectomorph or lean person: younger,

[3] William H. Sheldon, *Atlas of Man: A Guide for Somatotyping the Adult Male at all Ages* (New York: Harper and Row, 1954).

[4] William Wells and Bertram Siegel, "Stereotyped Somatotypes," *Psychological Reports* 8 (1961): 77–78.

taller than the mesomorph, more ambitious, tense and nervous, less masculine, suspicious of others, pessimistic, quiet, stubborn and inclined to be difficult.

It is interesting to note that the silhouette figures presented to the subjects of the study were depicted with the same heights. Yet the observers saw endomorphs as shortest and ectomorphs as tallest. This may be due to the closeness with which the words "short-and-fat" and "tall-and-thin" are associated in our outlooks. Just as salt-and-pepper are almost always presented or found together, tall-and-thin and short-and-fat may be expected to be found together.

Another comment of more than passing interest is that the silhouettes which were used to typify the categories of body types were all male. Many of the characteristics associated with the types were those usually associated with males in general. Recently some initial research has been done on silhouettes of typical female body types and the personality traits attributed to them. Since it is certainly no longer only a "man's world" the nonverbal dimensions of female appearances need to be observed and recorded. Some of you "people watchers" may want to do further research.

Another approach to the messages our body shapes send out was accomplished in reverse—from verbal descriptors to nonverbal realities.[5] A self-description test listed adjectives to be chosen and assigned to such things as feelings, study and work habits, sociability, and general attitudes. The test was administered to people of various

[5] John B. Cortes and Florence M. Gatti, "Physique and Self-Description of Temperament," *Journal of Consulting Psychology* 29 (1965): 34–39.

body shapes. When the results of the verbal test were correlated with actual measurements of body builds a very high relationship was found. This means that it might be possible to have a good idea of what a person's body shape is from the answers that person gives on the self-description test before the person is actually seen. Or it may mean that the expectations we have for certain body types are a "self-fulfilling prophecy."

Now that the early study of body shapes and corresponding personality traits has been given some respectability, we can expect more studies of the kind discussed above. Some of the future studies might begin to get at the circumstances by which body shape and personality or temperament coincide. Does the personality come entirely from within a given body shape or is it a product of the reaction outsiders have to the body shape? Or could it be some combination of both?

Sources of Meaning in Our Physical Appearances

In a radio interview some time ago, Jimmy Durante, whose comedy career went from vaudeville through movies and television, was asked how he became a comedian. He replied that his very large and always conspicuous nose, which became a part of his comedy routines, was the major factor. Durante explained that his nose seemed to grow to maturity long before the rest of his body and made him the brunt of cruel jokes by his playmates. He developed a style of survival whereby he would joke about his nose before anyone else would. Eventually his own joke anticipated all the possible jokes others could make and this left others with nothing to add. Where his nose might have been a source of rejection by others, Durante's compensating humor became a source of acceptance.

Perhaps the process which saved Durante's sense of self-esteem from utter ruin and which steered him into a very successful comedy career is at the base of all appearance-related behavior. The essence of this process is that a person whose appearance prompts insults and other rejecting behavior from those around him, finds a way to make his personality desirable to others. Thus, the potentially rejecting others accepted Jimmy Durante and always wanted him around them because of his great wit and the warmth it represented.

There's also another process which may be at work in relating physical appearances to behavior. Perhaps when someone *looks* funny he or she is expected to *be* funny. Then the expectation becomes a pressure to conform and the individual reacts positively to the pressure by becoming funny.

These processes are not just peculiar to the development of comic personalities but to the development of those general personalities attributed to the three basic body types discussed earlier. If we expect fat people to be easy-going and jolly and lean people to be nervous and mean the expectations can become demands. When a person is bombarded all his or her life with these demands, a personality may develop to respond favorably to the demands. Therefore, the receivers of the nonverbal message may be the real determinants of what messages are transmitted. We may even ignore or filter out unexpected messages in the same way we "listen through" static on the radio.

The role of expectation in determining the behavior of others appears to be quite prominent. What's more, expectations are often transmitted to the others nonverbally. The transmission is accomplished as follows: A encounters B and reads into B's appearance and actions certain expectations of behavior and language. B, in turn, reads A's nonverbal expectations or demands and behaves or speaks accordingly. A then concludes that anyone having B's appearance and actions can be expected to behave like B. He might even say "If you've met one B you've met them all."

APPEARANCES AS STIGMA

There's a danger that the discussion thus far might bury or obscure a very important consideration; namely, that there are many people who are unable or not allowed to develop personality skills sufficient to offset the rejection their appearances bring on. The rejection is so strong and so quick in these cases that a person remains unloved and unaccepted throughout his life. We are prone to listen for the successes such as Jimmy Durante's but apt to be ignorant of the failures. A great many cosmetic surgical operations are performed in this country to correct facial and other features that people feel will lead to derision and rejection. Some features cannot be changed, however.

Those physical attributes which discredit the person having them have been called "stigma" by Erving Goffman after the ancient Greek use of the word.[6] The Greeks used the word to

[6] Erving Goffman, *Stigma* (Englewood Cliffs, N.J.: Prentice-Hall, 1963).

refer to body signs that exposed something irregular and morally bad about the person having them. These "stigma" or signs were cut or burned into the body and indicated that the person so marked was a slave, a criminal, a traitor, or any other blemished personality to be avoided in public places. In modern times the stigma of old age is the most widespread. Old people are generally isolated and out of the view of young people. Our senior citizens are expected, from their appearances, to be senile and incapable of productive lives. Another group marked for life is the handicapped who are avoided or pitied by "normals" and are never expected to behave as whole persons.

In addition to visible stigma are those invisible stigma which people have and imagine others can detect. The stigma of drug addiction, homosexuality, a prison record, and mental hospitalization can result in styles of behavior designed to conceal them. These styles can become nonverbal messages to others which may indicate no more than that something is being hidden. Very often the behavior which conceals creates other problems. The shy and frightened girl at a party who works hard at concealing her discomfort may come across cool and aloof and thus be perceived as an unapproachable snob. This is especially damaging to the shy girl who simply doesn't know how to overcome her shyness but wants the company of other people. It is hard to "read" silence in another person and we often suspect the worst from a lack of responsiveness.

In people watching we will need to consider the ways in which real or imagined stigma affect the meaning of our appearances and actions as well as the meaning of the appearances and actions of others.

Some Interesting Experiments

There have been dramatic instances of the nonverbal exchange of expectations and behavior. Some of these have been summarized in Peter Farb's *Word Play*,[7] and they are described below.

Psychological experimenters who are supposed to be objective and uninvolved in their experiments unintentionally flash body signals which may be picked up by subjects in the experiment. For example, hidden cameras were able to observe that the sex of the experimenters can have an influence on the subjects' responses. While male and female experimenters were observed to be conducting experiments using identical procedures, the experimenters were aware of their own sex in relation to the subjects' sexes. Thus the male experimenters spent 16% more time with female subjects than with male subjects. Likewise, female experimenters spent 13% more time with male subjects than with female subjects. The camera also revealed that male experimenters smiled as much as six times more often with female subjects as they did with male subjects.

It would be hard to deny the influence such nonverbal communication has on the results of experiments. What is your reaction to a person who smiles approvingly as you do tasks for him or her?

Farb also related an episode in which psychologists watched movies of ex-

[7] Peter Farb, *Word Play* (New York: Alfred A. Knopf, 1973).

perimenters and subjects and were able to predict which experimenters would produce results in line with their self-interests. These viewing psychologists noticed nonverbal messages which told them which experimenters would obtain results from their subjects that they secretly hoped the subjects would yield. This nonverbal communication was entirely visual, or based on appearances and body language.

In another instance half of a group of experimenters was told that the rats it was using in its experiments would perform brilliantly. The other half was told to expect very poor performances from its rats. All rats were bred from the same ancestors and were therefore very similar in ability. The experiment involved teaching rats how to run a maze. The rats who were expected to behave best did behave best while those expected to behave poorly did behave poorly. Why? Possibly because the experimenters who were told their rats could be expected to perform outstandingly were gentler and friendlier to their animals and handled them more than the experimenters with the "poor" rats did. The experimenter influenced the outcome of the experiment.

If rats can pick up nonverbal cues, then humans certainly can. In fact, school children involved in a similar experiment gave outstanding performances where the teachers' expectations were high.[8] The teachers in the experiment were told that a group of students ranging from poor through average to outstanding would all show outstanding behavior in a forthcoming semester. The students complied with the teachers' expectations and all showed outstanding performance. Most of the teachers' expectations were expressed nonverbally, through smiles of encouragement, eye contact, pats on the back, and so forth.

The implications of these experiments can be quite severe; Farb has drawn some conclusions from a review of the findings:

> ... It has only recently become apparent that poor children—often black or Spanish-speaking—perform badly in school because that is what their teachers expect of them, and because the teachers manage to convey that expectation by both verbal and nonverbal channels. True to the teacher's prediction, the black and brown children probably will do poorly—not necessarily because children from minority groups are capable only of poor performance, but because poor performance has been expected of them. The first grade may be the place where teachers anticipate poor performances by children of certain racial, economic, and cultural backgrounds—and where the teachers actually teach these children how to fail.[9]

Messages in Clothing and Nudity

The next most visible aspect of human physical appearance after body shape and color is clothing or a lack of it. People watchers will want a way of organizing and viewing the various kinds of clothing they might observe being worn by human specimens. This section will provide a reasonable classification and some general ideas on the nonverbal communication aspects of clothing.

[8] Robert Rosenthal and Lenore Jacobson, *Pygmalion in the Classroom* (New York: Holt, Rinehart and Winston, 1968).

[9] See Farb, *Word Play*, chapter 10 for a discussion of this and other experiments involving nonverbal communication variables.

To begin with, clothing and the absence of it have provided many interesting stories and jokes, some of which relate to the subject of nonverbal communication. A famous children's story, "The Emperor's New Clothes," has been used to demonstrate our tendency to deny the reality of nudity and to avoid criticizing the taste of people of high status and wisdom. The story also serves to illustrate a general principle of nonverbal communication—that agreement on what is permitted to be acknowledged as seen can determine what it is we admit to seeing. In the story an emperor is fooled into thinking that he has been given elegant clothing which can be seen only by wise people with elegant tastes. To the unwise with poor taste the clothing is invisible. Though the emperor does not see the clothes his fear of identification as one of the unwise forces him to don the new clothes and to display them among the citizenry. The emperor's court and citizens also do not wish to be seen as unwise and proclaim that they can see the clothes and how elegant they are. However, a little child fails to follow these norms and has the courage to proclaim that the emperor is naked. The child's innocent observation becomes a turning point and others admit that the emperor indeed is naked. The emperor realizes it too but continues to promenade among his people rather than publicly acknowledge the truth. It may take a similar degree of courage for people watchers to convince others of what they see.

There's an old joke related to this topic which has some application to principles of nonverbal communication. It goes like this: A family is on a camping and hiking trip in the woods. While the family sets up camp, the youngest child wanders off on his own into the woods and unwittingly discovers an outing of nudists from a nearby colony. The boy races back excitedly to his family's encampment, telling his parents that he has just seen "a whole bunch of naked people." His father asks: "Well, what were they—men or women?" The puzzled child answers: "I couldn't tell without their clothes on."

Considering how much sharing of clothing styles has occurred among men and women in our culture in recent years, this joke is probably not as funny as it was originally. Nevertheless, it does illustrate one of the traditional functions of clothing—to distinguish men from women. Anthropology tells us that almost every ethnic or cultural group from the various inhabited climates has made some distinction between the clothing or body adornments of men and women.[10] Some of these distinctions are obvious, others are very subtle. In the United States, which traces its heritage to the repressive traditions of Christian Europe, clothing was designed simultaneously to conceal sexuality and to make it symbolically apparent. As a result, some of the obvious sexual differences can be found in the kind of undergarments and foundation devices each sex has worn. Pre-liberation women wore girdles and uplift bras to emphasize sexual attributes which appealed to men. Less obvious are the differences seen in the ways blouses, shirts, and jackets are buttoned. Men's shirts and jackets have the buttons on the right side and the buttonholes on the left. Women have the opposite

[10] Alfred L. Kroeber, *Anthropology* (New York: Harcourt Brace, 1948).

arrangement for buttons and button-holes. Note, too, that women wear shirts but men never wear blouses, or at least the words are not interchangeable. Furthermore, men wear trousers, pants, and slacks with functional fly fronts but never with side or back zippers, while women wear slacks but not trousers or pants (unless in pant suits) which may have front, side, or rear zippers.

These differences, however subtle or pronounced, have increased or diminished according to the historical period in which they have occurred. In the courts of eighteenth century Europe men's clothing included lace, wigs, and other relatively effeminate adornments. In fact, men were the first to wear high-heeled shoes. In the late 1920s and early 1930s women in the United States began to wear short, masculine hair styles and slacks and began to abandon such underpinnings as bras, corsets, and girdles. The recent liberated women's movement has been characterized by freer choices of clothing which ignore "traditional" male barriers. Hence, jeans and boots and bralessness are increasingly popular among women.

One can certainly consume a great deal of time wondering why these distinctions in clothing and body adornments are needed to reinforce the conspicuous and unambiguous sexual aspects of physical appearances. However, it is not our purpose here to explore these interesting questions but to get at the ways in which clothing functions as an aspect of nonverbal communication.

At the outset, it is beneficial to keep in mind a conflict that some anthropologists and psychologists have had over the function of clothing for human beings. The psychologists, as students of human biology, have maintained that humanity wears clothing in order to keep proper body temperatures—to keep the body warm in cold weather and cool in hot weather. Their position is that the wearing of clothing by humans is determined by the biological needs of the organism. This made a lot of sense, but was refuted by some powerful arguments advanced by anthropologists who were inspired by dramatic field observations such as those of Charles Darwin. Darwin, on a voyage around the harshly frigid tip of South America observed a native woman, wearing only a loin cloth, suckling a baby in a sleet storm.[11] The mother and baby appeared to be unaffected by the sleet which actually clung to both their bodies. Other anthropological observers have been amazed at the manual dexterity of female members of reindeer-herding tribes of Northeast Siberia who are able to sit around in circles on the ground in sub-zero weather threading needles and sewing with bared hands. Some anthropologists have concluded from these extreme examples that the wearing of clothing is determined more by cultural factors than it is by biological factors. Regardless of the validity of either of these positions we can certainly appreciate having clothing when there are flies and other pesky insects around, since we don't have the tails and quivering musculature that horses and other animals have to ward off these pests. Possibly clothes were originally functional, but when the

[11] Reported in *Charles Darwin's Diary of H.M.S. "Beagle,"* edited from the manuscript by Nora Barlow (Cambridge, England: The University Press, 1933).

first cave man attached a button to his animal skins, adornment was introduced and still persists.

Let's allow that there is some middle ground recognizing the correctness in the positions of both the anthropologists and the psychologists with regard to our reasons for wearing clothes. We can then conclude that what we decide to wear each day is motivated in part by our response to the weather and in part by the range of clothing styles our culture makes available to us. Of course, another important factor is the economic position we hold in our culture. If we have the financial means to maintain a large wardrobe, we have many choices. If we can afford only one or two clothing outfits then our decision is restricted if not, in fact, forced.

CLASSIFYING CLOTHING

We'll assume that the number of people you observe in people watching represent the full spectrum of choices available to our culture. How did these individuals choose the particular outfits they are wearing? When each dressed at the start of the day each was aware of some image he or she wanted to present. That image would be received as a message by others. Here are some classifications which may suggest the motives of the wearer or the assumptions of the observer.

Body Cover. In this classification we find the kind of casual clothing worn around the house or in the backyard but usually not in public. We wear this sort of clothing to provide minimal modesty. Comfort is more important here than color and style combinations. Buttons can be missing and the cloth

can be torn. We don't expect to be seen by any one other than very close friends and relatives. It's not our public clothing unless a fire or other emergency forces us out of the house in it. In emergencies such as this we'll grab anything that ensures our modesty and protects us from weather. People seen .in public in body cover clothing are considered eccentric unless their particular combination of apparel is not unlike that worn by many others. Since this class of clothing is not likely to be seen in public it does not have much message value and will not enter into people watching.

Uniform. This group of clothing is widespread in our general population. It includes the clothing of policemen, firemen, mailmen, soldiers and a variety of other persons we know to be "in uniform." The essential purposes of uniform are to bind their wearers together, to create solidarity and to set off one group of uniform wearers from another group of uniform wearers or from nonuniform wearers. Uniforms provide conspicuous messages. You can see a uniformed police officer a block away and summon his or her help. Soldiers can tell who their comrades are and who the enemy is from uniforms; likewise with athletes, hospital workers, and professional hostesses or stewardesses who can differentiate each other from clients and who can be easily spotted by clients.

But there's a subtler form of uniform. It's the form assumed by age groups and some occupational groups, by students and faculty, and a number of other groups which need to establish group membership identities. These uniforms are not identical as in the case of soldiers and policemen but are strikingly similar within any of these groups. The uniforms of this latter type may be consciously or unconsciously selected and sometimes result from a limited selection of clothes for certain age groups—the very old, or certain physical groups—the very tall and the very stout. In these instances people end up looking alike although they didn't start out with that intent.

Each generation of youth appears to have had its uniforms. You can see these in nostalgic films such as *American Graffiti* or in the musical *West Side Story*, set in the 1950s. Very often the uniforms of youth differ from one region of the country to another and even differ from one part of town to another. There appear to be differences between the uniforms of on-campus students and off-campus youth of the same generation. The knapsacks used for book carrying can have the unifying effect of a uniform.

People in certain professions appear to share similar clothing habits which are uniforms in a general sense. Construction workers have been identified by their hard hats but aren't there similarly uniform aspects in the dress of real estate brokers, bankers, automobile salesmen, teachers, and lawyers? You can often see these uniform features in newspaper and magazine ads which depict the persons at your service in these agencies and offices.

On a university campus, too, students in preprofessional schools often wear clothing which imitates their career models in the outside world. Engineering and business administration students generally dress differently from art students and "jocks."

Sometimes the uniform is elevated to a higher status than its wearer. There is something hallowed about a judge's robes and a priest's church garments. In the army soldiers are instructed to salute the rank shown by the uniform and not the man inside it, which is to say that regardless of one's feelings for the wearer the uniform itself demands respect.

Even to a nudist a uniform might be the complete absence of clothes. Thus, someone appearing in a nudist colony in a hat or a pair of socks might be considered to be "out of uniform."

Disguises and Costumes. These two classifications of clothing are generally similar but differ in small but significant ways. They are similar in that both are means a person could use to alter his or her normal or usual identity. They differ in that *disguises* are used to befuddle the viewer and to cause him or her to attribute *any* identity to the wearer other than the real one or to not notice the wearer at all. *Costumes* are worn to achieve the fullest effect of a specific role being played by the wearer.

A classic example of a disguise is the use of clothing, hairpieces, cosmetics, and jewelry by an undercover agent or fleeing criminal who attempts to conceal an actual identity from onlookers. Sometimes the disguise is used by ordinary people for harmless and legal reasons. The dark glasses, floral shirts, and novelty hats which adorn vacationing tourists may conceal the identities of some who do not wish to be spotted by clients, business associates, and other potential vacation spoilers. People whose curiosity drives them to "adult" bookstores and X-rated movies may also choose disguises to cover real identities.

The costume usually requires a greater involvement of self and a more prolonged or recurring use by its wearer than does the disguise. As an extension of one's self a costume gets put on carefully and is maintained constantly, never being allowed to fall into disarray. Damage to the costume is damage to the image being projected.

There are many examples of costumes used to assume a new identity for the specific purpose of presenting an appealing image. The suit and tie or the dress, hosiery and high heels worn by a job applicant may be uncomfortable for and untypical of the wearer but may be necessary to the projection of an acceptable image or message. Very often a person under pressure to look his or her best will even borrow or rent clothing which could aid in the creation and maintenance of the desired image. Prospective employers are often aware that the job applicant is "putting on" but are nevertheless very much interested in how well the applicant can present a desirable image, especially if the job calls for public relations. Sometimes the clothing of rituals, such as that worn in formal wedding ceremonies, can be considered costumes. The white gown of the bride is a symbol of purity worn for the sake of wedding ritual. Who gets married in a black gown? The expensive and sober outfit of the groom may project status and wealth as yet unattained while hiding the fact that currently he might be unemployed and penniless.

These instances indicate the overlapping areas to which the labels "costume" and "disguise" can be applied. Essentially, the image-making aspect of our apparel makes it a costume while the concealing aspect makes it a disguise. The value of this distinction to the reader of nonverbal messages rests in its potential for sharpening the awareness of possible motives in people's clothing selections. From this awareness could come an enriched reading of the messages in the adornments of ourselves and others.

The most obvious costumes are those worn by theatrical persons who assume roles as characters in dramatic and musical presentations and who attempt to project some dramatic impact to audiences. The backstage scene before the curtain opens is often a mad scramble for just the right amount of makeup or just the very part of clothing which could achieve the character being portrayed.

Nontheatrical costumes are worn by psychopathic personalities and normals and the two groups are not always easy to distinguish at a time in our culture which permits a wide range of attire. Some schizophrenics attach very peculiar and personal reasons to their costume selections. To disturb or ruffle these costumes is to invite violent reactions.

Transvestites, those persons of one sex who enjoy wearing the clothing of another sex for the conscious purpose of appearing to be of the clothing's sex, are also costume wearers. These costumes are carefully put on and maintained and may be so extremely identified with one sex or another as to be caricatures.

The nonpsychopathic and nontheatrical persons who wear costumes are relatively commonplace amongst us. For a variety of personal reasons not necessarily unhealthy a person might work very hard to create and maintain the costume's image. Every article of clothing, jewelry, and accompanying cosmetics must contribute to and support the image. Costume wearers can often be singled out from others by the time and effort they spend attending to themselves, straightening out clothing and combing hair more frequently than is warranted by the actual condition of hair and dress. It probably would be unwise to mess up even the costume of normals since this could be an attack on the person inside. A fundamental aspect of costumes is that the meaning to the individual wearing one is very personal. The message perceived by others cannot be expected to coincide with the personal meaning. Messages associated with costumes range from boldness to weirdness. What is important about costumes is that by changing costume, we can change our role and hence our "self."

The Unclassified. Not all clothing worn by people can be as neatly classified as the foregoing would suggest. Sometimes there are blends of uniforms, costumes, and body covers. For example, a campaign button, armband, or medallion may be the only element of a uniform or costume worn by a person. But regardless of the impreciseness of the categories offered above, most clothing is the deliberate effort of its wearer to transmit a message of some sort. The final test of meaning is in you, the beholder. What judgments do you make about persons in this or that outfit and what judgments do you want people to make of your outfits?

MESSAGES IN NUDITY

While nudity is not a commonplace occurrence, and therefore not some-thing likely to be encountered with any frequency during people watching, its message value is worth mentioning.

An idea of how we read an undressed person can be gotten from a consideration of a verbal problem we have in referring to it. There appears to be a significant difference between the uses of the words "nude" and "naked." Nude appears to be polite and usually refers to acceptable instances of undress. On the other hand "naked" is considered somewhat vulgar and usually refers to instances of improper undress. Nudes in art have been acceptable in polite society but naked men and ladies are shocking. In the rock musical *Hair* the performers were permitted to appear on stage nude—which meant, at least in Los Angeles, that the performers could assume statuesque poses while undressed but could not dance that way. Streaking is running naked from one place to another, not posing in the nude.

The differences in the words used obviously reflect differences in our perceptions of the undressed body. Sometimes the message of undress is respectable and sometimes it is not. From the standpoint of nonverbal communication the fact that the undressed body can have decent and indecent messages is worthy of some thought.

There's an interesting account of the efforts taken by a California prosecutor to prevent one form of nudity or nakedness—topless dancing in a nightclub.[12] The prosecutor's case claimed that this form of undress was

[12] See "Topless Dancing as a Form of Expression and Communication," in Haig Bosmajian, *The Rhetoric of Nonverbal Communication* (Glencoe, Ill.: Scott, Foresman, 1971), chap. 9.

a pornographic message, that is, it appealed to prurient interests and was intended to arouse immoral desires in the viewers. This claim worked against the prosecutor's case. Once the topless dancing was established to be a message or communication, it warranted the protection of the First Amendment of the U.S. Constitution. The prosecutor lost out because of the sacredness with which the courts have regarded free speech and its related forms. Since the high courts of this land have acknowledged the potential message value an undressed body may have we have included it as a way in which the body "says" things.

NO SHOES, NO SHIRTS, NO SERVICE

Across the country in the past few years there were, and still may be, a number of restaurants and stores which had signs on their front doors saying, "No shoes, no shirts, no service." The reasons given by the storekeepers pertained to the health and safety of customers. Local laws usually supported the propriety of these signs. However, some people thought the signs were discriminatory and that a certain segment of the population inclined to go shoeless and shirtless was being denied equal opportunities to shop and to dine. A play on the words of the sign led instant comedians to wonder if a person wearing *only* shoes and a shirt and nothing else would get service in any of these stores. At the present time, this possibility has not been tested.

What if the discriminatory theory regarding the intent of these signs were true? Is there a special group of people who have preferred to go shoeless and shirtless? Do the members of these groups have ideas and values which set them off from the mainstream of society? What do bare chests and bare feet say to us in general? These are questions which can be speculated on by people watchers.

Students in a course in nonverbal communication discussed this matter and developed an interesting exercise from it. The students began to think about groups of people they might like to exclude and groups they might like to include as customers in stores and restaurants they might own. One student suggested this sign for excluding women's liberation members: "No bras, no girdles, no service!" Another person suggested this sign for including people he likes: "No sandals, no beads, no service!" You might want to think of some and write them down among your people watcher notes. If you do so, you will begin to deal with the kinds of things that cartoonists and caricaturists do—the creation of the suggestion of a whole person from a few notable features.

Hair Today and Bald Tomorrow

Body and head hair have had various messages throughout the years. Greeks feared barbarians, whose very name meant hairiness and who were thought to be wild men who could not appreciate the fineries of civilization. Baldness on the head has never been desirable in Western culture, but shaven heads and faces have been mandatory in many Oriental cultures. The hair around the genital areas and armpits has often been considered taboo to display, except that popular nude pictorial magazines have been including pubic hair for realism.

Long hair has become acceptable and desirable and associated with "hip" people, while short, brush cuts are thought to be marks of square or conservative people. Many "mod" hairdos are designed to conceal that old indicator of advancing years and lack of virility, baldness. Incidentally, there was a time in the past thirty years when "long-hair" music was serious classical music. Now it is most likely to be "rock" or other popular music. Long hairs, as persons, were those musicians and intellectuals of past years who were too much into their music and studies to attend to and groom themselves.

Like clothing, hair styles can also be divided into classes. You might want to consider distinctions between hair styles as uniforms, disguises, and costumes. The wig technology of recent times has made all sorts of appearances possible.

Automobiles as Outer-Outer Garments

It is not too far out to think of the automobiles we select to drive as extensions of our skin and/or clothing. There was a time before the present era of relative affluence and abundance of goods when you could tell a person's status or the airs he was putting on by the make of car he drove. Cadillacs, Lincolns, Jaguars, and Mercedes were definitely upper class, or for those trying to pass as upper class. Down-to-earth people drove plain and simple cars such as Fords and Chevrolets.

Even after the wide distribution of all makes of cars brought on by a swollen middle class and easy payment plans, there still are differences in car-buying populations. Sports car drivers are probably younger and less conservative than luxury sedan buyers but that, too, depends on which make of either class is chosen. Owners of small imported cars may be very realistic and practical people responding to dwindling fuel supplies or they might be snobs in reverse showing off their contempt of luxury.

You might spend some time at the next social gathering you attend trying to determine who drives what kind of car. You can go further and notice what kinds of bumper stickers and decals appear on different makes of cars. Are pick-up truck and camper truck drivers a special lot?

Baubles, Bangles and Beads

The jewelry that people wear sends messages, too. Some lapel buttons and rings bearing symbols may indicate that the wearer is a member of an exclusive organization such as Masons or Knights of Columbus. The wearers, like the uniform wearers, may be expressing groupness but may also be excluding people from their inner sanctums. People can get turned off by the kinds of symbols you flaunt and not hear any of the words you are saying or, worse yet, not even give you a chance to speak. A wedding band often means the wearer is unavailable to would-be romantic partners; the same ring worn on the third finger *right* hand might indicate the death of a spouse. Very often jewelry is supportive of the total message the body shape, color, and clothing generate.

Posture

How the body is held as it stands, sits, or walks is a source of information about the mental attitudes of a person.[13] Stoop shoulderedness and downcast eyes are associated with depression and disappointment. The erect posture with head held up high conveys the feeling of well-being and self-satisfaction. Some posture, however, is a result of age, inheritance, or injury so care must be taken in its interpretation as a message.

Body Odors

When something leaves a very bad impression on us we may say "it smells" or "it stinks" even though it really has no odor for us. The figurative use of these expressions tells us something about odors as messages. If something bad can be assumed to have a bad odor, then a bad odor must indicate the presence of something bad. If the bad odor is thought to be coming from a person, then our judgment of the person may suffer.

If you consider how much advertising money and time is spent on room and body deodorants, reinforced by the consumer's positive response to the pressures to buy these, you must at least suspect that odors can be significant messages for persons. Perfumes, colognes, after-shave lotions, breath fresheners, underarm sprays and foot sprays are all concocted to give off pleasant and attractive odors. In fact, they are advertised to indicate that their frequent use will attract people to you even before you have spoken.

[13] The postural aspects of moods are neatly depicted in Albert Scheflen, *Body Language and the Social Order* (Englewood Cliffs, N.J.: Prentice-Hall, 1972). See Reading 5.2.

The implication of this emphasis on canned odors is that the natural odors of the human body, in this culture at least, are messages which need to be censored lest they result in the silent rejection of their bearers.

These natural body odors have been associated with uncleanliness, disease, and antisocial behavior on the contemporary American scene but are quite acceptable and even desirable in other cultures. The degree to which they are noticed seems to vary from culture to culture, too. When we Americans perfume our bodies we are attempting to broadcast our conformance to the odor norms of our culture. We are trying to give off the message of cleanliness and good health while inhibiting the body's natural messages which might cast us in a bad light and result in our rejection.

There are some odors which are all right if they come from food but repulsive if they come from people; for example, the odor of boiled eggs. But here's a story about another one. While visiting an Italian grocery in New York City one of the authors of this book noticed a smell in the store which struck him as disagreeable especially since he thought it was coming from the clerk behind the counter. It was one of those smells which could be human. When the author moved through the store and away from the clerk and counter the smell diminished in intensity. When he stopped at the counter to pay for some items he had selected, the smell was overwhelmingly disagreeable. He then noticed that the real source of the smell was a large provolone cheese aging in the open air on the counter. Being a cheese lover he began to savor the smell of the cheese which no longer was an undesirable one. The clerk suddenly became odorless. This episode dramatizes the idea that there are acceptable and unacceptable human odors in any given culture and that the meaning we attribute to an odor can attract or repel us. When the odor is repulsive and coming from a human being we avoid that person and may even make severely negative judgments about the person's habits and attitudes.

There are odors associated with certain age groups such as babies and young children. Babies usually smell from a mixture of formula or milk and baby oils and powders. If you visit an elementary school you can notice a collective odor consisting of apples from lunch bags, spilled milk, and the urine of young children who have not mastered the controls of adults. If you'll consider that babies and young children do not usually deodorize themselves beyond bathing it is no surprise that they might be more "natural" in their odors than are adults.

North Korean soldiers, who were vegetarians for economic reasons, claimed they could smell the strong body odors of nervous meat-eating American patrols which infiltrated their lines during the Korean War. During these night patrols were the Americans unwittingly transmitting nonverbal messages telling of their presence in spite of camouflage, darkness, and strict silence?

Bigoted people in our culture have always maintained that certain minorities smell bad to them. This kind of statement may belong to the same class of statements as the figurative "it stinks." On the other hand, there is reason to suspect that some ethnic groups do have eating and bathing habits which result in different smells. Of course,

the smells would come from any person sharing the same cultural habits and are not inborn. Furthermore, the evaluation of these smells is not absolute but rests with one's cultural values. It is simply a case of "one man's meat" being "another man's poison."

For an example of an ethnically determined odor problem, consider this problem encountered by a school teacher in a school located in a small Maltese community of Detroit, Michigan. People of Malta have traditions which go back to ancient times. One of these traditions is to anoint their bodies with olive oil. This organic oil quickly becomes rancid and may prove to be offensive to non-Maltese persons. Students in one class had been complaining of the odor given off by a Maltese student. The teacher was asked to intervene in the matter and decided to for the sake of the Maltese student's acceptance and the majority's comfort. A home visit was arranged to get to the source of the problem. With good intent the teacher brought along soap and gave a brief lecture on bathing to the Maltese family which appeared to welcome her help and advice though they were not fluent in English. They promised to use the soap and the bathing procedures on their child. The problem persisted after the teacher's visit. Another visit revealed that the family apparently had followed the teacher's instructions but had included the American-style bath with the traditional Maltese oil bath, restoring the odor problem. The ultimate solution was reached when the family agreed to abandon tradition in the interest of their child's acceptance and the accommodation of the majority population.

This story doesn't argue for the desirability of assimilation but does serve to indicate the extent to which the nonverbal message of odor can alienate people and prevent communication.

Sensitivity to the notion that we censor, monitor, and evaluate odors can help us to appreciate the possible impact these have on our interpersonal communication situations. Odors can have meanings in themselves or can greatly affect the opportunities for communicating with our fellow beings.

Kinesics: Actions Speak

In a chapter on what the body says it is necessary to talk about how the body moves and what that can tell us Charles Darwin speculated about body movement and what it conveyed as early as 1873,[14] and a variety of anthropologists have worked in the area in the meantime. The systematic and sustained work in the area of body movement began in 1952 with the publication of *Introduction to Kinesics* by Ray Birdwhistell, senior research scientist at the Eastern Pennsylvania Psychiatric Institute. Kinesics, according to Birdwhistell, is a systematic study of how human beings communicate through bodily movement and gesture.[15]

Birdwhistell began his pioneering effort following a field study of the Kutenai tribe of Western Canada in 1946. He was living among the Kutenai and noticed that their movements and facial expressions were quite different when they spoke Kutenai from when they spoke English. He began to suspect that nonverbal movement was cultural, and that some people were "bi-lingual" in body movement as well as in spoken language. Psychiatrists, psychologists, sociologists, and anthropologists have known for years that body motions had some sort of communicative significance, but they haven't been all that certain about what it was. There were some psychological studies of facial expressions done in the early 1900s. Early anthropologists such as Franz Boaz, Edward Sapir in the 1930s and Weston LaBarre and David Efron in the 1940s first suggested that body movements were cues to the unspoken communication of an individual, and that if we could read the cues properly, we could break the code and know from the body motions internalized and unexpressed communication. We would have insights into human behavior previously unknown even to the individual being observed.

Of course, people speak, move, and respond to one another constantly. A person cannot *not* behave and since all that behavior is potentially communication, we cannot not communicate. However, that doesn't mean that simply by observing someone's behavior we will know what is being communicated.

You don't have to be a behavioral scientist to understand some nonverbal behavior. A lot of it is simply common sense. You may be able to see tension in someone's posture, or anger in someone's flexing hands or sadness in someone's downcast head. This is known popularly as "body language"[16] and technically as kinesics. Birdwhistell says that words express the smallest part of our meaning. Most is communicated by body motion, posture, facial expression, and voice.

[14] Charles Darwin, *Expression of Emotions in Man and Animals* (Chicago: University of Chicago Press, 1965).
[15] Ray L. Birdwhistell, *Kinesics and Context* (Philadelphia: University of Pennsylvania Press, 1971).

[16] Julius Fast, *Body Language* (New York: Pocket Books, 1971).

Some of our gestures have clear and obvious meanings. Even though they are given without speaking, the meaning generally evoked in the observer is so clear and such a social convention that they probably more accurately are to be termed signals. Signals are immediate, and there is usually a one-to-one relationship between the signal and the meaning of the signal. Signals do not offer us much ambiguity. A good example of this kind of gesture is the hitchhiker's upraised thumb. This gesture, though unspoken, or nonvocal, has a conscious and well-understood meaning. Paul Ekman has categorized these gestures as "emblems." You may be able to think of several other emblems which express disbelief, disdain, or rejections.

Ekman has some other categories for body motion besides emblems.[17]

> *Illustrators:* accompany and complement the spoken word. Imagine responding to the question "Which direction?" without pointing. Pointing would be an illustrator.
> *Regulators:* control verbal interaction, letting people know when you're done talking or want to get into the conversation.
> *Affect displays:* indicate your emotional state. Smiling at someone in the supermarket would be an example of this as would clenching your fist in anger.
> *Adaptors:* body movements learned in childhood such as squinting or lip licking or leg kicking which may have some specific purpose and may not be noticed by a listener. A movement which served some instrumen-

[17] Paul Ekman and Wallace V. Friesen, "The Repertoire of Nonverbal Behavior: Categories, Origins, Usage, and Coding," *Semiotica* 1 (1969): 49–98.

tal purpose in early life may be continued in later life as a habit.

These classifications are, of course, merely a convenience. It would be possible to classify head nodding (indicating "yes") as an emblem, or to see it as an illustrator (accompanying "yes"), or as a regulator (signaling "I agree and want to talk now"). With the old question of what "part of speech" (noun, verb, adjective, etc.) a word was, we had to ask ourselves what the word did and how it was used. The same principle might be applied to kinesics. We have to look at the context of any particular movement and notice how the movement was used in order to understand what was meant by the movement.

Generally we are misled if we believe there is a point-to-point correspondence between a body movement and a meaning. This would suggest that each movement could be assigned a word and that each time that movement came up the label could be applied. It is not nearly so simple. When a person is making one motion with his hand, he is making another one with his foot. When a person is leaning forward in her chair she may be shaking her head and folding her arms. Normal behavior involves movement of various parts of the body simultaneously. Which movement does one take a cue from? This becomes even more difficult if the context of the communication is ambiguous and the person is behaving in such a way that we are getting mixed or contradictory nonverbal messages. What do we "pick up on" and what do we "choose to ignore"?

Since the area of nonverbal communication has become available for study a number of people who claim to be good readers of the nonverbal behavior of others have arrived on the scene. Perhaps you see yourself that way. All you have to do to test your ability is allow someone to think of several emotions and try to convey those emotions to you nonverbally while you make guesses about what is being portrayed. Compare your rate of error to your rate of success and it is likely to threaten your confidence about how good you really are. The exercise requires that the person try to communicate the emotion and in most of our day to day living the persons we observe are often attempting to *conceal* their emotions. We may do all right with happiness or anger, but how do we read jealousy or awe or envy or curiosity or confusion or anticipation? Moreover, we have reason to believe that different persons would register these inner emotional states differently if we were observing. What it comes down to is that most people are not nearly as good as they think they are at reading nonverbal cues. However, if we make an effort to observe the nonverbal behavior of others, most of us can increase our skills.

We need to look first at the context of the communication, to look at the variety of nonverbal cues being registered, consider the most likely range of possibilities that the combined nonverbal cues in that context would suggest, and attempt to empathize with the person exhibiting such behavior. ("If I were behaving that way nonverbally, what would I be feeling inside?") That may bring us closer to accuracy than the "this-means-that" (folded arms mean resistance) approach identified earlier, but we will still have to expect a certain margin of error.

Observing the nonverbal behavior of others will not make them "open books" to us. Most of us are simply not transparent enough to be seen through. On the other hand, while we are behaving, we are all exhibiting cues to what is going on inside of us. If a person wants to take the time and pays close attention, he/she may be able to make some very good guesses after a while. The insights or skills he/she gains with one person may be useful when he/she leaves that person and begins to observe someone else.

Summary

This chapter has given a representative sample of the kinds of things that make up physical appearance along with some indications of how these things convey meanings. People are usually perceived in totality and all at once, but in an order of increasing detail as they approach us. Messages can be read into body shapes, color, clothing, hair, and adornments. Indeed, the meanings of the individual and those who perceive him/her may not be parallel. Presumably some of the messages are intended and some are not. It is nearly impossible to present oneself or be perceived with no message value attached. This chapter may have increased your sensitivity to elements of appearance and the ways kinesic messages can be identified.

Reading 5.2
Interactions
Albert E. Scheflen

When two or more people come together, they engage in a common activity such as conversation or courtship. This activity forms a context for the relations, which become phases in the sequences of the activity. Each phase is a context for the particular kinds of communicative behavior that each participant contributes. Three kinds of activities will be described in this chapter: discourse, courtship, and quasi courtship.

Units of Discourse

We can describe units of speech behavior . . . only when we examine the behavior of one participant at a time. But communicational units ordinarily occur at the social level. Units of representational behavior, then, will include the behavioral contributions of all members.

Ordinarily a speaker orients his body and face to his auditors, and in this position he makes his point. It may

be a speech unit, a gesture, an actonic demonstration, or all of these simultaneously. In face-to-face conversations, the orientation of middle-class Americans is rarely eye to eye. Each fixates his central vision at a spot somewhere between the cheek and the shoulder of the other fellow, just out of the range for eye-to-eye gazing. When central vision is focused on the cheek-shoulder area of a vis-à-vis, the remainder of the upper body is visible in peripheral visual fields and will trigger an orienting reflex. Focal vision is then shifted to observe the moving part.

The accuracy of an orientation is worthy of comment. In an audience of forty or fifty people a speaker can "point" his head and eye convergence with sufficient accuracy to single out one auditor. This object of attention usually is aware that he is being addressed. Similarly, we can project our voices accurately enough to evoke a response from one person in a group— sometimes even if this person is behind us. With reasonably high-resolution motion pictures and a little practice, an observer can tell visually which participants are addressing each other. The interested reader should become acquainted with the careful experimental studies of Kendon on gaze in interaction (Kendon, 1965).

A listener may sit forward in his chair if he is contending for the floor or if he is of appreciably lower status, but he often sits back and addresses his eyes and face in the general direction of the speaker. A dominant listener may look the speaker fully in the face, but more often he looks just to the speaker's left or right, and he may look down if he is under criticism or look up to the ceiling, as speakers do, to indicate thoughtfulness.

Listeners are constrained at least to appear attentive. This they may do by remaining generally silent except for occasional questions or comments. They may also cock their heads to bring one ear closer to the speaker, and sometimes they point to their ear by placing their hand on the side of the jaw and extending an index finger. Sometimes listeners may even cup a hand behind an ear. In addition, they may adopt a bland and thoughtful countenance. However, listeners are also supposed to render comprehension signals from time to time. Head nodding is one way to do so, but equally successful are smiling and laughing at appropriate times, and supplying other demeanors appropriate to the speaker's statements. Some listeners fall into synchronous hand gestures and head movements with speakers—a behavior that often consists in supplying the same hand, head, and eye markers that the speaker is using (Condon and Ogston, 1966; Kendon, 1968; Scheflen, 1970).

Actually, listeners perform point-units. Many of these consist merely in reorienting their face-eye address with that of the speaker, without speaking.

Psychotherapists tend to minimize their activity in listening. They hold a dead pan and minimize comprehension signals, for example. Whitaker and Malone did this, but not as markedly as some therapists do. In their positions of listening and questioning, they performed as follows: They cocked their heads slightly and addressed Mrs. V. They suppressed virtually all body movement and facial expression in the dead pan that psychotherapists deliberately use to minimize influence on the speaker. They would occasionally *signal attentiveness*: lean the head forward; cock it, turning the ear; and use an overwide position of the eyelids.

But listeners may interrupt their silence and ask brief questions without abandoning the listening position. Whitaker, for example, repeatedly asked questions. He would extend his neck so that his head was high, jutted forward, and slightly cocked. He would direct his face, gaze, and eye focus to the addressee (Marge or Mrs. V.), and take his pipe out of his mouth and hold it forward. He would then articulate the question. At its termination he would raise his head still farther, jut his jaw slightly, and raise his eyebrows until an answer was begun. Then he would lower and retract his head and return his pipe to his mouth.

Modes of Reciprocal Speaking

Reciprocal speakers tend to look at each other's face in narratives. They do not, however, look in one another's eyes except in a direct, aggressive confrontation or in a sexual, courting exchange. If, in a group of males, one of greatly higher status or dominance is addressing the others, he may look directly at their faces even when he is listening. It is as though dominant males and those awarded the temporary status of speaker have charge of the gazing space directly in front of their faces.

However, speakers do not always look at the faces of their listeners. They may look down at their feet if they are speaking tentatively or hesitantly and at times when they subjectively report shame, guilt, or a fear of offending. The position of "head down" is sometimes a posture of submissiveness.

A speaker may also look upward, over the head of his listener. When he does so, he is likely to jut his jaw and bring his lower lip over the upper. He may even rub his chin or scratch the back of his head. Such posturing indicates thoughtfulness and may be associated with the subject's feeling of wishing to think about what he will say.

These forms of speaking address are associated with differences in voice projection, eye convergence, muscle tone, and paralanguage. In the usual mode of intimate or personal conversation, the eyes are converged appropriately for the distance between participants and the voice is projected directly to the listener. Birdwhistell (1963) calls this the interpersonal mode.

When the face and eyes are addressed to the floor, the speaker is likely to underproject the voice almost to inaudibility, and he may assume a hunched shoulder posture and a sagging of the musculature in general. When he speaks while looking over or beyond the shoulder of his listener, he is likely to converge his eyes at a point past the listener and overproject his voice outward to the "world at large." In this case, a speaker may bring back his shoulders and protrude his chest, and he may also lean backward and hold his head high. Birdwhistell (1963) calls these two modes, respectively, the intrapersonal and the extrapersonal.

In the simplest reciprocal relations, a speaker assembles a sequence of representational statements to which others indicate their comprehension or the lack of it by nodding, making facial displays, and commenting. The speaker may maintain his narrative position as he observes these indications, adding further point-units of speech or illustrations if these seem necessary.

In more formal presentations, time may be saved for questions, discussion, or rebuttal. A common format in Western meetings is a presentation, followed by several periods of comment, and then a period of debate or discussion. More complex formats are, of course, in use. Some provide for the exposition of a variety of viewpoints, and others make use of an agenda that permits a number of topics or matters to be brought up sequentially.

The role of speaker may also change hands. One person may take a position of narration for a while as the others listen; then another participant may take the floor and state a different position. This arrangement is characteristic of dialogue and negotiation.

If the utterance of one participant seems to elicit a response or a counterstatement from another participant, the sequence has an action-reaction format. If the first person then responds to what the second has said, a more complex sequence of interaction occurs (Menninger, 1958; Colby, 1960; Bales, 1950).

In fact, however, the structure of an interaction is governed by customary rules and agenda. Participants often take turns speaking according to such agenda, paying little or no heed to each other's statements, so interaction is minimal. Only the timing of their utterances is interactional. On other occasions, people do pay attention to each other, but the range of topics and ideas is governed by the agenda of the transaction. In this case the program of conversation follows the model of a game in which moves are contingent upon each other, but the allowable kinds and ordering of moves are governed by the rules.

Courtship Reciprocals

Some of the common activities of early courtship in America are courtship readiness, positioning for courtship, and actions of appeal or invitation.[1] Courtship behaviors occur after a participant has reached a specific state of readiness. People in high courtship readiness are often unaware of it, and, conversely, subjects who think they "feel" very sexually active often do not evidence courtship readiness at all. Courtship readiness is most clearly evidenced by a state of high muscle tone. Sagging disappears, jowling and bagginess around the eyes decrease, the torso becomes more erect, and pot-bellied slumping disappears or decreases. The legs are brought into tighter tonus, a condition seen in "cheesecake" and associated with the

professional model or athlete. The eyes seem to be brighter. Some women believe their hair changes. Skin color varies from flush to pallor—possibly depending upon the degree of anxiety. It is possible that changes in water retention and odor occur.

Preening often accompanies these organismic changes, sometimes only as token behaviors. Women may stroke their hair, or glance at their makeup in the mirror, or sketchily rearrange their clothing. Men usually comb or stroke their hair, button and readjust their coats, or pull up their socks. Some preening behaviors that have been observed in psychotherapy sessions are shown in Figure 1.

After the earliest steps, the courting partners assume postures that have a standard relationship. The partners turn their bodies and heads so as to face each other in a vis-à-vis or tete-à-tete configuration. They tend to lean toward each other and place their chairs or extremities in such a way as to block off others. Figure 2 shows the vis-à-vis positioning used in courtship. It also depicts the courtship position used when the parties open the position of the upper half of their bodies to include a third person, but form a closed circle with their legs. When

FIGURE 1. Some preening behaviors of male psychotherapists.

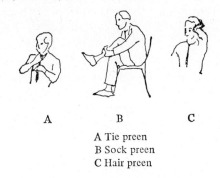

A Tie preen
B Sock preen
C Hair preen

[1] This section, on courting displays, and the next section, on quasi courting, are reprinted from an article by the author called "Quasi-Courting Behavior in Psychotherapy." This article was printed in *Psychiatry* 28: 245–57 (August 1965). This excerpt from that article is republished here with the kind permission of the William Alanson White Foundation, Inc.

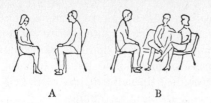

A   B

A With two people
B With third party present

FIGURE 2.   Positioning for courtship.

courting partners orient themselves vis-à-vis and come into closer physical proximity, they usually adopt an intimate mode of conversation.

The assumption of one participant of a vis-à-vis orientation with courtship readiness may be considered an invitation to court or to related activities. Other activities also appear to invite reciprocation in courtship. In addition to complimentary or invitational statements and soft or drawling paralanguage, characteristic bodily motions are seen. Flirtatious glances, gaze holding, demure gestures, head cocking, rolling of the pelvis, and other motions are well known. In women, crossing the legs, slightly exposing the thigh, placing a hand on the hip, and exhibiting the wrist or palm are invitational. Protruding the breast and slow stroking motions of the fingers on the thigh or wrist also are common. Some of these activities, seen in psychotherapy sessions, are illustrated in Figure 3.

Quasi Courtship

Two boys are wrestling. They may be fighting for domination or to defeat each other, but they also may have a quite different purpose. Their wrestling may not, even over years of repetition, progress to victory for either boy. Neither is hurt or humiliated.

Instead of showing anger, both may laugh and show evidence of considerable pleasure. None of the spectators even thinks of intervening. They seem to know from the beginning that injury and victory are not the aims of this interaction. Or two men approach each other in a barroom. They call each other the vilest names, exchange mock punches, then embrace and buy each other drinks. Animals also show such mock fighting (Bateson, 1955). Two dogs may rush at each other with such a show of ferocity that a spectator would expect them to tear each other apart; instead they romp off gaily together in play.

In such situations, two sets of behavior seem to be alike, but some signal occurs that lets those who know the rules distinguish between them. Some indication occurs that the activity is not a real fight; it is not to be taken literally.

Partners in a quasi courtship may make references to the inappropriateness of the situation for sexuality by reminding each other that other people are present or by reminders of taboos or ethical considerations. They may also remind each other that they

FIGURE 3.   Appealing or invitational behaviors of women patients.

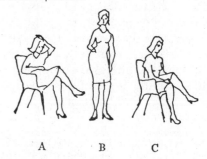

A   B   C

A Presenting the palm, with hair preening
B Rolling the hip
C Presenting and caressing the leg

are together to conduct the business at hand. In psychotherapy, the patient may be encouraged to feel her sexual feelings fully; yet she may be cautioned, by reference to the context, not to act them out. More often than not, such references are non-verbal. A gesture or a movement of the eyes or head toward the setting or toward others is as effective as any verbal statement about inappropriateness.

After the earliest steps in a courtship, the partners move into a vis-à-vis relationship of posture and adopt an intimate mode of conversation, excluding others from their relationship. In quasi courtship the relationship of postures is incomplete. The participants may face each other but turn their bodies so that they face partly away from each other, or they may extend their arms so as to encompass others. Or they may cast about the room with their eyes or project their voices so as to be clearly audible to third parties. This story of divided loyalties is told in Figure 4. In Figure 4A the woman, in vis-à-vis positioning with a man, turns in search behavior to another man, passing by. In Figure 4B, the couple on the right are in a semiclosed tete-à-tete position, but the woman is touching the other man with her ankle. This kind of division of the body in multiple simultaneous relationships, we have called splitting.

The behaviors may be modified so as to leave out characteristic courting elements. This is done by failing to complete typical courting actions or by conducting them only in certain communicative modalities so that the *Gestalt* required for a courting unit is not completed. For example, in courtship a man may lean forward, touch his partner, soften his facial expression, and, in soft paralanguage, verbalize his love. In quasi courting he may say the words while leaning slightly away from her, smile only by retracting the corners of his lips without crinkling his eyes, and use a matter-of-fact tone of voice.

Participants in quasi courting may try to reduce ambiguity and indicate non-courtship by lexical disclaimers. They may reassure the partners and others that their interest is not sexual. They may seem to court while talking about their love for another partner, or they may intellectualize the flirtation in a discussion, say, of great books.

It is logical that quasi-courting forms might differ between the classes, since their dating and courtship patterns are known to differ markedly. There is an American middle-class tendency to combine romantic love, which historically was a platonic concept, with active sexuality. It may be this combination that necessitates signals for differentiating courting and quasi courting. Qualifiers seem to be learned by middle-class children first in their relations with older relatives and later in the characteristic middle-class dating pattern with its ritualistic flattery, dance programs, and non-progressing court-

FIGURE 4. Multiple postural relationships in quasi courting.

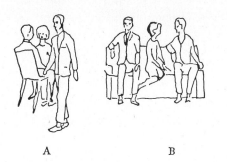

A   B

shiplike routines. But the non-upwardly mobile lower class, which separates romantic love and sexuality, has not developed a dating pattern of this kind and apparently lacks the pattern of quasi courting well known in the middle class.[2]

In the tradition-bound performances in a culture, a relatively few elemental units of behavior serve as basic building blocks for constructing complex and variegated patterns. An integration as complex as a long discourse, for example, is based upon a relatively small number of standard phonemes. In English, only forty-three such elements make up the thousands of morphemes (similar to words), which in turn are formed into such complex structures as sentences, conversation, and literature. In an analogous way, a few elements of courting behavior are put together in the complex pattern of courtship; these same elements, arranged in a different way and combined with "qualifiers," make up integrations that resemble courtship but have a quite different significance in an interaction.

Since quasi courting contains courtship elements, it is tempting to say that quasi courting is no more than aim-inhibited courtship. This idea is misleading, implying that interactants want to court or seduce and are merely dissuaded by circumstances or inhibition. On the contrary, quasi courting is a distinct element in American middle-class culture, learned separately and earlier than courtship and having a very different function. Once this situation has evolved, whatever the origins of quasi courting, a person "knows" at some level of consciousness that quasi courting elicits different behavior from courting. He can therefore intend to "quasi court" from the beginning of the relationship, and his behavior does not necessarily have to be attributed to any other intent.

Quasi courting is a complex of behaviors that resembles courtship. It can be distinguished from actual courtship by three major characteristics: (1) the integration of components, in which qualifiers state, in essence, "This activity is not to be taken literally as seduction"; (2) the contexts of appearance: quasi courting occurs in contexts in which courting or sexual behavior is inappropriate; (3) the ultimate progression of the behaviors in the interactional sequence determines whether the pattern is one of courtship or quasi courtship. The quasi-courtship pattern does not proceed to sexual consummation even in the later history of a given relationship.[3]

It is possible to postulate a state of quasi-courting readiness that includes a few aspects of courtship readiness but is observably different. For ex-

[2] For discussions of middle-class dating patterns see the following: D. D. Bromley and F. H. Britten, *Youth and Sex: A Study of 1300 College Students* (New York: Harper, 1938); Rayanne D. Cupps and Norman S. Hayner, "Dating at the University of Washington," *Marriage and Family Living* 9, 30–31 (1947); Winston Ehrmann, *Premarital Dating Behavior* (New York: Holt, 1959); C. Kirkpatrick and T. Caplow, "Courtship in a Group of Minnesota Students," *American Journal of Sociology* 51, 114–25 (1945); Robert T. Ross, "Measures of the Sex Behavior of College Males Compared with Kinsey's Results," *Journal of Abnormal and Social Psychology* 45, 753–55 (1956); Geoffrey Gorer, *The American People: A Study in National Character* (New York: Norton, 1948).

[3] This is why there is a serious risk of misinterpreting component behaviors of any pattern when they are observed out of context. If, for example, you hear only that two men exchanged kisses, without knowing that the context was a French military ceremony, you might wrongly interpret the kissing as homosexual. This is the shortcoming of the currently popular isolation-of-variables method of research, in which this or that element of behavior is studied as an isolated phenomenon.

ample, women may imitate the appearance of high muscle tone of courtship readiness by wearing nylon hose and high-heeled shoes, which throw the foot into flexion and tighten the hamstrings; or they may adopt a particular type of provocative, slightly bizarre attire and cosmetics, which give the impression of "sexiness." Such devices appear to solicit quasi courting rather than courting, and experienced men recognize that "sexy" women are not necessarily sexual.

Quasi courting occurs in nearly any situation—at least among the middle class—in which the members know each other and are engaged in a common objective. The sequence can be observed in the classroom, dining room, and meeting hall, and between parents and children, hosts and guests, teachers and students, and doctors and patients. It occurs between men and women and between people of the same gender. The intensity and duration vary from the briefest of kinesic interchanges (in formal activities such as psychotherapy) to the most elaborate, continuous, and intense rituals in situations such as the cocktail party. In the upper-middle-class social context, in fact, quasi courting takes on the quality of a deliberate game for enhancing attractiveness and social interest. Quasi courting across marital lines is common. It does not produce signs of anxiety or force interruption so long as certain rules are observed. Of course, the alarm bell rings when one party begins excluding others by seeking isolation.

Often, a quasi-courting relationship is at some point converted into an actual courtship. I have no observational data on this eventuality, but I would guess that some special signals or statements would be required to indicate the transition. On the other hand, a courtship may at some point be converted into a quasi courtship. This would be indicated by the addition of the qualifiers. But, by and large, in a quasi-courting sequence, the qualifiers are enacted from the beginning.

The occurrence of any deviance highlights and clarifies the lawfulness of the normal structure. For instance, an interactant may perform courting when it is inappropriate to do so, or perform overly intense quasi courting as a means of forcing another participant to withdraw from the relationship. Or the qualifiers may be deliberately kept unclear in order to produce an ambiguity between courtship and quasi courtship, thereby confusing the other participant or forcing him to declare his intentions.

Courtship displays are used, of course, in courtship, marriage, and certain other institutional procedures. Stylistic variants of these behaviors are employed in the theater and in modeling. Other stylized variants are used in prostitution and still others in homosexual relationships.

But most institutional procedures prohibit the use of full courtship reciprocals. Instead they employ quasi-courting variants. These presumably foster and maintain reciprocality during the transaction and from transaction to transaction in the institution. A particular quasi-courting variant, called rapport, is fostered and employed in psychotherapy. Another variant, flirting, is often used at social engagements for a variety of purposes. But some from of quasi courting is generally used in institutional proceedings of any duration in which men and women are both engaged.

References

Bales, R. F. *Interaction Process Analysis*. Cambridge, Mass.: Addison-Wesley, 1950.

Bateson, G. "The Message 'This is Play'." In Schaffner, B. (ed.) *Group Processes*, vol. II. New York: Macy, 1955.

Birdwhistell, R. L. "An Approach to Communication," *Family Process* I: 194–201 (Sept.) 1963.

Colby, K. M. *An Introduction to Psychoanalytic Research*. New York: Basic Books, 1960.

Condon, W. S., and Ogston, W. D. "Sound Film Analysis of Normal and Pathological Behavior Patterns," *J. Nerv. and Men. Dis.* 143: 338–347, 1966.

Kendon, A. "Some Functions of Gaze Direction in Social Interaction," *Acta Psychologica* 26:22–63, 1965.

———, *Personal Communication*, 1968.

Menninger, K. *Theory of Psychoanalytic Technique*. New York: Basic Books, 1958.

Scheflen, A. E. "Human Communication: Behavioral Programs and Their Integration in Interaction," *Amer. Behav. Scientist* 13: 44–55 (Jan.) 1970.

Action Steps: Applications

1. Meet in groups of eight to ten students. Have each group divided into two teams to play the game, "Charades." After each team has made a presentation, have each group reflect back to identify behaviors that were iconic, indexical, and symbolic.

2. Have each team make another presentation without using any hand or finger movement. Note difficulties involved and substitute behaviors employed.

3. Have each team make a third presentation in which only *iconic* signs are used. Note the difficulties encountered and possible efficiency achieved.

4. Outside class arrange an appointment with a student from another culture; agree that both of you will, for at least fifteen minutes, interact with each other using only nonverbal communication. To get started, you may verbally agree upon a topic such as sports or entertainment. After your period of nonverbal interaction, verbally discuss possible cultural similarities and differences in use of nonverbal signs.

5. Observe and compare perceptions of the nonverbal communication of selected groups of people. Note the use of eye contact, posture, facial expression, personal appearance, and gestures. Share reports of your observations with the class. Be sure to observe at least two different types of groups—for example, religious groups, business or professional, learning, entertainment (e.g., music groups), etc.

Chapter 6
Adapting Our Interpersonal Environment

W HEN WE MEET a person in our daily routine, we may decide to stop for a chat or a conference. Together we look at our surroundings and go into an ecological huddle; we look for a place suited to our purpose. We note or ask about their commitments to others; do they belong to a group or an organization that limits our chance to talk at this time? This questioning goes on without our thinking much about it because, as adults, we are accustomed to meeting limitations on our opportunities to talk with others; we have developed habits of accommodating our physical and social environments.

Our aim in this chapter is not to recount the obvious, nor is it to provide a catalog of environmental factors that may inhibit or promote interpersonal communication. Our purpose is to identify factors that most severely influence the communication process, calling attention primarily to those which, because they are so obvious or commonplace, may have been overlooked or given too little consideration. Our objective is to assist in the understanding of the process of interpersonal communication, by suggesting ways environmental problems may be handled with greater effectiveness.

Using Rooms, Chairs, Tables, and Time

Every teenager knows that there is a great deal of difference between being in one place or another with a boyfriend or a girlfriend. Walking home from school is one thing; "driving around" is another. Our interest is not to explore the sexual overtones of meeting in a secluded spot, but to illustrate, in an introductory way, the significance of "places" on interpersonal communication. Certain physical environmental factors obviously influence the process of interpersonal communication. Let's suppose you wish to "talk things over" with another person. The question arises: How can you best utilize the available environment? How can conditions be selected or arranged to serve your purpose best?

ROOMS AND PLACES

Different places have ways of giving us messages. Some places seem to say, "Sit down and enjoy yourself; talk things over if you wish." Other places are cold, formal, or barren, and contribute to difficulties in overcoming psychological distance between people. In many ways the physical elements influence the behaviors that can be expected in such a place.

When we wish to talk things over privately with another person, the size and shape of the room selected (or available) exercises significant influence. A large lobby in a hotel or dormitory suggests that strangers may meet, pass by each other, perhaps smile, or nod, but in general exchange only minimum courtesies—what Erving Goffman calls "civil inattention."[1] Here acquaintances may pause briefly for a greeting; friends may greet and show each other calm affection. Lovers warmly embraced will appear out of place.

Interpersonal face-to-face interaction is facilitated by a small room, one no larger than necessary to provide a feeling of comfort for a few persons. A larger room tends to suggest that other persons foreign to this particular grouping might enter and diminish the atmosphere of privacy. To some extent we tend to feel that if there are only two or three of us we should not "tie up" the amount of space afforded by a large room.[2] Mark Knapp (Reading 6.2) has called special attention to the significance of room furnishings, carpeting, and draperies.[3] There is some evidence that interpersonal communication is facilitated in rooms thought to be attractive; pleasing colors can enhance the effect of social interaction. For interpersonal communication we should seek a room that is not ordinarily used for some specific purpose such as table tennis or laboratory experiments. The usual behavior that occurs in such places tends to provide an atmosphere that distracts our attention, making it more difficult for us to note carefully both the verbal and nonverbal cues necessary for us to consider as we try to understand each other on something more than a surface level.[4]

By their very nature, rooms and places tend to imply a social contract between all persons who enter, a contract regarding the kind of interaction that is supposed to take place within their walls. Thus, semipublic (or semiprivate) places, such as cocktail lounges, have a special tone or atmosphere that suggests you may talk to your friends. But there is also a kind of piquant loneliness felt, such that if you have no friends, or none are present, you may talk to others who are similarly lonely. In such a place some persons are clearly observing the surface rule—talking with friends; others are more or less involved in hopes, fears, and actions that go beyond the surface rule—looking for a stranger with whom to be friendly.[5]

In our society restaurants provide a dilemma as a place for interpersonal communication. On the one hand, they are readily available and provide a minimal opportunity for interaction. On the other hand, there are interminable distractions—ordering food or drink; interruptions by waitresses or other

---

[1] E. Goffman, *Relations in Public* (New York: Basic Books, 1971), p. 209.

[2] Cf. A. H. Maslow and N. L. Mintz, "Effects of Esthetic Surroundings: I. Initial Effects of Three Esthetic Conditions Upon Perceiving 'Energy' and 'Well-Being' in Faces," *Journal of Psychology*, 41 (1956): 247–254.

[3] M. Knapp, "The Effects of Environment and Space on Human Communication," *Nonverbal Communication and Human Interaction* (New York: Holt, Rinehart and Winston, 1972), pp. 25–62.

[4] B. H. Westley and M. S. McLean emphasize the use of all sense modalities in "A Conceptual Model for Communications Research," *Journalism Quarterly*, 34 (1957): 31.

[5] Cf. Goffman, *Relations in Public*, pp. 106–107.

people passing by; unwanted noises from the kitchen, busboys, and recorded music. Despite these limitations, the availability of cafes or restaurants tempts us to use them for serious interpersonal talk; frequently, we find we are only partly able to accomplish this purpose.[6]

One of the advantages of being in the "management" class of persons working in many organizations is that for such people interpersonal communication is allowed, sometimes even encouraged. If an assistant manager is seen chatting with an employee, it is supposed that he or she is doing part of his/her job—"getting to know" the person, perceiving the employee's problems, gaining insight into his/her needs. An important status line in industry can be drawn on the basis of who may be allowed to "talk things over with others" or told to "get back to work." Persons who may be told to "get to work" may provide an outward show of activity while surreptitiously attempting to chat with other employees.[7]

In most rooms or places in our culture, interpersonal communication possibilities are institutionalized, that is, regulated and understood as conventional for that spot. Even if persons present are not quite aware of these conventions, they will sense something is amiss if norms are violated. For optimal use of the process of interpersonal communication, one should find a place where face-to-face encounters without interruptions or distractions are common occurrences. Perhaps the best place of all is the living room in your home. For a college student away from home, a dormitory room may have to suffice. The fact that you sleep there may make it an awkward place. However, the dormitory lobby is equally unsatisfactory in other ways. It is probably true that part of the loneliness expressed by many college students is caused by the lack of a place for personal, private communication that does not have overtones of other activities. They generally have no equivalent of a living room.[8]

There is a vast amount of literature on the alienation of young people, particularly college students who sometimes have a sense of loneliness and separation.[9] Little information is available about the impact on students of the unavailability of an equivalent of their living room at home—a place that offers a sense of appropriateness for interpersonal communication of a private or semipersonal nature. Their usual available spaces are a dormitory lobby or their sleeping-study room. Of even less attraction are semipublic places such as cafeterias, empty classrooms, or lawns.

Small wonder that college students away from home are lonely; they have no home, no place suitable for interpersonal communication. Lobbies, as we suggested earlier, are characterized by the interruptions of others walking by, coupled with a sense of a lack of privacy. If something important and personal is said in a low voice so that others nearby can't hear, the simple act of leaning forward to hear produces a feeling that others will interpret this closeness as

[6] Cf. E. Goffman, *Behavior in Public Places* (New York: Free Press, 1963), p. 52.

[7] Ibid., p. 56.

[8] See N. Sanford, *Self and Society* (New York: Atherton, 1966), pp. 48–51.

[9] See, for example, K. Keniston, *Young Radicals: Notes on Committed Youth* (New York: Harcourt Brace Jovanovich, 1968); see also G. B. Blaine, Jr., et al., *Emotional Problems of the Student* (Garden City, N.Y.: Doubleday, 1966).

out-of-place intimacy, inappropriate behavior in a semipublic lobby. And, as in some colleges, even if boys may invite girls to their rooms (or vice versa), there are often confusing overtones of sexual involvement. Even if such involvement is not objectionable, these rooms are bedrooms, with the suggestion present of very private behavior—sleeping, changing clothes, private body functions and odors. This is hardly the place to encourage mere acquaintances to test the ground for friendship; too much is implied regarding a highly personal relationship. The two available alternatives—lobby or sleeping quarters—tend to provide either too little or too much for the start of an informal friendship. In part, it appears to us that many college students are lonely because they have no place to overcome their loneliness. Why don't more dormitories have sitting rooms for students to use?

CHAIRS AND TABLES

Time after time we have walked by the open door of a college classroom, barren except for its disordered array of empty chairs with their little sidesaddle, armrest "desks"—a room empty save for two students, with chairs partly facing each other, each student trying to engage in interpersonal communication. With great concentration on each other they may be able to overcome the negative influence of the bare walls, empty chairs, and the feeling of the ambiguous presence of absent, unknown others. To some extent they may overcome the awkwardness of desk-chairs that suggest they should "take notes" on whatever is said.

Whether we are sharply aware of it or not, chairs and tables have a significant influence on the way we interact in face-to-face communication. Chairs have an effect in two respects: physical comfort and our psychological relationship to each other. In a similar fashion tables (including desks) provide physical convenience as well as psychological distance between us.

Chairs should be arranged in such a way that they encourage interpersonal communication, if that is the goal desired. They should be placed so that participants face each other and can easily see each other's eyes. An interpersonal encounter starts with the eyes. The eyes provide information to the important first impression and can indicate answers to such questions as, "Does he/she really want to talk to me?" "Is his/her intention friendly, serious, sincere?" In his history of frontier life, R. F. Adams provides an amusing illustration of this point:

> When nearin' 'nother person on a trail, etiquette required that a man approach within speakin' distance and pass a word before changin' his course unless, for a very good reason, he was justified in such a change. The West held that every person had the right to find out the intent of all other persons 'bout him. . . . If the stranger lit to cool his saddle, the other didn't stay mounted while carryin' on a conversation. The polite thing to do was dismount and talk with 'im face to face. This showed one wasn't lookin' for any advantage over the other.[10]

[10] R. F. Adams, *The Old-Time Cowhand* (New York: Macmillan, 1961), pp. 57–58.

There is a kind of "I-am-willing-to-talk-with-you" ritual that people use to start interpersonal communication. First they come into each other's presence. As they approach, their eyes are scanning the territory—the room, chairs, tables, and places where they may easily talk. When within a few paces of each other, their eyes connect. In the first flash of eye contact they recognize each other and *show this recognition*. Goffman, perhaps modern sociology's best-known "people watcher," thus describes the ritual for starting interaction:

> An encounter is initiated by someone making an opening move, typically by means of a special expression of the eyes. . . . The engagement properly begins when this overture is acknowledged by the other, who signals back with his eyes, voice or stance that he has placed himself at the disposal of the other for purposes of eye-to-eye activity. . . . There is a tendency for the initial move and responding "clearance" sign to be exchanged almost simultaneously.[11]

In another of his writings, Goffman suggests that "when one individual meets the eyes of another he can indicate a position (attitude), perceive the other's response to his taking this position, and show his own response to the other's response all in a brief moment."[12]

The importance of eye contact in interpersonal communication can hardly be overemphasized. It is so significant that if held slightly too long at a time, it can be taken as an intrusion on another's privacy. Staring or glaring can easily be taken as an offense.[13] It is somewhat amusing to observe that topless waitresses seldom look their customers in the eye; in close serving, clients frequently show courtesy by keeping their eyes focused elsewhere, mainly on other clients.[14] Additional evidence of the importance of eye contact for personal interaction may be obtained by observing those who are alienated from those around them, particularly persons who are mentally ill; they commonly express their alienation through avoidance of eye contact.[15]

For interpersonal communication to become optimal, the eye contact used at the beginning of the relationship must be maintained. The persons involved must have full access to each other's feelings as expressed in visual contact. Studies have shown that the arrangement of chairs in a discussion circle influences interaction; persons adjacent to each other tend not to address each other except for side comments, but tend to direct their remarks to persons whose eyes they can see.[16] In any interpersonal encounter the arrangement of chairs can have either a damaging or an enhancing effect. Part of the popularity of cocktail lounges in airline terminals may be attributed to the circular arrangement of chairs around tables as compared to the rows of chairs formally arranged in terminal waiting rooms. Such formal arrangement discourages interpersonal communication and heightens the traveler's isolated sense of loneliness—people, real people, are so near, yet so far.

[11] Goffman, *Behavior in Public Places*, pp. 91–92.
[12] Goffman, *Relations in Public*, p. 18 (fn.).
[13] For a detailed treatment of such effect, see ibid., pp. 45–46, 59–60, 126–132.
[14] Ibid., p. 45.
[15] See, for example, M. D. Riemer, "The Averted Gaze," *Psychiatric Quarterly*, 23 (1949): 108–115.
[16] For a report of experimental evidence, see B. Steinzer, "The Spatial Factor in Face-to-Face Discussion Groups," *Journal of Abnormal and Social Psychology*, 45 (1950): 552–555.

The *distance* between participants in interpersonal communication is also of special significance. Perhaps there is no specific optimal distance; it will likely vary with the participants' attitudes toward each other. If convenient or appropriate, they may move their chairs close enough to feel comfortable while talking with each other; the distance thus chosen may define their perceptions of their relationship, a point to be considered in more detail later. If the available chairs are not easily moved, the distance thus dictated will have subtle influence on the participants' interaction.

In their article (Reading 6.1), Edward and Mildred Hall have carefully observed the distances commonly used for different kinds of human interaction.[17] The Halls divide interaction space into four distances: intimate, personal, social, and public.[18]

Intimate distance, close phase (touching) is the distance for lovemaking, comforting, and protecting (also struggling or fighting). Intimate distance, far phase (6 to 18 inches) is too close for interaction unless the participants have an intimate relationship; it serves well for those who wish to comfort each other or get to know each other well.[19] It is thus limited to the interpersonal communication of those who wish to become psychologically close—at least for most middle-class Americans.[20]

Personal distance ranges from 18 to 30 inches (close phase) and from 30 to 48 inches (far phase). These distances are used for interpersonal communication by persons who are friendly and favorably inclined toward each other.[21] The far-phase limit (48 inches) is the distance used to keep another person "at arm's length away" and marks the distance at which the dominance of one person by another is less effective. Those who are not afraid of being dominated may move within this range; those who are afraid will not.[22]

Social distance, according to the Halls, ranges from 4 to 7 feet (close phase) and 7 to 12 feet (far phase). Close phase is the distance at which *interpersonal* interaction generally occurs. It is commonly used by acquaintances attending an informal social gathering and is the usual distance maintained by those who work together at impersonal tasks—executives and their secretaries, teachers and their students. Social distance, far phase, is ordinarily used for formal business or social interactions.[23] Incidentally, at this distance two people may work separately at different tables or desks.

Public distances, close phase (12 to 25 feet) and far phase (over 25 feet), are used on formal occasions involving public ceremonies. Public figures— kings, presidents, governors, celebrities—may occasionally maintain this non-involvement distance.[24] Conversely, politicians try to move in closer when seeking votes.

[17] See also E. T. Hall, *The Hidden Dimension* (Garden City, N.Y.: Doubleday, 1969), pp. 113–129.
[18] E. Hall and M. Hall, "The Sounds of Silence," *Playboy*, 18, No. 6 (June 1971).
[19] Hall, *Hidden Dimension*, pp. 117–118.
[20] Hall's studies deal primarily with middle-class subjects living in the northeastern United States. He suggests that great care should be exercised in any attempt to generalize his findings to other geographic areas or ethnic groups.
[21] Hall, *Hidden Dimension*, pp. 119–120.
[22] Ibid., p. 121.
[23] Ibid., pp. 121–123.
[24] Ibid., pp. 123–124.

Intimate Distance.

Hall's analysis of interaction distances provides special insight into the subtle influence of chairs and tables, particularly desks, on interpersonal communication. The uses of personal and social distances tend to vary from culture to culture, to some extent in a rather arbitrary fashion.[25] However, tables and desks almost universally provide distances that separate people psychologically and interfere with personal interaction. People ordinarily thought to be important usually have desks that keep visitors at the far phase (7 to 12 feet) of social distance. People talking across desks in modest offices are 9 to 10 feet apart. At this distance feedback from each other's eyes is significantly lost.[26] Not lost, however, is the impression of social distance separating the participants—a feeling that closeness, personal involvement, and a sense of interpersonal solidarity might be achieved only with special effort, if at all.[27]

Some chairs and tables (or desks) are personal territories, staked and claimed by an individual for his personal use. They may be the legal property

[25] See ibid., pp. 128–164. See also R. Birdwhistell's comments cited in a symposium reported in B. Schaffner, ed., *Group Processes* (New York: J. Macy, 1959), pp. 184–185.

[26] Hall, *Hidden Dimension*, p. 122.

[27] Cf. A. G. White, "The Patient Sits Down: A Clinical Note," *Psychosomatic Medicine*, 15 (1953): 256–257. See also K. B. Little, "Personal Space," *Journal of Experimental and Social Psychology*, 1 (1965): 237–247.

of a company or institution; but they are personal territory from 8:00 A.M. to 5:00 P.M., assigned to an individual for his/her use. If an acquaintance drops by, even an old personal friend, across that desk that person is a "visitor" no matter how warmly he/she is greeted. The flow of interpersonal communication is subtly influenced by such environmental conditions.[28] A university dean of our acquaintance comes out from behind his desk to meet his visitors and talks with them in a "conference corner" equipped with easy chairs, coffee table, side tables, and rug. Such practices are not unknown in industrial circles.[29]

TIME

Perhaps you have not thought of time as part of your physical environment. In our culture, however, we are quite accustomed to regulating our behavior in terms of the relative amounts of time required. For example, work crews avoid starting a new task in the late afternoon if it cannot be completed that day. We tend to schedule our day's events with full attention to the time available and the time required. Similarly, our use of the process of interpersonal communication is influenced by our sense of available time.

An event such as a wedding, a senior prom, or a celebration, such as a retirement dinner, may serve a special purpose and involve a ritualistic use of language; even so, such an occasion is essentially a "time-person-space" event, entailing special consideration of *when* certain persons are brought together to use designated space in a certain way. It will not serve your purposes for achieving interpersonal communication to violate the ritual connected with a special occasion; in effect, the purposes of the occasion will take precedence over your purposes of getting to know someone better. For example, smiling and exchanging confidences in church during a wedding ceremony will usually defeat such purposes. We could review the protocol for various occasions in this context, but that does not suit our purposes of describing the process of interpersonal communication. Many occasions involve primarily public communication, and our point is that violating the protocol involved is usually to misuse the interpersonal communication mode.

We tend to "tell time"—note its passage—in three ways: by use of clocks; by events that transpire (e.g., before or after lunch); and by the way people act. In an interpersonal encounter, the time available is frequently indicated by the way a person behaves. If he feels his time is being used for interaction that he doesn't desire, his hands may clasp and unclasp; his feet and legs move in subtle, inhibited "traveling" motions; his eyes wander to "not here, out there" distances; and his voice diminishes in interest-value cues. In nonverbal ways we are being told to move along. It is not by accident that a well-known beer advertisement proclaims that "If you've got the time, we've got the beer." Persons interested in initiating interpersonal communication might well take a lesson from this example.

The influence of the passing or availability of time on interpersonal

[28] Cf. Goffman, *Relations in Public*, pp. 28–32.
[29] Cf. Knapp, *Nonverbal Communication and Human Interaction*, pp. 25–36.

communication has not received great attention from scholars. We are aware of the obvious, but little more. We are aware of the importance of talking with people "in time," meeting people "on time," and being careful of the ways we "spend our time." But the full impact of these environmental factors on interpersonal communication has not been carefully studied. On the surface it appears that their influence is considerable.

When we wish to engage a person in conversation, there is a kind of "access ritual" used to establish that each is open to the other for at least a brief interchange.[30] Typically, the two persons face each other and their eyes lock for a brief moment. Usually, there is a smile of recognition, perhaps their eyes glisten or crinkle at the corners, and mutual pleasure is shown in some way. As they continue to show mutual willingness to talk with each other, a kind of "time-person-space" contract is subtly understood. If either "lacks the time at this time," a different agreement is necessary if further interaction is to take place.

The passage of time is viewed differently by various people. To some extent the way one views the use of time appears to be an arbitrary, individual matter. Even so the influence of time on human interaction deserves much more attention by scholars.

The practical point to be made on the basis of our observations is that when you desire to talk to someone in particular, you may easily overlook the fact that the other person may be viewing his/her time quite differently from the way you are viewing yours. He/she may wish to talk with you but have other commitments and needs for his time right now. Our recommendation is that as soon as the access ritual has taken place, you might well avoid misunderstanding and needless feelings of personal neglect or rejection if you courteously ask, "Are you sure you have time to talk with me? Perhaps there would be a better time for you?"

Adapting to Groups, Organizations, and Cultures

There are both things and people in the environment. Although other people may not always be present, much of our interpersonal communication takes place in the presence of persons other than the one or more with whom we are talking. These may be persons who can *overhear* what is said. Or, they may be members of a group, and for the most part we are actually talking with all of these group members. The presence of others, either those who overhear us or other members of a group with whom we interact, can have significant influence on our behavior in interpersonal communication.

Almost all our interpersonal communication is influenced to some extent by the fact that we and others are members of various organizations. When two people belonging to the same organization attempt to interact, the norms and

[30] Cf. Goffman, *Relations in Public*, pp. 73–90.

regulations of that organization have impact on the behavior of both people. The same is essentially true regarding the influence of a culture, although such influence may be relatively unnoticeable until we meet someone from a culture different from our own.

In this section we will discuss the influence of those who overhear as well as the factor of membership in groups, organizations, and cultures. Our objective is not to review the nature of groups, organizations, or different cultures, but to focus on primary ways they influence our interpersonal communication.

IN THE PRESENCE OF OTHERS

Interpersonal communication is a clear-cut enough form of behavior that a third person who is present must be either within the interaction or outside it.[31] Imagine yourself with a close friend, lying on a beach, gazing at the water, and intermittently chatting with one another. A kind of bond of mutual trust and obligation has been established. You have laid yourself open to confidences and special privileges. In so doing you have made yourself available, to some extent, to special requests or expectations. In addition, although you may feel quite secure that they won't occur, there is the possibility—though faint—of demands, threats, insults, and false information. In this kind of situation your openness or availability will change considerably if an unknown person sits down near you and your friend. Perhaps you will feel like leaving the beach, hoping your friend will go along. Such feelings will likely be subtly conveyed to your friend even though not verbalized; in turn, however, he/she may not understand their source and suspect that you do not enjoy his/her conversation. In this way your interpersonal communication can be influenced by the presence of others not participating; unless such influences are well understood by both you and your friend, miscommunication and misunderstanding may occur.

The primary effect of the presence of persons who may *overhear* interpersonal communication is inhibition of openness and personal disclosures necessary for building friendship. We may conduct business in the presence of others as long as it does not involve personal affairs. We may exchange greetings and impersonal information if it does not impinge on our private feelings. In a word, we may be courteous but not personal when persons are present with whom we cannot trust our personal views or feelings. The usual resolution to this problem, of course, is to find a "private space," a room where nonparticipants in the interpersonal exchange can be excluded. Walls, even though sometimes thin as paper, are a social convention that provide a necessary feeling of privacy and are felt by most of us to exclude fairly effectively the influence of those who may be on the other side.[32]

There is a considerable body of experimental research to show that we

---

[31] Cf. Goffman, *Behavior in Public Places*, pp. 102–104.

[32] Goffman suggests that "the work walls do, they do in part because they are honored or socially recognized as communication barriers," even though they may not actually deter others from overhearing our conversations. See Goffman, *Behavior in Public Places*, pp. 152–153.

tend to behave differently in the presence of even passive other persons.[33] Their presence tends to *impair* the learning of new material[34] but *facilitates* the performance of well-learned patterns of behavior.[35] In the presence of passive others, our motivation to do well or "look good" is increased[36] and the exposure of our ideas or feelings that might make us "look bad" is inhibited.[37] In addition, there is significant evidence that behavior which is ordinary or habitual is much more likely to occur in the presence of others than is behavior that we use only rarely or on special occasions.[38] Thus we may quite reasonably conclude that making new friendships, exchanging information about our private thoughts, and, in general, opening up ourselves to others will likely be inhibited if we attempt interpersonal communication in the presence of persons not included in the interaction.

IN AND OUT OF GROUPS

Probably no phase of human behavior has received more study and careful research than human interaction in small groups.[39] Literally thousands of experimental studies have been reported[40] and their results compared.[41] Our purpose will not be to review, however briefly, the dynamics of group interaction. Rather, we will focus on those particular ways interpersonal communication is influenced by groups of which a participant is a member. In taking this focus, we are viewing such groups as part of the social environment. Actually, a group's influence may be felt by persons engaging in interpersonal communication even though other members of the group are not present, that is, if one or both of the participants are members of the group.

Perhaps before progressing further we should give a brief definition of "group" as we are using it in this section. The most common definition of "small group" used today in research studies and sociopsychological literature involves two factors: (1) a small number of persons in interdependent role relations who (2) have a set of values or norms that regulate behavior of members in matters of concern to each other.[42] Thus, in a group, as we are using the term, each member is aware of each other member's belonging to the

[33] For a review of this literature, see R. B. Zajonc, *Social Psychology: An Experimental Approach* (Belmont, Calif.: Wadsworth, 1966), pp. 10–15.

[34] J. Pessin, "The Comparative Effects of Social and Mechanical Stimulation on Memorizing," *American Journal of Psychology*, 45 (1933): 263–270.

[35] B. O. Bergum and D. J. Lehr, "Effects of Authoritarianism on Vigilance Performance," *Journal of Applied Psychology*, 47 (1963): 75–77.

[36] See R. B. Zajonc, "Social Facilitation," *Science*, 149 (1965): 269–274.

[37] Cf. D. Seidman et al., "Influence of a Partner on Tolerance for Self-Administered Electric Shock," *Journal of Abnormal and Social Psychology*, 54 (1957): 210–212.

[38] See K. W. Spence, *Behavior Theory and Conditioning* (New Haven, Conn.: Yale University Press, 1956).

[39] See, for example, D. Cartwright and A. Zander (eds.), *Group Dynamics*, 3rd ed. (New York: Harper & Row, 1968).

[40] For a review, see J. E. McGrath and I. Altman, *Small Group Research* (New York: Holt, Rinehart and Winston, 1966).

[41] For a critical synthesis of this research , see G. Lindzey and E. Aronson (eds.), *The Handbook of Social Psychology*, Vol. 4 (Reading, Mass.: Addison-Wesley, 1969), especially pp. 1–283.

[42] Cf. K. Giffin, "The Study of Speech Communication in Small-Group Research," in J. Akin et al., (eds.), *Language Behavior* (The Hague: Mouton Press, 1970), pp. 138–162.

group and is concerned to some extent about his/her own behavior as it affects the group.

There are two major factors of group membership that influence the interpersonal communication of members: (1) *conformity* to the norms of behavior established by and for the group members and (2) *task or goal commitments* made by the group. These factors tend to influence the interpersonal communication of a group member even if he/she is talking with another person who is not a member of that group.

On the other hand, when a person is engaged in discussion with members of his/her own group, these two factors—conformity and goal commitments—exercise even greater influence. In such a circumstance, a third factor also has considerable influence on interpersonal communication: the size of the group, that is, the number of group members present. These three factors will be discussed briefly in this section—with due apology to the thousands of researchers who have devoted extensive time and energy to many other variables shown to have some relevance. We have made this selection in recognition of the time available to our readers; for those who have greater need or interest, we have prepared another book devoted to a detailed discussion of group interaction.[43]

Two other variables exercise great influence on the interpersonal behavior of members of groups: (1) the *power* of one person over another and (2) *personal attitudes* involving affection or hostility. However, these two variables are not in any sense uniquely a property of group interaction; they are the basic dimensions of any interpersonal relationship and may be easily observed in operation as two persons engage each other in interaction. They are a significant influence on the way a wife interacts with her husband or a child with his/her parent. They are, in fact, those primary variables that determine the specific nature of any interpersonal relationship. There is a vast amount of literature on these two factors in reported studies of small groups. *Power* or influence is frequently discussed as a function of difference in social status, and personal attitudes are often discussed under the rubric of *group cohesiveness*, sometimes that of *interpersonal attraction*. Because these two variables are not unique properties of groups and are pervasive in all interpersonal communication, we have chosen to discuss them in Chapter 7, "Developing Relationships."

Long ago, casual observation suggested that "birds of a feather flock together." However, the degree to which people *change* to be like others with whom they associate was only conjectured. In 1952 Solomon Asch experimentally derived solid evidence for one of the most disturbing of all facets of human behavior.[44] In Asch's primary experiment, college students were asked to look at a black line on a white card, then look at three other lines, and then pick the one of the three that was the *same length* as the first one shown. *One* of the "comparison" lines was *exactly the same length* as the original one. All lines were held in plain sight of the subjects. However, when the subject entered the experimental room several other students were present, and he was told that all present were there to perform the same task. Unknown to the "naive"

[43] B. R. Patton and K. Giffin, *Decision-Making Group Interaction* (New York: Harper & Row, 1978).
[44] S. Asch, *Social Psychology* (Englewood Cliffs, N.J.: Prentice-Hall, 1952).

subject, the other students present were Asch's confederates, "planted" there to lead the subject astray. The experimental session consisted of 12 trials. In each trial the confederates were asked to make their judgments *first*; they unanimously selected an incorrect line, erroneous by as much as 1¾ inches. All choices were given orally, *and after the others had individually voiced the unanimous but incorrect opinion*, the naive subject gave his.

Asch's results were astounding. Control subjects working alone achieved about 93 percent accuracy on the same-line judgments. However, naive subjects exposed to erroneous social influence achieved only 67 percent accuracy, a drop of 26 percent. In further experiments, confederates were instructed to give answers incorrect by as much as 7 inches, the original line being 10 inches and the confederates' "choice" being only 3 inches. The results were almost the same. Control subjects were 98 percent accurate. Naive subjects were 72 percent accurate—again a drop of 26 percent! Asch's comment was rather poignant:

> We are appalled by the spectacle of the pitiful women of the Middle Ages who, accused of being witches by authorities they never questioned, confessed in bewilderment to unthought-of-crimes. But in lesser measure we have each faced denials of our own feelings or needs.[45]

The work of Asch and others confirms the principle of social conformity in dramatic ways. The essential principle is that subjects agree to, or go along with, the conclusions of others—even decide to act upon them—even when such decisions are contrary to evidence staring them in the face. There is really no way of estimating how many people conform to others' decisions that are contrary to their own beliefs and values if no clear evidence is available. Additional experiments have shown that conformity tends to increase as the topic for judgment becomes more difficult.[46] As few as three confederates giving unanimous but incorrect answers can produce this effect. And experimental evidence is in no way limited to American college sophomores. Studies have shown that American military officers "yielded" (conformed to incorrect conclusions of experiment confederates) 37 percent; engineers, writers, scientists, and architects did about the same.[47] Norwegian students "yielded" 50 to 75 percent, and French students between 34 and 59 percent.[48]

It should be pointed out that in these studies the "groups" formed were not bound together by group norms or very much psychological cohesiveness; they were strangers prior to the experiments. Also, no attempts were made to use personal power or influence; no "leaders" or status persons were identified or chosen. Under conditions where group norms, cohesiveness, status persons, or leaders are involved, we could expect even greater degrees of social

[45] Ibid., pp. 450–451.
[46] P. Suppes and M. Schlag-Rey, "Analysis of Social Conformity in Terms of Generalized Conditioning Models," in J. Criswell, H. Solomon, and P. Suppes (eds.), *Mathematical Methods in Small Group Processes* (Stanford, Calif.: Stanford University Press, 1962), pp. 334–361.
[47] R. S. Crutchfield, "The Measurement of Individual Conformity to Group Opinion Among Officer Personnel," *Research Bulletin* (Berkeley: Institute of Personality Assessment and Research, University of California). See also R. S. Crutchfield, "Conformity and Character," *American Psychologist*, 10 (1955): 191–198.
[48] S. Milgram, "Nationality and Conformity," *Scientific American*, 205 (1961): 45–51.

What conformity pressures are evident?

conformity on the part of the group members. Some support for this conclusion is given in experiments where the experimenter (a sort of leader or status person) also made his/her choice known; when he/she chose the erroneous stimulus picked by his/her confederates, the naive subjects yielded about 60 percent![49] Studies of leadership and status influence support this line of reasoning.

Conforming to the behavior of other members of a group is not necessarily undesirable, even when such behavior violates evidence in front of you; when people start to rush out of a building, you may not see the fire but you may save your life if you leave rather than decide they are crazy. "Blind conformity"

[49] E. E. Jones, H. H. Wells, and R. Torrey, "Some Effects of Feedback from the Experimenter on Conformity Behavior," *Journal of Abnormal and Social Psychology*, 57 (1958): 207–213.

can sometimes have survival value, and its practice can easily be observed in the animal world: One dog barks at a stranger in the dark, and dogs blocks away pick up the cry. However, in many cases *blind* conformity to group norms can be less than a proper use of one's intelligence.

If a collection of people can be characterized as a group, certain norms and conformity behavior may be identified. The concept of group norms was derived from long usage in sociopsychological studies. It identifies the ways members of a group behave and ways that are thought by them to be proper. Norms may be viewed as a set of directions bestowed by the group on all its members concerning their behavior. Through interaction, members find out the group's standards. For example, a young woman elected by her sorority as a representative to the student council may find that such membership is important because it improves her status and provides opportunities for influence. To be an effective member of the student council, she must first determine what is expected of members. This natural "period of adjustment" accounts for the fact that freshmen in the U.S. Senate are seen, but rarely heard.[50]

The relationship between norms and communication has received considerable attention by students of group communication. Members who do not conform to group norms are initially the targets of greater amounts of communication, usually of an instructional nature; if they continue as nonconformists, the tendency is to give them rejecting communication and eventually little or none. The degree of rejection is a direct function of the cohesiveness of the group and the degree to which the nonconformist is deviant.[51] These results do not hold for just any collection of people, but for groups where belonging is attractive to its members. In some tightly knit, highly cohesive groups, a nonconformist is almost immediately rejected upon detection, in which case communication is both minimal and rejective.

Conformity to group norms is in actuality a yielding to group pressures, explicit or implicit. Conflict arises when the individual tends to react or respond in one way, but group pressures force him in another direction. Thus, when an individual has to express his opinion in a group on a particular issue and he knows his personal conviction is at variance with group attitudes, he may choose either to remain independent of group consensus and possibly suffer the consequences or to conform.

Conformity to the norms of a group by one of its members tends to extend beyond the boundaries of the group; it will influence his/her interpersonal communicative behaviors toward persons who are not group members. It can affect the way one perceives others; it can influence how one talks as well as what one says. In a recent issue of a popular magazine, there was a cartoon of a man talking to his wife, who entered politics. Her husband did not oppose her becoming a candidate, but he was appalled that she would enter the race against "a brother Elk."

[50] For a detailed review of these studies, see B. E. Collins and B. H. Raven, "Group Structure: Attraction, Coalitions, Communication, and Power," in Lindzey and Aronson, pp. 102–205; see especially pp. 168–184.

[51] S. Schacter, "Deviation, Rejection, and Communication," *Journal of Abnormal and Social Psychology*, 46 (1951): 190–207.

INTERPERSONAL COMMUNICATION IN ACTION

When a collection of people systematically gathers and forms a group, there is usually some common goal or task to be accomplished. If communication is poor within the group, there is no effective way of working toward the agreed-on task. A person will work for a group goal only if he/she believes that its achievement will satisfy his/her own wants. Individual studies of the relationship between worker morale and productivity emphasize the importance of the acceptance of group goals and the *perceived relevance* of group goals to individual wants. The members must, in other words, see group goals as personally satisfying. The group is constantly challenged by problems of task or goal commitment. The feeling that members have toward their goals will not only affect their interaction with each other, but also their interpersonal communication with persons outside the group.

Roles or role functions are commonly conceptualized in the literature on small groups as a set of behaviors related functionally to the goals of the group. Research on experimental groups has demonstrated that roles tend to appear in a relatively short time, require different but specifiable sets of behaviors, and have performance criteria set up by the group members. Factor analysis of a large number of alleged role functions has revealed three major factors:

1. *Individual prominence*—i.e., giving and receiving a higher amount of communication;
2. *Aiding group goal attainment*—i.e., presentation of "best ideas" and general suggestions for guidance of group thinking; and
3. *Sociability*—i.e., the characteristics of being well liked by members and demonstrating emotional stability.[52]

The relationship of these roles to communication is quite clear. The role of "prominent individual" correlates with the amount of talking and being talked to by other group members.[53] The amount of verbalization is well correlated with best ideas and guidance. However, individuals who achieve the sociability role (i.e., those who are well liked) generally do not give or receive as much verbalization and ordinarily do not present the best ideas for guidance of the thinking of the group.

Role behaviors customarily performed by a member in a group are frequently observed in his/her communication behavior with persons outside the group. This is especially true whenever the goals of the group are relevant to the outside interaction.[54]

The variable of group size, that is, the number of members present, may not have much effect on members' interaction outside the group; however, as members engage in interpersonal communication within the group, it has significant influences. Researchers have typically found that as the size of the group increases, the most active participant becomes more and more identifiable

[52] L. G. Wispe, "A Sociometric Analysis of Conflicting Role-Expectation," *American Journal of Sociology*, 61 (1955): 134–137.

[53] R. F. Bales and P. E. Slater, "Role Differentiation in Small Decision-Making Groups," in R. F. Bales et al., *Family, Socialization and Interaction Process* (New York: Free Press, 1955), pp. 259–306.

[54] See, for example, W. H. Crockett, "Emergent Leadership in Small Decision-Making Groups," *Journal of Abnormal and Social Psychology*, 51 (1955): 378–383.

as both a communication initiator and receiver; less participative group members become even less differentiated in communicative amounts.[55] As size increases, the degree of feedback decreases, producing loss of communication accuracy and increased hostility.[56].

One study examined some correlates of group size in a sample of groups ranging from two to seven members. These groups met four times to discuss problems in human relations. After each meeting, members were asked to evaluate group size as it influenced group effectiveness. Members of five-person groups expressed most satisfaction; members of larger groups felt their groups wasted time and that members were disorderly, aggressive, too pushy and competitive; members of groups with less than five members complained that they feared expressing their idea freely through fear of alienating one another.[57]

These inferences were limited to decision-making tasks. However, other studies with "opinion" tasks tend to confirm these results; they also show communication behaviors different for odd-numbered versus even-numbered groups in degrees of disagreement and antagonism. An even-numbered opinion split in a small group of two, four, or six members may produce impasse, frustration, and unwarrented hostility. This difficulty was most marked in groups of only two members, a fact that should have relevance for marriage partners.[58]

How does group size influence productivity in creative groups? One researcher found that larger groups produced a greater number of ideas, though not in proportion to the number of members; that is, there were diminishing returns from the addition of members. Perhaps as the size of the group increased, a larger and larger proportion of the group members experienced inhibitions that blocked participation. The researcher also noted that if he deliberately undertook to increase inhibitions by formalizing group procedures, the number of ideas contributed was reduced.[59] Reading 9.2 explores this topic further.

THE ORGANIZATION
AS SOCIAL ENVIRONMENT

There are many similarities between the ways our communication is influenced by our being members of groups and being members of organizations. In this discussion we will use the term *organization* to denote a combination of interrelated groups comprising an integrated social unity. This unit, like a group, has norms and conformity influence. In most organizations, those factors

[55] R. F. Bales, "The Equilibrium Problem in Small Groups," in T. Parsons, R. F. Bales, and E. A. Shils (eds.), *Working Papers in the Theory of Action* (New York: Free Press, 1953), pp. 11–161; and P. A. Hare, "Interaction and Consensus in Different Sized Groups," *American Sociological Review*, 17 (1952): 261–267.
[56] H. J. Leavitt and R. A. Mueller, "Some Effects of Feedback on Communication," *Human Relations*, 4 (1951): 401–410.
[57] P. E. Slater, "Contrasting Correlates of Group Size," *Sociometry*, 21 (1958): 129–139.
[58] R. F. Bales and E. Borgatta, "Size of Group as a Factor in the Interaction Profile," in P. A. Hare, E. F. Borgatta, and R. F. Bales (eds.), *Small Groups: Studies in Social Interaction* (New York: Knopf, 1955), pp. 396–413.
[59] C. A. Gibb, "Effects of Group Size and Threat Reduction upon Creativity in a Problem-Solving Situation," *American Psychologist*, 6 (1951): 324.

providing greatest impact on the communication behavior of their members are similar to those factors most influential in small groups: conformity and goal commitments. In actual operation, they take these forms: (1) an emphasis on achieving the organization's goals—"getting the job done"; (2) suppression of discussion of interpersonal problems; (3) insensitivity regarding one's impact on the feelings of those around him or her; (4) avoidance of taboo topics; and (5) creation of a climate of distrust. Perhaps we can make these concepts less abstract by reporting an interview held recently with one of our former students. Ten years ago Joe was hired as an executive trainee by a well-known corporation. He was interviewed a few months ago by one of the present authors in Chicago at a management institute. We later visited Joe's company at his invitation and surveyed conditions there.

In Joe's company, it is believed that important communication is that concerned with the company's objective: *getting the job done*. Joe's communication is designed to be rational, objective, unemotional. He believes that his personal effectiveness will decrease if interpersonal attitudes are exposed and discussed; the keynote is, "Let's keep feelings out of our discussions." Joe keeps his communication with others impersonal through the use of informal suggestions and little penalties.

The company's suppression of discussion of interpersonal problems has influenced Joe's interpersonal behavior. Joe has learned to hide, suppress, and disown his own interpersonal attitudes: "I didn't really mean it to sound that way." He has developed ways of keeping other people from discussing inter-personal problems: "Let's not get into personalities." Joe has difficulty in handling situations in which personal attitudes are expressed; afterwards he asks himself, "I wonder what he meant by that?" Joe avoids or refuses to consider new ideas involving human values: "I wouldn't want to get into that sort of thing." He tends to avoid *any* new idea for fear personal attitudes *might* become involved: "I never like to rock the boat." He avoids experimentation and risk-taking with new ideas that might involve value judgments: "Let's do it the safe way." He has become unaware of the impact on other people of his own inner emotions and feelings: "I wonder why he thinks I don't like him." In Joe's branch of the company, most interpersonal problems go unresolved; they tend to recur and have been increasing over time. One of Joe's employees said, "Those people at the front office certainly don't like each other."

Joe is quite unaware of the impact of his personal attitudes toward other persons; he is also poor at predicting the impact on himself of the personal attitudes of others toward him. Thus he occasionally shows the following:

1. Surprised confusion: "Why did he get sore over that?"
2. Frustration: "How can you talk with a guy like that?"
3. Heroic attempts at "objectivity": "My plan is really very simple."
4. Mistrust of others: "You just can't trust people like that."

Joe has adopted certain "play it safe" behaviors. He avoids intentional communication of his personal attitudes toward others. He ignores (or frowns at) communication of interpersonal attitudes by others. He tries to communicate "very clearly"; this means that he discusses only those ideas for which there is a clear company policy. He affirms values thought to be held by his superiors: "Yes, I think Mr. _____ would see it that way." He gives only tentative commitments to any direct question, especially one involving a new idea. He has gathered around him a group of employees whose communication behavior is similar to his own. His support of his superiors lacks "commitment from within," which might involve personal warmth. As you can see, Joe is not winning personal regard or trust for himself.

In Joe's situation, mistrust, conformity, conditional commitment, and dependence have operated in a circular fashion and now feed on themselves. The presentation of technical data is being substituted for the exploration of interpersonal problems. Careful, close supervision and "sticking to the rules" has replaced any real attempts at teamwork on decisions and policies. Joe resists any suggestion of organizational change unless it is proposed by a superior; in such a case he gives an indefininte "Sir, I believe so." Joe makes no decisions or changes until absolutely necessary, that is, only when a crisis occurs. In such cases (two witnessed), Joe's communication of emotion is high—too high for the situations; Joe's emotional outbursts are only temporarily fruitful. Joe mistrusts his superiors and peers, and his *modus operandi* has become defensive behavior designed to avoid any possible crisis.

Perhaps you may think that Joe's organization and its influence on his interpersonal behavior is unique or unusual. Our observation, as well as careful studies, show that it is rather ordinary for older, established organizations.[60] There are many points we could emphasize about organizational impact on interpersonal communication; however, we feel that they have been adequately identified in our description of Joe's company and his behavior. If you believe you need further evidence of these influences, we suggest you look closely at your own college or university. The odds are you will see supportive evidence all around you, with the exception of rare and special individuals—perhaps some of your instructors.

THE INFLUENCE OF ONE'S CULTURE

The norms and traditions of a culture not only influence the way people behave, but they affect the use of space, rooms, and chairs. In addition, viewpoints may differ regarding the use of time. Thus, we could have included a consideration of cultural differences in our discussion of the physical environment. We chose to discuss the cultural use of these variables in this section because the *use* of space and time are *behaviors*, "people variables" more than "object variables." People from one culture can move into another, and even if their cultural objects are left behind and they are confronted with new ones, they tend to *use* them according to old ways. In effect, they carry their cultural use of physical items around with them.

Perhaps our culture is, in the long run, the most important environmental

---

[60] Cf. C. Argyris, *Interpersonal Competence and Organizational Effectiveness* (Homewood, Ill.: Irwin, 1962), pp. 27–50.

Perhaps our culture is, in the long run, the most important environmental factor influencing our interpersonal communication.

factor influencing our interpersonal communication. Like our clothing, we tend to carry our culture around on our backs. As long as we interact only with persons from our own culture, this influence may pass unnoticed; however, when we attempt interpersonal communication with persons from Europe, the Near East, or the Orient, we usually notice important differences. Today many college students become personal acquaintances of students from other cultures, and many students visit foreign places. Cross-cultural differences have become—for many of us—not just an item of romantic interest, but a part of our immediate interpersonal communication environment.

It seems to us that the most important aspect of cultural influences on our interaction is those behaviors of persons from other cultures that may surprise us or make us feel awkward. Similarly, we are interested in identifying our own usual, habitual behaviors that may be misinterpreted by, or prove embarrassing to, persons from foreign lands. For these reasons we believe that your interests can best be served if, in this section, we focus on those cultural differences that relate directly to interpersonal communication. E. T. Hall, author of *The Hidden Dimension*, is the outstanding authority on this topic, and to a large extent our review relies on his careful observations.[61]

[61] E. T. Hall, *Hidden Dimension*.

Probably the most important cultural differences regarding the use of environmental factors are in the way people from Europe, the Orient, and America tend to utilize space.[62] Each individual surrounds himself/herself with a "bubble of privacy," a small space that he/she feels is his/her own little territory; others must gain permission to enter unless they are willing to be perceived as intruding. To an American, a short distance is necessary for this "bubble"—perhaps 2 to 3 feet.[63] To a German, this distance must be much greater. Space is felt as an extension of the ego and is implicit in a German's use of the term *lebensraum*, a concept almost impossible to translate directly because of the emotional feelings implied. Hitler was able to use this feeling as a lever to move the Germans to combat. If an American pokes his head into an office or inside the screen door of a home to chat briefly, he is considered still "outside"; not so to a German—his privacy has been intruded upon if you can *see* inside his room.[64]

The German's ego is, by American standards, quite tender, and he will preserve his privacy with great effort. During World War II, German prisoners were housed four to a small hut in one prison camp in the Midwest. Out of any materials they could scrounge, they each built internal partitions so that each could have his own tiny private space.[65] During the Allied occupation a few years later, when Berlin was in ruins and the housing shortage was indescribably acute, occupation authorities ordered Berliners with kitchens and baths to share them with neighbors. This arrangement had worked fairly well in Italy and France. The order had to be withdrawn in Germany when neighbors started killing each other over shared space.[66]

Americans keep the doors of office buildings open; Germans keep them closed. German doors are very important; they are usually quite solid, fit well, and are often double in public buildings. To a German a closed door does not mean that the person behind it is doing something he shouldn't; it is his way of protecting the privacy of the individual. Hall describes the problem in one American overseas company where the use of doors had created a situation severe enough to have him brought in as a consultant: the Americans wanted the office doors open and the Germans wanted them closed. Hall reports that "the open doors were making the Germans feel exposed . . . closed doors . . . gave the Americans the feeling that there was a conspiratorial air about the place and that they were being left out."[67] The point is that if you want to get to know a student from Germany, don't try to hold interpersonal communication with him in a crowded bus or restaurant; find a room and close the door!

In this context, the English are quite different (as they are regarding other factors). To an American, space is a way of classifying people; large homes and yards indicate important owners. The Englishman is born into a social class,

[62] See E. T. Hall and M. Hall, "Sounds of Silence."
[63] Goffman, *Behavior in Public Places*, pp. 98–99.
[64] Hall, *Hidden Dimension*, pp. 133–134.
[65] Ibid., p. 135.
[66] Ibid., pp. 135–136.
[67] Ibid., p. 136.

and space has nothing to do with it; a lord is a lord even if he lives in a one-room apartment.

An Englishman may never have a "room of his own." As a child he will likely live with siblings in a "nursery"; as a schoolboy he may live in a dormitory having large communal eating and sleeping rooms; as a businessman he will likely share office space with numerous colleagues. Even members of Parliament have no offices and often conduct their interviews in foyers or on terraces.[68] The English are often puzzled by an American's need for enclosed private space; the English need no such device to protect their egos. Their social status bequeathed by their parents is their permanent birthright.

The typical Englishman's attitude toward personal space is significant for interpersonal communication. When an American wants to be alone, he goes into some room and shuts the door; for him to refuse to respond to someone else in the same room is to render the "silent treatment," implying displeasure or lack of regard. When an Englishman wants to be alone, he simply quits talking. In so doing he means no interpersonal disrespect; he simply wants to be alone with his thoughts. Having never in his life used enclosed space or distance for this purpose, he is surprised when an American fails to understand this "common social convention." This factor holds much meaning for Americans wishing to hold interpersonal communication with the English: The more quiet or withdrawn the Englishman is, the more the American thinks something is wrong in the relationship, and the more he will press for assurances that all is well. The more he presses, the more he *intrudes* upon the Englishman's sense of privacy! Consequent tension will likely increase, lasting until one perceives the other's true intentions.[69]

To many Americans, the French appear to be from a world of their own; but they are fairly representative of that complex of cultures bordering the Mediterranean. In ways quite unlike the English and especially unlike Germans, they live, breathe, and eat in crowds. Crowded living is exemplified in their buses, trains, and cafés. They crowd themselves into small cars that contrast sharply in size with Detroit models. Their personal spheres of ego protection are relatively small.

In contrast to the Germans, their neighbors, the French hold their conversations outdoors. Their homes are for the family and are usually quite crowded. Their cafés are for socializing, and here also they are quite crowded and are sensually very much involved with one another. If you wish to enjoy interpersonal communication with a student from France or Italy, you can expect him or her to stand or sit quite close, to touch you from time to time,[70] and to expect your full attention.[71]

The Arabic culture of the Near East provides some contrasts of a paradoxical nature with respect to the use of space. In their public places, Arabs

---

[68] Ibid., p. 139.
[69] Cf. ibid., pp. 139–140.
[70] See Goffman, *Behavior in Public Places*, p. 101.
[71] Cf. Schaffner, ed., *Group Processes*, p. 184.

are compressed and almost overwhelmed with crowding, pushing, and shoving; however, inside their homes—at least in the upper and some middle classes—they rattle around in what suburban Americans would call too much space. The Arab's dream is of a home with unlimited internal space, high vaulted ceilings, few items of furniture to obstruct one's "moving around," and a limitless view *from a balcony*. This home, however, is simply a protective wall to shield the family from the outside world.[72]

Among Arab men in public, there is no privacy as Americans know it; in fact, Arabs do not even have a word for privacy.[73] In public, it is quite acceptable to push, shove, and intrude on what Americans and Europeans regard as their "bubble," or personal sphere. An American "Pardon me" is surprising and confusing to an Arab and, if meant as a request, is usually ignored. Hall describes a personal experience of having his privacy violated in a public place; later, in his discussion of the incident with an Arabic friend, the Arab regarded Hall's feelings as strange and puzzling. His conclusive comment to Hall was, "After all, it's a public place, isn't it?"[74]

Where then, is the Arab's sense of privacy—his spatial shield for his ego? It is somewhere inside the body. This may partially explain why severing of a thief's hand is standard punishment in Saudi Arabia.[75] Paradoxically, although an Arab's ego is not violated by touching and pushing, it is not thus protected from words; a verbal insult is not something taken lightly.[76]

Arabs tend to breathe on each other when they talk; this is not accidental, but a cultural pattern. To Arabs, smelling each other is a desirable way of being involved; good smells are pleasing and to smell one's friend, particularly his breath, is desirable. Arabs are careful about the way they smell; they take special pains to enhance body odors and to use them in building human relationships.[77] This is significant for Americans who want to achieve satisfactory interpersonal relations with persons from the Near East. Even more important, however, is that to "deny one's breath" (i.e., to refuse to interact closely enough so that your breath can be smelled) is to act as if you are ashamed! Arabs are quite willing to tell each other when their breath smells bad; but to avoid letting a frend smell your breath is to deny friendship![78] Can you imagine, then, that you, having been taught in America not to breathe in people's faces, are overtly denying your friendship to an Arab student, communicating shame to him when you are trying to be polite? If you really wish to be his friend, perhaps you might discuss these cultural differences with him.

At no time, in either public or private places, does an Arab like to be left by himself. He is used to crowds of people and a lack of physical privacy. How, then, does he achieve personal privacy, a sense of the integrity of himself as a person? Actually, it is easy: Like the Englishman, he just quits talking. If you

[72] Hall, *Hidden Dimension*, pp. 158–162.
[73] Ibid., p. 159.
[74] Ibid., p. 156.
[75] Ibid., p. 157.
[76] Ibid., pp. 157–158.
[77] Ibid., pp. 159–160.
[78] Ibid., p. 160.

inquire about his thoughts at this time he will regard you as a "pushy American"! Sometimes a member of an Arabic family may go for hours without saying a word, and no one in the family will think anything about it. Now imagine an Arab exchange student who visited a Kansas farm family; his hosts became angry at a long silence and withdrew—gave him the silent treatment. He was actually unaware of their anger until they took him to town and forcibly put him on a bus! He was on his way back to the university before he knew there was anything wrong![79]

Probably those representatives of the Orient most often encountered by Americans are the Japanese. Sitting closely together has special warm connotations to the Japanese. Deeply imbedded in their culture is the feeling of a family sitting closely together around the *hibachi*, the "fireplace." This feeling has even stronger emotional overtones than the American concept of the hearth.[80] Hall quotes an old Japanese priest:

> To really know the Japanese you have to have spent some cold winter evenings snuggled around the *hibachi*. Everybody sits together. A common quilt covers not only the *hibachi* but everyone's lap as well. In this way the heat is held in. It's when your hands touch and you feel the warmth of their bodies and everyone feels *together*—that's when you get to know the Japanese. That's the real Japan.[81]

An American student may be surprised, even confused, by the emotional show of warmth on the part of a friendly Japanese student. In such a situation you may wish to take extra pains to overcome what, to a Japanese, may appear to be cold disinterest—the usual American use of interpersonal distance. But by the time these two persons get this spatial distance worked out to their satisfaction, a paradoxical problem may arise. It has to do partially with the Japanese way of regarding space and objects; but it realizes its full potential in the way the Japanese approach topics of special interest.

There is an ethic in the Japanese culture that encourages them *to help a friend discover something for himself* rather than tell him bluntly something he should know. This leads the Japanese to approach a subject *indirectly* rather than head-on. One American banker who had spent years in Japan voiced his greatest sense of frustration with the Japanese: "They talk around and around and around a point and never get to it."[82] They behave somewhat like a rancher "rounding up" cattle; the Japanese round up more or less related ideas until this "herd," with its size, shape, and related proportions, is obvious to you or anybody—but this takes some time and patience. This way of behaving is illustrated dramatically in the way they treat space: They emphasize centers of population growth and ignore the areas between; they name intersections (growth centers) rather than the streets leading to them; and houses are numbered in the order they are built (grow) rather than along a linear distance.[83] These factors cause travelers inestimable problems, but very well

[79] Ibid., p. 159.
[80] Ibid., p. 150.
[81] Ibid., pp. 150–151.
[82] Ibid., p. 151.
[83] Ibid., pp. 149–150.

illustrate the way Japanese feel about relationships between objects, people, and ideas. People in close contact get to know each other well; peripheral areas relate somewhat. An area of concentration on the periphery will have *its own center* and focus; thus each "center" will have its own sense of unity and integrity. Similarly, with ideas, the circle or area is of greater importance than the linear or logical relationship between concepts. And the *feeling* one has about ideas is of greater value than the logical connections between ideas.

In talking with a Japanese friend, exercise time and patience; look for the feeling tones expressed rather than the logical rationale. Don't worry about "coming to the point," but sense your and his/her feelings about the general area of discussion as well as your feelings toward each other. And don't be surprised if you seem to sense an unexpected feeling of warmth and closeness. As the old priest said, "this is the real Japan!"

In this section on foreign cultures we would be remiss if we spoke only of space and interpersonal distance and failed to mention eye contact. One's way of using the eyes in interpersonal communication is one of the most dramatic differences between cultures and carries considerable impact.

To get along without private rooms and offices, the English have developed skill in paying strict attention, listening carefully, and, from about a distance of 6 to 8 feet, looking you directly in one eye—or so it will feel to you.[84] In fact, an Englishman will likely fix an unwavering gaze on you—*and blink his eyes to let you know he has heard you!* Once you have come to understand these social conventions, their meaning and source or derivation, you may come to use them—even appreciate their value in a crowded room. To misunderstand them is to increase confusion and minimize interpersonal understanding.

In like manner, as a Frenchman talks with you he really looks at you—in one eye, then the other eye, and then up and down. All French, especially the women, have grown accustomed to being looked at and will feel you are being cold or distant if you don't look at them in a direct manner.[85]

Arabs seem to be *unable* to talk without *facing* you at close range (1 to 2 feet); to talk to a person while viewing him peripherally is regarded as impolite.[86] While talking, Arabs will look at you in a way that may seem to approach a stare or glare; sometimes this searching gaze appears to beseech or demand more attention than you wish to give. Arabs frequently complain that Americans are aloof, "don't care."[87] Their searching gaze may at times seem hostile or challenging; some Arabs barely avoid fights with Americans because of the intensity and possible implications of this behavior.[88] If you have a friend from the Near East, think carefully before you take offense at his close and intense look into your eyes as he talks with you; show him you mean to be his friend by looking him directly in the eye even though such behavior may seem awkward or uncomfortable to you at first. If you really want to be his friend and make him feel "at home" with you, this effort will have its reward.

[84] Ibid., pp. 142–143.
[85] Ibid., p. 145.
[86] Ibid., pp. 160–161.
[87] Ibid., p. 161.
[88] Ibid., pp. 161–162.

Although we have stressed differences between the American culture and those of Europe, the Near East, and the Orient, another of our purposes has been to give you some appreciation of the way your own American culture has conditioned you to the use of physical space in interpersonal behavior. From this discussion you should have gained some deeper understanding of the influence of one's culture on the use of the environment in interpersonal communication.

As you can easily see from your observation of Americans, not all of them are alike; neither are *all* English, French, Arabs, or Japanese. The behaviors we have described apply in a general way, but will not be depicted by each individual. Even so, we believe that they apply well enough to be of value in your attempts to improve your interpersonal communication with persons from various cultures.

Summary and Preview of Readings

In this chapter we have discussed environmental factors, physical and social, that have particular influence on interpersonal communication.

An enclosed space, a room or place where an atmosphere of privacy prevails, can favorably influence interpersonal communication. A room of modest size and pleasant furnishings and attractive colors can have a positive effect. Tables and chairs can be helpful in terms of personal comfort and convenience; but they can have a deleterious effect as psychological barriers. Restaurants and lobbies are usually available as places to attempt interpersonal communication, but they ordinarily lack a psychological atmosphere conducive to sharing personal information. In many cases they provide so many distractions that emotion cues and nonverbal messages are difficult to perceive.

Chairs and tables must not be allowed to interfere with eye contact as we attempt to engage others in interaction. Messages carried by perceiving each other's eyes are perhaps almost as important as the verbal interchange; certainly these messages influence the interpretation of relationships between people. In our discussion of chairs and tables, we noted the four "interaction distances" identified by the Halls; these were briefly described, as were their relative values for interpersonal communication.

The way participants feel about the passage of time can significantly influence interpersonal communication; feelings of limited time or time poorly spent can subtly demolish the anticipated value of such interaction. Special occasions are essentially "time-person-place" arrangements wherein these environmental factors are controlled for specific purposes.

The social environment influences interpersonal communication in terms of four social contexts: the presence of other persons not currently engaged in the interaction, participants who are members of certain groups, interaction within an organization, and interpersonal customs within a culture.

Interaction within the presence of others who are not involved will likely be inhibited or limited; this will be particularly true if the participants hold allegiance of some sort to those who overhear.

Membership in groups tends to influence the interaction of members both in and out of the group. Members tend to conform to group norms and adhere to group goal commitments; these factors may severely limit the interpersonal communication behavior of group members, even when talking with nonmembers. Within the group itself, interaction is significantly influenced by the size of the group (i.e., the number of persons attempting to interact).

Interaction within the boundaries of most older, established organizations will likely be influenced by these norms or practices: an emphasis on achieving the organization's goals, suppression of discussion of interpersonal problems, insensitivity to one's influence on the feelings of others, avoidance of taboo topics, and creation of a climate of distrust.

There are significant cultural differences among Americans, Europeans, Arabs, and Japanese. Those cultural differences having the most significant influence on interpersonal communication are social customs regarding use of space, interpersonal distance (sense of physical closeness), and the use of eye contact. These customs are not uniform for all members of these cultures; but the degree of difference among cultures is stable enough to be important as you try to improve your interpersonal communication with persons from other cultures.

In the first article that follows, "The Sounds of Silence," Edward Hall and Mildred Hall describe the influence of space, time, and body movement on interpersonal communication. They provide a rather careful analysis of the use of distances—from "intimate" to "public"—along with a description of the personal "bubble" of privacy each of us desires and protects.

In his article "The Effects of Environment and Space on Human Communication," Mark L. Knapp analyzes the effects on interaction of spatial relationships between or among people. He provides an excellent discussion of houses, rooms, tables, desks, and chairs. Of particular interest to many of you will be his comments on population density as it applies to human interaction.

The Sounds of Silence

Edward Hall and Mildred Hall

Bob leaves his apartment at 8:15 A.M. and stops at the corner drugstore for breakfast. Before he can speak, the counterman says, "The usual?" Bob nods yes. While he savors his Danish, a fat man pushes onto the adjoining stool and overflows into his space. Bob scowls and the man pulls himself in as much as he can. Bob has sent two messages without speaking a syllable.

Henry has an appointment to meet Arthur at 11 o'clock; he arrives at 11:30. Their conversation is friendly, but Arthur retains a lingering hostility. Henry has unconsciously communicated that he doesn't think the appointment is very important or that Arthur is a person who needs to be treated with respect.

George is talking to Charley's wife at a party. Their conversation is entirely trivial, yet Charley glares at them suspiciously. Their physical proximity and the movements of their eyes reveal that they are powerfully attracted to each other.

José Ybarra and Sir Edmund Jones are at the same party and it is important for them to establish a cordial relationship for business reasons. Each is trying to be warm and friendly, yet they will part with mutual distrust and their business transaction will probably fall through. José, in Latin fashion, moved closer and closer to Sir Edmund as they spoke, and this movement was miscommunicated as pushiness to Sir Edmund, who kept backing away from the intimacy, and this was miscommunicated to José as coldness. The silent languages of Latin and English cultures are more difficult to learn than their spoken languages.

In each of these cases, we see the subtle power of nonverbal communication. The only language used throughout most of the history of humanity (in evolutionary terms, vocal communication is relatively recent), it is the first form of communication you learn. You use this preverbal language, consciously and unconsciously, every day to tell other people how you feel about yourself and them. This language includes your posture, gestures, facial expressions, costume, the way you walk, even your treatment of time and space and material things. All people communicate on several different levels at the same time but are usually aware of only the verbal dialog and don't realize that they respond to nonverbal messages. But when a person says one thing and really believes something else, the discrepancy between the two can usually be sensed. Nonverbal communication systems are much less subject to the conscious deception that often occurs in verbal systems. When we find ourselves thinking, "I don't know what it is about him, but he doesn't seem sincere," it's usually this lack of congruity between a person's words and his behavior that makes us anxious and uncomfortable.

Few of us realize how much we all depend on body movement in our conversation or are aware of the hidden rules that govern listening behavior. But we know instantly whether or not the person we're talking to is "tuned in" and we're very sensitive to any breach in listening etiquette. In white middle-class American culture, when someone wants to show he is listening to someone else, he looks either at the other person's face or, specifically, at his eyes, shifting his gaze from one eye to the other.

If you observe a person conversing, you'll notice that he indicates he's listening by nodding his head. He also makes little "Hmm" noises. If he agrees with what's being said, he may give a vigorous nod. To show pleasure or affirmation, he smiles; if he has some reservations, he looks skeptical by raising an eyebrow or pulling down the corners of his mouth. If a participant wants to terminate the conversation, he may start shifting his body position, stretching his legs, crossing or uncrossing them, bobbing his foot or diverting his gaze from the speaker. The more he fidgets, the more the speaker becomes aware that he has lost his audience. As a last measure, the listener may look at his watch to indicate the imminent end of the conversation.

Talking and listening are so intricately intertwined that a person cannot do one without the other. Even when one is alone and talking to oneself, there is part of the brain that speaks while another part listens. In all conversations, the listener is positively or negatively reinforcing the speaker all the time. He may even guide the conversation without knowing it, by laughing or frowning or dismissing the argument with a wave of his hand.

The language of the eyes—another age-old way of exchanging feelings—is both subtle and complex. Not only do men and women use their eyes differently but there are class, generation, regional, ethnic and national cultural differences. Americans often complain about the way foreigners stare at people or hold a glance too long. Most Americans look away from someone who is using his eyes in an unfamiliar way because it makes them self-conscious. If a man looks at another man's wife in a certain way, he's asking for trouble, as indicated earlier. But he might not be ill-mannered or seeking to challenge the husband. He might be a European in this country who hasn't learned our visual mores.

Many American women visiting France or Italy are acutely embarrassed because, for the first time in their lives, men really look at them—their eyes, hair, nose, lips, breasts, hips, legs, thighs, knees, ankles, feet, clothes, hairdo, even their walk. These same women, once they have become used to being looked at, often return to the United States and are overcome with feeling that "No one ever really looks at me anymore."

Analyzing the mass of data on the eyes, it is possible to sort out at least three ways in which the eyes are used to communicate: dominance *vs.* submission, involvement *vs.* detachment and positive *vs.* negative attitude. In addition, there are three levels of consciousness and control, which can be categorized as follows: (1) conscious use of the eyes to communicate, such as the flirting blink and the intimate nose-wrinkling squint; (2) the very extensive category of unconscious but learned behavior governing where the eyes are directed and when (this unwritten set of rules dictates how and under what circumstances the sexes, as well as people of all status categories, look at each other); and (3) the response of the eye itself, which is completely outside both awareness and control—changes in the cast (the sparkle) of the eye and the pupillary reflex.

The eye is unlike any other organ of the body, for it is an extension of the brain. The unconscious pupillary reflex and the cast of the eye have been known by people of Middle Eastern origin for years—although most are unaware of their knowledge. Depending on the context, Arabs and others look either directly at the eyes or deeply *into* the eyes of their interlocutor. We became aware of this in the Middle East several years ago while looking at jewelry. The merchant suddenly started to push a particular bracelet at a customer and said, "You buy this one." What interested us was that the bracelet was not the one that had been consciously selected by the purchaser. But the merchant, watching the pupils of the eyes, knew what the purchaser really wanted to buy. Whether he specifically knew *how* he knew is debatable.

A psychologist at the University of Chicago, Eckhard Hess, was the first to conduct systematic studies of the pupillary reflex. His wife remarked one evening, while watching him reading in bed, that he must be very interested in the text because his pupils were dilated. Following up on this, Hess slipped some pictures of nudes into a stack of photographs that he gave to his male assistant. Not looking at the photographs but watching his assistant's pupils, Hess was able to tell precisely when the assistant came to the nudes. In further experiments, Hess retouched the eyes in a photograph of a woman. In one print, he made the pupils small, in another, large; nothing else was changed. Subjects who were given the photographs found the woman with the dilated pupils much more attractive. Any man who has had the experience of seeing a woman look at him as her pupils widen with reflex speed knows that she's flashing him a message.

The eye-sparkle phenomenon frequently turns up in our interviews of couples in love. It's apparently one of the first reliable clues in the other person that love is genuine. To date, there is no scientific data to explain eye sparkle; no investigation of the pupil, the cornea or even the white sclera on the eye shows how the sparkle originates. Yet we all know it when we see it.

One common situation for most people involves the use of the eyes in the street and in public. Although eye behavior follows a definite set of rules, the rules vary according to the place, the needs and feelings of the people, and their ethnic background. For urban whites, once they're within definite recognition distance (16–32 feet for people with average eyesight), there is mutual avoidance of eye contact—unless they want something specific: a pickup, a handout or information of some kind. In the West and in small towns generally, however, people are much more likely to look at and greet one another, even if they're strangers.

It's permissible to look at people if they're beyond recognition distance; but once inside this sacred zone, you can only steal a glance at strangers. You *must* greet friends, however; to fail to do so is insulting. Yet, to stare too fixedly even at them is considered rule and hostile. Of course, all of these rules are variable.

A great many blacks, for example, greet each other in public even if they don't know each other. To blacks, most eye behavior of whites has the effect of giving the impression that they aren't there, but this is due to white avoidance of eye contact with *anyone* in the street.

Another very basic difference between people of different ethnic backgrounds is their sense of territoriality and how they handle space. This is the silent communication, or miscommunication, that caused friction between Mr. Ybarra and Sir Edmund Jones in our earlier example. We know from research that everyone has around himself an invisible bubble of space that contracts and expands depending on several factors: his emotional state, the activity he's performing at the time, and his cultural background. This bubble is a kind of mobile territory that he will defend against intrusion. If he is accustomed to close personal distance between himself and others, his bubble will be smaller than that of someone who's accustomed to greater personal distance. People of North European heritage—English, Scandinavian, Swiss and German—tend to avoid contact. Those whose heritage is Italian, Spanish, Russian, Latin American or Middle Eastern like close personal contact.

People are very sensitive to any intrusion into their spatial bubble. If someone stands too close to you, your first instinct is to back up. If that's not possible, you lean away and pull yourself in, tensing your muscles. If the intruder doesn't respond to these body signals, you may then try to protect yourself, using a briefcase, umbrella or raincoat. Women—especially when traveling alone—often plant their pocketbook in such a way that no one can get very close to them. As a last resort, you may move to another spot and position yourself behind a desk or a chair that provides screening. Everyone tries to adjust the space around himself in a way that's comfortable for him; most often, he does this unconsciously.

Emotions also have a direct effect on the size of a person's territory. When you're angry or under stress, your bubble expands and you require more space. New York psychiatrist Augustus Kinzel found a difference in what he calls Body-Buffer Zones between violent and nonviolent prison inmates. Dr. Kinzel conducted experiments in which each prisoner was placed in the center of a small room and then Dr. Kinzel slowly walked toward him. Nonviolent prisoners allowed him to come quite close, while prisoners with a history of violent behavior couldn't tolerate his proximity and reacted with some vehemence.

Apparently, people under stress experience other people as looming larger and closer than they actually are. Studies of schizophrenic patients have indicated that they sometimes have a distorted perception of space, and several psychiatrists have reported patients who experience their body boundaries as filling up an entire room. For these patients, anyone who comes into the room is actually inside their body, and such an intrusion may trigger a violent outburst.

Unfortunately, there is little detailed information about normal people who live in highly congested urban areas. We do know, of course, that the noise, pollution, dirt, crowding and confusion of our cities induce feelings of stress in most of us, and stress leads to a need for greater space. The man who's packed into a subway, jostled in the street, crowded into an elevator and forced to work all day in a bull pen or in a small office without auditory or visual privacy is going to be very stressed at the end of his day. He needs places that provide relief from constant overstimulation of his nervous system. Stress from overcrowding is cumulative and people can tolerate more crowding early in the day than later; note the increased bad temper during the evening rush hour as compared with the morning melee. Certainly one factor in people's desire to commute by car is the need for privacy and relief from crowding (except, often, from other cars); it may be the only time of the day when nobody can intrude.

In crowded public places, we tense our muscles and hold ourselves stiff, and thereby communicate to others our desire not to intrude on their space and, above all, not to touch them. We also avoid eye contact, and the total effect is that of someone who has "tuned out." Walking along the street, our bubble expands slightly as we move in a stream of strangers, taking care not to bump into them. In the office, at meetings, in restaurants, our bubble keeps changing as it adjusts to the activity at hand.

Most white middle-class Americans use four main distances in their business and social relations: intimate, personal, social and public. Each of these distances has a near and a far phase and is accompanied by changes in the volume of the voice. Intimate distance varies from direct physical contact with another person to a distance of six to eighteen inches and is used for our most private activities—caressing another person or making love. At this distance, you are overwhelmed by sensory inputs from the other person— heat from the body, tactile stimulation from the skin, the fragrance of perfume, even the sound of breathing— all of which literally envelop you. Even at the far phase, you're still within easy touching distance. In general, the use of intimate distance in public between adults is frowned on. It's also much too close for strangers, except under conditions of extreme crowding.

In the second zone—personal distance—the close phase is one and a half to two and a half feet; it's at this distance that wives usually stand from their husbands in public. If another woman moves into this zone, the wife will most likely be disturbed. The far phase—two and a half to four feet— is the distance used to "keep someone at arm's length" and is the most common spacing used by people in conversation.

The third zone—social distance—is employed during business transactions or exchanges with a clerk or repairman. People who work together tend to use close social distance—four to seven feet. This is also the distance for conversations at social gatherings. To stand at this distance from someone who is seated has a dominating effect (e.g., teacher to pupil, boss to secretary). The far phase of the third zone— seven to twelve feet—is where people stand when someone says, "Stand back so I can look at you." This distance lends a formal tone to business or social discourse. In an executive office, the desk serves to keep people at this distance.

The fourth zone—public distance— is used by teachers in classrooms or speakers at public gatherings. At its farthest phase—25 feet and beyond— it is used for important public figures. Violations of this distance can lead to serious complications. During his 1970 U.S. visit, the president of France, Georges Pompidou, was harassed by pickets in Chicago, who were permitted to get within touching distance. Since pickets in France are kept behind barricades a block or more away, the president was outraged by this insult to his person, and President Nixon was obliged to communicate his concern as well as offer his personal apologies.

It is interesting to note how American pitchmen and panhandlers exploit the unwritten, unspoken conventions of eye and distance. Both take advantage of the fact that once explicit eye contact is established, it is rude to look away, because to do so means to brusquely dismiss the other person and his needs. Once having caught the eye of his mark, the panhandler then locks on, not letting go until he moves through the public zone, the social zone, the personal zone and, finally, into the intimate sphere, where people are most vulnerable.

Touch also is an important part of the constant stream of communication that takes place between people. A light touch, a firm touch, a blow, a caress, are all communications. In an effort to break down barriers among people, there's a recent upsurge in group-encounter activities, in which strangers are encouraged to touch one another. In special situations such as these, the rules for not touching are broken with group approval and people gradually lose some of their inhibitions.

Although most people don't realize it, space is perceived and distances are set not by vision alone but with all the senses. Auditory space is perceived with the ears, thermal space with the skin, kinesthetic space with the muscles of the body and olfactory space with the nose. And, once again, it's one's culture that determines how his senses are programmed—which sensory information ranks highest and lowest. The important thing to remember is that culture is very persistent. In this country, we've noted the existence of culture patterns that determine the distance between people in the third and fourth generations of some families, despite their prolonged contact with people of very different cultural heritages.

Whenever there is great cultural distance between two people, there are bound to be problems arising from differences in behavior and expectations. An example is the American couple who consulted a psychiatrist about their marital problems. The husband was from New England and had been brought up by reserved parents who taught him to control his emotions and to respect the need for privacy. His wife was from an Italian family and had been brought up in close contact with all the members of her large family, who were extremely warm, volatile and demonstrative.

When the husband came home after a hard day at the office, dragging his feet and longing for peace and quiet, his wife would rush to him and smother him. Clasping his hands, rubbing his brow, crooning over his weary head, she never left him alone. But when his wife was upset or anxious about her day, the husband's response was to withdraw completely and leave her alone. No comforting, no affectionate embrace, no attention—just solitude. The woman became convinced her husband didn't love her and, in desperation, she consulted a psychiatrist. Their problem wasn't basically psychological but cultural.

Why has man developed all these different ways of communicating messages without words? One reason is that people don't like to spell out certain kinds of messages. We prefer to find other ways of showing our feelings. This is especially true in relationships as sensitive as courtship. Men don't like to be rejected and most women don't want to turn a man down bluntly. Instead, we work out subtle ways of encouraging or discouraging each other that save face and avoid confrontations.

How a person handles space in dating others is an obvious and very sensitive indicator of how he or she feels about the other person. On a first date, if a woman sits or stands so close to a man that he is acutely conscious of her physical presence—inside the intimate zone—the man usually construes it to mean that she is encouraging him. However, before the man starts moving in on the woman, he should be sure what message she's really sending; otherwise, he risks bruising his ego. What is close to someone of North European background may be culturally distant to someone of Italian heritage. Also, women sometimes use space as a way of misleading a man and there are few things that put men off more than women who communicate contradictory messages—such as women who cuddle up and then act insulted when a man takes the next step.

How does a woman communicate interest in a man? In addition to such familiar gambits as smiling at him, she may glance shyly at him, blush and then look away. Or she may give him a real come-on look and move in very close when he approaches. She may touch his arm and ask for a light. As she leans forward to light her cigarette, she may brush him lightly, enveloping him in her perfume. She'll probably continue to smile at him and she may use what ethologists call preening gestures—touching the back of her hair, thrusting her breasts forward, tilting her hips as she stands or crossing her legs if she's seated, perhaps even exposing one thigh or putting a hand on her thigh and stroking it. She may also stroke her wrists as she converses or show the palm of her hand as a way of gaining his attention. Her skin may be unusually flushed or quite pale, her eyes brighter, the pupils larger.

If a man sees a woman whom he wants to attract, he tries to present himself by his posture and stance as someone who is self-assured. He moves briskly and confidently. When he catches the eye of the woman, he may hold her glance a little longer than normal. If he gets an encouraging smile, he'll move in close and engage her in small talk. As they converse, his glance shifts over her face and body. He, too, may make preening gestures—straightening his tie, smoothing his hair or shooting his cuffs.

How do people learn body language? The same way they learn spoken language—by observing and imitating people around them as they're growing up. Little girls imitate their mothers or an older female. Little boys imitate their fathers or a respected uncle or a character on television. In this way, they learn the gender signals appropriate for their sex. Regional, class and ethnic patterns of body behavior are also learned in childhood and persist throughout life.

Such patterns of masculine and feminine body behavior vary widely from one culture to another. In America, for example, women stand with their thighs together. Many walk with their pelvis tipped slightly forward and their upper arms close to their body. When they sit they cross their legs at the knee or, if they are well past middle age, they may cross their ankles. American men hold their arms away from their body, often swinging them as they walk. They stand with their legs apart (an extreme example is the cow-

boy, with legs apart and thumbs tucked into his belt). When they sit, they put their feet on the floor with legs apart and, in some parts of the country, they cross their legs by putting one ankle on the other knee.

Leg behavior indicates sex, status and personality. It also indicates whether or not one is at ease or is showing respect or disrespect for the other person. Young Latin-American males avoid crossing their legs. In their world of *machismo,* the preferred position for young males when with one another (if there is no older dominant male present to whom they must show respect) is to sit on the base of their spine with their leg muscles relaxed and their feet wide apart. Their respect position is like our military equivalent; spine straight, heels and ankles together—almost identical to that displayed by properly brought up young women in New England in the early part of this century.

American women who sit with their legs spread apart in the presence of males are *not* normally signaling a come-on—they are simply (and often unconsciously) sitting like men. Middle-class women in the presence of other women to whom they are very close may on occasion throw themselves down on a soft chair or sofa and let themselves go. This is a signal that nothing serious will be taken up. Males, on the other hand, lean back and prop their legs up on the nearest object.

The way we walk, similarly, indicates status, respect, mood and ethnic or cultural affiliation. The many variants of the female walk are too well known to go into here, except to say that a man would have to be blind not to be turned on by the way some women walk—a fact that made Mae

West rich before scientists ever studied these matters. To white Americans, some French middle-class males walk in a way that is both humorous and suspect. There is a bounce and looseness to the French walk, as though the parts of the body were somehow unrelated. Jacques Tati, the French movie actor, walks this way; so does the great mime, Marcel Marceau.

Blacks and whites in America—with the exception of middle- and upper-middle-class professionals of both groups—move and walk very differently from each other. To the blacks, whites often seem incredibly stiff, almost mechanical in their movements. Black males, on the other hand, have a looseness and coordination that frequently make whites a little uneasy; it's too different, too integrated, too alive, too male. Norman Mailer has said that squares walk from the shoulders, like bears, but blacks and hippies walk from the hips, like cats.

All over the world, people walk not only in their own characteristic way but have walks that communicate the nature of their involvement with whatever it is they're doing. The purposeful walk of North Europeans is an important component of proper behavior on the job. Any male who has been in the military knows how essential it is to walk properly (which makes for a continuing source of tension between blacks and whites in the Service). The quick shuffle of servants in the Far East in the old days was a show of respect. On the island of Truk, when we last visited, the inhabitants even had a name for the respectful walk that one used when in the presence of a chief or when walking past a chief's house. The term was *sufan,* which meant to be humble and respectful.

The notion that people communicate volumes by their gestures, facial expressions, posture and walk is not new; actors, dancers, writers and psychiatrists have long been aware of it. Only in recent years, however, have scientists begun to make systematic observations of body motions. Ray L. Birdwhistell of the University of Pennsylvania is one of the pioneers in body-motion research and coined the term kinesics to describe this field. He developed an elaborate notation system to record both facial and body movements, using an approach similar to that of the linguist, who studies the basic elements of speech. Birdwhistell and other kinesicists such as Albert Scheflen, Adam Kendon and William Condon take movies of people interacting. They run the film over and over again, often at reduced speed for frame-by-frame analysis, so that they can observe even the slightest body movements not perceptible at normal interaction speeds. These movements are then recorded in notebooks for later analysis.

To appreciate the importance of nonverbal communication systems, consider the unskilled inner-city black looking for a job. His handling of time and space alone is sufficiently different from the white middle-class pattern to create great misunderstandings on both sides. The black is told to appear for a job interview at a certain time. He arrives late. The white interviewer concludes from his tardy arrival that the black is irresponsible and not really interested in the job. What the interviewer doesn't know is that the black time system (often referred to by blacks as C. P. T.—colored people's time) isn't the same as that of whites. In the words of a black student who had been told to make an appointment to see his professor: "Man, you *must* be putting me on. I never had an appointment in my life."

The black job applicant, having arrived late for his interview, may further antagonize the white interviewer by his posture and his eye behavior. Perhaps he slouches and avoids looking at the interviewer; to him, this is playing it cool. To the interviewer, however, he may well look shifty and sound uninterested. The interviewer has failed to notice the actual signs of interest and eagerness in the black's behavior, such as the subtle shift in the quality of the voice—a gentle and tentative excitement—an almost imperceptible change in the cast of the eyes and a relaxing of the jaw muscles.

Moreover, correct reading of black-white behavior is continually complicated by the fact that both groups are comprised of individuals—some of whom try to accommodate and some of whom make it a point of pride *not* to accommodate. At present, this means that many Americans, when thrown into contact with one another, are in the precarious position of not knowing which pattern applies. Once identified and analyzed, nonverbal communication systems can be taught, like a foreign language. Without this training, we respond to nonverbal communications in terms of our own culture; we read everyone's behavior as if it were our own, and thus we often misunderstand it.

Several years ago in New York City, there was a program for sending children from predominantly black and Puerto Rican low-income neighborhoods to summer school in a white upper-class neighborhood on the East Side. One morning, a group of young black and Puerto Rican boys raced down the street, shouting and screaming and overturning garbage cans on their way to school. A doorman from an apartment building nearby chased them and cornered one of them inside a building. The boy drew a knife and attacked the doorman. This tragedy would not have occurred if the doorman had been familiar with the behavior of boys from low-income neighborhoods, where such antics are routine and socially acceptable and where pursuit would be expected to invoke a violent response.

The language of behavior is extremely complex. Most of us are lucky to have under control one subcultural system—the one that reflects our sex, class, generation and geographic region within the United States. Because of its complexity, efforts to isolate bits of nonverbal communication and generalize from them are in vain; you don't become an instant expert on people's behavior by watching them at cocktail parties. Body language isn't something that's independent of the person, something that can be donned and doffed like a suit of clothes.

Our research and that of our colleagues has shown that, far from being a superficial form of communication that can be consciously manipulated, nonverbal communication systems are interwoven into the fabric of the personality and, as sociologist Erving Goffman has demonstrated, into society itself. They are the warp and woof of daily interactions with others and they influence how one expresses oneself, how one experiences oneself as a man or a woman.

Nonverbal communications signal to members of your own group what kind of person you are, how you feel about others, how you'll fit into and work in a group, whether you're assured or anxious, the degree to which you feel comfortable with the standards of your own culture, as well as deeply significant feelings about the self, including the state of your own psyche. For most of us, it's difficult to accept the reality of another's behavioral system. And, of course, none of us will ever become fully knowledgeable of the importance of every nonverbal signal. But as long as each of us realizes the power of these signals, this society's diversity can be a source of great strength rather than a further—and subtly powerful—source of division.

The Effects of Environment and Space on Human Communication

Mark L. Knapp

> Every interior betrays the nonverbal skills of its inhabitants. The choice of materials, the distribution of space, the kind of objects that command attention or demand to be touched—as compared to those that intimidate or repel—have much to say about the preferred sensory modalities of their owners.
>
> —Ruesch and Kees

The ultimate influence on students of the student–teacher dialogue in America's classrooms is unknown. Few would disagree that this particular communication context is an extremely critical one for many students.

What is the nature of the environment in which this important dialogue takes place? What difference does it make?

Most American classrooms are rectangular in shape with straight rows of chairs. They have wide windows which allow light to beam across the student's left shoulder. This window placement determines the direction students will face and thus designates the "front" of the classroom. Most classroom seats are also permanently attached to the floor for ease of maintenance and tidiness. Most classrooms have some type of partition (usually a desk) which separates teacher from students. Most students and teachers can provide a long list of "problems" encountered in environments designed for learning. Such complaints center around poor lighting, acoustics, temperature which is too hot or too cold, outside construction noises, banging radiators, electrical outlets which do not work, seats which do not move, gloomy, dull, or distracting color schemes, unpleasant odors, and so on. Why do they complain? Because they recognize that such problems impede the purpose for gathering in these rectangular rooms—which is to increase one's knowledge through effective student–teacher communication. The whole question of the influence of the classroom environment on student and teacher behavior remains relatively unexplored. One research project, however, provides us with some initial data on student participation in various classroom environments.[1]

Sommer selected six different kinds of classrooms for his study. He wanted to compare the amount of student participation in the different kinds of classrooms and to analyze the particular aspects of participatory behavior in each type. The types of classrooms included seminar rooms with movable chairs—usually arranged in the shape of a horseshoe; laboratories (complete with Bunsen burners, bottles, and gas valves) which represented an extreme in straight row seating; one room which was windowless, and one

which had an entire wall of windows. Undergraduate students acted as observers to record participation by the students. A distaste for the laboratory rooms and the windowless room was demonstrated through several attempts by instructors and students to change rooms or hold classes outside. Comparisons between rooms showed that in seminar rooms fewer people participated, but for longer periods of time. There were no differences between open and windowless rooms with respect to participation behavior.

When seminar rooms were analyzed separately, Sommer noted that most participation came from students seated directly opposite the instructor. Students generally avoided the two chairs on either side of the instructor—even when all other seats were filled. When a student did occupy the seat next to the instructor, he was generally silent throughout the entire period. In straight row rooms, the following observations were made: (1) Students within eye contact range of the instructor participate more. (2) There is a tendency for more participation to occur in the center sections of each row and for participation to generally decrease from the front to the back. This tendency, however, is not evident when interested students sit in locations other than those which provide maximum visual contact with the instructor. (3) Participation decreases as class size increases.

A related research project offers additional support for Sommer's observations on participation in straight row classrooms.[2] Adams and Biddle noted a remarkably consistent pattern

[1] R. Sommer, *Personal Space* (Englewood Cliffs, N.J.: Prentice-Hall, 1969): 110–19.

[2] R. S. Adams and B. Biddle, *Realities of Teaching: Explorations with Video Tape* (New York: Holt, Rinehart and Winston, 1970).

of interaction in Grades I, VI, and XI which indicated most student participation comes from students sitting in the center of the room. Sixty-three percent of the 1176 behaviors observed came from students located in three positions, one behind the other, down the center of the room. Almost all pupil-initiated comments came from the shadowed area in Figure 1. In no instance did teachers select special students for placement in these locations. As the authors point out, "it is now possible to discriminate an area of the classroom that seems to be literally and figuratively the center of activity."

Sommer concludes his observations on classroom behavior and environmental influences by saying:

> At the present time, teachers are hindered by their insensitivity to and fatalistic acceptance of the classroom environment. Teachers must be "turned on" to their environment lest their pupils develop this same sort of fatalism.[3]

The preceding discussion of the classroom was used as an illustrative example of a specific context in which the *spatial relationships, the architecture,* and *the objects* surrounding the participants influenced the type of interaction which occurred. Before we examine each of these areas in greater detail, we should recognize that even geographic location and climate may have some bearing on how we interact with our fellow men.

Geography and Climate

For many years, behavioral scientists have hypothesized that those who

[3] Sommer, *Personal Space*, p. 119.

FIGURE 1.   Zone of participation.

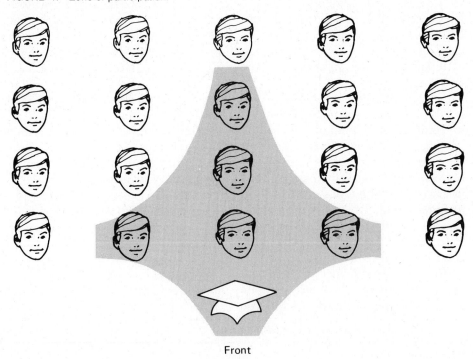

Front

choose to live in urban rather than rural areas will have fewer close personal relations. In the United States, however, there is less and less evidence to support this theory. Greater mobility and the influence of the mass media tend to offset the possibility that these differences exist. There is evidence to suggest, however, that the more physical mobility you have in a city, the less social intimacy you will have within your own neighborhood. If you are a resident new to the community, you will very likely associate with your neighbors more than do the old residents who know more people in other parts of town. And if the neighborhood is fairly homogeneous in terms of religious beliefs, social class, political attitudes, etc., these close relationships will tend to persist.

Some descriptive research, comparing characteristics of city and rural environments, reveals additional differences in city and country life—from which one may develop hypotheses concerning the effects of differing environments on the interaction patterns of the inhabitants. For instance: (1) there appears to be more political and religious tolerance in cities than in rural areas; (2) there appears to be less religious observance in cities than in rural areas; (3) there are more foreign immigrants in cities than in rural areas; (4) there is more change in cities and more stability in the country; (5) there is a higher level of education in cities than in rural areas; (6) there are fewer married people in the cities than in rural areas; (7) there is a lower birth rate in cities than in rural areas; (8) there is more divorce in cities than in rural areas; (9) there is more suicide in cities than in rural areas. In slums or ghettos in urban areas, one often finds a social climate which encourages or fosters unconventional and deviant behavior—or at least tolerates it. Thus, slum areas show a high incidence of juvenile delinquency, prostitution, severe mental illness, alcoholism and drug addiction, physical and mental disability, and crimes of violence.

Some have even speculated on the effects of the climate on man's behavior. There is considerable skepticism of this work—partially because climate (and moon positions and sun spots) seem too mystical to explain man's behavior, and partially because research studies conducted to date have generally used inadequate methods of scientific inquiry and control. Several pre-twentieth century authors hypothesized a relationship between climate and crime. More recently, the National Advisory Commission on Civil Disorders reported, in 1968, that the hot summer nights added to an already explosive situation which eventually resulted in widespread rioting in ghetto areas: "In most instances, the temperature during the day on which the violence erupted was quite high."[4] Griffitt varied heat and humidity under controlled laboratory conditions for students and confirmed a relationship to interpersonal responses. As temperature and humidity increased, evaluative responses for interpersonal attraction to another student decreased.[5] There may be more truth than fiction in the familiar explanation for a particularly unpleasant encounter, "Oh,

[4] U.S. National Advisory Commission on Civil Disorders, "Report of the National Advisory Commission on Civil Disorders" (Washington, D.C.: U.S. Government Printing Office, 1968): 71.
[5] W. Griffitt, "Environmental Effects of Interpersonal Affective Behavior: Ambient Effective Temperature and Attraction," *Journal of Personality and Social Psychology 15* (1970): 240–44.

he was just hot and irritable." Some research would even suggest air conditioning improves both student and teacher performance and attitudes toward the tasks they perform.

In the early twentieth century, Huntington advanced a seemingly bizarre theory that for mental vigour, an average outdoor temperature of 50 to 60 degrees is better than one above 70 degrees.[6] McClelland, in his analysis of folk stories in primitive societies, found that achievement motivation was highest in areas where the mean annual temperature ranged between 40 and 60 degrees Fahrenheit.[7] He also concluded that temperature variation was important in determining achievement motivation with at least fifteen degrees daily or seasonal variation needed for high achievement motivation. Lee speculates that tropical climates produce mental and physical lethargy:

> Some loss of mental initiative is probably the most important single direct result of exposure to tropical environment. . . . Certainly, the usual pattern of life in tropical countries is more leisurely and less productive of material goods than that which is found in most temperate latitudes, and a case can be made for at least some influence of climate in this respect. Man in the temperate zones has built up his civilization around the important demands created by cold weather for securing food and shelter in advance. In so doing, he has developed a culture in which activity and making provision for the future have high social values. In tropical populations, on the other hand, climate provides neither the social nor the psychological drive for activity and saving

beyond the needs of the more or less immediate future. This difference in "spontaneous" activity marks one of the most important conflicts at the personal level between temperate and tropical modes of behavior.[8]

A final note—hardly worth reporting were it not for the fact that this author was born in July—some researchers have even argued that American babies born in the North, in the summer months, have slightly higher I.Q. scores in later life than those born at other times!

These reports on geography and climate provide us with little reliable and valid information. The fact that geographical location and atmospheric conditions do exert some influence on human interaction seems to be a reasonable assumption. The exact nature of this influence, under what specific conditions this influence occurs, and the degree of influence are still unknown.

The Architecture and Objects Around Us

At one time in America's history, banks were deliberately designed to project an image of strength and security. The design frequently included large marble pillars, an abundance of metal bars and doors, uncovered floors, and barren walls. This style generally elicited a cold, impersonal reaction from visitors. Not too many years ago bankers perceived a need to change their environment—to present a friendly, warm, "homey" image where people would enjoy sitting down and openly discussing their financial prob-

[6] E. Huntington, *Civilization and Climate* (New Haven: Yale University Press, 1915).
[7] D. McClelland, *The Achieving Society* (New York: Van Nostrand Reinhold, 1961).

[8] D. Lee, *Climate and Economic Development in the Tropics* (New York: Harper & Row, 1957), p. 100.

lems. The interiors of banks began to change. Carpeting was added; wood was used to replace metal; cushioned chairs were added; potted plants were used in some cases for additional "warmth," along with other, similar changes designed to create the same effect. This is but one example of a situation in which it was recognized that oftentimes the interior within which interaction occurs can significantly influence the nature of the interaction. Night club owners and restaurateurs are aware that dim lighting will provide greater intimacy and will cause patrons to linger longer than they would in an interior with high illumination and no soundproofing.

Sometimes we get very definite person-related messages from home environments. Our perception of the inhabitants of a home may be structured before we meet them—whether we think they decorated their house for themselves, for others, for conformity, for comfort, etc. We may be influenced by the mood created by the wallpaper, by the quality and apparent cost of the items placed around the house, and by many, many other things. Most of us have had the experience of being ushered into a living room which we perceive should be labeled an "unliving" room. We hesitate to sit down or touch anything because the room seems to say to us, "This room is for show purposes only; sit, walk, and touch carefully; it takes a lot of time and effort to keep this room neat, clean and tidy; we don't want to clean it after you leave." The arrangement of other living rooms seems to say, "Sit down, make yourself comfortable, feel free to talk informally, and don't worry about spilling things." Interior decorators and product promotion experts

often have experiential and intuitive judgments about the influence of certain colors, objects, shapes, arrangements, etc., but there have been few attempts to empirically validate these feelings. Perhaps the best known empirical research into the influence of interior decoration on human responses were the studies of Maslow and Mintz.[9]

Maslow and Mintz selected three rooms for study—one was an "ugly" room (designed to give the impression of a janitor's storeroom in disheveled condition); one was a "beautiful" room (complete with carpeting, drapes, etc.), and one was an "average" room (a professor's office). Subjects were asked to rate a series of negative print photographs of faces. The experimenters tried to keep all factors, such as time of day, odor, noise, type of seating, and experimenter, constant from room to room so that any results could be attributed to the type of room. Results showed that subjects in the beautiful room tended to give significantly higher ratings to the faces than did participants in the ugly room. Experimenters and subjects alike engaged in various escape behaviors to avoid the ugly room. The ugly room was variously described as producing monotony, fatigue, headache, discontent, sleep, irritability, and hostility. The beautiful room, however, produced feelings of pleasure, comfort, enjoyment, importance, energy, and desire to continue the activity. In this instance, we have a well-controlled study which offers

[9] A. H. Maslow and N. L. Mintz, "Effects of Esthetic Surroundings: I. Initial Effects of Three Esthetic Conditions Upon Perceiving 'Energy' and 'Well-Being' in Faces," *Journal of Psychology* 41 (1956): 247–54. Also: N. L. Mintz, "Effects of Esthetic Surroundings: II. Prolonged and Repeated Experience in a 'Beautiful' and 'Ugly' Room," *Journal of Psychology* 41 (1956): 459–66.

some evidence of the impact of visual-esthetic surroundings on the nature of human interaction. Similar studies have tested recall and problem solving in rooms similar to those used by Maslow and Mintz. In both cases, more effective performance is found in rooms which are well appointed or "beautiful."[10]

Some pencil and paper research even associates specific colors with specific human "moods." Wexner presented eight colors and 11 mood-tones to 94 subjects. The results (see Table 1) show that for some mood-tones a single color is significantly related; for others there may be two or more colors.[11]

A real problem in interpreting such research concerns whether people pick colors which are actually associated with particular moods or whether they are responding using learned verbal stereotypes. Another problem with some of the color preference research concerns the lack of association between colors and objects. Pink may be your favorite color, but you may still dislike pink hair. Nevertheless, we cannot ignore the body of educational and design literature which suggests that carefully planned color schemes seem to have some influence on improving scholastic achievement. Obviously, we cannot make any final judgments about the impact of color on human interaction until behavioral studies link dif-

Table 1 Colors Associated with Moods

Mood-Tone	Color	Frequency of Times Chosen
Exciting-Stimulating	Red	61
Secure-Comfortable	Blue	41
Distressed-Disturbed-Upset	Orange	34
Tender-Soothing	Blue	41
Protective-Defending	Red	21
	Brown	17
	Blue	15
	Black	15
	Purple	14
Despondent-Dejected-Unhappy-Melancholy	Black	25
	Brown	25
Calm-Peaceful-Serene	Blue	38
	Green	31
Dignified-Stately	Purple	45
Cheerful-Jovial-Joyful	Yellow	40
Defiant-Contrary-Hostile	Red	23
	Orange	21
	Black	18
Powerful-Strong-Masterful	Black	48

ferently colored environments with different types of verbal behavior or communication patterns. In short, what configuration of circumstances is necessary for environmental color to affect human interaction to any appreciable degree? Another study tested the effects of rooms of different sizes (150 cubic feet vs. 1600 cubic feet), different shapes (circular vs. rectangular), and different reverberation times (.8–1.0 seconds vs .2–3 seconds) upon a speaker's rate and intensity in reading aloud.[12] Generally, the data suggest that rate and intensity of reading were affected by the size of the room and the reverberation time—but not by the shape. Rate seemed to be slower in the larger and less reverberant rooms; vocal intensity was greater in smaller and less reverberant rooms; and intensity consistently increased as

[10] H. Wong and W. Brown, "Effects of Surroundings Upon Mental Work as Measured by Yerkes' Multiple Choice Method," *Journal of Comparative Psychology* 3 (1923): 319–31; and J. M. Bilodeau and H. Schlosberg, "Similarity in Stimulating Conditions as a Variable in Retroactive Inhibition," *Journal of Experimental Psychology* 41 (1959): 199–204.

[11] L. B. Wexner, "The Degree to Which Colors (Hues) Are Associated with Mood-Tones," *Journal of Applied Psychology* 38 (1954): 432–35. Also, see D. C. Murray and H. L. Deabler, "Colors and Mood-Tones," *Journal of Applied Psychology* 41 (1957): 279–83.

[12] J. W. Black, "The Effect of Room Characteristics Upon Vocal Intensity and Rate," *Journal of the Acoustical Society of America* 22 (1950): 174–76.

the subject read through the twelve phrases provided in the less reverberant rooms.

The architecture and arrangement of objects in various man-made structures can suggest who shall meet whom, when, where, and perhaps for how long. In other words, objects can control actions.

> The life of domestic animals is, among other things, controlled through the erection of fences, flap doors, or the placement of food and water in particular locations. Although the control of human situations is implemented through verbal and nonverbal actions, manipulation of barriers, openings, and other physical arrangements is rather helpful. Meeting places can be appropriately rigged so as to regulate human traffic and, to a certain extent, the network of communication.[13]

In some cases, human interaction is inhibited or prohibited by environmental cues. Fences separating yards create obvious barriers—even if they are only waist high.

An experiment conducted in a doctor's office suggests that the presence or absence of a desk may significantly alter the patient's "at ease" state.[14] With the desk separating doctor and patient, only 10% of the patients were perceived "at ease," whereas removal of the desk brought the figure of "at ease" patients up to 55%. There seems to be little doubt that the location of a television set in a room has a definite influence on the positioning of chairs, and, in turn, on the pattern of conversations which occur in that room.

Less obvious barriers also exist. For instance, if you find a delicate objet d'art placed in front of some books in a bookcase you will likely feel hesitant about using the books. In at least one case, a furniture designer has deliberately designed a chair to exert disagreeable pressure on a person's spine when occupied for more than a few minutes. The Larsen Chair was originally designed to keep patrons from becoming too comfortable and remaining in seats which could be occupied by other customers.[15] Hotel owners and airport designers apparently are already aware of the "too comfortable" phenomenon. Thus, seating arrangements are deliberately made uncomfortable for long seating and conversations so patrons will "move along" and perhaps drift into nearby shops where they can spend some of their money. Some environments seem to have an unwritten code which prohibits interaction. The lone men entering, sitting, and leaving "girlie" movies without a word are a case in point.

Other environmental situations seem to facilitate interaction. Homes placed in the middle of a block seem to draw more interpersonal exchanges than those located in other positions on the block. Houses which have adjacent driveways seem to have a built-in structure drawing the neighbors together and inviting communication. Cavan reports that the likelihood of interaction between strangers at a bar varies directly with the distance between them.[16] As a rule, a span of three bar stools is the maximum distance over which patrons will attempt to initiate an encounter. Two men conversing

[13] J. Ruesch and J. Kees, *Nonverbal Communication* (Berkeley: University of California Press, 1956), p. 126.
[14] A. G. White, "The Patient Sits Down: A Clinical Note," *Psychosomatic Medicine* 15 (1953): 256–57.

[15] Sommer, *Personal Space*, p. 121.
[16] S. Cavan, *Liquor License* (Chicago: Aldine Publishing Co., 1966).

with an empty bar stool between them are likely to remain that way since they would be too close if they sat next to each other. However, if a man is talking to a woman and there is an empty stool between them, he will likely move onto it—to prevent someone else from coming between them. Some recent designs for housing elderly people have taken into consideration the need for social contact. These apartment dwellings have the doors of the apartments on a given floor open into a common entranceway. The probabilities for social exchange are then greatly increased over the situation in which apartment doors are staggered on either side of a long hallway so that no doorways face one another.

The whole question of physical proximity has received much attention from researchers concerned with human interaction. Stouffer comments:

> Whether one is seeking to explain why persons go to a particular place to get jobs, why they go to trade at a particular store, why they go to a particular neighborhood to commit a crime, or why they marry the particular spouse they choose, the factor of spatial distance is of obvious significance.[17]

Several studies have confirmed Stouffer's remark. For instance, students tend to develop stronger friendships with students who share their classes, or their dormitory or apartment building, or who sit near them, than with others who are geographically distant. Workers tend to develop closer friendships with those who work close to them. Some research concludes that increased proximity of white

persons and blacks will assist in reducing prejudice.[18] Several studies show an inverse relationship between the distance separating potential marriage partners and the number of marriages. For example, in New Haven in 1940, Kennedy reports 76% of the marriages were between persons living within twenty blocks of each other and 35% were between persons living within five blocks of each other.[19] Obviously, proximity allows us to obtain more information about the other person, but some have even suggested that proximity, in and of itself, may facilitate attraction to another person—apart from any information it may provide about the other person. The inescapable conclusion seems to be that as proximity increases, attraction is likely to increase. One might also posit that as attraction increases, proximity will tend to increase.

Perhaps the most famous study of proximity, friendship choice, and interpersonal contact was conducted by Festinger, Schachter, and Back in a housing development for married students.[20] Concern for what the authors called "functional distance" led to the

[17] S. A. Stouffer, "Intervening Opportunities: A Theory Relating Mobility and Distance," *American Sociological Review* 5 (1940): 845–67.

[18] M. Deutsch and M. Collins, *Interracial Housing: A Psychological Evaluation of a Social Experiment* (Minneapolis: University of Minnesota Press, 1951). It is interesting that some attack social legislation designed to eliminate segregation because it does not change attitudes but only forces civil obedience. This study, and others, suggest there are times when bringing those of different races together in close proximity will indeed bring about corresponding, positive attitude changes. Caution should be exercised in the generalization of such an idea, however. If the two groups are extremely polarized, proximity may only serve to magnify the hostilities.

[19] R. Kennedy, "Premarital Residential Propinquity," *American Journal of Sociology* 48 (1943): 580–84.

[20] L. Festinger, S. Schachter, and K. Back, *Social Pressures in Informal Groups: A Study of Human Factors in Housing* (New York: Harper & Row, 1950). For another interesting example of how architecture structures interaction, see R. R. Blake, C. C. Rhead, B. Wedge, and J. S. Mouton, "Housing Architecture and Social Interaction," *Sociometry* 19 (1956): 133–39.

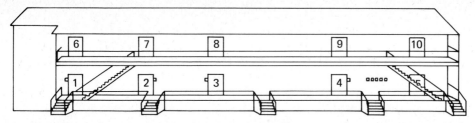

FIGURE 2.

uncovering of some data which clearly demonstrated that architects can have a tremendous influence on the social life of residents in these housing pro-

mined by the number of contacts that position and design encourage—e.g., which way apartments face, where exits and entranceways are located, location of stairways, mailboxes, etc. Figure 2 shows the basic design of one type of building studied.

The researchers asked the residents of seventeen buildings (with the design of Figure 2) what people they saw most often socially and what friendship choices they made. Among the various findings from this study, the following are noteworthy: (1) There seemed to be a greater number of sociometric choices for those who were physically close to one another—on the same floor, in the same building, etc. It was rare to find a friendship between people separated by more than four

or five houses. (2) People living in apartments 1 and 5 gave and received from the upper floor residents more sociometric choices than the people living in any other apartment on the lower floor. (3) Apartments 1 and 6 exchanged more choices than apartments 2 and 7. Similarly, apartments 5 and 10 exchanged more choices than apartments 4 and 9. Although this represents the same physical distance, functional distance differed. (4) Apartment 7 chose 6 more than it chose 8; apartment 9 chose 10 more than it chose 8. This relationship did not hold true for corresponding first floor apartments. (5) Because of the mailboxes, apartment 5 chose more upper level friends—more of those choices being apartments 9 and 10. There are many ways of making friends, but functional distance seems to be highly influential—and functional distance is sometimes the result of architectural design.

Action Steps: Applications

1. Note the environmental factors in your classroom. Can you determine the nature and extent of their influence on interaction in class? Discuss this issue with one or two of your classmates. Later, note any environmental influences at work in that discussion.
2. Think of the most successful discussion in which you have participated: Did it have an assigned leader? Was some organizational plan followed?

Was everyone in the group active? Was the group able to achieve consensus? Determine some criteria for measuring the success of a group experience.

3. Attend a meeting in an organization outside of class (campus, church, community). Analyze the interaction in terms of the communication variables suggested in this chapter.

4. In Knapp's article, "The Effects of Environment and Space on Human Communication," he discusses the influence of seating arrangements on behavior in small groups. Observe at least two meetings of a local campus policy-making or problem-solving group. Determine the degree that the seating arrangements affect the interaction.

5. Observe with care the cultural differences suggested by Hall and Hall in people's use of eye contact, postures, and spatial distances. Share the reports of your observations with the class.

6. Many of your class activities have involved discussion in small groups. Evaluate these discussions, trying to find out why some were more successful than others. Consider both the factors that helped and the factors that hindered discussion.

Chapter 7
Developing Relationships

I N MANY CASES, people attempt to build rewarding relationships with whomever happens to be nearby—members of the immediate family, school classmates, college roommates, the man or woman next door. Such relationships appear to be based on convenience; often they are not stable or rewarding. In some cases, the relationship may have started well and brought early signs of interpersonal reward; then, after a time, it became rigid, sterile, unrewarding. For the most part, in developing our interpersonal relationships, we tend to do the best we can, riding our emotional storms, accommodating others whenever possible or when we feel like it, and hoping for the best.

Our complex, mobile, automated society has produced a heightened condition of impersonality. As a result, we see a new emphasis on seeking warm, personal relationships. The yearning for closer personal ties is a major theme of our times. Without reservation we can conclude that for people today, the most significant phase of the process of interpersonal communication is developing and maintaining warm, personal relationships.

As two people interact, the relationship between them tends to stabilize, "freeze," become rigid and unchangeable. To improve an existing relationship or to achieve the most satisfying potential from a developing one, we must analyze it, evaluate it, and, if need be, change it if at all possible. In this chapter we focus on the process of analyzing, evaluating, and changing an interpersonal relationship.

A relationship may be analyzed in terms of its basic patterns of interaction and degree of rigidity. Both are important to your understanding if changes or improvements are to be sought. As you interact with another person, it is likely that you gain a general impression of "where you stand" with him or her. You seem to be fairly close, sympathetic with each other, and seem to like each other. Generally you cooperate, confide, and respect each other's wishes. The questions we are raising are these: Can the primary behavioral dimensions of a relationship be defined and identified? In how many *different* ways do people relate to each other? How many of these are really *important*, significant? In a given situation, can these be observed and the *intensity* of each estimated?

Dimensions of a Relationship

Three decades of research support the conclusion that any interpersonal relationship has three primary dimensions: (1) the degree of involvement, (2) the emotional tone or feelings, and (3) the amount of interpersonal control.[1]

INTERPERSONAL INVOLVEMENT

The degree of involvement in a relationship refers not only to the *amount* of interaction between the participants, but also to the importance each attaches to this interaction. If two people seldom see or talk to each other and, when they do, simply exchange impersonal greetings, the degree of their mutual involvement with each other is small. This is especially true if they do not notice that for days they don't see each other. For example, you may have a classmate who ordinarily sits on the opposite side of the room. Did he attend class yesterday? If you can't remember, your degree of involvement in this relationship is low, even if you tend to see and talk to each other two or three times a week. Conversely, you and your father may live in different distant cities, see each other twice a year, and communicate only four or five times a year, and still have a high degree of involvement in your relationship. If each idea he presents, each sentence he speaks or writes, is given careful thought and attention, then your degree of involvement is high.

The degree of involvement is closely related to the amount of personal information exchanged. To be involved with someone you must know some things about him/her that matter to you, things that are significant. If your involvement with another person is to be high, you and that person will have to reveal significant parts of yourselves to each other. There are fairly dependable research data showing that when self-disclosure is high, interpersonal involvement is heightened.[2]

Scholars who are studying the development of interpersonal relationships are generally agreed upon three principles according to Michael Roloff in his summary of their research:

1. A relationship requires sharing of information by the persons involved.
2. As information is shared, participants make more discriminating predictions about one another's responses.
3. As more discriminating predictions are made, the relationship becomes more valuable to the participants.[3]

Essentially four requirements must be met if a relationship is to develop: self-

[1] For a review of this body of research, see Kim Giffin and Bobby R. Patton, *Personal Communication in Human Relations* (Columbus, Ohio: Merrill, 1974), pp. 55–60; for further corroboration by a more recent study see Myron Wish, Morton Deutsch, and Susan J. Kaplan, "Perceived Dimensions of Interpersonal Relations," *Journal of Personality and Social Psychology*, 33 (1976): 409–420.

[2] W. Barnett Pearce and Stewart M. Sharp, "Self-disclosing Communication," *Journal of Communication*, 23 (1973): 409–425.

[3] Michael E. Roloff, "Communication Strategies, Relationships and Relational Change," in Gerald R. Miller, *Explorations in Interpersonal Communication* (Beverly Hills, Calif.: Sage Publications, 1976), pp. 173–194.

disclosure by both participants, positive interpersonal perceptions, sharing of information about one another's self-concepts, and predictions made and fulfilled regarding desirable responses to each other.[4]

Suppose, for example, that you (a woman) meet someone on the tennis court. You like his looks. This personal information initiates a degree of involvement on your part. You chat awhile and you like the sense of personal values implied by the conversation: He expresses regard for friends, appreciation of personal skill and achievement, and interest in conversing with you. You play tennis for an hour and receive an impression of honesty in keeping the score, determination to do one's best, and fairness in judging out-of-bounds serves. At lunch you are impressed by his courtesy and consideration for others, cleanliness in eating habits, and friendliness in meeting your needs or wishes. During the next half hour you hear of his hopes for graduation, ambition to be a pediatrician, frustration over required courses, and sadness over the recent loss of a grandfather. If over the ensuing days such self-disclosure continues and you can continue to be interested in such personal information, involvement in the relationship will increase. In addition, disclosure of the way he *feels about you* can lead to greater involvement. If he shows interest in and respect for your hopes, ambitions, values, and frustrations, your degree of involvement will be heightened, and the relationship will be of greater importance both to you and to him.

As people interact and disclose items of personal information to each other, they tend to reach little agreements on what is important and what is not. Out of this sharing comes a working consensus of mutual sympathy and consideration. There is also a tendency to close the gaps between their individual differences of opinion. In essence, *involvement* in a relationship means that participants interact in ways that are important to each other. As involvement is increased, the other two dimensions of a relationship become important: *control* and *affect* (emotional tone). In an established relationship, the degree of involvement is usually quite stable. The amount of interaction may vary from day to day, but such variations are expected and routine. In such a relationship control and affect are of greatest concern.

THE EMOTIONAL TONE

Behavior related to *affect*, or emotional tone, in a relationship involves expressions of warmth, acceptance, and love, as well as hostility, rejection, and hate. It is frequently characterized by such positive terms as "friendship," "emotionally close," "sweetheart," and such negative terms as "dislike," "coldness," and "anger."

---

[4] See the following four studies: I. Altman and D. A. Taylor, *Social Penetration: The Development of Interpersonal Relationships* (New York: Holt, Rinehart and Winston, 1973); S. W. Duck, *Personal Relationships and Personal Constructs: A Study of Friendship Formation* (New York: Wiley); C. R. Berger and R. J. Calabrese, "Some Explorations in Initial Interaction and Beyond: Toward a Developmental Theory of Interpersonal Communication," *Human Communication Research*, 1 (1975): 99–112; and G. R. Miller and M. Steinberg, *Between People: A New Analysis of Interpersonal Communication* (Palo Alto, Calif.: Science Research Associates, 1975).

Affectionate behavior on the part of one person tends to produce affectionate responses on the part of the other.

In a relationship, affectionate behavior on the part of one person tends to produce affectionate responses on the part of the other; on the other hand, hostile behavior tends to produce hostility. Behavior that can be characterized as severe hostility nearly always produces resentment, dislike, and anger; over time, many people learn to hate. We may thus conclude that interpersonal affect behavior falling on our affection–hostility continuum ordinarily elicits similar responses.[5] Affection elicits affection in response; hostility elicits hostility.

CONTROL: DOMINANCE–SUBMISSION

Dominant behavior in a relationship tends to produce submissive responses; this, of course, is only true if interaction continues.[6] If dominant behavior by one person continues and resistance is shown by the other person, the relationship may very likely be terminated. If a power struggle continues in a relationship, this struggle may last for days, months, or even years. In some families it may never be resolved; it may lead to the use of manipulative games or strategies that continue endlessly.[7] Whereas the appetite for sex or comfort is limited, the appetite for power can be limitless.[8]

---

[5] T. Leary, *Interpersonal Diagnosis of Personality* (New York: Ronald, 1957).

[6] T. Leary, "The Theory and Measurement Methodology of Interpersonal Communication," *Psychiatry*, 18 (1955): 147–161.

[7] For a discussion of such tactics and strategies, see G. R. Bach and Peter Wyden, *The Intimate Enemy* (New York: Morrow, 1968).

[8] For a discussion of the principle, see Silvano Arieti, *The Will To Be Human* (New York: Quadrangle Press, 1973): see especially Chapter 8.

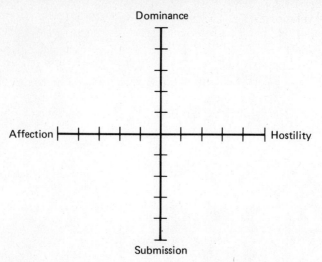

Dominance

Affection ├──┼──┼──┼──┼──┼──┼──┼──┼──┤ Hostility

Submission

FIGURE 7.1. The D-A-S-H paradigm of interpersonal relationships.

Submissive behavior in a relationship tends to elicit domination by the other person.[9] If you are dominated, it is not entirely the other person's fault. Submission reinforces dominating behavior, and vice versa.

THE D-A-S-H PARADIGM

These three dimensions of a relationship: involvement, emotional tone, and degree of control, can be analyzed in terms of a model, or paradigm. Drawing from the research of scholars in a variety of fields,[10] we suggest that an established relationship can be diagrammed in terms of two areas: amount of dominance–submission and amount of affection–hostility. By placing these four elements on an axis, we then have the D-A-S-H paradigm (Figure 7.1).

The value of the D-A-S-H paradigm as we attempt to analyze our own interpersonal relationships is that it makes our work easier and more efficient. It gives us primary targets for our analysis. Instead of saying to ourselves such things as, "We are usually friendly toward each other but I always feel uncomfortable and my feelings get hurt," we can review our interpersonal behavior with another person *in toto*. In so doing we can usually arrive at a satisfactory summary of the relationship in terms of the two dimensions: Am I *generally* dominant or submissive? Are we mostly affectionate or hostile (or in between)? In arriving at answers to these questions we review prior interpersonal behavior and observe more carefully interaction events as they transpire from day to day. We look for evidence of our tentative conclusions—smiles, disagreements, squeezes of a held hand, a smile unreturned, frowns, "hard looks," and many other such behaviors that Erving Goffman calls "tie-signs"—indica-

[9] See Leary, "Theory and Measurement Methodology," pp. 155–161.
[10] For a detailed discussion of the origins of this model, see Kim Giffin and Bobby R. Patton, *Fundamentals of Interpersonal Communication* (New York: Harper & Row, 1976), pp. 186–189.

tions that the relationship is affectionate or hostile, that we are dominating or being dominated.[11]

The D-A-S-H paradigm can be useful to you as you attempt to summarize your relationship with another person. The *essential* characteristics of any interpersonal relationship can be graphed on this model. For example, relationships between you (Y) and any other person (P) might be summarized in terms of the degree of *dominance, submission, affection,* or *hostility* shown by the distance of Y or P from the center of the D-A-S-H axis.

As you have been reading along, undoubtedly you have also been thinking about one of your own interpersonal relationships. Perhaps it is the one you have with your father. After giving it some thought, you may conclude that your relationship with him involves considerable mutual affection but contains some dominating efforts by your father to which you give small tokens of submission.

As you consider your relationship with another person, graph it as best you can on a D-A-S-H model. Reflect for a while; compare this relationship with other relationships of your own or with some you have observed on the part of other couples or groups. Make a tentative assessment and plot it on a graph. Then pay special attention to interaction events that transpire between you and the other person over a number of days. See if your tentative summary tends to be supported; if not, change it to comply with your observations.

Stages of Relationship Interaction

In Chapter 3 we introduced the concept of ERP (estimated relationship potential) when we encounter new people. Based upon this perceived potential for satisfying our needs, a relationship may develop into one of intimacy and love. Mark L. Knapp has identified ten stages that depict how relationships are built, maintained and terminated.[12]

The first five stages are described as processes of "coming together":

1. *Initiating.* As described in our discussion of ERP, individuals meeting for the first time "size each other up" as they tend to talk on casual, nonthreatening topics. The nonverbal signals of mutual attraction and liking are particularly important.
2. *Experimenting.* In this stage commonalities and norms are sought out. "Oh, you went to Ohio State, then maybe you know . . . ?" "Have you ever been to that new disco south of town?" Some degree of uncertainty is reduced as we gather more data on the relationship potential.
3. *Intensifying.* Mutual involvement and risk characterize this stage. Touching behaviors now complement the verbal messages that start to talk of

[11] E. Goffman, *Relations in Public* (New York: Basic Books, 1971), pp. 194–199.
[12] M. L. Knapp, *Social Intercourse from Greeting to Goodbye* (Boston: Allyn and Bacon, 1978), pp. 17–28.

sharing perceptions and experiences. The relationship becomes one of "close friends" with sexuality introduced as a factor in the relationship, if appropriate.

4. *Integrating.* The two individuals merge in such a way that the two "I's" become a "we." They are now viewed as a couple by their friends; signs of this stage include exchanging rings, dressing in a coordinated fashion, and the sharing of common property.

5. *Bonding.* The final stage of "coming together" formalizes a public commitment as with a marriage. A contract of explicit and implicit rules and regulations is agreed upon as the couple makes their integration fixed and more predictable.

These stages of "coming together" are sequential and build on one another. Either party may choose not to progress from one stage to another, and most relationships are frozen permanently in the second or third stage of development. We do not have the time, energy, inclination, or capability of becoming integrated with many people in a lifetime. With our greatly lengthened life spans (our life expectancy has doubled in less that a hundred years), the possibilities for and demands on long-term relationships are greater than ever before. As Carl Rogers has pointed out, "The flaws in a relationship which might be endured for ten years will not be endured for fifty. The number of elements that can change lives and make a relationship unstable is multiplied . . ."[13]

Unless the couple is able to continue to grow together and adjust in a continually changing environment, the relationship may start to "come apart." While neither person has permanent control or power over the other, each person has the power of choice of whether to preserve the relationship. Knapp has identified the following five processes of "coming apart":

1. *Differentiation.* "Literally, to differentiate means to become distinct or different in character. Just as integrating is mainly a process of fusion, differentiating is mainly a process of disengaging or uncoupling."[14] Usually conflict and fighting develop as personal differences and individuality are asserted. The degree of the commitment is tested.

2. *Circumscribing.* Strategies are developed by both parties for the amount and quality of the information exchanged. Touchy topics are avoided as the communication becomes more superficial and "safe." At parties, a great deal of effort may be made to be highly social and to cover up the relationship problems, but when alone, "the two people exhibit mutual silence, empty gazes, and a general feeling of exhaustion."[15]

3. *Stagnating.* During this stage of "marking time," all the messages are carefully thought out, and very little of substance is discussed. This time period may be long or short, depending upon the degrees of pain and the alternatives available to the current relationship.

[13] C. R. Rogers, *On Personal Power* (New York: Delta, 1977), p. 43.
[14] Knapp, *Social Intercourse,* p. 23.
[15] Ibid., p. 24.

People must be authentic if their relationship is to grow.

4. *Avoiding*. As the name suggests, the people now attempt to avoid face-to-face interaction. Physical separation and avoiding giving rewards to the other are attempted.
5. *Terminating*. As with the death of a person, the death of a relationship is typically a time of pain and feelings of loss. Distancing in both a physical and a psychological sense occurs, as does "disassociation," as the individuals move to lives without each other.

These stages are sequential, but the amount of time spent in any one stage may vary greatly among couples or even between the two people involved in the relationship. However, the stages are reciprocal in that the behavior of one of the persons will pull the other to behave in a similar manner.

Another model for noting the sequences in a relationship has been suggested by Friedman, Giffin, and Patton.[16] They have proposed the "A-frame" as a model means of achieving authenticity in a relationship. They identify five processes, each divided into two parts, one focusing on the *self* and the second focusing on communication with *others*:

1. *Awareness* is the process by which individuals grow to know with finer accuracy and subtlety what they themselves and others believe, feel, and do.
2. *Acceptance* is the degree to which people perceive and express worth in themselves and others.

[16] P. Friedman, K. Giffin, and B. R. Patton, "The A-Frame: Processes of Authentic Communication." Presented at the November, 1978 meeting of the Speech Communication Association.

3. *Actualizing* is the spontaneous, open sharing of one's ideas and feelings in the process of moving deeper and closer to another.
4. *Assertion* is the exercise of influence or control over one's own behavior or situation when something of personal significance merits expression.
5. *Aiding* is the process whereby a personal problem is examined and worked through to a satisfying resolution.

These five processes may go on simultaneously and be repeated throughout the life of a relationship; for the process to promote maximum growth, the participants must be authentic with each other and themselves. The stages are sequential in the sense that aiding, for example, cannot be accomplished until the other processes are operative.

Punctuation of Interaction

As you attempt to summarize your relationship with another person, you may find some difficulty with what has been called the "punctuation" of ongoing interaction behavior.[17] As we interact with others we are usually aware of little interaction events, encounters, or communication sequential units. For example, we meet, they smile, we respond, they tell us some news, we show what we think of it, we talk, then we note we must move along to do other things; so we show our pleasure regarding this meeting and we say we will meet again at some specified time. What happened first, second, third, and so on may be viewed collectively as an interaction unit or encounter.

In an ongoing series of such events or encounters, we tend to find one event overlapping with another. We may "pick up where we left off" or relate back to some midpoint item. It may be difficult, even a bit arbitrary, to decide when any particular sequence of communicative acts started—who did what first, who "responded" to whom, and so on. Even so, as we reflect back on such happenings, we usually have an impression of what behavior preceded another and what response it received. The way we reflectively or cognitively break up a series of ongoing, recurring actions into units may be termed our *punctuation* of such an ongoing series. Although the concept of "punctuation" may seem to you to be vague or complex, we bring it up because it can have considerable significance as you attempt to analyze your relationship with another person. The way you punctuate your interaction with him/her can make a difference in the way you view the relationship.

The punctuation made by one of the interacting persons may be quite different from that made by the other person in the relationship; differences in punctuation can thus produce confusion and misunderstanding. Consider a couple having marital difficulties. Suppose that the husband generally shows passive withdrawal and then reentry into the communication situation. In explaining the couple's disagreements and frustrations, he will indicate that

[17] Cf. P. Watzlawick, J. H. Beavin, and D. D. Jackson, *Pragmatics of Human Communication* (New York: Norton, 1967), pp. 80–93.

withdrawal is his only defense against her nagging. He will indicate that she nags, he withdraws; he goes back into the situation, she nags, he withdraws. The wife's interpretation of the interaction sequences, however, will very likely be that he withdraws and she has to nag to get him back into talking with her. Their two interpretations have been identified as follows:

1. "I withdraw because you nag."
2. "I nag because you withdraw."[18]

Seldom, however, do people recognize such a problem or talk about these things. The point to be noted is that in analyzing your relationship with another person, your own punctuation of communication events or encounters should be noted and shared as accurately as possible. We suggest that you seek help, if needed and possible, of a trusted observer outside the relationship.

Determining the Degree of Rigidity in a Relationship

The degree of rigidity, the established routine, is an important consideration in analyzing your relationships. It provides a basis for estimating the possibility of change and improvement, a primary issue in a relationship's value to us.

Timothy Leary and his associates, known at that time (1957) as the Kaiser Foundation Group, suggested the principle of *interpersonal behavior reflex*.[19] In his studies of interpersonal communication, Leary arrived at this conclusion: A large percentage of interpersonal behaviors simply involve a reflex—an automatic response.[20] Such behaviors are so automatic that they are often unconscious and even at variance with the individual's own perception of them; they are involuntary responses to the behavior of the other person.

As we have noted, affectionate or hostile behavior tends to evoke similar behavior. If one person in a relationship is highly affectionate toward the other, that other person ordinarily responds with at least moderate affection. In like manner, hostility generally generates hostility. On the other hand, dominant or submissive behavior tends to produce its *reciprocal*. Ordinarily, if a relationship survives over time, dominant behavior elicits passive or submissive responses. The reverse is also true: Passivity tends to reinforce and thus produce dominant behavior on the part of the other person. Of course, in the event two dominant people try to relate to each other, a power struggle usually ensues; it may last for years and may often involve manipulative games. If neither person's behavior changes, the relationship may dissolve because *reciprocal* responses cannot be established.

To a large extent the effect of one person's behavior can be explained,

---

[18] Ibid., p. 56.
[19] For a brief summary and evaluation of the work of this group, see R. C. Carson, *Interaction Concepts of Personality* (Chicago: Aldine, 1969), pp. 103–116.
[20] Leary, "Theory and Measurement Methodology," pp. 147–161.

even predicted, on the basis of these principles: Affection or hostility elicits *similar* behavior, and dominance or submissiveness elicits *reciprocal* responses. As two people interact, one person's behavior produces responses by the other; these responses in turn produce responses on the part of the first person. Responses produce responses that produce responses. As time goes on, the two persons tend to work out a "shared definition" of their relationships.[21] The "starting" behavior may be forgotten; perhaps it was never consciously perceived or analyzed; or perhaps it was misperceived because of an erroneous expectation. Nevertheless, once in motion, responses to responses tend to produce what may be called a "lockstep" effect. Once such a lockstep series has been established, change is difficult to achieve. A singular response, once given, tends to elicit a singular response from the other person, and the lockstep effect goes into full swing. On the other hand, many persons have a wider *repertoire* of responses and can appropriately react in different ways to different interpersonal behaviors. *The range of a person's response repertoire will tend to determine the degree of rigidity of his/her interpersonal relationships.* As we view two persons interacting, the degree of rigidity in their relationship to each other will be a function of the variety in the response repertoires of the two individuals.

To test the degree of rigidity in one of your own interpersonal relationships, you can "try out" new responses to the other person's behavior. Be prepared for his/her surprise—even shock, confusion, or disgust! Note the degree to which you are able to use a wider repertoire of responses; note, also, the other person's responses, especially any new ones. This procedure can give you some kind of index of the degree of rigidity in the relationship.

Manipulative Relationship Styles

Everett Shostrom analyzed the role-playing and rigid patterns in male–female relationships and explored the unconscious foundations of these patterns in people's personalities.[22] He describes certain characteristic relationship styles as exploitative or manipulative. In Shostrom's diagram (see Figure 7.2), six relationship patterns are identified in which the participants are not really relating to each other; instead, they are leaning on one another, avoiding each other, or competing with each other out of personal inadequacy. The diagram shows couples at polar extremes in their capacities to express *strength* or *weakness, anger* or *love.* These dimensions equate closely with the dimensions of *emotional tone* and *control* cited in the previous section. When a couple, either consciously or unconsciously, allows their relationship to become locked or frozen in one of these ways, it becomes one of leaning rather than relating.

Note the six pairs:

1. The Nurturing Relationship: Mother and Son. In this relationship pattern, the *weak* man has chosen unconsciously his opposite, the *strong,*

---

[21] E. Goffman, *Behavior in Public Places* (New York: Free Press, 1963), p. 96.
[22] E. L. Shostrom, *Man the Manipulator, the Inner Journey from Manipulation to Actualization* (New York: Arlington Press, 1967) and E. L. Shostrom and James Kavanaugh, *Between Man and Woman* (Los Angeles: Nash, 1971).

FIGURE 7.2. The pair relationships. (From *Between Man and Woman*, copyright © 1971 by Everett Shostrom and James Kavanaugh, by permission of Nash Publishing Corp.)

motherlike woman. Strengths and weaknesses then become reciprocally exaggerated as the pattern persists. Later in the relationship, should either or both person's self-perception change, major perception adjustment is required.

2. The Supporting Relationship: Daddy and Doll. This relationship pattern is the gender reversal of the mother/son relationship because, in this case, the man displays strength and the woman weakness. As Shostrom and Kavanaugh state:

> Each is a kind of cultural distortion of masculinity and femininity. The man appears to be strong. He is suave, intelligent, cool, charming, personable, usually

successful, apparently confident and in control of every situation. In the stereotype, he sits calmly with his pipe in his mouth surveying the world and his little doll is more than willing to sit on his lap and accept his help and direction. Actually, he is not as strong as he is uninvolved in the relationship. His doll is his mannequin who frames his masculinity well, who, in a sense, establishes and supports it. She is not a person to him as much as she is an expensive plaything. He does not reveal to her his weakness, since his image depends on his revelation of strength. In reality, the doll is usually a much stronger person. She controls the relationship by exaggerating her weakness and dependency. She can whine and pout and smile her way into power. She is usually sexy to behold in a kind of hybrid cross between Lolita and Marilyn Monroe. Very often, however, she is not really involved sexually. She would be inclined to feign an orgasm because her image would demand that she have one. But she is not at all "letting go" in the relationship. She is holding the reins tight with childish manipulation. The daddy and his doll actually avoid each other; they pass in the hall, they do not make contact as persons.[23]

3.   The Challenging Relationship: Bitch and Nice Guy.   Shostrom and Kavanaugh characterize this relationship as "the real prototype of the unhappy American marriage."[24] The bitch exaggerates her expression of anger and the nice guy exaggerates his expression of love. The bitch tends to deny her need to love and be loved as a defense against the vulnerability she feels in love, and the nice guy is out of touch with his anger or assertiveness; from his needs to be liked and accepted, he is indirect in his hostility and often needles his bitchy wife.[25]

4.   The Educating Relationship: Master and Servant.   This master/slave relationship reflects the old cultural stereotype of the strong, unyielding male and the helpless, weak, obedient woman. This relationship has little ambiguity; the male feels strong and "masculine" and the woman is dependent and devoted. This relationship differs from the daddy/doll relationship in that the master is demanding whereas the daddy is protective, and servants are more capable than dolls.[26]

5.   The Confronting Relationship: Hawks.   Hawks are fierce competitors who both want to control and dominate the relationship.

Hawks are fierce competitors and the energy of competition comes from their own denial of weakness or tenderness. They fight with words, they struggle for status, they strive to prove superiority. Sex is a contest, life is a chess game. They ridicule and taunt, test and prove, scream and criticize. They blame their partners for what is missing in themselves. Each day is another contest in which the competition of the preceding day is still unresolved. *When love leaves, competition arrives.*[27]

[23] From the book *Between Man and Woman*, copyright © 1971 by Everett Shostrom and James Kavanaugh, by permission of Nash Publishing Corp.
[24] Ibid., p. 149.
[25] Ibid., pp. 149–165.
[26] Ibid., pp. 167–186.
[27] Ibid., p. 190.

6. The Accommodating Relationship: Doves. Doves are the victims of our culture, which has taught people to be "nice" and polite at any cost, even at the loss of one's identity. Doves have learned to deny their true feelings, to not talk back, argue, or fight. Peace is more important than true feelings. They were taught to "control" themselves, to be kind, docile, and cheerful. Artificiality, dullness, and guilt are results. Such people don't experience love, but only play a part.[28]

Relationship "Games"

In his popular book *Games People Play*, the late Eric Berne analyzed relationship patterns in term of "games."[29] The term *game*, however, is somewhat misleading. Typically, a game is thought to imply two sides who follow mutually agreeable and coordinated sets of rules. Berne's "games" tend to operate as the victimization of one party by fraudulent, manipulative means by the other party.

A typical game as analyzed by Berne is one he calls *Corner*. Berne shows that it essentially consists of a delayed refusal to follow another's ploy to produce a show of affection. In this game, a wife suggests to her husband that they go to a movie; he agrees. She makes an "unconscious" suggestion that maybe they shouldn't because the house needs painting. He has previously told her that they don't have the money to paint the house right now; therefore, this is not a "reasonable" time to relate such an expensive consideration to the price of a movie. The husband responds rudely to the house-painting remark. His wife is "offended" and says that because he is in a bad mood, she will not go to the movie with him and *suggests that he should go alone.* This is the critical artificial ploy of the game. He knows very well from past experience that he is not supposed to take this suggestion seriously. What she really wants is to be "honeyed up" a bit, told everything will be all right. Then they could go off happily to the movie together. *But he refuses* to show her this affectionate attention. He leaves, feeling relieved but looking abused; she is left feeling resentful. In this instance the husband won this game because all he did was to do as she suggested—literally. Berne's conclusion is: "They both know this is cheating but since she said it, she is cornered." This is a cruel game played to achieve a *show* of affection; its target is manipulation or control of another person, and its interpersonal attitude beneath the surface—no matter who wins—is not affection but *hostility.*

Why Don't You—Yes But (YDYB), another game identified by Berne, is said to be a prototype for transactional analysis. It is initiated when A (the perpetrator) adopts a docile stance toward B (the victim) by presenting some life problem in such a manner that B is induced to offer advice, that is, to adopt a managerial counterstance. A responds to this advice by saying, "Yes, but . . . ," and adding to that some information that renders B's advice irrelevant,

[28] Ibid., pp. 213–234.
[29] E. Berne, *Games People Play* (New York: Grove Press, 1964).

erroneous, or gratuitous. If A's deflationary comment has been skillfully contrived and delivered, however, B will come back with an alternative solution, still believing that he/she has sincerely been offered the managerial position. A shoots him down again. This may go on for several "rounds," until B finally realizes that he/she has been defeated, as manifested perhaps by an exasperated silence or a weak acknowledgment that A "sure has a tough problem there." A has demonstrated B's inadequacy, and B confirms it by assuming a self-effacing position complementary to the competitive position to which A has already switched. Note that A's competitive position is reciprocal to B's original managerial one. In the face of his/her "demonstrated" lack of talent for the managerial role, B is literally forced out of it. Needless to say, this reversal can be, and often is, deployed in a group setting, where there are several potential victims and where an even sweeter competitive victory can be fashioned by the skillful player.

Berne cites the game *If It Weren't For You (IWFY)* as the most common one played between spouses. In this game the blame for inaction is shifted to the partner in such a way as to become both an excuse and an accusation. For example, Mary complains that her husband so restricts her social activities that she has never learned to dance. However, once the excuse of the husband's supposed restrictions are removed, she discovers that she actually has a morbid fear of dancing. Thus, Mary has been hiding her true self behind a "It's not that I'm afraid; it's that he won't let me." A common application of this game is in terms of "If it weren't for you, I'd be out having fun."

The title of the game *Now I've Got You, You Son of a Bitch (NIGYSOB)* reveals immediately that it is one involving an aggressive payoff. The perpetrator of *NIGYSOB* initiates the game by placing himself/herself in circumstances (often by adopting a strongly self-effacing position) that invite competitive exploitation from his/her victim. The victim, if he/she is unwise or unsophisticated in these matters, sooner or later accepts the proffered agreement and initiates a program of exploitation. At some point, however, the person teased to attack becomes careless and/or the perpetrator suddenly shows increased vigilance, and the invited exploitation is thereby publicly revealed in all its nakedness. The perpetrator, with a suitable show of rage and indignation, assumes his/her justly deserved aggressive *NIGYSOB* position. The victim, if the reversal has been carried off smoothly, retires to the only remaining position—withdrawn, bitter rebelliousness or guilty self-effacement. It should be noted that sometimes the victim in this reversal is not quite as "innocent" or passive as this account suggests. In some instances he/she may be playing according to a coordinate set of rules, which would make the transaction a more complicated, two-handed one—in effect, a true sadomasochistic game.

These four examples should be sufficient to illustrate the manner in which games can be used in relationships for fraudulent satisfactions at the expense of the other person. Other games described by Berne fit similar patterns; they include *Try and Collect, Frigid Woman, Schlemiel,* and *See What You Make Me Do.* Berne's work is valuable in showing us how we may unconsciously manipulate other people.

Evaluating and Improving
a Relationship

To assess one of your own interpersonal relationships, we suggest you first determine its nature. The issue then becomes: Are you happy with what you have? In the long run, only you can describe what is satisfying to you. For example, you may feel that you need to be dominated, told what to do; that without such direction your life is too puzzling, that problems overwhelm you. The questions still remain: By what process do you arrive at such a decision? How does a person evaluate a relationship? What procedures are involved?

CALCULATING THE COST/REWARD RATIO

We have previously introduced the concept of social exchange, or cost/reward ratios for calculating an estimated relationship potential (ERP). As you determine the cost/reward ratio of a relationship and note the degree of causal connections between your behavior and that of the other person, you have three possible alternatives. First, you may terminate the relationship if you see fit; you avoid or at least stop seeking out this person. Second, you may maintain the relationship as it is, perhaps fairly satisfied with it as it exists. Third, you may give serious thought and effort toward improving the relationship. This decision will be made on the basis of your estimates of the cost/reward ratio and the alternative relationship opportunities available to you.

IMPROVING THE RELATIONSHIP

Obtaining the cooperative help of the other person in the relationship is usually about the only way possible to achieve any significant change. The lockstep of patterned responses to responses usually dooms to failure the lone effort of a single member of the relationship. Together with the other person, you may "try out" new behaviors and note the responses. Deliberate role-playing may be useful; however, be careful of adopting roles that are not true to your own personal feelings. In most cases, artificiality in interpersonal behavior can create greater problems than the original undesirable behavior.

The other person in your relationship may resent the idea that any changes are needed. You may make the mistake of trying to point out to him/her the need for such changes. If such changes are discussed, the person is likely to fear exposure of his/her ideas and feelings. What he/she actually fears, of course, is possible damage to his/her self-image as a result of such exposure. If you try to point out the behaviors that are causing difficulty, it will tend to increase his/her anxiety. Many times this is what people do who want to be helpful but who are not knowledgeable.

What can you do to be helpful? Research findings in clinical counseling settings show the value of such attitudes and abilities as accurate empathy, nonpossessive warmth, and genuineness.[30]

[30] C. B. Truax and R. R. Carkhuff, *Toward Effective Counseling and Psychotherapy* (Chicago: Aldine, 1969).

Accurate empathy is the ability to sense the other person's view of the world as if that view were your own. However, to demonstrate accurate empathy requires ability to *communicate* this understanding to the other person.[31] You need to be sensitive to his/her current feelings and emotions, even his fear of letting you develop a closer relationship with him/her. You do not need to *feel* the same fear or anxiety that the other one does, but you must have an *awareness* and *appreciation* of these emotions. Such empathy is communicated by the language you use and also by your vocal qualities and behavior. Your posture, gestures, and entire attitude should reflect the other person's point of view and depth of feeling. Your behavior must show awareness of shifts in his/her emotional attitudes, his/her subtle fears and anxieties. At all times the message of accurate empathy is: "I am with you; I understand."

Nonpossessive warmth is a demonstration of unconditional positive regard, involving caring about the other person without imposing conditions. The attitude you communicate should be warm acceptance; there should be no expression of dislike, disapproval, or *conditional* warmth in a selective or evaluative way. You will need to show willingness to share the other person's joys and aspirations as well as his anxiety and despair. It may be difficult for you to understand how you can really show warmth and affection for a person who has ways or habits you dislike; this is indeed a serious problem and becomes the heart of the matter in trying to be helpful to others. What is actually required is caring about that person's potential, a warm feeling about the person *as a person*—a human being. It is imperative that the other person feels you will be *for* him or her, even through failed attempts to change. He or she needs to feel that you care about him in spite of your dislike of some of his behavior.

The attitude described here may not be clear to you; indeed, in working with problems in human relations it is the most complicated concept we have faced. However, it is also the most important. Let us note it once again: *Nonpossessive warmth* involves unconditional caring about a person *as a person with valued potential* irrespective of some behaviors you do not like. Consider a female's response to a male. You must show that you care for him even though you may not care for some of his ways. This caring is much like the loyalty and affection shown by supporters of a football team even when that team is having problems and losing games; these fans want the team to win, but they still love it when it loses—they love it for trying and for its *potential*. If you wish to help another person, you must show him acceptance as a human being who has both human frailties and human potential.

Genuineness consists of being open and frank at all times; it involves being yourself. You must be willing not only to express your feelings, but never to deny them.[32] There must be no facade, no defensive communication, no show of emotion followed by denial of that emotion. Your responses to the other person must be sincere, never phony. It does not mean that you need to show

---

[31] Ibid., p. 46.
[32] Ibid., p. 58.

Accurate empathy, nonpossessive warmth, and genuineness permit relationships to change and improve.

all your feelings or emotions; but once a feeling or emotion is shown, it must not be denied—your behavior must be consistent. You need not disclose your total self, but whatever is shown must be a real aspect of yourself, not behavior growing out of defensiveness or an attempt to manipulate the other person. Glib attempts to persuade or efforts to convince him/her are dangerous pitfalls. A "professional" facade—"Now, let us take our medicine"—can be disastrous.

In view of the preceding discussion of nonpossessive warmth, it should be noted that your show of warmth must be genuine. The requirements involved in showing nonpossessive warmth make it extremely difficult to help another person if you really do not care about him/her. What you think are clever strategies will likely be viewed with suspicion. You must learn to be true to yourself if you wish to be helpful to others.

Summary and Preview of Readings

In this chapter we have suggested that a significant phase of the interpersonal communication process is developing, maintaining, and improving a warm personal relationship. In recent years we have seen a new emphasis on seeking such a relationship with at least one other person.

To improve an existing relationship or to achieve the most satisfying potential of a new one, we must analyze it, evaluate it, and, if need be, change it.

A relationship can be analyzed in terms of its (1) basic patterns of interaction and (2) degree of rigidity. Interaction behavior has three basic dimensions: (1) degree of involvement, (2) emotional tone, and (3) amount of interpersonal control.

In an established relationship in which the degree of involvement has stabilized, the other two dimensions are of greatest concern. Such a relationship can be described in its *essential characteristics* by determining the interpersonal behavior of the two persons on two independent, bipolar dimensions: *dominance–submission* and *affection–hostility*. We presented these two dimensions as forming an axis in a D-A-S-H paradigm.

In determining each person's degree of *dominance* versus *submission* and amount of *affection* versus *hostility* in a relationship, we noted that affectionate or hostile behavior on the part of one participant tends to elicit *similar* behavior on the part of the other. Conversely, dominant behavior tends to produce its *reciprocal*, submissive behavior, and submissiveness tends to encourage dominance. Taken together, these two principles tend to produce a "lockstep" effect of responses that produce responses. Once set in motion, such a behavior pattern is difficult to change. The possibility of change can be estimated by noting the variety of the participants' response repertoire—to what extent they tend to respond differently to different behaviors.

Evaluation of a relationship is accomplished by calculating the ratio of individual costs to personal rewards and by comparing this ratio to estimates of relationship potential for any available alternative relationships. Decisions to terminate a relationship are based primarily on the cost/reward ratio, but may also consider the potential value of available alternate relationships. A decision to attempt to improve a relationship is ordinarily based on a comparison of what exists with an ideal version of what might be.

Improving a relationship ordinarily requires a determined effort on the part of both members. Procedures for improvement include optimum use of the process of interpersonal communication, special emphasis on self-disclosure followed by feedback, and working with the other person. Cooperation of the other person may be facilitated by showing accurate empathy, nonpossessive warmth, and genuineness.

Relating to others is a basic key to a satisfying life. It can aid personal growth, confidence through self-acceptance, and beneficial cooperation through shared responsibility with others. To negotiate satisfactory conditions with our social and physical environment, we must achieve cooperative, agreeable relationships with a number of our associates. Furthermore, to achieve a deeply satisfying opinion of our selves, it is essential to achieve a warm, personal relationship with at least one other person. Satisfactory relationships are the basic goal of interpersonal communication and the true test of the process.

In the article that follows, Charles Brown and Charles Van Riper show the value of interpersonal communication in achieving a rewarding, meaningful relationship. They identify and expand upon certain communication behaviors useful in developing relationships. In addition, they emphasize the importance of self-acceptance, acceptance of others, frankness and openness in interaction, and community through shared authority.

Writing from a highly personal perspective, Carl Rogers, in the second reading, tells us what it is like "being in relationship." He stresses the interface of *real* interpersonal communication and *real* relationships as growth promoting in yourself and in others.

Reading 7.1

The Role of Speech in Human Relationships

Charles T. Brown and Charles Van Riper

Each person has but one short life to live and somehow feels, deep within him, that it might just be possible to live a rich, rewarding, and meaningful existence. Somehow each of us senses—daily, perhaps—that he has great potential for inner growth, and that his life need not be casual, passive, and wasteful. Each of us yearns to fulfill that potential. But how?

It is our view that fulfillment, or its failure, is a function of speech communication, that a dull, fearful, and angry life is the consequence of living in a self-prison without satisfactory relationships. The imprisoned person tends to become cynical, hostile, envious, and trapped in projective emotions that deter contact with himself and relations with others. He lacks the capacity to turn his dreams into reality. How can we learn to function so that our dreams will lead to inner changes, and those changes into new dreams? That is the central question for every human being. In the past, before our way of living estranged the child from his parents, this was not true. The boy walked in his father's footsteps, the girl in her mother's. But now each person must make his own footprints.

Two things mark your life as a consequence of your heritage. First, you live in conflict between internal-

| INTERPERSONAL COMMUNICATION IN ACTION

ized and externalized authority. Students ask again and again, "How can I know whether I am developing my potential or merely acting out what has been programmed into me?" The very asking of this question suggests the second inheritance, the central problem of estrangement. Separated from a knowledge of your own feelings and from any close identification with a parent-model—even though you love your parents—you are placed at the mercy of your use of language, the instrument of both consciousness and community.

Language as an Instrument of Consciousness

Verbal behavior is consciousness. If the nerves that join the two hemispheres of the brain are severed, the unfortunate victim can describe the action of only one side of his body—if he is right-handed, only the right side of his body; if left-handed, only the left side.[1] We have awareness of our bodies only to the extent that stimuli from parts of the body reach and are translated into words at the language centers of the brain. Awareness is verbal behavior. Thus only to the degree that we can speak about ourselves are we able to know ourselves. More obviously, only as we can talk to and about other people can we know other people and have what we call "relationship." Only to the degree that we can talk about our total environment—from the clothes that cover our bodies to the stars that surround our universe—are we able to create satisfactory relationships in our homes and

[1] Bernard Campbell, *Human Evaluation* (Chicago: Aldine, 1966), chapter 10.

our environments. This is why we must learn to speak in new ways.

The same perspective about the role of language in life is seen in all psychotherapy. The person is encouraged to talk and to listen to what he says. Regardless of theory and method, the therapist tries to get the client to sense when his feelings revealed nonverbally match his stated awareness of them. In one way or another all therapists borrow from Freud's discovery that the sufferer is out of touch with his basic feelings. A Rogerian (i.e., Carl Rogers) therapist supports the speaking client emotionally, hoping to lower his anxiety so he can recognize the truth or the delusion in what he says. A gestaltist like Fritz Perls tries to help the client know when his nonverbal behavior (his voice or mannerisms) matches or belies his verbalizations. If he is a rational therapist, like Robert Ellis, he argues with the client to help him see when he is logical and illogical, on the theory that we square away when we are rational in our argument. The "operant psychologist" reinforces constructive (in his judgment) talk or behavior. As different as these therapeutic procedures are, they all use speech as the controlling instrument. Man is as he thinks and, insofar as he thinks consciously, he uses the instrument of speech.

Over the past quarter century, under the name of "general semantics," much has been written about the relationship between words and health. And a person must be unrelated to his own experience if he fails to recognize that the major differences between his good and bad moments are determined by the way he talks to himself about what is happening to him. Sometimes we do not speak the truth about our experience, but instead lie to ourselves and even to others, romantically and sentimentally. Sometimes we nurse our wrath, or wear ourselves out fighting windmills. Sometimes we escape through gossip, or wit, or rationalization. Man the symbol-maker can either say it "like it is" or in many ways find distorted language to make himself believe he can create a pseudo reality. But in speech there is also growth. Growth comes when we talk honestly about our feelings, the basic source of our self-awareness. Out of such honest talk there always develops a value scheme that matches reality—then we have our stuff together. This book is about the role of human speech in human growth.[2]

The scientific and intellectual historian James Harvey Robinson observes

> that we rose from the ape because, like him, we kept monkeying around, meddling with everything about us. True, there is a difference, because, although the ape meddles he forgets, and we have learned, first to meddle, and then to meddle and remember, and then to meddle and record.[3]

The poor ape can't do this because he has no speech. Man's evolution is inextricably entwined in verbal language, spoken and written. Take this tool away and man is not man, for he is not conscious of himself.

Consciousness may concern both our outer and inner worlds. Insofar as we evolved out of Greece we talk about external perceptions. Insofar as we evolved out of the Old Testament we talk close to our feelings. Aeschylus, the Greek, speaking of a mountain said what he saw: "the mighty summit, neighbor to the stars." Byron, with the visual image as his source, expressed not so much what he saw, but what he felt:

> The monarch of mountains,
> They crowned him long ago,
> On a throne of rocks, in a robe of
>   clouds, with a diadem of snow.

And Coleridge, out of the same image, said:

> Like some sweet beguiling melody,
> So sweet, we know not we are listen-
>   ing to it.

"The Greeks soar but keep their feet on the ground," said the poet Landor. "Our poets leave the earth far behind them," said Edith Hamilton. The Greek in us demands a reality in touch with the earth. The Hebrew in us demands the relevance of our feelings, echo upon echo upon echo. There are real values in either of these orientations, and the marriage of the two produces a kind of consciousness and awareness peculiar to our age.

Language as the Instrument of Community

Through language we build human community. How does this come about? In learning language we first learn how to listen. A baby thus understands much before he speaks. As he learns to talk, he is as likely to speak to himself or to his playthings as to the

---

[2] We do not wish to deemphasize the importance of other forms of human expression, from painting to working out a math problem. Yet the artist who cannot or will not describe "his thing" not only fails to communicate with many people, but usually also lives a life poorly related to other human beings. We have known brilliant mathematicians who, as teachers, could not verbalize their operations. They were isolates, happy only in their isolation.

[3] Irving Dilliard, *Papers and Addresses of Learned Hand* (New York: Vantage Books, 1950), p. 116.

other persons present. In the maturing process, he finally learns to speak in the presence of others. So doing, he may in fact be talking only to himself, though it may be to others or with them. Such monologues do not bring people together in a common deep emotion or under a common influence. Perhaps this is an early stage in speech development, and at one time the community of man may have been composed of monologists. The endlessly talkative patients in a mental hospital may be reenacting this earlier stage. Ludwig Van Bertalanffy, a general systems theorist, biologist by training, says that as a person disintegrates he falls back through the historical stages by which man's mind has evolved.[4] So, once upon a time, we may have all been monologists.

Down through the ages one important function of man's speech has been to gain some kind of control over another person. Aristotle said the study of speech was a study of the available means of persuasion. When you try to persuade somebody, you try to get him to see as you do or do what you want him to do. Governments have mastered their own people and as entities have conquered and enslaved each other down through the ages in this way. With a scarcity of food and essential tools yet to be invented, the use of other persons in order to survive has been the rule.

Therefore, speech historically has been viewed as a strategy, and strategy, as we see in any modern sport, is designed to beat the other person. Rulers and priests glorified themselves, threatened and frightened the

masses of men, and if successful, made the people like it, all through speech.

One way of attempting to do this is to make demands and threats, but most persuasion is more subtle, strategy veiling the demand or threat. You try to get the other person to *want* to see or do as you say. You try to build your case on his needs, feelings, and values, to let him see that any disagreement with you is error on his part. You rarely say, "I need your services so that I may achieve what *I* want." The purpose of persuasion is kept hidden when at all possible. As one of our professors used to say: "Persuasion is done by means of suggestion. You try to get the other person to think through his neck." In short, don't let him use his brain.

If man had remained projective in mind, this use of speech in power relationships would probably have continued to be broadly effective. But the coming of the private mind, given impetus by the faith and the verbalized feelings of the Hebrews and the spiritual preoccupation of the Christian doctrine, shifted a share of authority to the individual. Now we have to have a completely new way of perceiving the role of speech in community life. If we are not going to be held together by power or strategy, we must be held together by mutual dependence, by the expressed commonality of shared needs.

In persuasion, one communicant, the persuader, has been seen as the speaker with authority. The other has been viewed as the recipient, the listener without authority. The new concept of mutual interaction in communication, with both persons jointly participating as speaker and listener, with both simultaneously speaking and

[4] Ludwig Van Bertalanffy, *Robots, Men, and Minds* (New York: George Braziller, 1967), Part One.

listening—to themselves and each other—has come into being only recently, but it is flourishing. Consider how effective it might be in modern marriage, when interpersonal communication begins to fail. If the majority of marital unions are highly distressing, this is due, at least in part, to the partners' language habits. They still feel compelled to use the power strategies of persuasion on each other, and distrust and conflict are inevitable.

The concepts of Buber, with his "I" and "thou," have gradually filtered through the culture so we all know that speech has many uses beyond the control of another person. The human-potentials movement, dealing in sensitivity awareness, has evolved out of the same perspective. Modern schools of psychotherapy, growing out of the sickness generated by private awarenesses and strategic speech; humanistic psychology, with its emphasis upon the integrity of the individual; and transactional psychology, built on the concept that any two interacting persons mutually change each other—all these movements are leading to the canons of a speech of relationship. While speech has always been the instrument of community, as the concepts of community change, so must speech change. On the edge of tomorrow, if we make it through today, is the community based on a speech of relationship.

The Principles of a Relationship Speech
OPENNESS (NOT STRATEGY)

The essential principle of a speech of relationship is this: that one reveals, not conceals. If a person prizes himself as unique, yet is not open, others will tend to stereotype him and so misjudge him. If he behaves in such a way that the response he arouses excites his self-doubts, or estranges him from himself and others, he is not responded to as he desires to be. Since language is the instrument of consciousness, openness in speech is necessary if one is to know one's own uniqueness. Most important of all, if the real source of our creativity or uniqueness comes from our response to our own feelings, then we have to be open in our verbalizations in order to understand the patterns of expression that reflect our own special selves.

We know ourselves, not to the degree we talk, but to the degree we listen to ourselves. Here is our answer to the student who asks: "How do I know whether I am developing my potential or responding as others have programmed me to respond?" If you do not listen to the feelings expressed in your speech to others, you cannot know the answers to the question, and if you will not be open with them, you will not express the feelings that lead to the knowledge you seek. So if someone opts for strategy and closedness in his speech he must expect not to know himself or his potential. Speech that leads us to ourselves and others should disclose, not enclose.

We are not saying that a closed person cannot ever demonstrate any potential, as judged by his output or the judgment of others. In all professions and in all walks of life we find a few exceptions. We have also known far too many who were only half-achievers, because they did not know who they were and did not dare to know. But in either case, successful or unsuccessful in the eyes of the others, those who do not become acquainted with themselves do not fully enjoy themselves or feel a sense of their own significance. Many so-called "successful" people are often lonely or bored, strangers to themselves.

Nor are we suggesting a philosophy of openness that means indiscriminately saying everything to everybody. Our sex relations belong to those we are sexually related to. They need not be shared verbally with everyone. Our financial arrangements belong to those with whom we are financially related. The words of our friends should often not be repeated. If our communication is to produce the relationships of a cohesive community, we must have this underlying ethic: *that we do not say that which is destructive to community relationship.* Gossip is often an unhealthy way of creating one relationship by betraying another. Gossip may be an easy way of taking care of our own problems, but in the end it will create only self-doubts and suspicions. We should be eager to learn all we can about any relationship, but we must have a basic loyalty to it. What we speak openly about in one relationship we need not speak about in another relationship— if in doing so we betray another person. The question is always, What are we doing to the person most intimately affected? And if we betray another, who will never know it, to that degree we have sealed off any chance of real depth in that relationship.

Self-acceptance. As a subprinciple of the principle of openness, we note that all speech and listening are done in an attitude of self-acceptance. By this we mean that in either initiating a statement or responding to one, the communication (verbal and nonverbal) is done in good faith and with the support of one's self. This is perhaps the most crucial of the principles of the speech of relationship. If distrust or anxiety keeps us from speaking and listening openly, it emerges from our feeling that we are not being accepted. Thus self-acceptance is not entirely in our own hands.

In every communication we are acutely aware of the need for acceptance by the other person. As we search for this information, we are less concerned with *what* the other says than with the way he says it.[5] We seek clues in his eyes and posture and voice, for these he cannot monitor as easily as he can his choice of words. When our listener shows he does not accept us, we hesitate, our tongue cleaves to the roof of our mouth, or we speak untruthfully. Yet he will have his troubles in accepting us if we cannot accept ourselves enough to remain open to him.

Acceptance of the Other. The above sounds like a paradox, and in a sense it is. (If we are completely self-accepting we get a response that says we should not be.) But a second subprinciple—that one's openness requires acceptance of the other person—helps break the vicious cycle. Acceptance results in what we call empathy, the act of listening to the other to sense how he wishes to be heard. This confirms him and thus he tends to confirm us, and thus we are led to further self-confirmation. Self-acceptance and acceptance of the other are therefore interactive.

We give self-acceptance more im-

[5] Robert Rosenthal and Lenore Jacobsen, *Pygmalion in the Classroom* (New York: Holt, Rinehart and Winston, 1968).

portance than acceptance of others because we have been impressed by William James's concept of the "heave of the will"—the act of taking the initiative. You cannot be responsible for the behavior of the other person. Open as you may be to him, you cannot be guaranteed that he will accept you. As the studies of Sidney Jourard and others show, the best way to encourage openness in another is to be open ourselves. But sometimes this doesn't work. We fail, and become afraid of further failure. That is why the "heave of the will" is so important. If we are constantly beset by the threat of failure, then we will never make the first move. If we do not initiate openness, regardless of its effect, we can be open only to those who show trust in us.

But the person who is open and accepts another gains more than greater faith in himself. He gains new knowledge about himself and the other. If you will learn to listen to the other person as he wishes to be heard, you learn, in effect, to speak as the other speaks. Doing this without awareness or consciousness of self, you imaginatively adopt this view for a moment. Upon returning to self-awareness, you then have two kinds of knowledge: what the statements of the other say about *him* and what they say about *you*.

THE MIRROR RESPONSE

The second major principle of a speech of relationship, standing as a corollary to openness, is this: one must be responded to in order to become aware of oneself. Just as you must have a mirror to know your own face, so you need a response, verbal and nonverbal, from the other person to know what you mean. It is deceptively easy to believe you can become aware of yourself by yourself. But just as children reared by wolves never matured emotionally or intellectually into persons, so a person who talks about himself cannot mature emotionally and intellectually. In part, this is because we need interaction with others to arouse ourselves emotionally. Conversations with oneself can get terribly dull. Since the other person is different from us he will respond to us in ways that give us new insights for our own self-communication.

But there is more to it than that. We actually change a little every time we speak to another person. Identity involves playing different roles.[6] We talk differently to different people. Some students, in their search for honesty, conceive of these role changes as signs of phoniness. But while we cannot be all things to all people—we are not chameleons—neither can we be one thing to all people. If we try to do this we will acquire a tense rigidity that is certain to lead to further alienation. In effect, we are saying that our various potentials express themselves in different roles. Or, if you like, different people trigger different sets of our own potentials.

Certainly our flexibility of approach, necessary to growth, will have some central, constant tendencies. Those we will not change, no matter whom we communicate with. Indeed we discover ourselves in this way. You may consistently refuse the role of the formal gentleman or lady, or the snob, or the homosexual, or the thief, or the preacher, or the servant. You may consistently choose to be kind, or inconsiderate, or competitive, or respect-

[6] Kenneth J. Gergen, "Multiple Identity," *Psychology Today* 5 (1972): 31.

ful with everyone. But you may also choose to be serious with some, clownish with others, intimate with some, distant with others, and so on. The other person with whom you interact changes your thinking about yourself, but the central core of your identity changes little if at all. You merely discover facets of it that you had not known before. Such discoveries about different aspects of your identity are in large measure brought about by those you choose to associate with, for they help you to know *you*. The psychologist Sidney Jourard says that if a person is to have any insights into his identity and its potentials, he must have at least one other person to whom he may talk with complete candor.[7]

Communication of Relationship and Shared Authority

If we examine these two principles together we see that the speech of relationship has one obvious difference from that of persuasion: the authority it exercises is not an exploiting of one person's power over another, but instead is shared. Perhaps the significance of this is best seen in our second principle, which acknowledges that self-awareness is dependent upon information from the other—the mirror. While we live in an age when most people are keenly aware of the boundaries of their own egos, they unfortunately are not yet equally aware that anyone's ego is dependent on other egos for its development. Thus the more isolated and belligerent of our

young people—understandably feeling as they do—need to examine the preceding principles with care if they hope to continue to grow. If you cannot discover your powers alone, and if you, like most other persons, feel some deep need for personal authority, the basic condition for human relationship is that of shared authority. Our only hope is to find community in a shared authority.

The Communicative Process of Shared Authority

The above solution for easing the loneliness and anger of youth must doubtless sound impossible to students caught up in those feelings. It seems to ask for faith in people in whom you have no faith, for belief in what you do not believe. But this is not true. We do not ask the impossible. We only suggest that you try the experiences of the course for which this text is designed. Some progress toward insight and in the alleviation of alienation and hostility can be attained even in a single semester. As we understand it, the communicative process, like something of a miracle, does its work in the following sequence:

1. The assignments will increase your acquaintance with yourself, others, and your universe. We never cease to marvel at the fact that many of our beginning students have not talked much, if at all, about themselves and their relationships. Having grown up estranged, they have used speech almost exclusively as an instrument of social utility: "Let's go to dinner." "How about a cigarette?" "Did the mail come?" Since there must be some re-

[7] Sidney Jourard, *The Transparent Self* (Princeton, N.J.: Van Nostrand, 1964), and *Disclosing Man to Himself* (Princeton: Van Nostrand, 1968).

lationship, they argue about this or that, or discuss the latest automobile designs, or listen appreciatively, with others, to music. If you are typical, you have seldom made comments about yourself, or others, or the way you see things around you. Thus you have sealed yourself off from your world—at the conscious level. In this class we hope you will do otherwise.

2. Acquaintance at the verbal level leads to understanding. It is almost a truism that getting acquainted with someone takes away the feeling of strangeness and the vanishing of strangeness is replaced by understanding. Talking about anything changes it from the strange to the familiar.

3. Understanding leads to acceptance. We reject what is strange or does not belong to us, and at the heart of our rejection is fear and anxiety. As we become truly acquainted, we lose our fears—unless the new has been thrust upon us before we are ready for it. Thus you will not be asked to become acquainted faster and more deeply with yourself or with others than you are able to endure. As debilitating stage fright shows, people are often forced to speak in public before they are ready, and the result is intense fear and rejection instead of acceptance. In our classes there have been times when the only way we could desensitize such a person was by having him write at the board while we lectured, or by involving him in a casual dialogue before the class. But the principle remains—that out of acquaintance and understanding grows acceptance.

We have learned the validity of this from our personal experiences too. As professors, we sometimes feel hostility or anxiety in dealing with a student. But after we have worked with him

long enough and hard enough to feel we were beginning to understand him, our negative attitudes have always changed to acceptance and confirmation. If you really try to understand another person, you will find that sooner or later he becomes included in your world of concern.

4. Acceptance leads to a growth in the relationship with others, and, as a bonus, to a growth within the self. As we begin to know the other person, and to accept him in his uniqueness, new feelings of personal security and new insights about ourselves develop.

Implementing These Insights

You may have felt that these principles and this background information are too abstract to guide you in the vital changes you feel you would like to make in yourself if only you could. Very well, since a global approach might overwhelm you, we offer a simple diagram as a guide.

	Feelings	Awareness	Significance
Self			
Others			
Universe			

. . . We have discovered that when students are given the opportunity to understand and explore and discuss the contents of each cell they cannot help showing growth, sometimes in spite of their disinclinations or initial fears.

The key that unlocks the latent potential of this grid is *speech*, and it is our hope that you may try to express in words your feelings and your awareness and your sense of the significance of yourself, your fellows, and your universe. To learn to talk about the important things in your life is almost like learning to talk all over again, and it is hard to learn this kind of speaking by yourself, alone. You need comrades and teachers who are also learning. If at first you feel that this novel way of talking holds some threat because it is unfamiliar, all we can say is that the students we have taught have found the experience not only meaningful but exciting.

Reading 7.2
Being in Relationship
Carl R. Rogers

Just as it was an awesome thing to face a sea of a thousand faces so early in the morning, so I have the same feeling, something akin to panic, whenever I start a chapter. . . . What possible way is there in which I can make real *contact* with a multitude of unknown readers, whose background, expectations, and attitudes are all unknown to me? Especially is this concern a deep one when I want to talk about interpersonal relationships. I don't believe a scholarly, abstract chapter will make that contact. Furthermore, I have no desire to instruct my readers, or impress you with my knowledge in this field. I have no desire to tell you what you should think or feel or do. How can I meet this dilemma?

The only solution I have come up with is that perhaps I can share something of myself, something of *my* ex-

From Carl R. Rogers, *Freedom to Learn*, 1969, pp. 231–237. Reprinted by permission of Charles E. Merrill Publishing Company, Columbus, Ohio.

This paper is a revised version of a highly personal talk I gave to a recent conference of the American Personnel and Guidance Association in Dallas. I was dumbfounded that the auditorium, holding several thousand persons, was crammed full at 8:30 in the morning (!) to hear a talk on interpersonal relationships.

perience in interpersonal relationships, something of what it has been like to me, in communication with others. This is not an easy thing to do. But if I can do it, if I can share something of myself, then I think you can take what I say, or leave it alone. You can decide whether it is relevant to your own job, your career, your profession, your life. You can respond to it with the reaction, "That's just what *I've* felt and what *I've* discovered," or equally valuable, "I feel *very* differently. My experience has taught me something entirely different." In either case, it may help you to define *yourself* more clearly, more openly, more surely. That I *do* regard as worthwhile, and as something I hope I can facilitate.

So I'm going to share with you a somewhat miscellaneous bag of learnings, things I have learned or am learning about this mysterious business of relating with other human beings, about communication between persons. I'm going to share some of my satifactions and my dissatisfactions in this area. The reason I call it a mysterious business is that interpersonal communication is almost never achieved except in part. You probably never feel fully understood by another, and neither do I. Yet I find it extremely rewarding when I have been able, in a particular instance, truly to communicate myself to another. I find it very precious when, for some moment in time, I have felt really close to, fully in touch with, another person.

I Like to Hear

So the first simple feeling I want to share with you is my enjoyment when I can really *hear* someone. I think perhaps this has been a longstanding characteristic of mine. I can remember this in my early grammar school days. A child would ask the teacher a question and the teacher would give a perfectly good answer to a completely different question. A feeling of pain and distress would always strike me. My reaction was, "But you didn't *hear* him!" I felt a sort of childish despair at the lack of communication which was (and is) so common.

I believe I know why it is satisfying to me to hear someone. When I can really hear someone it puts me in touch with him. It enriches my life. It is through hearing people that I have learned all that I know about individuals, about personality, about psychotherapy, and about interpersonal relationships. There is another peculiar satisfaction in it. When I really hear someone it is like listening to the music of the spheres, because beyond the immediate message of the person, no matter what that might be, there is the universal, the general. Hidden in all of the personal communications which I really hear there seem to be orderly psychological laws, aspects of the awesome order which we find in the uni-

verse as a whole. So there is both the satisfaction of hearing this particular person and also the satisfaction of feeling oneself in some sort of touch with what is universally true.

When I say that I enjoy hearing someone I mean, of course, hearing deeply. I mean that I hear the words, the thoughts, the feeling tones, the personal meaning, even the meaning that is below the conscious intent of the speaker. Sometimes, too, in a message which superficially is not very important, I hear a deep human cry, a "silent scream," that lies buried and unknown far below the surface of the person.

So I have learned to ask myself, can I hear the sounds and sense the shape of this other person's inner world? Can I resonate to what he is saying, can I let it echo back and forth in me, so deeply that I sense the meanings he is afraid of yet would like to communicate, as well as those meanings he knows?

I think, for example, of an interview I had with an adolescent boy, the recording of which I listened to only a short time ago. Like many an adolescent today he was saying at the outset of the interview that he had no goals. When I questioned him on this he made it even stronger that he had no goals whatsoever, not even one. I said, "There isn't anything you want to do?" "*Nothing* . . . Well, yeah, I want to keep on living." I remember very distinctly my feeling at that moment. I resonated very deeply to his phrase. He might simply be telling me that, like everyone else, he wanted to live. On the other hand he might be telling me, and this seemed to be a distinct possibility, that at some point the question of whether or not to live had been a real issue with him. So I tried to resonate to him at all levels. I didn't know for certain what the message was. I simply wanted to be open to any of the meanings that this statement might have, including the possible meaning that he might have at one time considered suicide. I didn't respond verbally at this level. That would have frightened him. But I think that my being willing and able to listen to him at all levels is perhaps one of the things that made it possible for him to tell me, before the end of the interview, that not long before he had been on the point of blowing his brains out. This little episode constitutes an example of what I mean by wanting to really hear someone at all the levels at which he is endeavoring to communicate.

I find, in therapeutic interviews, and in the intensive group experiences which have come to mean a great deal to me in recent years, that hearing has consequences. When I do truly hear a person and the meanings that are important to him at that moment, hearing not simply his words, but *him*, and when I let him know that I have heard his own private personal meanings, many things happen. There is first of all a grateful look. He feels released. He wants to tell me more about his world. He surges forth in a new sense of freedom. I think he becomes more open to the process of change.

I have often noticed, both in therapy and in groups, that the more deeply I can hear the meanings of this person the more there is that happens. One thing I have come to look upon as almost universal is that when a person realizes he has been deeply heard, there is a moistness in his eyes. I think in some real sense he is weeping for

joy. It is as though he were saying, "Thank God, *somebody* heard me. Someone knows what it's like to be me." In such moments I have had the fantasy of a prisoner in a dungeon, tapping out day after day a Morse code message, "Does anybody hear me? Is there anybody there? Can anyone hear me?" And finally one day he hears some faint tappings which spell out "Yes." By that one simple response he is released from his loneliness, he has become a human being again. There are many, many people living in private dungeons today, people who give no evidence of it whatever on the outside, where you have to listen very sharply to hear the faint messages from the dungeon.

If this seems to you a little too sentimental or overdrawn, I would like to share with you an experience I had recently in a basic encounter group with fifteen persons in important executive posts. Early in the very intensive sessions of the week they were asked to write a statement of some feeling or feelings which they had which they were *not* willing to tell in the group. These were anonymous statements. One man wrote, "I don't relate easily to people. I have an almost impenetrable facade. Nothing gets in to hurt me but nothing gets out. I have repressed so many emotions that I am close to emotional sterility. This situation doesn't make me happy but I don't know what to do about it." This is clearly a message from a dungeon. Later in the week a member of my group identified himself as the man who had written that anonymous message, and filled out in much greater detail his feelings of isolation, of complete coldness. He felt that life had been so brutal to him that he had been forced to live a life without feeling, not only at work, but in social groups, and saddest of all, with his family. His gradual achievement of greater expressiveness in the group, of less fear of being hurt, of more willingness to share himself with others, was a very rewarding experience for all of us who participated.

I was both amused and pleased when, in a letter a few weeks later he included this paragraph. "When I returned home from (our group) I felt somewhat like a young girl who had been seduced but still wound up with the feeling that it was exactly what she had been waiting for and needed! I am still not quite sure who was responsible for the seduction—you or the group, or whether it was a joint venture. I suspect it was the latter. At any rate I want to thank you for what was an intensely meaningful experience." I think it is not too much to say that because several of us in the group were able genuinely to hear him, he was released from his dungeon and has come out, at least to some degree, into the sunnier world of warm interpersonal relationships.

I LIKE TO BE HEARD

Let me move on to a second learning which I would like to share with you. I like to *be heard*. A number of times in my life I have felt myself bursting with insoluble problems, or going round and round in tormented circles or, during one period, overcome by feelings of worthlessness and despair, sure I was sinking into psychosis. I think I have been more lucky than most in finding at these times individuals who have been able to hear me and thus to rescue me from the chaos of my feelings. I have been fortunate in finding individuals who have been able to hear my meanings a little more deeply than I have known them. These individuals have heard me without judging me, diagnosing me, appraising me, evaluating me. They have just listened and clarified and responded to me at all the levels at which I was communicating. I can testify that when you are in psychological distress and someone really hears you without passing judgment on you, without trying to take responsibility for you, without trying to mold you, it feels *damn good*. At these times, it has relaxed the tension in me. It has permitted me to bring out the frightening feelings, the guilts, the despair, the confusions that have been a part of my experience. When I have been listened to and when I have been heard, I am able to reperceive my world in a new way and to go on. It is amazing that feelings which were completely awful become bearable when someone listens. It is astonishing how elements which seem insoluble become soluble when someone hears; how confusions which seem irremediable turn into relatively clear flowing streams when one is understood. I have deeply appreciated the times that I have experienced this sensitive, empathic, concentrated listening.

I have been very grateful that by the time I quite desperately needed this kind of help, I had trained and developed therapists, persons in their own right, independent and unafraid of me, who were able to go with me through a dark and troubled period in which I underwent a great deal of inner growth. It has also made me sharply aware that in developing my style of therapy for others, I was without doubt, at some unconscious level, developing the kind of help I wanted and could use myself.

WHEN I CANNOT HEAR

Let me turn to some of my dissatisfactions in the realm. I dislike it in myself when I can't hear another, when I do not understand him. If it is only a simple failure of comprehension or a failure to focus my attention on what he is saying, or a difficulty in understanding his words, then I feel only a very mild dissatisfaction with myself.

But what I really dislike in myself is when I cannot hear the other person because I am so sure in advance of what he is about to say that I don't listen. It is only afterward that I realize that I have only heard what I have already decided he is saying. I have failed really to listen. Or even worse are those times when I can't hear because what he is saying is too threatening, might even make me change my views or my behavior. Still worse are those times when I catch myself trying to twist his message to make it say what I want him to say, and then only hearing that. This can be a very subtle thing and it is surprising how skillful I can be in doing it. Just by twisting his words a small amount, by distorting his meaning just a little, I can make it appear that he is not only saying the thing I want to hear, but that he is the person I want him to be. It is only when I realize through his protest or through my own gradual recognition that I am subtly manipulating him that I become disgusted with myself. I know too from being on the receiving end of this how frustrating it is to be received for what you are not, to be heard as saying something which you have not said and do not mean. This creates anger and bafflement and disillusion.

WHEN OTHERS DO NOT UNDERSTAND

The next learning I want to share with you is that I am terribly frustrated and shut into myself when I try to express something which is deeply me, which is a part of my own private, inner world, and the other person does not understand. When I take the gamble, the risk, of trying to share something that is very personal with another individual and it is not received and not understood, this is a very deflating and a very lonely experience. I have come to believe that it is that experience which makes some individuals psychotic. They have given up hoping that anyone can understand them and once they have lost that hope then their own inner world, which becomes more and more bizarre, is the only place where they can live. They can no longer live in any shared human experience. I can sympathize with them because I know that when I try to share some feeling aspect of myself which is private, precious, and tentative, and when this communication is met by evaluation, by reassurance, by denial, by distortion of my meaning, I have very strongly the reaction, "Oh, what's the use!" At such a time one knows what it is to be *alone*.

So, as you can see, a creative, active, sensitive, accurate, empathic, nonjudgmental listening, is for me terribly important in a relationship. It is important for me to provide it. It has been extremely important especially at certain times in my life to receive it. I feel that I have grown within myself when I have provided it. I am very sure that I have grown and been released and enhanced when I have received this kind of listening.

I Want to Be Real

Moving on to another area of my learnings, I find it very satisfying when I can be real, when I can be close to whatever it is that is going on within me. I like it when I can listen to myself. To really know what I am experiencing in the moment is by no means an easy thing but I feel somewhat encouraged because I think that over the years I have been improving at it. I am convinced, however, that it is a lifelong task and that none of us ever is really able to be comfortably close to *all* that is going on within his own experience.

In place of the term *realness* I have sometimes used the word *congruence*. By this I mean that when my experiencing of this moment is present in my awareness, and when what is present in my awareness is present in my communication, then each of these three levels matches or is congruent. At such moments I am integrated or whole, I am completely in one piece. Most of the time of course I, like everyone else, exhibit some degree of incongruence. I have learned, however, that realness, or genuineness or congruence—whatever term you wish to give to it—is a fundamental basis for the best of communication, the best of relationships.

What do I mean by being real? I could give many examples from many different fields. But one meaning, one learning is that there is basically nothing to be afraid of when I present myself as I *am*, when I can come forth nondefensively, without armor, just me. When I can accept the fact that I have many deficiencies, many faults, make lots of mistakes, am often ignorant where I should be knowledgeable, often prejudiced when I should be openminded, often have feelings which are not justified by the circumstances, then I can be much more real. And when I can come out wearing no armor, making no effort to be different from what I am, I learn so much more—even from criticism and hostility—and I am so much more relaxed, and I get so much closer to people. Besides, my willingness to be vulnerable brings forth so much more real feeling from other people who are in relationship to me, that it is very rewarding. So I enjoy life *much* more when I am not defensive, not hiding behind a facade, just trying to be and express the real me.

COMMUNICATING THE REALNESS IN ME

I feel a sense of satisfaction when I can dare to communicate the realness in me to another. This is far from easy partly because what I am experiencing keeps changing in every moment, partly because feelings are very complex. Usually there is a lag, sometimes of moments, sometimes of days, weeks, or months, between the experiencing and the communication. In these cases, I experience something, I feel something, but only later do I become aware of it, only later do I dare to communicate it, when it has become cool enough to risk sharing it with another. Yet it is a most satisfying experience when I can communicate what is real in me at the moment that it occurs. Then I feel genuine, and spontaneous, and alive.

Such real feelings are not always positive. One man, in a basic encounter group of which I was a member, was talking about himself in ways which seemed to me completely false, speaking of the pride he took in maintaining his front, his pretense, his facade, how skillful he was in deceiving others. My feeling of annoyance rose higher and higher until finally I expressed it by simply saying, "Oh, nuts!" This somehow pricked the bubble. From that time on he was a more real and genuine person, less a braggadocio, and our communication improved. I felt good for having let him know my own real angry feeling as it was occurring.

I'm sorry to say that very often, especially with feelings of anger, I'm only partly aware of the feeling at the moment, and full awareness comes later. I only learn afterward what my feeling was. It is only when I wake up in the middle of the night, finding myself angrily fighting someone, that I realize how angry I was at him the day before. Then I know, seemingly too late, how I might have been my real feeling self; but, at least, I have learned to go to him the next day, if need be, to express my anger, and gradually I'm learning to be more quickly acquainted with it inside myself. In the last basic encounter group in which I participated, I was at different times very angry with two individuals. With one, I wasn't aware of it until the middle of the night and had to wait until morning to express it. With the other, I was able to realize it and express it in the session in which it occurred. In both instances, it led to real communication, to a strengthening of the relationship, and gradually to a feeling of genuine liking for each

other. But I am a slow learner in this area.

ENCOUNTERING REALNESS IN OTHERS

It is a sparkling thing when I encounter realness in another person. Sometimes in the basic encounter groups which have been a very important part of my experiences these last few years, someone says something which comes from him transparently and whole. It is so obvious when a person is not hiding behind a facade but is speaking from deep within himself. When this happens I leap to meet it. I want to encounter this real person. Sometimes the feelings thus expressed are very positive feelings. Sometimes they are very decidedly negative ones. I think of a man in a very responsible position, a scientist at the head of a large research department in a huge electronics firm, very "successful." One day in such a basic encounter group he found the courage to speak of his isolation, to tell us that he had never had a single friend in his life. There were plenty of people whom he knew but not one he could count as a friend. "As a matter of fact," he added, "there are only two individuals in the world with whom I have even a reasonably communicative relationship. These are my two children." By the time he finished he was letting loose some of the tears of sorrow for himself which I am sure he had held in for many years. But it was the honesty and realness of his loneliness which caused every member of the group to reach out to him in some psychological sense. It was also most significant that his courage in being real enabled all of us to be more genuine in our communications, to come out from behind the facades we ordinarily use.

MY FAILURES TO BE REAL

I am disappointed when I realize—and of course this realization always comes afterward, after a lag of time—that I have been too frightened or too threatened to let myself get close to what I am experiencing and that consequently I have not been genuine or congruent. There immediately comes to mind an instance which is somewhat painful to reveal. Some years ago I was invited to spend a year as a Fellow at the Center for Advanced Study in the Behavioral Sciences at Stanford, California. The Fellows are a group chosen because they are supposedly brilliant and well-informed scholars. It is doubtless inevitable that there is a considerable amount of one-upmanship, of showing off one's knowledge and achievements. It seems important for each Fellow to impress the others, to be a little more assured, to be a little more knowledgeable than he really is. I found myself several times doing this same thing—playing a role of greater certainty and of greater competence than I really felt. I can't tell you how disgusted with myself I was as I realized what I was doing. I was not being me; I was playing a part.

I regret it when I suppress my feelings too long and they burst forth in ways that are distorted or attacking or hurtful. I have a friend whom I like very much but who has one particular pattern of behavior that thoroughly annoys me. Because of the usual tendency to be nice, polite, and pleasant I kept this annoyance to myself for too long a time. When it finally burst its bounds it came out not only as annoyance but as an attack on him. This was hurtful and it took us time to repair the relationship.

I am inwardly pleased when I have the strength to permit another person to be his own realness and to be *separate* from me. I think that is often a very threatening possibility. In some ways I have found it sort of an ultimate test of staff leadership and of parenthood. Can I freely permit this staff member or my client or my son or my daughter to become a separate person with ideas, purposes, and values which may not be identical with my own? I think of Kahlil Gibran's poem on marriage, which includes the lines:

But let there be spaces in your togetherness,
And let the winds of the heavens dance between you.

Love one another, but make not a bond of love:
Let it rather be a moving sea between the shores of your souls. . . .

Give your hearts, but not into each other's keeping.
For only the hand of Life can contain your hearts.
And stand together yet not too near together:
For the pillars of the temple stand apart,
And the oak tree and the cypress grow not in each other's shadow.[1]

From a number of these things I have been saying I trust it is clear that

[1] Reprinted from *The Prophet,* by Kahlil Gibran, with permission of the publisher, Alfred A. Knopf, Inc. Copyright 1923 by Kahlil Gibran; renewal copyright 1951 by Administrators C.T.A. of Kahlil Gibran Estate, and Mary G. Gibran.

when I can permit realness in myself or sense it or permit it in the other, I find it very satisfying. When I cannot permit it in myself or fail to permit a separate realness in another it is to me very distressing and regrettable. I find that when I am able to let myself be congruent and genuine it often helps the other person. When the other person is transparently real and congruent it often helps me. In those rare moments when a deep realness in one meets a deep realness in the other it is a memorable "I-thou relationship," as Martin Buber, the existential Jewish philosopher, would call it. Such a deep and mutual personal encounter does not happen often but I am convinced that unless it happens occasionally we are not human.

Unleashing Freedom for Others

There's another learning. I like it when I can permit freedom to others, and in this I think I have learned, and developed considerable ability. I am frequently, though not always, able to take a group, a course, or a class of students, and to set them psychologically free. I can create a climate in which they can be and direct themselves. At first, they are suspicious; they're sure that the freedom I'm offering them is some kind of a trick, and then they bring up the question of grades. They can't be free because in the end I will evaluate them and judge them. When we have worked out some solution, in which we have all participated, to the absurd demand of the University that learning is measured by grades, then they begin to feel that they are really free. Then curiosity is unleashed. Individuals and groups start

to pursue their own goals, their own purposes. They become explorers. They can try to find the meaning of their lives in the work they're doing. They work twice as hard in such a course where nothing is required as in courses with requirements. I can't always achieve this atmosphere and when I cannot, I think it is because of some subtle holding back within myself, some unwillingness for the freedom to be complete. But when I can achieve it, then education becomes what it should be, an exciting quest, a searching, not an accumulation of facts soon to be outdated and forgotten. These students become persons living in process, able to live a changing life. Of all the learnings I have developed, I think this climate of freedom which I can frequently create, which I can often somehow carry with me and around me, is to me one of the most precious parts of myself.

Accepting and Giving Love

Another area of my learning in interpersonal relationships has been slow and painful for me. It is more warming and fulfilling when I can let in the fact, or permit myself to feel, that someone cares for, accepts, admires, or prizes me. Because, I suppose, of elements in my past history it has been very difficult for me to do this. For a long time I tended almost automatically to brush aside any positive feelings which were turned in my direction. I think my reaction was, "Who, me? You couldn't possibly care for me. You might like what I have done or my achievements but not *me*." This is one respect in which my own therapy helped me very much. I am not always

356 | INTERPERSONAL COMMUNICATION IN ACTION

able even now to let in such warm and loving feelings from others, but I find it very releasing when I can do so. I know that some people flatter me in order to gain something for themselves. Some people praise me because they are afraid to be hostile. Some people, in recent years, admire me because I'm a "great name," or an "authority." But I have come to recognize the fact that some people genuinely appreciate *me*, like me, love me, and I want to sense that fact and let it in. I think I have become less aloof as I have been able really to take in and soak up those loving feelings.

I have found it to be a very enriching thing when I can truly prize or care for or love another person and when I can let that feeling flow out to him. Like many others, I used to fear that I would be trapped by this. "If I let myself care for him he can control me, or use me, or make demands on me." I think that I have moved a long way in the direction of being less fearful in this respect. Like my clients I, too, have slowly learned that tender, positive feelings are *not* dangerous either to give or receive.

Here I could give examples from my own experiences, but, as I thought this over, it seemed to me that it would be almost too personal and might reveal the identities of others, so I'm going to give an illustration in which I have helped two other people to go even further than I could, I think, in the giving of love. The story has to do with two friends, both of them priests, whom I will call Joe and Andy. Joe participated in a basic encounter group that I conducted and he was deeply affected by it. Later, Andy was also a member of a group with which I was associated. Some months later, I received this letter from Andy. It said:

Dear Carl:

I've been trying to get a letter off to you ever since the workshop. I keep thinking I'm going to have some leisure time when I can sit down and really collect my many impressions of those three days. I can see that the leisure time is a dream so I'd like to get at least a note to you.

Perhaps, I can best tell you what that workshop meant by describing an incident that happened not too long after.

Joe [the other priest] had been working with a severely neurotic woman with schizophrenic tendencies, very suicidal and very guilty. She had spent a fortune on psychiatrists and psychologists. One afternoon he asked me to come down to her home with him to meet her, sing and play my guitar and talk. As Joe hoped, it turned into a basic encounter. At one point, she said that her hands really contained her. When she is angry, her hands are angry; when she is happy, her hands are happy; when she is dirty, her hands are dirty. As she was speaking and gesturing, she was sitting near me on the couch. I had the sudden urge to take her hand, I just couldn't buy the concept that she was dirty. So I did. Her first reaction was "Thank you." Then she went into a type of seizure, shaking and crying. We learned later she was reliving a frightening and traumatic experience from her past. Joe had his arm around her shoulders. I held onto her hand for dear life. Finally, she relaxed. She put my hand in hers, turned it over and looked at it. She remarked, "It is not cracked and bleeding, is it?" I shook my head. "But it should be, I'm so dirty." About ten minutes later in the course of the encounter, she reached out and took my hand.

A while later her little girl, a third grader, was screaming. The girl is very emotional and has a lot of problems. I excused myself and went in to see her.

I sat on her bed, talked with her and sang. Before long I had her in my arms, holding her and kissing her and rocking her. When she quieted down, I put her under the covers and got her Mom. She told me later that when she kissed Mary good night, on a new inspiration, she leaned over and kissed her again on the cheek. "This was for Father Andy." Mary looked up, smiled, and said, "You know Mommy, he loves me kind of special, doesn't he?" Then she turned over and went to sleep.

I wanted to tell you about these incidents, Carl, as the workshop with you helped me to respond in each case freely and trustingly with my own instinctive reactions, I have had the words for years. In theory, I have strongly held that that is how I think a man—a Christian—a priest most truly acts. But I have had a hard struggle getting to the point where I could be that free, without hesitation or worry. I left your workshop *really* knowing that I couldn't just say to people that I love them or that they are loveable, especially when they need to be shown this. Since then, many times, I have in some way or another *shown* where before I would have *said*. This has brought much more joy and peace to many like this mother and daughter and to myself.

So often I think gratefully about our group. As you might imagine, I can quite vividly remember the love and warmth of the members of the group as I was struggling so hard to be truly honest with myself and you. For an experience like that, it is difficult to say thank you. May a life more free, more honest, and more loving say it for me. I still get tears in my eyes when I think of the last few hours, all of us sharing deeply and warmly, without any urgency of ourselves. I can't ever remember being so deeply touched by anything—nor have I felt more true love for a group of people. I could go on but I think you see how truly grateful

I am for the workshop, for the group, for you. I just pray that I can help give to others what you and the others gave me. Thank you.

I'm not at all sure that I could have gone as far as those two men did, but I'm very pleased that I have a part in helping someone go beyond where I am. I think it is one of the exciting aspects of working with younger people.

It is also very meaningful to me that I can vouch for the truth of this account. Since the time of this letter I have come to know both Andy and Joe much better. I have also had the privilege of becoming acquainted with the woman whose psychological life they quite literally saved. So I feel confirmed in my view that prizing, loving feelings are *not* basically dangerous to give or receive, but are instead growth-promoting.

I AM MORE ABLE TO APPRECIATE OTHERS

Because of having less fear of giving or receiving positive feelings, I have become more able to *appreciate* individuals. I have come to believe that this is rather rare. So often, even with our children, we love them to control them rather than loving them because we appreciate them. I have come to think that one of the most satisfying experiences I know—and also one of the most growth-promoting experiences for the other person—is just fully to *appreciate* this individual in the same way that I appreciate a sunset. People are just as wonderful as sunsets if I can let them *be*. In fact, perhaps the reason we can truly appreciate a sunset is that we cannot control it. When I look at a sunset as I did the other evening I don't find myself saying, "Soften the orange a little on the right hand corner, and put a bit more purple along the base, and use a little more pink in the cloud color." I don't do that. I don't *try* to control a sunset. I watch it with awe as it unfolds. I like myself best when I can experience my staff member, my son, my daughter, my grandchildren, in this same way, appreciating the unfolding of a life. I believe this is a somewhat oriental attitude, but for me it is the most satisfying one.

So in this third area, prizing or loving and being prized or loved is experienced by me as very growth-enhancing. A person who is loved appreciatively, not possessively, blooms, and develops his own unique self. The person who loves nonpossessively is himself enriched. This at least has been my experience.

I Value Interpersonal Communication and Relationships

Let me close this chapter by saying that in my experience real interpersonal communication and real interpersonal relationships are deeply growth-promoting. I enjoy facilitating growth and development in others. I am enriched when others provide a climate which makes it possible for me to grow and change.

So I value it very much when I am able sensitively to hear the pain and the joy, the fear, the anger, the confusion and despair, the determination and the courage to be, in another person. And I value more than I can say the times when another person has truly been able to hear those elements in me.

I prize it greatly when I am able to move forward in the never-ending attempt to be the real me in this moment, whether it is anger or enthusiasm or puzzlement which is real. I am so delighted when a realness in me brings forth more realness in the other, and we come closer to a mutual I-thou relationship.

And I am very grateful that I have moved in the direction of being able to take in, without rejecting it, the warmth and the caring of others, because this has so increased by own capacity for giving love, without fear of being entrapped and without holding back.

These, in my experience, are some of the elements which make communication between persons, and *being in* relationship to persons, more enriching and more enhancing. I fall *far* short of achieving these elements, but to find myself moving in these directions makes life a warm, exciting, upsetting, troubling, satisfying, enriching, and above all a worthwhile venture.

Action Steps: Applications

1. Select one of your most important interpersonal relationships and analyze it as suggested in this chapter. Use the D-A-S-H model; check your analysis by noting your own and the other person's behaviors in

a number of subsequent encounters. If you trust the other person sufficiently, talk over your conclusions with him/her. Note especially your "punctuation" of interaction events.

2. In one of your interpersonal relationships, attempt to broaden your "response repertoire." Try to respond in various ways (new to you) to the other person's behaviors. Note the subsequent responses. Determine if possible the degree to which the "lockstep" effect influences your and the other person's behaviors.

3. To give you more personal insight into helping others, we offer the following suggestion. Determine which one of your friends or classmates would like to work with you on improving his/her ways of relating to others; this person will likely be one who has participated with you on one of the applications or learning experiences previously suggested in this book. Have that person meet with you and a third person for lunch. During this time have your friend do his/her best to employ effective interpersonal communication with this third person, while you act primarily as an observer. Later meet with your friend and give open, frank, honest feedback on his behavior while talking at lunch. Then ask your friend to evaluate your communication behavior during the present discussion with respect to his/her perceptions of your empathy, nonpossessive warmth, and genuineness. Discuss these aspects of yourself with him/her at some length, being careful to listen more than talk. Later, when you are alone, reflect on this feedback, recalling as best you can your own interpersonal communication behavior. Decide what specific behaviors you would like to change. Then arrange another sequence of experiences with two other persons. See if you can achieve feedback that is more desirable from your own point of view.

4. Identify the person who has shown you the greatest amounts of empathy, warmth, and genuineness while working with friends or classmates on applications and learning experiences suggested in this book. Ask him or her to meet with you and a third person for lunch. During this lunch period, do your best to use effective interpersonal communication with the third person, while your special friend acts mainly as an observer of your communication behavior. At a later meeting with your friend, ask him/her for open and honest feedback regarding your behavior. Now, note very carefully your personal feelings as you listen to this friend criticize your effectiveness. Note any feelings of yours that are negative or evasive. Note: Do you look your friend in the eye as you receive this feedback? Note carefully any defensive communication on your part, identified either by you or by your friend. Thank your friend sincerely for his/her efforts to be of help to you. At a later time—the next day or in days to follow—determine for yourself your own capability for accepting and utilizing such help from other people.

5. Plot the changes that you would like to make in yourself on the diagram form presented in Reading 7.1. Meet in small groups (4–6 students)

and discuss the changes that you are comfortable sharing with others. Are you able to be more open in a group than you were in earlier groups? How does it feel when you share openly?

6. Eric Berne's "games," discussed in this chapter, stand in contrast to the "realness" expressed by Carl Rogers. Analyze your own significant relationships past and present. To what extent have you been real or played games with each other? What influence did this factor have on the nature of the relationship?

Chapter 8
Special Problems in Interpersonal Communication

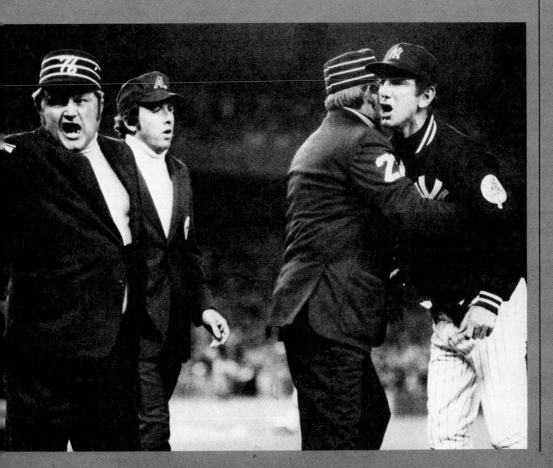

FOR THE PAST seven chapters we have focused attention on the process of interpersonal communication with chapters and readings devoted to key ingredients in the process. In addition to being aware of the process, we must also overcome any barriers or special problems that impede our abilities to achieve successful human interaction. Four significant problem areas will be discussed: (1) defensiveness and distrust, (2) "gaps" between people, (3) complacency and lack of communication skills, and (4) flight vs. fight behaviors. To the extent that these problems can be avoided or resolved, our interpersonal communication can be greatly enhanced.

Defensiveness and Distrust

Probably the foremost problem in relating well to other people is distrust—and its counterpart, defensive interpersonal behavior. The basic cause of defensiveness is inherent in one's unmet interpersonal needs. We need supportive feedback from valued others to achieve a satisfactory self-image. When this need remains unmet, a general feeling of anxiety is produced. Unresolved anxiety generates defensive tactics when we are with other people. Defensive behavior may simply be a show of fear, including postural, facial, or verbal signals that warn the other person to be careful. Or defensive behavior may involve small signs of a desire to withdraw: verbal hesitancies, stepping backward, turning sideways, or simply paying more attention to some other person. These defensive behaviors are real and not devious; thus, the other person perceives them directly as signs of anxiety or fear.

A more disagreeable strategy of defensiveness is the deliberate distortion of the message received. All of us have heard exchanges such as this: (She) "Will you please shut the door; I feel cold." (He) "Why don't you just say you don't want me coming in and bothering you?"

A most serious form of defensive strategy is direct, personal attack. A severe problem arises when the person attacked is unaware that in some way he or she is perceived as a threat; in such a case he or she will probably view the attack as pure, unprovoked aggression.[1] This type of behavior can be

---

[1] P. Watzlawick, J. H. Beavin, and D. D. Jackson, *Pragmatics of Human Communication* (New York: Norton, 1967),pp. 80–93.

complex. Recently one of our students went home to visit her parents, who were having marital strife. At the time of her arrival, her mother was "leaving" to go to her mother's home. The mother asked the girl to go with her, and upon their arrival at the grandmother's home, the girl telephoned her father that they had arrived safely. Her mother asked her why she had done so; the girl replied, "I knew he would be worried." Her mother accused: "Why have you turned against me?" In talking about the incident, the girl interpreted her mother's attack as unprovoked aggression, although she made some allowance for her mother's highly emotional condition at that time. Even so, her resentment of her mother's attack was unresolved.

COMMUNICATION BEHAVIORS THAT GENERATE DEFENSIVENESS

Sometimes we find ourselves distrusting a person without quite knowing how it came about. Knowledge about communication behavior that tends to produce or increase distrust may help us forestall our signal reactions of defensiveness. Investigation of such incidents has identified the following contributory conditions, or causes of defensive behavior:

1. Evaluative expressions, manner of speech, tone of voice, or verbal content, perceived by the receiver (listener) as criticism or judgment, will produce defensive behavior.
2. Communication perceived by the recipient as an attempt to control him/her will produce defensiveness. (It is interesting to note that if speech can be said to be a social "tool," the implication is that the recipient has been "tooled.")
3. Stratagems that are perceived as clever devices produce defensiveness; partially hidden motives breed suspicion. Persons seen as "playing a game," feigning emotion, withholding information, or having private access to sources of data will stimulate defensive responses.
4. An appearance of lack of concern for the welfare of a person will heighten his/her need for defensiveness. Such "neutrality" may be necessary at times, but people strongly need to be perceived as valued persons. A clinically detached or impersonal manner (not caring) is usually feared and resented.
5. An attitude of superiority arouses defensive behavior; any behavior that reinforces the recipient's feelings of inadequacy is a source of disturbance.
6. Dogmatism is a well-known stimulus of defensive behavior; if you know something "for certain," it is wise to determine whether or not anyone else wants to hear it from you, and whether they want your answer to be offered tentatively or with final certainty.[2]

When people are perceived to be attempting to manipulate us, we tend to be suspicious and defensive behavior increases.

[2] J. R. Gibb, "Defensive Communication," *Journal of Communication*, 11 (1961): 141–148.

REQUISITE CONDITIONS FOR
REDUCING DEFENSIVE BEHAVIOR

Over a quarter century ago Carl Rogers began to report a movement toward a nondirective approach to psychotherapy. These practices culminated in his client-centered approach. The relevant point here is his emphasis on the patient's need for personal trust in the therapist. Rogers emphasized acceptance or psychological safety in psychotherapy groups.[3]

Rogers's approach was a forerunner of Jack Gibb's concept of supportive climate in the communication process. Starting a long-range research effort in 1953, Gibb focused his efforts on the reduction of defensive behavior in groups. This defensive behavior seemed to be caused, in part, by lack of interpersonal trust. In later work he began to focus on trust and its development, associating trust with interpersonal acceptance.[4] According to his findings, cited earlier in Reading 3.2, defensive behavior is reduced by interaction that is perceived by the individual as:

1. Descriptive rather than evaluative or critical
2. Oriented toward solving mutual problems rather than toward personal control
3. Spontaneous rather than strategic
4. Empathic rather than neutral
5. Indicative of an attitude of equality instead of superiority
6. Expressive of provisionally held viewpoints instead of dogmatic certainties.[5]

Additional studies by Gibb tend to corroborate these findings.[6]

EFFECTS OF REDUCING DEFENSIVENESS

As interpersonal trust increases, interpersonal relationships change so that there is:

1. Increased acceptance of legitimate influence by others
2. Decreased suspicion of motives of others
3. Increased tolerance for deviant behavior of others
4. Increased stability when one is not trusted by others
5. Shifting of emphasis to control over the interaction process rather than control over individuals
6. Further increase in interpersonal trust.[7]

[3] C. R. Rogers, *Client-Centered Therapy* (Boston: Houghton Mifflin, 1951), pp. 515–520.
[4] J. R. Gibb, "Climate for Trust Formation," in L. P. Bradford et al. (eds.), *T-Group Theory and Laboratory Method* (New York: Wiley, 1964), pp. 279–309.
[5] Gibb, "Defensive Communication," p. 148.
[6] J. R. Gibb, "Dynamics of Leadership," *Current Issues of Higher Education* (Washington, D.C.: American Association for Higher Education, 1967).
[7] Cf. Kim Giffin, "Interpersonal Trust in Small-Group Communication," *Quarterly Journal of Speech*, 53 (1967): 224–234.

Changes in personality characteristics are not easy to produce; changes in behavior that seem to indicate changes in personality structure may be only temporary. Even so, studies tend to indicate that, as defensive behavior decreases and interpersonal trust increases, two important personality changes can occur: (1) We tend to achieve heightened feelings of personal adequacy (improved self-image), and (2) we achieve easier acceptance of our temporary feelings of internal conflict (less anxiety). Reducing defensive behavior and increasing interpersonal trust appear to be extremely valuable goals in terms of effective interpersonal communication.

TRUST IN INTERPERSONAL COMMUNICATION

Trusting behavior in the communication process can be defined as reliance on the communication behavior (speaking and/or listening) of a person while you are attempting to achieve a desired but uncertain objective in a risky situation. A theoretical formulation of the trust paradigm in the communication process includes both *inter*personal and *intra*personal trust:[8]

1. Trust of a speaker by a listener, called "ethos" by Aristotle and "source credibility" by C. Hovland, I. L. Janis, and H. H. Kelley[9]
2. Trust of a listener by a speaker, called "sense of psychological safety" by Rogers,[10] "perceived supportive climate" by Gibb,[11] and "speech confidence" (rather than "anxiety") as described by Giffin and Bradley[12]
3. Trust of oneself as a speaker—a person's perception of himself/herself as a communicator capable of achieving a desired goal in a situation perceived as risky or threatening (the opposite of speech anxiety)
4. Trust of oneself as a listener—a person's perception of himself/herself as a listener capable of achieving a desired goal in a situation perceived as risky or threatening.

Trust both influences and is influenced by various elements in the communication process. For example, our trust of a person is influenced by his/her reliability as we perceive it. On the other hand, the degree of trust we have for this person influences the communication behavior of both of us as well as the results of our interaction. The relationship between these variables is reflexive: As trust increases, certain interaction patterns change; in turn, their change tends to increase the degree of interpersonal trust.

The manner in which one person's perception of another influences personal trust has been of major concern to many scholars; however, interest has been focused primarily on the first element of the trust paradigm we

[8] Ibid.

[9] C. Hovland, I. L. Janis, and H. H. Kelley, *Communication and Persuasion* (New Haven, Conn.: Yale University Press, 1953), p. 21.

[10] Rogers, *Client-Centered Therapy*, p. 41.

[11] J. Gibb, "Climate for Trust Formation," in L. P. Bradford et al. (eds.), *T-Group Theory and Laboratory Method* (New York: Wiley, 1964), p. 298.

[12] K. Giffin and K. Bradley, "Group Counseling for Speech Anxiety: An Approach and a Rationale," *Journal of Communication*, 19 (1969): 22–29.

Trust is important in all stages of a relationship.

described: trust of a speaker by a listener (ethos or source credibility). Although the evidence is not entirely clear, trust of a speaker appears to be influenced by a listener's perceptions of the following characteristics of a speaker:

1. Expertness relevant to the topic under discussion; this expertise may be in the form of quantity of pertinent information, degree of ability or skill, or validity of judgment.
2. Reliability; this may be perceived as dependability, predictability, consistency, or intentions of the trusted person regarding the goals or objectives of the person doing the trusting.
3. Dynamism; that is, behavior perceived as more active than passive and more open or frank than closed or reserved.[13]

Further evidence has been obtained to demonstrate that these three dimensions constitute the attitude elements of personal trust.[14] These three characteristics of a person are perceived directly by another person, and each may influence interpersonal trust. If you wish to have others trust you, you should adopt behaviors that will demonstrate that you are expert, reliable and dynamic.

SELF-CONCEPT AND TRUST IN OTHERS

One's cognition of oneself is obtained, in part, by personal sensory perception and also, in part, by checking with other people. According to this

[13] K. Giffin, "The Contribution of Studies of Source Credibility to a Theory of Interpersonal Trust in the Communication Process," *Psychological Bulletin*, 68 (1967): 104–120.
[14] K. Giffin, *An Experimental Evaluation of the Trust Differential: Research Monograph R/19* (Lawrence: Communication Research Center, University of Kansas, 1968).

line of reasoning, a person needs to communicate with others to verify his/her own view of himself/herself. However, if there is considerable question in our mind about our social capabilities, we are not likely to expose ourselves via communication with others. In fact, we will most likely fear communication situations. Research evidence tends to support this line of reasoning.[15]

Both Heider's balance theory and Festinger's theory of cognitive dissonance would lead us to suspect that a person with a high concept of self would not fear exposure in his/her interaction with others, and even if an attack on his/her self-image occurred, he/she would likely disparage the source of the attack. Very likely he/she would filter such information, accepting only that with which he/she tended to agree. Exactly the same reasoning would lead us to suspect that a person with a *low* concept of self would reject information that would tend to raise the concept. There is research support for this line of reasoning. A. E. Bergin has demonstrated that when (1) a person's self-concept is low and (2) the information received from another person is favorable about his/her behavior, he/she will tend to resolve this dissonance *by discrediting the source.*[16] An experiment by Deutsch and Solomon indicated that persons with low concept of self tend to accept only information congruent with their concept; such subjects *view low* evaluations of themselves from others more favorably than high evaluations.[17]

In our culture, having a low concept of self is not a pleasant experience. Confirmation of it, even if valid, is likewise not pleasant. Thus, the individual with low self-esteem will pay more attention to information that confirms his low concept, but not be happy about it. He/she actually *fears confirmation of his/her fears.* In terms of interpersonal relationships, the protection of one's self-image is closely linked with trust of those with whom one interacts. Self-confidence in interpersonal relations can be conceptualized as willingness to expose one's self-concept to evaluation by others.

In a summary of the literature on self-concept, Roger Brown concluded that there is a strong relationship between a broad conception of oneself and one's conception of others with whom one interacts (i.e., if I like people, I tend to like me).[18] Recent research has provided direct evidence in support of this line of reasoning.[19]

Rogers has argued that when an individual interacts with trusted others, he is able to form new and more favorable perceptions of himself; that is, he can afford exposure of his self-concept for possible self-evaluation.[20] There is limited research evidence that exposure of oneself can help to increase one's trust of his/her listeners.[21]

[15] H. Gilkinson, "A Questionnaire Study of the Causes of Social Fears Among College Speech Students," *Speech Monographs*, 10 (1943): 74–83. See also E. Bormann and G. Shapiro, "Perceived Confidence as a Function of Self-Image," *Central States Speech Journal*, 13 (1962): 253–256.

[16] A. E. Bergin, "The Effects of Dissonant Persuasive Communications upon Changes in a Self-Referring Attitude," *Journal of Personality*, 30 (1962): 423–438.

[17] M. Deutsch and L. Solomon, "Reactions to Evaluations by Others as Influenced by Self-Evaluations," *Sociometry*, 22 (1959): 93–112.

[18] R. Brown, *Social Psychology* (New York: Free Press, 1965), p. 650.

[19] Rogers, *Client-Centered Therapy*, pp. 515–524.

[20] Rogers, *On Becoming a Person*, pp. 39–58.

[21] Giffin, "Studies of Source Credibility," 104–120.

In view of the findings cited, the following principles may be stated: (1) Self-confidence in a given interpersonal communication situation is a function of perceived acceptance by valued others. (2) There is an interaction between three types of trust, all three of which are functionally related to self-confidence in a given interpersonal communication situation: (a) trust of oneself, (b) trust extended toward others, and (c) perceived evidence of trust extended by others.

INCREASING ONE'S TRUST OF OTHERS

If speech anxiety and tendency toward withdrawal from communication situations are related to one's trust of others, it is a natural question to ask: How can one's trust of others be increased?

It should be acknowledged that, in some cases, increasing a person's trust of others may be dangerous; some dupes are altogether too trusting. However, if a person is abnormally distrustful of other persons, that is, if he/she has unrealistic or irrational fear of others in social or communicative situations, then attempts on his/her part to increase his/her general level of trust of other people seem warranted. By achieving a more objective perception of others, one can hope to raise his/her own self-concept and reduce his/her speech anxiety.[22]

Interpersonal trust can be achieved in a climate of perceived acceptance of the individual by others with whom he/she interacts. Personal change in a socially desirable way, and in a way desirable for the individual, requires a climate of acceptance and support. This climate of acceptance is sometimes found in t-groups (sensitivity training groups) and in therapy groups. From his work with normal subjects who were attempting to make their interpersonal relations more effective, Gibb drew the following conclusion:

> A person learns to grow through his increasing acceptance of himself and others. Serving as the primary block to such acceptance are the defensive feelings of fear and distrust that arise from the prevailing defensive climates in most cultures. In order to participate consciously in his own growth, a person must learn to create for himself, in his dyadic and group relationships, defensive-reductive climates that will continue to reduce his own fears and distrusts.[23]

It seems somewhat obvious that a key variable in increasing a person's trust of others is the behavior of those others. Studies show that counselors vary as to characteristics of accurate empathy, nonpossessive warmth, and genuineness. A large number of studies have demonstrated that counselors who show above average amounts of empathy, warmth, and genuineness have above average success with psychoneurotic clients in psychiatric hospitals, psychiatric outpatient clinics, veteran's clinics, college counseling centers, and juvenile

---

[22] See evidence cited by K. Giffin and M. Heider in "A Theory of the Relationship Between Speech Anxiety and the Suppression of Communication in Childhood," *Psychiatric Quarterly Supplement*, 2 (1967): 311–322.

[23] Gibb, "Climate for Trust Formation," p. 279.

institutions. These studies include both individual and group counseling approaches.

The following line of reasoning thus emerges: (1) Speech anxiety involves low concept of self and distrust of others. (2) Irrational distrust of others is significantly reduced by interaction with others and by counselors who show empathy, warmth, and genuineness; thus the inference can be drawn that an environment which can measurably increase interpersonal trust is one in which a person is shown high degrees of these elements of rapport.

This inference makes logical sense; an anxious person can cope more easily with a communication environment in which he receives empathy, warmth, and genuineness. Successful coping with this communication environment may provide additional interpersonal confidence.

"Gaps" Between People

It is unthinkable that a man, alone in the forest, chancing upon a person being mauled by a bear, or one who has deeply chopped his foot with an axe, would not lend help. Yet similar instances of unconcern for others have occurred repeatedly in the crowded city. A young woman named Kitty Genovese was attacked by a maniac at 3:00 A.M. Thirty-eight of her neighbors heard her screams and cries for help. No one came. No one even bothered to call the police. In another instance a seventeen-year-old Manhattan boy was stabbed in the stomach while riding a commuter train. Eleven persons watched his assailants leave and the boy bled to death without anyone's offering assistance. An eighteen-year-old switchboard operator was beaten and raped in her place of work. She ran naked into the street, screaming for help, but the rapist, in view of forty observers, tried to drag her back into the building until two policemen interrupted the violent scene. What is the difference between the city street and the lonely forest? If no one else is present, the individual will take responsibility. One person does not wait to see what others will do because there is no one for whom to wait. In the crowd responsibility is so diffused that no one takes action. "Surely," the feeling is, "if it were really serious, someone would make a move." And so pedestrian traffic will flow around a heart attack victim or one who is suffering from insulin shock. "Drunk!" is the excuse for shrugging off involvement.[24]

Much has been said about the loneliness within a large city. A person who speaks to a stranger may be thought to be a "screwball" or worse. This aloneness in the presence of others can also be seen in the impersonal nature of living in an apartment building where even next-door neighbors are not known well enough to call by name. A major problem is that of overcoming barriers between people, including those from different reference groups, different generations, and different cultures.

[24] H. W. Bernard and W. C. Huckins, *Dynamics of Personal Adjustment* (Boston: Holbrook Press, 1971), p. 29.

BARRIERS BETWEEN MEMBERS OF DIFFERENT REFERENCE GROUPS

In order to be adequate socially we must achieve personal beliefs, attitudes, and convictions that help us to function well with those people who surround us. Conflicts over norms of behavior and belief usually prove to be threatening. If our personal standards and norms conflict seriously with those of people in our immediate environment, the experience is likely to be painful because our very basis of existence is at stake.

When we identify with a group, such as the people in our community, we almost inevitably adopt and defend the standards and behavior of that group. A group with which we identify is sometimes called a *reference group.* This process of identification introduces a certain degree of narrowness or distortion into our perceptual field; limiting and distorting our perception of "foreigners" (persons not in our reference group) then becomes a major source of breakdown in communication.

Because each of us accepts his/her own perceptions as "reality," the customs and attitudes of our own reference group are judged to be superior when they are different from those of other groups. Other people and other groups are then judged according to these standards. Americans commonly place a high value on houses with modern plumbing; as a result, many Americans consider the Germans superior to the French. If you say, "Well, they are!" then you have illustrated the point at issue—you have made a judgment based on a standard derived from your American reference group.

A boy called George has identified with a predelinquent gang. He has a different system of prestige values from Charles, who has identified with the Boy Scouts. Not only do the two boys admire different institutions, but they also respect different individuals and types of "success." It is not enough to say that they "don't talk the same language." Such may be the case and, if so, communication is hampered; but even if they know and agree on the same meanings for words, their system of values is different. Charles will think the predelinquent boy is wrong, and George will judge Charles to be naive and ignorant. This kind of problem is not uncommon; in fact, two such boys may even live on the same city block. Even so, bridging the communication gap in this rather common setting is not at all easy.

In the larger social sense, the insular thinking just described is one of the principal barriers to intercultural cooperation. People of almost all cultures sincerely desire a better world and a better society; the barrier consists of lack of agreement among the various groups as to what constitutes a good society. Members of each culture consider their own version of society fundamentally right because it (more or less) satisfies their personal needs as they see them. Thus, they believe that the better society can arise only from a further development and modification of their own. This is true for Iranians, Hindus, Mexicans, Eskimos, Russians, and Americans.[25] When members of different

---

[25] A. W. Combs and D. Snygg, *Individual Behavior*, rev. ed. (New York: Harper & Row, 1959), pp. 341–344.

reference groups or subcultures try to communicate, it frequently seems that their actions are chiefly intended to hinder or obstruct another group's efforts to create their version of a "better" world.

How can such gaps ever be bridged? In a way, every individual bridges a similar gap whenever he tries to contact and "get to know" any other single individual. We start by accepting and even adopting a few behaviors of others that help us to satisfy some personal need. As we accept or adopt behaviors, we later modify our attitudes, beliefs, and value systems. For example, the white man's alcohol was a boon from heaven in the eyes of the Plains Indians, who viewed the world as a place where a man became great ("successful") and held power over others through dreams and delirium. On the other hand, the Hopi, living in a world of fragile order and regularity where a small mistake could bring personal hardship, saw alcohol as a great menace and rejected it.

The process of acceptance of the ways, attitudes, and beliefs of others is speeded up if the other person has some acceptable source of status, or if the behavior satisfies some immediate and important personal need.[26] New ways of doing things that otherwise fit our customary pattern of behavior are easily accepted and adopted. Once the change is made, we quickly find additional reasons why it was a good idea; we thus reduce the cognitive dissonance imposed by the new behavior.[27]

The primary tool for bridging gaps between reference groups is, of course, getting the group to look at each other without perceptual distortion. *The real barrier is the a priori notion that just because a person is a member of another group his/ her behavior and his/her beliefs will be inferior.* People who fail to conform to our standards tend to be viewed as ignorant or perhaps evil. Such prejudgment— judgment without taking an objective, open-minded, inquisitive look to see first and decide later—is properly called prejudice. No people of any nation, religion, or group have been entirely free of this problem. Even teachers who ordinarily are severe critics of their own educational system will have difficulty giving objective consideration to the suggestions of those who are not a part of the system. Objectivity, however, is the true basis of tolerance and makes possible the bridging of gaps between members of different reference groups.

GAPS BETWEEN DIFFERENT CULTURES AND MINORITY SUBCULTURES

We have been aware of the problem of communication between segments of cultures or subcultures ever since it was discovered in Boston that Lowells talked only to Cabots and Cabots talked only to God. Today the need for communication between members of different subcultures is urgent. Our primary concern in this section is with interpersonal communication barriers between representatives of different cultures or subcultures; such problems are brought to light at the "interface" between cultural groups.

[26] R. Linton, *The Cultural Background of Personality* (New York: Appleton, 1945), pp. 39–74.
[27] S. Feldman, *Cognitive Consistency* (New York: Academic, 1966), pp. 43–57.

Communities that pride themselves on tolerance and the absence of prejudice almost always have only a few members of a minority group in their midst. Minority groups become threatening to majority groups only when they are large or powerful. When a group feels threatened, its members tend to accentuate or idealize their own characteristics. This has two negative effects on their perceptual processes: (1) Their perceptions tend to be focused on the object of threat so that it is difficult to see broadly and clearly, and (2) they tend to be much more rigidly defensive of their existing perceptions.[28] As a general principle, the psychological effects of intergroup threat or conflict are felt at the lower socioeconomic levels, especially if persons at these lower levels are the victims of domination or aggression within their own group.[29] For example, in the South, the most violent reactions to school integration occurred among the "poor white" economic classes.

The point of greatest potential for bridging intercultural gaps is at the interface between cultures, that is, the personal, face-to-face interaction between official and unofficial representatives of those cultures. Foreign travelers are generally better educated, more broadly experienced, and feel less personally threatened by representatives of the other culture. At this interface, a common language capability is helpful but not crucial. For example, in the earlier periods of World War II, American and Russian soldiers found ways of overcoming the language problem. The need for action in a common cause made individuals from the different cultures important to each other. There was also a certain pleasure in getting acquainted with new allies, and the Americans admired the great physical stamina and courage of the Russians.

What is severely needed by intercultural representatives at this interface is objectivity of perception. Intercultural conflict is always carried on by individuals who think of their antagonists as *members of the other group* rather than as individual human beings. Intergroup conflict at the cultural interface can be diminished by increasing the capability of members to differentiate one another as individuals.[30]

Increased interaction between such representatives is helpful; it fosters the ability of these persons to see each other as individuals rather than as blacks or whites, Germans or Jews, Russians or Americans.[31] A very interesting procedure developed by R. D. DuBois has been shown to be an effective means of promoting better relationships between representatives of different groups. Instead of talking about intergroup or intercultural problems and differences, they are asked to talk about pleasant childhood memories.[32] Members of both groups talk about their experiences in smelling and tasting enjoyable foods, playing games, and participating in athletic events. After awhile they feel as if they have had similar experiences, somewhat similar childhoods, and are, first

[28] Combs and Snygg, *Individual Behavior*, pp. 165–189.
[29] D. Snygg, "The Relative Difficulty of Mechanically Equivalent Tasks: 1. Human Learning," *Journal of Genetic Psychology*, 47 (1935): 299–320.
[30] B. Kutner, C. Wilkins, and P. Yarrow, "Verbal Attitudes and Overt Behavior Involving Racial Prejudice," *Journal of Abnormal and Social Psychology*, 47 (1952): 649–652.
[31] J. W. Thibaut and J. Coules, "The Role of Communication in the Reduction of Interpersonal Hostility," *Journal of Abnormal and Social Psychology*, 47 (1952): 770–777.
[32] R. D. DuBois, *Get Together, Americans* (New York: Harper & Row, 1943).

Fences may serve as symbolic gaps between neighbors.

of all, all members of the human race. Shared experiences make possible a common feeling; furthermore, shared experiences provide a more personal, human view of a member of another group or culture.

The objective view of one another, a view focused on the other person as an individual human being rather than as a specimen of a strange cultural type, is the basis for effective interpersonal communication between representatives of different cultures. Such effective communication behavior is highly useful in reducing intergroup conflict for the following reasons: (1) It maximizes human capability for tolerance of differences and acceptance of new or different folkways and attitudes, and (2) it minimizes the degree of fear and feelings of threat imposed by the other group, race, or culture.

We cannot afford to be parties to the discrimination that creates and reinforces the low self-concept of others. We believe that it is simply beneath one's dignity to do less than wholly accept and respect (not just tolerate) a fellow human being; prejudices and discrimination hamper one's chances for self-actualization (see Chapter 9) as well as impose psychological distress on others.

Complacency and Lack of Communication Skills

Throughout this book we have emphasized that it would be impossible for most of us to exist very long in this society without participating in a number of relationships with varying degrees of intimacy. Although the nature and intensity of these relationships vary from person to person and from situation to situation, they are almost as much a part of our lives as the clothes we wear and the air we breathe. Why then do we feel that many people are complacent about their interpersonal communication abilities?

Regretfully, there is a general unconscious denial by most people of needs for improvement in interpersonal communication skills. William V. Haney conducted a survey including over 6,000 people, asking them anonymously how they assessed their communication performance as compared with others in an organizational setting. He noted:

> ... The main conclusion of the study was that virtually everyone felt he was communicating *at least as well as* and, in many cases, *better than* everyone else in the organization ... Most people readily admit that their organization is fraught with faulty communication but it is almost always "those other people" who are responsible.[33]

We believe at least two factors should be considered regarding this complacency. Recall Proposition 5: "In interpersonal communication, the sender and the receiver are interdependent." If this proposition is true (and we believe it is), then the success or failure of communication is a joint responsibility. Neither the receiver nor the sender has total control over the process, so success cannot be measured solely by how well someone listens or speaks. Therefore, it is extremely difficult and often futile to assess individual blame in the communication process, because one person's performance is so intertwined with that of the other.

A second factor that contributes to complacency is the absence of feedback concerning our interpersonal communication abilities. As students you have no doubt received ample feedback concerning your writing competencies, but how much feedback have you received on your interpersonal communication competencies? Our interpretation of the response of others is often too general and too abstract to reflect directly and specifically on our communication. If something is clear and logical to me, the other person must see it the same way.

The overriding problem is that when a person is unable or unwilling to acknowledge a deficiency, he/she is not going to change. If, in trying to improve yourself you aim at nothing, you are pretty apt to hit it. Hopefully in your study of interpersonal communication, you have set some goals for yourself. Remember Proposition 4: "The choices that a person makes reflect the degree of that person's interpersonal communication competencies." In Chapter 1 we presented an overview of the competencies demanded by effective interpersonal communication. Now we shall consider these competencies in greater detail.

John M. Wiemann has studied extensively the topic of communicative competency and has observed:

> ... The competent interactant is other-oriented to the extent that he is open (available) to receive messages from others, does not provoke anxiety in others by

---

[33] W. V. Haney, *Communication and Organizational Behavior* (Homewood, Ill.: Irwin, 1973), pp. 181–182.

exhibiting anxiety himself, is empathic, has a large enough behavioral repertoire to allow him to meet the demands of changing situations, and, finally, is supportive of the faces and lives his fellow interactants present.[34]

Let us consider the factors involved in Wiemann's five dimensions:

1. *Affiliation/support.* Such nonverbal behaviors discussed in Chapter 5 as eye contact, head nods, smiles, and standing close show the degree of liking and support. Verbal behaviors include "owning" our perceptions about another, choosing words that indicate the nature of the relationship (e.g., "Professor" or "Sir"), and appropriate sharing of the amount of speaking time.
2. *Social relaxation.* The behavior cues that allow the other person to relax include general postural movements such as leaning and rocking, a relaxed rate of speech, and an absence of speech hesitations and disfluencies.
3. *Empathy.* Empathic listening is indicated by head nods and verbal listener responses. Statements of feeling such as "I know how you feel" and responding with appropriate and reciprocal signs of feeling are important.
4. *Behavioral flexibility.* The competent communicator must be able to adapt his/her behavior as the situation within an encounter changes and, as he/she moves from encounter to encounter. The competent individual is able to be assertive if needed, or serve as a passive observer if appropriate.
5. *Interaction management.* Wiemann cites five rules that typically apply to face-to-face encounters: (1) Interruptions of the speaker are not permitted, (2) one person talks at a time, (3) the speaker turns must interchange, (4) frequent and lengthy pauses should be avoided, and, (5) an interactant must be perceived as devoting full attention to the encounter.[35]

While such a description of behaviors must be viewed as tentative, we believe that such research is important. We know that some people are quite effective in certain capacities (such as conducting a meeting), while weak in others (such as sharing feelings with an associate). The Action Steps at the end of each chapter have been designed to give you experiences across the spectrum of communication expectations. We shall discuss ways to improve our interpersonal competence more fully in the next chapter.

Flight *vs.* Fight Behaviors

Pressure and stress are symptomatic of the times and conditions in which we live. Living in close proximity to masses of people, and having direct,

[34] J. M. Wiemann, "Explication and Test of a Model of Communicative Competence," *Human Communication Research*, 3 (1977): 198.
[35] Ibid., pp. 60–70.

immediate access to all the problems of the world by means of our mass media contribute to the pressures we feel. Some psychologists believe that a certain amount of pressure, stress, or discomfort is necessary for action. An unsatisfied need provokes a drive that moves a person to act until the need is satisfied.[36]

The problem for all of us is not to attempt the impossible and to eliminate pressure, but to recognize it as a fact of everyday living and to learn how to deal with it. Although a certain amount of dissatisfaction or pressure may be necessary for action to be initiated, it is important to recognize excess pressure that hinders or results in inappropriate behavior. Certain internal changes take place that prepare the body for action when stress and pressure are high. Physically we are ready for "flight or fight," but our conscious processes are not promoted.[37]

Flight and fight represent two extreme patterns of reactions to stress situations. The typical reactions vary from individual to individual and from situation to situation. Extreme flight or withdrawal from interaction can result in feelings of alienation, the topic of Reading 8.1.

At the other end of the continuum is fight behavior, choosing to engage in conflict. Conflict is inevitable in ongoing relationships, and is a topic worth serious consideration, The choice to engage in conflict does not require a decision to flail, to destroy, or even to win. In many ways if a person wins an argument and another person loses, the relationship suffers. Reading 8.2, "Types and Sources of Conflict," discusses aspects of this behavior.

We may choose to withdraw from an encounter, or we may choose to engage in conflict. The key issue is understanding that we have a choice and knowing what the consequences are. Occasional withdrawal in order to conceptualize more effective ways of dealing with the situation may be appropriate behavior. It is only when a person uses flight to the exclusion of other methods, as when a person habitually withdraws, that should warrant concern. To the extent that a person knows what he/she does and chooses responsibly to do it, he/she controls his/her own behavior.

Summary and Preview of Readings

Of the many potential problems in interpersonal communication, at least four are important enough to deserve special consideration. In this chapter we discussed: (1) defensiveness and distrust, (2) "gaps" between people of different backgrounds, (3) complacency and lack of interpersonal communication skills, and (4) flight *vs.* fight orientations.

We suggested ways defensive behavior can be increased as well as reduced. We also suggested that cultural prejudice and gaps between groups and between cultures are natural but not necessary. Certain ways of overcoming prejudice are available to those who wish to reduce these barriers. Such an achievement is rarely easy; in any case it takes determination and strong resolve.

[36] Bernard and Huckins, *Dynamics of Personal Adjustment*, p. 184.
[37] Ibid., p. 193.

We noted that many people are unaware of substantial parts of what they communicate and the way in which others respond to them because of the absence of specific feedback, poor habits, and our informal learning systems. We cited five categories of behaviors that can be related to a person's interpersonal competencies: showing affiliation/support, social relaxation, empathy, behavior flexibility, and interaction management. An effective control of our interpersonal communication is indispensable for managing our social encounters and developing our sense of self-sufficiency.

The final topic of flight *vs.* fight reactions to stressful situations will be developed more fully in the two readings that follow. The first reading describes the way individuals are sometimes influenced to withdraw from interaction with others. The process is discussed in terms of social alienation as well as speech anxiety, and indicates some close relationships between the two concepts. In addition, the reading suggests that such withdrawal can be the result of prior communication experiences, particularly continued communication denial.

The second reading is devoted to the fight end of the reaction continuum, analyzing conflict. The reading outlines the sequence typically associated with the development and resolution of conflict. The conflict process is depicted as well as characteristics of relationships that are associated with various degrees or kinds of conflictive behavior.

Feelings of Alienation

Kim Giffin and Bobby R. Patton

In comments on current social problems, the term "alienation" is frequently used. Sometimes these comments are about the "alienated teenager" or the "alienated generation." Since there are many persons in our society who appear to hold negative attitudes toward other persons in their immediate social environment, the problem deserves special consideration.

In common parlance the term "alienated" usually refers to persons who are estranged or withdrawn from other persons whom they would ordinarily be expected to associate with or to admire—even to love. A student who has turned away from his teachers—that is, who has ceased to talk with them in the way that they expect or desire—may sometimes be called "alienated."

From *Fundamentals of Interpersonal Communication* (2d ed.) by Kim Giffin and Bobby R. Patton. Copyright 1976. Reprinted by permission of Harper & Row.

The Problem of the Alienated Person

The term "alienated" has two usages pertinent to our discussion. The first simply refers to a person who withdraws from or avoids another person or persons. This withdrawal behavior has been identified as *social alienation*, and is defined by Hajda, a representative authority in this area, as follows:

Alienation is an individual's feeling of uneasiness or discomfort which reflects his exclusion or self-exclusion from social and cultural participation. It is an expression of non-belonging or non-caring, an uneasy awareness or perception of unwelcome contrast with others. It varies in scope and intensity. It may be restricted to a few limited situations, such as participation in a peer group, or it may encompass a wide social universe, including participation in the larger society. . . . In this sense, alienation is a general social phenomenon, a feeling that may be experienced in some fashion by any member of a given society. It cannot be understood apart from its opposite, the feeling of belonging, sharing, or participation which follows from the individual's inclusion or integration into the social collectivities.[1]

Although here we will be using the term "alienation" to refer to social alienation, it should be noted that common usage of the term often connotes an implication of *mental* disturbance. This connotation comes from the technical use of the term in psychiatry. In their *Psychiatric Dictionary*, Hinsie and Campbell give the psychological definition of *mental alienation* as follows:

> The repression, inhibition, blocking or dissociation of one's own feelings so that they no longer seem effective, familiar or convincing to the patient.[2]

Thus whenever a person is said to be alienated, there is a connotative suggestion of personal maladjustment.

Alienation does not mean simple disagreement with another person, even if the disagreement is violent, as long as interaction continues. When one ceases overt communication with another person or persons and withdraws from interaction, social alienation, in the sense we are using the term, has occurred. In this way we can become alienated from a person or a group—a brother, sister, mother, father, husband, wife, teacher, peer group, school, reference group, or even an entire culture or social system. Alienation thus involves a conclusion that one's attempts to communicate

with a person (or persons) are pointless. At this point functional withdrawal from interaction begins.

Alienation of a person from another can be partial; one can be convinced that he/she will be denied the opportunity for communication on certain topics or at certain times or under certain conditions. As long as he/she is allowed to communicate on most topics most of the time, the degree of alienation is only slight. The severity of alienation increases as a person perceives an increase in the number of times his/her communication is denied.

Alienation can occur between a person and one or more other people. Complete alienation from one other person may not matter very much; complete or nearly complete alienation from many others can make life miserable. William James once said, "No more fiendish punishment could be devised, even were such a thing physically possible, than that one should be turned loose in society and remain absolutely unnoticed by all members thereof."[3]

Alienation does not occur between a person and someone whom he/she has never known. It does occur most noticeably when a person withdraws from interaction with someone he/she has known well, such as a parent, wife, or husband.

As described above, alienation from another person does not necessarily mean neurotic behavior; when confronted with denial of one's attempts to communicate, it is perfectly rational to conclude (1) "He won't talk with me (on those topics, now, or under those conditions)" or (2) "It is not worth my

[1] J. Hajda, "Alienation and Integration of Student Intellectuals," *American Sociological Review*, 26 (1961):758–759.
[2] L. E. Hinsie and R. J. Campbell, *Psychiatric Dictionary*, 3rd ed. (New York: Oxford University Press, 1960), p. 26.

[3] Quoted by R. D. Laing, *The Self and Others: Further Studies in Sanity and Madness* (London: Tavistock, 1961), p. 89.

time to try to talk with him (on those topics, now, or under those conditions)." Neurotic alienation begins when *reality* is ignored—that is, when the above conclusions are drawn in the face of identifiable evidence to the contrary. It becomes critical when a person denies his/her own feelings that are at the same time expressed in obvious behavioral ways.

Of course, social alienation is not the same as mental alienation. However, it is sometimes viewed by parents and even by others in society as mental disturbance. This confusion in thinking occurs as follows: (1) The socially alienated person may appear to parents to be repressing, inhibiting, blocking, or denying expected or desired warm feelings about them, and (2) these expected or desired feelings no longer seem to be operative in producing "appropriate" responses to the overtures of the parents. This breakdown of such a relationship can be analyzed in terms of communication theory; that is, it constitutes a refusal to utilize a communication channel generally thought to be available and useful. An important question for the student of communication behavior is thus exposed: What kinds of communication behavior tend to produce alienation?

Tangential questions are as follows: Is it possible that "the alienated" are realistically responding to communication events in an intelligent way? Can such alienating communication events be described in a way that will provide insight and understanding of this problem? Are "the alienated" mistakenly withdrawing from social interaction that would be very useful to them? Have parents or teachers or other important persons unknowingly or thoughtlessly provided excellent causes for such social withdrawal?

An exploratory study of this problem was made through analyses of interviews with college students who appeared to be alienated from teachers and peer groups. The data tend to indicate that certain prior communication events have transpired. These events can be identified as misuse or misunderstanding of one or more of the basic principles of interpersonal communication.[4] We will give this problem detailed consideration here, because we have found that young people of our acquaintance are concerned about it.

Speech Anxiety

In the study of speech communication, tendencies to withdraw from interpersonal communication have been variously called communication apprehension,[5] reticence,[6] and speech anxiety.[7] Essentially such tendencies are a response to interaction conditions that produce fear or tension.[8] This attitude is a situation-specific anxiety, and it will be identified here as *speech anxiety*.[9]

A major part of our research work in the Communication Research Cen-

[4] For a more detailed report of studies completed and those in progress, see K. Giffin, "Social Alienation by Communication Denial," *Quarterly Journal of Speech*, 56 (1970): 347–357.

[5] J. C. McCroskey, "Measures of Communication-Bound Anxiety," *Speech Monographs*, 37 (1970):269–277.

[6] G. M. Phillips, "Reticence: Pathology of the Normal Speaker," *Speech Monographs*, 35 (1968):39–49.

[7] K. Giffin and S. M. Gilham, "Relationships Between Speech Anxiety and Motivation," *Speech Monographs*, 38 (1971):70–73.

[8] M. Heider and K. Giffin, *The Influence of Situation Variables on Reported Approach or Avoidance of Communication Interaction, Research Report R-37* (Lawrence: Communication Research Center, University of Kansas, 1971).

[9] Cf. D. H. Lamb, "Speech Anxiety: Toward a Theoretical Conceptualization and Preliminary Scale Development," *Speech Monographs*, 39 (1972):62–67.

ter at the University of Kansas has been focused on persons who exhibit tendencies toward general withdrawal from social interaction. For eight years we have offered such students a special program designed to improve their interpersonal communication behavior and reduce their speech anxiety.[10] Students are identified for invitation to participate in this program on the basis of high degree of speech anxiety.[11] The most marked difference in behavior of these students (in comparison with the average University of Kansas freshman or sophomore), however, is not a poor ability to communicate, but the tendency to avoid or withdraw from interaction situations. Our research efforts have identified what might be termed a speech anxiety syndrome for students exhibiting withdrawal tendencies. They have a significantly higher-than-average degree of speech anxiety. They have lower self-image and lower trust of others,[12] as well as higher motivation to avoid failure and lower motivation to achieve success.[13] They also indicate that they have experienced significantly greater suppression of their childhood communicative efforts by their parents[14] and a significantly greater-than-average degree of communication denial from persons held by them to be important.[15]

The introspective pattern of low self-image, low trust of others, high speech anxiety, high motivation to avoid failure, low motivation to achieve success, along with indications of parental suppression of communication and communication denial by important others, all point to the probability of a significantly high degree of social alienation—and this is what we have found.[16]

It is tempting to guess that the reported childhood communication suppression and/or experience of communication denial have produced this syndrome. This, of course, we have not experimentally verified; we have only established significant correlation coefficients. However, because it would be unethical to produce experimentally such an undesirable syndrome, we will continue to pursue this problem mainly through case studies and clinical reports. In the meantime, we suspect that the causal relationship does exist.

[10] For further details see K. Giffin, *A Program in Counseling for Speech Anxiety* (Lawrence: Communication Research Center, University of Kansas, 1967).

[11] See K. Giffin and G. Friedrich, *The Development of a Baseline for Studies of Speech Anxiety, Research Report 20* (Lawrence: Communication Research Center, University of Kansas, 1968).

[12] K. Giffin, M. Heider, B. Groginsky, and B. Drake, *A Study of the Relationships Among Four Variables: Speech Anxiety, Self-Concept, Social Alienation, and Trust of Others, Research Report 24* (Lawrence: Communication Research Center, University of Kansas, 1970).

[13] See K. Giffin and S. Masterson, "A Theoretical Model of the Relationships Between Motivation and Self-Confidence in Communication," in L. Thayer, ed., *Communication Spectrum* (Flint, Mich.: International Communication Association, 1968), pp. 311–316; see also K. Giffin and S. M. Gilham, *A Study of the Relationships Between Speech Anxiety and Two Types of Motivation: (1) Motivation to Achieve Success, and (2) Motivation to Avoid Failure, Research Report 24* (Lawrence: Communication Research Center, University of Kansas, 1969).

[14] See K. Giffin and M. Heider, "A Theory of the Relationship Between Adult Speech Anxiety and Suppression of Communication in Childhood," *Psychiatric Quarterly Supplement, 11* (1967), 311–322; see also M. Heider, "An Investigation of the Relationship Between Speech Anxiety in Adults and Their Indication of Parental Communication Suppression During Childhood," unpublished M. A. thesis, University of Kansas, 1968.

[15] See K. Giffin and B. Groginsky, *Research Report 20,* and K. Giffin and B. Groginsky, *Research Report 31* (Lawrence: Communication Research Center, University of Kansas, 1969).

[16] K. Giffin and B. Groginsky, *A Study of the Relationship Between Social Alienation and Speech Anxiety, Research Report 27* (Lawrence: Communication Research Center, University of Kansas, 1970).

Communication Behaviors Related to Social Alienation

It has been our experience that an understanding of the ways in which basic principles of interpersonal communication may be ignored or violated can lead to a better understanding of one's feelings of alienation. In addition, such insights can provide the basis for changes in one's communication behavior that may lead to the reduction of the feeling of alienation. Your own insights and your changes in use of interpersonal communication techniques may or may not change the behavior of those persons from whom you feel alienated, but such additional insight can at least help you to understand yourself and others better.

The first principle of interpersonal communication that appears to be related to social alienation is this: We communicate on two levels. The first level is that of message sending; the second level is that of providing information about the message. When the message itself is in conflict with, or contradictory to, the communication about the message, a natural response is confusion and at least a partial attempt at withdrawal from further interaction. If parents say, "We really do love you, John," *but say it in a way that shows distrust, suspicion, anger, or hostility,* social alienation is a reasonable result (from John's point of view).

The second principle that appears to be related to alienation is that in an interpersonal situation one cannot refuse to communicate. A refusal to interact with another person is a communication in and of itself. When another person simply refuses to talk to you (perhaps for a reason thought to be excellent by that person), the message given to you is conclusive: He/she does not wish to talk with you. Such a conclusion provides an excellent reason for withdrawal from later interaction unless it is absolutely necessary.

The third related principle is that nonverbal communication ultimately establishes the nature of an interpersonal relationship. Many times we actually receive verbal messages from another person telling us how he/she perceives our interpersonal relationship with him/her: "I like to be with you," or "I enjoy talking with you." Sometimes we believe what we hear; however, *if the other person's nonverbal behavior is in conflict with such a verbal message, we usually recall the old adage that "actions speak louder than words."* In the final analysis, a person's perception of his/her relationship with another is determined by the latter's nonverbal communication. In many interviews we have been told by students that "my parents said they loved me, but they didn't act like it." Such behavior appears to us to be reasonable justification for diminishing interaction.

The fourth related principle is that the degree to which two persons similarly perceive their relationship will heavily influence the interpretation of communication between the two. Different perceptions of their relationship by two persons can lead to serious and even violent disagreement between them regarding what one has really "said" to the other. There is a case study of a husband and wife who frequently participated in violent quarrels. One day the husband received a phone call from a friend who was in town for a few days. The husband immediately invited the friend to stay at their home. When he told his wife, a bitter quarrel arose over the desirable and undesirable characteristics of this friend. Finally the wife agreed that an invitation to the friend was the appropriate and natural thing, but she concluded with this comment: "Well, you may be right, but you are wrong because you are arguing with me." In actual fact the real conflict was over the husband's right to take such initiative without consulting his wife; this concerned their perceptions of the nature of their interpersonal relationship. In their quarrel this couple committed a common mistake in their communication. They *argued* about the characteristics of a third person while actually *disagreeing* about their treatment of each other, failing completely to resolve the confusion between their two perceptions of their interpersonal relationship.[17]

At this point we can briefly summarize the potential impact of the four principles of interpersonal communication given: In an interpersonal situation, nonverbal communication usually establishes the nature of an interpersonal relationship, which in turn heavily influences interpretations of communication by both persons in the relationship.

Alienation by Communication Denial

The initiation of any communication act carries with it an implied request: "Please validate me." This plea can be in the form of a request for recognition of one's ideas as worthwhile. Even in such a case, however, there is an ob-

[17] Watzlawick, Beavin, and Jackson, *Pragmatics of Human Communication*, pp. 80–81.

vious implication regarding the value of oneself personally.

There are three ways in which a person can respond to the implied request for validation of another person: (1) agreement—a person or his/her idea is responded to as somewhat worthwhile or valid; (2) disagreement—the person or his/her idea is responded to as more or less invalid; and (3) denial of the existence of the question. This denial (that is, an attempt to refuse to give any response at all) not only denies the existence of the request "Please validate me," but by implication denies the existence of the other person on a functional, interpersonal, or communicational level.

Little Johnny, age five, comes home from kindergarten and says, "I have a girl friend." His mother says, "Eat your soup, Johnny." This constitutes a denial of Johnny's capability of discussing girl friends (at that time)— perhaps an event of no great consequence. Ten years later John says, "Dad, Joe Smith is taking his folks' car to the school picnic Saturday." Dad says, "Finish your homework, John." This is an example of a denial of John's right to talk about using the family car—that is, a denial of John's existence on this communicational level. Two such instances in ten years are inconsequential; two instances per day for ten years is another matter. Also, denial of communication on one isolated topic may not pose a severe threat to an individual's self-validation. Remember, however, that the question of his validity is implied with every statement John ever makes, and that in any interpersonal situation the other person cannot refuse to respond to it: A refusal becomes at least a temporary or partial denial of John's self-identity.

The impact of such denial depends upon the value a person places on the other person or persons, perhaps upon the value he places upon his relationship with them. Consistent and continued denial of a child by his parents can cause severe damage. Ronald Laing has given the following description of what happens when a child is denied in this manner:

> The characteristic family pattern that has emerged from the study of families of schizophrenics does not much involve a child who is subjected to outright neglect or even to obvious trauma, but a child whose authenticity has been subjected to subtle, but persistent, mutilation, often quite unwittingly.[18]

In another paragraph Laing poignantly describes the effect on the child:

> The ultimate of this is ... no matter how a person feels or how he acts, no matter what meaning he gives his situations, his feelings are denuded of validity, his acts are stripped of their motives, intentions and consequences; the situation is robbed of its meaning for him so that he is totally mystified and alienated.[19]

In commenting on our society, Martin Buber wrote as follows:

> At all its levels, persons confirm one another in a practical way, to some extent or other, in their personal qualities and capacities, and the society may be termed human in the measure to which its members confirm one another. . . . The basis of man's life with man is two-fold and it is one; the wish of every man to be confirmed as what he is even as what he can become, by men, and the innate capacity of man to confirm his fellow men in this way; that this capacity lies so immeasurably fallow

constitutes the real weakness and questionableness of the human race; actual humanity exists only where this capacity unfolds.[20]

We should note that the implied request, "Validate me," may be put by an individual, a group, a subculture, or even a nation; the responses—agreement, disagreement, or denial of existence—may be made by another individual, a group, a subculture, or a nation. Perhaps not in the last year, but certainly in previous years, most of us have seen an adult black person attempt to ask a sincere, intelligent question about how to perform a part of his job, only to be given a response of this order: "Bring me that board over there!" Looking backward, it seems to the present writers that much of the observed communication of white people with black people has carried a denial of the latter's capability to interact with others as fully worthwhile human beings.

There are two major ways in which an individual can respond to the denial described: (1) He can refuse to accept it as a denial, or (2) he can accept the idea that he does not exist on that communication level. Communication behaviors exhibiting a refusal to accept such a denial include (1) repetition of the request, (2) escalation of the tone or manner of the request, and (3) overt verbal communication about the denial.

Repetition of the request simply involves continuation of any verbal communication with its attendant implied request, "Please validate me." Escalation can involve changes in vocal tone or intensity, threatening posture, vio-

[18] Laing, *The Self and Others*, p. 91.
[19] Ibid., pp. 135–136.

[20] M. Buber, "Distance and Relation," *Psychiatry*, 20 (1957):97–104.

lent gestures, or, on a larger scale, demonstrations, riots, etc. Overt communication about the denial would likely be something like this: "Dad, why don't you talk with me about my using the family car on the picnic?" It should be noted that such overt communication is rarely initiated by the person in the weaker, "one-down" position who feels threatened, and, of course, such denial of one's existence (on any level) by a valued other will produce a feeling of threat.[21]

Acceptance of the implication of denial of oneself is more common than many people believe; many persons accept the idea that they are unworthy of talking to "better" people, people with more influence, more education, more experience, or just more self-assurance. This phenomenon is not uncommon; the acceptance of this implication is frequently a constituent of the process of social alienation.[22]

The "Double Bind"

A particularly interesting problem arises when communication denial occurs and at the same time the denied person cannot withdraw from a situation because of the value he/she places on a potential relationship with that specific other person. In an analysis of the communication environment of schizophrenia, Bateson and his associates[23] coined the term "double bind" to identify a communication situation in which these elements occur:

1. For certain important reasons a person cannot withdraw from the scene; for example, for his own moral reasons he must continue to try to talk things over with his parents, or for his own religious reasons he must continue to try to talk with his wife.

2. Messages are sent by the other person on the verbal and nonverbal levels that are internally contradictory; that is, the subject is validated by a verbal message and invalidated by nonverbal behavior—those cues as to how he is to interpret the verbal message.

3. His attempts at overt communication about the contradiction are denied; that is, he is not allowed to initiate discussion about the internal contradiction posed between the verbal message that validates him and the nonverbal communication that invalidates him.

An attempt to justify the denial of opportunity to communicate about this contradiction—that is, denial of opportunity to engage in overt communication about it—is frequently based on rather unreasonable grounds. Moral ground-rules may be invoked: "It is not right (moral) for you to question your mother this way." Such morality is seldom expressed in overt verbal communication; rather, the horrified stare or the hurt expression usually carry the message of infraction of moral boundaries. In other cases an ethic is invoked; for example, in business circles it is sometimes claimed to be unethical to "deal in personalities." Thus, a request for overt communication about the contradiction may be construed as an attack on the other person's status or position of authority.

[21] Watzlawick, Beavin, and Jackson, *Pragmatics of Human Communication*, pp. 86–90.
[22] Laing, *The Self and Others*, pp. 135–136.
[23] G. Bateson et al., "Toward a Theory of Schizophrenia," *Behavioral Science*, 1 (1956):251–264.

Once again, refusal of overt communication about the contradiction will likely be indicated by a cold stare or nervous fidget rather than by forthright verbal communication. If for his own reasons a person cannot "leave the field" and is also denied the opportunity to initiate overt communication with the other person, he is confronted with an undecidable problem. If he additionally feels it is morally wrong to question the source of this contradiction—for example, if he actually believes it is immoral to question his mother about her confusing messages—he truly is in a double bind. If he acts upon the apparent implication of the verbal message ("You are a worthwhile person," or "You have a good idea"), he will run the risk of antagonizing his mother. On the other hand, if he accepts the apparent implication of his mother's vocal tone and general manner, he will infer that she thinks his idea is worthless, and thus, again, he will run the risk of antagonizing her by acting as if his mother did not "properly" care about her son. The point is, he is in trouble; he is "damned if he does and damned if he doesn't."

There is no way out of this dilemma; the doorways out—leaving the field or initiating overt communication—have been closed. In such a case the individual usually does one of three things: (1) He scans the interpersonal horizon—that is, his mother's behavior—for some message or clue that he must have missed or overlooked; (2) he ignores all or most of her communication from her; that is, he interprets all or most of her communication as confusing and of slight value or meaning; (3) he may overreact, jumping inside his skin when his mother says, "How's my

boy tonight?" Such is the way in which the double bind can produce an unhappy relationship between two more or less well-meaning people who, according to the notions of many of us, should mean a great deal to each other.

It is of the highest importance to note that the double bind is not one of life's ordinarily difficult situations in which one must choose between two mutually exclusive but equally desirable alternatives—for example, choosing between getting married or staying single—where both alternatives hold attraction, but once one is chosen, the other cannot then be enjoyed. The double bind is not the same dilemma; it is not a case of simply finding out that you cannot have your cake and eat it too. Rather, in the case of the double bind, *both choices are poor.* The double bind *bankrupts choice itself;* neither alternative is tenable and the dilemma is complete—the situation is a true paradox.

Matina Horner made an insightful examination of such a condition:

A bright woman is caught in a double bind. In achievement-oriented situations she worries not only about failure but also about success. If she fails, she does not live up to her own standards of performance; if she succeeds she is not living up to societal expectations about the female role. College women students who feared success aspired to traditional female careers: housewife, mother, nurse, schoolteacher. Girls who did not fear success aspired to graduate degrees and careers in such scientific areas as math, physics, and chemistry.[24]

Where double binding is of long-lasting duration, it will produce habitual suspicion regarding the general

[24] M. Horner, "A Bright Woman Is Caught in a Double Bind," *Psychology Today* (1969):36–38, 62.

nature of human relationships. This suspicion leads to a self-perpetuating pattern of mistrust of communication. It can lead to alienation, not only toward others, but eventually toward oneself.[25]

There may be times when we cannot or should not respond to the overtures of another person. At times we may be tired, mentally exhausted, or have nothing to say that has not already been said over and over. At other times, for our own survival or peace of mind we may deem it necessary to ignore the presence of another person. Even so, the point to be noted here is that in such a case we should be aware of what is happening: If we are with other persons, and they believe we are aware of their presence, to ignore them is to deny their implicit requests for validation as persons. Even more, to remain silent in response to an *overt request* to talk with us is prima facie evidence that, for us, they do not, at this time, functionally exist.

Interpersonal Communication with Alienated Persons

There are few things more difficult than to try to overcome the effects of misuse of interpersonal communication principles outlined above; interaction with persons who have been alienated from their social enviornment is never easy. Of course, the primary requirement is that someone must want to make the effort. It is also helpful to provide the alienated person with insight into the process that has contributed to the alienation; sometimes this insight plus that person's own attempts to reach out and establish new contacts with people around him/her tend to reduce the problem. Most certainly, covert denial of communication must be avoided if interaction with alienated persons is to be achieved.[26]

It has been our observation that people who alienate people and then are surprised at their alienation do not seem to understand the basic principles of interpersonal communication. One can raise the following questions: When people alienate other people in the ways described above, are they really surprised by the results? Or are they perhaps subconsciously aware of what they are doing?

It should be emphasized that the purpose of the present analysis has not been to untangle the problems of all teenagers, much less the snarls of the generation gap. Our purpose here has been simply to shed light on the way in which some persons are alienated from those who seem to be surprised when it happens. It is our belief that new insight into such a problem shows ways in which the problem can be reduced. Our suggestions regarding ways in which basic principles of interpersonal communication have been ignored or violated identify possible changes in communication behavior that can sometimes provide more desirable results—warmer and more satisfying interpersonal relationships.

---

[25] D. Jackson, "Psychoanalytic Education in the Communication Processes," *Science and Psychoanalysis*, 5 (1962):129–145.

[26] K. Giffin and K. Bradley, "An Exploratory Study of Group Counseling for Speech Anxiety," *Journal of Clinical Psychology*, 25 (1969):98–101.

Reading 8.2
Types and Sources of Conflict

Alan C. Filley

As humans we live our lives within a web of social relationships, most of which seem almost mechanical in their predictability and smoothness of function. We seek, establish, and maintain predictable patterns in our lives to avoid the anxiety of the unpredictable; such patterns, once established, require little conscious choice as they operate. We have predictable patterns for interacting with our family, for going to work in the morning, for performing in a job, for shopping at the market, and for socializing with others. Yet, because we are not solely mechanical, because we are social creatures in a social system, these patterns are not absolutely predictable.

We must also reckon with the elements of chance. While we can predict the movement of the solar system with relative certainty, we can only speak of the likelihood or probability of driving to work or of greeting the guard at the entrance. An accident or illness may have occurred to alter our usual routines. Finally, as human animals, we introduce a third element into our social systems, that of freedom (Boulding, 1964). We are capable of planning, of holding in our minds some picture of the future, and of altering our usual patterns of behavior.

Within our various social relationships are some which involve real or perceived differences between two or more parties. Where the interests of the parties are mutually exclusive— that is, where the gain of one party's goal is at the cost of the other's, or where the parties have different values—then the resulting social interaction between the parties contains fertile ground for conflict.

It is our freedom which allows us to learn about our own social systems. We are able (1) to discover those elements of our systems which increase the likelihood of conflict, (2) to develop contingency plans when chance occurrences create disruptions, and (3) to produce and to improve systems for resolving conflict which maximize the benefits and minimize the costs to the parties involved. In this first chapter we shall be concerned with those characteristics of a system which increase the likelihood of conflict and with the system of conflict production. Such discussion permits us to organize in ways which minimize conflict, if that is the desired goal. Furthermore, by knowing the natural system of conflict production, we may adjust actions or conditions before conflicts take place, rather than wait for conflicts to develop before taking action. . . .

Either because it may not be useful to avoid conflicts or because conflict develops as an unanticipated outcome, the resolution of conflict becomes necessary. We shall examine the various systems of resolution and suggest how they may be applied.

Kinds of Conflict

Not all conflicts are of the same kind. Some, for example, follow definite rules and are not typically associated with angry feelings on the part of the parties, while others involve irrational behavior and the use of violent or disruptive acts by the parties. As a first step, therefore, we shall distinguish between conflicts which are *competitive* and those which are *disruptive*. In competitive situations there can be a victory for one party only at the cost of the opponent's total loss and the way in which the parties relate to each other is governed by a set of rules. The parties strive for goals which are mutually incompatible. The emphasis of each party is upon the event of

winning, rather than upon the defeat or reduction of the opponent. The actions of each party are selected using criteria based on the probability of leading to successful outcomes, and the competition terminates when the result is obvious to both sides (Rapoport, 1960).

In the disruptive conflict, on the other hand, the parties do not follow a mutually acceptable set of rules and are not primarily concerned with winning. Instead, they are intent upon reducing, defeating, harming, or driving away the opponent. The means used are expedient, and the atmosphere is one of stress, anger, or fear. In extreme cases, the parties in disruptive conflict will abandon rational behavior and behave in any manner necessary to bring about the desired outcome, the goal of defeat.

Experience tells us that conflicts are usually distributed along a continuum between those that are competitive and those that are disruptive. Anger arises in a game and causes disruption. A competitor changes his behavior from a rational pursuit of a strategy of winning to an irrational act of aggression. Thus, the motives of the parties and the degree of strategic control which each exhibits are important factors in determining the degree to which a conflict is competitive or disruptive.

For a further elaboration of the kinds of conflict, we may describe the interaction between the parties according to (1) their mutuality of interests and (2) their perception of resource availability. As seen in Table 1, when parties seek real or perceived scarce resources (for example, victory or a share of a fixed sum) and when they have a mutuality of interests, the relationship is one of competition. When

Table 1 Elements of Conflict

	Like Interests	Unlike Interests
Seek Scarce Resources	Competition/games	Fights/disruption
Seek Abundant Resources	Problem solving	Disagreement/debate

they seek real or perceived scarce resources and have unlike interests, their relationship is likely to be characterized by fighting and disruption. When the parties seek abundant resources but have dissimilar interests, their interaction will contain disagreement. Finally, when the parties seek abundant resources and have similar interests, they will most probably resort to problem solving.

Competition, disruption, and disagreement all imply a win-lose outcome (or at least some degree of winning or losing by each of the parties). Problem solving, on the other hand, implies the development of an outcome which provides acceptable gain to both parties. Thus, if the focus of competition changes from a win-lose game to a situation involving enhancement of skill or knowledge by the parties, it becomes problem solving since the parties are now, in effect, asking each other, "How can we interact in a manner which increases the benefit to both of us?" Likewise, if opposing parties in a fight realize the mutuality of their interests and the existence of abundant resources or if debaters change their emphasis from argument to the achievement of a correct solution, then their interactions will also shift to a problem-solving mode.

The point in this classification scheme is that conflict has been defined in terms of incompatible goals and different values, but that such differences are frequently *perceived rather than real*. If opposing parties can change their perceptions of resources from scarce to abundant and can recognize the mutuality of their interests, it is often possible to change from a form of conflict to a form of problem solving.

We may summarize the characteristics of a conflict situation as follows:

1. At least two parties (individuals or groups) are involved in some kind of interaction.
2. Mutually exclusive goals and/or mutually exclusive values exist, in fact or as perceived by the parties involved.
3. Interaction is characterized by behavior designed to defeat, reduce, or suppress the opponent or to gain a mutually designated victory.
4. The parties face each other with mutually opposing actions and counteractions.
5. Each party attempts to create an imbalance or relatively favored position of power vis-à-vis the other.

The Values of Conflict

Conflict, a social process which takes various forms and which has certain outcomes, itself is neither good nor bad. The conflict process merely leads to certain results, and the value of those results as favorable or unfavorable depends upon the measures used, the party making the judgment, and other subjective criteria. Let us consider some of the possible positive values of conflict.

THE DIFFUSION OF MORE
SERIOUS CONFLICT

Competitive situations such as games provide conflict processes and outcomes which are governed by rules. These types of conflicts seem to provide entertainment value and tension release to the parties. Winning and losing are identified as events and may have little effect on the self-perception of any player. That is, to lose in a competitive event does not suggest that an individual is less important, has less status, or is less valued as a person. In addition, in competitive situations aggressive behavior can be channeled along socially acceptable lines.

Viewed another way, conflict processes which are institutionalized (that is, for which acceptable resolution procedures have been established) function as preventive measures against more destructive outcomes. Grievance systems, for example, permit the step-by-step adjudication of differences to avoid major clashes between parties such as labor and management. Similarly, systems which provide for participation by the members of an organization in decision making, while they are positively associated with the number of disputes between parties, are negatively associated with the number of major incidents between them (Corwin, 1969). Thus, it might be accurate to say that intimacy between parties tends to result in disagreements which, in turn, reduce the likelihood of major fights and disruption.

THE STIMULATION OF
A SEARCH FOR NEW
FACTS OR SOLUTIONS

As pointed out earlier, at least some aspects of our social systems are automatic and predictable. Where social systems are functioning mechanically, however, there is little likelihood of creativity or change. On the other hand, when parties are involved in a disagreement the process may lead to a clarification of facts, thus facilitating the resolution of conflict. For example, if a wife tells her husband, "You are not doing your share of the housework," and the husband replies, "Yes, I am," then little may be resolved. However, if the husband replies, "What statements or behavior of mine have led to your conclusion that I am not assuming enough responsibility at home?" then the interaction is changed from a conflict to a problem-solving situation based on clarification of facts.

In another way, conflict can stimulate the search for new methods or solutions. When parties are in conflict about which of two alternatives to accept, their disagreement may stimulate a search for another solution mutually acceptable to both. In like manner, when both parties view themselves as seeking to gain an adequate share of scarce resources, they may actually find that their needs or goals can be met simultaneously with the development of creative solutions which neither had previously considered.

As these situations suggest, conflict can create tension which is reduced through problem solving. The tension acts as a stimulus to find new methods for its own reduction. This is the difference between *confrontation* and the way in which confrontation is resolved. The confrontations between labor and management, between students and college administrators, or between blacks and whites act as stimuli for change, stimuli which may lead to disruption or overt hostility or which may lead to new relationships between the parties and creative solutions to problems.

AN INCREASE IN GROUP COHESION AND PERFORMANCE

Conflictive situations between two or more groups are likely to increase both the cohesiveness and the performance of the groups, although we must be careful to distinguish between effects during the conflict and those after the winner and loser have been identified. During the conflict members of each group close ranks and are united in their efforts. Members' evaluations of their own group improve (Blake and Mouton, 1961c); and each group judges its own solution as best. The positions of opponents are evaluated negatively, and there is little effort to understand them. Questions asked opponents are designed to embarrass or to weaken them rather than to generate facts and understanding. Perceptions of the group's own position are distorted, as is recognition of areas of common agreement with the opposing group. Even when the adversary's position is thought to be well understood by members of one group, research has shown that a real understanding is blocked by identification with the position of one's own group. In these circumstances intergroup resolution of conflict increases in difficulty since groups are most likely unaware of the distortions in factual knowledge that exist between them (Blake and Mouton, 1961a).

During the competitive period, levels of work and cooperation within each group are high. When competing groups select representatives to deal with other groups, they choose task leaders (hard-driving individuals who keep their own group on course) rather than individuals skilled in social facilitation. During conflict such leaders exhibit high loyalty to their group and tend to conform to group expectations rather than to focus upon the assigned problem (Blake and Mouton, 1961b).

Such conditions appear to be desirable, for the most part, and probably account for the popular belief that competition is valuable as a stimulus to work groups. But what actually happens when one group is declared the victor and the other the vanquished? For one thing, the leader of the winning group increases in status, while the leader of the losing group decreases in status. The leader in the losing group is blamed for the loss. The atmosphere in the groups also changes. The rate of tension, problem avoidance, fighting, and competitive feelings will increase in the losing group and decrease in the winning group. If the loss can be blamed on conditions beyond the control of the group, the result may be increased cohesion in the losing group (Lott and Lott, 1965). If the group does assume responsibility for the loss, it often analyzes the situation and prepares itself to fight better the next time. In contrast, the winning group merely says, "We did a good job. Let's knock off" (Blake and Mouton, 1961c, p. 432). Thus, heightened cooperation and effort by group members during the conflict may actually decrease once the conflict is resolved.

THE MEASURE OF POWER OR ABILITY

Conflict provides a readily available method of measurement. If the ground rules for victory or defeat are identifiable to both parties, then the winner of a game or sports event can be easily determined. Such literal interpretation has cognitive value. In addition, while not precisely measurable, the relative power between parties may be identified through conflictive situations. Coercion, control, and suppression require clear superiority of power of one party over another, whereas problem solving requires an equalization of power among the parties. Thus, a party wishing to avoid overt suppression of the opponent must take action to provide a favorable power balance; suppression of the opponent can be avoided by employing problem-solving methods which insure a balance of power.

From the preceding discussion it should be clear that conflict is a process which itself is neither good nor bad, but which has elements and outcomes which may be judged favorably or unfavorably by those participating in or evaluating it. We shall now turn to the conflict process itself.

The Conflict Process

Conflict is defined in this book as a process which takes place between two or more parties.[1] By *parties* we may be referring to individuals, groups, or organizations. The six steps in the process are depicted in Figure 1.

1. Antecedent conditions are the characteristics of a situation which generally lead to conflict, although they may be present in the absence of conflict as well.

[1] This section draws from the work of Pondy (1967, 1969); Corwin (1969); Walton and Dutton (1969); Fink (1968); and Schmidt (1973).

2. Perceived conflict is a logically and impersonally recognized set of conditions which are conflictive to the parties.
3. Felt conflict is a personalized conflict relationship, expressed in feelings of threat, hostility, fear, or mistrust.
4. Manifest behavior is the resulting action—aggression, competition, debate, or problem solving.
5. Conflict resolution or suppression has to do with bringing the conflict to an end either through agreement among all parties or the defeat of one.
6. Resolution aftermath comprises the consequences of the conflict.

We shall now consider each part of the conflict process in more detail. An understanding of the factors that lead to conflict is necessary if its occurrence is to be minimized.

The Antecedent Conditions of Conflict

Listed below are nine characteristics of social relationships that are associated with various kinds or degrees of conflictive behavior.

1. Ambiguous Jurisdictions. Conflict will be greater when the limits of each party's jurisdiction are ambiguous. When two parties have related responsibilities for which actual boundaries are unclear, the potential for conflict between them increases. Conversely, when role definitions are clear, each party can expect a certain type of behavior from the other, and fewer opportunities for disagreement occur. For example, the argument of a married couple about who should

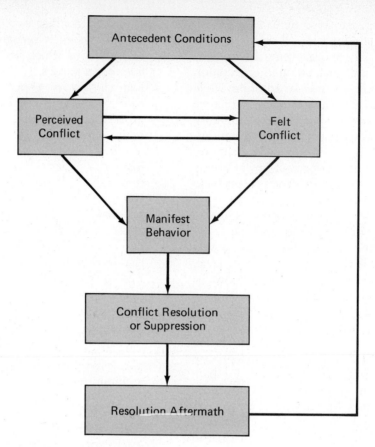

FIGURE 1. The conflict process.

make decisions relating to household chores or the selection of evening entertainment was resolved by an agreement that on alternate days one of them would make all decisions and would be responsible for the success or failure of the decisions. On a more complex level, large organizations will define boundaries of individual responsibility through such tools as organization charts and job descriptions.

2. Conflict of Interest. Conflict will be greater where a conflict of interest exists between the parties. One such situation is a competition for scarce resources. For example, one summer a married couple found themselves arguing about the use of the only air-conditioned room in their apartment, which also contained the television set. The woman was attending graduate school and the man was working; in the evening he wanted to watch baseball games on television and she wanted to use the room for study, complaining that the noise of the television prevented her from concentrating. Another situation involves a case where the gain of one group is at the expense of another group. For example, Walton, Dutton, and Cafferty (1969) describe such an incident in which a maintenance department is evaluated on the basis of equipment perform-ance. However, the equipment per-formance in a department served by maintenance is not part of the main-tenance evaluation. The second de-partment makes demands upon main-tenance to increase its own performance record but in so doing reduces the rating of the maintenance department by interfering with the repair of other equipment.

3. Communication Barriers. Con-flict will be greater when barriers to communication exist. It appears that if parties are separated from each other physically or by time—for ex-ample, day shift versus night shift—the opportunity for conflict is in-creased. One explanation for this is the increased possibility of misunder-standing between the parties. Yet, as will be discussed shortly, the degree of knowledge which one party has about another is shown to be associated with conflict (Walton, Dutton, and Cafferty, 1969). It seems more likely that space or time separations create natural groupings which promote separate group interests rather than advance a common effort toward joint goals.

4. Dependence of One Party. Conflict will be greater where one party is dependent upon another. Where parties are dependent, they must rely on each other for perform-ance of tasks or for the provision of resources. Thus, the opportunity for conflict to occur is increased. For ex-ample, a supervisor who depends upon the preparation of a cost effectiveness report by a subordinate in order to make a marketing decision may mon-itor the subordinate's progress. Closer supervision in itself contributes to the

potential for conflict between the par-ties, as does their dependence upon each other.

5. Differentiation in Organiza-tion. Conflict will be greater as the degree of differentiation in an orga-nization increases. Where people work together in complex organizations, there is evidence (Corwin, 1969) that measures of conflict are related to the number of organizational levels, the number of distinct job specialties rep-resented, and the degree to which labor is divided in the organization. The reasons may well relate to condi-tions already discussed. For example, the number of levels of authority may create difficulties of communication, conflicts of interest, difficult depend-ency situations, or jurisdictional dis-putes. In any case, the greater the degree of differentiation, the greater the potential for conflict.

6. Association of the Parties. Conflict will be greater as the degree of association of the parties increases. *Degree of association,* as used here, refers both to the parties' partic-ipation in decision making and to in-formal relations between them. Where parties make decisions jointly, the op-portunity for conflict is greater, which may explain the reluctance of some managers to involve others in decision making. However, since groups often make superior decisions, the failure to utilize the potential of groups in de-cision making may be costly in terms of inferior judgments as well as in terms of employee dissatisfaction. An alternative logic would suggest that where participative decision making is used, the parties will need skills in conflict resolution. General conflict measures are positively associated with the degree of participation, although major incidents of conflict decrease as participation increases (Corwin, 1969).

The above holds true for informal associations as well. Interaction and the degree of knowledge which parties have about each other are also related to rates of conflict.

7. Need for Consensus. Conflict will be greater where consensus between the parties is necessary. When all parties must agree on a decision, at least to the point that no individual feels the decision is unacceptable, it is not surprising that disagreements will occur. Thus, it is possible to avoid conflict by having mechanisms such as voting, coin flipping, or adjudication to make decisions without the confrontation of consensus. As we shall see later, however, such mechanisms themselves are not without undesirable consequences.

8. Behavior Regulations. Conflicts will be greater where behavior regulations are imposed. Regulating mechanisms include standardized procedures, rules, and policies. Regulating mechanisms seem to do two things at the same time. On the one hand, they reduce the likelihood of conflict since they serve to make relationships predictable and reduce the need to make arbitrary decisions. On the other hand, they increase the degree of control over parties, and this control may be resisted. If the adherence to or the imposition of rules becomes discretionary, further sources of disagreement are created. Furthermore, if the parties have high individual needs for autonomy and self-control, it is likely that the presence of regulating procedures will lead to conflict.

9. Unresolved Prior Conflicts. Conflicts will be greater as the number of unresolved prior conflicts increases. As will be discussed later, the type of conflict resolution utilized will affect the resolution aftermath. Thus, prior experiences of the parties will themselves create antecedent conditions. Suppression of conflict by the use of power, or compromises to which the parties are uncommitted, create conditions and expectations which may lead to behavior conducive to further conflict.

The antecedent conditions need not lead directly to conflict, but they are certainly conditions which create opportunities for conflict to arise. Further development of overt conflict depends upon the perception of conditions which exist and the attitudinal characteristics of the parties.

Perceived Conflict

Perceptions of the conditions which exist between the parties may enhance the likelihood of conflict or may reduce it. The failure to identify potentially conflictive conditions may prevent conflicts from developing. In many cases, however, it is the inaccurate or illogical perception of the situation which leads to overt conflict between the parties. Perceptual processes contribute to conflict in two ways. First, they provide an accurate or inaccurate assessment of the conditions which exist. This occurs when, for example, clear jurisdictions are perceived as ambiguous or when similar interests are perceived as conflicting. Second, they affect the extent to which the parties see the situation as one threatening a potential loss. The latter occurs when each party fails to recognize the availability of solutions which will satisfy the needs or requirements of both parties.

In the case of the couple in conflict about the use of the air-conditioned room containing the television set, the perceptions of one air-conditioned room and one television set were accurate. In fact, overt conflict resulted from this perception of the situation, and the conditions of dissimilar interests and scarce resources led to fighting behavior, as would be expected. Yet the perception of the problem could be and, in fact, was changed to suggest that the common interest was to find a way so that the wife could study in a quiet air-conditioned room and the husband could hear and watch the ball game in the air-conditioned room. Solutions to the conflict could be interpreted as unlimited when one considers not just the actual materials involved but the available combinations of these materials. In this particular case, the changed perceptions led to overt problem-solving behavior rather than conflict. The husband watched the game on television with the sound off and listened to the game through earphones. The wife then studied with her back to the television set.

Conflicts may also be perceived when antecedent conditions do not exist (Pondy, 1967). Such situations occur when the parties do not understand each other's actual positions or when either of the positions taken is based upon a limited knowledge of the facts. Both cases lend themselves to resolution by discussion between the parties

to clarify the facts. In such situations, the difficulty lies not so much in the perceptual process and its clarification as it does in the attitudinal issues which arise when the parties become angry, mistrustful, or defensive. If these negative attitudes can be controlled, the eventual resolution is facilitated by discussion and clarification.

For example, if two arts administrators are planning a summer concert for a community and both agree that the objective is maximum entertainment value for the greatest number of people in the community, then the selection between two alternatives can be made easily by obtaining facts about the appeal of each to various client groups and by choosing the alternatives with the most appeal. Or, when two fishermen state potentially conflictive preferences for fishing deep or fishing shallow, the logical process is one of asking why each prefers his strategy and of determining more facts, in hope of finding a goal compatible to both fishermen and to their mutual goal of catching fish.

Finally, initial perceptions of conflict may result in conflict-avoiding processes. Two important methods which lead to this outcome are the suppression mechanism and the attention-focus mechanism (Pondy, 1967). The former occurs when individuals ignore conflictive situations that involve low potential loss or are viewed as minimally threatening (Blake, Mouton, and Shepard, 1964). The attention-focus mechanism occurs because parties can selectively perceive conflictive conditions and make choices about those to which they wish to attend.

It is likely that individuals attend more readily to those conflictive conditions which are perceived to have readily accessible processes for resolution or for which readily accessible outcomes are available.' There also seems to be a preference for attending to those conflictive situations involving relatively fewer negative attitudes. Thus, the parties in a labor-management disagreement may focus on issues which lend themselves to established grievance systems or arbitration procedures and effectively ignore fundamental differences which cannot be handled routinely in the usual way. They may also be reluctant to deal with issues provoking anger and hostility and instead restrict attention to matters which do not create such feelings.

From the above discussion it may be seen that perceptual processes can act to create conflict or to avoid existing conflictive situations. The third important ingredient in the development of overt conflict or problem-solving behavior consists of the feelings or attitudes of the parties.

Felt Conflict

Feelings and attitudes, like perceptions, may create conflict where rational elements would not suggest that it must arise; feelings and attitudes also play a part in avoiding conflict where it might be expected to occur. The most important consideration in determining the outcome of the conflict is whether the situation is personalized or depersonalized. Personalized situations are those in which the whole being of the other party is threatened or judged negatively. Depersonalized situations are those in which the behavior of the other party, or the characteristics of the relationship, are *de-scribed* as creating a problem, rather than judged as being responsible.

To illustrate, feelings or expressions of feelings which say "You are bad" are personalized; feelings or their expression which say "What you believe is different from what I believe" are depersonalized. Similarly, the statement "You threaten me" is personal, while "Your behavior leads to fear on my part" is depersonalized. Personalized situations create tension and anxiety; depersonalized situations lend themselves to problem solving. We shall see later how much the language that parties use with each other can affect the personalized or depersonalized nature of the situation.

Feelings and attitudes which set the stage for overt behavior also arise out of characteristics of the individual personality. There is not as much likelihood of overt conflict when parties who are yielding or anxious to please are dealing with parties who are dominant or self-seeking, as there is when the parties are both of the dominant type. A married couple in which one partner is dominant and the other is submissive will experience less overt conflict than one in which both are dominant or both are submissive.

The feelings and attitudes about the mutuality of the relationship will further affect eventual behavior. Where the parties value cooperation and believe that success in their relationship involves the attainment of the needs of both, the situation is less conflictive than when the parties value competition and believe that one can win only at the other's expense. Such attitudes not only affect their perceptions of the situation but also determine the way in which they will judge the availability of solutions. Again, mutuality of interests and scarcity of resources relate in part to the initial feelings and attitudes of the parties.

Finally, trust between the parties can strongly affect the outcome of a potentially conflictive situation. Trusting attitudes elicit recognition of the mutual vulnerability of the parties, which occurs in part through the sharing of information between them. Vulnerability is also exhibited through the sharing of control by the parties. In the absence of such trust, a party is more likely to withhold information in order to avoid the danger of having the other party use the information against him. If a party does give information, however, he is likely to distort it in order to maintain his own advantage. Similarly, each nontrusting party will try to maximize his control over the other and to minimize the control of the other over himself. Thus, the presence of trust may prevent potentially conflictive situations from arising, while its absence may create conflict where actual conditions do not seem to warrant it.

No attempt is made here to determine the origins of the attitudes and feelings held by the parties. Undoubtedly some are cultural, while others have their origin in developmental experiences, perceptual processes, or personal experiences. Whatever the source, these feelings become important determinants of the development and resolution of overt conflict between the parties.

Manifest Behavior

The actual overt behavior of the parties, based upon antecedent conditions, perceptions, and attitudes, may be exhibited as conflictive or problem solving. Where there is a conscious (though not necessarily deliberate) attempt by one party to block the goal achievement of another party, the behavior may be considered to be conflictive (Pondy, 1967). Thus, when one party accidentally blocks the goal attainment of another, it is a chance occurrence in a social system. But when one party knowingly interferes with another, conflict is said to occur.

On the other hand, when the parties make conscious attempts to achieve the goals of both by supportive efforts, the behavior is that of problem solving. As with conflict behavior, the accidental achievement of both sets of goals is a chance occurrence; the deliberate effort to achieve them is overt problem-solving behavior. Parenthetically, it may be noted that the methodology of conflict is learned early in life and is well practiced. Competition, dominance, aggression, and defense are part of an established process unconsciously learned in the family, in the school, and in other social institutions. Problem solving, on the other hand, appears to be learned less frequently through developmental experiences. Conscious effort is generally required to develop and practice problem-solving skills.

Manifest conflict-resolution or problem-solving behavior may be described according to the degree to which it is programmed or unprogrammed. Programmed behavior follows specified or anticipated patterns in order to achieve outcomes readily identifiable by the parties. Its effectiveness is determined by the breadth of alternative behaviors available for utilization by the parties. For example, the skill of a chess player depends upon his ability to choose appropriately from among a wide variety of strategic moves. Similarly, the simulation of war through war games is designed to increase the variety of strategies and tactics available to the participants and to anticipate action-reaction sequences. Thus, programmed behavior is rational behavior.

Unprogrammed behavior in conflict resolution or in problem solving does not follow known patterns and is governed more by emotion. The appearance of anger, aggression, apathy, or rigidity in conflictive situations reduces each party's effectiveness in gaining a relative advantage and makes it difficult for both to terminate the interaction. For that reason, it is useful to program the conditions surrounding the relationship when it is not possible to program the actual action-reaction sequences. For example, where the boundaries between the parties cannot be made unambiguous, it is more useful to provide mechanisms for resolving boundary issues than it is to leave such resolution to chance. Such is the case when two departments with overlapping responsibilities establish a coordinating committee to deal with unanticipated issues that could potentially lead to conflict between them.

In like manner, problem solving may be handled on an unprogrammed emotional basis or it may be handled rationally. Communal or cooperative groups, united by strong emotional ties, often attempt to use consensual methods in their interactions. While the problem resolutions may be acceptable, the lack of programming and the scarcity of consciously identified alternative behaviors make such processes lengthy and susceptible to failure (Filley, 1973).

Finally, manifest behavior may be identified as that of an individual or that of a group. In this book we shall not distinguish between the two as parties in overt conflict unless making specific references to one or the other. Behavior between groups rather than individuals does not alter the basic pattern in the conflict process itself.

Conflict Resolution or Suppression

The next step in the conflict process is that of conflict resolution or suppression. Although the activity here is directed at ending the manifest conflict, in many cases it may resemble a continuation of the manifest conflict or problem-solving activity. It is distinguishable from such manifest behavior by the process of conflict reduction rather than conflict elevation. In competition, the resolution process is simple and programmed: Rules specify the outcome. In less programmed and more disruptive conflicts, resolution involves the imposition of a deliberate strategy of conflict reduction. . . .

Resolution Aftermath

Usually the resolution of conflict leaves a legacy which will affect the future relations of the parties and their attitudes about each other. Perhaps the most neutral in its effects is the end of a simple competitive situation viewed impersonally as an event. In such cases the value of the competitive process probably outweighs the attitudes about the final victory or defeat.

More often, however, the outcome of a conflict leaves the parties with positive or negative changes in resources and with attendant feelings which are also positive or negative.

As pointed out earlier in this chapter, a clear defeat may leave a party with antagonistic or self-destructive feelings that merely set the stage for further conflict. Losers intend to win on the next encounter and such determination necessarily is accompanied by less cooperation, less trust, more personalization of the role of both parties, and distorted communication between the parties.

Where the resolution is one of compromise, the agreement often involves some form of future reciprocity. The parties become bound together by some kind of antagonistic cooperation. Often both parties will judge that they have given more than they have received; and, although neither party loses all, they both may have feelings of defeat (Burke, 1970). Parties will prepare themselves for a better bargain in the next encounter and, as in the previous case, will exhibit less trust, more personalization, and more frequent distortions in communication. Perhaps most important, they will often tend to manifest a low level of commitment to the compromise agreement (Blake, Mouton, and Shepard, 1964).

Finally, where problem solving results in an integrative outcome which is viewed as a win by both sides, the parties are brought closer together. Cooperation increases, future issues are depersonalized, trust is enhanced, and communication is accurate and complete. Problem solving is likely to leave the parties with a high level of commitment to the agreement.

To summarize, we have outlined the sequence associated with the development and resolution of conflict. Antecedent conditions, plus perceptions and attitudes, generate manifest behavior of a conflictive or problem-solving nature which is followed by some mechanism for ending the overt behavior. The resolution may be one which increases the likelihood of future conflicts or one which contributes to future harmony and cooperation. . . .

References

Blake, R. R., and J. S. Mouton. "Comprehension of own and outgroup positions under intergroup competition." *Journal of Conflict Resolution* 5 (1961a): 304–10.

Blake, R. R., and J. S. Mouton. "Loyalty of representatives to in-group positions during intergroup competition." *Sociometry* 24 (1961b): 177–83.

Blake, R. R., and J. S. Mouton. "Reactions to intergroup competition under win-lose conditions." *Management Science* 7 (1961c): 420–35.

Blake, R. R., J. S. Mouton, and H. A. Shepard. *Managing Intergroup Conflict in Industry*. Gulf, 1964.

Boulding, K. B. "A pure theory of conflict applied to organizations." In *The Frontiers of Management Psychology*, G. Fish, ed., Harper & Row, 1964.

Burke, R. J. "Methods of resolving superior-subordinate conflict: The constructive use of subordinate differences and disagreements." *Organizational Behavior and Human Performance* 5 (1970): 393–411.

Corwin, R. G. "Patterns of organizational conflict." *Administrative Science Quarterly* 14 (1969): 507–21.

Filley, A. C. "Organization invention: A study of utopian organizations." Wisconsin Business Papers No. 3. Bureau of Business Research and Service, University of Wisconsin-Madison, 1973.

Fink, C. F. "Some conceptual difficulties in the theory of social conflict." *Journal of Conflict Resolution* 13 (1968): 413–58.

Lott, A., and B. E. Lott. "Group cohesiveness as interpersonal attraction: A review of relationships with antecedent and consequent variables." *Psychological Bulletin* 64 (1965): 259–309.

Pondy, L. R. "Organizational conflict: Concepts and models." *Administrative Science Quarterly* 12 (1967): 296–320.

Pondy, L. R. "Varieties of organizational conflict." *Administrative Science Quarterly* 14 (1969): 499–506.

Rapoport, A. *Fights, Games, and Debates.* University of Michigan, 1960.

Schmidt, S. M. "Lateral conflict within employment service district offices." Unpublished doctoral dissertation, University of Wisconsin-Madison, 1973.

Walton, R. E., and J. M. Dutton. "The management of interdepartmental conflict: A model and review." *Administrative Science Quarterly* 14 (1969): 73–84.

Walton, R. E., J. M. Dutton, and T. P. Cafferty. "Organizational context and interdepartmental conflict." *Administrative Science Quarterly* 14 (1969): 522–43.

Action Steps: Applications

1. With one of your classmates take a "trust walk." Do it this way: close your eyes and have the other person lead or guide you out of the room and out-of-doors and around at least two objects such as a building and a tree; on the return trip have the other person close his/her eyes and you guide him/her. During this walk note very carefully two things: (1) ways in which the other person "takes care of you" and actually shows that he/she cares about you, and (2) your own thoughts and feelings while the other person is dependent upon you. Discuss these observations with a small group of your classmates after they have returned from a similar "trust walk." Determine for yourself the extent to which you have perhaps previously been needlessly distrustful of other people or careless about trust placed in you by others.

2. Obtain permission to observe a routine problem-solving discussion such as that which frequently occurs in a dormitory or student living group, or in a student organization. Note carefully any defensive behavior which occurs; note also the immediately preceding interaction which seemed to generate this defensiveness, and compare it with Gibb's findings reported in this chapter. Share your observations with a small group of your classmates.

3. Determine in your own mind the degree to which you feel alienated from some particular person who is supposed to be (expected by society to be) important to you. This may be a wife, husband, mother, father, sister, brother, teacher, counselor, adviser, or department chairman. Arrange a meeting with such a person and note very carefully any evidences of *communication denial* on the part of this person; note also the nature of your responses to such denial. Carefully but deliberately attempt to discuss with this person your perception of his/her com-

munication denial and what the two of you might be able to do about it. Share your findings with your classmates.

4. If for any reason (geographic distance or no feeling of alienation on your part) you cannot comply with suggestion 3 above, select a member of another race and follow the instructions given.

5. Observe a campus group in at least two of their meetings and note the types of manipulative behavior and conflicts evidenced. Discuss these observations with the other members of your class.

6. Meet with one of your classmates and attempt to determine the amount of understanding that is going on between you. Focus precisely on selected parts of your interaction at first; then try to arrive at an overall assessment of your discussion with this other person.

7. Analyze a recent conflict situation in which you have been involved according to Filley's description of the process in Reading 8.2. How did you feel about the resolution of the conflict? Share your learnings with a group of classmates.

Chapter 9
Applying Principles of Interpersonal Communication

BASIC TO THE IMPROVEMENT of your interpersonal communication is a sincere desire to become a better person—"better" according to your own criteria gained from personal experience. Embodied in this concept of a better person is the possibility of your becoming the very best person you can within your own biological capabilities and psychological potential. This improvement not only includes becoming the best you have ever dreamed of for yourself, but also involves, as we see it, the vision of becoming something even better—a person who desires eventually to *transcend* your present highest hopes for yourself.

When we speak of improving ability in interpersonal communication, we do not have in mind a person who just talks better; rather, we envision a better person talking. Improvement in interpersonal communication involves achieving a healthier, more functional personality. We might look at a person engaged in business; let's think of this person in the role of a manager. As this person strives to improve his/her interactions with others in the organization, he/she is striving to become a better person. In writing on the process of manager development in the *Harvard Business Review*, Paul Brouwer makes this point: Improvement in one's management behavior requires improvement in the whole person. Management development is self-development.[1]

Improvement in interpersonal communication is not just the acquisition of a skill, such as learning to type or to use shorthand. It involves the psychological interior of a person, his/her way of thinking about himself/herself as well as his/her way of relating to others.

In Chapter 2 we suggested that our need for interpersonal communication is two-fold: first, for self-development and, second, for negotiation with others to control our physical and social environment. Our primary need is the first—self-development; improved achievement in negotiating with others follows from changes in ourselves. These changes in ourselves may be identified as personal growth. The first thing involved is a change in the image of our potential, at least to the extent that we can envision or imagine ourselves being different—not just doing something *in addition* to what we do already. Personal growth inherently involves changes in self-concept. Similarly, improvement in interpersonal communication also involves changes in one's self-concept.

---

[1] P. J. Brouwer, "The Power to See Ourselves," *Harvard Business Review*, 42 (1964): 156–163; see especially pp. 158–159.

INTERPERSONAL COMMUNICATION IN ACTION

Great people have always held a concept of themselves as unique, set apart from the ordinary—Michelangelo, fighting political pressures to achieve his art; Beethoven, composing even when deaf; Milton, writing even though blind. Such people had a vision of themselves fulfilling their destiny. The difference between a great person and one who is not great is not always ability, for many clerks have keen intelligence; it is not ambition, for many ambitious people somehow defeat themselves. The primary difference is in self-concept: How valuable is my life? What do I want to do with it? What must I do to be myself?[2]

The Process of Self-actualization

We have emphasized throughout this book that interpersonal communication is a dynamic process, not an achievement or a goal to be secured. Similarly, self-actualization is not an accomplishment; rather it is a process of becoming and a way of dealing with life. Probably the best-known advocate of this emphasis is Abraham Maslow, and the key concept he employs is *self-actualization*, the process of becoming that which is inherent in one's potential.[3] According to Maslow, self-actualization involves "acceptance and expression of the inner core of self," and putting into operation "these latent capacities and potentialities." Achievement in the sense of personal accomplishment is also involved in this concept—achievement according to one's unique innate capabilities.[4]

Carl Rogers has contributed significantly to the movement toward humanistic emphasis in psychology. From his personal experience he has come to place special emphasis on a person's being of value to other people.[5] A relationship with another person in such a way that both persons benefit is essential to Rogers's thinking about a fully functioning, self-actualized person.[6]

SELF-ACTUALIZATION AND INTERPERSONAL COMMUNICATION

Inherent in the *process* of self-actualization is interpersonal communication. For a person to get to know himself well, to understand how he/she might become better, to envision himself/herself *being* better, and to change his/her ways almost always requires interaction with helpful others.[7] This is especially true when one is trying to improve his/her ways of relating to other people.[8]

[2] Cf. C. R. Rogers, "Toward Becoming a Fully Functioning Person," in *Perceiving, Behaving, Becoming: A New Focus for Education: 1962 Yearbook* (Washington, D.C.: Association for Supervision and Curriculum Development, 1962), pp. 21–33.

[3] See A. H. Maslow, *Toward a Psychology of Being* (New York: Van Nostrand Reinhold, 1962).

[4] See A. H. Maslow, *The Further Reaches of Human Nature* (New York: Viking, 1971), p. 43.

[5] See C. R. Rogers, *Freedom to Learn* (Columbus, Ohio: Merrill, 1969), pp. 231–237.

[6] See, for example, his treatment of this principle in C. R. Rogers, *Becoming Partners: Marriage and Its Alternatives* (New York: Delacorte, 1972).

[7] See, for example, the evidence summarized in C. B. Truax and R. R. Carkhuff, *Toward Effective Counseling and Psychotherapy* (Chicago: Aldine, 1967).

[8] Cf. R. R. Carkhuff, *Helping and Human Relations*, Vol. 1 (New York: Holt, Rinehart and Winston, 1969).

Inherent in this process is disclosure of one's thoughts and feelings to another person.[9] According to Sidney Jourard, the process of self-actualizing includes self-disclosure, feedback from a trusted person, self-examination, and personal change.[10]

For self-actualization, Jourard emphasizes disclosure of one's thoughts and feelings to a trusted listener.[11] In one of his earlier writings, Jourard gives this illustration of an interchange between a person and someone he trusts:

> I have never told this to a soul, doctor, but I can't stand my wife. My mother is a nag, my father is a bore, and my boss is an absolutely hateful and despicable tyrant. I have been carrying on an affair for the past ten years with the lady next door, and at the same time I am a deacon in the church.[12]

Jourard has the doctor respond in a sympathetic manner, making no particular evaluation except to appreciate that all this poses a problem.

Such self-disclosure may take the form of statements about oneself; however, much more valid and useful are actions. In either case the true feelings must be displayed; the use of masks, subterfuge, and deceit must be minimal. Achieving this level of disclosure is not easy, and for some it may take special instruction and the assistance of trained persons.[13]

Our twentieth-century society tends to strip each of us of our personal identity characteristics. Organizations and bureaucracies seem to be intent on reducing each of us to an interchangeable unit. This "sociological sheepshearing" is often accomplished by removing or ignoring all identifiers not needed to help us fit a certain slot: student, teacher, doctor, patient, and so on. In most cases this procedure starts with "admissions" and is called "training."[14] When this process is completed, quite often a person does not know what he/she is really like—what his/her own feelings and desires actually are—or if he/she has any! Jourard argues in *Disclosing Man to Himself* that interpersonal communication, involving self-disclosure and feedback, can recapture for people this ability to know themselves.[15]

FEEDBACK: AN ESSENTIAL ELEMENT

Self-actualization requires feedback from a person you trust. Validation of your self-concept can produce belief in yourself.[16] It can supply encouragement and support when most needed. On the other hand, negative feedback

[9] See S. M. Jourard, "Growing Awareness and the Awareness of Growth," in H. A. Otto and J. Mann (eds.), *Ways of Growth* (New York: Grossman, 1968), pp. 1–15.

[10] See S. M. Jourard, *The Transparent Self* (New York: Van Nostrand Reinhold, 1964); see especially pp. 19–30.

[11] S. M. Jourard, *Disclosing Man to Himself* (New York: Van Nostrand Reinhold, 1968), p. 47.

[12] Jourard, *The Transparent Self*, p. 21.

[13] See, for example, the results of an experimental study by J. W. MacDoniels, "Factors Related to the Level of Open Expression in Small Group Laboratory Learning Experiences," unpublished doctoral dissertation, University of Kansas, 1972.

[14] Jourard, *The Transparent Self*, p. 149.

[15] Jourard, *Disclosing Man to Himself*; see especially pp. 43–51.

[16] Z. A. Pepitone, "An Experimental Analysis of Self-Dynamics," in C. Gordon and K. J. Gergen (eds.), *The Self in Social Interaction* (New York: Wiley, 1968), p. 350.

can stimulate self-examination; the twin needs of self-esteem and self-evaluation can produce dissonance that leads to a desire for personal change.

Self-actualization requires *vision* on the part of the individual involved—vision in the older, perhaps Biblical, sense of creative imagination. Nowhere in the literature of the human potential movement have we seen this concept of vision better portrayed than in *Man's Search for Meaning* by Victor Frankl.[17] During World War II, Frankl, a Jew, was in a Nazi prison camp. He saw relatives and friends tortured and killed; he went through years of extreme physical and psychological suffering. His book is a psychological treatise on what keeps a person going under such conditions and how some survive and some do not. After describing an almost endless series of debasing and traumatic experiences, Frankl approaches the question of why some men gave up—"broke"—and others did not. The difference between these men was that some were able to *transcend* the most pitiful conditions and horrible experiences. It required a vision of oneself being able to suffer anything and live through it:

> Any attempt at fighting the camp's psychopathological influence on the prisoner by psychotherapeutic or psychohygienic methods had to aim at giving him inner strength by pointing out to him a future goal to which he could look forward. Instinctively some of the prisoners attempted to find one on their own. . . . I remember a personal experience. Almost in tears from pain (I had terrible sores on my feet from wearing torn shoes), I limped a few kilometers with our long column of men from the camp to our work site. Very cold, bitter winds struck us. I kept thinking of the endless little problems of our miserable life. What would there be to eat tonight? If a piece of sausage came as extra ration, should I exchange it for a piece of bread? Should I trade my last cigarette, which was left from a bonus I received a fortnight ago, for a bowl of soup? How could I get a piece of wire to replace the fragment which served as one of my shoelaces? Would I get to our work site in time to join my usual working party or would I have to join another, which might have a brutal foreman? What could I do to get on good terms with the Capo, who could help me to obtain work in camp instead of undertaking this horribly long daily march?
>
> I became disgusted with the state of affairs which compelled me, daily and hourly, to think of only such trivial things. I forced my thoughts to turn to another subject. Suddenly I saw myself standing on the platform of a well-lit, warm and pleasant lecture room. In front of me sat an attentive audience on comfortable upholstered seats. I was giving a lecture on the psychology of the concentration camp! All that oppressed me at that moment became objective, seen and described from the remote viewpoint of science. By this method I succeeded somehow in rising above the situation, above the sufferings of the moment, and I observed them as if they were already of the past. Both I and my troubles became the object of an interesting psychoscientific study undertaken by myself.[18]

Under other, much more pleasant conditions, Brouwer analyzed the characteristics of people that make some of them good managing executives and cause others never to make it. He came to the same conclusion: The major

---

[17] V. E. Frankl, *Man's Search for Meaning* (Boston, Mass.: Beacon, 1963).
[18] Ibid., pp. 116–117.

difference lies in self-concept—vision of themselves meeting the requirements of the job![19]

It is our belief that any attempt to improve a relationship with another person—a parent, teacher, wife, husband, friend—requires this same kind of vision of ourself *behaving* in a new way, acting in a different manner. If it doesn't come to us easily, we must think about it and try hard. As Frankl said about those men who survived the prison camp by gaining a concept of themselves being different from their former selves—some of them had to work at it![20]

In his book on becoming partners in a marriage, Carl Rogers reports a case of a young married couple who became involved in a "triangle."[21] The husband, Roy, fell in love with another young woman, and the survival of his marriage was seriously at issue. Through talking with others and his wife, Roy achieved a vision of himself being open and sharing with his wife—being her true friend and companion in ways never before achieved. Rogers quotes Roy's evaluation of their new relationship as follows:

> There has always been movement and development in our marriage but never like the last two years—moving from a small town to a large city, children both in school, women's liberation, sexual liberation in the youth culture—all have had a profound impact. As the kids grew, Sylvia increasingly began to search out her own identity. I really affirmed that. I wanted a stimulating relationship of co-equals. Increasingly we spent time together talking—exploring wishes—my listening and drawing out her thinking about herself and what she wanted to become. It works. Now she does this for me too. It's great to have someone to help you explore your own mind.[22]

As we see it, personal growth involves self-disclosure in words and actions, feedback from a trusted person, self-evaluation, a vision of what one might become, attempts to achieve those changes, followed by further feedback, self-evaluation, and so on. This use of interpersonal communication can provide a self-revelation, *not just what you are, but a vision of what you can become.* It can stimulate self-improvement by stirring your imagination, opening new horizons, new ideas, new appreciation of the needs of others, along with a desire to meet those needs. This process of "getting involved" with others can give you a new vision of yourself relating to them in new ways.[23]

Jourard has presented some evidence that through the process of interpersonal communication involving self-disclosure to trusted others, a person can achieve a healthier personality; by contrast, he shows that nondisclosers tend to get sick—alienated, mentally disturbed.[24]

Breuer, a Viennese physician, escaped fame only by a small margin. He discovered that when his hysterical patients *talked about their suppressed feelings,* their hysterical symptoms disappeared. Breuer backed off from reporting discoveries that would have made him Freud's colleague in psychiatry's hall of

[19] Brouwer, "The Power to See Ourselves," pp. 162–163.
[20] Frankl, *Man's Search*, pp. 123–127.
[21] Rogers, *Becoming Partners*, pp. 53–70.
[22] Ibid., pp. 54–55.
[23] Cf. Jourard, *Disclosing Man to Himself*, p. 47.
[24] Cf. ibid., pp. 37–51.

By self-disclosure to trusted others, a person can achieve a healthier personality.

fame. Apparently he became scared because some of his female patients (in Victorian time) disclosed themselves to be quite sexy; worse yet, they felt quite sexy toward him! From such discoveries, however, Freud did not flinch. He found that neurotic people were struggling toward being themselves, admitting their feelings to themselves, and being known fully to others.[25] Without some

[25] Cf. Jourard, *The Transparent Self*, pp. 21–22.

opportunity to let their true selves develop and be known to others, these persons allowed their problems to multiply and become severe. And, indeed, we sometimes find ourselves surprised to encounter and confront an infant inside the skin of someone playing the role of an adult!

Throughout recorded time there has existed a struggle between the self-actualizers and the nondisclosers. We now know the nonself-actualizers as persons who tend to hide their thoughts and ideas, people who wear masks and distort reality. In severe cases they actually achieve cognitive separation from reality—they become sick. In the past decade we have heard much about a "sick society," containing people who would keep their consciousness within limits of traditional views—the status quo. This struggle is now sharper than ever before; as we write this book we feel we are on the side of those who try to find reality through self-disclosure plus feedback from honest people.

Making Optimal Use of the Process of Interpersonal Communication

Actualizing people are flexible in their use of interpersonal communication as the situations change; they have a choice. Their security comes from the confidence that they can interact effectively with others when and if there is a need to do so. Because they are confident, they no longer have to prove their ability to relate or to verify that they are acceptable. The avenues to self-actualization are so varied that we can only suggest some typical suggestions and guidelines. These suggestions will constitute a partial, but only partial, summary of some of the points made throughout this book.

Obviously, you as an individual must use sound judgment in applying the suggestions. Interpersonal communication should never be mechanistic or routine. A suggestion that might be generally useful may not apply specifically to your own communication with your father, mother, teacher, or particular friend. The value of the suggestions presented is to increase your awareness of choice in interpersonal encounters. The educated person should be cognizant of the communication choices available and the potential consequences.

1. NOTE VERY HONESTLY YOUR OWN INTERACTION NEEDS

Many of our individual needs can only be satisfied through social interaction; these include our personal development, personal growth, clarification of our relationships with others, and ways of negotiating our disagreements.

In our personal development we must deliberately search for new ways of gaining social approval. As our social environments change, we need to check on those elements in them that earn approval. Just as we should avoid straight, narrow, ritualized ways of behaving, we should also avoid trying to hide a part of ourselves or acting as if we are something we are not. An open, frank, and genuine approach to others in our communication is our best avenue of self-identity.

We must build confidence in our ability to achieve and maintain self-esteem. This is accomplished as we expose a bit of ourselves to someone and note and evaluate the feedback we receive. As we find that we can profit from such exposure and feedback, we then disclose ourselves a little more. When we find a person we can trust to be open, frank, and accepting, we can gain honest and genuine feedback. As we communicate in this fashion with another, we may achieve the pleasure of shared personal growth. When we find that we can be comfortable in shared silence, we have achieved a level of interpersonal growth that is fully worth the effort.

When we have associated with other individuals over a period of time, there is a temptation to take the relationships for granted. In a work group, it is often useful to ask the other people how they feel about the way the members work together. A conflict area or basis of confusion may be revealed. We should seek to establish a pattern whereby every now and then we seek to clarify our relationships with those with whom we come into constant contact.

We should negotiate disagreements by attempting to achieve a level of mutual satisfaction. Ethically, we should avoid deliberate efforts to manipulate or distort the perceptions of others. They may see things differently than we do, but we should allow this to occur and attempt to understand it. The bases for our varying perceptions should be communicated and mutual revision accomplished, particularly if our needs and desires are obscuring reality! A compromise is sometimes necessary; usually it can be achieved satisfactorily through open, accurate, and honest exposure of the different viewpoints.

2. TRY TO ACHIEVE ACCURATE PERCEPTIONS OF OTHERS

We should attempt to avoid use of pigeonhole categories and oversimplification in our perceptions of other people. We must expect and note complexities and differences instead of simple similarities. We should expect our perceptions of another person to change from time to time and avoid "once-and-for-all" conclusions. Two-valued orientations, such as "clean–dirty" or "young–old," and status perceptions, such as "high–low," should not filter our views of others.

It is important to watch for subtle cues as we try to get to know others better. It will be necessary to look beyond such surface characteristics as use of cosmetics, long hair, and dress; as we avoid misleading stereotype casting we should watch closely for visual expressions and slight changes in posture and eye contact that give us more significant messages. Such nonverbal communication can help us understand the emotions and true feelings of the other person. We may deliberately have to explore the ways he/she wishes to relate to us, or the "game" he/she is attempting to play.

It is important that we try to understand the ways we ordinarily orient ourselves toward others. Our orientation may serve our own personal needs for interaction, but greater flexibility may serve them even better. One of the major considerations is to determine if our willingness to interact with others is congruent with our desire to be included in their activities. Occasionally we find an unhappy person who, for one reason or another, is unwilling to include others in his/her life or activities, and who simultaneously feels that others seem to pass him by. The golden rule would seem to apply, for if we wish others to include us in their activities, we will have to show the same interest in including them in ours.

We must determine if we are willing to share control of a group in which we participate. We must see if our desire to control others is balanced by a willingness to be controlled at times by them. If we attempt to control others and feel that we can be happy only if we are in control of the situation, we may find conflict with those who are unwilling to let us control all the time. It is probably beneficial to adopt a balanced approach—to be willing to be controlled as well as to take control when others seem to feel that it is appropriate.

Similarly, we should determine if our needs to receive attention and affection are approximately equal to our tendencies of showing affection to others. The area is critical in interpersonal orientations. In our culture many of us, especially males, find it difficult to show affection toward others. At the same time, however, most men and boys find it pleasant and rewarding to receive attention and affection. The point is this: If we want affection from others, we will probably have to be willing to show it toward them at appropriate times. Such displays of affection may be so foreign to our habits of thinking as to be awkward or even embarrassing, but they may be necessary if our interpersonal relations are to be mutually pleasant and satisfying.

If we feel that we are left out of groups or given too little affection by others, we can do the following:

1. Make a special effort to include others in our circle of associates.
2. Show more readiness to accept the leadership and suggestions of others.
3. Sincerely show others the genuine affection we feel for them.

We must try to make our behavior toward others congruent with the interpersonal behavior we would like to have them extend to us.

3. BE CAREFUL IN THE SENDING AND RECEIVING OF VERBAL MESSAGES

If we are to gain maximum information from our interactions, we have to avoid making fast assumptions that we "know what he/she means." Whereas verbal communication provides clues to the other person's intended meanings, we should ask for additional information when the clues are in conflict or if we are unsure of what is intended. We must make every attempt to make certain that our conceptual maps are known to one another and that they fit the territory they profess to represent.

We should pay special attention to the intended meaning of another person when he/she uses words describing such strong feelings as love, dislike, hurt, sympathy, understanding, and fear. When a person says that he/she is "unhappy" with someone, we must not automatically assume we know what he/she means. Our own experiences and feelings may make empathy difficult.

Sudden shifts in the levels of abstraction should be noted. Suppose we ask a friend, "Did you have a good time at the party last night?" and he responds, "I met a lot of new people." We asked for an evaluative response and received a statement of fact, so what conclusions can we draw?

Because language can be used as an instrument for interpersonal manipulation, we should be alert to the ways we are influenced and persuaded. Consider the ways many adults talk to children. Basic premises are implied but not stated openly; value systems are evoked but not discussed; and general statements are made about observed data, behaviors, and events but are not allowed to be questioned.

Such uses of language are manipulative and produce responses that may be unthinkingly submissive, resentful, alienated, or hostile. Interpersonal relationships are damaged rather than improved. Although it may be true that language is a social tool, care must be exercised that you or someone else is not thus "tooled."

Listening to others ordinarily requires deliberate effort. It should include a sincere attempt to understand the viewpoint of the other person: his/her value system; the source of his/her basic premises that frequently are implied but not openly stated; his/her generalized notion of observable facts, including his/her limited ability to observe objectively—sometimes called "personal prejudice"; and his/her limited linguistic ability to express his/her ideas in ways easily understood by others.

True listening is hard work. We may decide that in many cases it may not be worth all that much effort; but to make such a decision with full knowledge of the potential loss of understanding is one thing, and to allow such loss through neglect is quite another. When we really desire a lasting relationship with someone, listening to him/her is a necessary investment.

The point of this discussion is this: a rewarding relationship with another person seldom occurs by chance; we can't expect such a relationship to "just happen." If we really want to enjoy being with another person, we have to *work at* "being with" him or her. A starting point is to try to listen, to hear with "ears like theirs" instead of ours.

4. BE ALERT TO THE IMPACT OF NONVERBAL MESSAGES

Because nonverbal messages ultimately define a relationship, it is important to be aware of the messages that we both send and receive. The key is that, because most nonverbal messages are unconscious, they are less likely to lie. We may, in fact, learn a great deal about ourselves if we sense that our bodies are generating tension or expressing pressures.

Similarly, we should be alert to incongruent messages. If we perceive a disparity between words and actions, we should probe deeply to find out the bases for such incongruency.

We suspect that the person whose words do not match the nonverbal messages may find close and meaningful relationships with others difficult to maintain. We are more transparent than we think, and it is difficult to fool people about our feelings for very long.

5. CONSTANTLY CONSIDER ENVIRONMENTAL CONDITIONS

Teachers of public speaking have for many years requested students to note the requirements of the "occasion" or the situation confronting a speaker. In like manner, in an interpersonal situation the other person expects us to interact in certain ways; these expectations will be related to the specific environment and the chain of events or interactions that have led to this specific encounter. We typically respond without reflecting on the basis for our situational conditions.

Here we are concerned with situations that call for discriminating choice, for fine distinctions. For example, you are going to accuse your roommate of misusing your typewriter; at the time you meet him he is standing on a street corner talking to an acquaintance. "Now is probably not the right time to bring it up, but . . ." is a poor way to deal with the situation if we want optimum response. There may never be a perfect time to open a discussion about personal disagreements, but the usual mistake is that they are not brought up under optimum conditions. A presentation of such problems should take advantage of conditions that are at least somewhat favorable.

Certain situational guidelines are available for work in groups. You should hope to work with groups that provide optimum conditions for accomplishing a given task as well as maintaining positive group relations:

1. The group task should be clear and relevant to your interest.
2. There should be the possibility for you to achieve a desirable status in the group.
3. The group's norms should be known and acceptable to you.
4. The power structure of the group should offer you an opportunity to participate in controlling other members as well as being controlled and influenced.
5. Group cohesiveness should be present or potentially possible.
6. Leadership roles should be shared and they should be reasonably attractive to you; that is, few members should exhibit excessive anxieties or a need to dominate others.

In joining and working with groups, it may take some time to learn each of these group characteristics, and when you have done so, some elements may not be to your liking because, like individuals, no group is perfect. However, if you are to work well with the group and achieve satisfaction, you will want most of the characteristics just listed to be present or attainable.

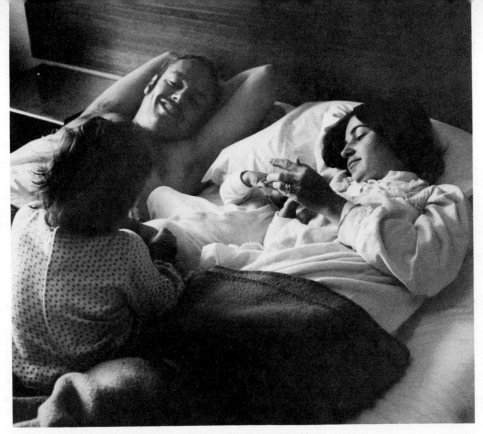

People who look for happiness and success are likely to find it.

We believe that it is important for people to seek and find enjoyment in their daily interactions. Pleasant things occur during a working day that merit reflection. As we have noted, human perception is such that people tend to find what they seek. If they look for rejection and failure, they will probably find it. If they are alert for evidences of happiness and success, those are likely to be found. The point is that an optimistic viewpoint is more beneficial to effective communication and self-actualization than a pessimistic one predictive of defeat. The self-fulfilling prophecy can create or inhibit opportunities for social participation. Optimism helps create the courage to tackle problems and stirs the confidence of others.

6. BUILD THE BEST POSSIBLE HUMAN RELATIONSHIPS

Without allowing ourselves to become dupes for "confidence men," we should strive to increase our trust in other people. Increased trust in ourselves is vital; we must be willing to expose our thoughts and ideas to others and listen to their responses to these ideas. Our trust of others will increase as we learn to profit from their responses. An open and frank expression of what we think and how we feel about it will be an excellent start toward increasing interpersonal trust.

Our confidante or confidant must be selected with care. By easy stages, we can achieve greater candor and disclosure of our feelings—our fears, anxieties, hopes, and pleasures. We should not worry about "saying things just right"; the other person's responses should guide us in determining how well we have expressed ourselves. As trust increases, we learn that the correction of misinterpretation is not only possible but relatively easy; it does require, however, that we listen carefully to the person's responses and reflections on our thoughts.

The most valuable thing for us to learn as our trust of others increases is that *we do not ordinarily lose self-esteem by self-disclosure and relevant feedback*; rather, the opposite is true. The surest way to increase self-esteem is to listen and to evaluate feedback about ourself from someone we trust, making changes in our behavior when desirable and possible. In this way increased interpersonal trust serves our own personal needs and purposes.

The opportunities for experiencing relationships with others are more abundant than ever before. The numerous opportunities make it possible that a classmate or friend may share the risk of the first steps; but this must be a case of an equal helping an equal.

Summary and Preview of Readings

This chapter has focused on improving interpersonal communication by becoming a better person. A challenge was presented to fulfill your own human potential, not by just adding a few behaviors to those already practiced, but by achieving a new vision of yourself as a human being and then working toward self-actualization in terms of that vision. Special emphasis was placed on *self-disclosure* to a trusted person and utilization of *feedback* thus obtained.

Self-disclosure requires interpersonal trust. In the communication setting, trust of a speaker is influenced by our perception of his/her expertness, reliability, and dynamism. Trust of a listener is influenced by our perception of his/her accurate empathy, nonpossessive warmth, and genuineness. Our trust of ourselves, trust of others, and perceived trust *by* others are all interrelated; as one goes up or down, the others appear to be influenced.

Increased trust of others can be beneficial if one guards against being a dupe—offering trust when there is solid evidence that it will be misused. To increase our trust of others, we must increase both our interaction and our self-disclosure. Usually these overtures will achieve rewarding responses from others; if they do not, we must find associates who respond with consideration, sincerity, and warmth.

The final section of this chapter presented direct suggestions for improving interpersonal communication. These incorporated a brief review of the essential elements of the process of interpersonal communication. The key to improvement is to activate some plan, as the result of reflection and interaction with honest others, and begin to work on it. We must realize that any changes or growth require time, so we must take the small day-to-day steps of slowly developing our communication skills. In whatever area we feel inadequate, we must take the planned time to build small increments of interpersonal competence and be momentarily satisfied with small gains.

The first reading that follows—"Personal Relationships and Sex Role Playing," by Janet Saltzman Chafetz—deals with the sex roles that all of us have been conditioned to play and the impact they have on our personal relationships. Many of our behaviors are so ingrained that we're not aware that often we are merely acting out roles. Hopefully, that reading will stimulate your thinking concerning the impact that sex-role stereotyping has made on your life, and it may suggest potential changes in your ways of relating to other people.

A great deal of our time is spent in small groups as we work with other people in attempts to solve mutual problems. The second reading—"Interpersonal Behavior in Groups"—categorizes and analyzes the behavior of people in the small group situation.

The final reading—"Surviving on the Job," by David W. Johnson—shows how our interpersonal skills, such as interviews, determine to a great extent our success in acquiring and performing a job. He provides a useful summary of the interpersonal skills that are likely to be needed in your working environment.

In the preceding pages we have presented many ideas we think are important. Throughout the book, we have attempted to suggest choices available to you to help overcome communication obstacles. Basically, the framework we have provided is meant to serve as a starting point for serious thinking about the aims and consequences of your communication behaviors. It is our hope that these ideas will have a particular relevance to *you* and that theory will be turned into practice.

Personal Relationships and Sex Role Playing

Janet Saltzman Chafetz

The intimate relationships of most people with other humans are among the most important aspects of their lives, if not the single most important one. Such relationships are undoubtedly colored strongly by sex roles, yet, ironically, this is precisely the subject about which social science has the least unbiased relevant research information available. Nonetheless, no discussion of sex roles can ignore their impact on interpersonal relationships. This chapter is an attempt to explore the issues, despite the relative paucity of relevant data. The basic question is: To the extent that males and females fulfill their respective sex role stereotypes, what are the implications for a variety of relationships?

Because few people of either gender "live up to" their stereotypes totally, the relationships discussed in the following pages will necessarily be exaggerated. The issue is not how many people really behave in these ways.

Rather, we can more profitably ask what aspects of our relationships reflect, however dimly, the processes hypothesized as resulting from the pressures exerted by sex role stereotypes. Beyond that more cannot be said, in the absence of research evidence.

Theories of Human Relations

Dick and Jane interact with a myriad of people of both genders, and they do so in a variety of ways. Human relationships have long been categorized as falling into one of two broad types: primary and secondary. Secondary relations are those ritualized interactions between two or more individuals playing specific roles who come into contact for a limited purpose. The interactions that normally occur between salesclerk and customer, teacher and student, doctor and patient, are all examples of secondary relations. One can rather easily predict the content of such exchanges, since they are generally prepatterned to a substantial degree, the behaviors are limited in scope, and emotional responses are minimal. Primary relations are exactly the opposite. They consist of interactions among people in a broad spectrum of ways and settings in which some degree of emotional commitment is usually present. Relationships between lovers and/or spouses, friends, and children and parents, are all primary in nature. Naturally, the line between the two types is not clear-cut: many secondary relations shade into primary ones, while in some circumstances primary relations partake of secondary elements. The focus in this chapter is chiefly on primary relationships among adults.

The same individual is never precisely the same in relationship to a number of other individuals, although there is a tendency toward consistency. We have all experienced the feeling that the Dick or Jane we know is "not the same person" as that same Dick or Jane is to someone else. The stoical, silent Dick we know is loquacious, sensitive Dick to somewhat else; scatter-brained outgoing Jane to someone else is that bright but somewhat shy Jane we know. Are Jane and Dick hypocrites, hiding their "true selves" from us, someone else, or both? Probably not; they are merely performing in response to different circumstances, as well as differing perceptions and expectations of themselves. Stated in another way, we all have a very large repertoire of behaviors; other people elicit some elements of it, but not all. It is probably the case that no other person ever elicits the entire range of behaviors from another, regardless of how close the two may be or how long they have known one another. In primary relations, however, a substantial proportion of that repertoire is often revealed. Sooner or later there will still come that time when we scratch our heads and wonder why Jane or Dick "acted out of character," i.e., showed us some part of their behavior repertoire we had not seen before.

Sex role playing constitutes one among several important factors that influence the behaviors an individual will exhibit in a given relationship. As a feminine person, Jane will tend to display somewhat different behaviors to males who might be romantic partners than to females or even to other categories of males. Some of this difference may be a conscious effort to fulfill certain assumed expectations; for example, she may "play dumb" to attract a certain male whom she believes feels threatened by bright females. This is called "impression management" (Goffman, 1959). More important, however, are those behaviors she does not consciously manipulate. She may actually *be* rather dependent *vis-à-vis* a given male, while fairly independent with her female friends. This results from the fact that she has somewhat different self-concepts when she is with that male and with her friends which developed because she was sanctioned differently by them; she was "punished"—rebuffed or affection withdrawn—when she acted in an independent manner with her potential mate, but "rewarded" for the same efforts with her friends. Because the "definition of the situation" differed in the two instances, the behaviors rewarded differed, and the situations came to constitute self-fulfilling prophecies. The key is the nature of these situational definitions, and the point is that they are more or less strongly influenced by sex role stereotypes.

There are a number of other social-psychological theories dealing with human interaction which may help us understand the possible effects of sex role stereotypes on various human relationships. People who remain in a close primary relationship either originally agree on most issues deemed important by those involved or evolve into such agreement over time. Stated another way, individuals who continue to participate in a close relationship feel the same way about most fundamental things (Newcomb, 1961). Thus, for instance, a female who rejects the traditional feminine role (or a war, or a political ideology) is not apt to be found in a stable, long-term relationship with a male who accepts that role as appropriate; sooner or later the "imbalance" will become too uncomfortable or "dissonant," and if neither changes, the relationship will usually terminate. Thus, there are basically two possibilities when a fundamental lack of agreement exists: the relationship may end, or one or both individuals' attitudes may change. Indeed, the feminine sex role encourages women not to become too committed to any attitudes that may conflict with those of a mate, that is, women are encouraged to defer to a male's opinion. Thus there is a built-in tendency for this kind of circumstance not to reach the point of real conflict in that particular type of relationship.

Which of these two possibilities in fact occurs in the face of conflict depends in large measure on the quantity and quality of other satisfactions being derived from a relationship. Exchange theory (Homans, 1961; Thibault and Kelley, 1959) postulates that in any human interaction the participants receive certain "rewards" and pay certain "costs." For an interaction to continue, the rewards must be equal to or greater than the costs for the parties involved. According to this approach, the motivation for people to remain in a relationship exists when there is a "net profit" or, minimally, no loss. The only exception is when individuals who are experiencing a loss nonetheless remain in a relationship because the alternatives appear even more costly (Thibault and Kelley, 1959). For instance, a wife who is quite unhappy in her marital relationship may fail to seek a separation or divorce if she thinks that the resultant loneliness, lack of father-presence, and so forth will be worse (more costly) than the current misery.

The key to this approach resides in what people define as rewarding and what as costly. Such definitions are undoubtedly strongly influenced by sex role stereotyping. Females are systematically taught that one of the most important rewards they can receive is an overt display of warmth and affection; the withdrawal of this constitutes a cost. Past a very early age, males are not taught to value overt affection and, indeed, may even be taught it is "unmanly." It is not surprising that they are frequently embarrassed by, or at least oblivious to, the little signs of affection deemed so important by most females. One might say that giving these signs constitutes a cost for many males. Our folklore is full of jokes which center on precisely this phenomenon: husband forgets wife's birthday, their anniversary, the morning goodbye kiss, to compliment her new dress or a new recipe she has tried. Marriage manuals routinely contain advice to the male not to forget "afterplay" in sex, namely, a display of affection and warmth that is no longer explicitly directed at sexual fulfillment. Females are also taught to value dependency—

psychological and financial—*vis-à-vis* males, for whom support may well come to constitute a cost.

Males, on the other hand, are systematically taught to value more concrete rewards, such as money or service, as well as power or dominance and prestige. Using the marital relationship as an example, Dick's rewards consist of such things as an orderly and well-kept home (children quiet, dinner ready, socks clean), an ear that will listen, a mouth that will compliment, and, perhaps more importantly, an overall impression that he is dominant (Laws, 1971, p. 507). Conversely, all these things may be said to constitute costs for many wives. Our folklore reflects this as well, with endless stories about the wife who manipulates her spouse while making it appear that he is dominant and competent.

This chapter analyzes the ways in which people seek to have their needs met by others and the effects that sex role stereotypes have on this process. Fulfillment of such needs certainly constitutes a reward, but it might well entail a cost for the interaction partner. The thesis to be developed is that sex role stereotypes tend to decrease the ability of individuals to achieve need satisfaction (rewards) and increase the costs of granting such satisfaction to others. In short, sex roles encourage the dissolution of a variety of types of interpersonal relationships.

Interpersonal Relations Between the Genders

In our society there is an ever-present tendency for relationships between a male and a female to either become "romantic" (i.e., sexual in the broadest sense of the word) or to dissipate; platonic or nonromantic relationships are seemingly very unstable. This phenomenon results from a limited and limiting view of love fostered by Hollywood, television, true-romantic-type magazines, and indeed, our entire culture. Before male-female relationships of any type can be understood, it is crucial to examine our culturally accepted notion of this emotion.

Our language has but one word to cover a multitude of different emotional states: "love." We must then add adjectives to distinguish between the love parents and children have for one another from the love that is characteristic of close friends or romantic love, or, in some instances, forego the use of the word. We further distinguish between "infatuation," as a supposedly temporary, totally sexually based kind of romantic love; "liking," which is nonsexual love; and "TRUE LOVE," which is held out as the highest pinnacle of human emotion and sexuality and excuses all sins we may commit in its name.

Perhaps because we basically have only one word for all these various emotions, we tend to treat love as a zero-sum game. A zero-sum game is any situation in which one person's gain automatically entails another's loss. If, for instance, one gains to the hypothetical value of $+1$, the "opponent" loses to the value of -1, totaling zero when summed. In terms of love, this means the following. We begin with the very dubious assumption, rarely made explicit, that each person has a fixed, finite quantity of that emotion available to give. TRUE LOVE is assumed to take virtually all of it. Thus, if a person also "loves" someone else (not to mention many others), be it child, friend, or another romantic partner, he or she is automatically assumed to be giving less to the "legitimate" recipient. The result is a feeling called jealousy which is generally excused by society unless it is manifested in a fashion that is too dangerous (e.g., murder). Even then, . . . it is often excused. We frequently hear about the "problems" a new father experiences as his wife "withdraws" some of her love to focus it on the new child. It is not unusual for people to be jealous of a spouse's or lover's same-sexed friends. Mother-in-law "problems," about which so many jokes abound, are often reflecting the same phenomenon. Most serious are the problems that develop around one spouse's sexual and/or emotional "unfaithfulness" to the other. Why do we say that a married person who engages in sexual intercourse with another to whom she or he is not married is "cheating"? The very word carries the connotation that the "cheating" spouse is taking something that rightfully belongs to the cheated-upon person; one's gain constitutes the other's loss.

The emotion we call love is not a zero-sum game. We are just not that limited in our emotional energies. Humans are capable of loving many others at the same time as well as serially (and, in fact, often do so). Indeed, it is unlikely that any one individual can ever fill all of another person's emotional needs. To gain a full life and have a variety of their needs met, humans must develop deep emotional commitments to more than one individual and in more than one way.

PLATONIC RELATIONSHIPS

The widespread if subtle acceptance of a zero-sum concept of love helps to ensure that many loving relationships, especially platonic love for a member of the opposite sex, will be less re-warding and long-lived than they might otherwise be. Most Americans suspect that platonic relationships between a male and a female are something other than they appear. Husbands or male lovers, even more than their female counterparts, are apt to react to such relationships on the part of their mates with suspicion and jealousy. They are apt, in other words, to interpret such a friendship in terms of an increase in the cost of the relationship and a diminution of the rewards, thus creating an element of instability in both relationships. According to tradition and the masculine mystique, wives and female lovers are property not to be shared with others. Any hint of such sharing places the male in particular in an extremely embarrassing situation among his peers and undercuts his own feelings of masculinity. In most societies few insults are worse than accusing a man of being cuckolded by his wife or girl-friend; it is grounds for divorce in virtually every state even when no other grounds exist, although adultery is not always automatic grounds for a wife seeking divorce. Moreover, jealousy and a zero-sum concept of love (i.e., strict monogamy) cannot possibly be inherent in our species, given all the societies in which polygamy and polyandry have functioned.

Thus any attempt at a close platonic relationship between a male and a female will elicit suspicions if either is romantically committed to someone else. If, however, they are not committed to others, such a relationship will create ungrounded assumptions arising from stereotyped notions of how the sexes "ought" to relate to one another. Both male and female sex role stereotypes encourage individuals to define members of the opposite gender in broadly sexual terms. Females are taught to view males primarily as potential mates or husbands, namely, the objects of TRUE LOVE. Males learn to view females primarily as sex objects to be exploited if possible, married if necessary.

Indeed, it is not altogether unfair to view our cultural notions pertaining to sex, especially for males, in terms of war. Sex is often used as a method of proving dominance rather than a means of communication and mutual pleasure. In extreme cases we call this "rape," but the same general mentality exists in much of what passes for "normal" sexual activity, especially for males (Millett, 1970, p. 44). For many men the way to end an argument is to initiate sex. Our slang terms relating to sexual intercourse also generally reflect this attitude. "Screwing" refers both to copulation and exploitation, and one can be "laid" in bed or "laid out" in a fight; "balled" in love or "balled out" in punishment; "fucked" sexually or in terms of being "taken" or exploited; "banged" in bed or with a gun. The male sexual organ is also characterized by slang expressions emphasizing dominance: a "cock" is a fighting bird; a "prick" is something that produces pain.

In short, the one way in which neither sex is taught to view the other is as potential friends and peers. Thus in any platonic relationship there is a built-in dynamic encouraging one or both participants to redefine the situation by "falling in love." Generally, either both do, in which case TRUE LOVE results, or one alone does, in which case the relationship becomes uncomfortable and is usually abruptly terminated.

Even though platonic relationships between males and females tend to be short-lived and unstable, they cast a very interesting light on contemporary sex role phenomena. Typically, the relationship begins with the male approaching a female he knows in order to confide something and/or seek advice. Or he asks her for a date and they then discover that, although they are not sexually attracted, they do like one another. In either case the stereotypical prerogative of male initiation of cross-gender interaction is maintained, even when the purpose is clearly not sexual or romantic. Many males confide things to female friends they would never broach with other males. Basically the masculine stereotype discourages males from speaking openly with one another about their fears, anxieties, or weaknesses. It fosters intellectualizing, bravado and competitiveness among males, all of which are directly antithetical to more intimate personal exchanges. As a result, males often seek the ear of a nonthreatening female for such purposes. But notice how strongly the two sex role stereotypes are reflected in this. His expectation is that she will function basically as a compassionate, even ego-boosting listener and make few such demands in return; she usually supports such expectations. If, perchance, she attempts to elicit the same attention from him that she gives to him, she will often find a bored expression, an attempt to change the subject, or a quick excuse for leaving. His rewards are obvious, his costs few. Her motivations are more difficult to comprehend. Probably she remains in it because her ego is boosted simply by virtue of the fact that a member of the superior caste has "chosen" her—for whatever purpose. Moreover, she is being given the opportunity to perform the kinds of expressive functions she has been taught to value so highly.

ROMANTIC RELATIONSHIPS

However influential sex roles are in shaping platonic relationships, they are that much more powerful in their effects on romantic male-female interactions. It is probably the case that truly open and honest communication, mutual respect, and the concomitant emotions of warmth and deep affection can only result from interaction among equals (O'Neill and O'Neill, 1972). Yet the genders are anything but equal in this society and most others. To put it bluntly, in most such relationships the male has considerably more power, resulting from his provider function, from those myriad personality differences instilled in the two genders by socialization and, if need be, from his superior physical strength. Sexual attraction, protectiveness, dependency, and a host of other emotions can all develop among people who are unequal (even masters and slaves in times past sometimes held such feelings for one another), but not the TRUE LOVE or the equalitarian, companionate marriages lauded in the media and found so rarely in reality (Gillespie, 1971; Safilios-Rothschild, 1972). As long as our culture maintains two different and unequal sex role stereotypes that enable people to explore a mere half of their human potential, interpersonal relations, and most especially those between males and females, will fall far short of our ideal norms concerning love relationships (Firestone, 1970, chap. 6).

Compounding the inequality of the genders is the fact that our sex role stereotypes have left virtually the entire realm of emotional expression and human caring to femininity. It is difficult to imagine a genuine loving relationship involving the stoical, unemotional, instrumentally oriented, dominating, aggressive, and competitive creature of the masculine stereotype. Moreover, both males and females view a husband's primary function as that of provider; there is no socially defined and sanctioned expectation that he confide, comfort, or share, and without these there is scarcely "love." It is, of course, equally difficult to imagine a male developing deep respect for the scatterbrained, passive, dependent, vain creature who would be "feminine."

Regardless of how contradictory sex roles are to establishing a love relationship, when Dick and Jane come together they generally share many, if not most, of the stereotypical notions of masculinity and femininity. In turn, these shape their expectations of one another and themselves. On the one hand, if they live up to these expectations, their behavior will often prove costly to one another because of the types of considerations discussed above. On the other hand, if either one fails to live up to these expectations, that failure may be defined as a cost or a diminution of rewards by the other. Dick may have a very real need to express his emotions, maybe even to cry; he may have dependency needs and a whole host of other traits that belie his masculinity. And Jane really may not be all that passive; moreover, she might be a straight A student and very competitive and aggressive. As their relationship deepens and a broader range of their behavior repertoires is revealed (often long after marriage), they begin to see signs of these unexpected traits in one another.

From that point that relationship may go in a number of directions. It may simply end as one or both find that the costs of having their expectations unmet is too high. When this occurs people later look back and wonder what it was they ever saw in him or her. Such a response usually results only if the pair has not yet made a binding commitment to one another, but the relatively high divorce rate today attests to the fact that it may occur even after such a commitment has been made. If, however, the mutual "profits" derived from other aspects of the relationship are great enough, the couple may grope toward redefining those expectations and ultimately rejecting society's stereotypes. Although this solution may bring with it real human growth and a more satisfying relationship, it is painful, and because of this, it is perhaps not too widespread. Probably the most common solution if the two are married, and especially if they have children, is the sort of compromise that eventually shatters whatever emotional ties may have existed: they simply attempt to ignore the discrepancies and work around them.

Let us explore this last option more closely. Dick and Jane are unwilling or unable to reject the stereotypes they have internalized and strike out as "deviants" in relatively uncharted directions; they are also unwilling to separate (because of "the children," the new house, their religion, whatever). At this point they turn to manipulation, play-acting, withdrawal, and a variety of means of displacement in an attempt to have their needs and expectations met. Let us suppose that Jane is really a very aggressive and competitive person. She cannot directly manifest these traits and still appear "feminine" to herself and her mate. What she can and does do, often quite unconsciously, is express these personality attributes by nagging, flattering, and manipulating Dick; she uses "feminine wiles" to get her way (Hacker, 1951, p. 65). She nags him to do better on the job, pushing him ever harder to "succeed" while belittling his efforts. She does this not so much because of the new car she claims to want as for the vicarious thrill of experiencing competition and success through him.

Hanna Papanek (1973) has recently coined the term "two-person career" in examining the vicarious ways in which wives share their husbands' occupational fortunes. Were she out competing in the world herself, she would have no need to displace her needs by badgering her husband. Or maybe Jane likes to dominate. She cannot go out and obtain a position of power; moreover, Dick refuses to be directly dominated. Her response is to develop timely "headaches" when he wants to engage in sex; she openly flirts with his best friend at a party; she belittles him in public or gives away the punch line to the joke he is telling. In short, those unpleasant qualities of nagging, whining, manipulating, perhaps even frigidity attributed so often to wives result largely from the fact that in trying to conform to their sex role stereotype many Janes find that they are left without direct expression of much of their personality (Greer, 1970, especially pp. 281–89). Ironically, the state of being married, to which they have devoted so much of their attention since youth, is a highly disadvantageous one for most females, who nonetheless spend their lives thinking "if only (I was different, he was different, etc.) life would be bliss." Research has repeatedly shown that wives are more unhappy in their marriages than husbands (Bernard, 1971).

What is Dick doing in response to Jane's behavior and to his own unsatisfied needs? In the first place, unlike Jane, Dick never expected his entire life to revolve around the marital relationship. Thus he is psychologically in a position to use both her behavior and his needs as a justification for various forms of withdrawal. He withdraws affection from her; spends his time at home glued to the TV, a book, the newspaper, a hobby; stays late at work or takes a second job. All of these can be forms of withdrawal from an unpleasant relationship. Ultimately he spends less and less time at home and more time with "the guys" or a succession of girl friends who "understand him" and his needs. Another reaction Dick may have is to engage in never-ending "put-downs," denigrating his mate's abilities and intellect and thus her "right" to belittle or even disagree with him. In turn, this behavior feeds back and exacerbates his wife's nagging and whining. It is also not uncommon for him to react to his mate with various degrees of physical violence or threats of violence. This is most frequent among those in the lower classes (Komarovski, 1967, p. 227).

In all of this Dick has one strong advantage over Jane. He, unlike she (if she is a housewife), has the world outside the home in which to seek satisfaction of his needs. Given the current isolated nuclear family structure, if he can't satisfy her needs she has very few options. In the relatively

happy circumstance that they "deviate" from their sex roles in congruent fashion—for instance, he by being dependent, she by being domineering—they can switch roles. In doing so, however, they will frequently reap the sneers and scorn of others. Mostly, the war between the sexes goes on in millions of homes, each skirmish helping to ensure that the next will be worse (Jones, 1970). A vicious circle develops in which her unpleasant behavior elicits withdrawal, denigration, or violence from him, which in turn results in worse behavior by her and more reaction by him. Communication, respect, and affection are all casualties of trying to live within the straitjacket of the sex role stereotypes.

While the picture just presented may represent something of an extreme, elements of it are undoubtedly present in a very large proportion of marriages. Given this, one can only view the relatively high divorce rate with optimism. If nothing else, it represents an attempt on the part of millions to opt out of relationships that bring out the worst human traits and seem to grant so little by way of rewards for so many (Scanzoni, 1972, chap. 4). From this point of view divorce is hardly the "failure" it is frequently pictured. Rather, it may represent significant human growth for one or both of the former spouses.

There are also many cases where the partners comfortably conform to the relevant sex role stereotype, and he, she, or they have so strongly internalized them that the kinds of displacements suggested above do not occur. If both have done so, conflict is probably minimal, but so too are genuine sharing and two-way communication; the masculine role particularly, has hardly prepared a male to enter a close, open relationship, nor would the power differential encourage it. The situation in which both sex role stereotypes are conformed to is probably increasingly rare in today's world of flux, although it might possibly have been the norm in more traditonal times and places. Such a relationship would tend to be quite stable. If only the female has truly internalized her role, her partner will face different kinds of problems than those already discussed. Instead of a bitchy, nagging, manipulative spouse, he will find himself saddled with a human being who is virtually totally dependent upon him for the fulfillment of all her needs, for making all the decisions, and so on. Moreover, such a wife will be of little help to him in coping with whatever insecurities he may have. What starts out to be an ego trip quickly becomes a heavy burden for many modern men. Few honest males today would deny that such overwhelming responsibility is exremely difficult and unpleasant, as well as constricting to their own lives. If only the male has fully internalized his role, his mate is likely to respond in the manner delineated earlier and become manipulative and nagging in an effort to extract more open affection and attention, as well as more power in the decision-making process.

In general, the less similar the daily activities and interests of the male and female (or of any two people) (i.e., the more stringent the sexual division of labor), the more difficult communication and understanding between the two are likely to be. Perhaps ironically, males have been found to be more willing to engage in household and child-rearing activities than females are willing to allow them to do so, especially as the years go by in a marriage (Safilios-Rothschild, 1972, p. 67). By the time children arrive, most couples have developed a fairly precise and stereotyped division of labor that often serves to encourage further deterioration in the relationship. Wives and mothers jealously guard the only realm of activity that is socially defined as their legitimate preserve, resisting any but the most minimal efforts by their husbands to engage in them ("because they are inept"). After a while the husband who has been ejected from the kitchen and nursery no longer offers his services at all. This provides his harried wife with an excuse to play the "martyr" and proclaim his lack of appreciation for her efforts, and him with the opportunity to complain about the disorganized state of their home. Again, we have come full circle to find her complaining and him withdrawing.

At this point the natural question arises concerning the possibility of a long-term loving relationship between a male and female working out happily. Such a relationship is possible, but probably only if the two are willing to engage in the difficult tasks of overcoming many aspects of the traditional sex role stereotypes and striking out in new directions that allow both to explore their human potential more fully. A first but by no means sole requisite for this is equality between the two parties, and one important road to equality is for the female to be actively engaged in self-fulfilling activities outside the home. Research has consistently indicated that working wives, especially those with a "career" as opposed to a mere "job," have more power in the decision-making process *vis-à-vis* their mates than housewives (Scanzoni, 1972, p. 69). It is reasonable to assume also that such women will find more direct fulfillment of their own personal needs and develop more self-confidence, both of which are necessary to a mature relationship.

The basic fact remains that females and males who attempt to conform to their sex role stereotypes enter romantic relationships with one another based on the supposition that their partner will behave in certain predictable ways. They also assume that such behaviors will serve to fulfill one another's needs. This assumption is largely false, given the fact that feminine needs involve receiving affection, while the masculine stereotype by and large discourages the open expression of emotion. In addition, females expect more personal gratification from a marital relationship than do males, who look more to their work for life satisfaction (Safilios-Rothschild, 1972, p. 67).

It is increasingly unlikely today that either partner truly conforms to these stereotypes and hence to the other's expectations. Nor is our accepted courtship system, . . . likely to reveal many of these disparities until after a binding commitment between the pair has taken place. When you add to this the fact that many males have the opportunity to grow and change in their daily contact with the world, while many females find themselves mentally shrinking in the isolation of their homes and the heavy menial requirements of housework, the probability of any real understanding between the two shrinks even further. The result is millions of families in which frustrated women who feel unappreciated, unloved, and impotent face hostile men who feel exploited as "meal tickets" and react by withdrawing psychically and physically from the relationship. As often as not, they maintain this way of life for the dubious "sake of the children."

Parents and Children

Soon after an American couple marries, pressure by parents and friends to produce children begins, to become a clamor within a few years. As Ellen Peck puts it, people don't ask *if* you are planning to have children, they ask *when* (1971, p. 171). The childless couple is almost as socially deviant as the husbandless woman. Couples who choose not to ever have children are labeled selfish, immature, immoral, or just plain peculiar. Most, of course, desire children; even if the husband does not, his wife has learned to view this as her primary mission in life. Among those who don't, most eventually succumb to the pressure and have them anyway.

Once a couple conforms in this respect, the same society that encouraged their parenthood and prides itself on being so child-centered proceeds to do very little by way of manifesting any further interest in the child. Unlike most European societies, we have no children's allowance (except the humiliating A.F.D.C.); few inexpensive, well-run child-care centers; little provision for ensuring adequate health care for children; and a penchant for turning down school bond issues. In short, once a couple has had a child it becomes solely their responsibility and, in reality, *hers*. This is not an irrelevant fact, given estimates that for a family to raise two children, send them to college, and forego the wife's potential income costs between $80,000 and

$150,000! Before the society will intervene in any way the parents must abuse the child to the point of near murder, a not infrequent and rapidly increasing occurrence.

Most couples probably need to make less adjustments to marriage than they do to parenthood (Lopata, 1971, chap. 4). Husband–wife roles may flow fairly smoothly from the girl friend–boy friend ones. This is especially true if, as is typically the case today, the female continues to work or go to school and if the couple lives in an apartment where housekeeping chores are relatively minimal. The assumption of father and mother roles, however, is usually a completely new experience, and it often entails radical adjustments in both of their individual lives as well as in the nature of their interaction. For those who planned the pregnancy, the news is often greeted with euphoria. The husband becomes extremely attentive to his spouse and to her "mystical" condition. Indeed, females often desire pregnancy precisely to elicit such attention. Very soon after the birth, if not somewhat before, this starts changing. He begins to resent the intrusion of the newcomer on his previously exclusive "turf"; she generally ceases employment (at precisely the time expenses have increased) and begins to perceive the realm of the house and child as more or less exclusively hers—in short, it is at this juncture that she turns into the traditional housewife (Gavron, 1966, p. 135). All of the problems enumerated in the preceding section either surface at this time or are exacerbated if they were manifested previously. Far from "bringing a couple closer together," as myth would have it, the arrival of a child strains any but the most solid

relationships between parents (Peck, 1971, pp. 15–16 and 20 ff.).

MOTHER–CHILD RELATIONS

Young Jane begins learning the mother role when she receives her first doll at about age 2 or 3. If she has a younger sibling, she is probably encouraged to aid in its care. As just about the single most important aspect of the total feminine role complex, motherhood is romanticized and taught to a greater or lesser extent from early youth (Peck, 1971, p. 18 ff.). MOTHERHOOD IS FULFILLMENT! shout the media, the "helping professions," Madison Avenue, and the corporations which see babies as consumers and a high birth rate as a business bonanza. As a social role motherhood is relatively precisely defined, and its obligations are broadly agreed upon by members of the many diverse subcultures that comprise American society. Mother is expected to be responsible for the daily physical and health care of the child from birth until at least adolescence. She is responsible for monitoring the child's emotional and intellectual development. She is expected to function as the chief mediator between the family on the one hand, and school, church, and the families of the child's friends on the other. Particularly during the preschool years, she is chiefly responsible for amusing the child or seeing to it that someone else does. Above all, mother is held to be the major emotional mainstay of the child: the constant provider of unconditional affection, understanding, and moral support. These things are expected of mothers regardless of their education, social class, interests, abilities, mental health, and so forth.

The theoretical basis of these social expectations is the simple fact that, usually, it was the woman's body that carried and eventually gave birth to the child. Myth has it that the process of being pregnant and giving birth magically results in instant "mother love," namely, an overwhelming desire to nurture and care for all the needs of her offspring for the next 15 or 20 years of life (Lopata, 1971, p. 35). If, indeed, "nature" provided such an urge we could scarcely account for the large numbers of mothers who neglect, abuse, and abandon their children, not to mention the even larger number who peform their maternal tasks poorly. Nor could we account for the deep "maternal" love people of both genders often develop for children they did not physically conceive. The fact of the matter is that a *social* injunction is placed on virtually all females to be mothers, to do the required types of things and develop the "appropriate" emotions, as outlined above (Peck, 1971, chap. 5). The context in which the role of motherhood is normally played in contemporary America is that of the small, isolated nuclear family with only two or three children. When grandparents are present in middle-class white families, they tend to be excluded from serious participation in family life. Moreover, most "experts" and public opinion maintain that the only way in which one can adequately play the mother role, especially when children are young, is for the specific woman who is the mother to be constantly accessible, that is, not employed outside the home. This again is enjoined without regard to the particular mother's interests or abilities, unless she is poor.

The ramifications of these circumstances for children and for mother–child relations (not to mention the mothers themselves) are relatively disastrous. Until quite recently in history most people lived in extended families consisting usually of at least three generations, a number of adults of both sexes, and a number of children of various ages and both genders. A child was reared in a microcosm of the world in which it would probably live as an adult. It had a variety of role models and a variety of inputs to its developing behaviors and attitudes. With a number of adults and older children to share the responsibility, a young child was not an overwhelming burden to any one individual; its many needs could be easily met because there were many people to meet them. If the biological mother lacked in any way the interest or ability to fulfill the many and varied responsibilities entailed in child rearing, there were always others to make up for the deficiency. Larger families precluded concentrating close attention and scrutiny on every move of the child; they discouraged an intense, all-consuming interest in any one individual. In this way they encouraged cooperativeness and discouraged extreme ego-centeredness. Moreover, they necessitated active contributions on the part of all but the very youngest, thus giving all family members functional roles and a concomitant sense of importance. In fact, the very concept of "childhood" as a distinct stage during which individuals are treated in a markedly different manner from adults is only a few centuries old at most (Firestone, 1970, chap. 4).

By contrast, the modern middle-class mother has little choice but to lavish attention on her few children, and she is strongly encouraged by society to focus on the most minor details of their daily existence. Barraged by a constant stream of "expert" opinions on child development, she scrutinizes every aspect of the child's life, apprehensive lest she damage its psyche or fail to recognize and correct some "abnormality." Ironically, in the process she works harder than her predecessors, with their larger families and lack of modern conveniences. The children, in turn, have few other adults present during their waking hours to turn to or emulate. They exist, by and large, in a world of children their own age and even sex which bears little resemblance to that which lies outside the home, and they have few if any functional roles to fulfill to give them a sense of worth. Young mothers, bound to children during virtually all their waking hours and almost alone responsible for fulfilling all their needs (as well as performing all the other household duties) quite frequently find themselves harried, exhausted, and frustrated. They periodically explode with anger for minor infractions of rules by their offspring and subsequently feel guilty at their own reactions. Survey the mid-afternoon or late-morning scene at any supermarket and you will see this drama endlessly played. Years later, these same mothers are reluctant to allow their children the independence that spells the end of their only major functional role in life.

But the problem only begins here for many women. The same aggressive, dominant, ambitious wife who must live vicariously through her husband because she is prohibited by her sex role from direct and constructive expression of these traits will do the same to her children—and especially her male offspring. If she can dominate no one else, she can at least wield power over her young (Sexton, 1969, chap. 3). Little Dick *must* be the best athlete, get top grades, be most popular, in short, *succeed;* little Jane *must* be the prettiest girl in her class with the best wardrobe, best in dancing and piano lessons, have the most dates, and so forth. Mother vests all of her pent-up energies and needs on her two or three children, dragging them from one organized activity to another, lavishing attention on their "progress" that is reminiscent of a horticulturist in a hothouse. She ends up putting incredible pressure on them to be not themselves but some version of her own dreams. Her self-definition becomes that of her offspring (the final insult occurs when her husband begins referring to her as "mother" or "mom"). Dick can't grow up to be a plumber rather than a lawyer, nor can Jane marry the former rather than the latter; it would reflect badly on mother. She comes to expect that the costs in terms of work and "sacrifice" for her children will be repaid in terms of rewards accrued from a vicarious thrill in their successes.

In the past decade middle-class adolescents (and even younger children) have found their own ways of striking back at all this close scrutiny and pressure. They have committed suicide, run away from home, and become juvenile delinquents in unprecedented numbers; they have turned to an escapist drug culture; they have created an entire youth culture designed to flout the most cherished ambitions of the adult world. Far from being the result of a "permissive" upbringing, these phenomena have resulted from a pressure-cooker environment in which they are pressured to perform well a series of nonfunctional activities. Without the daily inputs of a variety of adults, without the independence that can only arise from a studied *lack* of attention to all aspects of their daily existence, without meaningful roles to fulfill during the many years before they finish school, youths have a difficult time trying to develop a clear sense of themselves as self-reliant, independent, responsible human beings with some sense of purpose in life (Friedan, 1973, chap. 12; Grønseth, 1971–72, p. 13).

Motherhood cannot be an all-encompassing activity, for the sake of both the mothers and the offspring. Quantity of attention (past some absolute minimum) is simply not an important consideration in how children "turn out." A few hours a day of intensive, loving, high "quality" attention to a child by a mother who is happily growing and fulfilling herself the rest of the time is worth infinitely more than the never-ending hours of incessant bickering that passes for child rearing in so many homes today. Try as they might, researchers have failed to document any substantial differences in adjustment, happiness, and so forth between children of working mothers and those of housewives. In fact, it seems to be the case that children of nonworking mothers who wish they *were* working suffer the most, and youngsters whose mothers work are generally more self-reliant than others (Bird, 1968, p. 182; Friedan, 1963, p. 186). If mother love means anything, it must involve encouraging a child to fulfill its own potential—not to live the life its mother would have liked to live had she not been bound by social convention. It means raising a child who is capable of functioning without her (by providing a model of an independent person) and then encouraging that offspring to do just that. It is difficult to imagine how our current family structure, combined with our definitions of motherhood and of the feminine sex role, can function to permit that kind of mother love to thrive.

FATHER–CHILD RELATIONS

The role of fatherhood is very dissimilar to that of motherhood in three crucial ways. First, it is a very minor part of the total masculine role constellation; it ranks relatively low on the list of priorities a male is likely to have, and he is not strongly sanctioned socially for playing this role either well or poorly. Second, our society does not have a precise, agreed-upon definition of the components of this role, beyond the ever-present obligation to "provide" in economic terms. Finally, almost nothing in the prefatherhood learning of most males is oriented in any way to training them for this role (Brenton, 1966, p. 130 ff.). They are actively discouraged as children from play activites involving baby surrogates, and, except in rare instances of large families with few or no older sisters, they are not usually required to help much in the daily care of younger siblings. In short, a new father has only the vaguest idea of what he is expected to do and how he ought to do it, and often his commitment to the role in the first place is marginal.

Females are prompted in part to have babies because society has continually informed them that their primary function in life is motherhood. Males are under little such direct social pressure to become parents, except as it is exerted through their wives. It is not surprising, then, that males are generally somewhat less enthusiastic about the prospect of parenthood (Peck, 1971, p. 19) and may in fact face it with grave trepidation. They may fear the added financial obligation and the decreased freedom to come and go at will, as well as a decline in attention from their wives. Counterbalancing this is the vague notion, especially within some ethnic subcultures and the lower classes, that to father a child "proves" one's potency, hence one's "masculinity." Indeed, much opposition to vasectomy or male sterilization results from an erroneous confusion (not altogether at the intellectual level) of male fertility and sexual potency. Related to this is the masculine emphasis on "productivity"; fathering children comes to be viewed as a kind of sexual productivity, and later the offspring themselves may be viewed as products more or less "owned" by the father.

In the past fatherhood was a rather more clearly defined role than today. Father was the chief disciplinarian; mother's threat of "wait 'till your father comes home and hears of this" was enough to quell the most obstreperous child. Today mother is more willing and father less so to engage in such tasks; discipline is no longer a critical component of the father role as distinct from parenthood in general. Before the Industrial Revolution, father was also the chief mentor of his sons, passing on his craft or trade through an apprenticeship program begun early in the child's life. In the remote and complex work world of postindustrial society this task has been virtually abandoned, devolving instead on for-

mal institutions, most notably schools. In simpler times father the fount of all knowledge, the mary educator of his children. To his well-educated spouse is usually more available and as well equipped as he to answer children's questions, if indeed anyone in the family is capable of so doing.

In recent decades countless popular articles and books have encouraged father to be a "pal" to his children—especially his sons, who spend their days in a virtually maleless environment. Simultaneously, the "experts" have warned him not to be "*too much* of a pal"—to remain authoritative and, when needed, capable of discipline. He is enjoined to somehow avoid both being an ogre and being "permissive," yet he is given little time or opportunity to learn how to walk this tightrope (Brenton, 1966, pp. 120–21). His major responsibility remains his work, and now he has even greater financial needs than before he had children. For the up-and-coming middle-class businessman or professional, this means that he will rarely even see his young children awake. The working-class father, pressured by financial need to work overtime or at a second job, will also rarely see his children. Yet when such fathers find that their eight-year-old sons are incapable of throwing a ball decently or are too "tied to mother's apron strings," they react with guilt and a sudden burst of attention. Even then they are hampered by their sex role. The "masculine mystique" has discouraged males from learning to relate to people, including children, in a compassionate, warm, open, affectionate manner. The instrumental orientation they have been taught all their lives leads them to praise their children's successes but ill equips them to sympathize with their bumbling errors. They are thus able to offer "conditional affection" only.

Moreover, if father is not very successful at work, he (like his mate) is apt to pressure his children, especially the males, to succeed in order to enjoy a vicarious compensation for the failures and frustrations he has experienced. Caught in the "success ethic" himself, he is likely to stress achievement more strongly than just about anything else (Brenton, 1966, p. 138 ff.), thus perpetuating this component of the masculine mystique. When father proudly proclaims "This is *my* son," he is engaging in that "ego trip" that says, "If I have succeeded in nothing else, look at what I have produced." In the process he forgets that he took little part in the actual upbringing of the child, not to mention the fact that the child was the one who actually accomplished whatever it was that elicited the outburst.

By and large most fathers, especially in the white middle class, probably relate very little to their children during infancy and early childhood, perceiving them as more or less of a nuisance (Peck, 1971, chap. 6). Later, often much to the anger of the mother, they may return slightly from their withdrawal. They take the children (usually the sons) to interesting places and engage them briefly in the kind of exciting play for which the harried and exhausted mother has little time or energy. They buy them special things (not their everyday needs like clothes and school supplies). They occasionally "flirt" with and heap praise upon their dressed-up daughters (one of the few things many fathers actually do with daughters). They teach their sons sports and hobbies. They badger them to succeed in school and in sports and tend to reward them only contingent upon such success. In short, fathers do not actively partake of the petty, daily problems and needs of their offspring; they remain tangential to the intimate lives of their children, involved only in the "special" moments of excitement or disaster. In most cases, fathers refuse to even engage in physical contact with their sons past infancy, preferring the handshake to the kiss. All too often a divorce between the parents reduces the quantity and quality of the father's interaction with his children little, if any (assuming they all remain in the same geographical vicinity), and occasionally even increases it because of the guilt involved.

Motherhood is often said to have a humanizing effect on women because of their intimate daily contact with a developing child, with all its strengths and frailties. To the extent that fathers do not actively engage themselves in their children's daily growth process, in the minor changes in their offsprings' abilities and activities, the experience of paternity will not result in their own human growth. Once again the sex role stereotype is responsible for a vicious and unrewarding circle: ill equipped by the masculine stereotype to deal with children on a deep emotional ("expressive") level, caught in an often all-consuming devotion to work and economic success, the father fails to involve himself in his child's life to the extent necessary to ultimately develop the more humane and compassionate aspects of his personality which might, in turn, make him better able to relate to his offspring. The nature and costs of both sex role stereotypes, combined with the isolated nuclear family structure characteristic of this society, have thus resulted in parent–child relations that fall far short of our cherished social ideals and, in the process, create numerous problems for the next generation of adults.

Same-sexed Friendships

It might seem that if sex role stereotypes are irrelevant to any type of interpersonal relationship, it would be in friendships between members of the same gender. The fact that this is not the case underlines the all-pervasive quality of such stereotypes in virtually every aspect of human existence.

MALE FRIENDSHIPS

From early childhood males are encouraged to form friendship and peer groups with other members of their gender, and to cooperate with other males for the achievement of mutually desired goals, often in competition with other all-male groups. . . . the play activites of young males foster the formation of such relationships, and they scarcely end at adolescence. "Bonded males," or all-male groups, as Lionel Tiger (1970) argues, persist throughout life, be they for work, war, sport, poker, or "drinking buddies." Moreover, a rudimentary kind of superior "caste consciousness" that begins in childhood encourages males to shun the companionship of females for ordinary friendship purposes. It is not unusual for females to be informed more or less explicitly by male colleagues or fellow students that they have enough (male) friends; what they want is a sexual partner, or nothing. When they find their family life becoming unpleasant, males look to other males even more for companionship, often developing a virtual woman-hating fraternity (Fast, 1971, chap. 2).

The same masculine stereotype that encourages male friendships, however, often seriously limits the scope and content of such relationships (Booth, 1972, p. 186), as suggested in the discussion above of male–female platonic relationships. Male friendships are characterized by a kind of rough-and-ready camaraderie. Males will usually be found *doing* something together (fishing, bowling, tinkering with machinery, working). When they are "merely" talking to one another it will usually be on a "light" subject (sports, some "dish" who works in the office), or they may engage in generalized "bitching" about their mates; other topics are approached in an abstract, intellectualized manner. What they are very rarely found doing is talking to one another on an intimate basis about their deepest needs and insecurities. As one male put it who was attempting to organize a men's consciousness-raising group similar to those existing among feminists:

> A salient observation . . . involved an increasing awareness of how annoying the employment of men's values can be. Among such traits observed were dominating, interrupting, condescension, disrespect, aggression, obsession with sex, ego, intellectualization, put downs, and a lack of empathy, emotion, openness, warmth and contact with persons as human beings, rather than as competitors for power and position (Farrell, 1971–72, pp. 21–22).

Two major aspects of the masculine sex role discourage intimacy among American males. First, they are taught it is "unmanly" to show most emotions or to express dependency needs. Second, the aggressiveness and power orientation of the masculine role encourages males to view each other as competitors for status, and one hardly reveals weakness to a competitor. "One-upmanship" is primarily a masculine game. A pervasive fear of being labeled "homosexual" that is particularly endemic to American males exacerbates these tendencies further; a male who approaches another male on too intimate a basis fears being interpreted as making an improper "pass" (Fast, 1971, pp. 19 and 104–7).

I recall a very amusing incident nearly ten years ago that helps to highlight this national male phobia. Six people were temporarily traveling together; four males, myself, and another female. We reached a city where cheap hotel space was very scarce, so we decided to spend the night crammed into one room. There were only two double beds, and we drew lots to see who was to sleep on the floor and who was to get which beds. Two male American college students who were traveling together for the entire summer drew the lots that gave them one double bed. We awoke to find both, fully dressed, virtually falling off opposite sides of the bed. The very next evening we had occasion to watch two French males, about the same age and patently not homosexual, share a single bed when other facilities were unavailable. They awoke in their underclothes, tangled around one another, and thought it quite funny.

The old adage that males will talk to one another in quite explicit terms about females they don't care for but say little if anything about those they love is also indicative of the level of communication in all-male groups.

Sexual prowess is acceptable conversation, emotional commitment is not; the former grants prestige, the latter, if anything, takes it away. The many hours that males spend in one another's presence are rewarding in that they serve primarily to satisfy their needs for amusement, the accomplishment of instrumental goals, and prestige. Status and prestige, however, are relative; by definition someone is always on the bottom. Those males whose prestige among their peers is low are thus impelled to look to the lower caste to resurrect their bruised egos, a role most females know only too well. At any rate, the nature of males' expectations of one another makes it appear far too costly to attempt to push such relationships to a deeper level (Fasteau, 1972). Thus many are left with unmet emotional needs which, as we have seen, are not easily satisfied in their long-term relationships with females, either.

FEMALE FRIENDSHIPS

Females face almost exactly the opposite problems from males in their friendships. They have a more difficult time forming relationships with members of their own sex and do so with less frequency than males, but when they succeed such friendships are qualitatively deeper and more intimate (Booth, 1972). In a study of the aged, Marjorie Lowenthal and Clayton Haven (1968) found that females were more likely to have a confidant than males, and that the younger the respondents the more pronounced the differences between males and females in this regard. Moreover, among women husbands were least frequently mentioned as confidants, while among males wives were most frequently designated (p. 28). The nature of such female friendships is strongly rooted in the sex role stereotype.

Girls are not encouraged to participate in games that foster cooperation and camaraderie. More importantly, from adolescence females are taught that their major task is to outshine other members of their gender sufficiently to attract and then hold the best possible mate. In centering the female's self-definition around that of the male she will eventually attract and wed, the feminine sex role encourages a kind of constant competition between all members of the sex; the most important aspect of their entire lives rests directly on a never-ending war of all against all. We have all heard repeatedly that women "hate" other women. Unlike the kind of competition fostered among males, this does not in the least entail group cooperation for the purpose of competing. Indeed, best friends among young females often specifically and explicitly exempt the realm of "boys" from their friendship. Males will usually avoid dating a friend's girl friend, to preclude rejection by peers. Females are bound by no such code. From early childhood females learn to size themselves up relative to other females, especially in appearance and "charm," and this habit becomes lifelong for most (Pogrebin, 1972). Matrons enter a party and, while their spouses eyeball the opposite sex, they scrutinize the "competition," namely, members of their own gender, always insecure lest they lose their mate to a better looking woman. The clothing and cosmetic industries have been extraordinarily successful in extracting huge sums of money from females for constant fashion changes precisely because of this mentality.

The isolation caused by this orientation is further encouraged by the isolation of the daily activities of the housewife. Each little nuclear family lives in its own "cell"—be it a 3-room apartment or a 20-room mansion—and each is more or less self-contained as to the tools and appliances needed for its functioning. Housewives need not cooperate with any other females to accomplish their daily tasks, except perhaps in rare emergencies. The result is that for many the only females they know are the wives of their husband's friends and the mothers of their children's playmates, with whom they may not have much in common personally. Tied to their homes and to a heavy, time-consuming schedule of household and child-rearing duties, many women have little opportunity to meet other females who share their own interests and points of view, as distinct from those of other family members. It is here that the female's submergence of her own identity in those of her husband and offspring becomes most evident and most costly.

Against all these odds, most females do get to know other females and form close friendships. Housewives often find that they have a lot in common with their husband's friends' wives and their children's playmates' mothers, if for no other reason than that they are all in the same leaky boat. Especially as children grow older, females get out of the house and join voluntary organizations where they meet others with similar interests. Increasingly they go to school or to work and find friends there. Because the feminine sex role stereotype encourages women to express their emotions, needs, and problems without feeling threatened, when and if they get beyond worrying about competition over appearance and males the way is clear for a deep intimate association. Females talk to females about the males they love—not about those with whom they have had fleeting and casual relations. They discuss their own dreams and insecurities, their marital and even sexual problems (often to the profound embarrassment of their mates, if they discover it). The kaffeeklatsch, afternoon of shopping, or weekly bridge game is often an excuse to gather and talk rather than an activity for its own sake. The telephone has greatly aided such interaction among isolated housewives and, in the process, has spawned its share of male jokes about the female's presumably excessive use of that instrument.

Ironically, some of those very qualities that handicap females most in the world of work and in interactions with males enable them to experience far richer interactions with others of their own gender. Precisely because of their insecurities and general feelings of inferiority and incompetence, it is possible for power plays, dominance, ego trips and abstracted intellectualizing to be absent from their interactions, while openness, empathy, and compassion can readily flourish. However, all of this is possible only *if and when* they surmount the initial hurdle of competing over appearance and male attention. Nowhere is this more evident than in the relative ease with which the growing numbers of feminist "rap groups" have been able to elicit their members' deepest feelings, compared to the great difficulty experienced by the few male groups that have attempted to do the same.

. . .

Conclusions

This depressing litany of the effects of sex role stereotyping on a wide variety of primary relationships and on human sexual expression is somewhat exaggerated. This has been done in part as a response to the pervasive romanticization of such relationships. However, there can be little doubt that to varying degrees we all relate to other humans in a much constricted manner because of those cultural definitions of masculinity and femininity which have been emphasized and reinforced throughout our lives. We are none of us free to develop truly multifaceted personalities and behavior repertoires in relationship to a number of significant others. Nor are we free to develop our full potential as humans *vis-à-vis* other humans. Another conclusion may also be drawn from this discussion. It would appear that where femininity exacts a high price in the realm of functioning in instrumental roles outside the context of the home, masculinity extracts its greatest toll in the development of rewarding interpersonal relationships within and outside of the family. Were this book written a decade ago, it may well have ended on this bleak note. However, a number of recent developments encourage hope that the heavy burdens of the sex role status quo are beginning to decrease. . . .

References

Abbott, Sidney, and Love, Barbara. *Sappho Was a Right-on Woman: A Liberated View of Lesbianism.* New York: Stein and Day, 1972.

Aldrich, Ann. *Take a Lesbian to Lunch.* New York: MacFadden Bartell, 1972.

Bernard, Jessie. "The Paradox of the Happy

Marriage." In Vivian Gornick and Barbara Moran, *Woman in Sexist Society*, pp. 145–62. New York: Signet Books, 1971.

Bird, Caroline. *Born Female: The High Cost of Keeping Women Down*. New York: David McKay Co., 1968.

Booth, Alan. "Sex and Social Participation." *American Sociological Review* 37 (April 1972): 183–93.

Brenton, Myron. *The American Male*. Greenwich, Conn.: Fawcett Publications, Inc., 1966.

Damon, Gene, "The Least of These: The Minority Whose Screams Haven't Yet Been Heard." In Robin Morgan (ed.), *Sisterhood Is Powerful*, pp. 279–306. New York: Vintage Books, 1970.

Davis, Alan. "Sexual Assaults in the Philadelphia Prison System." In John Gagnon and William Simon (eds.), *The Sexual Scene*, pp. 107–24. Chicago: Aldine Publishing Co., 1970.

Farrell, Warren, T. "Male Consciousness-Raising from a Sociological and Political Perspective." *Sociological Focus* 5 (Winter 1971–72): 19–28.

Fast, Julius. *The Incompatibility of Men and Women*. New York: Avon Books, 1971.

Fasteau, Marc. "Men: Why Aren't We Talking?" *Ms.* (July, 1972): 16.

Firestone, Shulamith. *The Dialectic of Sex*. New York: Bantam Books, 1970.

Friedan, Betty. *The Feminine Mystique*. New York: Dell Publishing, 1963.

Gagnon, John, and Simon, William. "Introduction: Deviant Behavior and Sexual Deviance." In Gagnon and Simon (eds.), *Sexual Deviance*, pp. 1–12. New York: Harper & Row, 1967.

Gavron, Hannah. *The Captive Wife: Conflicts of Household Mothers*. London: Routledge and Kegan Paul, 1966.

Gillespie, Dair L. "Who Has the Power? The Marital Struggle," *Journal of Marriage and the Family* 33 (August 1971): 445–58.

Goldman, Joyce. "Women of Bangladesh." *Ms.* (August, 1972): 84–88.

Goffman, Erving. *The Presentation of Self in Everyday Life*. Garden City, N.Y.: Doubleday Anchor Books, 1959.

Greer, Germaine. *The Female Eunuch*. New York: McGraw-Hill Book Co., 1970.

Grønseth, Erik. "The Husband Provider Role and Its Dysfunctional Consequences." *Sociological Focus* 5 (Winter 1971–72): 10–18.

Hacker, Helen M. "Women as a Minority Group." *Social Forces* 30 (1951): 60–69.

Hedblom, Jack, "Social, Sexual, and Occupational Lives of Homosexual Women." *Sexual Behavior* 2 (October 1972): 33–37.

Homans, George. *Social Behavior: Its Elementary Forms*. New York: Harcourt, Brace and World, 1961.

Hooker, Evelyn. "The Homosexual Community." In John Gagnon and William Simon (eds.), *Sexual Deviance*, pp. 167–184. New York: Harper & Row, 1967.

Jones, Beverly. "The Dynamics of Marriage and Motherhood." In Robin Morgan (ed.), *Sisterhood Is Powerful*, pp. 46–61. New York: Vintage Books, 1970.

Koedt, Anne. "Can Women Love Women?" *Ms.* (Spring 1972): 117–121.

Komarovski, Mirra. *Blue Collar Marriage*. New York: Vintage Books, 1967.

Laws, Judith Long. "A Feminist Review of Marital Adjustment Literature: The Rape of the Locke." *Journal of Marriage and the Family* 33 (August 1971): 483–516.

Lopata, Helena. *Occupation: Housewife*. New York: Oxford University Press, 1971.

Lowenthal, Marjorie Fiske, and Haven, Clayton. "Interaction and Adaptation: Intimacy as a Critical Variable." *American Sociological Review* 33 (February 1968): 20–30.

Marmor, Judd. " 'Normal' and 'Deviant' Sexual Behavior." *The Journal of the American Medical Association* 217 (July 12, 1971): 165–70.

Martin, Del, and Lyon, Phyllis. "Lesbian Love and Sexuality." *Ms.* (July 1972): 74–77 and 123(a).

Martin, Del, and Lyon, Phyllis. *Lesbian/Woman*. New York: Bantam Books, 1972(b).

Millett, Kate. *Sexual Politics*. Garden City, N.Y.: Doubleday, 1970.

Nadle, Marlene. "Prostitutes." In Sookie Stambler (ed.), *Women's Liberation: Blueprint for the Future*, pp. 51–56. New York: Ace Books, 1970.

Newcomb, T. M. *The Acquaintance Process.* New York: Holt Rinehart & Winston, 1961.

O'Neill, Nena, and O'Neill, George. *Open Marriage: A New Life Style for Couples.* New York: M. Evans & Co., 1972.

Papanek, Hanna. "Men, Women, and Work: Reflections on the Two-Person Career." *American Journal of Sociology*, 78 (January 1973): 852–72.

Peck, Ellen. *The Baby Trap.* New York: Pinnacle Books, 1971.

Pogrebin, Letty Cottin. "Competing with Women." *Ms.* (July 1972): 78–81 and 131.

Reiss, Albert J., Jr. "The Social Integration of Queers and Peers." In John Gagnon and William Simon (eds.), *Sexual Deviance,* pp. 197–228. New York: Harper & Row, 1967.

Safilios-Rothschild, Constantina. "Companionate Marriages and Sexual Inequality: Are They Compatible?" In Safilios-Rothschild (ed.), *Toward a Sociology of Women,* pp. 63–70. Lexington, Mass.: Xerox College Publishing, 1972.

Scanzoni, John. *Sexual Bargaining: Power Politics in the American Marriage.* Englewood Cliffs, N.J.: Prentice-Hall, 1972.

Sexton, Patricia Cayo. *The Feminized Male.* New York: Vintage Books, 1969.

Shelley, Martha. "Lesbianism and the Women's Liberation Movement." In Sookie Stambler (ed.), *Women's Liberation: Blueprint for the Future*, pp. 123–29. New York: Ace Books, 1970.

Shelley, Martha. "Women of Lesbos." In *Up Against the Wall, Mother: On Women's Liberation.* Beverly Hills, Calif.: Glencoe Press, 1971.

Simon, William, and Gagnon, John. "The Lesbians: A Preliminary Overview." In Gagnon and Simon (eds.), *Sexual Deviance,* pp. 247–82. New York: Harper & Row, 1967.

Simon, William, and Gagnon, John. "Psychosexual Development." In Gagnon and Simon (eds.), *The Sexual Scene,* pp. 23–41. Chicago: Aldine Publishing Co., 1970.

Strong, Ellen. "The Hooker," In Robin Morgan (ed.), *Sisterhood Is Powerful,* pp. 289–97. New York: Vintage Books, 1970.

Thibault, J. W., and Kelley, H. H. *The Social Psychology of Groups.* New York: John Wiley & Sons, 1959.

Tiger, Lionel. *Men in Groups.* New York: Vintage Books, 1970.

Interpersonal Behavior in Groups

Bobby R. Patton and Kim Giffin

We spend a great amount of our lives in groups of various sorts—the family, friends, teams, work groups, and so on—but rarely do we take the time to stop and observe what is going on within the group; what do the members' behaviors mean? One of our main goals here is to note and categorize some of the behaviors in order that we might become better observers and better participants.

Agenda and Hidden Agenda

In our emphasis on decision-making groups we have stated that a primary reason for people's meeting and forming a group is to accomplish some publicly stated and agreed-upon task. This advertised business is often called the *agenda*, the purpose for which a group meets. A "task force" may be formed to analyze a community problem and recommend courses of action.

A university committee may study graduation requirements with thoughts of revision. A student-faculty committee may meet to decide on entertainment for a homecoming program. This acknowledged purpose of meeting is the formal agenda for the group.

If the task is clear, the procedures established, the leader competent, and the members committed, it would seem that the group would work logically and progressively to an intelligent consensus. We all know, however, that groups do not always follow logical, progressive patterns to intelligent conclusions. Harsh feelings, emotional harangues, irrelevant issues, and factional squabbles impede progress and distract from the task to be accomplished.

Such indirect problems of behavior are manifestations of what have been called by Bradford *hidden agenda*. According to him,[1]

[1] L. P. Bradford, "The Case of the Hidden Agenda," in *Group Development*, Selected Reading Series One (Washington, D.C.: National Training Laboratories and National Education Association, 1961), p. 60.

Unlabelled, private and covered, but deeply felt and very much the concern of the group, is another level. Here are all of the conflicting motives, desires, aspirations and emotional reactions held by the group members, sub-groups, or the group as a whole that cannot be fitted legitimately into the accepted group task. Here are all of the problems which, for a variety of reasons, cannot be laid on top of the table.

The motivational drives of individual members, discussed in the previous chapter, may emerge as hidden agenda. If the individual's agenda are at variance with the group agenda, dissensions are likely to appear. A hostility toward the pattern of leadership, lack of group recognition ("They ignored my comment!"), or implicit attacks upon value orientations can cause a member to try to change the group's direction, regardless of the desirability or logic of the diversion.

The group as a whole may also have certain hidden agenda. Resentment over absent members or tension at the presence of new members may reflect on the total group. As Bradford states further:[2]

> The group may have hidden agendas about its task. If the task is seen as too difficult; if it suggests consequences that might be harmful to the group; if it has been pressed on the group by some outside group or individual who is disliked by the group; if it is solely the leader's task—the group's hidden agenda may be to slow down on the task. While this is never brought out on the surface, the group has many ways of running away from its job. One pattern of flight may be that of endless discussion over unimportant details, another, through listing on the black board endless lists

that could better be done by one person later. Escape into discussion of principles or into esoteric arguments is very common. Anecdotal periods that delay work are found in many groups.

Hidden agenda may be a real barrier to group productivity. Each member should recognize the fact that the group is always working on two levels at once and be able to diagnose what the genuine problems are. Sometimes it is desirable to get the hidden agenda to the surface; at other times they are best ignored. There can be no substitute for sensitivity and good judgment.

Perceptions Within the Group

The criteria, or "scales," we use in judging people are important factors in our ability to work with others. Most people have favorite yardsticks that they apply to everyone. Anxious patients in psychotherapy may see everyone as threatening; to these individuals, people do not seem to have faces or personalities and are only so many danger signs. On the other hand, patients may begin by seeing everyone as wonderful, but see themselves as no good at all. During successful therapy such patients begin slowly to recognize real people, and distinctive characteristics replace the blob-faces and the one-dimensional personalities. Seeing real differences in others is a sign of a functioning individual.

A popular scale for judging others is prestige. People who overemphasize prestige respond to the roster of members in a group by trying to discover *important* members. In introducing themselves such persons let it be known that they are members of influential families, belong to well-known student

[2] Ibid., p. 67.

organizations and living groups, or are generally important on the campus, and so on, feeling the need to hint at prominent connections.

Another overworked measure of people is money. Some of the cues we use to determine the financial status of our fellow students are the ways they dress, the places they live, or the cars they drive.

Other people quickly respond to indices of power. Small boys coming to new neighborhoods have to prove themselves in a series of fights until it is clear who can lick whom. In a classroom discussion or debate the power struggle is more subtle, but it's there: someone senses a power vacuum and moves in to give direction, and usually someone else responds with a counterproposal. The debate is ostensibly on the merits of the proposal, but under the surface of words and logic, at the hidden-agenda level, it is a competition for power. Often there is a third fellow who is so politically sagacious that he moves in to take over. To some members of the group this is not surprising: they are hypersensitive to power dimensions and have watched these struggles from the first moment. Other members have no idea that any competition for power and leadership is in progress.

Another overused scale is intelligence or education. It is a safe guess that some students quickly size up the IQs of their group and conclude that only two or three members are worthy of attention, the rest being all ordinary or less. Still another very influential dimension is sex: for some members a group consists of a few who might be attractive lovers and all the others, who don't count. To some persons the all-important question is "Who is sincere?" and the only behavior they care about is "leveling," the scale running from guile or hypocrisy to candor.

Any measuring rod may take a legitimate place in sizing up new acquaintances; the trouble usually lies in placing too much reliance on *one* dimension and neglecting others. Obvious differences in age, sex, race, or nationality do not tell us much about other important personal dimensions, such as whether a person is warm or cold, deep or shallow, or creative or plodding.

One of the most important facts about our classroom experience is that the overused dimensions do not indicate which members will contribute most to a group's productivity. Those who turn out to be most valuable cannot be predicted from prestige, power, money, sex appeal, or intelligence. We should not place great reliance upon these useless measuring sticks. Instead, we need to look more closely at such dimensions as self-awareness, ability to listen, balance, insight, and breadth of social acceptance.

We used to think, in our naive way, that the act of perception consisted of two independent things: the perceiver and the thing perceived. The act of perception simply meant "seeing what was there." One of the important advances in the behavioral sciences has been the recognition that perceivers are not just passive "cameras" taking pictures, but individuals taking active parts in perception. Perceivers see what experience has conditioned them to see.

We enter a room to join a new group of six persons sitting around a table. What do we "see" beyond the mere fact that there are six human beings? Do we all see the same picture, either individually or collectively? A European notes that there are six Americans, by their dress and speech. A Southerner notes that one person might be a light-skinned black. An older woman notes the youth of the group. What perceiver, then, "sees what is there"? Nobody, of course. Each of us perceives what our past has prepared us to perceive; we select and distinguish, we focus on some subjects and relationships, and we blur others; we distort objective reality to make it conform to our needs or hopes or fears or hates or envies or affectations.

As we observe groups, we reflect the same subjective influences: not merely do our eyes and brains register some objective portrait of other persons or groups, but our very act of seeing is warped by what we have been taught to believe, by what we want to believe, and by what we need to believe.

These varied perceptions contribute to communication difficulties within a group. We may not be disagreeing about the same thing but about different things; we are not looking at the same people in the conference room; we don't see people as they are, but as what they mean to us.[3]

Some of the most serious distortions in perception of new acquaintances come from their chance resemblance to people who were once important to us. This is the process that Freud called transference. A gray-haired woman in a group may be seen as a mother-symbol: those who enjoyed childhood dependence on their own mothers expect a similar acceptance for her, and those who found their own mothers hateful will anticipate that kind of personal relationship and perhaps guard against it. A dominant male may be a father-figure against whom men who have never worked out their parental conflicts will rebel. An older man may be perceived as a godlike person who has the power to solve all our problems. These are familiar transference patterns, but there are many others. The young man with horn-rimmed glasses resembles a fellow we used to know; until we learn otherwise, we expect him to behave as our earlier acquaintance did. We may feel let down because he does not exhibit the lively sense of humor we imagined he would have or relieved because he is not so critical as we had feared. Often we attribute to "intuition" those immediate flashes of feeling about new acquaintances that lead us to feel that they will prove trustworthy, malicious, superficial, or kind. Actually, those strong impressions can be shown on analysis to arise from some resemblance, in physique, speech, manner, or relative position, to someone whom we earlier knew as trustworthy, malicious, superficial, or kind.

First impressions, in addition to what they tell us about others, tell us about ourselves. A genuine dislike for an exhibitionistic person may suggest how strictly we forbid expression of our own exhibitionist drives, whereas a feeling of attraction to such a person may suggest that we would like to live out our own drives in this direction. Rather than dismiss the value of first impressions, we should attempt to determine the bases of our reactions and remain tentative in our evaluations.

[3] See W. V. Haney, "Perception and Communication," in *Communication and Organizational Behavior: Text and Cases* (Homewood, Ill.: Irwin, 1967), pp. 51–71. Also reprinted in *Basic Readings in Interpersonal Communication*, K. Giffin and B. R. Patton (eds.), (New York: Harper & Row, 1971), pp. 137–169.

Defensive and Supportive Behavior

If an individual anticipates or perceives threat in a group, he is likely to behave defensively. Gibb studied this phenomenon for eight years and delineated two communication climates, one threatening, or defensive, and the other nonthreatening, or supportive.[4] He states.[5]

The person who behaves defensively, even though he also gives some attention to the common task, devotes an appreciable portion of his energy to defending himself. Besides talking about the topic, he thinks about how he appears to others, how he may be seen more favorably, how he may win, dominate, impress or escape punishment, and/or how he may avoid or mitigate a perceived or an anticipated attack.

He cited certain behaviors as contributory to defensiveness:[6]

1. *Evaluation* by expression, manner of speech, tone of voice, or verbal content, perceived by the listener as criticism or judgment, will produce defensive behavior.
2. Communication perceived as an attempt to *control* him will produce defensiveness; it is interesting to note that if speech is said to be a social "tool," the implication is that the recipient has been "tooled."
3. *Stratagems* that are perceived as clever devices produce defensiveness; partially hidden motives breed suspicion. Persons seen as "playing a game," feigning emotion, withholding information, or having private access to sources of data will stimulate defensive responses.
4. An appearance of *neutrality* or lack of concern will heighten the need of defensiveness. A clinically detached or impersonal manner (not caring) is usually feared and resented.
5. Conveying an attitude of *superiority* arouses defensive behavior; any behavior that reinforces the recipient's feelings of inadequacy is a source of disturbance.
6. *Dogmatism* is a well-known stimulus of defensive behavior; if you know something "for certain," it is wise to determine whether or not anyone else wants to hear it from you and whether they want your answer to be offered tentatively or with final certainty.

Defensive behavior in one member of a group is likely to provoke defensiveness in others. A vicious circle is begun and becomes increasingly destructive as people stop listening to what is being said. Gibb noted:[7] "As a person becomes more and more defensive, he becomes less and less able to perceive accurately the motives, the values, and the emotions of the sender." Gibb's analysis of tape-recorded discussions showed a positive correlation between defensive behavior and losses of efficiency in communication. Thus distortions became greater when defensive behaviors were demonstrated in the groups.[8]

The reverse was also true. In a supportive, nonthreatening climate,

---

[4] J. Gibb, "Defensive Communication," *Journal of Communication* 11 (September 1961): 141–148. Also reprinted in *Basic Readings in Interpersonal Communication*, K. Giffin and B. R. Patton (eds.), (New York: Harper & Row, 1971), pp. 366–374.
[5] Ibid., p. 141.
[6] Ibid., pp. 142–148.

[7] Ibid., p. 142.
[8] Ibid., pp. 146–148.

receivers of messages were less likely to read into the message distorted meanings arising from projections of personal anxieties, motives, and concerns. As defenses were reduced, listeners were better able to concentrate on the intended cognitive meanings, content, and structures of the messages.

Trust seems to be at the heart of the supportive climate. Research in industry has demonstrated that high trust tends to stimulate high group productivity.[9] Haney suggests reasons why communication practices are generally effective in a trusting, supportive organizational climate:[10]

> First of all the members of such an organization, relatively speaking, have no ax to grind, nothing to be gained by miscommunicating deliberately. The aura of openness makes possible candid expressions of feelings and ideas. Even faulty communication does not lead immediately to retaliation, for others are not prone to presume malice on the offender's part, but instead "carry him," compensate for his errors. "That's not what he means to say." Moreover, a lapse in communication is viewed not as an occasion for punishment, but as an opportunity to learn from mistakes. Obviously, effective communication will do much to reinforce and enhance an existing trusting climate and the reverse is also true.

The implications of this material should be obvious to all groups. Defensiveness interferes with communication within a group and makes it difficult if not impossible to deal with tasks in any effective measure.

According to Gibb, defensive behavior is reduced by interaction that is perceived as:[11]

> Descriptive rather than evaluative or critical
>
> Oriented toward solving mutual problems instead of toward personal control
>
> Spontaneous rather than strategic
>
> Empathic rather than neutral
>
> Indicative of an attitude of equality instead of superiority
>
> Expressive of provisionally held viewpoints instead of dogmatic certainties.

Additional studies have corroborated these findings.

Task, Maintenance, and Self-oriented Behavior

One way of viewing the behavior of individuals in a group is determining what its function, or purpose, seems to be.[12] When a member says something, is that member trying to promote accomplishment of the group task, to maintain relationships among members, or to meet a personal need or goal?

If the primary *task* of the group is to deal with a common problem, certain behaviors can be categorized in terms of roles that facilitate and contribute to the decision-making activities. A given member may enact a wide range of such roles in a meeting, be-

[9] R. Likert, *New Patterns in Management* (New York: McGraw-Hill, 1961), pp. 101–105.
[10] Haney, "Perception and Communication," p. 13.
[11] J. Gibb, "Climate for Trust Formation," in *T-Group Theory and Laboratory Method: Innovation in Re-education*, L. B. Bradford, J. Gibb, and K. D. Benne (eds.), (New York: Wiley, 1964), pp. 279–309.
[12] These three broad groupings were originally cited by the National Training Laboratory in Group Development. See K. D. Benne and P. Sheats, "Functional Roles of Group Members," *Journal of Social Issues* 4 (1948): 41–49.

having relevantly to the group's ful-fillment of its task in the following ways.

1. *Initiating.* Starts the group along new paths, such as by proposing the task or goal or by suggesting a plan of attack for handling a problem.
2. *Clarifying and elaborating.* Inter-prets issues and helps clear up ambiguous ideas or suggestions; focuses attention on the alter-natives and issues before the group.
3. *Seeking information or opinions.* Requests the facts and relevant information on the problem; seeks out expressions of feeling and values; asks for suggestions, estimates, ideas.
4. *Giving information or opinion.* Of-fers facts and information needed by the group; is willing to state beliefs and offer suggestions and ideas.
5. *Evaluating.* Helps establish standards for judgment; offers practical concerns such as cost, operations, and implementation of a proposal.
6. *Coordinating.* Shows relationships between ideas and may restate suggestions to pull them to-gether; summarizes and offers potential decisions for the group to accept or reject.
7. *Consensus testing.* Asks to see whether the group is nearing a decision; sends up a "trial bal-loon" to test a possible conclu-sion.

Types of behavior relevant to the group's remaining in good working order, having a good climate for task work, and having good relationships that permit maximal use of member resources—*group maintenance*—in-clude:

1. *Harmonizing.* Attempts to recon-cile disagreements; reduces ten-sion; gets people to explore dif-ferences.
2. *Gate keeping.* Helps to keep com-munication channels open by suggesting procedures that per-mit sharing remarks; facilitates the participation of everyone in the decisions.
3. *Encouraging.* Is warm, friendly, and responsive to others; indi-cates by a remark or by nonver-bal communication (nodding, smiling) the acceptance of others' contributions.
4. *Compromising.* Offers compro-mises that may yield status when one's own idea is involved in a conflict; admits errors and is will-ing to modify beliefs in the in-terest of group cohesion or growth.
5. *Standard setting and testing.* Tests whether a group is satisfied with its procedures; points out the norms that have been set for evaluating the quality of the group process.
6. *Relieving tension.* Introduces humor or other relief in a tense situation; helps relax the group.

Every group needs both task and maintenance to accomplish its prob-lem-solving mission; both types of be-havior make positive contributions to the group's productivity. There are other forces active in groups that dis-turb the work. These underlying emo-tional issues produce a variety of emo-tional behaviors that may interfere with or prove destructive to effective group functioning. We have discussed some of the underlying causes of such problems. A member may respond to group problems in the following *self-oriented* ways.

1. *Fighting and controlling.* Asserts personal dominance and attempts to get own way regardless of others. Fighting may be the reaction of hostile aggression toward the aspects of the problem that appear to be blocking our progress. Deep in our biological natures lies a suppressed tendency to be angry, to retaliate, to hurt, to punish. This is one emotional mode of responding to a problem. Aggression may actively strike out, or it may be passive and appear as a resentful refusal to apply effort to the solution of the problem. Unfortunately, the fighting response tends to elicit the same response from other members of the group.[13]

2. *Withdrawing.* Tries to remove the sources of uncomfortable feelings by psychologically leaving the group. This flight is the tendency of a person confronted by a problem to want to run away from it. The student who is failing to solve his college-work problems can escape to beer parties and bull sessions. The urge to flee, like the urge to fight, is a social reality in the group situation. A whole group may flee by tacitly agreeing not to talk about certain subjects.[14]

3. *Dependency and counterdependency.* Reacts to people as authority figures. When certain persons are confronted with a problem, their natural reaction is to wait for someone, a leader, to lead them to the solution. In all of us there seems to be a wish for a savior who is all-knowing and all-powerful. Perhaps this wish for a perfect leader is reflected in the companion emotion, an unwillingness to use the imperfect leadership resources available, particularly within ourselves, when confronted with a problem. Dependency may manifest itself in the guise of its opposite, counterdependency, by a rejection of the efforts of anyone who is seen as an overt leader or authority figure.[15]

4. *Fixation.* Responds to a problem by unwarranted rigidity and persistence in a stereotyped response. Fixation is particularly apt to be present when a group is confronted with a problem of great magnitude that appears impossible to solve. In such a case there will be repeated attempts to use solutions that are ineffective in achieving the desired goals.[16]

This list of self-oriented behaviors could easily be expanded to include such defense mechanisms as *projection* and *alienation.* The main point, however, is to bring to our awareness the reality of emotionality as it affects the progress of groups.

[13] A. Zaleznik and D. Moment, *The Dynamics of Interpersonal Behavior* (New York: Wiley, 1964), pp. 161–172.

[14] G. Egan, *Encounter: Group Processes for Interpersonal Growth* (Belmont, Calif.: Brooks/Cole Publishing, 1970), pp. 336–358.

[15] Zaleznik and Moment, *Dynamics of Interpersonal Behavior.*

[16] D. Krech, R. S. Crutchfield, and N. Livson, *Elements of Psychology* (New York: Knopf, 1969), pp. 426–428.

Response to Group Pressure

Much of the behavior of people in groups is the result of group pressures. The psychological pressure to fulfill the expectations of other group members provides the conformity dimension of the group. Yet, as has been suggested, for there to be conformity, there must be conflict:[17] "conflict between those forces in the individual which tend to lead him to act, value, and believe in one way and those pressures emanating from the society or group which tend to lead him in another way."

Although there are numerous individual motives to account for the attention we pay to the expectations of others, the basic one seems to be that we care about what other members of the group think of us. Kiesler and Kiesler suggest that the individual motives for fulfilling others' expectations fall into three categories. As the group generates normative pressures, a person responds as he does because:[18]

1. The others will accept and like him, or will not reject him.
2. The group goal will be successfully attained.
3. The continuation of the group will be assured. People may also fulfill others' expectations as a by-product of informational, or cognitive, needs. Thus, if the group has an informational function, the others' expectations can serve as a guide for:
   1. Gaining "correct" information about reality.
   2. Validating one's own opinions and making sure they are consistent with the opinions of others.
   3. Evaluating oneself and others.

The roles forced upon individuals are products of the interaction between his interpersonal orientations, the situational elements, and the demands of the group. The behavior is influenced by the individual's knowledge of the role, his motivation to perform the role, his self-concepts, and the other people in the group. Because each individual has a unique set of drives, attitudes, cognitions, and orientations, the ways in which he performs his various roles may be unique.

Insight into the various types of conformity behavior can be gained from looking briefly at one of Asch's experiments.[19] In his experiment a group of seven to nine college students were instructed to announce publicly the length of one of three unequal lines. All but one of the students were confederates of the experimenter and were instructed each to give the same incorrect response. The experimental student sat near the end of the row, so that his announced decision would come after most other members'. Thus, the subject found himself a minority of one in the midst of a unanimous majority.

Of the students in the experimental group who were subjected to group pressure, only one fourth of them consistently rated the lengths of the lines correctly, whereas nearly perfect

[17] D. Krech, R. S. Crutchfield, and E. L. Ballachey, *Individual in Society* (New York: McGraw-Hill, 1962), p. 506.

[18] C. A. Kiesler and S. B. Kiesler, *Conformity* (Reading, Mass.: Addison-Wesley, 1970), p. 33.

[19] S. E. Asch, "Effects of Group Pressure upon the Modifications and Distortion of Judgments," in *Readings in Social Psychology*, G. Swanson et al. (eds.), (New York: Holt, Rinehart and Winston, 1952), pp. 2–11.

reports were given by individuals in a control group free of any group pressure. The remaining three quarters of the experimental group made errors in the direction of the views of the majority. There was, however, great variation in the number of errors in this group, ranging from total adherence to the group views to very few errors.

Further analysis of the behavior of students who conformed revealed three categories of reactions:

Perceptual distortion. Some of the students were unaware that their estimates had been influenced and distorted by the group.

Judgmental distortion. Some of the students perceived the lengths correctly but decided that their perceptions were less accurate than those of other members of the group and decided to "go along." Thus they doubted their own perceptual capabilities.

Distortion of action. Some of the students perceived correctly and actually believed that they were correct, but they wanted to avoid being different from the others. Thus they conformed to the group's erroneous decisions rather than voice a difference.

Students who resisted group pressures were also able to be categorized into three groups:

Those who were confident of their perceptions.

Those who believed strongly in the importance of independent judgments.

Those who believed in taking effective action in the situation.

Rather than moralize over the merits or demerits of conformity behavior, let us merely note that individuals in both groups satisfied their own personal needs: The conformists had goals of involvement with the group that transcended their own perceptual difference, while the independent ones had different behavioral goals set for themselves.

Summary

We have been concerned with some of the behavior typically present in a decision-making group, and this behavior may be summarized as follows.

A group is always responding on two levels: to the public agenda, or business of the meeting; and to the hidden agenda, which represent the motives, desires, aspirations, and emotional reactions of the members.

Group perceptions may be noted in terms of what factors in the group serve to impress: prestige, power, and education; or the more important dimensions of self-awareness, the ability to listen, and the breadth of social acceptance.

A group may exhibit defensive behaviors, which diminish its effectiveness, or supportive behaviors based on mutual trust.

Behaviors may be classified according to primary function: accomplishing a *task*, *maintaining* group relationships, or being *self-oriented,* indifferent to the best interests of the group.

Responses to group pressure in terms of *conformity* or *independent action* provide another key to group accomplishment.

Such behavior, whether noted in others or in ourselves, can assist analysis and diagnosis of problem-solving group interaction. None of the variables may be considered alone, since each influences all the others.

Surviving on the Job

David W. Johnson

My Interpersonal Skills Determine My Career Success

The success of your career depends largely on your interpersonal skills. Finding and holding a job depends largely on how well you can work cooperatively with other people. Promotions and raises depend on your ability to work cooperatively with fellow employees. People who cannot cooperate, provide leadership, communicate, build meaningful relationships, and manage conflicts helpfully are not promoted, rewarded, or even kept in an organization.

Having the technical skills needed to do your job is not enough to be successful. Likewise, having necessary organizational skills, such as reliability (arriving on time, consistently coming to work) and responsibility (having good work habits and following through on assigned tasks), are important, but they are not enough to make you successful. *The most important skills for the success of your career are the interpersonal*

From David W. Johnson, *Human Relations and Your Career*, © 1978, pp. 336–345. Reprinted by permission of Prentice-Hall, Inc., Englewood Cliffs, New Jersey.

skills needed for cooperating with your fellow employees.

Every career requires you to work for and with other people. To complete your work and to achieve your organization's goals, you have to interact with other people. Coworkers, supervisors, suppliers, and customers cannot be avoided. To be a success, you have to be able to build good relationships. Interpersonal skills are an absolute necessity for a successful career.

Are You Born with Interpersonal Skills, or Are They Learned?

Is the ability to be liked by other people born in some people and not in others? Is getting along with other people born in some people and not in others? Are you either likeable or unlikeable from the moment of your birth? From the instant of your conception, are you either skilled in getting along with other people or likely to have trouble in relating to other people? Some people believe that interpersonal skills are inherited. They assume that if they do not have such skills now they never will. "This is it, this is me, I can never change!" is their motto. They do not try to improve their interpersonal skills, because they do not believe it is possible to do so.

What do you believe? Do you believe that you were born with your interpersonal skills? Do you believe that when you are hired to do a job the needed interpersonal skills will magically appear? Do you believe that interpersonal skills are a gift given by fate to some people and not to others?

Actually, nothing could be farther from the truth. All interpersonal skills are learned. Some of your interpersonal skills you learned from your parents; others you learned from your older brothers, sisters, and friends. And still others you learned from your teachers and other authority figures in your life. Some of your interpersonal skills you learned as a child, others as a teenager. And still others will be learned while you are an adult. All of your life, you will be learning interpersonal skills and perfecting ones you already know. You learn interpersonal skills just as you learn any other skill. And you keep on learning them all your life.

The success of your career depends on your interpersonal skills. Nothing is more important for your career than mastering the interpersonal skills discussed in this book. And these skills can be learned now, to prepare for success in the future.

The Beginning: The Job Interview

Your career begins with a job interview. An interview is an opportunity that may open a gate to a job. It is during the interview that a potential employer may judge your ability to get along with your fellow employees. And it is during the job interview that you can demonstrate your interpersonal skills to a potential employer.

The job interview is a formal conversation in which two people seek to learn more about each other. The job interview has two objectives:

1. To give the employer information about you.
2. To give you information about the employer and the organization.

As the applicant, you both give and seek information. You prepare for the interview, therefore, by reviewing what you need to share with the interviewer and by reviewing what you wish to find out about the organization.

"This person has the skills for the job, but can he get along?" This question is in the mind of every employer who interviews you. And it is the answer to this question that this book specifically focuses on. There are other aspects of the job interview that are discussed in other courses. In this book, we concentrate on the part of the job interview that focuses on the question, "Can you get along with others? Do you fit in with the other people in our organization?"

The average job interview lasts from ten to fifteen minutes. Most employment interviewers agree that they usually make their decision to hire a person within the first five minutes of the interview. Since the results of the interview will determine whether or not you are hired, you need to be able to create an immediate positive impression. How do you do this? Here are some helpful hints.

The most important information

about yourself relates to your goals, assets, and credentials. This information should be presented in the first five minutes of the interview. An important asset to be emphasized is your interpersonal skills. You should be prepared both to talk about your interpersonal skills and to demonstrate them during the interview. It is important that you know your credentials and assets so thoroughly that you can discuss them without having to stop and think about what to say or how to say it. During this book, the discussion of your assets with your fellow group members has been emphasized, to help you prepare a short statement about your goals, credentials, and assets for your job interviews. During the job interview, you have to see yourself as a good worker and as a competent and skilled person. Be proud of yourself. Be proud of what you can offer the employer. You should be ready to answer such questions as, "Why do you believe you should be hired by this company?" and "Where do you expect to be in this company in ten years?" Do not undersell yourself. The interviewer wants to know what assets you can contribute to the organization. And she wants to know about your goals and credentials. You need to be able to discuss yourself without fake modesty. If you cannot discuss your assets, credentials, and goals realistically, review the second chapter of this book.

During the job interview, remember that when you are hired to do a job you are hired to be part of a cooperative effort to achieve organizational goals. The interviewer is looking for a person who can fit in with the other employees and for a person who can contribute to the overall effort to achieve the organization's goals. Your ability to cooperate is important. And your ability to provide leadership to help the organization achieve its goals and maintain good relationships among employees is also important. During your interview, use words such as *cooperation* and *teamwork*. Let the interviewer know that you see yourself as being part of a cooperative effort, as helping to achieve the organization's goals. And let the interviewer know you see yourself as helping maintain good working relationships among employees.

Your communication skills are of great importance during the interview. Review the communication skills discussed in this book, and be sure to use them during the interview. Both sending and listening skills are of great importance during the job interview. The more skilled in communicating you are during the interview, the more likely you will be to get the job.

The first impression you make is the most important part of the interview. First impressions do count, no matter what your qualifications are. Plan the communication of a favorable first impression. This includes your greeting, your actions during the interview, your appearance, and your exit from the interview.

YOUR GREETING

When you enter the interview, walk in briskly. Shake hands firmly. Say "thank you" when the interviewer indicates where you should sit. When the interviewer says "How are you?" you should reply "Fine, thank you," even if you have a bad headache.

YOUR ACTIONS DURING THE INTERVIEW

Sit in your chair in such a way that you look alert. Look the interviewer in the eye without staring. Do not chew gum. Speak clearly without hiding your mouth with your hand. Use complete sentences, and avoid slang. Do not interrupt the interviewer, but *do* allow yourself to be interrupted. Avoid disagreeing with the interviewer. Do not smoke during the interview, because some interviewers do not like smokers. And the interviewer may suspect that if you are such a heavy smoker that you have to light up during a short interview, your smoking may interfere with your work. Good posture is important, so do not slump carelessly in the chair. Show that you are interested in the job—look and sound enthusiastic. You can do this by having done some research on the organization before the interview. For example, read their annual report. Find out things about the organization and mention them in the interview. By mentioning what you know about the organization, you communicate interest and enthusiasm.

YOUR APPEARANCE

Your appearance communicates a great deal about you. Have clean fingernails, dentally checked teeth, shined shoes, and clean breath (no smoking or drinking before the interview). Wear deodorant. Look clean, fresh, and neat. Consider how your appearance reflects the job you are applying for. If you are applying for a job in a department store, dress fashionably. If you are seeking a managerial job, dress conservatively. If you are seeking a job as a mechanic, dress in clean work clothes. Carefully choose the most appropriate clothes you have. If you are not sure what to wear, observe the persons working for the organization. Note what they are wearing. Then wear something similar. Do not wear clothing that requires your attention, such as a dress that looks good only if you stand or sit in a certain way, a shirt that will not stay tucked into your trousers if you move about, or garments with zippers that come open if you forget to hold your breath. Choose clothing that is comfortable, that you can forget about, so you can concentrate on the interview. Take your appearance seriously. It is an important nonverbal communication about you as a person. And it greatly influences the first impression you make on the interviewer.

YOUR EXIT

Thank the interviewer. Leave promptly when the interview is over. Walk out briskly.

During the interview, you must convey your ability to get along with fellow employees and customers. This means communicating your interpersonal skills and your commitment to form and maintain good relationships. During the interview, you should also communicate that you are able to fit in with what the organization wants from its employees. Communicate your organizational skills of dependability and reliability. Communicate that you have few personal problems that could interfere with your work. And communicate your knowledge of the job and your ability to do the job.

Since the interview takes place between you and another person, your interpersonal skills will greatly influence its outcome. Before going into a job interview, practice demonstrating the interpersonal skills covered in this book. They will help you get the job you want.

Growing on the Job

The longer you have the same job, the better you will do it. But your real growth on the job does not come from increasing your technical skills. Your real growth on the job comes from increasing your skills in working cooperatively with other people. You grow on the job as you improve your interpersonal skills, as you improve your relationships with your fellow employees.

Mastering interpersonal skills does not end when you finish this book or your training. Your interpersonal skills will improve as long as you are alive. No matter how old you are, no matter how long you have worked, your interpersonal skills can still be improved. As you meet more and more people within the organization, learn new ways to provide leadership and increase cooperation among fellow employees, you will grow on the job. You will grow on the job as you become more skillful in managing conflicts and as your relationships with your fellow employees deepen. Your growth depends on continuing to improve your interpersonal skills and on improving your relationships with your fellow employees.

Improving your technical and organizational skills is important. But do not forget that the organization you work for is a network of interpersonal relationships aimed at achieving goals. As you improve your interpersonal skills, you improve the organized efforts of the people you work with.

Your organization is held together by the ability of employees to work with each other. Your organization survives by employees cooperating with each other. Therefore, as your interpersonal skills improve, so does your ability to contribute to the organization.

Other People: You Can't Work Without Them

Other people are a key factor in your success or failure on the job. They can help you do a good job, or they can make you do a bad job. Other people can make your job fun and interesting, challenging and rewarding. It is other people who make your career meaningful. If you like your fellow employees and they like you, going to work is something you look forward to. If you dislike your fellow employees and they dislike you, going to work is something you dread. In the long run, it is your interpersonal relationships at work that make your career satisfying and successful. Your interpersonal skills are the most important aspect of your career.

There are a series of interpersonal skills you need to master if your career is to be successful:

1. *Setting realistic goals.* You need to be aware of your goals, assets, and credentials. And you need to be able to communicate them to potential employers. Your goals need to be flexible so they can be modified to overlap with the goals of the organization you work for.
2. *Cooperating and leading.* Your career depends on your ability to work cooperatively with other people. The very nature of an

organization demands cooperation among employees. And cooperation takes leadership. An essential part of cooperating is helping the organization achieve its goals and maintain good working relationships among employees.

3. *Communicating.* Sending and receiving messages is an essential aspect of any job. Managing your feelings is an essential aspect of any job. And communicating your feelings is an important interpersonal skill. The more skilled in communicating you are, the more successful your career will be.

4. *Forming good relationships.* Your self-awareness, self-acceptance, and ability to let yourself be known are essential aspects of forming good relationships on the job. You also need to be able to get to know others. You need to be skilled in building and maintaining trust. The ability to appreciate yourself and appreciate diversity among fellow employees is also important. Forming good relationships on the job is one of the most rewarding aspects of your career.

5. *Managing conflicts.* Being able to manage conflicts like an Owl is an important interpersonal skill. Conflicts will inevitably occur. You need to be able to define them constructively. You need to initiate helpful conversations about the conflict, arrive at joint definitions, disagree without rejecting the other person, accept disagreement without feeling rejected, see the conflict from the other person's viewpoint and arrive at a solution that leaves both you and the other person satisfied. Managing conflicts is probably the most difficult aspect of maintaining good relationships on the job. It takes all the interpersonal skills discussed in this book to manage conflicts successfully.

All these interpersonal skills have been discussed in this book. Experiences have been structured so you could learn the skills. You have practiced most of the skills. You may find you wish to repeat many of the lessons. You may want to reread many of the chapters of the book. You will want to keep practicing the skills until they are so automatic that they are your natural way of acting.

It is your relationships with other people that make your career seem worthwhile and enjoyable. Keep improving your interpersonal skills. And enjoy your relationships with the people you interact with during your career!

Action Steps: Applications

1. Meet with one of your close friends and, in more detail than you have ever done before, describe the kind of person you would really like to be. Listen carefully to his/her feedback; request it in more depth and more detail than usual. Note its effect on you and discuss this with your friend.

2. With one of your close friends, reverse the procedure described above; this time you take the role of listener and encourage your friend to describe the kind of person he/she would like to be. As best you can, help this friend to gain an imaginary picture or "vision" of himself/herself actually behaving in ways that meet and even transcend his/her hopes or aspirations. With your friend discuss the value of this interaction.

3. Meet with two or three of your best friends and, with their help, attempt to create a climate of acceptance and trust formation. No one should behave in ways that are insincere; do not try to show feelings that are not genuine. However, special efforts should be made to be as accepting of one another as possible without being artificial. Talk about your personal aspirations for becoming a better person. After some time spent in this way, together assess the degree of interpersonal trust among all of you. Has it increased? If so, do you and they think the experience has been valuable? Together decide to what extent attempts should be made, through similar experiences, to increase one's trust of others not present. Discuss with them where "one should draw the line" in increasing one's interpersonal trust.

4. Analyze the sub-groups in which you have participated in class. When were there hidden agenda? What conformity pressures have been present? Did defensive behaviors diminish as the semester progressed? Evaluate these groups in terms of Reading 9.2 and the checklist in Appendix A.

5. Meet with a group of people of your gender. Discuss pressures you feel from sex-role stereotyping and differences in your communication with people of the opposite sex. For example, how do you change your vocabulary with people of the other sex? Do you play any special "games"? Compare the conclusions of your group with the generalizations of a group made up of the other sex.

6. Role-play a job interview with classmates as observers. Using the suggestions offered in Reading 9.3, determine how you can improve your communication skills in a job interview.

Appendixes

Appendix A
Participating in a Small Group

A S WE DISCUSSED in Chapter 4 and in Reading 9.2, one of the important contexts of interpersonal communication is the small group. The small group process typically comprises two types of activities: solving problems and relating interpersonally. The first is a task-oriented behavior; it includes identifying and analyzing a mutual problem, evaluating possible ways of solving it, and preparing for the implementation of a selected solution. The second involves acting in a decently human way, by listening to how others feel about *their ideas*, not just noting those ideas, and by listening to how they feel about *us*, not just to how they feel about *our* ideas.

Because of the significance of groups to our lives, we have included this checklist of behaviors that can be observed in groups. This list may be helpful as you examine your own and others' interpersonal communication in the small group setting.

Checklist of Behaviors
in the Small Group*

A. Orientations and attitudes:
1. Personal needs for identity, recognition, or security.
2. Prejudices or biases involving interpersonal attitudes.
3. Severely competitive orientations.
4. Need to dominate others (lack of opportunity for some members to avoid being overly dependent).
5. Overly defensive behavior.

B. Interpersonal behavior:
1. Apparently inaccurate interpersonal perceptions (as when one member thinks some other member is threatening him).
2. Lack of attraction by the group for some members.
3. Unreasonable conformity to group pressures.
4. Lack of communication or poor or ineffective communication.
5. Personal hidden agenda.

C. Lack of identification of group task or problem:
1. Lack of mutual concern or lack of any concern.
2. Lack of cohesiveness in the group regarding the task.
3. Inability to overcome confusion regarding the task or problem.

D. Inability to analyze a problem:
1. Failure to compare what *is* with what is *desired*.
2. Inability to agree on the scope of the problem.
3. Inability to agree on the intensity or severity of the problem.
4. Lack of information on *impelling* forces (forces increasing the need of a change).
5. Lack of information on *restraining forces* (forces resisting the desired change).
6. General lack of factual information regarding the problem (too much reliance on unverified opinions, guesses, suppositions).

E. Inability to evaluate proposals:
1. Lack of identification of possible solutions (inexperience in area; lack of creative thinking).
2. Poor identification of the criteria by which the group could evaluate a proposal: Does it meet the problem as analyzed by the group? Is there any evidence that it would really work? Are there serious disadvantages, such as cost or danger?
3. Inability to agree on a group decision.

F. Inability to implement group decision when reached:
1. Inability to sort and allocate relevant group resources.
2. Inability to agree upon individual group members' responsibilities.
3. Inability to persuade others (outside the group) to give support, approval, assistance.

* From B. R. Patton and K. Giffin, *Decision-Making Group Interaction* (New York: Harper & Row, 1978), pp. 232–233. This book may be consulted for detailed discussion of the ideas cited.

G. Group member problems with role functions:
   1. Inability to agree on who can perform the needed leadership functions.
   2. Poor relationship between a member's personality and his role requirements.
   3. Neglect of either task or maintenance functions.
   4. Inappropriate or ineffective attempts at performing leadership functions.
H. Difficulties caused by group characteristics:
   1. Group is too large or too small.
   2. Lack of attractiveness of group members for each other (poor cohesiveness).
   3. Lack of attractiveness of status or prestige of group (poor cohesiveness).
   4. Dysfunctional group norms (such as tardiness, absenteeism, all members talking at once, discourtesy).
   5. Disagreement concerning an individual's status or power (perhaps a power struggle is evident).
   6. Lack of member commitment to group tasks or problems.
   7. General apathy, poor motivation on part of members to be helpful to one another.
I. Inability to handle or resolve conflict:
   1. Inability to discriminate between honest disagreement over the nature of the problem or the value of a possible solution and interpersonal dislike.
   2. Inability to handle cognitive dissonance (such as inability to be comfortable with honest, reasonable disagreement on problem or task issues).
   3. Inability to produce attitude congruence (agreement) through communication.
J. Inability to use appropriate discussion modes:
   1. Inability to choose alternative appropriate formats for group thinking (such as brainstorming, leaderless discussion, sub-grouping, committees).
   2. Inability to structure discussions (such as making a complete problem analysis before arguing for or against a specific proposal).
   3. Inability to build and achieve group acceptance of agenda.
   4. Poor use of possible communication channels, or "nets," as when the leader responds to each member's comments.

Appendix B
The Preplanned Message: Techniques of Advocacy

T HE FOCUS OF this book has been upon the spontaneous interaction between people. We recognize, however, that there are situations in all of our lives that require that we preplan and structure a message for oral presentation. We believe that it is possible and important to develop such skills and to use them in an ethical manner that does not distort reality or, in effect, manipulate our listeners. The ethics of the interpersonal encounter that we have discussed apply equally to the public speech.

Employing Techniques of Advocacy*

When we become an advocate, a significant change occurs in our role of interacting with others. While we are investigating a problem, we attempt to

* This material is drawn from B. R. Patton and K. Giffin, *Decision-Making Problem-Solving Interaction* (New York: Harper & Row, 1978), pp. 187–208.

keep an open mind; when we become committed to a specific course of action, we are inclined to disregard contrary points of view and data. Such behavior can be dangerous, but it is difficult to avoid. Eventually we must satisfy the demands of our own logic and conscience and offer the essence of our thinking to others as honestly and as clearly as we can. To *you*, then, we offer this advice.

As an advocate you must deal with persons who do not share your concern or your commitment. Your task is not simple: You must convince them that they *ought* to be concerned, that your analysis of the problem is valid, and that your chosen solution is the logical one to satisfy the need. Although your first problem may be only to get their attention (we'll have further suggestions about this later), your real objective is to *prove* to them that, first, they share with you a problem and, second, your chosen solution is the one they would choose if they gave the problem adequate consideration, as you have done.

We used the word *prove*. This concept requires special attention. *You prove something to someone only when you have convinced him/her to his/her own satisfaction.* This means that you have to start where the other is: think as he/she thinks, consider his/her biases or prejudices, and work from there. The task of proving something to someone requires that you compare your *assumptions* with his/hers and start your advocacy by dealing with *his/her* assumptions, not just your own. You cannot move into a position of advocacy by assuming that others share the concern of your group, even if they ought to (as you see it); in addition, you cannot afford to *assume* that they will think as you do or even trust you.

As we consider major elements in your role as an advocate, we need a term to use in identifying those persons who are the target of your advocacy. We shall call them your *listeners,* although many may not listen very well, and although as an advocate you may employ such media as newspapers, brochures, and pamphlets, interviews with public officials, and spoken and visual messages to conferences, committees, and civic groups. For our purposes we shall call all persons whose help you are trying to enlist in solving a community or social problem your listeners, because in large measure, unless you are already prominent as a leader of social reform, your most important role as an advocate will be in face-to-face verbal presentations to small groups. Certain characteristics of persons in these audiences should be your very first concern. In order of importance, the first is their attitude toward the problem, situation, or condition about which you and your group are concerned.

USING PRINCIPLES OF ATTITUDE CHANGE

Attitude is a predisposition to behave in a particular way with respect to a specified set of conditions or circumstances. Not all your listeners will have the same attitude toward the specific problem: some will have no attitude at all, having paid no attention to this particular situation; others will have given it their consideration and decided that nothing of significance is wrong; still others will have already become mildly convinced that in this specific situation all is not well. In essence, some of your listeners may reflect no attitude, some will have unfavorable attitudes of varying intensity, and perhaps some will have favorable attitudes of minor intensity. What principles of attitude change can be of help to you in your task as an advocate?

In the first place, you will need to form some estimate of your listeners' attitudes toward the condition or situation about which you are concerned. We shall call this situation or condition the *attitude object*. In a general way you can assess people's attitudes by observing their behavior. Appearances, however, may be deceptive: In a well-known study, La Piere traveled across the United States in the early 1930s with a Chinese friend and his wife; in only *one* of 251 instances were they denied service in hotels, restaurants, and public places; yet when the same persons were subsequently surveyed, 92 percent said they would *not* accept members of the Chinese race in their establishments.[1]

Other studies have shown similar results. The expressed attitudes in the early 1950s were not consistent with behavior in a study of service for a party for two whites and one black.[2] The party was served in eleven taverns and restaurants; however, later responses to calls to the establishments ranged from mildly favorable to outright refusal. In a later study white students were questioned regarding their attitudes toward blacks; when asked if they would be willing to be photographed sitting with a black, the expressed attitudes and behavior tended to agree but were not highly consistent.[3]

The verbal expression of an attitude is called an opinion. It is somewhat risky to infer attitudes (predispositions to act) from opinions, because many circumstances can cause a person to express an opinion inconsistent with his/her real attitude, such as pressure from groups of which a person is a member and the influence of status persons who may be listening. Even so, in a general way opinions do reflect attitudes. It can be of value to you as an advocate to ask representatives of your listeners for their opinions regarding the condition you perceive as a problem.

Attitudes have three essential characteristics or dimensions: *direction* (favorable, neutral, unfavorable), *intensity* (strength with which they are held, from great intensity to almost none), and *saliency* (the perceived importance to the individual). For example, a young man and a woman acquaintance both may have an unfavorable attitude toward the draft (direction); both may strongly adhere to these views (intensity); the man, however, probably will attach more importance to the draft as an attitude object (salience). For our purposes here we shall be interested primarily in direction and intensity; in addition, highly salient attitudes are usually held with great intensity.

Attitudes are influenced by our experiences, including the attachments we form for other people. All of your listeners will be members of many small groups—as, for example, work groups, bridge clubs, bowling teams, and churches. The attitudes of others with whom we associate tend to influence our own. In an intensive four-year study of the entire student body of Bennington

[1] R. T. La Piere, "Attitudes vs. Actions," *Social Forces* 13 (1934): 230–237.
[2] B. Kutnev, C. Wilkins, and P. Yarrow, "Verbal Attitudes and Overt Behavior Involving Racial Prejudice," *Journal of Abnormal Social Psychology* 47 (1952): 649–652.
[3] M. L. De Fleur and F. R. Westie, "Verbal Attitudes and Overt Acts: An Experiment on the Salience of Attitudes," *American Sociological Review* 23 (1958): 667–673.

College, Newcomb found that such "reference groups" influenced changes in students' attitudes.[4]

The amount of information an individual has about an *attitude object* influences to some extent the nature of his attitude. This is particularly true in terms of its *intensity* but not generally true regarding the *direction* (whether favorable or unfavorable). When people are well informed they tend to have more intense attitudes; these attitudes may, however, be either for or against that about which they are informed.[5] Such information about his/her listeners can be of real service to an advocate.

At this point we can review our suggestions regarding the attitudes of your listeners: (1) It is very important to try to ascertain their attitudes regarding the problem in question, and (2) you may seek to do this by observing relevant behavior, sampling their opinions, and noting the amount of information they probably have regarding the problem. In this way you will consider your possible behavior in the light of general principles of attitude change.

Some of you may have read some studies of attitude change or have had some experiences in influencing people. You may have been highly successful in managing a candidate for office at Girl's State or in sales work. In one way or another you may have formed the opinion that people are thoughtless dupes who can be manipulated at will by those who have a little bag of tricks. In some instances this seems to be the case, but in general it is not. For the most part, once an attitude has been formed toward an attitude object, people do not easily change; attitudes tend to persist over long periods of time. You will need to be aware of those factors that cause their retention. The most important one appears to be a tendency of people to seek out information they think will be consistent with their currently held attitudes; we call this behavior *selective exposure*. Much research has demonstrated the tendency of people to form friendships, join organizations, and subscribe to newspapers and magazines that reinforce previously obtained attitudes.[6] When people cannot avoid being exposed to information inconsistent with their attitudes, they tend to pay more attention to that with which they agree.[7] There is some evidence that they tend to avoid information that is inconsistent with presently held attitudes;[8] however, research data on this point is not entirely consistent, and some scholars oppose this conclusion.[9] Often persons unconsciously distort their perceptions of

[4] T. M. Newcomb, "Attitudes Development as a Function of Reference Groups: The Bennington Study," in E. E. Maccoby, T. M. Newcomb, and E. L. Hartley (eds.), *Readings in Social Psychology* (New York: Holt, Rinehart and Winston, 1958), pp. 265–275.

[5] See, for example, G. Nettler, "The Relationship Between Attitudes and Information Concerning the Japanese in America," *American Sociological Review* 11 (1964): 177–191.

[6] See J. Mills, E. Aronson, and H. Robinson, "Selectivity in Exposure to Information," *Journal of Abnormal Social Psychology* 59 (1959): 250–253.

[7] H. Gilkinson, S. F. Paulson, and D. E. Sikkink, "Conditions Affecting the Communication of Controversial Statements in Connected Discourse: Forms of Presentation and the Political Frame of Reference of the Listener," *Speech Monographs* 20 (1955): 253–260; also see L. K. Canon, "Self-Confidence and Selective Exposure to Information," in L. Festinger, *Conflict, Decision and Dissonance* (Stanford, Calif.: Stanford University Press, 1964), pp. 83–95.

[8] For an evaluation of research on this issue see C. A. Kiesler, B. E. Collins, and N. Miller, *Attitude Change* (New York: Wiley, 1969), pp. 223–224.

[9] See J. L. Freedman and D. Sears, "Selective Exposure," in L. Berkowitz (ed.), *Advances in Experimental Social Psychology* (New York: Academic, 1966), Vol. 1.

information received so as to perceive it as consistent with their attitudes (even when it is not).[10] Sometimes, if the information is such that it cannot be ignored or distorted, and it is extremely inconsistent with currently held attitudes, people will simply derogate the information source, perceiving it as dishonest.[11]

All the factors that tend to increase the persistence of an attitude, once acquired, have direct bearing on your task as an advocate. You may now be wondering how anybody's attitudes, once firmly entrenched, ever are changed. We know, however, that under certain circumstances they do change.[12]

The most important factors in changing attitudes are (1) the relationship of new information to attitudes currently held, (2) the way in which the information source is perceived, and (3) the nature of the new information itself. We shall deal with each of these factors in some detail.

HOW DO YOUR VIEWS COMPARE WITH THOSE HELD BY YOUR LISTENERS?

More specifically, you have developed an opinion regarding an issue, and you have taken a stance regarding it. As you present this information to your listeners, how does it compare with their current attitudes?

There is more than one theory of attitude change; however, the general approach that has been of extraordinary value and produced substantial and provocative data is generally known as *consistency theory*. We introduced this concept in Chapter 3 and noted that the essential premise of this theory is that persons tend to seek a reduction of feelings of dissonance between inconsistent attitudes,[13] and a balance between,[14] or congruence of,[15] their attitudes toward related attitude objects such as persons, things, behavior, or other parts of their environment. For example, two such attitudinal objects might be "I am a heavy smoker," and "Heavy smokers tend to get cancer." Consistency theory postulates that the human being has a powerful need to achieve consistency between attitudes toward objects or ideas that seem to be related. If such inconsistencies are not reduced or kept at a minimum, psychological tension results, and the individual tends to change one or both, until a "balance" or congruence is achieved.[16] Osgood and his associates have presented some evidence that the more intense a person's attitude is toward one of the attitude objects, the less will he/she be likely to change his/her attitude toward that object as he/she

[10] See E. Cooper and M. Jahoda, "The Erosion of Propaganda: How Prejudiced People Respond to Anti-Prejudice Propaganda," *Journal of Psychology* 23 (1947): 15–25.
[11] See D. K. Berlo and H. E. Gulley, "Some Determinants of the Effect of Oral Communication in Producing Attitude Change and Learning," *Speech Monographs* 25 (1957): 10–20.
[12] For a comprehensive review and criticism of existing theories of attitude change see C. H. Kiesler, B. E. Collins, and N. Miller, *Attitude Change*.
[13] See L. Festinger, *A Theory of Cognitive Dissonance* (New York: Row, Peterson, 1957).
[14] See F. Heider, "Attitudes and Cognitive Organization," *Journal of Psychology* 21 (1946): 107–112.
[15] See C. E. Osgood and P. H. Tannenbaum, "The Principle of Congruity in the Prediction of Attitude Change," *Psychology Review* 62 (1955): 42–55.
[16] See, for example, the review of consistency theories by W. J. McGuire, "The Current Status of Cognitive Consistency Theories," in S. Feldman (ed.), *Cognitive Consistency* (New York: Academic, 1966), pp. 1–46; E. Aronson, "Dissonance Theory: Progress and Problems," in R. P. Abelson et al. (eds.), *Theories of Cognitive Consistency* (Chicago: Rand McNally, 1968), pp. 5–28.

tries to bring the two related attitudes into congruence; he/she will, more likely, change the one that is held with less intensity.[17]

In a general way the degree of attitude change increases as the degree of inconsistency between two related attitudes is increased. However, there is a limit to the degree of inconsistency a person can tolerate and respond to by changing attitudes. If the inconsistency is great, selective perception or source derogation is more likely to result. More specifically, if you present a message that is extremely divergent from attitudes currently held by your listeners, less attitude change is likely to occur, and your listeners will turn away from you. Listeners appear to have an area, or "latitude," of acceptance around an attitude they hold, a range of positions that are near their own but different to some degree, all of which are tolerable or acceptable to them. They also seem to have an area, or latitude, of rejection, a range of positions that are objectionable. Somewhere in between the two areas there may be one toward which they feel no commitment.[18] Very simply, a person tends to be quite tolerant of attitudes relatively close to his/her positions. Now suppose you tell a man your attitude, which is very different from his; suppose he has earlier perceived your position as (probably) close to his, but now he sees it as severely deviant. In this case he is likely not to change his attitude but to be even more negative or opposed to yours than he was before.[19] You must also be on guard against an additional factor: if your listener perceives your stance or position as being in his latitude of rejection, he is likely to see it as *much more extreme* than will those who see it as within their range of acceptance or noncommitment.[20] This is an important factor, because it can sometimes explain a disconcerting attack by someone whom you thought to be only mildly opposed to your position.

At this point we may summarize the ways in which you can apply the information we have presented regarding attitudes and attitude change. First, you must make the best assessment you can of the attitudes of your various listeners toward your position as an advocate; you may do this by observing their behavior and sampling their opinions. But be careful: At times you may be in for surprises. Second, you may have great difficulty in getting people's attention. If they initially see your position as somewhat different from their own, they may avoid you and your message; in addition, they may distort their perception so that they see you as agreeing with them; and some others may derogate you as a source of information, concluding (more or less sincerely) that you are ignorant, dishonest, or both. It is no great wonder that some advocates of commendable programs have sometimes turned to the manipulation of news media, the capricious use of social pressures, and even the

---

[17] C. E. Osgood, "Cognitive Dynamics in the Conduct of Human Affairs," *Public Opinion Quarterly* 24 (1960): 341–365; also P. H. Tannenbaum, "The Congruity Principle Revisited: Studies in the Reduction, Induction, and Generalization of Persuasion," in L. Berkowitz (ed.), *Advances in Experimental Social Psychology* (New York: Academic, 1967), Vol. 3, pp. 270–320.

[18] For an extensive discussion of these issues see C. W. Sherif, M. Sherif, and R. E. Nebergall, *Attitude and Attitude Change* (Philadelphia: Saunders, 1965).

[19] Empirical support of this principle is presented in O. J. Harvey and J. Rutherford, "Gradual and Absolute Approaches to Attitude Change," *Sociometry* 21 (1958): 61–68.

[20] See C. I. Hovland, O. J. Harvey, and M. Sherif, "Assimilation and Contrast Effects in Reactions to Communication and Attitude Change," *Journal of Abnormal Social Psychology* 55 (1957): 244–252.

THE PREPLANNED MESSAGE: TECHNIQUES OF ADVOCACY

malicious use of economic forces. The task of the advocate is not an easy one, even, or especially, if he/she is quite sincere. Third, if your position is seen by your listeners as signally different from their own, you must be careful not to present your message in its most extreme form; if it is perceived by them as falling within their latitude of rejection, speak very softly, and don't be surprised if you are attacked with greater fervency than your position really warrants in your eyes. Fourth, to the extent that you can show that your position is near to that held by your listener, you should do so; try to identify those listeners who perceive your position as falling near or in their latitude of acceptance, and show them the various elements of similarity between your position and theirs, placing less emphasis on those areas of disagreement. These suggestions can serve you well as an advocate, but they cannot guarantee you success; one reason for this is that your listeners will be influenced by their perception of *you* as well as by their perception of the position or attitude that you advocate.

DO YOUR LISTENERS TRUST YOU?

In all likelihood this question is the most important of the series we are asking you to consider as you assume the role of advocate. Literary masterpieces, historical accounts, and our collective experiences tell us that people listen to those they trust and reject the ideas of those viewed with suspicion. Time and again we see or hear of incidents in which people rejected an advocate's message because "his actions spoke louder than his words."

Students of speech communication have long been aware of the importance of a listener's trust of a speaker. In their scholarly writings they have identified this concept as *ethos* and have carried out significant research to identify the perceived characteristics of an advocate that influence this trust. Almost without exception studies of ethos have demonstrated its power as a force for attitude change.

Ethos may be defined as the attitude toward the source of a message or communication held at a given time by a receiver. *Initial ethos* is the attitude toward a source prior to his act of communicating; this attitude may be modified by the contents and nature of the message as well as by other behavior of the communicator. In passing we should note that the perceived source of a message may be one person or a group or a subculture of which that person or group is a member. To wit, as an advocate you may be helped or hindered by the ethos of your group, that is, the attitude toward you derived by your listeners from their perception of your associates. This may in part be unfair, but it is real.

Perceptions of communication sources that influence attitude change have been given much attention by researchers. Aristotle identified these elements as *intelligence, character,* and *good will.*[21] The Yale studies of source credibility identified essentially the same variables, but they were called *expertness, trust-*

[21] L. Cooper, *The Rhetoric of Aristotle* (New York: Appleton, 1932), p. 92.

worthiness, and *intentions* (receiver-perceived) *toward the receiver.*[22] In a series of modern factor-analysis studies researchers found three factors, which they called *competence, trustworthiness,* and *dynamism.*[23] The first two corresponded almost exactly with Aristotle's theoretical constructs of intelligence and character; the third was present, although weak and unstable. In a special series of studies designated to test the effect of perceived dynamism (activeness versus passiveness) of speakers, McCroskey found it to be interactive with the other two factors and concluded that dynamism is important but is mainly perceived as reflecting on the competence of the speaker.[24] In another series of factor-analysis studies of the perceived characteristics of individuals in groups which influence the degree of interpersonal trust between group members, Giffin found the same three factors, although once again dynamism was the weakest of the three.[25]

We can see that trusting a speaker is an attitude heavily influenced by at least two, and probably three, types of characteristics perceived by the listener: the speaker's *expertness* on relevant (to them) issues, his/her *reliability* as an information source, and his/her *dynamism,* or activeness, as perceived in a general way. We emphasize these perceived characteristics because you, as an advocate, will need to take stock of them. You will need to estimate the ways in which your listeners perceive you with respect to these three characteristics.

The usual experimental research on this topic has selected sources with different levels of initial ethos, attributed an identical message to them for comparable groups of listeners, and measured the differences in attitude change. Various studies have demonstrated that the listener's perceptions of such speaker characteristics as education, experience, and reputation influence the degree of attitude change.[26] In some cases these results were obtained irrespective of the quality of the message.[27] In a few cases characteristics that were logically *irrelevant* to the message topic (such as race and political-party affiliation) were shown to be influential.[28] In two studies it was demonstrated

[22] C. I. Hovland, I. L. Janis, and H. H. Kelley, *Communication and Persuasion* (New Haven: Yale University Press, 1953), Ch. 2.

[23] D. K. Berlo, J. B. Lemert, and R. J. Mertz, *Dimensions for Evaluating the Acceptability of Message Sources,* Research Monograph, Department of Communication (East Lansing: Michigan State University, 1966).

[24] J. C. McCroskey, "Scales for the Measurement of Ethos," *Speech Monographs* 30 (1968): 57–64.

[25] K. Giffin, *An Experimental Evaluation of the Trust Differential: Research Monograph R/19* (Lawrence: The Communication Research Center, The University of Kansas, 1968).

[26] F. Haiman, "An Experimental Study of Ethos in Public Speaking," *Speech Monographs* 16 (1949): 190–202. E. Strother, "An Experimental Study of Ethos Related to the Introduction in the Persuasive Speaking Situation," unpublished doctoral dissertation, Northwestern University, 1951. C. I. Hovland and W. Weiss, "The Influence of Source Credibility on Communication Effectiveness," *Public Opinion Quarterly* 15 (1951): 635–650. H. C. Kelman and C. I. Hovland, "Reinstatement of the Communicator in Delayed Measurement of Opinion Change," *Journal of Abnormal Social Psychology* 48 (1953): 327–335. J. S. Kerrick, "The Effect of Relevant and Non-Relevant Sources on Attitude Change," *Journal of Social Psychology* 47 (1958): 15–20. E. Aronson and B. W. Golden, "The Effect of Relevant and Irrelevant Aspects of Communicator Credibility on Opinion Change," *Journal of Personality* 30 (1962): 135–146. J. C. McCroskey, "Experimental Studies of the Effects of Ethos and Evidence in Persuasive Communication," unpublished doctoral dissertation, Pennsylvania State University, 1966.

[27] See K. Anderson and T. Clevenger, Jr., "A Summary of Experimental Research in Ethos," *Speech Monographs* 30 (1963): 59–78.

[28] See Aronson and Golden, *op. cit.,* and Kerrick, *op. cit.* (both in note 26).

that listeners' perceptions of a person who *introduces* a speaker influence the degree of attitude change achieved by the speaker.[29] The *appearance* of the source also has been experimentally determined to make a difference.[30] In addition, *endorsement* by respected persons has been shown to increase ethos and the degree of resultant attitude change.[31] Politicians frequently have contended that they cannot be too careful in protecting their image in the eyes of their public; experimental studies confirm this precept.

You as an advocate may enhance your influence with your listeners if they perceive you as an intelligent, informed, experienced person with a reputation for honesty and reliability. Any actions you can take to enhance this image should be beneficial, especially if they demonstrate that you are an active, dynamic person. In addition, you should be aware that even apparently irrelevant factors, if viewed negatively, may be damaging. To whatever extent it is within your control you should seek to be introduced and endorsed by persons viewed in a favorable way by your listeners. Your manners, dress, and appearance also should be considered in terms of those viewed positively by the persons you hope to influence.

Besides the factors influencing your listeners' perceptions of you before you present your message there are at least two variables in your manner of presentation that can add to your ethos: the evidence (data) employed to support your position and the oral and visual aspects of your presentation. If you merely *assert* that a problem exists or that a specific proposal will solve that problem, you are relying upon your ethos to convince your listeners (unless they happen to agree already). The use of such claims unsupported by data relies upon your listeners' perception of *you* as a *warrant* for belief. If you draw extensively upon your ethos, you may, like a money borrower, overextend your credit. In a series of experimental studies McCroskey has shown that the use of data (evidence) can maintain and sometimes increase a speaker's ethos; this is especially true if the evidence is new to the listener.[32]

There is empirical evidence to show that people's opinions of the personality characteristics of speakers are significantly influenced by their vocal characteristics.[33] Moreover, their judgments of social status are similarly influ-

[29] See J. C. McCroskey and R. E. Dunham, "Ethos; a Confounding Element in Communication Research," *Speech Monographs* 30 (1966): 456–463; and P. D. Holtzman, "Confirmation of Ethos as a Confounding Element in Communication Research," *Speech Monographs* 30 (1966): 464–466.

[30] See J. Mills and E. Aronson, "Opinion Change as a Function of the Communicator's Attractiveness and Desire to Influence," *Journal of Personality and Social Psychology* 1 (1965): 173–177; and N. Fensterheim and M. E. Tresselt, "The Influence of Value Systems on the Perception of People," *Journal of Abnormal Social Psychology* 48 (1953): 93–98.

[31] I. G. Harvey, "An Experimental Study of the Influence of the Ethos of the Introducer as It Affects the Ethos and the Persuasiveness of the Speaker," unpublished doctoral dissertation, University of Michigan, 1968.

[32] J. C. McCroskey, "Studies of the Effects of Evidence in Persuasive Communication," *Speech Communication Research Laboratory Report SCRL 4-67* (East Lansing: Department of Speech, Michigan State University, 1967).

[33] G. W. Allport and H. Cantril, "Judging Personality from Voice," *Journal of Social Psychology* 5 (1934): 37–55.

enced.[34] Other studies have indicated that the oral and the visual aspects of a speaker's presentation can significantly raise or lower his/her ethos.[35]

To apply these findings, let us suppose that you as an advocate have a moderately high ethos in the eyes of your listeners; let us also suppose that you are introduced and sponsored by a person whom your listeners regard favorably, and that your manners, dress, appearance, and vocal-visual presentation are such that your listeners are favorably impressed. We shall also assume that you support your claims with new and logically relevant data. We predict that your listeners' attitude (trust) of you would be diminished somewhat as you advocated a position contrary to the one they hold but that they would be moved to a more favorable attitude toward your position. Your ultimate success will also be influenced by other factors, one of which is the logical sense you make to your listeners; bear in mind that no amount of ethos will convince the ordinary person that he/she should do something that he/she firmly perceives as harmful to himself/herself and his/her interests.

DO YOU MAKE SENSE TO YOUR LISTENERS?

As you become an advocate of the position you have adopted, you present the thinking you have previously done. This means that you *re-present* to your listeners the essential elements of your thought process. Your focus is on their thinking as much as on your own, and you literally recreate your earlier analysis of the problem and your evaluation of the alleged solutions.

In presenting your earlier thinking you should not needlessly waste the time of your listeners: you need not replay every misunderstanding and misconception you earlier encountered. We might look at an analogy: You may have personally explored the fishing possibilities of some nearby lake; in telling someone where to catch fish in that lake you wouldn't tell all about the places you tried where you were unsuccessful. However, if some of these unfruitful spots in the lake are reputed to be good ones, or if your friend has earlier viewed them as having some potential, you would certainly tell him of your exploration in which you found them completely useless. In like manner, in telling your listeners of your exploration of a problem you would give some consideration to the alleged solutions thought by them to be valuable. You would warn them against these undesirable conclusions, giving the reasons you have earlier identified.

Your first concern will be to gain the attention of your potential listeners. Obviously, if they don't pay any attention to you, they will never be influenced by your message. You *must* get their attention, but in so doing you should not

---

[34] L. S. Harms, "Social Judgments of Status Cues in Language," unpublished doctoral dissertation, Ohio State University, 1959.

[35] H. Winthrop, "Effect of Personal Qualities on One-Way Communication," *Psychology Reports* 2 (1956): 323–324; see also J. C. McCroskey, "Studies of the Effects of Evidence in Persuasive Communication," *Speech Communication Research Laboratory Report SCRL 4-67* (East Lansing: Department of Speech, Michigan State University, 1967).

in any way diminish your ethos; in fact, in any way possible you should try to enhance it. Have you had an exciting, recent experience somewhat related to the problem? For example, perhaps you have just spent three months working in a ghetto, an asylum, or a "free university"; or perhaps you have recently helped a friend suffer through a drug crisis. In such fashion you should look for something that is in itself exciting to your listeners; in addition, if possible, it should have direct relevancy to the problem with which you are concerned.

Your second concern should be the problem itself. We presume that your listeners are not of your persuasion, that the attendant situation or condition is not viewed by them as it is by you. They, of course, may not even be aware of the existence of a problem; some of them may know of its presence but be unconcerned, unaware that it involves some characteristic that is dangerous or potentially damaging to their interest. Your task is to demonstrate to them that some interest of theirs is in jeopardy, that there is a situation that constitutes a clear and present danger. This step is imperative; no matter how workable or valid your chosen solution, if your listeners do not believe that they have a problem, they are not very likely to change their behavior. Your keynote is this: there is a clear and present danger, and they cannot afford to let it go unattended. And, of course, you must then support this claim.

Your support of the "need to do something" claim rests on your ability to show your listeners that there is a distinct difference between what *is* and what they *want*. Martin Luther King's persuasive effectiveness lay in his ability to *demonstrate* to the nation that the situation they thought existed (and wanted) did not, in fact, exist. You must do the same by presenting the thinking you have done earlier.

Suppose your listeners note the situation but think it is not bad, perceiving no clear and present danger to any interest or ethic to which they are committed. This is a severe handicap and one almost insurmountable, as has been discovered by some disadvantaged minority groups. You have one possible approach: try to get them actually to experience the situation, to see, for example, how it feels to be black, to "take a walk in the other person's shoes." They may, in effect, change their minds about the *need* to do something about the condition in question.

As you try to convince your listeners that a clear and present danger exists, you are likely to use what psychologists call a *fear appeal*.[36] A seminal study by Janis and Feshback demonstrated that with high school freshmen[37] minimal fear arousal of tooth decay was more persuasive than high fear arousal. Although subsequent research has produced conflicting results,[38] there is sufficient reason to conclude that an extreme effort in fear arousal can produce

[36] For an extended discussion see W. J. McGuire, "The Nature of Attitudes and Attitude Change," in G. Lindzey and E. Aronson (eds.), *Handbook of Social Psychology* (Reading, Mass.: Addison-Wesley, 1969), Vol. 3, pp. 136–314 (see especially pp. 203–205).
[37] I. L. Janis and S. Feshback, "Effects of Fear-Arousing Communications," *Journal of Abnormal Social Psychology* 47 (1953): 78–92.
[38] See, for example, the review of research by I. L. Janis, "Effects of Fear Arousal on Attitude Change; Recent Developments in Theory and Experimental Research," in L. Berkowitz (ed.), *Advances in Experimental Social Psychology* (New York: Academic, 1967), Vol. 3, pp. 166–224.

excessive anxiety along with a negative attitude toward the source of the persuasive attempt. This can be especially true if you have only moderate ethos,[39] or if your listeners are generally high in chronic anxiety, are persons who tend to avoid, misperceive, or deny the presence of threatening conditions.[40]

In essence we advocate that you demonstrate to your listeners that a clear and present danger exists; you must do so if you want them to support your chosen solution to a problem. However, extreme appeals to fear-arousal should be used only with care and attention to your listeners.

Your third major concern will be a presentation of the solution of the problem. Your thinking about the workability of your plan should be emphasized. In addition you should be aware of the significance of any potential disadvantages. Do your listeners think its costs may be excessive? Do they perceive that something important to them may be endangered by your proposal? These questions must be satisfied in the view of your listeners if they are to accept your plan.

You must present data (evidence) to support both your claims—that a problem exists and that your plan will meet it.[41] However, it is especially important that you use data to show that potential arguments *against* your proposal are invalid. An early study demonstrated that presenting both arguments, pro and con, with the weight on the evidence supporting the main thesis, is significantly more effective with persons having at least a high school education.[42] Further research has supported this principle, showing that an advocate who refers to possible counterarguments and refutes them immunizes his listeners against opponents of his/her plan and gains a long-term persuasive advantage.[43]

DO PERSONS YOUR LISTENERS TRUST SUPPORT YOUR POSITION?

At first glance this question may appear to you to be a subissue of the question dealt with in the preceding section, "Do you make sense to your listeners?" In fact, it has been traditional for persuasion theorists to treat testimony or support of an argument by authority as a "logical appeal," or appeal to the reasoning of the listener. However, in recent years a different approach has been advanced by Kelman, one that relies more heavily upon psychological factors than upon logic or reasoning processes.[44] Probably both

[39] See M. A. Hewgill and G. R. Miller, "Source Credibility and Response in Fear-Arousing Communications," *Speech Monographs* 32 (1965): 95–101.

[40] See M. J. Goldstein, "The Relationship Between Coping and Avoiding Behavior and Response to Fear-Arousing Propaganda," *Journal of Abnormal Social Psychology* 59 (1959): 247–252.

[41] See R. S. Carthcart, "An Experimental Study of the Relative Effectiveness of Four Methods of Presenting Evidence," *Speech Monographs* 22 (1955): 227–233.

[42] C. I. Hovland, A. A. Lumsdaine, and F. D. Sheffield, "The Effects of Presenting One Side Versus Both Sides in Changing Opinion on a Controversial Subject," in T. M. Newcomb et al., *Readings in Social Psychology* (New York: Holt, Rinehart and Winston, 1947), pp. 566–577.

[43] For a general review of research on this principle see W. J. McGuire, "Inducing Resistance to Persuasion; Some Contemporary Approaches," in L. Berkowitz (ed.), *Advances in Experimental Social Psychology* (New York: Academic, 1964), pp. 191–229.

[44] H. C. Kelman, "Compliance, Identification, and Internalization: Three Processes of Attitude Change," *Journal of Conflict Resolution* 2 (1958): 51–60.

theories have merit, but the psychologically based approach has received more research support.[45]

In the first place, there is little doubt that people are influenced by the judgment of others. In some cases these others may be persons whose opinions are held in high regard'. In many other cases they may not be viewed as expert but simply as close friends or members of a salient reference group. In the first instance we could properly identify the influence as a logical or reasoning process, as follows: The conclusion advocated is supported by experts; positions supported by experts are desirable; therefore, I should adopt this conclusion. However, studies have shown that the *expertness* of the "expert" is not the only (or sometimes the primary) consideration: his/her *trustworthiness* is of overriding significance, sometimes producing a boomerang effect of negative, instead of positive, influence.[46] Thus the effect of support from "authorities" relies quite heavily upon psychological forces. The dynamics involved include the personal characteristics of the "expert," not just what he/she says; thus, all the factors of *ethos* (perceived expertness, reliability, and dynamism) are influential. In this sense we may view the use of "authorities" in support of an advocate's position as closely akin to an appeal to ethos.

In essence this is the position taken by Kelman in his theory of social influence.[47] His approach is particularly useful in explaining the influence of "nonexpert" opinions of friends or co-members of reference groups.[48] Kelman has identified three different ways in which attitudes are formed or changed: *compliance* with attitudes held by others, in order to achieve a favorable reaction from them, *identification* with the attitudes of others, in order to establish or maintain a satisfying interpersonal relationship, and *internalization* of attitudes of others, in order to achieve a congruence of new information within one's own (internal) attitude system. The concepts of compliance and identification suggest the potential value of an advocate's citing the attitudes of persons who both support his/her position and are *trusted* by his/her listeners.

We suggest that you demonstrate to your listeners that your position is supported by persons held by them (your listeners) to be experts on the subject *provided those "experts" are viewed by your listeners as reliable and having favorable intentions.* We also suggest that you show that persons *significant* to your listeners favor your proposal; this significance may be based either upon such persons' ability to give your listeners some desired reward, status, advancement, affection, recognition, and so forth, or upon their ability to provide or sustain a relationship (such as group membership) that is desired by your listeners.

[45] See B. E. Collins and B. H. Raven, "Group Structure: Attraction, Coalitions, Communication, and Power," in G. Lindzey and E. Aronson, *Handbook of Social Psychology* (Reading, Mass.: Addison-Wesley, 1968), Vol. 4, pp. 102–204; see especially pp. 176–178.

[46] See H. C. Kelman and C. I. Hovland, "Reinstatement of the Communicator in Delayed Measurement of Opinion Change," *Journal of Abnormal Social Psychology* 48 (1953): 327–335.

[47] H. C. Kelman, "Processes of Opinion Change," *Public Opinion Quarterly* 25 (1961): 57–78.

[48] For an extended description and evaluation of Kelman's approach see C. A. Kiesler, B. E. Collins, and N. Miller, *op. cit.,* pp. 330–342; also see W. J. McGuire, "The Nature of Attitudes and Attitude Change," in G. Lindzey and E. Aronson, *op. cit.,* pp. 158 and 179–182.

IS YOUR POSITION CLEARLY
PRESENTED TO YOUR LISTENERS?

This question addresses itself both to the organizational characteristics of your presentation and to the language you employ. There is a heavy tradition in the requirements of unity, coherence, and emphasis in message preparation; moreover, there are numerous research findings to support the suggestion that your message should be well organized.[49]

There is some evidence that you may be more effective as an advocate if you present your message as an objective, informed analysis of your topic rather than as a head-on attempt to change the opinions of your listeners.[50] In this chapter we have suggested that in your presentation you generally follow the analytical-inductive approach used earlier in your thinking: analysis of the problem followed by evaluation of alternative alleged solutions, giving reasons for the adoption of your choice and giving some consideration to other approaches thought by your listeners to be potentially valuable. In addition to support for this general approach[51] there is evidence to support the suggestion that you should give primary emphasis and first consideration to your chosen solution as you compare it with objectionable (to you) alternative alleged solutions to the problem.[52]

The need for clarity of language is legendary; our daily experience supports this demand. At least one study has shown that brevity or economy of language is related to increased attitude change,[53] and additional research has demonstrated the value of emphasis, especially by means of repetition of a major idea.[54]

To enhance message clarity we suggest that you give your listeners an opportunity for questions. Of course, you run the risk that some opponent of your plan may voice dissension or even attack. You must be prepared to meet such a situation without loss of your ethos; no response on your part should show that you are not to be trusted. Research evidence shows, however, that if you can maintain an image of being well informed and highly reliable, when listeners participate in the problem-solving process they have a clearer understanding of the problem and its solution, demonstrate a subsequent higher

[49] See R. C. Smith, "Effects of Speech Organization Upon Attitudes of College Students," *Speech Monographs* 18 (1951): 292–301; and F. Thompson, "An Experimental Investigation of the Relation of Effectiveness of Organizational Structure in Oral Communication," *Southern Speech Journal* 26 (1960): 59–69.

[50] C. A. Kiesler and S. B. Kiesler, "Role of Forewarning in Persuasive Communication," *Journal of Abnormal Social Psychology* 68 (1964): 547–549.

[51] See A. R. Cohen, *Attitude Change and Social Influence* (New York: Basic Books, 1964), pp. 11–12.

[52] See N. Miller and D. T. Campbell, "Recency and Primacy in Persuasion as a Function of the Timing of Speeches and Measurements," *Journal of Abnormal Social Psychology* 59 (1959): 250–253; and N. H. Anderson and A. A. Barrios, "Primary Effects in Personality-Impression Formation," *Journal of Abnormal Social Psychology* 63 (1961): 346–350.

[53] J. D. Ragsdale, Jr., "Effects of Selected Aspects of Brevity on Comprehensibility and Persuasiveness," unpublished doctoral dissertation, University of Illinois, 1964.

[54] See R. Ehrensberger, "An Experimental Study of the Relative Effectiveness of Certain Forms of Emphasis in Public Speaking," *Speech Monographs* 12 (1945): 94–111.

commitment, and manifest greater behavioral change.[55] Whatever you do, keep cool. Do not try to "beat" your opponent; try, instead, to maintain the trust of those who are listening.

ACHIEVING COMMITMENT THROUGH SMALL BEHAVIORAL CHANGES

Throughout this discussion we have implied that you may win commitment through re-creation of your prior thinking for those whose support is needed to implement the change you desire. Of course, empirical evidence supports this approach.[56] However, there is another, perhaps even better way to achieve commitment on the part of others.

Numerous studies suggest that if you want to achieve behavioral change on the part of others, you should seek to change their behavior in some small way consistent with your long-range goal.[57] A study conducted by Freedman and Fraser is illustrative.[58] Housewives were asked to put a small sign in a window entreating others to keep California beautiful; at a later time, in comparison with other (nonexperimental) housewives, these subjects were much more willing to place a large sign on their lawn proclaiming the same message. Freedman and Fraser concluded that if you want a person to do a big favor for you, ask him to do a small favor first. It is, of course, no accident that political candidates try to get you to wear their campaign buttons. Even more commiting is handing them out to others. Public behavior has been found by researchers to be particularly committing.[59] In an industrial setting Lieberman studied ordinary workers who were promoted to two types of position, shop steward (a union man) and foreman (a company man). He found that the behavior and attitudes of the men changed to fit the position. This was not very surprising; but when they were demoted back to the common labor pool, their behavior and attitudes reverted back as well.[60]

The principle is fairly clear: If you want to change a person's behavior greatly, start by changing it a little. It is not uncommon for an old campaigner to ask his/her listeners to raise their hands in response to a question, write

[55] See, for example, studies reported by K. Lewin, "Group Decision and Social Changes," in T. M. Newcomb and E. L. Hartley (eds.), *Readings in Social Psychology* (New York: Holt, Rinehart and Winston, 1947), pp. 330–344; and E. B. Pelz, "Discussion, Decision, Commitment and Consensus in Group Decision," *Human Relations* 8 (1955): 251–274.

[56] There is conclusive evidence that attitudes are correlated with behavior; see C. A. Kiesler, B. E. Collins, and N. Miller, *op. cit.*, pp. 22–38; on the other hand, there are only a handful of studies that demonstrate that attitude change is followed by behavioral change; see L. Festinger, "Behavioral Support for Opinion Change," *Public Opinion Quarterly* 28 (1964): 404–407 (see especially pp. 406–407); also see the review of research on this issue in C. A. Kiesler, B. E. Collins, and N. Miller, *op. cit.* (in note 8), pp. 37–38.

[57] For a summary of these findings see C. A. Kiesler, *The Psychology of Commitment* (New York: Academic, 1971), pp. 14–17.

[58] J. L. Freedman and S. C. Fraser, "Compliance Without Pressure: the Foot-in-the-Door Technique," *Journal of Personality and Social Psychology* 4 (1966): 195–202.

[59] See M. Deutsch and H. B. Gerard, "A Study of Normative and Informational Social Influence upon Individual Judgment," *Journal of Abnormal and Social Psychology* 51 (1955): 629–636; also see C. I. Hovland, E. H. Campbell, and T. C. Brock, "The Effects of 'Commitment'," in C. I. Hovland et al. (eds.), *The Order of Presentation and Persuasion* (New Haven: Yale University Press, 1957), pp. 23–32.

[60] S. Lieberman, "The Effects of Changes in Roles on the Attitudes of Role Occupants," *Human Relations* 9 (1956): 385–402.

down his/her office address, hand out his/her name cards, put on a bumper-sticker, and so on. The practice has real merit, but we must caution you that, if you ask a person a small favor and he/she *refuses*, you may be in real trouble the next time you try to influence his/her behavior.[61]

We urge you as an advocate to use this approach but to exercise caution in it. If you ask your listeners to do some small favor, they must respond affirmatively if the approach is to work in your favor. No matter what an avowed opponent does—whether he calls you names, attacks your ethics, even tells lies about you—you must make every effort to present yourself as a dynamic person of intelligence and sound character, reliable and with the best interests of your listeners uppermost. Remember, you may lose an argument and still win the respect and commitment of your listeners and stand a good chance of turning every reprehensible act of your opponent into money in your ethos bank.

[61] See the summary of this problem in C. A. Kiesler, *op. cit.* (in note 57), pp. 164–167.

Postscript

I N THE PLAY *Our Town,* Thornton Wilder develops a scene in which young Emily Webb, who has died prematurely at the age of 26, is allowed to return to earth from heaven for one day. She chooses her twelfth birthday. To her father and mother this is just another day in their lives, but to Emily it is the only day that she has. With her new insights Emily is distressed by the family's lack of genuine communication and by the distracted, matter-of-fact manner of her mother. Finally in desperation she cries out:

> "Oh Mama, just look at me one minute as though you really saw me . . . just for a moment now we're all together. . . . Let's look at one another."

Like Emily, our time on earth is also limited. We should not have to accept indefinitely the alienations, the undue hostilities, the misunderstandings, and the distrust and impersonality between people of good faith. It is our hope that through improved interpersonal communication each of us can contribute toward a world in which we can, like Emily Webb in Grover's Corners, New Hampshire, "look at one another."

Indexes

Name Index

Subject Index

Ethos, 474–477. *See also* Source credibility
  initial, 474
Evaluation, 168, 365, 449–450
Evaluating, 451
Exchange theory, 424–425. *See also* Cost/
  reward ratio
Exercises
  awareness, 89–105
  environment as nonverbal communication,
    315–316
  face awareness, 100
  "Hand dialogue," 100–102
  "I can't–I won't," 97–98
  "I have to–I choose to," 97
  "I'm afraid–I'd like to," 98–100
  "I need–I want," 98
  interpersonal conflict, 404–405
  interpersonal skill, 460–461
  language, 211–212
  listening to self, 91–92
  nonverbal, 266
  "Parent dialogue," 95–97
  perception, 171–172
  relationship-oriented, 359–361
  self-concept, 104–105
  "Symptom dialogue," 102–103
  "Symptom-other dialogue," 103–104
  for understanding interpersonal
    communication, 47–48
  "Yes-No," 92–95
Existential topics, 202–204
Experience, in formation of self, 51–53
Experimenting, 323
Eyes. *See* Eye contact
Eye contact, 40, 110, 224–226, 271–272, 292,
    296–298
  emotional states and, 225
  interpersonal relationships and, 225–226

Face
  awareness of, 100
  features of, 110–111
Facial expressions, 224–226
  emotional states and, 225
Families, 433–439
Fear appeal, 478–479
Feedback, 4, 188, 410–414
  conflicting and cognitive consistency, 66
  direct, 63–64
  evaluative, 63–64
  indirect, 63–64
  nonevaluative, 46
  nonverbal communication and, 232
Feelings, 346
Fighting, controlling and, 452
FIRO, 130–131
First four minutes, 200–211
First impressions, 120–121, 146–148, 448, 457.
    See also Impression formation
Fixation, 452
Frame of reference, 161–162

Freedom, 356. *See also* Independence from
  others
Friendships
  female, 440–442
  male, 439–440
  same-sexed, 439–442
Furniture, effects of on communication,
    271–272, 274–275, 313–314

Games (transactional analysis), 331–332
Game theory, 76, 129
Gatekeeping, 451
General semantics, 14, 178–180, 339–340
General systems, 341
Genuineness, 60, 334–335, 353–356. *See also*
  Congruence
Geography, 308–310
Gestures, 111–112, 226–230
  categorization of, 221, 256
  emotional states and, 228–229
  functions of, 227
  signaling via, 229
Ghetto English, 182
Glossolalia, 194–196
Goals
  group, 279, 283
  influence on communication, 279–284
  setting of, 283–284
  size of group and, 279, 283–284
Greeting, job interview and, 457
Group cohesiveness, interpersonal conflict and,
    394
Group pressure, response to, 453–454
Groups
  guidelines for work in, 418
  interpersonal behavior in, 445–454
  participating in small, 465–467
Guilt, 163–164

Habitual patterns, 62
Halo effect, 18
Hands, awareness of, 100–102
Harmonizing, 451
Hearing, 349–353. *See also* Listening
Heightism, 140
Here-and-now, 204–205
Hidden agenda, 445–446
Hobbies, 207
Human relations, theories of, 422–425
Humor, 206–207

Iconic signs, 219–220, 223, 227, 229–230
Identification, 480
Identifying data, 201–204
Identity, 344–345
Identity formation, 53
Illustrators, 221, 256
Implicit personality theory, 138, 149
Impression formation, 108, 133–151
  accuracy of, 114–116
  role of cognitive dissonance in, 121
Impression management, 423

National Advisory Commission on Civil Disorders, 309
Needs, 414–415
  effects on perception, 141
  interpersonal, 130–131
  mutuality of, 16
  sex role stereotypes and, 425
Neutrality, 168–169, 365, 449–450
Non-possessive warmth, 333–334
Nonverbal communication, 9, 22, 40, 110–114, 208, 214–266, 295–305, 417–418
  classification of, 112, 221–232
  in classrooms, 306–308
  conscious control of, 217
  dimensions of, 221
  distance in, 313–315. See also Personal space
  feedback and, 232
  functions of, 216
  personal appearance and, 222–223
  sequences of, 214–215, 224
  smiling as, 225
  stages of, 230–231
Norms, 372
  expectancies of, 66
Nudity, 250–251

One-way communication, 7, 37
  morale and, 37
Openmindedness, 127–128
Openness, 170–171, 342–343
Operant psychology, 339
Opinion, definition of, 470
Order effects, 134, 144–145
Organizational communication, 284–286
Others
  acceptance of, 343–344, 346
  presence of effects on communication, 277–278

Paralanguage. See Metacommunication
Parents, 432–439
Perception, 9, 415–416
  analogy of the box and, 162
  bargaining in, 77–78
  communication and, 152–172
  constructs and, 32–33
  cultures and. See Culture
  differing stimuli and, 154–155
  distortion of, 77–78, 165–166, 352, 373–374, 473
  environments and, 155
  evoked sets and, 157–158
  first impressions in. See First impressions
  group communication difficulties and, 448
  internal states and, 156–157
  learning and, 155
  model of, 153–158
  need and motivation in, 162
  objectivity of, 160, 375
  process of, 108–127
  reality and, 159–162
  reciprocity of, 125–127

selection and, 153–154
selective. See Selective perception
sensory receptors and, 155–156
stability and, 35, 149
stimuli and, 171
within the group, 446–448
Perceptual accentuation, 140–142. See also Selective perception
Perceptual distortion. See Perception, distortion of
Perceptual screen, 11
Personal appearance, 222–223, 234–238
  meaning of, 241–243
Personal constructs, 32–33
Personal development, 11, 50–72
Personal growth, 340, 359, 412
  confirmation and, 71
Personal space, 288–291, 298–299, 301. See also Distance zones
Personal statements, 339–340
Personality topics, 202–204
Person perception, 157, 164–165. See also Perception
Persuasion, 341–342
Phatic communion, 70
Phoniness, 60–62
Physical appearance. See Personal appearance
Physical reality, 65
Physical senses, 64, 110–114
Placating, 23–24
Porpoises, 216
Posture, 226–230, 253. See also Body language
  effect on interaction, 227
  emotional states and, 227
Power, 279
  attraction in groups and, 447
  interpersonal conflict and, 394–395
  relationships in, 341
Pragmatics, 218
Preplanned message, techniques of advocacy and, 468–483
Prestige, attraction in groups and, 446–447
Primacy effect, 134, 144–148
Prisoner's dilemma, 128
Problem orientation, 168, 450
Problem solving, 392–393, 395, 401–403
  cooperation in, 74–75
  disagreement in, 75–76
  trading help and resources in, 76–78
Process, 4–5, 20
Projection, 452
Provisionalism, 168–169, 450
Psychotherapy, 349–350
  Gestalt, 339
  perception and, 446
  rational emotive, 339
  Rogerian, 339
  types of, 339
Pygmalion effect. See Self-fulfilling prophecy

Quasi courtship, 262–265